A Century *of* Developmental Psychology

A Century *of* Developmental Psychology

EDITED BY

ROSS D. PARKE

PETER A. ORNSTEIN

JOHN J. RIESER

CAROLYN ZAHN-WAXLER

American Psychological Association
Washington, DC

Published by the
American Psychological Association
750 First Street, NE
Washington, DC 20002

Copies may be ordered from
APA Order Department
P.O. Box 2710
Hyattsville, MD 20784

In the UK and Europe, copies may be ordered from
American Psychological Association
3 Henrietta Street
Covent Garden, London
WC2E 8LU England

Typeset in Goudy by Easton Publishing Services, Inc., Easton, MD

Printer: Braun-Brumfield, Inc., Ann Arbor, MI
Cover and Jacket Designer: Anne Masters, Washington, DC
Technical/Production Editor: Miria Liliana Riahi

Library of Congress Cataloging-in-Publication Data

A Century of developmental psychology / edited by Ross D. Parke . . . [et al.].
    p.   cm.
    Includes bibliographical references and index.
    ISBN 1-55798-233-3—ISBN 1-55798-238-4 (pbk.)
    1. Developmental psychology—History.   I. Parke, Ross D.
    BF713.C4   1994
    155'.09—dc20
                                                            94-4484
                                                            CIP

British Library Cataloguing-in-Publication Data
A CIP record is available from the British Library

Printed in the United States of America
First Edition

CONTENTS

v

CONTRIBUTORS

Karen E. Adolph, Emory University

Harry Beilin, City University of New York

Victor W. Bergenn, Council on Educational Psychology, New Jersey

Inge Bretherton, University of Wisconsin, Madison

Emily D. Cahan, Harvard University

Robert B. Cairns, University of North Carolina

William R. Charlesworth, University of Minnesota

Thomas C. Dalton, California Polytechnic State University

Robert N. Emde, University of Colorado

John H. Flavell, Stanford University

Joseph A. Glick, City University of New York

Joan E. Grusec, University of Toronto, Canada

Robert A. Hinde, St. John's College and Medical Research Council Group on the Development and Integration of Behaviour, England

Frances Degen Horowitz, City University of New York

Jerome Kagan, Harvard University

Kurt Kreppner, Max Planck Institute for Human Development and Education, Germany

Lewis P. Lipsitt, Brown University

Eleanor E. Maccoby, Stanford University

Peter A. Ornstein, University of North Carolina

Ross D. Parke, University of California, Riverside

Herbert L. Pick, Jr., University of Minnesota

John J. Rieser, Vanderbilt University

Judy F. Rosenblith, Wheaton College

Robert S. Siegler, Carnegie Mellon University

Esther Thelen, Indiana University

Peeter Tulviste, University of Tartu, Estonia

James V. Wertsch, Clark University

Sheldon H. White, Harvard University

Carolyn Zahn-Waxler, National Institute of Mental Health

PREFACE

Developmental psychology has a long but somewhat neglected history. This volume seeks to address that omission by examining the legacy of the most influential pioneers in our field and the current relevance of their thinking.

In its earliest days, developmental psychology was closely linked with mainstream psychology. Indeed, two of the founding fathers of the American Psychological Association (APA), G. Stanley Hall and M. M. Baldwin, were renowned developmentalists. Then, for a long while, many developmentalists operated outside the central concerns of the mainstream of psychology. But increasingly, we have returned to a central place in psychology. We believe this to be to our benefit as developmental psychologists and to the benefit of those in other subfields as well.

The recent 100th anniversary of the founding of the APA provided a unique opportunity for developmentalists to take stock of the progress of the field. The articles in this book appeared originally in centennial issues of *Developmental Psychology*. This book brings these articles together under one cover and prefaces them with a historical overview chapter that traces not only thematic changes over the past 100 years but also shifts in theoretical, developmental, and methodological assumptions.

Our thanks go to Karin Horspool for her assistance in the preparation of the first chapter and the introductory material. Preparation of the volume was supported in part by NSF grant BNS 89 19391. Finally, thanks to Liliana Riahi for her skill and patience in guiding this volume through the final editorial process.

Ross D. Parke
Peter A. Ornstein
John J. Rieser
Carolyn Zahn-Waxler

1

THE PAST AS PROLOGUE: AN OVERVIEW OF A CENTURY OF DEVELOPMENTAL PSYCHOLOGY

ROSS D. PARKE, PETER A. ORNSTEIN, JOHN J. RIESER, and
CAROLYN ZAHN-WAXLER

The approach of the 21st century heralds a new and exciting era for psychology and particularly for developmentalists, whose investigations will be enriched by new findings emerging from such fields as behavioral genetics, cognitive science, cultural studies, sociology, epidemiology, history, psychiatry, and pediatrics. With more than 100 years of psychology behind us, this seems to be a propitious time to take stock of our progress and to acknowledge the debt that we owe to our forebears.

This volume contains a series of readings by prominent developmentalists, each of whom focuses on a key pioneer or pioneers in the field. The major goal of the book is to articulate the ways in which these theorists

Portions of this chapter are based on a paper presented by the first author as a Division 7 invited address at the annual meeting of the American Psychological Association, Washington, D.C., August, 1992.

Thanks to Robert Hinde and Judy Rosenblith for their constructive comments on an earlier version of the manuscript. Preparation of this chapter was supported, in part, by NSF grant no. BNS 8919391 and SBR 9308941 to Parke. Thanks to Karin Horspool, Chris Strand, and Jane-Ann Phillips for their assistance in the preparation of the manuscript.

have influenced current theory and research in developmental psychology and to provide an assessment of their contribution to the field in light of our current knowledge. Our hope is to stimulate interest in the history of developmental inquiry—a topic that has been neglected—and also to remind us that questions in the field are often recurring ones.

As the chapters that follow illustrate, issues often disappear and reappear in slightly different guises at various stages of the field's history. All raise issues that have reemerged on the contemporary scene. The claim is not that developmentalists simply recycle problems, but that progress often proceeds to a point and comes to a halt. Developments in other fields, new conceptualizations and formulations of a problem, and, of course, new methodological and design advances are often necessary for the reemergence of a set of ideas. By stimulating interest in the historical roots of our discipline, we hope both to sharpen our appreciation of our forebears and to develop a source of hypotheses that may now be ripe for investigation in the current scientific climate.

One of the major messages of these chapters is to remind the reader of the complexity that characterizes the theoretical positions of the earlier contributors to our field. Often, only a sketchy outline of a theorist's central thesis survives in our collective historical memory. The qualifications and nuances that frequently were integral to the original work become obscured across time. Only a "caricature" of the original theoretical position is all that remains. Although many times, caricatures of theoretical positions are useful as points of departure for the next paradigm shift in the Kuhnian sense, they leave us with an incomplete and sometimes distorted sense of our own past. The chapters in this volume help to correct many of our misconceptions of past theorists or, at least, to underscore the forgotten complexities of their thinking.

A caveat is in order. The purpose of these chapters is to whet the reader's appetite for further exploration. Clearly, no more than this can be accomplished in the brief overviews that the chapters offer. At the same time, if this modest goal is achieved, the book will have achieved its purpose.

Chapters in this volume feature the following theorists: Darwin, Hall, Baldwin, Binet, Dewey, Freud, Spitz, Piaget, Watson, Gesell, McGraw, Vygotsky, Stern, Werner, Bayley, Bowlby, Ainsworth, Sears, Bandura, and E. J. Gibson. In the final section, prominent developmental scientists provide a series of reflections on the future of the field. Each of these chapters originally appeared in *Developmental Psychology* as a series of articles celebrating the American Psychological Association's (APA) centennial.

This introductory chapter sets the stage for the rest of the book by offering an overview of the major themes and issues that have challenged our forebears. A series of recurring issues—theoretical, developmental, and methodological—that theorists in all eras over the past century have addressed are discussed. By choosing three time points—the beginning years of developmental psychology, the 1950s, and the present era—we hope to illustrate the ways in which there has been both constancy and change in psychologist's views on the central issues of the field. We argue that, in many regards, there have been major strides in the subtlety of the distinctions and in the sophistication of the measurement and design brought to bear on developmental questions. At the same time, there is much consistency between the perspectives on the major developmental themes of our ancestors of a century ago and the views of contemporary theorists. Just as in the case of the developing organism, change occurs within the context of stability and constancy.

Our thesis is that the agenda of contemporary developmental psychology has more in common with the field's agenda near the turn of the century than with the agenda of the more recent times of the 1950s and 1960s. Our argument is that the more recent past, with its narrow emphasis on experimental child psychology and social learning theory, was a sharp departure from the origins of the field. As Cairns (1983) noted, "An overview of the past suggests that today's investigators are as much determined by history as they are makers of it. The major issues of the present appear to be, in large measure, the same ones that thoughtful contributors to the science have addressed in the past" (p. 90).

Why are we returning to the concerns of our more distant past? First, our forebears were wise in their choice of questions and raised enduring issues. Second, developmentalists took some detours in the enthusiasm for establishing a separate science on the basis of positivistic principles. To a large degree, the field's behavioristic focus promoted a proliferation of excellent methods and technological advances that, in some regards, have led us to reask the old questions and address them in more sophisticated ways.

This chapter is organized in three parts. First, the major thematic shifts in the content of our concerns are noted. Second, a dimensional analysis to support our argument is offered. (These dimensions are content-free issues of theory, method, and developmental assumptions that can be used to characterize the field at any point in historical time.) Third, a set of issues that need more attention in the future is outlined.

CONTENT-BASED CONCERNS

One Hundred Years Ago

What were the major substantive themes of a century ago? Five major themes stand out. First, emotional development was a major preoccupation. Darwin is perhaps the most celebrated example of someone who anticipated both the need for the careful documentation of emotional expressions and the need to study the functional role of emotion in social interaction. Darwin, as Charlesworth (chapter 2, this volume) and Ekman (1974) noted, was ahead of the field by nearly one century in his careful documentation of the features of emotional expressions in infants and adults in response to different stimuli, in different types of individuals (brain damaged, retarded), and in different cultures (Darwin, 1872). In addition, Freud, as Sulloway (1979) argued, was in many regards a closet Darwinian—a biologist of the mind who laid the groundwork for a host of issues surrounding the study of emotion. These include issues of the unconscious influence of emotion on both social and cognitive functioning and of the interpersonal regulation of emotion, especially interpersonal conflict in family contexts.

A second major theme was the biological basis of behavior. Two issues were of concern: the relationship between evolution and development, first outlined by Darwin (1859) and developed later by Hall (1904) in his treatment of recapitulation theory and by others (Preyer, 1888–1889), and the relationship between nature and nurture and their relative contributions to development. These concerns are evident in the legacies of Darwin and Freud, as well as in that of the important but largely forgotten early theorist Wilhelm Preyer. The evolutionary views of Darwin are well known, as are the Darwinian-influenced stands of Hall and Freud, but Preyer—an ardent student of his times—was also "evolutionary in his outlook and committed to the clarification of the relations between ontogeny and phylogeny, between nature and nurture" (Cairns, 1983, p. 46). Of course, many of these early views were wrongheaded, in part because of the limited understanding of genetics and resulting commitment to Lamarkian principles. However, the goal of embedding the emerging science of development in its biological roots was clear and is central to our enterprise today.

A third theme in our field's early history was cognitive development. Although Piaget is usually considered to be the founder of cognitive development, this credit ought to be shared with other early contributors. As others have shown (Cahan, 1984; Cairns, 1983; Cairns & Ornstein, 1979), many of Piaget's stage notions and mechanisms of development were outlined in Baldwin's writings at the turn of the century. Another figure who anticipated Piaget's ideas and other modern developmental issues was Binet. According to Binet, "cognitive development is a constructive process, the purpose of cognitive development is adaptation to the physical and social worlds, children assimilate new experience to existing ways of thinking, and intelligence pervades all activities, simple as well as complex" (Siegler, chapter 6, this volume, p. 186). Binet also recognized the qualitatively different nature of adult and child thinking. Like Piaget, Binet recognized the value of verbal probes and the diagnostic importance of children's errors. In contrast to Piaget, however, he did not believe that development proceeded in a stagelike fashion. But it was Piaget, not Binet, who developed the ideas and, most important, fashioned ways of testing these positions.

There has been a recent revival of interest in Binet, a surprisingly modern cognitive developmentalist who anticipated many of the themes of our era. For example, Binet published articles on prose memory (Binet & Henri, 1894), on the effects of suggestibility on children's memory (Binet, 1900), and on how expertise in mental calculation can provide information about memory limits. As Siegler (chapter 6, this volume) noted, this early activity was a direct challenge to Wundt's (1907) pessimism concerning the possibility of a science of cognitive development. Wundt stated,

> It is an error to hold, as is sometimes held, that mental life of adults can never be fully understood except through the analysis of the child's mind; the exact opposite is the case. (p. 336)

Or as Kessen (1983) noted, "Tichener, like his mentor Wundt, thought an experimental psychology of children is impossible" (p. viii). As the early demonstrations and arguments of Baldwin, Binet, and Piaget anticipated, both Wundt and Tichener were clearly mistaken, and the beginnings of a flourishing science of cognitive development were clearly established, at least in outline form, nearly one century ago.

A fourth and closely related theme was that conscious and unconscious processes can be differentiated. Both Binet and Freud dealt with this issue. Baldwin wrote about how conscious acts, with practice and time, become unconscious and how awareness and intentionality develop in step with cognitive development (Cairns, 1983).

A fifth theme was the role of the self in development. The self figured prominently in our field's early years, especially in the hands of J. Mark Baldwin. Although the lineage was not direct but probably mediated through sociologists Cooley and G. H. Mead, it became a prominent theme again in the past decade—as exemplified in the work of Lewis and Brooks-Gunn (1979), Harter (1983), and others.

These themes waxed and waned throughout the 50 years that followed. Watson (1913) addressed issues of emotion, psychoanalysis kept alive concerns about motivation and unconscious processes, and the nature–nurture debate continued to flourish—often with disastrous political and social overtones in the 1930s. However, under the dominance of behaviorism and other forms of learning theory, many of the early concerns were shunted aside and thus became nearly nonexistent in the more recent past.

Content Concerns of the 1950s and 1960s

What were the major themes of the 1950s and 1960s? Learning theory in various forms dominated psychology and, to a large degree, shaped the concerns of developmental psychology. This influence assumed two forms. One was the long period of time during which attempts were made to test a series of assumptions derived from psychoanalytic (Freudian) theory, but cast in (Hullian) learning theory language. Led by Robert Sears and his colleagues (Sears, Maccoby, & Levin, 1957; Sears, Rau, & Alpert, 1965), these activities occupied us as a field for 30 years.

The second was the rise of an experimental child psychology as a way of testing applications of Hull–Spence theory to relatively simple learning situations, such as form and color discrimination (see Lipsitt & Cantor, 1986, for a review). One focus of these efforts was the exploration of *mediational variables* stemming largely from the translation of the Hullian concept of the fractional anticipatory goal response into a verbal mediational mechanism. Salient examples of this influence were the efforts by Kuenne (1946) and Kendler and Kendler (1962) to extend Spence's treatment of discrimination learning, which had been based on the assumption that the choice of one or another member of a stimulus pair was a function of differences in positive and negative response strength. In contrast, both Kuenne and Kendler and Kendler argued that the performance of children of different ages would differ, depending on whether or not words were used as mediators between the presented stimulus and the subsequent overt response.

Although subsequent research raised questions about the age-related progression in verbal mediation charted by Kendler and Kendler and pointed out the role of other (e.g., attentional) mediators, support was found for the interpretation of task performance in mediational terms (see Cairns & Ornstein, 1979; Stevenson, 1972). One consequence of this extension of the Hull–Spence framework was the explicit treatment of cognitive phenomena, albeit in stimulus–response (S–R) mediational terms, phenomena that would later be interpreted in terms of hypotheses and strategies.

Another aspect of the experimental child psychology movement was the growth of interest in operant analyses of children's behavior. Skinner's (1938) operant conditioning techniques were used to examine conditioning in neonates and older children, to explore the impact of social reinforcers on the production of social responses (e.g., vocalization, smiling), to examine schedules of reinforcement, and as tools for the exploration of other phenomena such as size constancy (for an overview, see Hulsebus, 1973). At a broader level, considerable interest was generated in the analysis of behavior in everyday settings according to Skinnerian principles (e.g., Bijou & Baer, 1964). This, in turn, gave rise to the now familiar and highly influential behavior modification movement.

The 1950s and 1960s also provided the groundwork for the emergence of the vigorous contemporary investigation of infant sensory and perceptual development. Three lines of inquiry formed the basis for the current work on these issues. One was the nativist–empiricist controversy (Gottlieb, 1983) about the degree to which the organization of minds and brains depended on experience; a second emerged from Hebb's (1949) analysis of neural nets, namely, the role of learning in perceptual development; and

6   *ROSS D. PARKE ET AL.*

a third was the idea that mental life did not arise with the onset of symbolic language but is built on understandings that emerged during infancy (Bruner, 1968; Gibson and Walk, 1960; Piaget, 1952). In the 1960s and 1970s, the study of infant looking and reaching behavior provided workable methods to gain insights into the cognitive understandings of preverbal infants (Cohen & Salapatek, 1975; Yonas & Pick, 1975).

By way of illustration, we consider a few examples of each. Riesen's (Riesen & Aarons, 1959; Riesen, Kurke, & Mellinger, 1953) experimental studies of the visual development of cats and monkeys were early experimental attempts to investigate nature–nurture issues. Later, Hubel and Wiesel (1965) and their colleagues devised new methods to probe the receptive field characteristics of specific neurons. In turn, these methods, were used to investigate the specific effects of visual experience on development, for example, through experimental studies of strabismus.

Hebb's theory helped inspire work by Fantz, Salapatek, Haith, and others on the nature of visual scanning in human infants as a route to understanding their pattern perception (Salapatek & Kessen, 1966). A major idea was that records of visual scanning behavior could be used to infer infants' shape discrimination. Fantz (1961, 1963) devised a preferential looking method from which a perceptual discrimination was inferred when an infant visually fixated one stimulus more reliably than a second stimulus that was also available. A second idea depended on measuring which features of pattern were fixated by infants while looking at pictures (e.g., Salapatek, 1975). One of the ideas motivating this work was that the motor-scanning patterns themselves were learned and that the resulting *cell assemblies* may have provided a physiological basis for later object recognition.

The era also spawned the use of objective methods to investigate the cognitive understandings of preverbal infants. The Gibson and Walk (1960) studies of the visual cliff behavior of 6–12-month old human infants is one illustration of this, and Bruner's (1970) studies of infant reaching and detour behavior is another example.

Contemporary with this research on preverbal infants was work on the language development of toddlers and young children initiated by Roger Brown, together with his students and colleagues. The work took place within the context of interest in syntactic structures as mediators of complex utterances (Chomsky, 1957), and a monumental summary was published by R. Brown (1973).

Little effort was made during this period to address the themes of emotion, consciousness, intentionality, or social relationships. Moreover, in spite of some work on the effects of early experience on later behavior, there was still relatively little effort devoted to the biological underpinnings of development. Finally, with the exceptions noted above, the study of cognitive development was largely confined and constrained by the traditional S–R learning orientation of the era. Only in the more recent past have these themes come into the forefront of developmental research activity.

Content Concerns of the Contemporary Period

Perhaps the major set of shifts that characterize the current era is the revival of interest in emotional development, the biological bases of behavior, and the emergence of social relationships, as well as the revitalized effort to study children's cognitive capacities. The most unanticipated theme is the continuing discovery of the precocity of infants and young children— not only cognitively but also socially and emotionally.

Biological Bases of Behavior

The increasing interest in the biological underpinnings of behavior in infancy and in adolescence is of considerable importance. Of the forms that this interest has taken, five are discussed here. The first form is evident in the current interest in the patterning of psychophysiological responses associated with different emotions and different social situations, such as the separation of a child from the mother or the entrance of a stranger into the room (Field, 1987). These studies provide additional evidence in support of the specificity-of-emotion hypothesis (i.e., that different emotions may have different elicitors and distinct psychophysiological patterns) (Campos, Barrett, Lamb, Goldsmith, & Stenberg, 1983). They also provide another index of emotional responsivity in different situations.

The second form of recent interest in the biological bases of behavior is the renewed interest in behavioral genetics. This return to biology has resulted, in part, from advances in the field of behavior genetics that have produced a more sophisticated understanding of the potential role that genetics can play not only in the onset of certain behaviors but in the unfolding of behavior across development (Plomin, DeFries, & McLearn, 1990). This work has generally taken the form of determining the possible genetic origins of certain traits, such as extroversion and introversion, and other aspects of temperament, as well as the age of onset of emotional markers, such as smiling and fear of strangers. Recently, Plomin and DeFries (1985) found that identical twins exhibit greater concordance than fraternal twins in the time of onset and amount of social smiling. Similarly, identical twins are more similar in social responsiveness than fraternal twins (Plomin, 1986). At the same time, behavior genetic researchers are documenting the clear and necessary role of the environment in this process. Plomin's reformulation of genetic questions has led to a call for studies of nonshared environment effects and represents a good example of how behavior genetics has stimulated new designs for the assessment of both genetic and environmental influence. Rather than returning to an old-fashioned nature–

nurture debate, the new behavior genetics is spurring the development of better measures of the environment that will enable us to assess the interactions of nature and nurture in more meaningful ways. Clearly, environmental influences matter; they simply need to be measured better. One of the ironies of recent years is that some of the most compelling evidence that environmental effects are important comes from behavior genetics. At the same time, advances in the measurement and conceptualization of *specific* environmental influences has come largely from the work of socialization scholars interested in parental disciplinary styles and socialization techniques and who generally use between-family rather than within-family designs (Baumrind, 1973; Radke-Yarrow & Zahn-Waxler, 1985). In fact, the reorientation of research to a nonshared emphasis remains controversial and there is considerable debate about the implications and interpretation of nonshared effects (Baumrind, 1993; Hoffman, 1991; Scarr, 1992, 1993).

The third focus in the area of biological bases for behavior is found in the studies of hormones and behavior, especially during infancy and adolescence (e.g., Gunnar, 1987). The fourth factor is work on brain development in cognitive neuroscience (Diamond, 1990; Greenough, Black, & Wallace, 1987).

Finally, the resurgence of interest in the use of evolutionary approaches to the study of human development represents a return to biological themes, as well as a return to Darwin's early efforts to apply evolutionary principles to human behavior (Hinde, 1991; MacDonald, 1987), as in the recent integrative work of Belsky, Steinberg, and Draper (1991), who offered an evolutionary theory of socialization, whereas Charlesworth (1987) applied this approach to intelligence and adaptation. Although controversial (Hinde, 1991), this theorizing clearly illustrates one of the myriad ways in which psychologists are returning to questions that were raised by our forebears. This return is evident not only in developmental psychology but in other areas, such as social psychology, as well as in work on the origins of anger and jealousy (Buss, 1989; Buss, Larsen, Westen, & Semmelroth, 1992).

Emotional Development

Perhaps the most dramatic shift in content-based interest in the past 25–30 years has been the renewed interest in the development of emotions in infancy. Topics such as social smiling, stranger anxiety, and fear of heights were of interest in the 1960s (Gibson & Walk, 1960; Spitz, 1950), but "the motivation for conducting such studies was to use emotions to index something else—usually perceptual or cognitive process" (Campos et al., 1983, p. 786). The timing of development of emotions and the role of emotions in social interaction were of little interest at that time. A dramatic change has occurred since then, and in the 1980s, the role of affect became an issue of increasing concern throughout psychology (e.g.,

Campos et al., 1983). The developmental origins of both the production and recognition of emotions, as well as the role of emotional expressions in the regulation of social interaction, are central concerns of current developmental psychologists, especially of infancy researchers.

In light of research by Ekman (Ekman & Friesen, 1978) and Izard (1982), the older assumption that facial response patterns are not specific to discrete emotional states is being discounted. Evidence suggests that facial expressions may be, at least in part, governed by genetically encoded programs—an implication of the finding of universality in facial expression recognition (Ekman & Friesen, 1978).

The recognition of the role of emotional expressions in the regulation of social behavior is one of the most important shifts in recent years. The extensive studies of face-to-face interaction of parents and infants (e.g., Brazelton, Koslowski, & Main, 1974; Stern, 1977, 1985; Tronick, 1989) illustrate how parents and infants modify their patterns of stimulation in response to each other's emotional signals.

The social regulatory effects of emotions have been demonstrated through the notion of *social referencing* (Campos & Stenberg, 1981). Social referencing labels the tendency to seek out emotional information from a significant other and to use that information to make sense of an event that is otherwise ambiguous or beyond the person's own intrinsic appraisal capabilities (Campos & Stenberg, 1981). Investigators have shown that infants' reactions to novel toys (Klinnert, 1981), the visual cliff (Sorce, Emde, Klinnert, & Campos, 1981), and adult strangers (Feinman & Lewis, 1981) can be modified by the nature of the mother's facial expressions. Positive emotional expressions (e.g., happiness) elicit approach behavior, and negative emotional displays (e.g., fear) lead to avoidance. Moreover, social referencing is sensitive to the prior relationship that the infant has established with the referencing agent—an additional measure of the close ties between emotions and social relationships (Dickstein & Parke, 1988). This work illustrates the reemergence of interest in the interplay between cognition and emotion, as expressed by the role of appraisal in this process (Campos, Campos, & Barrett, 1989). Such a focus is consistent with the revival of interest in children's understanding of emotion (Harris, 1989).

Most recently, the range of emotion studies has expanded to include self-conscious emotions such as shame, guilt, pride, empathy, and envy—topics that were anticipated by Freud and others but were of little interest for many years (Eisenberg, 1992; Lewis, 1992; Zahn-Waxler & Kochanska, 1990). Thus, it is evident that there has been a resurgence of interest in various aspects of emotional development, including the role of emotions in the regulation of social behavior.

Social Relationships

A third content area that is a current focus is social interactive processes and the ways in which these face-to-face processes emerge into the formation of social relationships (Hartup & Rubin, 1986; Hinde, 1979; chapter 22, this volume). A prominent issue of the current era continues to be the understanding of social interaction patterns among infants, children, and their social partners. In some ways, this interest was anticipated in the earlier concerns with the effects of social feedback on infant social responsiveness. However, the emphasis on the mutual regulation of the partners' behavior, the descriptive concerns, and the quantification of the tempo and flow of the interactive interchange clearly separates the current work from its earlier antecedents (Cohn & Tronick, 1987; Field, 1991). The concern is beyond the process of interaction per se; it includes an interest in using interaction as a window on understanding the nature of social relationships between children and their social partners (Hartup & Rubin, 1986; Hinde, 1979; chapter 22, this volume).

The most ambitious theoretical effort in the understanding of the nature of early relationships is reflected in the work on infant–parent attachment. Although the theoretical roots of this work extend back to the 1950s and 1960s in the writings of Bowlby (1951, 1958, 1969), the sustained empirical effort on behalf of this theoretical position began in the early 1970s (Ainsworth, 1973; Ainsworth, Bell, & Stayton, 1972; Ainsworth, Blehar, Waters, & Wall, 1978) and has continued in the 1980s and 1990s (Bretherton, chapter 15, this volume; Eliker, Englund, & Sroufe, 1992; Main & Weston, 1981; Sroufe, 1983; Sroufe & Fleeson, 1986).

Moreover, there is an increasing appreciation of the range of characters who play a prominent role in children's social relationships. The definition of family has expanded to include a focus not only on the mother–infant dyad but on the role of fathers, siblings, and grandparents in the child's development as well (Dunn & Kendrick, 1982; Parke & Tinsley, 1984, 1987; Tinsley & Parke, 1987).

There is also a growing appreciation of the embeddedness of children and families in a variety of social systems outside the family, including peer-, school-, and kin-based networks (Bronfenbrenner, 1986, 1989; Cochran & Brassard, 1979; Parke & Ladd, 1992), which has led to an interest in peer and other relationships outside the family (Asher & Coie, 1990). This focus on relationships is part of a more general reorientation away from a focus on the individual as the unit of analysis to dyadic and larger units of analysis.

Cognitive Development

As part of our vigorous study of cognitive development, researchers have returned not only to issues of the description and explanation of knowledge acquisition, but to issues of consciousness, reflection, intention, motivation, and will (Flavell, chapter 20, this volume), children's theory of mind (Wellman, 1990), and the emergence of expectations in the first

3 months of life (Haith, Hazan, & Goodman, 1988). Finally, there is a reemergence of interest in the interplay between conscious and unconscious processes—another indication of a willingness to tackle problems that preoccupied our field's founders but that were set aside for nearly a century. Several investigators (Greenwald, 1992; Kihlstrom, Barnhardt, & Tataryn, 1992) have developed methods that permit examination of the impact of unconscious processes on a variety of cognitive and perceptual processes and allow methodical defensible excursions into such classic clinical issues as repression and self-deception. These methods could be adapted usefully for developmental studies and would provide interesting approaches to a range of current issues, from eyewitness testimony to early affective memories, that, in turn, would have important implications for the understanding of effects of early experience and of such specific issues as attachment.

The Discovery of Precocity

Beginning in the 1960s with the work of Thomas Bower, Jerome Bruner, Robert Fantz, Eleanor Gibson, and Richard Walk, the past several decades have witnessed a remarkable set of demonstrations of the abilities of infants to behave in ways that imply an understanding of physical and perceptual phenomena at ages younger than believed possible in earlier eras. Examples include Baillargeon's (1993) work on object permanence, as well as Spelke's (1988) studies of the understanding of surfaces and static objects.

Less attention, however, has been devoted to children's ability to understand social relationships in early childhood. A good example is Dunn's (1988) work on the emergence of social understanding, which suggested that children learn a variety of social rules, such as those pertaining to ownership and responsibility, as early as 2 years of age. As early as 16 months of age, mothers and children engaged in "moral dialogues" about rules, with children often nodding, shaking their heads, or providing verbal answers to their mothers' inquiries about rules.

However, a word of caution is necessary. As Fischer and Bidell (1991) and others (e.g., Fogel & Thelen, 1987) indicated, the interpretation of these achievements is, to a considerable extent, task dependent and may require greater attention to the nature of the tasks that children confront. Thus, by simplifying the tasks, the children's performance may be enhanced.

This analysis is consistent with much of the recent literature in cognitive development that indicates that children's performance in a wide range of tasks varies markedly from context to context. It can be illustrated readily with the Piagetian framework in which performance on such classic problems as class inclusion and transitive reasoning depends markedly on the materials, wording of the examples and instructions, and supports provided for remembering (e.g., see Donaldson, 1978; P. H. Miller, 1983; Siegler, 1991). Within the traditional transitive reasoning problem, even

4- and 5-year-olds can perform well if they are provided with training that permits them to remember the premises of the problem under consideration (Bryant & Trabasso, 1971). Additional examples come from research on the development of memory which indicates that young elementary school children's strategic efforts vary considerably as a function of characteristics of the to-be-remembered materials, opportunities for extended study, and so on (Folds, Footo, Guttentag, & Ornstein, 1990; Ornstein, Baker-Ward, & Naus, 1988).

These demonstrations raise additional questions about the assessment of children's capabilities because the very assessment reached will be conditional upon the parameters of the situation in which the children are observed. Thus, to return to the example of transitive inference: Can preoperational children demonstrate this skill? The answer is certainly "Yes" if the assessment is made under conditions in which memory for the premises of the problem is guaranteed. But the answer is equally certainly "No" if the problem is arranged in the traditional Piagetian manner. At one level, the answer chosen is linked to theoretical assumptions about the component subskills that a child must master to be viewed as able to engage in transitive forms of reasoning. For example, Piagetians adopt a "high threshold" for crediting a child with skill and may feel that demonstrations of transitive reasoning must be made in situations without props or supports. At another level, however, it is clear that both the "yes" and "no" answers are correct and that an adequate description of cognitive competence and development requires multiple measurements in settings that differ in the extent to which they support children's performance.

All of this leads to a significant change in the way in which one thinks about development. The question of development may not be "Can children do?" because it is increasingly evident that children can perform a variety of tasks at very young ages. Rather, the question ought to be "Under what task conditions can a child demonstrate a particular capacity?" There is also a need to give more consideration to what constitutes a definition of a particular capacity. What are the minimal aspects needed to satisfy the requirements for inclusion as an example of the capacity? If one does not pay closer attention to these definitional issues, there is a danger of comparing capacities that are, in fact, different, rather than being instances of the same phenomenon. In turn, this suggests the need for a much better psychology of tasks and testing contexts. The development of a taxonomy of tasks and how these particular versions relate to the central constructs of interest would go a long way to resolving some of the current disputes.

At the same time, a recasting of the major problem of development may be needed from one of acquisition of a basic set of skills or abilities into a question of knowledge of application rules. Knowing when to apply knowledge to solve a problem may be as important as knowledge per se.

DIMENSIONS OF DEVELOPMENTAL THEORY AND RESEARCH

Next, we turn to a series of dimensions that are relatively independent of content. The usefulness of these dimensions is based on the assumption that, at any point in the development of a field of inquiry, both theory and research can be organized around a series of themes or dimensions that reflect the central concerns of the era. These dimensions can be organized into three major groups. The first encompasses general theoretical assumptions that apply to any area of psychological inquiry and relate to developmental psychology. These include such themes as the nature of explanatory models, the aim and scope of theory, the universality of theory, the role of secular influences in theory, and theory's relationship to other disciplines. The second includes issues that are of concern mainly to developmentalists. These include such issues as the discontinuous versus continuous nature of development, the period of development of interest, the degree of plasticity across development, the directionality of influence, and the unit of analysis. The third consists of several methodological issues of concern to developmental and nondevelopmental investigators. These issues include the nature of designs (longitudinal vs. cross sectional), experimental versus nonexperimental approaches, choice of research context, the nature of data collection strategies, and the level of analysis (molecular vs. molar). These dimensions will be defined and examined in terms of their usefulness in organizing the nature of the changes that have occurred in the past 100 years. Examination of the ways in which the field has shifted in its reflection of these content-free dimensions provides greater insight into the status of the field and moves it beyond a mere content-based description of theory and research in development over the past century. A schematic summary of these dimensions and the associated shifts is provided in Table 1.

GENERAL THEORETICAL DIMENSIONS

Nature of Explanatory Models

The study of development may be characterized by the types of models of development endorsed by theorists. These rival perspectives have been termed *mechanistic* and *organismic* world views or models (Overton & Reese, 1973). The importance of such perspectives flows from the assumption that the choice of explanatory model determines a variety of theoretical decisions and the nature of testable hypotheses.

A century ago, theorists such as Baldwin, Hall, and Binet endorsed an organismic world view. For example, Baldwin took a clear stand against

TABLE 1
Dimensions of Theory and Research in Developmental Psychology

Dimensions	Turn of the Century	1950s and 1960s	Present (1990s)
General Theoretical Dimensions			
Nature of explanatory models	Predominantly organismic	Predominantly mechanistic	Predominantly organismic; some mechanistic
Principal explanatory processes	Evolutionary principles	Social, environmental; learning principles	Affective, biological, cognitive, social; interactional processes
Aims of theory	Explanation and description	Prediction and control	Explanation and description
Scope of theory	Broad	Very broad	Limited
Universal versus culture-bound nature of explanations	Universal	Universal	Culture bound; universal
Status of secular influences on development	Limited	Limited	Extensive
Relationship to other disciplines	Extensive	Limited links	Many links
Applied versus nonapplied orientation	Both	Nonapplied	Both
Developmental Dimensions			
Developmental as continuous versus discontinuous	Discontinuous	Both	Predominantly continuous; some discontinuity
Focal period of development	Childhood	Early Childhood	Life span
Role of critical periods	Accepted	Accepted	Limited
Direction of influence	Unidirectional	Unidirectional	Bidirectional
Unit of analysis group	Individual, dyad	Individual	Individual, dyad, triad
Methodological Dimensions			
Nature of designs: cross sectional versus longitudinal	Both	Cross sectional	Both
Experimental versus nonexperimental	Both	Experimental	Both
Setting: Laboratory versus field	Multiple settings	Laboratory	Multiple settings
Data collection strategy (self-report; observations)	Multiple strategies	Nonsequential observations	Multiple strategies
Level of analysis	Molar	Molecular	Molar and molecular
Selection of samples	Samples of convenience	Convenience sample, random assignment to experimental conditions	National surveys; multicultural samples

the usefulness of mechanistic world views and in favor of an organismic position. As Cairns noted,

> His [Baldwin's] aim was to outline a "system of genetic psychology" that would attempt to achieve a synthesis of the current biological theory of organic adaptation with the doctrine of the infant's development (Baldwin, 1895, p. vii, cited by Cairns, 1983, p. 54).

In Baldwin's view, mechanistic or atomistic methods were inappropriate for the task. Binet and, later, Piaget similarly took a constructivist stance and endorsed an organismic view of development.

The major dissenter in the early years of the discipline was, of course, J. B. Watson. In his effort to make a clear break with our introspectionist past, he posited that development was a mechanistic process that could be reduced to simple units of behavior that combine together through learning principles. These views continued, in various guises, to dominate developmental psychology—at least in North America—for the next 60 years in spite of the continuing activity of organismically oriented theorists such as Piaget in Europe and Gesell in the United States.

The 1950s and 1960s were dominated by the mechanistic model, although the organismic viewpoint also had advocates. Proponents of behaviorist or neobehaviorist theories (e.g., Gerwirtz, 1965; Kendler & Kendler, 1962; Lipsitt, 1963; Rheingold, 1956) were active scientific leaders and producers. Similarly, social learning theories (Bandura & Walters, 1963) proliferated during this period, but there were exceptions, as Piaget's theory was beginning to influence (Flavell, 1963) American psychology, and Kessen (1967) offered an organismic analysis of infant cognitive and perceptual development.

In the 1980s and 1990s, the situation has changed, with various versions of an organismic viewpoint clearly emerging. Bowlby's ethologically oriented attachment theory is a major example (Ainsworth, 1973; Sroufe & Fleeson, 1986). A second major theoretical development of current importance is the ecological perspective of Bronfenbrenner (1979, 1986), which is consistent with another general trend toward a systems theory viewpoint (Belsky, Rovine, & Fish, 1989; Ramey, MacPhee, & Yeates, 1982; Sameroff, 1983). All these views are clearly organismic in orientation. The 1990s clearly belong to the organismically oriented theories—a return to our roots. At the same time, information-processing approaches to cognitive development (Klahr, 1989; Siegler, 1991) rely in part on a mechanistic perspective, which suggests that we are entering a more eclectic era, one not characterized by a single viewpoint.

Types of Principal Explanatory Processes

Every era is characterized by different sets of explanatory principles or processes that serve as the focus for explaining the emergence and maintenance of behaviors under question. These include biological, cognitive, affective, perceptual, learning, and social interactional processes. Although in every era some attention is given to all of these processes, some preferred processes gain prominence in different periods of investigation. Major shifts have occurred in the processes invoked to explain behavior over the past century.

Two of the major explanatory processes from earlier times are considered here. First, a century ago, there was a strong sense of biological determinism in some form of evolutionary progression. For Hall, this was the biogenetic law that "ontogeny recapitulates phylogeny." Baldwin, in contrast, reversed the order and proposed that changes in ontogeny may precede and shape phylogeny. Baldwin proposed circular reactions and imitation—two loose predecessors of reinforcement and observational learning—as mechanisms for acquisition and change across development. Watson's later introduction of conditioning notions exerted a great deal of influence over the next 80 years but was unavailable as an integrative tool at the turn of the century.

Second, in the 1960s, there was a major focus on general processes of S–R associationism that were thought to account broadly for perception, thinking, and social behavior. An important debate of the times concerned whether S–R associationism was the only type of learning or whether the type of information to be learned mattered. Postman (1955) developed the former point of view, which emphasized the general nature of learning processes and stated that they served to integrate and enrich one's knowledge of objects. Gibson and Gibson (1955) developed the latter view emphasizing the importance of understanding the tasks and their context and focusing on cases of perceptual learning resulting in learning to discriminate alternative instances of things, not to integrate them.

In the realm of social development, the same learning principles predominated in the early 1960s. One group of researchers (e.g., Gewirtz, 1965; Rheingold, 1956) believed that contingent reinforcement from social agents shapes the form and frequency of social responses like smiling and vocalizing. Closely related were social interactionists who believed that similar processes operated under naturalistic conditions (e.g., Schaffer & Emerson, 1964).

The 1990s are more eclectic in terms of the processes that are invoked to explain developmental changes. Current explanations draw upon a wide range of explanatory processes. First, a widespread assumption is that processes operate within a context defined by an individual's situation, understanding of the task and situation, and base of knowledge. Second, genetic influences on development are more widely recognized (Plomin, 1989). Third, emphasis on biological constraints on behavioral development has flourished. For example, developmental implications of immature sensory systems have been related to the social world of infants (e.g., Banks and

Salapatek, 1983), the implications of immature limb systems have been related to locomotion (Thelen & Ulrich, 1991), and the implications of an immature cortex have been related to infant search behavior (Diamond, 1990, 1992; Goldman-Rakic, 1987). Fourth, concepts of temperament, which is presumed to be biologically based at least in part, are given more recognition (Bates, 1987; Kagan & Snidman, 1991). Fifth, affective processes are viewed as important modifiers of infant social (and cognitive) development (Campos, Campos, & Barrett, 1989). Sixth, both perceptual and cognitive processes are invoked to explain the occurrence of social behaviors (Campos et al., 1983). Finally, social interactional processes have been given a central explanatory role in the emergence and maintenance of social behavior (Parke & Tinsley, 1987; Schaffer, 1984). The diversity of explanatory processes of development is one of the hallmarks of the 1980s and 1990s.

Within the cognitive arena, a variety of information-processing mechanisms have been proposed as substitutes for the Piagetian processes of assimilation and accommodation as mediators of developmental change. Thus, in his neo-Piagetian theory, Case (e.g., 1985) focused on the development of automaticity as a mechanism for overcoming capacity limitations in the processing space required to conduct intellectual operations. Other potential mediators of change include transformation rules that govern the modification of existing skill structures (Fischer & Farrar, 1987; Fischer & Pipp, 1984); self-modifying production systems that are subject to generalization as a function of experience (Klahr, 1984; Klahr & Wallace, 1976); and competition among various rules and concepts that results in the "evolution" of adaptive strategy choices (e.g., Siegler, 1991; Siegler & Jenkins, 1989). In addition, other theorists (e.g., Keil, 1984) distinguish between general and domain-specific cognitive skills and emphasize that learning and development may be constrained by the organizational structure of specific knowledge domains. Thus, no single explanatory process dominates the current era.

Aims of Theory

Theories across various disciplines vary in terms of goals. Description, prediction–control, and explanation are three different goals. Within developmental psychology, the ecological approach (Barker, 1968) is largely descriptive. Other approaches are aimed at increasing the level of predictability of behavior or at modifying the extent to which behavior can be brought under control. For example, Skinnerian approaches and behavior modification theories (Bijou & Baer, 1961) have prediction and control as their primary goals. Finally, explanation is the goal of the grand theories of Freud and Piaget, as well as of recent theories of infant social development, such as Bowlby's attachment theory (Bowlby, 1969, 1973, 1980).

The ethological approach (Hinde, chapter 22, this volume) focuses on both description and explanation.

Within developmental psychology, the relative emphasis on these three goals has shifted. In the early days of the discipline, explanation was a central goal, especially of the grand theorists such as Freud, Baldwin, and later Piaget. Description was also a common practice. Darwin, in view of his own early training in geology and botany, understood well the value of a descriptive database from which a theory could be built. G. Stanley Hall, who relied largely on questionnaires, was a committed devotee of description, although of a different sort than Darwin. He published 194 questionnaires between 1894 and 1915 (White, chapter 3, this volume). His first paper, titled "The Contents of Children's Minds," predated his questionnaire phase but set the stage for his commitment to a descriptive phase of science. The range, as well as the methodological precision, of his work was impressive and included diverse issues as dolls, toys, and playthings to emotions and will and common traits and habits.

During the nineteenth century, some embryologists were struck by the morphological similarity between human embryos and other animal species during the different stages of prenatal development. Examples of the "gill slits" structures appearing early in the embryonic stage are well known. Such similarities in structures led some scientists (e.g., Preyer, 1895) to speculate that human ontogenesis recapitulated phylogenesis. An important implication of this was that studies of phylogenesis could replace studies of human development. Later, De Beer (1940) pointed out that the physical similarities were superficial. Although they may indeed have reflected ancestral relations, the structures were not the same, and little could be learned about one from systematic studies of the other.

Again, Watson (1913) was the early exception to a descriptive orientation with his focus on prediction and control as the guiding aims of behaviorism. In the 1960s, a great deal of research activity was devoted to the study of factors that could exercise control over children's behavior, such as smiling and vocalizing (e.g., Gewirtz, 1965). Within learning studies, a similar focus on stimulus events or reinforcing consequences that controlled subjects' responses was common (Lipsitt, 1963). The goals of description and explanation received less attention.

In the current period, concern with both description and explanation has increased. A primary goal of Bowlby's attachment theory (1969, 1973, 1980) was to provide a descriptive account of the ways in which children manage the naturally occurring events of separation and loss. Similarly, the goal of recent ethologically influenced studies of the emergence of emotional expressiveness in infancy has been largely descriptive (e.g., Izard & Malatesta, 1987). The ecological orientation of Bronfenbrenner (1979) has led to an increased concern with a description of social contexts and settings that children may encounter during development. Likewise, the ecological orientation of Gibson & Gibson (1955) has led to an emphasis on the description of stimulus information and analysis of the physical contexts of perceptual and perceptual-motor learning (Pick, chapter 8, this volume).

Descriptive studies have appeared in other areas of development as well, including language (R. Brown, 1973), cognitive development (Rogoff, 1991), and parent–infant interaction (see Maccoby & Martin, 1983; Osofsky, 1987). However, implicit in this work has been the assumption that description is a first step in a multistage process. Explanation follows as a next step in theory development. For example, explanatory theories of infant personality development have emerged and range from psychoanalytically oriented (Mahler & Pine, 1975) and psychoanalytic–ethological positions (Bowlby, 1969) to family systems (Lewis, 1982) and transactional positions (Sameroff & Chandler, 1975).

The focus is also on explanation in current accounts of cognitive development, a number of which may be viewed as efforts to integrate Piagetian and information-processing principles (see Sternberg, 1984). Case's (e.g., 1984, 1985) theory, for example, retained the Piaget-like stages but used automatization of cognitive processing (and the corresponding reduction in resources that are needed for task execution) as one of the potential mechanisms underlying developmental progression and change.

Scope of Our Theories

A century ago, theorists in the grand tradition assumed that large portions of the developmental landscape could be accounted for in terms of a limited number of general principles. In other words, their scope was very wide. Watsonian behaviorism is one example, as are Freud's and Piaget's attempts to account for affective development and psychopathology on the one hand and cognitive development on the other. Gesell's theory of motor development is another example. In spite of the broad scope of these perspectives, there was a tendency to seize upon a central set of concerns—affective, cognitive, and motoric—and develop a theory around this pivotal issue.

The ancestor who perhaps most clearly anticipated current trends is J. Mark Baldwin, who, in contrast with many of the theorists in the grand tradition, did not compartmentalize social and cognitive development. Instead, he was one of the earliest theorists to recognize the interplay between cognitive and social development—as his volume *Social & Ethical Interpretations of Mental Development: A Study in Social Psychology* (1897) attested. More than many of our forebears, Baldwin, recognizing the need to integrate behaviors across domains of development, seemed surprisingly modern in his outlook.

In the 1950s and 1960s, the influence of wide-scope theorizing was still evident, in the form of either some version of behaviorally oriented learning theory (e.g., Hull, 1943), or some combination of psychoanalytic theory and learning approaches (e.g., Sears, Maccoby, & Levin, 1957), or later social learning theory (Bandura & Walters, 1963). The revival of interest in Piagetian theory (Flavell, 1963) during the 1960s in North American psychology was consistent with the long-standing commitment to the search for a few principles that would explain large domains of development.

Since that time, there has been a retreat from wide-scope theorizing. As Kessen (1982) observed, "At an accelerated rate, child psychologists as a society of colleagues have moved away from the general process, general-principle specification of their intellectual task. More and more, we have turned from the search for singular general laws of development" (p. 36). In the past 25–30 years, the degree of specialization has increased sharply; in place of grand theories, a variety of minitheories aimed at limited and specific aspects of development have emerged. However, there is evidence of an attempt to link together these minitheories. The idea of *general processes* as explanations of development has been given up because we have learned that they are not so general; instead, it is increasingly evident that they depend on the specifics of the situation, the task, and the subjects' understanding of the task or situation (Flavell, 1985, chapter 20, this volume; Siegler, 1991). There is a recognition that the domains of childhood—social, emotional, physical, health, and cognitive aspects—are interdependent, and it is recognized that they overlap and influence each other mutually.

By way of examples, first, there is a growth of interest in the interplay between social and cognitive development, especially in factors associated with the socialization of cognition. Thus, current research focuses on parents' abilities to provide supportive contexts for the emergence and growth of their children's cognitive skill. Concepts such as *scaffolding* (Wood, Bruner, & Ross, 1976) and the Vygotskian *zone of proximal development* (Vygotsky, 1978; see also Rogoff, 1991; Van der Veer & Valsiner, 1991) reflect the current commitment to analyzing the impact of the changing social context on cognition and development. A specific example of this approach is seen in recent efforts (e.g., Fivush & Hammond, 1990; Hudson, 1990) to relate children's early memory development to different maternal styles of talking about the past.

Second, and closely related, is the increase in interest in the role of cognitive factors in the explanation of social processes. For example, the recent work on working models within the attachment paradigm is a search for an explanation of how the expectations and social rules acquired in the context of the parent–child relationship become guides or maps that the child imposes on other social relationships (Bretherton, chapter 15, this volume; Bretherton & Waters, 1985). In the domain of children's aggression, Dodge (1986) offered a social information-processing analysis that has successfully accounted for children's aggression toward their peers.

Third, the course of physical development and locomotion are being related to growth in perceptual and affective understanding (e.g., Bertenthal & Campos, 1990). Fourth, recent work on language, communication, and perceptual development is often studied in the context of social development (Bruner, 1983; Nelson, 1987). Finally, work on the interplay between malnutrition and cognitive development is another example of the erosion of the barriers between domains of developmental inquiry (Ricciuti, 1970, 1980).

Universal Versus Culturally Bound Nature of Explanations

A century ago, the assumption that processes were universal was the dominant view. This does not imply that theorists were unaware of cross-cultural variation. Rather, they viewed other cultures as living laboratories that could provide opportunities to evaluate the operation of fundamental laws of development. Freud's use of anthropological data is a prime example of the eagerness of our ancestors to seek confirmation of their theories in often primitive understanding of other cultures (Freud, 1919). Darwin (1872) used cross-cultural data to evaluate the universality of emotional expressions—not unlike the recent study by Ekman (1992) of emotional expressions in Sumatra. In the 1960s, it was widely assumed that our theories were universally applicable, and relatively little attention was given to contributions of culture to our explanations. However, in the 1980s and 1990s, more attention has been given to cross-cultural work in development (Field, Sostek, Vietze, & Leiderman, 1981; Rogoff, 1991). These works provide important reminders that the generalizations concerning development derived from studies of American samples may, in fact, not be valid in some other cultural contexts.

One example would be the cross-cultural studies of infant–parent attachment, in which wide disparities were found in the distribution of infants in terms of their attachment classifications. Although the measures show securely attached infant–mother relationships in 57% of American samples, the rate drops to 33% in samples tested in northern Germany (Grossman, Grossman, Spangler, Suess, & Unzner, 1985). Another example would be the common finding that American father–infant relationships are often characterized as being dominated by playful interaction (Lamb, 1977a, 1977b; MacDonald & Parke, 1986; Power & Parke, 1982). However, in Sweden, Lamb, Frodi, Hwang, Frodi, and Steinberg (1982) found few differences between mothers and fathers in their level of playful interaction. These findings of limited generality are not restricted to cross-national studies. A series of studies in the 1970s by Tulkin and Kagan (1972) concerning social class differences in parent–infant interaction seriously challenged the generality of findings even within one cultural or national context. These authors found clear social class differences in the ways in which mothers treated their infants: Lower class mothers, in contrast with middle-class mothers, were less verbal in their interactions, a finding revealed by many other studies as well.

Ironically, researchers may soon be in the position of knowing more about cultures outside of our own country than about intracultural differences in the United States. Although there have been modest advances in understanding the development of children of different races and ethnic heritage, there is a serious gap in the descriptive base that can be used to begin to develop a clear profile of similarities and differences across children of different background in our own country. There is even less understanding of the processes that may account for the patterns of similarities and differences. This state of affairs was documented by Graham (1992) in her review of trends in published research on African–Americans in APA journals between 1970 and 1989. In spite of a brief burst of activity in the early 1970s, there has been a near-linear decline in such studies published in six APA journals in this 20-year period. In *Developmental Psychology*, only 4.6% of the articles published focused on African–American subjects, and there was a decline from the early 1970s from 8% to 2.6% in the period between 1985 and 1989. Other APA journals fared even worse: *Journal of Personality and Social Psychology* had only 1.6% of its articles involving African–American subjects. The recent special issue of *Child Development* (McLoyd, 1990), however, was a sign that this situation may be in the process of being corrected.

As Graham (1992) noted, this lack of a strong empirical base has resulted in "sets of isolated and outdated findings, often of questionable methodological soundness." Graham suggested several reasons for this, including "fears associated with conducting socially sensitive research," which entails ethical and moral risks. Also there are *bandwagon effects*, that is, "the tendency for particular issues to rapidly emerge as timely to dominate an empirical literature for some period and to just as quickly fade from view" (p. 637). For example, the study of black English vernacular in the early 1970s led to a host of studies that aided in clarifying the "differences versus deficits" viewpoints, but then quickly faded. Shifts in the *Zeitgeist* within the discipline may also account for some of the decline. For instance, the search for cognitive processes that are apparently universal may undermine the search for diversity. These same arguments can be made about a variety of groups: Asian–Americans, Hispanic–Americans, and Native Americans. One exception is the work on achievement among Asian–American children (Steinberg, Dornbusch, & B. B. Brown, 1992).

These variations across ethnic lines represent important opportunities to explore the universality of processes and to provide naturally occurring variations in the relative salience of certain key determinants of social–

emotional and perhaps cognitive development as well, such as interactive style, beliefs, and values. Most important, these studies may provide a better basis for guiding policies, programs, and culturally sensitive interventions on behalf of children. As our own culture becomes increasingly diverse, it becomes important that we begin to make a serious commitment to an exploration of this diversity, both theoretically and through systematic empirical inquiry. The search for a balance between processes that are universal and those that are particular to cultures and racial and ethnic groups probably represents one of the greatest challenges of the 1990s.

Status of Secular Influences on Development

Just as awareness of the limitations imposed by culture has increased, so has appreciation of the role of secular changes in development. In some ways, this issue is similar to the cross-cultural generality issue, but with the question phrased in a horizontal rather than in a vertical direction. In other words, how have historical conditions in a variety of spheres—medical, educational, economic, political, and social—shifted, and, in turn, what impact have these shifts had on children's development? Historical analyses can have several functions. First, history can provide unique opportunities to assess the generalizability of our explanatory principles in different historical periods. Historical variations such as war, famine, or economic depression represent important and powerful natural experiments that permit opportunities for theory and model testing, often under conditions that are much more drastic than developmental researchers could either ethically or practically engineer or produce in either the laboratory or the field.

In the early years of our science, this was not a prominent issue. There is little doubt that historical conditions shaped choices of problems and theoretical interpretations. The most celebrated example is, of course, the frequent allegation that Freudian theory was shaped, to a large degree, by conditions in Victorian Vienna at the turn of the century. However, there seemed to be little awareness of the need to factor this issue into theories of development.

With the exception of some of the early life-span theorists, the issue is a relatively late-developing one. Even in the 1950s and 1960s, there was little recognition that cohort effects were important to consider. However, within the past 25 years, researchers (Elder & Rockwell, 1979) have shown a growing awareness of this issue in the face of increasing evidence that secular change is an issue that may be important for understanding development.

These trends are readily illustrated by the changes that have taken place in medical and hospital practices: Less maternal medication is administered during labor and delivery (Brackbill, 1979); the number of cesarean-section deliveries has increased dramatically (Bottoms, Rosen, &

Sokol, 1980); the survival rates of low-birth-weight infants have risen greatly (Goldberg & DeVitto, 1983); and liberalized hospital visitation practices for fathers and siblings have altered the early context of the mother and newborn. These factors have contributed to marked alterations in the level of father participation in early infancy (Parke & Tinsley, 1984, 1987), which in turn may produce shifts in the developmental patterns of infants in contrast to those reared more by mothers alone. In the economic sphere, maternal employment has risen sharply, with a consequent modest increase in rates of father participation with infants (Parke & Tinsley, 1984; Pleck, 1985). Closely linked with the change in maternal employment is a rapid rise in the proportion of infants in out-of-home care (Clarke-Stewart, 1989). This change alone has altered the social development of infants and children, especially their sociability and interactive competence with peers (Belsky, Steinberg, & Walker, 1982; Phillips, McCartney, & Scarr, 1987). However, evidence is emerging that day care, especially if it begins in infancy, may be associated with shifts in the quality of infant–parent attachment (Belsky, 1986; Belsky & Rovine, 1988). The debate over this issue is not yet resolved (Phillips, McCartney, Scarr, & Howes, 1987).

Shifts like these in the secular sphere appear to be altering the nature of development. It is important to determine whether secular shifts produce changes in the timing of onset of developmental phenomena or whether the developmental processes themselves are significantly altered. According to one view, the underlying processes that govern social development remain unchanged or unaltered by secular trends (Bijou & Baer, 1961). A second view is that changes occur in the rates of certain behaviors or in the pace at which certain developmental landmarks are reached, but no change occurs in the organization of underlying processes. Still another view is that secular change is in part responsible for changes in the reorganization of underlying processes of development (Riegel, 1972, 1975, 1976). All three of these formulations may be correct, each applicable to some spheres of development and not to others.

Horowitz (1987) distinguished between universal and nonuniversal behaviors that may help articulate those aspects of behavior that are likely to be affected by historical factors and those that are not:

> Two types of universals in development are being proposed. Universal I involves behavioral characteristics that have a course of development that is laid down in the phylogenetic inheritance of the organism—shaped . . . by the eons of evolutionary history. The behavioral expression of these universals cannot occur in the absence of a normal species-typical environment. However, given that environment, what will be expressed is largely the same in every normal human organism. (p. 145)

Horowitz further distinguished a type II universal, which is one in which the probability of expression and development is also high but somewhat less than "one." It is more subject to variability in environmental conditions and plastic elaboration than is the case for universal I type behaviors. Many of the behaviors we identify as universally human are of this type. For example, erect locomotion, the capacity to learn language and sensori-motor skills in the first two years of life. (p. 146)

In contrast, nonuniversal behaviors "encompass all those behaviors that are the result of learning opportunities determined by cultural values and variations in functional environments" (Horowitz, 1987, p. 149). At this stage, sensitivity to this issue far outstrips understanding of the ways in which development is altered.

Relationship to Other Disciplines

It is not surprising that, as an emerging discipline, developmental psychology was an interdisciplinary enterprise in the beginning. Philosophy, biology, pedagogy, and sociology all influenced the early theorists. Hall was particularly influenced by philosophy, religion, education, and (of course) evolutionary biology. Baldwin reached out to sociology, whereas Freud incorporated anthropological insights into his writings. At the same time, there was a strong push to disassociate the emerging field from its roots—especially its philosophical roots—and to establish the new field as a separate discipline, especially a scientific one. Perhaps, Watson's (1913) manifesto, "Psychology as a Behaviorist Views It," marks a clear break with the introspectionist past and represents a dramatic example of this attempt to start a separate and distinctive science of behavior.

Not only are barriers falling across content domains within our own discipline, but a rise in interdisciplinary cooperation is evident as well. In comparison with the 1960s, there are indications of a marked increase in interdisciplinary cooperation. This is evident in links with the field of pediatrics in both training (Parmalee, 1982; Tinsley & Parke, 1984) and research (Goldberg & DeVitto, 1983; Ricciuti & Breitmayer, 1988). Because of increased interest in developmental psychopathology, collaboration between child psychiatry and developmental researchers has increased (Sameroff & Emde, 1989). There are also increased links with sociology and psychology, as exemplified by collaborative work on day care, divorce, and timing of parenthood (e.g., Furstenberg, Brooks-Gunn, & Morgan, 1987; Hoffreth & Phillips, 1987). Geneticists, neurologists, and psychophysiologists are now collaborating with developmental psychology researchers (Field, 1987; Gunnar, 1987; Plomin, 1990), and developmentalists and historians are increasingly aware of each other (Elder, Modell, & Parke, 1993). The 1980s and 1990s represent a rich context for interdisciplinary research in development. In some regards, the complexities of development are best addressed from a perspective of multiple disciplines—and it is, in fact, likely that the interesting issues and questions of the 1990s will arise at the boundaries between disciplines.

Applied Versus Nonapplied Orientation

The task of applying developmental psychology to practical problems has been an issue of long-standing concern to developmentalists, as exemplified by the Watson and Gesell excursions into the child advice movement and as evident in G. Stanley Hall's early writings about the child study movement. As White (chapter 3, this volume) noted:

> The movement reflected the rise of "whole-child professions" at the turn-of-the-century renegotiation of American social contracts distributing responsibilities for the socialization of children among families, professionals and government institutions. (p. 113)

Sears (1975), in his classic "Your Ancients Revisited" history of our field, amply documented how the institutional location of much of child development in schools of home economics and education shaped the field's continuing commitment to the application of knowledge on behalf of children and families.

In spite of a long-standing commitment to the application of knowledge about development to solving applied problems, researchers showed less interest in these issues in the 1960s. However, by the 1990s, several trends converged to redirect attention to applied concerns. First, the nature of research problems had shifted toward an increased emphasis on mental health and social relevance (Sroufe & Rutter, 1984). Second, populations had changed to focus on at-risk infants and children such as premature babies and handicapped babies, as well as at-risk parent groups such as poor and young mothers (Field, 1991; Warren, in press). Third, research settings had shifted to include hospitals, institutions, and day-care centers. Fourth, such large-scale intervention projects such as Head Start had shifted their focus to the earliest years of development. Fifth, schools were changing as developmentalists applied recent advances in cognitive science and technology to improve children's classroom learning (A. L. Brown & Reeve, 1987; Lepper & Gurtner, 1989). Finally, there was a rise of interest in the application of research for guiding the formation of social policy (Stevenson & Siegel, 1984; Thompson, 1990).

DEVELOPMENTAL DIMENSIONS

Developmental Orientation: Continuous Versus Discontinuous Change

In considering dimensions that are unique to developmental issues, one of the major questions that confronts developmental psychologists is that of how to characterize the nature of change across development. Some take a discontinuous view in arguing that development occurs in a series of discrete steps or stages, with the organization of behavior being qualitatively different at each new stage. Others view development as a process of steady quantitative change in which development is a continuous process whereby each new event or change builds upon prior experiences in an orderly way (for discussions, see Rutter, 1987; Wohlwill, 1973).

Our founders were stage-oriented theorists. J. Mark Baldwin conceived of mental development moving through epochs or stages—reflexive, sensorimotor, and ideomotor stages progressing to symbolic and ideational transformations. Advanced stages included prelogical, logical, and hyperlogical. Similarly, G. Stanley Hall, a recapitulationist, was a firm advocate of stage notions, which represent stages of human evolution. Along with Freud and Piaget, the early years of our discipline were clearly committed to stagelike conceptions of development.

Generally, advocates of mechanistic models, such as learning theorists, view development as a continuous process. To the extent that Hullian-influenced experimental child psychology and social learning theory characterized the 1960s, we would suggest that this era endorsed a continuous view of development. Freudian theorists, who advocated a discontinuous view of development, were still influential, but in a lesser way. In the 1960s, remnants of psychoanalytic thinking were still evident (Sears, Maccoby, & Levin, 1957; Sears, Rau, & Alpert, 1965), as was allegiance to a modified stage view of development. Although the influence of Freudian theory was waning, the impact of Piagetian theory was beginning to be felt in developmental psychology in the 1960s, especially in the domain of cognitive development (Flavell, 1963) and in infant social (Hunt, 1961) and cognitive development (Kessen, 1967) as well.

In the 1990s, in terms of the continuity-versus-discontinuity issue, developmentalists have retreated from the predominant theoretical positions of Piaget and Freud and have become less interested in strong forms of discontinuity that are organized around stage constructs. In the Piagetian case, the evidence is not consistent with the view that, within a given stage, there are similarities in performance on a variety of tasks that, presumably, share characteristics of that stage and that reasoning changes from stage to stage in a qualitative manner (see Brainerd, 1978; Flavell, 1971, 1982, chapter 20, this volume). As a result, the strong forms of the stage argument have few supporters. Rather, there is growing recognition that the course of development may vary markedly even for presumably related concepts. But there is also recognition that the entire issue of qualitative or quantitative change may depend on one's point of observation. As Siegler (1991) indicated, "when viewed from afar, many changes in children's thinking appear discontinuous; when viewed from closeup, the same changes often appear as part of a continuous, gradual progression" (p. 50).

These changes in conceptualization about the course of development relate to a group of relatively new positions that suggest the importance of focusing simultaneously on both domain-specific and general cognitive skills. Thus, as Flavell (chapter 20, this volume) noted, a viewpoint is emerging that suggests that

> development is specific in many respects but that it contains general properties (Case, 1987; Fischer & Farrar, 1987; Halford, 1993). They assume that there is a regular probably maturation-based increase with age in some aspect of the child's information processing capacity, such as the child's processing speed or processing efficiency. This, in turn, is thought to make possible new and more complex forms of cognition in all content domains because the child can now hold in mind and think about more things at once. Conversely, capacity limitations may constrain and limit the possible forms of cognition the child can enact. These capacity limitations and their progressive reduction with age act as governors and enablers of cognitive growth, making for important across-domain similarities in the child's functioning at each point in development. (p. 574)

Progress may be forthcoming in this area as new theoretical approaches are applied to the problem. For example, Van der Maas and Molenaar (1992) proposed a revised model based on a catastrophe theory that permits identification of a genuine stage transition. Their recent success in applying this approach to the transition in cognitive development from Piaget's preoperational to concrete operational stage suggests that the approach may have promise.

However, the debate is by no means settled. Rather, the formulation of the issues has been transformed into more than a dichotomous debate. The issue has been recast in terms of (a) the forms of continuity and discontinuity, (b) the behaviors that may show one or the other form over time, (c) the mechanisms that are involved, and (d) the role of constitutional factors (Rutter, 1987). As Rutter noted, "much has still to be learned about what happens to the organism as a result of experiences, and hence much uncertainty remains about the processes involved in continuity and discontinuity" (p. 286). The new openness to the possibilities is the hallmark of the debate in the 1990s.

Focal Periods of Development

Each era can be characterized in terms of the period of development that is emphasized. At the turn of the century, there was considerable debate about the most important period of development. Some (e.g., Freud, 1919) emphasized infancy as the focal period, whereas others (e.g., Hall, 1904) saw adolescence as the period that deserved the most sustained attention. Although Hall (1922) published a volume on senescence, the later part of the life span did not receive serious attention by developmental researchers in the early period. From the 1960s to the present, the infancy period has been rediscovered as an important phase of development. Other periods, especially middle childhood (Collins, 1984) and adolescence (Lerner & Foch, 1987), are beginning to challenge the emphasis on infancy, and the treatment of infancy as an isolated period of development is beginning to shift.

Researchers in the 1980s and 1990s have taken seriously a life-span perspective (Baltes, 1987). In part, this view emerges from a recognition that the social context provided by caregivers varies as a function of the location of the adults along their own life course trajectory (Parke, 1988). The earlier view was that variations in parenting behavior are relatively independent of adult development. Evidence of this shift comes from a variety of sources, including studies of the impact of the timing of parenthood and the effects of maternal (and paternal) employment, and of the impact of job satisfaction and involvement on infant development (see Parke & Tinsley, 1984, 1987, for reviews). In addition, there has been a serious return to the study of aging (Baltes, 1987; Salthouse, 1985), especially of explorations of speed of processing, memory, and intelligence (e.g., Hertzog, 1989; Perlmutter, 1985; Shaie, 1989; Zacks & Hasher, 1988), and to studies of social behavior (e.g., Brubaker, 1990) as well.

Role of Critical Periods

A century ago, there was considerable interest in the effects of early experience on later development, both on the animal front and in the psychopathology domain. Several early researchers (Romanes, 1884; Spalding, 1873) took strong stands on the primacy and critical effects of early experience on later development (Cairns, 1983). Carlson (1902) demonstrated that physiological structures of the visual system of birds could be altered by variations in stimulation. Similarly, strong advocates of critical period effects were found in Freud, who emphasized the infancy period, and in Hall, who saw adolescence as a formative period.

Consistent with the shift toward a life-span view is the reevaluation of the role of critical periods in development. In the 1960s, considerable evidence supported the critical period hypothesis as it related to infant social development. Several lines of research converged in support of this viewpoint for both animal (e.g., Harlow & Harlow, 1962; Sackett, 1968) and human (Yarrow, 1961, 1964) studies. However, it soon became apparent that simple yes-or-no questions about whether experience played a role in particular domains were too simple. The important issues were to understand the processes through which experiences exerted their influence on structure and function and when they exerted that influence.

In the realms of sensory and perceptual development, there has continued to be interest in plasticity and the degree to which organisms are more responsive to experiences at some (relatively critical) ages than at others. Many of the investigations were focused on low-level sensory functions through experimental studies of animals. Many important examples were conducted on the development of binocular vision with cats and monkeys (for example, Blakemore, 1976; Hubel and Wiesel, 1965). Gottlieb (1976) reported experimental studies of animals, but his investigations were on sensory–motor development of more complex pattern production—the development in birds of species-specific songs. The results of these comparative studies indicate that the timing of experience does indeed matter. But it is not always the case that earlier experience is better than later experience—"when" experience exerts its greatest impact varies across behaviors or functions and species.

Investigation of the effects of experience on development, to determine whether an experience matters, how it matters, and when it matters, are sometimes conducted with animals through logically straightforward experimental manipulations of experience in which a class of experience is available during some ages and not others. In addition, two other methods are sometimes used: *enrichment* experiments and *naturally occurring groups* experiments.

The enrichment method involves experimental administration of extra amounts (that is, beyond the amount ordinarily available) of experience that are thought to have positive effects on development. With this method, children are randomly assigned to a group either with "normally" occurring amounts of experience or "enriched" amounts of experience. In her case study of twins, McGraw (1935) enriched the sensory–motor experiences of one twin but not the other and reported corresponding differences in their athletic skill. Zelazo, Zelazo, and Kolb (1972) followed McGraw's work by demonstrating that exercise of the infantile step reflex during the first months of life facilitated its maintenance in the infant's repertoire beyond the age at which it typically disappears; in addition, infants in the "enriched" group walked at slightly earlier ages than those in the other group (see also Thelen, 1989). In the 1960s, Burton White (1970) conducted a well-known enrichment study of sensory–motor development.

The naturally occurring groups method consists of identifying groups of individuals who are "deprived" of some class of experience because of their circumstances or as a result of an experimenter's intervention. For example, studies of persons with visual impairment are sometimes used as a step toward investigating the role that visual experience may play in nonvisual development (e.g., Rieser, Guth, & Hill, 1986; Rieser, Hill, Talor, Bradfield, & Rosen, 1992).

Banks, Aslin, and Leston (1975) used this method to investigate whether human binocular development depended on binocular vision during a critical time in early life. To do this, they identified a group of adults whose eyes had been severely misaligned (they were either cross eyed or walleyed) at some point in their lives, at which time they did not receive normal binocular input to the visual system. The subjects differed in the age at which they experienced abnormal binocular input because of the eye misalignment, before which they had experienced normal vision. For some, abnormal eye alignment had been noted very early in life, whereas for others, it had started at different ages in childhood or adulthood. Similarly, the subjects differed in the age at which the eye misalignment was corrected, undergoing the relevant surgeries at different ages in infancy, childhood, or adulthood. The results indicated that the timing of binocular experience did matter: The adults with normal binocular experience during infancy and early childhood showed better binocular vision than others.

However, since the 1960s, important challenges have been mounted that bring into serious question the critical period hypothesis with regard to the development of infant social behavior. First, later research seriously challenged one of the central postulates of a critical period view of development, namely, that certain periods of development are of particular importance and that the individual who does not receive an appropriate experience during this phase will suffer permanent deficits. Research has strongly challenged this view by showing that monkeys reared in total social isolation for the first 6 months of life can be rehabilitated (Novak & Harlow, 1975). Similarly, evidence at the human level has continued to accumulate and to challenge the assumption of nonreversibility (Clarke & Clarke, 1976; Kagan & Klein, 1973). A similar conclusion is evident from more recent studies of infant–parent attachment. Studies have shown that early attachment relationships show a high level of stability across the first few years of life (Sroufe & Fleeson, 1986). Other evidence suggests that the classification of attachment in infancy shifts across time as a result of changes in family circumstances (Lamb, Thompson, Gardner, Charnov, & Estes, 1984). These findings suggest the modifiability of attachment relationships.

However, some evidence suggests that a modified version of sensitive, if not critical, periods is likely to emerge in contrast to a view of unlimited plasticity across development (Bornstein, 1989). As noted above, Banks et al. (1975) have shown that the attainment of normal binocular depth perception depends upon early (prior to age 3) opportunities for bifovial fixation; and Rieser et al. (1992) have demonstrated that adult skill in spatial representation of the environment seems to require early perceptual learning experiences that involve the coordination of sensory experiences resulting from movement that is self-produced. Moreover, J. S. Johnson and Newport (1989), examining the development of competence in a second language, found evidence for a sensitive period in grammatical mastery. The question for the 1990s is to discover which aspects of behavior are likely to be altered by environmental events at specific points in development, and which aspects remain more plastic and open to influence across wide spans of development.

The Direction of Influence: Unidirectional Versus Bidirectional

An issue of continuing concern for developmental psychologists has been the role of the child in his or her own development. In the social and socialization domains, this is often expressed in terms of the directionality of influence. With few exceptions, our founders viewed the child as influenced largely either by innate biological forces or by environmental factors. In the social realm, for example, Freud and Watson both provided a picture of the passive child who was either buffeted by internal drives and instincts or molded by external contingencies. The direction of influence was clearly unidirectional, with adults shaping the child's outcomes. On the cognitive side, there was more variability. Hall saw an inevitability in the way in which children's intellectual development would proceed that was constrained by his recapitulationist views of development. Other earlier thinkers were less committed to a passive view of the child. J. Mark Baldwin, Binet, and later Piaget were all champions of the child as an active, constructive participant in his or her own development.

In the 1950s and 1960s, in both the social and cognitive spheres, there was a clear return to views of the passive child. Children learned as a result of feedback and support from the external environment, a view underscored by the nature of the paradigms—of conditioning, discrimination or learning, and so on—that were popular in the recent era of experimental child psychology. In this same period, most approaches to social development included a unidirectional model whereby parents influenced their children's development; the children's contribution to their own socialization was rarely recognized.

In the current era, our views are very different. One of the lasting legacies of the Piaget revival in the 1960s and 1970s was the reevaluation of the child's role in his or her own cognitive progress:

> As Piaget correctly taught us, their [children's] cognitive structures dictate both what they accommodate to [notice] in the environment and how what is accommodated to is assimilated [interpreted]. The active nature of their intellectual commerce with the environment makes them to a large degree the manufacturers of their own development. (Flavell, chapter 20, this volume, p. 570)

It was a view that was reinforced by Eleanor Gibson's (1969) emphasis on children as active learners who search for information that is relevant to their task and who work to become sensitive to it (Gibson and Spelke, 1983; Pick, chapter 18, this volume).

On the social side, under the influence of Bell's (1968) classic paper, the historical imbalance was corrected and the children's contribution to their own socialization came to be widely accepted. In part, this shift occurred because of the experimental analyses of infant and child competencies of the 1960s, which demonstrated the wide range of capacities as well as the readiness of the infants and toddlers for social interaction (Schaffer, 1971). A new phase is now being increasingly recognized. In the enthusiasm to correct a historical imbalance, researchers focused on the child's impact on the parent instead of the more appropriate focus on the reciprocal nature of the interactive process. The current *Zeitgeist*, however, has clearly shifted to the study of the reciprocity of interaction. The ways in which parents and children mutually regulate each other are of central interest (Parke, 1978; Parke & Tinsley, 1987; Schaffer, 1984; Tronick, 1989).

The Individual Versus Other Units of Analysis

Every era can be characterized by the units of analysis that are preferred for empirical and theoretical work. Individuals, dyads, triads, and polyadic units (e.g., families) are groupings that can be used.

Historically, in the beginning of our field, the unit of analysis was typically the individual. For example, whether for purposes of cognitive or of social developmental analysis, the unit of concern was typically the individual for our forebears, such as Hall, Freud, and Piaget. However, two exceptions should be noted. First, J. Mark Baldwin envisioned the dyad as the proper unit of analysis for understanding social interaction, and later, Vygotsky championed the view of "mental functioning as a kind of action" (Wertsch, 1991) that may be exercised by individuals or by dyads or larger groups. His view is one in which mind is understood as "extending beyond the skin. Mind, cognition and memory . . . are understood not as attributes or properties of individuals but as functions that may be carried out intermentally or intramentally" (Wertsch & Tulviste, 1992, p. 549).

In the 1950s and 1960s, a very different picture emerged that was more consistent with the views of Hall and Freud than of Baldwin and Vygotsky, with a focus on the individual as the unit of analysis. Thus:

> Accounts of psychological development have for the most part been individually based. Their concern has been with the child as such; it is the child who is regarded as the basic unit of study, everything outside his skin being considered extraneous, even antithetical—forces that may have an impact on the child but that are not an inherent part of his developmental progress. (Schaffer, 1984, p. 11)

This description captures well the 1950s and 1960s, when the unit of analysis was generally the individual. Typically, the child was examined to assess his or her response to input from social agents in the environment.

The unit was not simply the individual but often only the infant or child. Adults, of course, should be expected to behave differently toward infants as a function of their own developmental progress. However, researchers had little interest in how the adult social agents who populate the child's world change developmentally, or in how their developmental changes shape the form and frequency of the social input they provide to children. They were interested in the effects of different kinds of child-rearing practices (Sears, Maccoby, & Levin, 1957) but had little interest in the reasons for individual differences across adults in their choices of practices. Shifts in family circumstances, life events, occupational changes, or even simply age differences across adults were rarely examined. The 1960s were individualistic and child-oriented years. Units of analysis beyond the individual were seldom investigated and were rarely the object even of theoretical inquiry.

Consider several of the changes that have occurred in the 1980s and 1990s. First, researchers now have an increased appreciation of adult development and of how shifts in adult development shape the course of the adult role as socializer of the child's development (Elder, 1984; Parke, 1988). This expansion of the cast of individuals from the child to the adult was encouraged, in part, by the life-span developmental theorists (Baltes, 1987). Researchers began to conceptualize the unit of analysis as dyads within the family system, such as the parent–child dyad, the husband–wife dyad, and the sibling–sibling dyad (Belsky, 1984; Cowan et al., 1985; Parke, 1988; Parke & Tinsley, 1987). Moreover, units beyond the dyad have been recognized as important as well. Several researchers have recently begun to investigate triads (Hinde & Stevenson-Hinde, 1988; Kreppner, 1988), as well as the family, as units of analysis (Reiss, 1981). It is clear that units of social analysis that extend beyond the individual were increasingly recognized by the 1990s (Parke, 1988; Sigel & Parke, 1987).

In the 1990s, this shift toward units beyond the individual is evident in cognitive as well as social development and is due in part to the revival of interest in Vygotsky. Such terms as *socially shared cognition* (Resnick, Levine, & Teasley, 1991), *socially distributed cognition* (Hutchins, 1991), and *collaborative problem solving* (Rogoff, 1991) reflect the increasing awareness that cognition can be a social as well as an individual enterprise.

SHIFTS IN METHODOLOGICAL ORIENTATION

In addition to shifts in theoretical assumptions, the past century has witnessed a variety of shifts in methodological approaches to development. First, there has been an increased commitment both to longitudinal research designs and to cross-sectional approaches. Second, there appears to be a return to the methodological pluralism of the turn of the century. In contrast to the dominance of the experimental approaches in the 1960s, the 1980s and 1990s have been characterized by an openness to multiple strategies, including laboratory-based experimental studies as well as a variety of nonexperimental approaches (Parke, 1989). Third, the research settings have changed from a near exclusive focus on the laboratory context in the 1960s to an increased use of natural settings for the conduct of research (Bronfenbrenner, 1979). Again, this represents a return to the earlier appreciation of the need for a range of research contexts that characterized the beginning of the field. Finally, attitudes toward sampling issues have changed, with a greater appreciation of the importance both of subgroup differences and of representative samples.

Nature of Designs: Cross Sectional Versus Longitudinal

At the turn of the century, the predominant approach was a cross-sectional one, in spite of the call for longitudinal studies to help evaluate the hypothesized impact of early experience on later development (Mills, 1898). It was not until the 1920s and 1930s that the great longitudinal investigations of this century began at Berkeley and at the Fels Research Institute.

By contrast, in the 1960s, cross-sectional designs were common and longitudinal studies were relatively uncommon. For example, there were a number of studies on the effects of various types of reinforcers on significant aspects of infant social behavior, such as smiling and vocalizing. Weisberg (1963) showed that rates of smiling and vocalizing could be modified for various combinations of visual, tactual, and auditory feedback. Others obtained similar results (Brackbill, 1958; Etzel & Gewirtz, 1967; Wahler, 1967). Little interest was evident in issues of stability of or change in development across time. One exception was the early charting of the course of infant–parent attachment relationships by Schaffer and Emerson (1964), who studied a group of infants over an 18-month period.

In the 1980s and 1990s, the proportionate use of longitudinal designs increased markedly, motivated in part by an increased interest in issues of developmental stability and change. Two types of longitudinal studies are evident. Short-term longitudinal studies, in which a particular issue is traced over a short period of a few months to a year, are currently popular (Clarke-Stewart & Hevey, 1981; Crockenberg, 1981; Hetherington & Clingempeel, 1992). These studies are of value for detecting short-term stability or for tracking development across a period of assumed rapid change in an emerging developmental process or structure.

Short-term longitudinal studies have been conducted to investigate whether different skills emerge at similar times. Lockman (1984) conducted one such study, which was framed as a test of some of Piaget's ideas about mental representations. Lockman observed detour behavior longitudinally in infants from an age slightly before starting to walk until somewhat after walking skillfully. He created two detour situations that were identical in most regards: In the detour-reaching situation, an object was lifted over a barrier, and infants had the chance to reach around the barrier to retrieve the object; in the detour locomotion situation, an object was lifted over the barrier, and infants had the chance to walk around the barrier to retrieve the object. Lockman found that the infants succeeded at reaching around the detour well before they started walking at all. After beginning to reach, infants needed several months of reaching experience before they started to detour by reaching around the barrier. Although they were skillful detour reachers when they started to walk, infants needed several months of walking experience before they started to detour by walking around the barrier.

In addition, short-term longitudinal studies have been conducted to investigate the role played by specific categories of experience in perceptual-motor development. Zelazo et al.'s (1972) study of the step reflex and later development of locomotion is one illustration of this. Bertenthal and Campos's (1990) investigations of the relation of locomotor experience and skilled spatial orientation in infancy constitute other examples.

Many of the current longitudinal studies have a long-term character and have continued from infancy through childhood and into adolescence. For example, a number of investigators have followed families from infancy to the preadolescent or adolescent years (Lewis & Feiring, 1988; Sameroff, 1987; Sroufe, 1983). This strategy has permitted a more definitive evaluation of a variety of theoretical issues, especially those concerning the impact of early experience, including the role of sensitive and critical periods on later development. This increase in the amount of longitudinal research does not imply that it is the dominant research strategy. Indeed, in the area of cognitive development, longitudinal investigations are rare, with the exception of research directed to continued analysis of the Fels and Berkeley growth studies (e.g., McCall, Appelbaum, & Hogarty, 1973), as well as evaluations of the cognitive (usually IQ) consequences of intervention programs for at-risk children (e.g., Lazar & Darlington, 1982). A notable exception is the longitudinal exploration of children's memory and cognition from age 5 through the elementary school years that is currently being conducted at the Max Planck Institute for Psychological Research in Munich (e.g., Weinert & Schneider, 1989). Nonetheless, because of the expense and difficulty of longitudinal research, cross-sectional designs still predominate among developmental researchers. Often researchers will use both strategies, and in an area that is not yet well developed either theoretically or empirically; cross-sectional studies often precede the pursuit of an issue longitudinally. A commitment to multiple design strategies rather than a near-exclusive reliance on a single design is most characteristic of the current era.

Experimental Versus Nonexperimental Approaches

Both experimental and nonexperimental approaches flourished a century ago. Representative of the nonexperimental approach were, of course, G. Stanley Hall and Freud, who both relied on field-based self-reports of various types. Nevertheless, we should remember that Binet was an early experimental child psychologist who designed and conducted a variety of memory suggestibility experiments. At the same time, he recognized the need for convergent methodological approaches to apply to the same set of problems. "Our psychology is not yet so advanced" that we can limit our analyses to information attained in the laboratory (Binet quoted in Cairns, 1983). It is interesting that Binet's demonstrations of the feasibility of an experimentally based science of child development predated Watson's more famous experiments on conditioning of emotion by nearly 20 years. "Binet was the first to provide convincing evidence for the proposition that a science of human development was possible" (Cairns, 1983, p. 51).

In the 1960s, investigators relied largely on experimental approaches, especially laboratory experiments. Few field experiments, natural experiments, or nonexperimental field studies appeared in the 1960s. Again, this trend has some exceptions, but these were relatively isolated examples outside the main tradition of the times. One notable exception was Rheingold's (1956) study of the effects of extra mothering on institutionalized infants—an example of a field experimental approach. Another exception was Skeels's (1966) study of infants who were adopted out of institutions; this may be viewed as an example of a natural experimental strategy, although the work is often criticized for methodological weaknesses. Nonexperimental approaches were not widely used during the 1960s.

How should we characterize the 1990s—30 years later? Again, a greater openness to multiple strategies is evident. A variety of approaches can be found, including laboratory-based experimental studies (Kuchuk, Vibbert, & Bornstein, 1986) and field-based experimental studies (Easterbrooks & Goldberg, 1984; Parke, MacDonald, Beitel, & Bhavnagri, 1988).

Research Settings: Laboratory Versus Field

Although experimental approaches are used most often in laboratory settings, it is important to recognize that choice of setting and method are, in fact, independent (Parke, 1979a). Therefore, in this section, we focus on the selection of the context within which the research is to be conducted, including field as well as laboratory settings. Both field- and laboratory-based studies were evident at the turn of the century in the hands of Hall and Binet. In the 1960s, the vast majority of research projects were conducted in laboratory settings. The choice of the laboratory context was consistent with the theoretical focus of the day on the S–R framework, which led to testable propositions that, experimentally, could be evaluated best under controlled conditions. This preference was particularly evident in the experimental child tradition (see Lipsitt & Cantor, 1986, for a review) but was evident in the social learning theory tradition as well (Bandura & Walters, 1963). The early studies of social reinforcement of infant social responses were generally laboratory based (Rheingold, Gewirtz, & Ross, 1959), as were the influential nonhuman primate studies by Harlow (Harlow & Zimmerman, 1959). However, one can find exceptions, such as Schaffer and Emerson's (1964) study of the development of attachment in the home and Rheingold's (1956) investigation of social responsiveness in institutionalized babies.

The choice of naturalistic contexts for the assessment of behavior has become increasingly evident in the 1980s and 1990s. What are the origins of this shift? In the past two decades, psychologists have become concerned about the limited ecological validity of traditional methodologies, particularly of reliance on the laboratory context as the sine qua non for the study of social development and socialization. In fact, a "mythology of childhood," to borrow Alfred Baldwin's (1967) phrase, has evolved in which a set of effects noted in the laboratory is assumed to occur also in naturalistic socialization contexts and to be an accurate account of how the child develops. One result of this myth has been a confusion between necessary and sufficient causality; the laboratory experiments suggest only that certain variables are possible contributors to social–cognitive development. However, the extent to which these hypothesized processes are in fact necessary for adequate socialization is left unanswered. To the extent that the aim is a technological one, in which the most effective techniques for modifying behavior in clinical and educational contexts are sought, the ecological validity can be ignored. Similarly, if the concern is to evaluate the adequacy of a theoretically derived prediction concerning the operation of a developmental process, this may not be an issue. However, if the concern is with the generalizability of the hypothesized or observed processes that have been discovered in the laboratory to natural social settings, direct assessment of the extent to which these processes operate in naturalistic contexts is necessary. This framing of the ecological validity debate does not deny the importance of the laboratory context as a highly relevant and useful setting for the testing of hypotheses concerning development. Rather, it suggests that the additional step of testing laboratory-derived propositions in naturalistic contexts be undertaken before any claims concerning the boundaries of generalizability are made.

Under the influence of increasing criticism concerning the ecological validity of laboratory paradigms (Bronfenbrenner, 1979, 1989; Cole, Hood, & McDermott, 1978; Parke, 1976), as well as an increasingly sophisticated appreciation of the importance of contextual factors for understanding social behavior (Pervin, 1978) and the value of different settings for different research goals (Parke, 1979a), a more eclectic era was ushered in. Instead of the sole commitment to a single setting, the 1980s was a period during which multiple contexts came to be commonly used to investigate children's development. The laboratory is still a context for the evaluation of well-specified theoretical propositions concerning development. However, other settings, such as homes (Waters & Deane, 1986; Zahn-Waxler & Radke-Yarrow, 1982), hospitals (Field, 1991; Parke & O'Leary, 1976), day-care settings (Belsky, 1986; Howes & Olenick, 1986), schools (A. L. Brown & Campione, 1990), and physicians' offices (Whitt & Casey, 1982), are used as well. Moreover, consistent with earlier eras (Gesell, 1928), a resurgence of interest in controlled naturalistic contexts, such as a laboratory apartment that approximates a home situation, has occurred (Radke-Yarrow, 1989, 1991). This proliferation of settings reflects a recognition of the value of different contexts both for different research purposes and for different stages of evaluation of a research paradigm.

Data Collection Strategies

One of the most significant shifts in the past 100 years has been in the choice of data collection strategies used to assess development. Two trends can be detected: (a) a return to the use of verbal reports and (b) a rise in the use of observational strategies.

A century ago, a number of data collection strategies were used, including the questionnaire (Hall) and interview (Binet), as well as observational techniques (Darwin, Preyer, Baldwin). There was little agreement about the most appropriate strategy, and many investigators used a variety of approaches, depending on the question. For example, Binet was well aware of the value of different methods for different issues. The use of self-report strategies were, of course, soundly criticized by Watson and later behaviorists. More recently, retrospective reports of child rearing (Sears, Maccoby, & Levin, 1957) were severely criticized as being unreliable and open to bias and distortion. With the advent of the 1960s and the rise of experimental approaches, self-report strategies were seldom used.

In the last two decades, a return to our roots has been evident in the rise of the use of verbal reports and in an increase in observational strategies.

Protocol Analysis

One use of self-reports is in the analysis of subjects' thinking as they attempt to solve various types of problems. A frequently used method involves presenting children with a problem and asking them to verbalize whatever they are doing as they work toward the solution. The resulting verbal protocol then becomes a valuable source of information about individual subjects' hypotheses and strategies (see Ericsson & Simon, 1980).

Analysis of such "talk-aloud" data has permitted the identification of a developmental progression in the types of rehearsal strategies used by children of different ages and of the linkage among these techniques and corresponding changes in actual memory performance (Ornstein & Naus, 1978). Other examples of the successful use of protocol analysis are seen in the documentation of children's changing hypotheses about the properties of objects (e.g., size, weight) that are critical for balancing on a balance scale (Karmiloff-Smith & Inhelder, 1977), as well as in their discovery of effective arithmetic and memory strategies (McGilly & Siegler, 1990; Siegler & Crowley, 1991; Siegler & Jenkins, 1989).

Parental Reports

There has been a resurgence of interest in the value of parental self-report strategies. These methods assume various forms, including parental interviews and questionnaires, parental diaries, and playback techniques (i.e., presenting videotapes of parents' behavior to them to obtain their responses) (Maccoby & Martin, 1983; Zahn-Waxler, Radke-Yarrow, Wagners, & Chapman, 1993), as well as new approaches to parental attitudes and beliefs (Goodnow, 1988; Goodnow and Collins, 1991).

Under the weight of considerable criticism concerning the limitations of self-report strategies, especially retrospective accounts, these approaches were relatively unfashionable during the past two decades (see Robbins, 1963). In spite of these criticisms, there are clear advantages to the techniques, and many issues of current interest (e.g., the nature and extensiveness of and satisfaction with infant's social networks) cannot be investigated without recourse to such procedures.

As Maccoby and Martin (1983) wrote:

> Using parents as informants has great potential advantages. For assessment of behavior that varies considerably across situations or behavior that is usually not displayed in public, reliable observational data are difficult to obtain and parent interviews are often the only viable alternative. Parents have an opportunity to observe their children and the patterns of interaction in their families over extended periods of time in a broad range of situations. Thus by virtue of their daily participation in the family system, parents have access to a truly unique body of information about the family, and it is reasonable to tap into this information by questioning them. (p. 16)

A number of significant changes have occurred since the 1960 era that have blunted many of the earlier criticisms. Parent reports are now used primarily for obtaining concurrent, not retrospective, information about family interaction (Maccoby & Martin, 1983). Instead of asking parents to make trait attributions such as "dependent" or "difficult," many researchers ask parents to provide detailed descriptions of specific behaviors, which are presumably less open to subjective interpretation and bias and, therefore, yield more reliable as well as valid ratings. Researchers (Zahn-Waxler et al., 1993) have trained mothers to act as observers of their own and their children's behavior, which has led to advances in our understanding of behavior in naturalistic settings and to avoiding distortions in behavior which may accompany the presence of unfamiliar observers.

Another major advance that has occurred, in part because of renewed attention to the value of self-report data, is the recognition of the importance of parental belief systems in understanding parent–child development (Goodnow, 1984; Goodnow & Collins, 1991; Parke, 1978; Parke & Tinsley, 1987; Sigel, 1985). Parental beliefs are another characteristic of the child's caregiving environment, and many researchers have articulated and demonstrated empirical and theoretical relationships among parent beliefs, parent behavior, and child development. Various studies have confirmed that parent beliefs can affect child rearing, socialization, the quality of the "home as a learning environment" (J. E. Johnson & Martin, 1983; Skinner, 1985), and, subsequently, child language and cognitive and social development (Dix & Grusec, 1985; S. A. Miller, 1988).

Parents have complex sets of belief systems concerning child development (Goodnow & Collins, 1991; McGillicuddy-DeLisi, 1982), and these beliefs appear to guide parents' behavior with regard to their children. Earlier, Parke (1978) suggested that parents' reports of their own behavior did not always match investigators' observations of parent behavior and that parents' reports and observational data were two independent sources of data. According to this view, both are necessary to understand the antecedents and consequences of parenting behavior. Recently, researchers have begun to look to parent beliefs and attitudes "as 'the missing link' in their accounts of parent–infant relationships" (Goodnow, 1984, p. 193).

In summary, self-report strategies are being used more widely, and recent innovations are making these approaches more effective than in earlier eras.

Observational Strategies

The use of observational methods as an approach to gathering data about infant social behavior has been a growth industry (Bakeman & Gottman, 1986; Sackett, 1979); closely linked with this shift has been an increase in the choice of naturalistic contexts for observation of behavior, a shift noted in the preceding section. Moreover, the sophistication of observational methodologies has increased sharply in the past decade. In part, this change has resulted from advances in technology that permit the collection of sequentially ordered data, as well as advances in portable videotape equipment that provides high-fidelity recording in field settings. In addition, advances in both video and computer technology have permitted the analysis of behavior at a microanalytic level. This last kind of advance is clearly evident in work on the development of facial expressions (Ekman & Friesen, 1978; Izard & Malatesta, 1987).

Data-coding strategies have shifted as well. The analysis of frequency counts of parent and infant behavior and the use of time sampling techniques have decreased. Part of the reason for the decline in the use of these approaches is that the data collected in this fashion are *not* truly interactive, because they permit no statements concerning the manner in which the infant and parent activities are coordinated. Instead, to provide more accurate representation of social interactive processes as dynamic and reciprocal, investigators are increasingly using approaches that capture the sequential and time-dependent order of interaction between partners. This approach is increasingly feasible because of the availability of statistical techniques, such as sequential analyses (Bakeman & Gottman, 1987; Sackett, 1987) and time series analysis (Cohn & Tronick, 1987; Gottman, 1981; Lester, Hoffman, & Brazelton, 1985).

Another noteworthy trend reflects in part the openness of researchers to multimethod strategies, as opposed to strict adherence to one approach. The use of global ratings is increasingly common and, in some cases, serves as a protective net against failure to detect interesting patterns that may not appear at the microanalytic level. The usefulness of macro- and microlevels of analysis for different questions is being recognized (Cairns & Green, 1979). Evidence, not just speculation, may be driving the field to this new openness to a wide range of methods. Some researchers have found that ratings of parental behavior yield better prediction of later social behavior (Bakeman & Brown, 1980) and later cognitive assessments (Jay & Farran, 1981) than more microanalytic and more expensive measures of parent–child interaction.

Further delineation of the types of questions for which various levels of observational analyses are most useful would constitute a major methodological contribution. In the final analysis, the basis for selecting a data collection strategy and for choosing a level of analysis should be the nature of the problem, the status of theory in the area, and the stage of development of the research program. In the early stages of an investigation or in a theoretically underdeveloped area, a time-sampling strategy may be most appropriate. After preliminary work has been completed, selection of a more detailed and sophisticated but more expensive sequential analytic strategy may be appropriate (Power & Parke, 1982). Clearly, simply moving to a more molecular or more abstract level of analysis should not be the goal; rather, comparative analysis of the usefulness of different strategies for specific problems needs to be done carefully before any particular level or type of analysis is preferentially advocated.

Other types of analytic strategies are changing the type of research that is being executed in the 1990s. In part to capture the commitment to multimeasure research projects, the use of structural-modeling and path-modeling approaches has increased (see Connell, 1987, for a review). Similarly, logit analyses are increasingly common (Bakeman, Adamson, & Strisik, 1988; Green, 1988) in developmental psychology in general.

Level of Analysis

In each era, the choice of level of analysis reflects the types of constructs that are preferred. At some points in time, researchers prefer molar constructs and, at other points, molecular constructs. The 1960s was a period in which a molecular level of analysis was in vogue. Small units of behavior that could be easily observed and measured were preferred. Reliance on molecular analysis is consistent with the mechanistic view that was dominant in the period.

In contrast, the 1990s can be characterized by endorsement of both molecular and molar constructs. Although the data collection strategies have shifted, a significant commitment to molecular analysis of discrete responses has remained (e.g., vocalizations, changes in facial muscles, direction of gaze), especially in research on social interaction (e.g., Field, 1982; Osofsky, 1979, 1987; Parke, 1979b). At the same time, there is an influential move to work with more molar constructs, such as attachment (Park & Waters, 1988; Sroufe & Fleeson, 1986; Sroufe & Waters, 1977) and relationships and traits (Hartup & Rubin, 1986). Similarly, in the study of emotions, both molecular and molar levels of analysis are evident (Izard & Malatesta, 1987). Again, the issue is specification of the linkage among these various levels of conceptualization (see Hinde, 1979; chapter 22, this volume; Sroufe & Waters, 1977, for more on this issue).

Selection of Samples

An important change has taken place in the choice of samples. Both at the turn of the century and in the 1960s, highly selected samples of unknown representativeness were considered satisfactory. In part, this was due to a focus on the search for experimentally derived, process-oriented laws of development, as well as to reliance on experimental designs involving random assignment of child subjects to experimental conditions. It was largely assumed that preexisting individual differences were "error variance." A variety of conditions have conspired to increase awareness of the limitations of samples, including awareness of cultural and historical diversity, as well as the increasing interest in testing multivariate models of development.

These shifts in awareness regarding sampling issues have led to an increase in interest in large representative national samples. Although this has typically been the domain of sociologists and survey researchers, in the early 1990s, developmentalists have shown an increased awareness of the potential value of supplementing their usual small-sample strategies with these large-sample approaches. The most prominent example is the rise in the use of the National Longitudinal Study of Youth (NLSY) for the examination of developmental issues, including divorce, achievement, and day care (Brooks-Gunn, Phelps, & Elder, 1991). These surveys have several advantages, including a large number of subjects, more representative samples, a multifaceted range of variables, and the longitudinal nature of the design. In turn, these characteristics permit testing of more complex models of development that require large numbers of subjects. In addition, these studies allow the examination of connections across content-based domains, as well as encourage and permit interdisciplinary cooperation. Finally, they permit testing of the cultural generality of the models.

It should be underscored that these approaches are not free of methodological limitations. Often the measures are limited to only a few items that must be relied on to operationalize the construct of interest. Moreover, the impact of repeated testing may present problems. In addition, the reliance on easily administered tests, which are often based on self-reports, may limit the value of the approaches. However, recent waves of the NLSY have included cognitive and social measures that are based on observed performance rather than on self-reports. In any case, the increased use of these large-scale data bases was a new and emerging trend in the 1980s and will likely continue in the present decade.

Newer, more innovative approaches that combine levels of sampling are becoming increasingly common as well. As a supplement to a large-scale survey approach, researchers are selecting a subsample of subjects for more intensive examination of a particular process of interest. For example, Bietel and Parke (1990) conducted a survey of 300 families to assess maternal attitudes toward father involvement in infant care. To supplement this approach, in which a self-report questionnaire was used, a subsample of 40 families was observed in their homes as a way of validating the self-report data. Similarly, Hetherington, Reiss, and Plomin (1994) generated a nationally representative sample of stepfamilies, and in a second stage of their work, they observed these families in interaction tasks in the home. These combined approaches increase both the generalizability of findings and, at the same time, allow us to illuminate basic social processes.

Future Challenges

Several issues are foreshadowed by our review of the history of the field, and other issues are salient today in spite of their lack of historical precedence. Some important directions for the future are discussed in the following sections.

Toward a Developmental, not Just a Child, Psychology

One of the continuing concerns that our discipline faces is how to conceptualize developmental shifts. We have already discussed the concept of stages and the limited support for this concept. However, we still need better theories about the developmental points that are likely to be most productive for us to examine. Two sources of guidance may be helpful in the future. Periods of neurological organization that can be usefully described may be helpful. For example, the 3-month shift in synaptic growth is one point of entry that may prove useful. Also, Diamond's (1992) work on the development of object permanence and delayed response tasks in monkeys suggested that the maturation of the frontal lobe plays a central role in monkeys' ability to perform these tasks. Her work suggests that human infants' abilities may be based on similar underlying frontal lobe processes. Her predictions of the timing of these accomplishments for monkeys and humans implies that cognitive–developmental neuroscience may be useful for understanding the possible neural mechanisms and that maturational changes in neural development can serve as a useful guide for pinpointing likely points of interesting developmental change.

Recent work on changes in hormonal levels during adolescence and the accompanying shifts in social and cognitive functioning (Paikoff & Brooks-Gunn, 1991) represents another promising avenue for exploring the relationships between biological change and developmental functioning. These biologically based processes are probably universal and fundamentally similar across individuals in all cultures (Liben, 1987) and could appropriately be described as "developmental" acquisitions (Siegler, 1991). In developmental neuroscience terms, Greenough et al. (1987) labeled these as experience-expectant processes.

In the enthusiasm to discover universals of development, however, developmental researchers often overlook the fact that development is contextually and culturally embedded. As a result, children do not all encounter the same set of events at the same time or in the same sequence. According to this perspective, it is not the maturationally based changes alone, but also the culturally controlled social agenda that determines the timing of the child's entry into various social settings, such as the transition to elementary school or junior high school, that will shape the child's development. For example, the impact of the school experience on memory and cognitive development was demonstrated by Morrison's (1991) exploration of the performance of children who are nearly matched for age, but whose birth dates fall on either side of the cutoff date for school entry.

In addition, a series of nonnormative as well as normative transitions shapes children's developmental trajectories. Much has been learned about development, especially about coping and adaptation capacities, by focusing on development during transitions in children's lives. The kinds of change that occur during these individually based experiences is probably akin to Greenough et al.'s (1987) experience-dependent processes. One other issue about transitions needs to be noted, namely, the need to focus on adult as well as on child transitions. One need not be a committed life-span theorist to recognize that it is critical to understand how adults change across development, in terms of their biologically based shifts or the normative and nonnormative transitions that they undergo. Increasingly, to understand children's development, it is important to understand the course of adult lives. More work is needed on the intersection of developmental changes in children and adults. Development, in fact, may be viewed best as a set of multiple developmental trajectories, and our task as developmentalists is to discover how the interplay between different trajectories of children and adults accounts for outcomes (Parke, 1988).

Finally, it is clear that the perspectives of biological and culturally determined transitions are not independent. In fact, advances in the field are likely to come by recognition of the interplay between these two domains. Cowan (1991) has suggested that biological reorganization can cause major life shifts—a standard view. In addition, stressful life transitions can produce changes in hormonal and immune system functions; in this case, biological shifts are the consequence of transitions. Alternatively, "biological functions participate in interactive systems that amplify or reduce the impact of environmental, psychological or behavioral events. . . . Both temporary and long-lasting biological characteristics of the organism are involved in determining the timing, duration and adaptational outcomes of each life transition" (Cowan, 1991, p. 23).

Also, a better theory of tasks is needed. As noted earlier, a vocabulary for describing tasks in terms of dimensions would be helpful in cross-investigation comparisons and would permit us to organize the developmental changes better.

Toward a Better Theory of Contexts

One of the most pressing issues that our field faces is the development of a better theory of contexts, although this is a rather difficult task because the term "context" is used in many ways by developmentalists. At the core, however, there appear to be two different senses of context, one dealing with the origins of the skills or abilities under consideration and the other with the characterization and diagnosis of those skills (see Morrison & Ornstein, in press). Thus, at one level, it is essential to consider the impact of the multiple contexts in which development occurs, such as the family and the school, and how these settings influence the development of the child. At another level, it is important to recognize that children's behavior and cognition vary to a considerable extent from context to context. A consequence of this context specificity is that the assessment or "diagnosis" of a child's abilities is dependent on the setting in which the observation is made; indeed, minor contextual changes may result in quite different impressions of skill (Ornstein et al., 1988).

Over the years, the development context has been explored from various perspectives. Barker's (1968) ecological psychology and Bronfen-brenner's (1979, 1989) social systems perspective represent two significant ways of studying the settings in which development occurs. Other approaches to this central developmental question are evident in comparative–cultural studies (Cole, Gay, Glick, & Sharp, 1971; Rogoff, 1991) and in parent–child interaction (e.g., Rogoff, 1991; Rogoff & Gardner, 1984) and microgenetic (e.g., Siegler & Crowley, 1991) studies that have been inspired by Vygotsky's (1978) consideration of the zone of proximal development. However, we are hampered by the lack of a commonly used set of dimensions that would allow us to characterize contexts along similar lines. Hinde's (1979, 1987) dimensions for characterizing relationships appear to hold promise as a way of specifying settings in terms of the kinds of relationships that exist within different contexts. These dimensions include content, diversity, quality, relative frequency and patterning of interactions, the direction of the relationship, the degree of commitment, the degree of intimacy, the mutual understanding of the relationship, and the structural properties (size and density). While this is not an exhaustive taxonomy, it is a useful starting point.

In contrast with the many explorations of the contexts in which development takes place, little attention has been directed to the assessment context. Although it is clearly recognized that children's behavior varies across settings, the implications of this variability for characterizing children's abilities and propensities have not typically been explored. Moreover, the minute variations in setting that can yield different estimates of a child's cognitive skills are not always appreciated. For example, even slight changes in the materials to be remembered and the conditions of presentation can mean the difference between children being judged as "strategic" or not in their approaches to a memory task (Ornstein et al., 1988). These contextual variations imply that adequate assessment of children's skills requires multiple measurement in contrasting settings and summarization in the form of profiles of performance (Folds et al., 1990). This view of cognitive diagnosis jibes nicely with emerging efforts to explore the zone of proximal development (e.g., A. L. Brown & Reeve, 1987) by measuring children's performance under conditions of task support.

Several other issues need attention, such as the need to expand the range of contexts. To date, researchers in our field have paid a disproportionate amount of attention to the family context, while paying less attention to other settings. At the same time, we know vastly more about peer contexts, schools, and day-care centers today than we did 1 century ago. Yet, we still are only beginning to understand work contexts. As Crouter

(1994) noted, "we will only fully understand work and family in settings when we pay equal attention to what is going on at work" (p. 22). Moreover, we need to return to the lessons of 100 years ago and address more attention to religious institutions as developmental contexts. In fact, a psychology and sociology of religion are emerging, and developmentalists have not played a major role in describing the influence of religion on or the links between religious and other significant contexts in children's lives.

Other issues include the bidirectional influence across settings. To date, most of our research has focused on family influence on children's adaptation to other settings. Less is known about the impact of extrafamilial contexts on family functioning than vice versa. Recent work on job loss, work stress, and school experience is beginning to correct this imbalance by showing clearly that experience of family members in outside contexts, in turn, can alter the nature of family functioning.

Better articulation is needed of the processes by which settings are linked. Several possibilities have been offered, including working models by attachment theorists and emotional regulatory processes, as well as family managerial processes. At this point, there is no consensus concerning the processes that are central and that can adequately account for transfer of behaviors across contexts.

CONCLUSION

One final issue needs to be addressed. There has been a proliferation of minitheories, rather than a single dominant position or theoretical framework, and each of these smaller scale theories accounts for only a limited set of issues. This domain-specific nature of theory is one of the hallmarks of our current period. The prevalence of minitheories represents a reaction to disenchantment with grand theories (e.g., of Freud, Hull-Spence, Piaget), both of a century ago and of our more recent past. Part of the reason for the current proliferation of smaller and more modest paradigms is the failure of a new overarching paradigm to emerge to replace the disfavored grand theories.

The next stage of our development as a field involves the creation of such a new overarching paradigm to help us continue these integrative efforts. There are signs that a new integration may be emerging in the form of a systems perspective that will bring together biological, social, cognitive, and emotional minitheories into a more coherent framework (Fogel & Thelen, 1987; Sameroff, 1983). Although the promise of a general dynamic systems theory is appealing and has been applied with considerable success to the motor development domain, especially by Thelen (1989), it remains to be seen whether the stringent requirements of this approach for precise parameter estimation and measurement can be met in other domains (Aslin,

1993). Whether we have reached the stage of being able to quantify social behavior or children's theories of mind with sufficient precision to make this approach useful, beyond being merely metaphoric, is an open question.

We are cautiously optimistic that a systems approach is a promising one and has proven useful both in organizing data and in pointing to new research directions in recent family research, as well as research on the organization and functioning of social contexts. Perhaps we need to develop a family of systems-theory level integrations that would be hierarchically organized and would represent the levels of analysis that are intrinsic to different areas of development, just as we have long recognized that biological, biochemical, and social levels of inquiry may each have their own set of integrative principles (Sameroff, 1983, 1987). Multiple integrative approaches may be needed to cover sections of the developmental terrain. The goal is to retain the advances that our retreat to minitheories has brought but, at the same time, to begin to put the "whole child" back together again. Our forebears had the vision to see this as the goal, and we may be in a better position to achieve it now than 1 century ago.

REFERENCES

Ainsworth, M. D. S. (1973). The development of infant–mother attachment. In B. Caldwell & H. Ricciuti (Eds.), *Review of child development research* (Vol. 3, pp. 1–94). Chicago: University of Chicago Press.

Ainsworth, M. D. S., Bell, S. M., & Stayton, D. J. (1972). Individual differences in the development of some attachment behaviors. *Merrill-Palmer Quarterly, 18*, 123–143.

Ainsworth, M. D. S., Blehar, M. C., Waters, E., & Wall, S. (1978). *Patterns of attachment.* Hillsdale, NJ: Erlbaum.

Asher, S. R., & Coie, J. (1990). *Peer rejection in childhood.* Cambridge, England: Cambridge University Press.

Aslin, R. N. (1993). The strange attractiveness of dynamic systems theory to development. In L. B. Smith & E. Thelen (Eds.), *A dynamic systems approach to development* (pp. 385–399). Cambridge, MA: MIT Press.

Baillargeon, R. (1993). The object concept revisted: New directions. In C. E. Granrud (Ed.), *Visual perception and cognition in infancy: Carnegie-Mellon Symposium on Cognition* (Vol. 23, pp. 265–314). Hillsdale, NJ: Erlbaum.

Bakeman, R., Adamson, L. B., & Strisik, P. (1988). Lags and logs: Statistical approaches to interaction. In M. H. Bornstein & J. Bruner (Eds.), *Interaction in human development* (pp. 241–260). Hillsdale, NJ: Erlbaum.

Bakeman, R., & Brown, J. V. (1980). Early interaction: Consequences for social and mental development at three years. *Child Development, 51*, 437–447.

Bakeman, R., & Gottman, J. M. (1986). *Observing interaction: An introduction to sequential analyses.* Cambridge, England: Cambridge University Press.

Bakeman, R., & Gottman, J. M. (1987). Applying observational methods: A systematic view. In J. D. Osofsky (Ed.), *Handbook of infant development* (2nd ed., pp. 818–854). New York: Wiley.

Baldwin, J. M. (1895). *Mental development in the child and the rare methods of processes.* New York: Macmillan.

Baldwin, J. M. (1897). *Social and ethical interpretations of mental development: A study in social psychology.* New York: Macmillan.

Baldwin, A. (1967). *Theories of child development.* New York: Wiley.

Baltes, P. B. (1987). Theoretical propositions of life span developmental psychology: On the dynamics of growth and decline. *Developmental Psychology, 23,* 611–626.

Bandura, A., & Walters, R. H. (1963). *Social learning & personality development.* New York: Holt, Rinehart & Winston.

Banks, M. S., Aslin, R. N., & Leston, R. D. (1975). Sensitive period for the development of human binocular vision. *Science, 190,* 675–677.

Banks, M. S., & Salapatek, P. (1983). Infant visual perception. In P. H. Mussen (Ed.), *Handbook of child psychology* (Vol. 2, pp. 435–572). New York: Wiley.

Barker, R. G. (1968). *Ecological psychology: Concepts and methods for studying the environment of human behavior.* Stanford, CA: Stanford University Press.

Bates, J. E. (1987). Temperament in infancy. In J. Osofsky (Ed.), *Handbook of infancy* (2nd ed., pp. 1101–1149). New York: Wiley.

Baumrind, D. (1973). The development of instrumental competence through socialization. In A. D. Pick (Ed.), *Minnesota Symposia on Child Psychology* (Vol. 7, pp. 3–46). Minneapolis: University of Minnesota Press.

Bell, R. Q. (1968). A reinterpretation of the direction of effects in studies of socialization. *Psychological Review, 75,* 81–95.

Belsky, J. (1984). The determinants of parenting: A process model. *Child Development, 55,* 83–96.

Belsky, J. (1986). Infant day care: A cause for concern? *Zero to Three, 6,* 1–9.

Belsky, J., & Rovine, M. J. (1988). Nonmaternal care in the first year of life and the security of infant–parent attachment. *Child Development, 67,* 157–167.

Belsky, J., Rovine, M., & Fish, M. (1989). The developing family system. In M. Gunnar (Ed.), *Minnesota Symposium in Child Psychology* (Vol. 22, pp. 119–166). Hillsdale, NJ: Erlbaum.

Belsky, J., Steinberg, L., & Draper, P. (1991). Childhood experience, interpersonal development and reproductive strategy: An evolutionary theory of socialization. *Child Development, 62,* 647–670.

Belsky, J., Steinberg, L., & Walker, A. (1982). The ecology of day care. In M. E. Lamb (Ed.), *Nontraditional families* (pp. 71–116). Hillsdale, NJ: Erlbaum.

Bertenthal, B., & Campos, J. J. (1990). A systems approach to the organizing effects of self-produced locomotion during infancy. In C. Rovee-Collier &

L. P. Lipsitt (Eds.), *Advances in infancy research* (Vol. 6, pp. 1–60). Norwood, NJ: Ablex.

Bietel, A., & Parke, R. D. (1990). *Maternal attitudes as determinants of paternal–infant involvement.* Unpublished paper, University of Illinois.

Bijou, S. W., & Baer, D. M. (1961). *Child development: A systematic and empirical theory* (Vol. 1). New York: Appleton-Century-Crofts.

Bijou, S. W., & Baer, D. (1964). Some methodological contributions from a functional analysis of child development. In L. P. Lipsitt & C. C. Spiker (Eds.), *Advances in child development and behavior.* New York: Academic Press.

Binet, A. (1900). *La suggestibilité* [The power of suggestion]. Paris: Schleicher Frères.

Binet, A., & Henri, V. (1894). La mémoire des phrases [The memory of prose]. *L'Année Psychologique, 1,* 24–59.

Blakemore, C. (1976). The conditions required for the maintenance of binocularity in the kitten's visual cortex. *Journal of Physiology, 261,* 423–444.

Bornstein, M. H. (1989). Sensitive periods in development: Structural characteristics and causal interpretations. *Psychologcial Bulletin, 105,* 179–197.

Bottoms, S. F., Rosen, M. G., & Sokol, R. J. (1980). The increase in the cesarean birth rate. *New England Journal of Medicine, 302,* 559–563.

Bowlby, J. (1951). *Maternal care and mental health.* Geneva, Switzerland: World Health Organization, (WHO Monograph Serial No. 2).

Bowlby, J. (1958). The nature of the child's tie to his mother. *International Journal of Psycho-Analysis, 39,* 350–373.

Bowlby, J. (1969). *Attachment and loss: Vol. 1. Attachment.* London: Hogarth Press.

Bowlby, J. (1973). *Attachment and loss: Vol. 2. Separation.* London: Hogarth Press.

Bowlby, J. (1980). *Attachment and loss: Vol. 3. Loss.* London: Hogarth Press.

Brackbill, Y. (1958). Extinction of the smiling response in infants as a function of reinforcement schedules. *Child Development, 29,* 115–124.

Brackbill, Y. (1979). Obstetrical medication and infant behavior. In J. D. Osofsky (Ed.), *Handbook of infant development* (pp. 76–125). New York: Wiley.

Brainerd, C. J. (1978). The stage question in cognitive developmental theory. *Behavioral and Brain Sciences, 1,* 173–213.

Brazelton, T. B., Koslowski, B., & Main, M. (1974). The origins of reciprocity: Early mother–infant interaction. In M. Lewis & L. A. Rosenblum (Eds.), *The effect of the infant on its caregiver* (pp. 49–76). New York: Wiley.

Bretherton, I., & Waters, E. (Eds.). (1985). Growing points in attachment theory and research. *Monographs of the Society for Research in Child Development, 50* (1–2).

Bronfenbrenner, U. (1979). *The ecology of human development.* Cambridge, MA: Harvard University Press.

Bronfenbrenner, U. (1986). Ecolology of the family as a context for human development: Research perspectives. *Developmental Psychology, 22,* 723–742.

Bronfenbrenner, U. (1989). Ecological systems theory. In R. Vasta (Ed.), *Six theories of child development* (pp. 187–249). Greenwich, CT: JAI Press.

Brooks-Gunn, J., Phelps, E., & Elder, G. (1991). Studying lives through time: Secondary data analysis in developmental psychology. *Developmental Psychology, 27,* 899–910.

Brown, A. L., & Campione, J. C. (1990). Communities of learning and thinking, or a context by any other name. In D. Kuhn (Ed.), *Developmental perspectives on teaching and learning thinking skills* (pp. 108–126). Basel, Switzerland: Karger.

Brown, A. L., & Reeve, R. A. (1987). Bandwidths of competence: The role of supportive contexts in learning and development. In L. S. Liben (Ed.), *Development and learning: Conflict or congruence?* (pp. 173–223). Hillsdale, NJ: Erlbaum.

Brown, R. (1973). *A first language: The early stages.* Cambridge, MA: Harvard University Press.

Brubaker, T. (Ed.). (1990). *Family relationships in later life.* Newbury Park, CA: Sage.

Bruner, J. (1968). *Processes of cognitive growth: Infancy.* Worcester, MA: Clark University Press.

Bruner, J. (1970). The growth and structure of skill. In K. Connolly (Ed.), *Mechanisms of motor skill development.* New York: Academic Press.

Bruner, J. (1983). *Children's talk.* New York: Norton.

Bryant, P. E., & Trabasso, T. (1971). Transitive inferences and memory in young children. *Nature, 232,* 457–459.

Buss, D. M. (1989). Conflict between the sexes: Strategic interference and evocation of anger and upset. *Journal of Personality and Social Psychology, 56,* 735–747.

Buss, D. M., Larsen, R. J., Westen, D., & Semmelroth, J. (1992). Sex differences in jealousy: Evolution, physiology and psychology. *Psychological Science, 3,* 251–255.

Cahan, E. D. (1984). The genetic psychologies of James Mark Baldwin and Jean Piaget. *Developmental Psychology, 20,* 128–135.

Cairns, R. B. (1983). The emergence of developmental psychology. In P. H. Mussen (Ed.), *Handbook of child psychology* (Vol. 1, 4th ed., pp. 41–102). New York: Wiley.

Cairns, R. B., & Green, J. A. (1979). How to assess personality and social patterns: Observations or ratings? In R. B. Cairns (Ed.), *The analysis of social interactions: methods, issues, and illustrations* (pp. 209–226). Hillsdale, NJ: Erlbaum.

Cairns, R. B., & Ornstein, P. A. (1979). Developmental psychology. In E. Hearst (Ed.), *The first century of experimental psychology* (pp. 459–510). Hillsdale, NJ: Erlbaum.

Campos, J. J., Barrett, K. C., Lamb, M. E., Goldsmith, H. H., & Stenberg, C. (1983). Socio-emotional development. In M. M. Haith & J. J. Campos (Eds.),

Handbook of child psychology: Vol. 2. Infancy and developmental psychobiology (pp. 783–916). New York: Wiley.

Campos, J. J., Campos, R. G., Barrett, K. (1989). Emergent themes in the study of emotional development and emotion regulation. *Developmental Psychology, 25*, 394–402.

Campos, J. J., & Stenberg, C. R. (1981). Perception, appraisal and emotion: The onset of social referencing. In M. E. Lamb & L. R. Sherrod (Eds.), *Infant social cognition: Empirical and theoretical considerations* (pp. 273–314). Hillsdale, NJ: Erlbaum.

Carlson, A. J. (1902). Changes in Nissl's substance of the ganglion and the bipolar cells of the retinal of the brandt cormorant phalacrocorax pencillaturs during prolonged normal stimulation. *American Journal of Anatomy, 2*, 341–347.

Case, R. (1984). The process of stage transition: A neo-Piagetian view. In R. J. Sternberg (Ed.), *Mechanisms of cognitive development* (pp. 19–44). San Francisco: W. H. Freeman.

Case, R. (1985). *Intellectual development: A systematic reinterpretation.* New York: Academic Press.

Case, R. (1987). Neo-Piagetian theory: Retrospect and prospect. *International Journal of Psychology, 22*, 773–791.

Charlesworth, W. R. (1987). Resources and resource allocation during ontogeny. In K. B. MacDonald (Ed.), *Sociobiological perspectives on human development* (pp. 24–77). New York: Springer-Verlag.

Chomsky, N. (1957). *Syntactic structures.* The Hague: Mouton.

Clarke, A. M., & Clarke, A. D. B. (1976). *Early experience: Myth & evidence.* London: Open Books.

Clarke-Stewart, K. A. (1989). Infant day care: Maligned or malignant? *American Psychologist, 44*, 266–273.

Clarke-Stewart, K. A., & Hevey, C. M. (1981). Longitudinal relations in repeated observations of mother–child interactions from 1 to 2½ years. *Developmental Psychology, 17*, 127–145.

Cochran, M. M., & Brassard, J. A. (1979). Child development and personal social networks. *Child Development, 50*, 601–616.

Cohen, L., & Salapatek, P. (1975). *Infant perception: From sensation to cognition: Vol. 1.* New York: Academic Press.

Cohn, J. F., & Tronick, E. Z. (1987). Mother–infant face-to-face interaction: The sequence of dyadic states at 3, 6, and 9 months. *Developmental Psychology, 23*, 68–77.

Cole, M., Gay, J., Glick, J. A., & Sharp, D. W. (1971). *The cultural context of learning and thinking.* New York: Basic Books.

Cole, M., Hood, L., & McDermott, R. P. (1978). Concepts of ecological validity: Their differing implications for comparative cognitive research. *Quarterly Newsletter of the Institute of Comparative Human Development, 2*, 34–37.

Collins, W. A. (Ed.). (1984). *Development during middle childhood.* Washington, DC: National Academy Press.

Connell, J. (1987). Structural equation modeling and the study of child development: A question of goodness of fit. *Child Development, 58,* 167–175.

Cowan, P. A. (1991). Individual and family life transitions: A proposal for a new definition. In P. A. Cowan & E. M. Hetherington (Eds.), *Family transitions* (pp. 3–30). Hillsdale, NJ: Erlbaum.

Cowan, C. P., Cowan, P. A., Heming, G., Garrett, E. V., Coysh, W. S., Curtis-Boles, H., & Boles, A. J. (1985). Transitions to parenthood: His, hers and theirs. *Journal of Family Issues, 6,* 451–481.

Crockenberg, S. B. (1981). Infant irritability, mother responsiveness, and social support influences on the security of infant–mother attachment. *Child Development, 52,* 857–865.

Crouter, A. (1994). Processes linking family and work: Implications for behavior and development in both setings. In R. D. Parke & S. Kellam (Eds.), *Exploring family relationships with other social contexts* (pp. 9–28). Hillsdale, NJ: Erlbaum.

Darwin, C. (1859). *The origin of species by means of natural selection.* London: John Murray.

Darwin, C. (1872). *The expression of emotions in man and animals.* London: John Murray.

De Beer, G. (1940). *Embryos and ancestors.* Oxford, England: Clarendon Press.

Diamond, A. (1990). Rate of maturation of the hippocampus and the developmental progression of children's performance on the delayed non-matching to sample and visual paired comparison tasks. *Annals of the New York Academy of Sciences, 608,* 394–426.

Diamond, A. (1992). Frontal lobe involvement in cognitive changes during the first year of life. In K. Gibson, M. Konner, & A. Petersen (Eds.), *Brain and behavioral development.* New York: Aldine.

Dickstein, S., & Parke, R. D. (1988). Social referencing: A glance at fathers and marriage. *Child Development, 59,* 506–511.

Dix, T. H., & Grusec, J. E. (1985). Parent attribution processes in the socialization of children. In I. Sigel (Ed.), *Parental belief systems: The psychological consequences for children* (pp. 201–233). Hillsdale, NJ: Erlbaum.

Dodge, K. A. (1986). A social information processing model of social competence in children. In M. Perlmutter (Ed.), *Minnesota Symposia on Child Psychology* (Vol. 18, pp. 77–126). Hillsdale, NJ: Erlbaum.

Donaldson, M. (1978). *Children's minds.* New York: W. W. Norton.

Dunn, J. (1988). *The beginnings of social understanding.* Cambridge, MA: Harvard University Press.

Dunn, J., & Kendrick, C. (1982). *Siblings: Love, envy and understanding.* Cambridge, MA: Harvard University Press.

Easterbrooks, M. A., & Goldberg, W. A. (1984). Toddler development in the family: Impact of father involvement and parenting characteristics. *Child Development, 55,* 740–752.

Eisenberg, N. (1992). *The caring child.* Cambridge, MA: Harvard University Press.

Ekman, P. (Ed.). (1974). *Darwin and facial expressions: A century on review*. San Diego: Academic Press.

Ekman, P. (1992). Facial expressions of emotion: New findings, new questions. *Psychological Science, 3,* 34–38.

Ekman, P., & Friesen, W. (1978). *Facial action coding system*. Palo Alto, CA: Consulting Psychological Press.

Elder, G. H. (1984). Families, kin and the life course: A sociological perspective. In R. D. Parke, R. N. Emde, H. P. McAdoo, & G. P. Sackett (Eds.), *Review of child development research: The family* (Vol. 7, pp. 80–136). Chicago: University of Chicago Press.

Elder, G. H., Modell, J., & Parke, R. D. (1993). *Children in time and place*. Cambridge, England: Cambridge University Press.

Elder, G. H., & Rockwell, R. (1979). The life course and human development: An ecological perspective. *International Journal of Behavioral Development, 2,* 1–21.

Elicker, J., Englund, M., & Sroufe, L. A. (1992). Predicting peer competence and peer relationships in childhood from early parent–child relationships. In R. D. Parke & G. W. Ladd (Eds.), *Family–peer relationships: Modes of linkage* (pp. 77–106). Hillsdale, NJ: Erlbaum.

Ericsson, K. A., & Simon, H. A. (1980). Verbal reports as data. *Psychological Review, 87,* 215–251.

Etzel, B. C., & Gewirtz, J. L. (1967). Experimental modification of caretaker-maintained high rate operant crying in a 6- and a 20-week-old infant: Extinction of crying with reinforcement of eye contact and smiling. *Journal of Experimental Child Psychology, 5,* 303–317.

Fantz, R. (1961). The origin of form perception. *Scientific American, 204,* 66–72.

Fantz, R. (1963). Pattern vision in newborn infants. *Science, 140,* 296–297.

Feinman, S., & Lewis, M. (1981, April). *Social referencing and second-order effects in 10-month-old infants*. Paper presented at the meeting of the Society of Research in Child Development, Boston.

Field, T. M. (1982). Affective displays of high-risk infants during early interactions. In T. Field & A. Fogel (Eds.), *Emotion and early interaction* (pp. 101–126). Hillsdale, NJ: Erlbaum.

Field, T. M. (1987). Affective and interactive disturbances in infants. In J. D. Osofsky (Ed.), *Handbook of infant development* (2nd ed., pp. 972–1005). New York: Wiley.

Field, T. (1991). *Infancy*. Cambridge, MA: Harvard University Press.

Field, T. M., Sostek, A. M., Vietze, P., & Leiderman, P. H. (Eds.). (1981). *Culture and social interactions*. Hillsdale, NJ: Erlbaum.

Fischer, K., & Bidell, T. R. (1991). In S. Carey & R. Gelman (Eds.), *The epigenesis of mind: Essays on biology and cognition*. Hillsdale, NJ: Erlbaum.

Fischer, K., & Farrar, M. J. (1987). Generalizations about generalization: How a theory of skill development explains both generality and specificity. *International Journal of Psychology, 22,* 643–677.

Fischer, K. W., & Pipp, S. L. (1984). Processes of cognitive development: Optimal level and skill acquisition. In R. J. Sternberg (Ed.), *Mechanisms of cognitive development* (pp. 45–80). San Francisco: W. H. Freeman.

Fivush, R., & Hammond, N. R. (1990). Autobiographical memory across the preschool years: Toward reconceptualizing childhood amnesia. In R. Fivush & J. A. Hudson (Eds.), *Knowing and remembering in young children* (pp. 223–248). Cambridge, England: Cambridge University Press.

Flavell, J. (1963). *The developmental psychology of Jean Piaget.* New York: Van Nostrand.

Flavell, J. H. (1971). Stage-related properties of cognitive development. *Cognitive Psychology, 2,* 421–453.

Flavell, J. (1982). Structures, stages and sequences in cognitive development. In W. A. Collins (Ed.), *Minnesota Symposia on Child Psychology* (Vol. 15). Hillsdale, NJ: Erlbaum.

Flavell, J. (1985). *Cognitive development* (2nd ed.). Englewood Cliffs, NJ: Prentice-Hall.

Fogel, A., & Thelen, E. (1987). Development of early expressive and communicative action: Reinterpreting the evidence from a dynamic systems perspective. *Developmental Psychology, 23,* 747–761.

Folds, T. H., Footo, M. M., Guttentag, R. E., & Ornstein, P. A. (1990). When children mean to remember: Issues of context specificity, strategy effectiveness, and intentionality in the development of memory. In D. F. Bjorklund (Ed.), *Children's strategies: Contemporary views of cognitive development* (pp. 67–91).

Freud, S. (1919). *Totem and taboo.* London: Hogarth Press.

Furstenberg, F. F., Jr., Brooks-Gunn, J., & Morgan, S. P. (1987). *Adolescent mothers in later life.* Cambridge, England: Cambridge University Press.

Gesell, A. (1928). *Infancy and human growth.* New York: Macmillan.

Gewirtz, J. L. (1965). The course of infant smiling in four child-rearing environments in Israel. In B. M. Foss (Ed.), *Determinants of infant behavior* (pp. 205–248). London: Methuen.

Gibson, E. J. (1969). *Principles of perceptual learning and development.* New York: Appleton-Century-Crofts.

Gibson, E. J., & Spelke, E. S. (1983). The development of perception. In P. M. Mussen (Ed.), *Handbook of child psychology* (Vol. 3, pp. 1–76). New York: Wiley.

Gibson, E. J., & Walk, R. D. (1960). The "visual cliff." *Scientific American, 202,* 2–9.

Gibson, J. J., & Gibson, E. J. (1955). Perceptual learning: Differentiation or enrichment. *Psychological Review, 62,* 32–41.

Goldberg, S., & DeVitto, B. A. (1983). *Born too soon.* San Francisco: Freeman.

Goldman-Rakic, P. S. (1987). Development of cortical circuitry and cognitive function. *Child Development, 58,* 601–622.

Goodnow, J. J. (1984). Parents' ideas about parenting and developing: A review of issues and recent work. In M. Lamb, A. Brown, & B. Rogoff (Eds.), *Advances in developmental psychology* (pp. 193–242). Hillsdale, NJ: Erlbaum.

Goodnow, J. (1988). Children's household work: Its nature and functions. *Psychological Bulletin, 103,* 5–26.

Goodnow, J., & Collins, A. (1991). *Ideas according to parents.* Hillsdale, NJ: Erlbaum.

Gottleib, G. (1976). Conceptions of prenatal development: Behavioral embryology. *Psychological Review, 83,* 215–234.

Gottlieb, G. (1983). The psychobiological approach to developmental issues. In P. H. Mussen (Ed.), *Handbook of child psychology* (Vol. 2, pp. 1–26). New York: Wiley.

Gottman, J. M. (1981). *Time series analysis: Introduction for social scientists.* Cambridge, England: Cambridge University Press.

Graham, S. (1992). Most of the subjects were white and middle class. *American Psychologist, 47,* 629–639.

Green, J. A. (1988). Loglinear analysis of cross-classified ordinal data: Applications in developmental research. *Child Development, 59,* 1–25.

Greenough, W. T., Black, J. E., & Wallace, C. S. (1987). Experience and brain development. *Child Development, 58,* 539–559.

Greenwald, A. (1992). New look 3: Unconscious cognition reclaimed. *American Psychologist, 47,* 766–779.

Grossman, K., Grossmann, K. E., Spangler, G., Suess, G., & Unzner, L. (1985). Maternal sensitivity and newborns' orientation responses as related to quality of attachment. *Monographs of the Society for Research in Child Development, 50,* (1–2, Serial No. 209).

Gunnar, M. R. (1987). Psychological studies of stress and coping: An introduction. *Child Development, 58,* 1403–1407.

Haith, M. M., Hazan, C., & Goodman, G. S. (1988). Expectations and anticipations of dynamic visual events by 3½-month-old babies. *Child Development, 59,* 467–479.

Halford, G. S. (1993). *Children's understanding: The development of mental models.* Hillsdale, NJ: Erlbaum.

Hall, G. S. (1904). *Adolescence: Its psychology and its relations to psychology, anthropology, sex, crime, religion and education* (2 vol.). New York: Appleton-Century-Crofts.

Hall, G. S. (1922). *Senescence: The last half of life.* New York: Appleton.

Harlow, H. F., & Harlow, M. K. (1962). Social deprivation in monkeys. *Scientific American, 207,* 137–146.

Harlow, H. F., & Zimmerman, R. R. (1959). Affectional responses in the infant monkey. *Science, 130,* 421–432.

Harris, P. L. (1989). *Children and emotion.* New York: Basil Blackwell.

Harter, S. (1983). Developmental perspectives on the self-system. In P. M. Mussen (Ed.), *Handbook of child psychology* (Vol. 4, pp. 275–286). New York: Wiley.

Hartup, W. W., & Rubin, Z. (Eds.). (1986). *Relationships and development*. Hillsdale, NJ: Erlbaum.

Hebb, D. (1949). *The organization of behavior: A neuropsychological theory*. New York: Wiley.

Hertzog, C. (1989). Influences of cognitive slowing on age differences in intelligence. *Developmental Psychology, 25*, 636–651.

Hetherington, E. M., & Clingempeel, W. G. (1992). Coping with marital transitions: A family systems perspective. *Monographs of the Society for Research in Child Development, 57* (2 and 3, Serial No. 227). Chicago: University of Chicago Press.

Hetherington, E. M., Reiss, D., & Plomin, R. (Eds.). (1994). *Separate social worlds of siblings: Importance of non-shared environment on development*. Hillsdale, NJ: Erlbaum.

Hinde, R. A. (1979). *Toward understanding relationships*. London: Academic Press.

Hinde, R. A. (1987). *Individuals, relationships and culture*. Cambridge, England: Cambridge University Press.

Hinde, R. A. (1991). When is an evolutionary approach useful? *Child Development, 62*, 671–675.

Hinde, R. A., & Stevenson-Hinde, J. (Eds.). (1988). *Relationships within families: Mutual influences*. New York: Oxford University Press.

Hoffman, L. W. (1991). The influence of the family environment on personality: accounting for sibling differences. *Psychological Bulletin, 110*, 187–203.

Hoffreth, S. L., & Phillips, D. A. (1987). Child care in the United States, 1970 to 1995. *Journal of Marriage and the Family, 49*, 559–572.

Horowitz, F. D. (1987). *Exploring developmental theories: Toward a structural/behavioral model of development*. Hillsdale, NJ: Erlbaum.

Howes, C., & Olenick, M. (1986). Child care and family influences on compliance. *Child Development, 57*, 202–216.

Hubel, D., & Wiesel, T. (1965). Binocular interaction in striate cortex of kittens reared with artificial squint. *Journal of Neurophysiology, 28*, 1041–1059.

Hudson, J. A. (1990). The emergence of autobiographical memory in mother–child conversation. In R. Fivush & J. A. Hudson (Eds.), *Knowing and remembering in young children* (pp. 166–196). Cambridge, England: Cambridge University Press.

Hull, C. L. (1943). *Principles of behavior*. New York: Appleton-Century-Crofts.

Hulsebus, R. C. (1973). Operant conditioning in infant behavior: A review. In H. W. Reese (Ed.), *Advances in child development and behavior* (Vol. 8, pp. 112–158). New York: Academic Press.

Hunt, J. McV. (1961). *Intelligence and experience*. New York: Ronald Press.

Hutchins, E. (1991). The social organizations of distributed cognitions. In L. B. Resnick, J. L. Levine, & S. D. Teasley (Eds.), *Perspectives on a shared cognition* (pp. 283–307). Washington, DC: American Psychological Association.

Izard, C. E. (1982). *Measuring emotions in infants and children.* Cambridge, England: Cambridge University Press.

Izard, C. E., & Malatesta, C. Z. (1987). Perspectives on emotional development: Part 1. Differential emotions theory of early emotional development. In J. D. Osofsky (Ed.), *Handbook of infant development* (2nd ed., pp. 494–554). New York: Wiley.

Jay, S., & Farran, D. C. (1981). The relative efficacy of predicting IQ from mother–child interactions using ratings versus behavioral count measures. *Journal of Applied Developmental Psychology, 2,* 165–177.

Johnson, J. E., & Martin, C. (1983). Parents' beliefs and home learning environments: Effects on cognitive development. In I. Sigel (Ed.), *Parent belief systems: The psychological consequences for children.* Hillsdale, NJ: Erlbaum.

Johnson, J. S., & Newport, E. L. (1989). Critical period effects in second language learning: The influence of maturational state on acquisition of English as a second language. *Cognitive Psychology, 21,* 60–99.

Kagan, J., & Klein, R. (1973). Cross-cultural perspectives on early development. *American Psychologist, 28,* 947–961.

Kagan, J., & Snidman, N. (1991). Temperamental factors in human development. *American Psychologist, 46,* 856–862.

Karmiloff-Smith, A., & Inhelder, B. (1977). If you want to get ahead, get a theory. *Cognition, 3,* 195–212.

Keil, F. C. (1984). Mechanisms in cognitive development and the structure of knowledge. In R. J. Sternberg (Ed.), *Mechanisms of cognitive development* (pp. 81–99). San Francisco: W. H. Freeman.

Kendler, H. H., & Kendler, T. S. (1962). Vertical and horizontal processes in problem solving. *Psychological Review, 69,* 1–16.

Kessen, W. (1967). Sucking & looking: Two organized patterns of behavior in the human newborn. In H. W. Stevenson, E. H. Hess, & H. L. Rheingold (Eds.), *Early behavior: Comparative and developmental approaches* (pp. 147–179). New York: Wiley.

Kessen, W. (1982). The child and other cultural inventions. In F. S. Kessel & A. W. Siegel (Eds.), *The child and other cultural inventions* (pp. 26–39). New York: Praeger.

Kessen, W. (1983). Preface to volume 1. In P. H. Mussen (Ed.), *Handbook of child psychology* (Vol. 1, pp. viii–x). New York: Wiley.

Kihlstrom, J., Barnhardt, T. M., & Tataryn, D. J. (1992). The psychological unconscious. *American Psychologist, 47,* 788–791.

Klahr, D. (1984). Transition processes in quantitative development. In R. J. Sternberg (Ed.), *Mechanisms of cognitive development* (pp. 101–139). San Francisco: W. H. Freeman.

Klahr, D. (1989). Information processing approaches. In R. Vasta (Ed.), *Six theories of child development* (pp. 183–185). Greenwich, CT: JAI Press.

Klahr, D., & Wallace, J. G. (1976). *Cognitive development: An information processing view.* Hillsdale, NJ: Erlbaum.

Klinnert, M. D. (1981). *Infants' use of mothers' facial expressions for regulating their own behavior.* Paper presented at the meeting of the Society for Research in Child Development, Boston.

Kreppner, K. (1988). Changes in dyadic relationships within a family after the arrival of a second child. In R. Hinde & J. Stevenson-Hinde (Eds.), *Relationships within families* (pp. 143–167). Cambridge, England: Cambridge University Press.

Kuchuk, A., Vibbert, M., & Bornstein, M. H. (1986). The perception of smiling and its experimental correlates in three-month-old infants. *Child Development, 57,* 1054–1061.

Kuenne, M. R. (1946). Experimental investigation of the relation of language to transposition behavior in young children. *Journal of Experimental Psychology, 36,* 471–490.

Lamb, M. E. (1977a). The development of mother–infant and father–infant attachments in the second year of life. *Developmental Psychology, 13,* 639–647.

Lamb, M. E. (1977b). Father–infant and mother–infant interaction in the first year of life. *Child Development, 48,* 167–181.

Lamb, M. E., Frodi, A. M., Hwang, C. P., Frodi, M., & Steinberg, J. (1982). Mother and father–infant interaction involving play and holding in traditional and nontraditional Swedish fathers. *Developmental Psychology, 18,* 215–222.

Lamb, M. E., Thompson, R. A., Gardner, W., Charnov, E. L., & Estes, C. (1984). Security of attachment as assessed in the strange situation: Its study and biological interpretation. *Behavioral and Brain Sciences, 7,* 127–147.

Lazar, I., & Darlington, R. (1982). Lasting effects of early education: A report from the Consortium for Longitudinal Studies. *Monographs of the Society for Research in Child Development, 47* (2–3, Serial No. 195).

Lepper, M., & Gurtner, J. (1989). Children and computers: Approaching the twenty-first century. *American Psychologist, 44,* 170–178.

Lerner, R. M., & Foch, T. T. (Eds.). (1987). *Biological and psychosocial interactions in early adolescence: A life span perspective.* Hillsdale, NJ: Erlbaum.

Lester, B., Hoffman, J., & Brazelton, T. B. (1985). The rhythmic structure of mother–infant interaction in term and preterm infants. *Child Development, 56,* 15–27.

Lewis, M. (1982). The social network systems model: Toward a theory of social development. In T. M. Field, A. Huston, H. C. Quay, L. Troll, & G. E. Finley (Eds.), *Review of human development* (pp. 180–214). New York: Wiley.

Lewis, M. (1992). *The development of shame.* New York: Basic Books.

Lewis, M., & Brooks-Gunn, J. (1979). *Social cognition and the acquisition of self.* New York: Plenum Press.

Lewis, M., & Feiring, C. (1988). Attachments as a measurement of a trait or of the environment. In J. Gerwitz & B. Furtines (Eds.), *Intersections with attachment.* Hillsdale, NJ: Erlbaum.

Liben, L. S. (Ed.) (1987). *Development and learning: Conflict on congruence.* Hillsdale, NJ: Erlbaum.

Lipsitt, L. P. (1963). Learning in the first year of life. In L. P. Lipsitt & C. C. Spiker (Eds.), *Advances in child development and behavior* (Vol. 1, pp. 147–195). New York: Academic Press.

Lipsitt, L. P., & Cantor, J. H. (Eds.). (1986). *Experimental child psychologist: Essays and experiments in honor of Charles C. Spiker.* Hillsdale, NJ: Erlbaum.

Lockman, J. J. (1984). The development of detour ability during infancy. *Child Development, 55,* 482–491.

Maccoby, E. E., & Martin, J. A. (1983). Socialization in the context of the family: Parent–child interaction. In E. M. Hetherington (Ed.), *Handbook of child psychology* (Vol. 4, pp. 1–102). New York: Wiley.

MacDonald, K. B. (1987). *Sociobiological perspectives on human development.* New York: Springer-Verlag.

MacDonald, K., & Parke, R. D. (1986). Parent–child physical play: The effects of sex and age of children and parents. *Sex Roles, 7–8,* 367–378.

Mahler, M., & Pine, F. (1975). *The psychological birth of the infant.* New York: Basic Books.

Main, M., & Weston, D. R. (1981). The quality of the toddler's relationship to mother and to father: Related to conflict behavior and the readiness to establish new relationships. *Child Development, 52,* 932–940.

McCall, R. B., Appelbaum, M. I., & Hogarty, P. S. (1973). Developmental changes in mental test performance. *Monographs of the Society for Research in Child Development, 38* (3, Serial No. 150).

McGillicuddy-DeLisi, A. V. (1982). The relation between family configuration and parental beliefs about child development. In L. M. Laosa & I. E. Sigel (Eds.), *Families as learning environments for children* (pp. 261–300). New York: Plenum.

McGilly, K., & Siegler, R. S. (1990). The influence of encoding and strategic knowledge on children's choices among recall strategies. *Developmental Psychology, 26,* 931–941.

McGraw, M. (1935). *Growth: A study of Johnny and Jimmy.* New York: Appleton-Century-Crofts.

McLoyd, V. C. (1990). The impact of economic hardship on Black families and children: Psychological distress, parenting and socioemotional development. *Child Development, 61,* 311–346.

Miller, P. H. (1983). *Theories of developmental psychology.* San Francisco: W. H. Freeman.

Miller, S. A. (1988). Parents' beliefs about their children's congitive development. *Child Development, 59,* 259–285.

Mills, W. (1898). *The nature and development of animal intelligence.* London: Unwin.

Morrison, F. J. (1991, April). Making the cut: Early schooling and cognitive growth. Paper presented at the meeting of the Society for Research in Child Development, Seattle, WA.

Morrison, F. J., & Ornstein, P. A. (1993). Cognitive development. In R. B. Cairns, G. H. Elder, E. J. Costello, & A. McGuire (Eds.), *Developmental Science*. Cambridge, England: Cambridge University Press.

Nelson, C. A. (1987). The recognition of facial expressions in the first two years of life: Mechanisms of development. *Child Development, 58,* 889–909.

Novak, M. A., & Harlow, H. F. (1975). Social recovery of monkeys isolated for the first year of life. *Developmental Psychology, 11,* 453–465.

Ornstein, P. A., Baker-Ward, L., & Naus, M. J. (1988). The development of mnemonic skill. In F. E. Weinert & M. Perlmutter (Eds.), *Memory development: Universal changes and individual differences* (pp. 31–50). Hillsdale, NJ: Erlbaum.

Ornstein, P. A., & Naus, M. J. (1978). Rehearsal processes in children's memory. In P. A. Ornstein (Ed.), *Memory development in children* (pp. 69–99). Hillsdale, NJ: Erlbaum.

Osofsky, J. D. (Ed.). (1979). *Handbook of infant development*. New York: Wiley.

Osofsky, J. D. (Ed.). (1987). *Handbook of infant development* (2nd ed.). New York: Wiley.

Overton, W. F., & Reese, H. W. (1973). Models of development: Methodological implications. In J. R. Nesselroade (Ed.), *Life-span developmental psychology: Methodological issues* (pp. 65–86). New York: Academic Press.

Paikoff, R. L., & Brooks-Gunn, J. (1991). Do parent–child relationships change during puberty? *Psychological Bulletin, 110,* 47–66.

Park, K., & Waters, E. (1988). Personality and social relationships. In S. Duck (Ed.), *Handbook of personal relationships*. West Sussex, England: Wiley.

Parke, R. D. (1976). Social cues, social control and ecological validity. *Merrill-Palmer Quarterly, 22,* 111–118.

Parke, R. D. (1978). Parent–infant interaction: Progress, paradigms and problems. In G. P. Sackett (Ed.), *Observing behavior: Vol. 1. Theory and applications in mental retardation* (pp. 69–94). Baltimore: University Park Press.

Parke, R. D. (1979a). Interactional designs. In R. B. Cairns (Ed.), *The analysis of social interaction* (pp. 15–35). Hillsdale, NJ: Erlbaum.

Parke, R. D. (1979b). Perspectives on father–infant interaction. In J. Osofsky (Ed.), *Handbook of infant development* (pp. 549–590). New York: Wiley.

Parke, R. D. (1988). Families in life-span perspective: A multilevel developmental approach. In E. M. Hetherington, R. M. Lerner, & M. Perlmutter (Eds.), *Child development in life-span perspective* (pp. 159–190). Hillsdale, NJ: Erlbaum.

Parke, R. D. (1989). Social development in infancy: A twenty-five year perspective. In D. Palermo (Ed.), *Advances in child development and behaviors* (pp. 1–30). New York: Academic Press.

Parke, R. D., & Ladd, G. (Eds.). (1992). *Family–peer relationships: Modes of linkages*. Hillsdale, NJ: Erlbaum.

Parke, R. D., MacDonald, K. B., Beitel, A., & Bhavnagri, N. (1988). The role of the family in the development of peer relationships. In R. D. Parke & R. J. McMahon (Eds.), *Social learning and systems approaches to marriage and the family* (pp. 17–44). New York: Breiner/Mazel.

Parke, R. D., & O'Leary, S. E. (1976). Father–mother–infant interaction in the newborn period: Some findings, some observations and some unresolved issues. In K. Riegel & J. Meacham (Eds.), *The developing individual in a changing world: Social and environmental issues* (Vol. 2, pp. 653–663). The Hague: Mouton.

Parke, R. D., & Tinsley, B. J. (1984). Fatherhood: Historical and contemporary perspectives. In K. A. McCluskey & H. W. Reese (Eds.), *Life span developmental psychology: Historical and generational effects* (pp. 203–248). New York: Academic Press.

Parke, R. D., & Tinsley, B. J. (1987). Family interaction in infancy. In J. D. Osofsky (Ed.), *Handbook of infant development* (2nd ed., pp. 579–641). New York: Wiley.

Parmalee, A. H., Jr. (1982, Fall). Teaching child development and behavioral pediatrics to pediatric trainees. *Society for Research in Child Development Newsletter* (1–2).

Perlmutter, M. (1985). Memory development across the lifespan. In P. B. Baltes, D. Featherman, J. R. Nesselroade, & H. W. Reese (Eds.), *Life span development and behavior* (Vol. 7). New York: Academic Press.

Pervin, L. A. (1978). *Current controversies and issues in personality.* New York: Wiley.

Phillips, D., McCartney, K., & Scarr, S. (1987). Child-care quality and children's social development. *Developmental Psychology, 23,* 537–543.

Phillips, D., McCartney, K., Scarr, S., & Howes, C. (1987). Selective review of infant day care research: A cause for concern. *Zero to Three, 7,* 18–21.

Piaget, J. (1952). *The origins of intelligence in children.* New York: International Universities Press.

Pleck, J. (1985). *Working wives, working husbands.* Beverly Hills, CA: Sage.

Plomin, R. (1986). *Development, genetics and psychology.* Hillsdale, NJ: Erlbaum.

Plomin, R. (1989). Environment and genes: Determinants of behavior. *American Psychologist, 44,* 105–111.

Plomin, R. (1990). *Nature and nurture.* Pacific Grove, CA: Brooks/Cole.

Plomin, R., & DeFries, J. C. (Eds.). (1985). *Origins of individual differences in infancy: The Colorado adoption project.* Orlando, FL: Academic Press.

Plomin, R., DeFries, J. C., & McClearn, G. E. (1990). *Behavior genetics: A primer* (2nd ed.). New York: Freeman.

Postman, L. (1955). Association theory and perceptual learning. *Psychological Review, 62,* 438–446.

Power, T. G., & Parke, R. D. (1982). Play as a context for early learning: Lab and home analyses. In I. E. Sigel & L. M. Laosa (Eds.), *The Family as a Learning Environment* (pp. 223–241). New York: Plenum.

Preyer, W. (1888–1889). *The mind of the child* (Vol. 2). New York: Appleton.

Preyer, W. (1895). *The mind of the child.* New York: Appleton-Century-Crofts.

Radke-Yarrow, M. (1989). Family environments of depressed and well parents and their children: Issues of research methods. In G. R. Patterson (Ed.), *Aggression and depression in family interactions* (pp. 169–184). Hillsdale, NJ: Erlbaum.

Radke-Yarrow, M. (1991). The individual and the environment in human behavioural development. In P. Bateson (Ed.), *The development and integration of behaviour* (pp. 389–410). Cambridge, England: Cambridge University Press.

Radke-Yarrow, M., & Zahn-Waxler, C. (1985). Roots, motives and patterns in children's prosocial behavior. In J. Reykowski, J. Karylowski, D. Bartal, & E. Staub (Eds.), *Origins and maintenance of prosocial behaviors* (pp. 155–176). New York: Plenum.

Ramey, C. T., MacPhee, D., & Yeates, K. O. (1982). Preventing developmental retardation: A general systems model. In L. Bond & J. Joffe (Eds.), *Facilitating infant and early childhood development*. Hanover, NH: University of New England Press.

Reiss, D. (1981). *The family's construction of reality*. Cambridge, MA: Harvard University Press.

Resnick, L., Levine, J., & Teasley, S. D. (1991). *Perspectives on socially shared cognition*. Washington, DC: American Psychological Association.

Rheingold, H. L. (1956). The modification of social responsiveness in institutional babies. *Monographs of the Society for Research in Child Development, 21* (63).

Rheingold, H., Gewirtz, J. L., & Ross, H. W. (1959). Social conditioning of vocalizations in the infant. *Journal of Comparative and Physiological Psychology, 52*, 68–73.

Ricciuti, H. N. (1970). Malnutrition, learning, and intellectual development: Research and remediation. In *Psychology and Problems of Society*. Washington, DC: American Psychological Association.

Ricciuti, H. N. (1980). Developmental consequences of malnutrition of early childhood. In M. Lewis & L. Rosenblum (Eds.), *The uncommon child: The genesis of development* (Vol. 3). New York: Plenum.

Ricciuti, H. N., & Breitmayer, B. (1988). Observational assessments of infant temperament in the natural setting of the newborn nursery. *Merrill-Palmer Quarterly, 34*, 281–299.

Riegel, K. F. (1972). Influence of economic and political ideologies on the development of developmental psychology. *Psychological Bulletin, 78*, 129–141.

Riegel, K. F. (Ed.). (1975). *The development of dialectical operations*. Basel, Switzerland: Karger.

Riegel, K. F. (1976). The dialetics of human development. *American Psychologist, 31*, 689–700.

Riesen, A., & Aarons, L. (1959). Visual movement, and intensity discrimination in cats after early deprivation of pattern vision. *Journal of Comparative and Physiological Psychology, 52*, 142–149.

Riesen, A., Kurke, M., & Mellinger, J. (1953). Interocular transfer of habits learned monocularly in visually naive and visually experienced cats. *Journal of Comparative and Physiological Psychology, 46*, 166–172.

Rieser, J. J., Guth, D. A., & Hill, E. W. (1986). Sensitivity to perspective structure while walking without vision. *Perception, 15,* 173–188.

Rieser, J. J., Hill, E. W., Talor, C. A., Bradfield, A., & Rosen, R. (1989, April). *The perception of locomotion and the role of visual experience in the development of spatial knowledge.* Paper presented at the meeting of the Society for Research in Child Development.

Rieser, J. J., Hill, E. W., Talor, C. R., Bradfield, A., & Rosen, R. (1992). Visual experience, visual field size, and the development of nonvisual sensitivity to the spatial structure of outdoor neighborhoods explored by walking. *Journal of Experimental Psychology: General, 121,* 210–221.

Robbins, L. C. (1963). The accuracy of parental record of aspects of child development and of child rearing practices. *Journal of Abnormal and Social Psychology, 66,* 261–270.

Rogoff, B. (1991). *Apprenticeship in thinking: Cognitive development in social context.* New York: Oxford University Press.

Rogoff, B., & Gardner, W. (1984). Adult guidance of cognitive development. In B. Rogoff & J. Lave (Eds.), *Everyday cognition: Its development in social context* (pp. 95–116). Cambridge, MA: Harvard University Press.

Romanes, G. J. (1984). *Mental evolution in animals.* New York: Appleton.

Rutter, M. (1987). Continuities and discontinuities from infancy. In J. D. Osofsky (Ed.), *Handbook of infant development* (2nd ed., pp. 1256–1296). New York: Wiley.

Sackett, G. P. (1968). The persistence of abnormal behavior in monkeys following isolation rearing. In R. Porter (Ed.), *The role of learning in psychotherapy.* London: Churchill.

Sackett, G. P. (1979). The lag sequential analysis of contingency and cyclicity in behavioral interaction research. In J. D. Osofsky (Ed.), *Handbook of infant development* (pp. 954–976). New York: Wiley.

Sackett, G. P. (1987). Analysis of sequential social interaction data: Some issues, recent developments and a causal inference model. In J. D. Osofsky (Ed.), *Handbook of infant development* (2nd ed., pp. 855–878). New York: Wiley.

Salapatek, P. (1975). Pattern perception in infancy. In L. Cohen and P. Salapatek (Eds.), *Infant perception: From sensation to cognition* (Vol. 1, pp. 133–248). New York: Academic.

Salapatek, P., & Kessen, W. (1966). Visual scanning of triangles by the human newborn. *Journal of experimental child psychology, 3,* 155–167.

Salthouse, T. A. (1985). *A theory of cognitive aging.* Amsterdam: North-Holland.

Sameroff, A. J. (1983). Developmental systems: Contexts and evolution. In W. Kessen (Ed.), *Handbook of child psychology* (Vol. 1, pp. 237–294). New York: Wiley.

Sameroff, A. J. (1987, July). *Social contexts of development.* Paper presented at the International Society for the Study of Behavioral Development Satellite Conference, Beijing, China.

Sameroff, A. J., & Chandler, M. J. (1975). Reproductive risk and the continuum of caretaking casualty. In F. D. Horowitz, M. Hetherington, S. Scarr-Sala-patek, & G. Siegel (Eds.), *Review of child development research* (Vol. 4, pp. 187–244). Chicago: University of Chicago.

Sameroff, A. J., & Emde, R. (Eds.). (1989). *Relationship disturbances in early childhood*. New York: Basic Books.

Scarr, S. (1992). Developmental theories for the 1990s: Development and individual differences. *Child Development, 63,* 1–19.

Scarr, S. (1993). Biological and cultural diversity: The legacy of Darwin for development. *Child Development, 64,* 1333–1353.

Schaffer, H. R. (1971). *The growth of sociability*. Harmondsworth, Middlesex, England: Penguin.

Schaffer, H. R. (1984). *The child's entry into a social world*. New York: Academic Press.

Schaffer, H. R., & Emerson, P. E. (1964). The development of social attachments in infancy. *Monographs of the Society for Research in Child Development, 29* (3, Serial No. 94).

Schaie, K. W. (1989). Perceptual speed in adulthood: Cross-sectional and longitudinal studies. *Psychology and Aging, 4,* 443–453.

Sears, R. R. (1975). Your ancients revisited: A history of child development. In E. M. Hetherington (Ed.), *Review of child development research* (Vol. 5, pp. 1–73). Chicago: University of Chicago Press.

Sears, R. R., Maccoby, E. E., & Levin, H. (1957). *Patterns of child-rearing*. Evanston, IL: Row, Peterson.

Sears, R. R., Rau, L., & Alpert, R. (1965). *Child-rearing and identification*. Stanford, CA: Stanford University Press.

Siegler, R. S. (1991). *Children's thinking* (2nd ed.). Englewood Cliffs, NJ: Prentice-Hall.

Siegler, R. S., & Crowley, K. (1991). The microgenetic method: A direct means for studying cognitive development. *American Psychologist, 46,* 606–620.

Siegler, R. S., & Jenkins, E. (1989). *How children discover new strategies*. Hillsdale, NJ: Erlbaum.

Sigel, I. E. (Ed.). (1985). *Parent belief systems: The psychological consequences for children*. Hillsdale, NJ: Erlbaum.

Sigel, I., & Parke, R. D. (1987). Conceptual models of family interaction. *Journal of Applied Developmental Psychology, 8,* 123–137.

Skeels, H. (1966). Adult status of children with contrasting early life experiences. *Monograph of the Society for Research in Child Development, 31* (3).

Skinner, B. F. (1938). *The behavior of organisms*. New York: Appleton-Century-Crofts.

Skinner, E. A. (1985). Determinants of mother-sensitive and contingent-responsive behavior: The role of child-rearing beliefs and socioeconomic status. In I. Sigel (Ed.), *Parent belief systems: The psychological consequences for children* (pp. 51–88). Hillsdale, NJ: Erlbaum.

Sorce, J. F., Emde, R. N., Klinnert, M. D., & Campos, J. J. (1981). *Maternal emotional signaling: Its effect on the visual cliff behavior of one-year-olds.* Paper presented at the biennial meeting of the Society for Research in Child Development, Boston.

Spalding, D. A. (1873). Instinct: With original observations in young animals. *Macmillan's Magazine, 27,* 282–293.

Spelke, E. S. (1988). Where perceiving ends and thinking begins: The apprehension of objects in infancy. In A. Yonas (Ed.), *Perceptual development in infancy: Minnesota Symposia on Child Psychology* (Vol. 20, pp. 197–234). Hillsdale, NJ: Erlbaum.

Spitz, R. A. (1950). Anxiety in infancy: A study of its manifestations in the first year of life. *International Journal of Psychoanalysis, 31,* 138–143.

Sroufe, L. A. (1983). Infant-caregiver attachment and patterns of adaptation in preschool: The roots of maladaptation. In M. Perlmutter (Ed.), *Minnesota Symposium on Child Psychology* (Vol. 16, pp. 41–81). Hillsdale, NJ: Erlbaum.

Sroufe, L. A., & Fleeson, J. (1986). Attachment and the construction of relationships. In W. W. Hartup & Z. Rubin (Eds.), *Relationships and development* (pp. 51–72). Hillsdale, NJ: Erlbaum.

Sroufe, L. A., & Rutter, M. (1984). The domain of developmental psychopathology. *Child Development, 55,* 17–29.

Sroufe, L. A., & Waters, E. (1977). Attachment as an organizational construct. *Child Development, 48,* 1184–1199.

Steinberg, L., Dornbusch, S., & Brown, B. B. (1992). Ethnic differences in adolescent achievement: An ecological perspective. *American Psychologist, 47,* 723–729.

Stern, D. N. (1977). *The first relationship.* Cambridge, MA: Harvard University Press.

Stern, D. N. (1985). *The interpersonal world of the infant.* New York: Basic Books.

Sternberg (Ed.). (1984). *Mechanisms of cognitive development.* San Francisco: W. H. Freeman.

Stevenson, H. W. (1972). *Children's learning.* New York: Academic Press.

Stevenson, H. W., & Siegel, A. (Eds.). (1984). *Child development research and social policy* (Vol. 1). Chicago: University of Chicago Press.

Sulloway, F. J. (1979). *Freud: Biologist of the mind.* New York: Basic Books.

Thelen, E. (1989). Self-organization in developmental processes: Can systems approaches work? In M. Gunnar (Ed.), *Minnesota Symposia in Child Psychology* (Vol. 22, pp. 77–117). Hillsdale, NJ: Erlbaum.

Thelen, E., & Ulrich, B. D. (1991). Hidden skills: A dynamic systems analysis of treadmill stepping during the first year. *Monographs of the Society for Research in Child Development, 58* (Serial No. 223).

Thompson, R. (1990). Vulnerability in research: A developmental perspective on research risk. *Child Development, 61,* 1–16.

Tinsley, B. J., & Parke, R. D. (1984a). Grandparents as support and socialization agents. In M. Lewis (Ed.), *Beyond the Dyad* (pp. 161–195). New York: Plenum.

Tinsley, B. J., & Parke, R. D. (1984b). The interrelationship between developmental psychology and pediatrics. In H. Fitzgerald & M. Yogman (Eds.), *Behavioral Pediatrics* (Vol. 2). New York: Plenum.

Tinsley, B. J., & Parke, R. D. (1987). Grandparents as interactive and social support agents for families with young infants. *International Journal of Aging and Human Development, 25,* 261–279.

Tronick, E. (1989). Emotions and emotional communication in infants. *American Psychologist, 44,* 112–119.

Tulkin, S. R., & Kagan, J. (1972). Mother–child interaction in the first year of life. *Child Development, 43,* 31–41.

Van der Maas, H. L., & Molehaar, P. C. (1992). Stagewise cognitive development: An application of catastrophe theory. *Psychological Review, 99,* 395–417.

Van der Veer, R., & Valsiner, J. (1991). *Understanding Vygotsky: A quest for synthesis.* Oxford: Basil Blackwell.

Vygotsky, L. S. (1978). *Mind in society: The development of higher psychological processes.* Cambridge, MA: Harvard University Press.

Wahler, R. G. (1967). Infant social attachments: A reinforcement theory interpretation and investigation. *Child Development, 38,* 1979–2088.

Warren, D. (in press). *Blindness in children.* New York: Cambridge University Press.

Waters, E., & Deane, K. (1986). Defining and assessing individual differences in attachment relationships: Q-methodology and the organization of behavior in infancy and early childhood. *Monographs of the Society for Research in Child Development, 50* (Serial No. 102).

Watson, J. B. (1913). Psychology as the behaviorist views it. *Psychological Review, 20,* 158–177.

Weinert, F. E., & Schneider, W. (Eds.). (1989). *The Munich longitudinal study on the genesis of individual competencies (LOGIC), Report No. 5: Results of Wave 3.* (Technical Report). Munich: Max Planck Institute for Psychological Research.

Weisberg, P. (1963). Social and nonsocial conditioning of infant vocalizations. *Child Development, 34,* 377–388.

Wellman, H. M. (1990). *The child's theory of mind.* Cambridge: M.I.T. Press.

Wertsch, J. V. (1991). *Voices of the mind: A sociocultural approach to mediated action.* Cambridge, MA: Harvard University Press.

Wertsch, J. V., & Tulviste, P. (1992). L. S. Vygotsky and contemporary developmental psychology. *Developmental Psychology, 28,* 543–553.

White, B. (1970). *Human infants: Experience and psychological development.* Englewood Cliffs, NJ: Prentice-Hall.

Whitt, J. K., & Casey, P. H. (1982). The mother–infant relationship and infant development: The effect of pediatric intervention. *Child Development, 53,* 948–956.

Wohlwill, J. F. (1973). *The study of behavioral development in children*. New York: Academic Press.

Wood, D., Bruner, J. S., & Ross, G. (1976). The role of tutoring in problem-solving. *Journal of Child Psychology and Psychiatry, 17*, 89–100.

Wundt, W. (1907). *Outlines of psychology*. New York: Stechert.

Yarrow, L. J. (1961). Maternal deprivation: Toward an empirical and conceptual re-evaluation. *Psychological Bulletin, 58*, 459–490.

Yarrow, L. J. (1964). Separation from parents during early childhood. In M. L. Hoffman & L. W. Hoffman (Eds.), *Review of child development research* (Vol. 1, pp. 89–136). New York: Sage.

Yonas, A., & Pick, H. L. (1975). An approach to the study of infant space perception. In L. Cohen and P. Salapatek (Eds.), *Infant perception: From sensation to cognition* (Vol. 2, pp. 3–32). New York: Academic Press.

Zacks, R. T., & Hasher, L. (1988). Capacity theory and the processing of inferences. In L. L. Light & D. M. Burke (Eds.), *Language, memory, and aging* (pp. 154–170). Cambridge, England: Cambridge University Press.

Zahn-Waxler, C., & Kochanska, G. (1990). The development of guilt. In R. Thompson (Ed.), *Nebraska Symposium on Motivation, 1988: Socioemotional Development* (pp. 183–258). Lincoln, NE: University of Nebraska Press.

Zahn-Waxler, C., & Radke-Yarrow, M. (1982). The development of altruism: Alternative research strategies. In N. Eisenberg (Ed.), *The development of prosocial behavior* (pp. 109–137). New York: Academic Press.

Zahn-Waxler, C., Radke-Yarrow, M., Wagners, E., & Chapman, M. (1993). Development of concern for others. *Developmental Psychology, 28*, 126–136.

Zelazo, P. A., Zelazo, N. A., & Kolb, S. (1972). Newborn walking. *Science, 177*, 1058–1060.

I

THE FOUNDING YEARS OF DEVELOPMENTAL PSYCHOLOGY

INTRODUCTION

THE FOUNDING YEARS OF
DEVELOPMENTAL PSYCHOLOGY

In this section, we examine the contributions of several founders of developmental psychology: Darwin, Baldwin, Hall, and Dewey. Many of the major issues that served to define the field of developmental psychology were laid out in the writings of these pioneers. Some (Kessen, 1965) have suggested that the beginnings of modern child psychology can be traced to the early theorizing observations and experimentation of Charles Darwin in the mid-to-late 1800s. In fact, Darwin is often treated as the intellectual parent of modern developmental science. However, this view is not immune from challenge, and in the opening chapter of this section, Charlesworth (chapter 2) argues that evolutionary biological theory may have had less direct impact on developmental psychology than has been traditionally assumed. Alternatively, Charlesworth suggests that the effects of Darwin's views are more often indirect than direct; he poses a mediational view by which Darwin's impact is traced through a variety of subsequent theorists and movements rather than representing a direct lineage from Darwin to modern views.

In chapter 3, White focuses on G. Stanley Hall, the first president of the APA and, in the view of many, the organizing force behind the emergence of psychology, especially of a developmentally oriented psychology, as a separate and distinctive discipline. Whereas it is sometimes thought that Hall's contribution was solely organizational, White reminds us of the variety of ways in which Hall contributed to the advancement of the science of development as well. In addition to Hall's well-known recognition of adolescence as a distinctive and influential period of development, White notes Hall's creative if somewhat methodologically limited use of the questionnaire as an important tool in the developmentalist's arsenal. Finally, Hall's later writings on aging anticipated modern concerns about both life-span developmental theories and issues of development and decline in the later years of the life cycle.

In chapter 4, Cairns presents a synthesis of the views of J. Mark Baldwin. This influential early theorist was a direct descendant of Darwin and contributed both to the early organization of psychology's emergence as a separate discipline and to its early theoretical developments. Baldwin was an early president of the American Psychological Association (APA) as well as the cofounder of the *Psychological Review*. Perhaps of greatest importance was the fact that Baldwin was one of the foremost early developmental theorists who anticipated many of the current social and cognitive themes of our field. Although his empirical contributions lagged behind his theoretical offerings, as Cairns argues, he laid the groundwork for the later theoretical contributions of Piaget (Cahan, 1984), Vygotsky (Valsiner & Van der Veer, 1988), and Kohlberg (Kohlberg, 1969). Moreover, Baldwin's recognition of the intimate interplay between social and cognitive development, his focus on the emergence of the self, and his call for analysis of individuals, dyads, and groups are all very modern in their emphasis. Although we are better equipped to address these issues empirically than Baldwin was, his articulation of the underlying theoretical concerns remains of considerable value to contemporary thinkers. In spite of his wide-range vision, it is important to note that some of his ideas, especially those concerning genetics and modes of intergenerational transmission, have not fared well and have been superseded by advances in modern behavior genetics.

John Dewey was a contemporary of Baldwin and Hall and represented another bridge between philosophy and the early emergence of psychology. Cahan (chapter 5) urges us to join her in redefining and rediscovering Dewey's contributions to developmental psychology's modern manifestation. Although Dewey is usually given more credit for his contributions to education than to psychology, he was in fact decidedly modern in his outlook on psychological issues. As Cahan notes, he recognized the interplay between development and secular change, the issue of ecological validity, and the view that development is not guided by a predetermined biologically programmed agenda but rather is influenced by culture and social context. As Hall did, Dewey raised important issues that bear reexamination concerning the interplay between moral and social development and modern science, especially the role of science in promoting human values and in improving the welfare of humankind.

In sum, these early theorists clearly laid the groundwork for a modern developmental science and anticipated both theoretical themes and empirical concerns of the contemporary era.

REFERENCES

Cahan, E. D. (1984). The genetic psychologies of James Mark Baldwin and Jean Piaget. *Developmental Psychology, 20,* 128–135.

Kessen, W. (1965). *The child.* New York: Wiley.

Kohlberg, L. (1969). Stage and sequence: The cognitive development approach to socialization. In D. Goslin (Ed.), *Handbook of socialization theory and research* (pp. 347–380). Chicago: Rand McNally.

Valsiner, J., & Van der Veer, R. (1988). On the social nature of human cognition: An analysis of the shared intellectual roots of George Herbert Mead and Lev Vygotsky. *Journal for the Theory of Social Behavior, 18,* 117–136.

2

CHARLES DARWIN AND DEVELOPMENTAL PSYCHOLOGY: PAST AND PRESENT

WILLIAM R. CHARLESWORTH

. . . man gains ideas, the simplest cannot help becoming more complicated; & if we look to first origin there must be progress.

Thus notes Darwin sometime during 1837–1838 in what has become known as his "B Notebook: Transmutation of Species" (Gruber, 1974, p. 441). This excerpt sums up the fate of most searches for origins, including those aimed at examining the impact great historical figures have on scientific disciplines. What appears simple as the search begins inevitably becomes complicated and often much less clear than expected. The struggle for clarity that ensues is often accompanied by the realization that it is impossible to isolate clear instances of historical causes for anything. When this happens the author's only hope is that out of this struggle, some form of progress will be made—if not historically, at least in the form of better understanding of the conceptual issues involved.

This chapter asks two questions. The first question is: To what extent and in what manner has the work of Charles Darwin influenced develop-

Reprinted from *Developmental Psychology*, 28, 5–16. Copyright 1992 by the American Psychological Association.

mental psychology? Only a partial answer to this question can be forth-coming in the space available. The second question is: What could account for the weak relationship between Darwin's ideas and theory and research in developmental psychology? Three such reasons are addressed—ideological, conceptual, and methodological. Discussion of these reasons is followed by an expression of hope for a new, more abundant synergism between evolutionary theory and developmental research. To help actualize this hope, current evolutionary concepts and those applying them to understand developmental problems are briefly mentioned.

HISTORY

A word of caution must be provided before the history of the relationship between Darwin and developmental psychology is examined. It has been traditionally accepted that Darwin's contribution to developmental psychology was clearly revolutionary. A closer look at what actually happened, however, reveals that the picture is more complicated: The causal connection between Darwin and developmental psychology is much less linear than originally thought. When one looks at Darwin's long-term impact on developmental psychology, it turns out that his promissory note has been much more ambiguous than that of other genealogical giants in the field. To complicate matters, one detects a lack of clarity as well as some ambivalence on the part of many developmentalists about Darwin's ultimate significance for their field. For these reasons, this article should be viewed as a tentative appraisal of some of the historical connections between Darwin's ideas and the field of developmental psychology.

As is generally recognized, developmental psychology has a rich history. Its precursors include eminent philosophers, pedagogues, and physicians whose thoughts and observations undoubtedly have had a cumulative impact on those establishing the science of child behavior and development in the 19th century. But such a prodigious gathering of approaches and disciplines over the centuries makes it difficult to identify direct ancestors of developmental psychology. Furthermore, the contributions of great minds such as Darwin's, no matter how original, are always embedded in a climate of intellectual, cultural, and socioeconomic processes surrounding them. Such Zeitgeist factors make it virtually impossible to eliminate other agents that may be causally involved in the early construction of a scientific discipline. When a great mind stretches across many disciplines, as Darwin's did, targeting its direct impact on a single scientific discipline is virtually an impossible task because such impact may be effected indirectly through adjacent disciplines.

The task with Darwin is even more complicated by the fact that both developmental psychology and Darwin got their start at approximately the same time in history. Concurring histories of two disciplines are difficult to separate if one wants to identify their causal interactions. Evidence that developmental psychologists and Darwin shared common ideas extends at least as far back as the late 18th century. This is exemplified in such figures as Tiedemann and Lamarck, both of whom had effects on Darwin and developmental psychologists.

Influences on Darwin

Before looking for Darwin's causal effect on developmental psychology, let us invert the historical question and look for the opposite, the latter's effect on him. Let us look for sources within the prehistory and history of developmental psychology that antedate (or are contemporaneous with) Darwin's efforts and therefore could have influenced his thinking. There is some indication that he was influenced by Hippolyte Taine and possibly indirectly by Dietrich Tiedemann (Gruber, 1974). But both influences seem to be limited pretty much to the writing of his baby diaries and to studies on facial expressions. Also, both appear to support Lamarck's idea of the inheritance of behavior patterns acquired earlier through experiences of ancestors. This idea was also entertained by Darwin, though it did not play a central role in the construction of his theory.

As far as can be determined, Darwin was interested in children and their development: As Beer (1985) notes, Darwin enjoyed reading biographies and autobiographies. There is no evidence, however, that the results of this interest contributed to the development of his theory. If we look at a concordance to Darwin's *The Descent of Man and Selection in Relation to Sex* (Barrett, Weinshank, Ruhlen, & Ozminski, 1987), the volume in which Darwin spends his major efforts on humans, references to children are extremely rare. Only 62 times do words having to do with children appear in the text's 243,178 words. This sparsity of allusion suggests that extant knowledge of children at the time did not contribute significantly to shaping his theory. As Darwin scholars (Gruber, 1974; Mayr, 1982) have pointed out, Darwin was influenced primarily by geological data, his own naturalistic observations of animals and plants, a wide assortment of reports from anthropologists, travelers, missionaries, animal breeders, and especially Malthus's theory on population size and environmental conditions.

At first glance, then, it appears that those studying children had little or no influence on the development of Darwin's theory and that his own firsthand observations of children seemed to be used more as grist for his already established theoretical mill than as a good reason to build a theory. For example, it appears that he used information on children to support his idea that many early behaviors were innate in the sense that they were phylogenetic adaptations of animal ancestors of humans. Their presence in children (in his eyes) confirmed the existence of an unbroken lineage between humans and these ancestors. As is now generally recognized, after the *Beagle* voyage, Darwin set out to solve the problem of how life in general changes in a continuous fashion over long periods of time. He did not set out to solve the developmental problem of how humans change over their lifetimes.

However, none of this means that Darwin was not influenced by ideas of development per se. As he himself points out (Darwin, 1859/1936), he was influenced early by Karl von Baer's contributions to embryogenesis, claiming that embryology had provided him with the best evidence of evolution. As Gould (1977) points out in his detailed explication of the relationship between phylogeny and ontogeny, Darwin and many others felt strongly that evolutionary processes were influenced by developmental mechanisms. Such feelings, however, did not lead to much. As Mayr and Provine (1980) point out, ". . . neither Darwin nor any of the great comparative embryologists could meaningfully synthesize embryology with evolution by natural selection" (p. 96). This is an important observation because as will be seen below, it bears on one of the key issues that separates evolutionary biology from many interested in human development ontogeny.

The second instance of Darwin's interest in the generic problem of development has to do directly with Lamarck. As is well known, Lamarck's theory held that habits (the giraffe stretching its neck) acquired during ontogeny were somatically transmitted across generations. This theory had a strong appeal for many evolutionists. It probably had an even stronger hold on those who felt that environmental factors played a larger role in the evolution of behavior than Darwin's natural selection theory admitted. Because environmental factors need time to achieve their effects, it is easy to imagine how developmentalists, especially, would be inspired by Lamarck: A lifetime of experiences surely would make a permanent difference on the body of an individual and hence on the transmission of future characteristics.

With the publication of Weismann's "Concept of Germ Plasm" in 1889, Lamarck's theory received a severe blow. Weismann distinguished between somatic cells that were altered during ontogeny by experience and germ plasm that was not, thereby ensuring immutable transmission of heritable traits across generations. This distinction carried the day and for most scientists gravely weakened Lamarck's hypothesis. Mendel's subsequent discovery of the laws of hereditary transmissions (cf. Dobzhansky, Ayala, Stebbins, & Valentine, 1977) rendered Lamarck's hypothesis even more questionable.

Without knowledge of Weissman and Mendel, Darwin can be excused for accepting Lamarckian transmission of traits as playing at least a partial role in bringing about evolutionary change. However, natural selection that influenced the frequency and distribution of germ plasm (not its content—

that was thought of as changing mostly at random) was for Darwin the major factor in bringing about such change. As will be discussed below, this factor appears to play an important role in the rejection of Darwin on the part of many developmental psychologists.

In conclusion, then, it appears that though Darwin was a partner in historical time with developmental psychology, there is no evidence suggesting that the formulation of his theory was influenced in any significant way by developmental psychologists or their precursors. The construction of his theory had other sources, a major one being Malthus's thesis, which was as far removed from developmental psychology as it is today.

Darwin's Impact on Developmental Psychology

It is traditionally recognized that Darwin had a revolutionary impact on much of Western thought, including the life sciences. This impact was viewed as especially strong in psychology. For example, Boring (1950) noted that the impact was "tremendous" in that it brought about Galton's work on individual differences and the inheritance of mental capacities as well launched the subdiscipline of comparative psychology in the work of Romanes. Other historians of psychology make similar claims. For example, Schulz (1981) sums up four general influences Darwin had on psychology: (1) a recognition that there was substantial continuity in mental functioning between animals and humans; (2) an emphasis on the importance of individual differences; (3) a focus on function as expressed in terms of adaptation to the environment, in contrast to a focus on structure in terms of detailed elements of the mind; and (4) a broadening of methodology, that is, extending it beyond the psychophysiology and experimental introspection of the day.

Let us examine each of these influences as they would apply to developmental psychology. Influence 1 is exemplified in early studies of chimp–child behavior and development, and Influence 2 can clearly be found in the work of Binet, Terman, and others. The strength of both influences, though, was not great because Influence 1 was limited to small samples and Influence 2 was left mostly to those interested in practical issues involving assessment and prediction. Neither influence represented a significant theoretical change in the field.

As for Influence 3, Darwin's notion of function had an impact on many psychologists at the time—Peirce, James, Dewey, Angell, Carr. But none of them were developmentalists. There is little evidence that developmentalists in general were committed to a functionalist account of development. The few who were, such as Piaget, were more influenced by Lamarck than by Darwin (cf. Ghiselin, 1986). The kinds of adaptation that developmentalists tend to be interested in include functionalist issues. To deal with such issues empirically, however, requires long-term naturalistic observation and description of behavior and its short- as well as long-term consequences, a methodological approach not adopted on any significant scale by developmentalists (see Charlesworth, 1979).

As for methodology, Influence 4, developmental psychologists have historically employed a wide range of methodologies—naturalistic observation, diaries, testing, interviews, questionnaires, learning–training experiments, intervention, and so forth. It is doubtful that Darwin alone contributed to such methodological pluralism in developmental psychology. If anything, he probably strengthened already existing naturalistic accounts of children. Such accounts, however, did not dominate the field. As developmental psychologists became more interested in scientific rigor, they became more experimental and test and interview oriented. As a result, developmentalist inclinations toward documenting naturally occurring behavior never got a strong foothold in their discipline.

Apart from psychologists' reactions to Darwin, Darwin's impact was also viewed as revolutionary by some developmental psychologists. In his introduction to a collection of readings in child psychology, Kessen (1965) gives Darwin credit for "dramatically" changing our notion of the child and notes that Darwin's "irreducible contribution . . . to the study of children was . . . in his assignment of scientific value to childhood" (p. 115). A section of five readings entitled "Darwin and the Beginning of Child Psychology" includes Darwin's biographical sketch of his infant son and excerpts by William Preyer, G. Stanley Hall, James Mark Baldwin, and Hippolyte Taine.

However, a close look at the readings does not suggest much of a revolution. None of the latter four are purely Darwin, and only one (Baldwin) makes reference to natural selection, Darwin's unique contribution to evolutionary theory. One gets the impression that these four writers had assimilated Darwin to their own creative ideas. Darwin's infancy paper (nine pages) is miniscule compared with the voluminous observations and descriptions of infants made by developmentalists at the time. In short, Darwin's impact seems weak, indirect, and somewhat distorted, having been passed through the lenses of those who were aware of him but hardly accommodated to his theory.

Wohlwill (1973) shared Kessen's view but with some reservations. He viewed Darwin as being

> seen as a point of departure from which the major lines of thought shaping the field depart—one moving via James Mark Baldwin and Claparade to Piaget; another via Preyer and Hall to Gesell; a third via Freud to Eriksen and the other branches of the neo-Freudian school. (p. 4)

Wohlwill's view, though, revealed some skepticism. "Yet if this picture is the truth, it is very far from being the whole truth" (p. 5).

Darwin's significant impact on the field of developmental psychology still appears to be shared by many. However, there is also a sizable number of writers who do not adopt the viewpoint that Darwin's viewpoint was revolutionary. We turn to them now in some detail because their position is not as well known as that of the others.

Let us turn first to collections of historical readings. In Shipley's (1961) list of 36 *Classics in Psychology*, nothing by Darwin is included. In Herrnstein and Boring's (1965) sourcebook in the history of psychology, out of 116 classical papers, 1 is by Darwin; 2 by Galton, a major Darwinian proponent; and 1 by Romanes, another major Darwinian proponent. In Dennis's (1972) 37 historical readings in developmental psychology, 1 reading is a four-page excerpt from Darwin's (1872/1965) *The Expression of the Emotions in Man and Animals*. Francis Galton has one entry on the history of twins and one on psychometric methods, the former making only passing reference to Darwin, the latter none. G. Stanley Hall has one entry on the content of children's minds and no reference to Darwin. "Darwinism in the Nursery," a treatise on the grasping reflex by Louis Robinson, was included because it was considered one of the few successful examples of recapitulation theory, a theory that Dennis notes "plays almost no part in the present book because there is little evidence to support it" (p. 148). Darwin and evolutionary theory are mentioned only occasionally in the other 32 chapters. These omissions of Darwin's work present a picture quite at variance with that of Kessen and others.

If we take a broader perspective by looking at interdisciplinary readings that address the question of evolution and behavior, we get a similar picture. In *Behavior and Evolution*, edited by Roe and Simpson (1958), a wide range of contributors address Darwin's contribution to their discipline. No developmental psychologist has a chapter in the book, although several writers do make remarks about human developmental psychology. The position of ontogeny within the evolutionary framework is specifically addressed in a chapter by R. W. Sperry, a neuroscientist. More recently, in *The Darwinian Heritage* (Kohn, 1985), 32 scholars from various disciplines examined Darwin's contributions. None of the chapters are devoted to human development, although several make reference to historical instances of the term *development* as it was used in various ways, most not consistent with present usage. Expressing a more continental European view of Darwin's impact, Reinert (1979) notes that Darwin did not have an impact on developmental theory or research as generally thought and especially not among many German researchers.

When we turn to theories, Baldwin (1967), in his classic contribution to theories in child psychology, does not mention Darwin as a major or minor contributor, nor does Baldwin mention the concept of evolution as a useful conceptual tool for developmentalists. Langer (1969) also makes no mention of Darwin, not even in the section dealing with biological systems. Also, in Lerner's (1983) more recent and intentionally diverse treatment of philosophical and historical dimensions of developmental psychology, Darwin's theory does not emerge as an important influence. This is true even when the focus is on organismic developmental theory, life span developmental psychology, and ecology, all potential targets of evolutionary theorizing.

We find similar indications of Darwin's lack of impact when we examine Carmichael's *Handbook* series. In the first edition of Carmichael (1946), a number of references are made to Darwin, many of which cite his brief sketch of his infant son's behavior, but no reference is made to evolution or natural selection in the index. The second edition (Carmichael, 1954) is not much different in this respect with the exception of a note that G. Stanley Hall, "the 19th-century evolutionist," gave "real impetus to the study of development" (p. 698). The third edition of the *Handbook* (Mussen, 1970), with several citations of Darwin, appears like the first two but has a distinctive chapter by Hess on ethology and its relationship to developmental psychology. Hess (1970) does a good job connecting ethology to evolutionary theory by stressing the fact that both relied heavily on innate behaviors as major constituents of animal behaviors that were as subject to natural selection as morphological features in general. Mostly, though, Hess stresses proximate behaviors and their eliciting conditions (e.g., imprinting) of interest to ethologists rather than ultimate factors (reproductive success, ecological selection pressures, etc.) of more concern to evolutionary biology. In the fourth, most recent edition of the Carmichael *Handbook*, Cairns (1983), in his thoughtful historical analysis of the emergence of developmental psychology, makes virtually no mention of Darwin's contributions.

If we look at several major instances of empirical child development research in the decades after the publication of Darwin's *Origins* . . . , we find little or at best mixed evidence that Darwin played a significant role in structuring the empirical research. William Preyer (1909/1895), one of the leading early baby observers and biographers of Darwin's time, cites Darwin a good many times but concentrates mainly on observational facts, making no attempt to establish their causal status within the greater evolutionary picture. One gets the impression that Preyer could have done his work whether or not he knew about Darwin. Milicent Shinn (1909/1893), also an eminent naturalistic observer and recorder of children's behavior, cites Darwin, noting in the process his emphasis on the instinctual and adaptive significance of reflexes and early behaviors. She, however, also cites Tiedemann, Preyer, Hall, Sully, and Sigismund, thus revealing that not only Darwin influenced the direction of her efforts and the interpretation of her findings.

More recently, Myrtle McGraw (1935), long interested in the biological foundations of child behavior, has a chapter entitled "Phylogenetic

Activities and the Effect of Exercise upon Them" in her classic study of Johnny and Jimmy. In it, though, she does not cite Darwin or evolution, even though she clearly demonstrates awareness of early species adaptations. Rather than relying on evolutionary theory, she relies on naturalistic observation to supply her with hints of explanations of behavior. Like Tinbergen and Lorenz, the two ethologists whom she acknowledged as her models, she put her main weight on current behavior. Also, she, like many child developmentalists, focused heavily on the effects of experience during ontogeny on behavior rather than on hypothetical effects of historical adaptations.

The 1872 publication of Darwin's *The Expression of the Emotions in Man and Animals* helped strengthen the belief among psychologists that Darwin's theory could deal with behavior and the proximate factors that influenced it. But even this volume did not have the kind of effect on psychology that the work of others (Fechner, Wundt, James, Hall, Cattell, Baldwin) who were more in the mainstream of psychology had at the time. As Ekman (1973), in *Darwin and Facial Expression: A Century in Review*, notes, Darwin's work on emotional expression failed to have an effect on the field of psychology. In the same volume, Charlesworth and Kreutzer (1973) reviewed over a hundred empirical efforts dealing with facial expressions in infants and children since Darwin's time and found that fewer than a third indicated any debt to Darwin. Other contributors to the Ekman volume independently concluded that a century of research in facial expressions after Darwin was not substantially influenced by Darwin's ideas.

More recent dissatisfaction with the notion that Darwin had a significant impact on child psychology is expressed in a symposium in which Ghiselin (1986) challenges the argument that Piaget was influenced by Darwin and points out how developmental psychologists were more influenced by Spencer, Haeckel, and Huxley. In the same symposium, Costall (1986) points out that Darwin's impact on developmentalist psychology was only partial and frequently misleading, and Charlesworth (1986) notes that Darwin's emphasis on adaptation (as an important concept associated with natural selection) "never became part of Darwin's legacy to developmental psychology" (p. 1).

Most recently, Morss (1990) makes a similar case in a much stronger and extensive manner. In a daring exposition of what he calls the "Darwinian myth" within developmental psychology, Morss does a step-by-step demolition of the notion of Darwin's reputed contribution to developmental psychology. Morss argues that developmentalists misconstrued or failed to read most of what Darwin said, adopting instead two pre-Darwinian beliefs—Lamarckianism and Haeckelian recapitulationism. This did not stop developmentalists, however, from jumping on Darwin's bandwagon with most other scientists.

In considering evidence for Darwin's weak impact, it should be kept in mind that psychology during the second half of the 19th century was coming into its own, having separated itself from philosophy and establishing itself as a unique and useful science. Connecting itself with another discipline was not a top priority for a young, vigorous science. That Darwin had a strong initial impact on everyone's thinking, including that of developmental psychologists, is clear. It appears, however, that such an impact did not alter the latter's empirical research or theorizing in any enduring manner.

In defense of those who failed to grasp the meaning and ramifications of what Darwin said, it should be noted that many others, including biologists, failed to understand clearly what Darwin actually said (Mayr, 1982). Actually, it took decades until Darwin's theory came into its own (Ghiselin, 1969; Mayr, 1982). Today, it is argued, as many sociobiologists do (Alexander, 1979; Wilson, 1975), that the revolutionary implications for studying human behavior from an evolutionary point of view are just starting to be realized. Why it is starting now and not earlier is undoubtedly due to many factors—some indigenous to biology itself (cf. Mayr, 1982; Odling-Smee, 1988), some to Zeitgeist factors, and perhaps some to a realization on the part of many behavioral scientists, including developmental psychologists, that the scope of their field is not being served well enough by extant theories.

Darwin's Intermediaries

In searching for Darwin's connections to developmental psychology, one does not have to trace connections back directly to Darwin. Many younger biologists, as well as major behavioral scientists, took him seriously. Given Darwin's emphasis on adaptation made possible by instinct (motivation) and amplified by habit (learning) and insight (cognition), many psychologists assimilated his ideas to their own. These include Morgan, McDougall, Hall, Baldwin, Freud, James, and many other functionalists. Interestingly, none of them (with perhaps McDougall as an exception) wrestled with the deeper implications of natural selection for theory and practice.

It should be kept in mind that these intermediaries were most probably already well informed of (some apparently deeply impressed by) Spencer's (1870) theory of evolution, which had much popular appeal during the second half of the 19th century. Spencer's efforts antedated Darwin's *The Origins* . . . by a number of years and had much more to say about topics of interest to psychologists than Darwin did. Reading Darwin may have simply reinforced some of the ideas that these psychologists had already picked up from Spencer.

In answer, then, to the first question posed at the beginning of this article—To what extent and in what manner did Darwin influence developmental psychology?—it appears that Darwin did have an effect but that it was far from revolutionary, as was originally thought. What effect his theory did have was clearly fragmentary because it almost completely lacked the theory's distinctive feature, namely, natural selection.

Let us turn now to possible reasons why Darwin's impact on developmental psychology was not strong enough to bring about a revolutionary change in the discipline, as some seem to claim.

REASONS FOR DARWIN'S WEAK IMPACT

Three reasons are proposed here for why Darwin had a weak impact on developmental psychology—ideological, conceptual, and methodological.

Ideological: Meliorism

The ideological reason, labeled *meliorism* (Charlesworth, 1986), derives from developmental psychologists' long history of concerns for the health, education, and welfare of children. These concerns today provide strong motivation for much child development research.

One of the assumptions of the melioristic approach is that efforts that are based on research to improve the lives of children will indeed be effective. Hence, theories that suggest that difficulties will be minimal in applying melioristic efforts to real-life cases will be viewed as more acceptable than theories suggesting otherwise. According to this point of view, environmentalist models postulating plasticity during early development, for example, would have a less difficult time in attracting research funding than behavioral genetic models. Approaches that assume strong biological determinism are attractive only if the underlying causal mechanisms are relatively easily accessible (phenylketonuria [PKU] research, for example) and hence subject to experimental control.

Exacerbating the problem posed by evolutionary theory's commitment to genetic determinism is the theory's recognition of the effect on individuals and populations of the various forces of natural selection. This phenomenon is stressed by the fact that evolution has been characterized by continuous extinctions of enormous numbers of organisms and species. The mechanism for these extinctions is natural selection operating daily on individuals, including the young. Given the pervasive and persistent power of selection, competition for survival is a paramount feature of life. The death of a child (through abortion or infanticide, accident, disease, or neglect) leaves a vacant habitat that is immediately occupied by another child—from the evolutionary perspective, a successful competitor.

Such a message is harsh: It smacks of social Darwinism at its most repugnant. Instead of affirming equality and democracy, it affirms inequality and aristocracy. Along with unconscious or conscious acts or omissions of acts, thousands of children each day fail permanently to reach maturity. This process of selection differentially affects particular populations of children—those born into poverty, those with physical–behavioral handicaps, those of the culturally less preferred gender, and so forth. There are many impersonal reasons behind such forms of selection—some are related to the resource-carrying capacity of the environment and the number of excessive births; others to the material and psychosocial burdens of warfare, natural catastrophes, and political upheaval; and still others to differences in the general competitive ability to acquire and retain vital resources (World Resources Institute, 1990). The selection scene is complicated by complex systemic factors that, when recognized, are seen as either undermining the efficacy of melioristic action or questioning its wisdom in terms of long-term effects—effects that not only may diminish the lives of other children but have a profound effect on the lives of unborn generations. The issues raised by Malthus and developed by Darwin underlie much of the novel force Darwin's theory of evolution brought to the world scene.

It should be pointed out, however, that the acceptance of natural selection as the dominant mechanism in evolution is not uniform amongst modern biologists. For example, Lewontin (1983), in a more extensive argument than can be done justice here, argues that Darwin's evolutionary theory's emphasis on internal genetic factors being operated on by external environmental factors make the organism the object of two major forces outside of itself. The effect of this emphasis is to deprive the organism and the ontogenetic processes that bring its various phenotypes into being of any significant causal status in the evolutionary process. Lewontin cites evidence showing that this is not the case: The organism plays a very significant role in shaping (if not creating) environments. That the organism and its influence are omitted in most current empirical considerations of Darwin's theory is, for Lewontin, a serious mistake. His point has merit in keeping balanced our view of evolutionary processes. It also serves the melioristic point of view, putting more causal status into ontogenetic processes and thereby into the hands of those who have a daily influence on such processes.

Nevertheless, even if natural selection's role is diminished by organism activity, and no matter how morally repugnant it may be, from the Darwinian point of view, it is a chief characteristic of life. The issues raised by Malthus and increasingly expanded on today by conservationists and ecologists will not go away. Resources, whether natural or artificially produced, are not infinite, and there is no reason to believe that what is available will be equally available to everyone. Differential rationing is continually taking place, whether consciously recognized or not. It would be surprising if it had no differential impact on world populations.

Adding such a painful view of the fate of many children to the fact of individual differences in ability to escape such a fate (one of Darwin's main points) makes evolutionary theory even less acceptable for many. Such a mixture is very depressing and, for some, a very dangerous view of the human condition. Unequal competitive abilities and differences in outcomes clearly do not fit into a just and egalitarian world scheme. It appears that for many, such a view should for moral reasons never enter the picture presented by developmental psychology. That most, if not all, introductory textbooks in developmental psychology (unlike biology texts—see Hardin & Bajema, 1978) do not include such a picture suggests that this moral stance is prevalent within the field.

The professional ethics of such a stance can be debated. In defense of it, one can argue that the natural selection hypothesis has not been convincingly proven to be operating amongst humans, hence designing research policy in light of it would be morally irresponsible. If the picture is accurate, one can still justify ignoring it because new advances in science and technology (as history has often shown, for example, in agriculture) may well alter life circumstances sufficiently to make it obsolete. For example, even if conditions are currently dismal because of the zero-sum status of many vital resources and uncontrollable increases in population size, technological innovation and improvements in public education (on birth control, environmental conservation, etc.) may alter this status.

Darwin's second major revolutionary book was *The Descent of Man and Selection in Relation to Sex* (1936), which first appeared in 1871. This book also has great ideological import, especially today, because one of its major themes is the role of reproductive differences between males and females in the evolution of the species. Sexual dimorphism in both anatomy and behavior, according to Darwin, serves a significant reproductive function in humans. Ignoring this fact in one's research considerations would be seen by Darwin as peculiar as ignoring individual differences because both sexual dimorphism and individual differences are deeply implicated in human evolution.

The general issue of generic human traits having been adaptive in the long run because they contributed to successful reproduction is part of the picture associated with gender differences. Generic human traits responsible for aggressive and dominant behaviors, cheating, and selfishness, as well as those associated with altruism and cooperation, have, according to Darwin, been selected over evolutionary time. As a consequence, they are an inevitable part of the current human genetic and hence phenotypic makeup. The phenotypic part cannot be escaped or altered without paying a reproductive penalty. In this sense, biology is destiny.

Given all this, it is easy to understand why Darwin would not be a developmentalist's first-choice theorist to guide child research. Also, it is easy to understand why those applying evolutionary biology to human behavior in general would be looked on as dangerous at worst or misleading and hence irrelevant at best. But there is more than ideological concern behind the developmentalists' ambivalence about evolutionary theory.

Conceptual: Phylogeny and Ontogeny

In addition to finding Darwin's theory unacceptable for ideological reasons, many developmentalists are aware of a conceptual problem in adopting an evolutionary perspective of child development: the problem of ontogeny and phylogeny.

As Patterson (1983) points out, until the 1840s both terms were synonymous for biological change in general. As a result of the work of von Baer, ontogeny became more associated with embryology. In subsequent years the term *development* became identified with ontogeny—the processes of an individual's change from the fertilized cell to adulthood. Phylogeny broke away from ontogeny in the 1860s when Haeckel used the term to account for species changes over evolutionary time, claiming (as already noted, incorrectly) that such species changes were inevitably reflected in the individual ontogenies of species members. Darwin himself was not inclined to draw any analogies between the terms (Gruber, 1974). Instead, he viewed them as separate but in critical interaction with each other.

Today, as evolutionary biologists and others point out, the synthetic theory of evolution views phylogeny and ontogeny as fundamentally different. Phylogeny deals with populations, and ontogeny deals with individuals. Phylogenetic implies long-term historical, intergenerational changes; ontogenetic implies short-term intraindividual changes. Only taxonomic groups such as species have phylogenies; only individuals have ontogenies. Phylogenies reflect material changes in deoxyribonucleic acid (DNA) and its distribution in populations; ontogenies reflect behavioral and psychological as well as physical changes in individuals. Natural selection factors change the gene pools of different generations; at a more microlevel, similar selection factors change the adaptive capacities of individuals and their gene representation in subsequent generations.

Given that Lamarck's idea of acquired traits being heritable was demolished and Haeckel's notion that ontogeny recapitulates phylogeny dismissed as a myth, it is easy to understand why most scientists would reject the idea of any meaningful connections between them that could be used for purposes of research. Despite such rejection, it was also obvious, if only from a rational point of view, that evolutionary changes depended on individual ontogenies for their representation in subsequent generations. On one hand, if an organism does not reach its reproductive age, its genes (unless it has many close relatives who do reproduce) will not be represented in the next generation. On the other hand, ontogenies cannot exist with the phylogenetic processes that produced the genetic material that make ontogeny possible. In short, phylogeny and ontogeny are not forces independent of or in competition with each other. They characterize the whole flow of life across geological time, phylogenies being long lines of successive ontogenies. What happens to the former may have effects on the latter and vice versa. If we want to know as much as there possibly is to know about a lineage and its origins, we have to know about the individuals and their life histories within it; and if we want to know about individuals and their histories, we have to know their lineage.

Not all developmentalists, however, agree that acknowledging this connection has scientific merit. Acknowledging it requires accepting genes as the crucial causal link between individuals and their lineage. Oyama (1985), for example, takes an extreme position in this regard, arguing that for all practical (research) purposes, phylogenetic (more correctly, genetic) determination stops at conception. The epigenetic processes that take over the activity of the zygote are from her point of view nonpredictive because the entry of novel environmental conditions and inevitable probabilistic interactions that follow introduce a high degree of unpredictability into the picture. Only careful experimental intervention (not historical speculation or hypothetical genetic influences) can make sense of these complex interactions and their phenotypic effects. In other words, knowledge of phylogeny and genetics is virtually useless in adding anything of significance to our understanding of how the phenotype comes into existence.

Gottlieb (1991) takes a similar but less extreme position in his discussion of the role experience plays in trait canalization. He acknowledges the role that genetic determination (read backwards to phylogenesis) plays in the canalization of traits but feels that this role (and the notion of a genetically determined reaction range) has been overrated and is now outmoded. A new model, the developmental systems view, gives less power to such determination, emphasizing instead novel, environmentally induced experiential factors.

Such a systems model serves as a valuable heuristic for developmental research. Claiming that the epigenesis involves the development of new structures and functions during individual development is by definition correct. However, the material basis and organizational structure of such systems are hardly limitless in their functional potential. No organisms or machines are made to do everything. No matter how hard one tries today to expand or improve early calculating machines, they can never be made to do what current computers can do. Similarly, a particular configuration of deoxyribonucleic acid that constitutes part of the human genome cannot be made to produce any phenotype that fits an experimentalist's fancy. When the experimenter does succeed, it is not without a great cost to other phenotypes. Most existing systems are very stable because their variants have failed many earlier selection tests. As for most human adaptations, many, if not all, of the most common of them, such as emotions and many social behaviors, are very old and stable because they have successfully passed numerous recurring environmental challenges.

It should also be stressed that not all stable human adaptations are infinitely malleable. There is a limit not only on adaptive phenotypic variations but on the number of developmental trajectories through which these variations come into existence. Ontogenies are not only constrained to variables dealing with early perception and imprinting: Many other interlocking systems contribute concurrently to channelizing ontogeny into fairly narrow straits. This has been well illustrated for developmentalists by Waddington's (1957) notion of canalization, the evolved homeostatic mechanism that keeps ontogeny on a species-typical track. As for the track's destination, according to evolutionary theory, the well-known conservative nature of ontogenetic processes ensures a positive reproductive outcome under natural conditions. Those that deviate too far from this track do not meet environmental (physical and social) preconditions for reproductive success and consequently are not represented in subsequent generations.

To complicate matters for developmental systems constructivists, as modern evolutionary biology demonstrates, ontogenies (life histories) appear to be subject to natural selection (Stearns, 1976). This means that it is the environment that ultimately structures ontogenies and imposes constraints on individual development and its outcomes: The genes, the random genetic material, have to submit, so to speak, to their environments, even when they are involved in the complex process of helping to create very complicated ontogenies such as human life histories.

Whatever position one takes toward genetic factors—overrating them as some sociobiologists do, underrating them as some developmentalists do, or rating them just right as perhaps the majority do—the fact remains that developmental researchers work with living individual organisms, not hereditary mechanisms, nor with lineages and populations. It is not surprising, then, that evolutionary speculation about different ancestors fighting it out in different environments now long gone is viewed as having little utility in guiding such research.

It should be noted that developmental psychologists ignoring the implications of evolutionary theory are not alone. There is evidence that early ethologists, also, were not uniformly inspired by evolutionary theory. As Burkhardt (1983) points out, although the founders of modern ethology, such as Konrad Lorenz, worked with the theory of evolution in mind, they got along well in their research for decades with only passing general reference to it. The point being made here is that a productive research effort can be expended on an empirical phenomenon without any specific reference to the preontogenetic origins of the phenomenon.

Methodological: Ultimate and Proximate Factors

As already intimated, the distinction between phylogeny and ontogeny poses not only conceptual problems but methodological ones as well. After deciding on a research domain, every researcher faces the practical problem of how to collect data and what kinds of inferences can be legitimately made from them. Here is where the distinction between proximate and ultimate factors enters the picture. Data collected from current events allow inferences about causality with much more legitimacy than data from more historical sources. Those proximate factors that can be controlled here and now are within practical reach of everyone. Like every approach, however, such an approach has a drawback: It produces a microscopic, highly delimited picture of a very complex, dynamic phenomenon driven by a multiple of unknown factors, some very remote in time. Sometimes the picture is so small that it has slim connections with anything else, except by means of general principles established in some other discipline (e.g., neurophysiology).

Those involved with ultimate (historical and broad ecological) factors have the opposite problem—no causality and a vast macroscopic picture that connects much over great expanses of time and space but has no reference to an individual in the process of everyday adaptation. Given a choice, developmentalists would rather struggle with microscopic proximate problems than engage in the comparative and often speculative task facing those who deal with the ultimate.

As one interested in phylogeny, Darwin, of course, dealt with ultimate factors, the major geological and biological events that transformed species over time. He was, though, very aware of proximate factors, as is evident in his daily experiments with earthworms (Darwin, 1890). Despite his close-up view of earthworm behavior, he, nevertheless, managed to give their behavior ultimate significance—"Worms have played a more important part in the history of the world than most persons would at first suppose" (p. 305). In light of this, it will be interesting when developmental psychologists make similar assertions about infants. This is not a playful challenge. One could ask the evolutionary (ultimate) question of what part has infancy played in the history of human phylogenesis, or one could ask the ontogenetic functional (proximate) question of what does being an infant do for the individual human. Cross-species comparisons of adaptive significance make such questions of historical significance and function plausible because some species have virtually no infancy period, and some have relatively long, expensive infancies. Answers to these questions can come about only when both phylogenetic and ontogentic thinking are united.

Let us consider now possible points at which evolutionary theory and developmental research can be united in a mutually beneficial manner.

NEW SYNERGISM

A major thesis of the present article is that knowledge of Darwin's contribution and its current elaborations can enhance developmental research, whereas the latter can assist the former by putting its hypotheses to competent test. In very general terms, enhancement consists of both clarifying and filling in empirical gaps in developmental research and establishing new connections with other domains. Asking why this should be done gets at least one important answer. One of Darwin's major achievements was expanding nomological nets across many disciplines. Because of this achievement, for the first time in history, geology and paleontology, organic evolution, ecology, animal behavior, and even human behavior, mind, and conscience became linked by faintly discernible laws of causal relationships. It is now up to scientists to examine these links, to make them more discernible, and to determine whether they are causal.

There are at least two conceptual matrices that have been generated by evolutionary theory that have not been fully exploited by developmentalists. The most familiar, historically labeled as *instincts*, deals with generic human traits; usually those that appear to have high adaptive value are species universal (infant–caretaker attachment, for example), thereby suggesting that they have had a long historical association with successful survival and reproduction. The concepts characterizing this matrix expand the current matrix of standard developmental concepts by including such factors as iterative (sequential) reproduction and its developmental implications, sexual dimorphism and attraction as reproductive strategies, developmental immaturity requiring prolonged parental care, infant–caretaker attachment, parent–child conflict, weaning, sibling rivalry, peer group formation, structure, and function, selfishness, the ontogeny of dominance and submission and competition and cooperation, conscience and its formation, learning as adaptation, niche construction during ontogeny, and the acquisition of deception as a competition strategy. Examples of these concepts and those working with them directly or indirectly include socialization, development, and personality (MacDonald, 1987, 1988); social evolution, family, and parent–child conflict (Trivers, 1985); evolution of various aspects of human development (Konner, 1981); sex, parenting, and family (Daly & Wilson, 1978); evolution of self-knowledge and deception (Krebs, Denton, & Higgins, 1988); sociobiological perspective on the development of human reproductive strategies (Draper & Harpending, 1988); morality and moral development (Alexander, 1987; Charlesworth, 1991); learning as an evolutionary adaptation (Plotkin, 1988); niche-constructing phenotypes during ontogeny and individual–environment coevolution (Odling-Smee, 1988); and childhood experience and reproductive strategies (Belsky, Steinberg, & Draper, 1991).

The second matrix bears more directly on the issue of individual (as contrasted with universal) traits and their role in natural selection, a topic long omitted from the great bulk of research in animal and human sciences. It deals with individual differences in such traits and the effect that these differences have on individuals relative to their social and physical environments. In other words, this matrix emphasizes vital functional relationships between individuals and ecological factors and requires measures of both individuals and such factors as the process of interaction itself. To date, some of these measures and relationships are represented by vast amounts of personality and demographic data not yet connected into any unified, meaningful picture. These phenomena include individual differences in infant and child mortality, quality of infant and child care and education, abuse, neglect, poor nutrition, accidents, and so forth, and their immediate effects on the health, lives, and development of children and the long-term effects on adaptations and reproduction as adults. These well-known aspects of childhood are to be viewed in terms of ecological, economic, human population, and cultural factors, however, not in traditional terms but in natural selection terms that include the effects on health, mortality, reproduction of resource availability, disparities of resource costs and benefits across populations (ethnic, socioeconomic, cultural) of children and families, and disparities in environmental risks to which different groups of children are exposed.

Parenthetically, it should be stressed that it is no longer satisfactory that developmentalists adopt only that part of biology dealing with proximate mechanisms (e.g., physiology, physical growth and development, endocrinology, neuroanatomy and neurophysiology, the traditional biology of most behavioral scientists) and totally disregard that part of biology that deals with ecological factors (social, physical, environmental). The lab coat and microscope used to isolate biological variables to generate universal principles are no more important to acquiring understanding of the biological nature of human development than walking shoes and a clipboard used to discover organism–environment connections to identify significant individual differences in adaptation and the nature of the microniches in which these differences become apparent.

Examples of current researchers who think in terms of this second matrix include, for example, those in the fields of general evolutionary and comparative aspects of behavior development (Burghardt & Bekoff, 1978); developmental evolutionary ecology of humans (Chisholm, 1988); natural selection, ecological instability, and child maltreatment (Burgess, Kurland, & Pensky, 1988); socialization and reproductive strategies (Belsky et al., 1991); resources and resource acquisition during ontogeny (Charlesworth, 1987); genetically organized life histories and environmentally contingent behavior strategies (Crawford & Anderson, 1989); personality differences and their evolutionary function (Buss, 1991); individual differences and similarities as evolutionary adaptations (Tooby & Cosmides, 1990); and personality and reproductive fitness (Eaves, Martin, Heath, Hewitt, & Neale, 1990).

As for developmental research enhancing evolutionary biology (synergisms benefit both parties), there is no better way to test and aid in the formulation of evolutionary hypotheses having to do with human behavior and then submit them to the best research tests available. Because most evolutionary biologists have not been trained as developmental psychologists and have no firsthand feel for the intricacies of developmental research, it is the developmentalists who have to do the job.

CONCLUSION

Darwin's achievement and the great body of research that has enriched it have shown that humans are kin to all living things by virtue of sharing a common stock of life hundreds of millions of years old. The significance of this achievement is enormous because it requires that we view ourselves and our development as being preformed (loosely or rigidly) by processes that antedate each individual's conception. According to evolutionary theory, the ultimate function of these processes is to ensure that we survive and successfully reproduce ourselves. It is with this in mind that we are led to recognize the necessity and power of genetic mechanisms and the forces of natural selection that have come to structure human existence.

The extreme epigenetic argument that development is so complex, so nonpredictable, and so conditioned by environmental factors that genetic influences (as the most recent deposits of evolutionary history) lose any meaningful force in shaping it cannot be used to deny this conclusion. We can, of course, choose to deny it, but if we wish to do so, we foolishly cut ourselves off from a great source of potential knowledge. We do not have to deny the nature and origin of genes to study epigenesis any more than we have to deny the nature and origin of building materials when we study the architectural process.

Those who are worried about recognizing the powers of natural selection claim that humans are not passive agents of environmental factors but active shapers of their environments. This claim is correct. Culture and technology are capable of altering all of human existence, including our biology. However, although a cultural innovation may be a positive, life-enhancing benefit for one group, it can be a great burden or danger to another. Because most groups are established because their members have common interests not shared with other groups, the hope for universal benefits as a result of one group's innovations is not encouraging. At present, humans have more material goods than at any time in history. That these goods are unequally distributed across the world's various populations, resulting in the deaths (or loss of reproductive opportunity) of millions of children annually, argues strongly for the continued operation of the kind of natural selection Darwin was talking about. Whether such selection will ultimately have an effect on the human gene pool cannot be predicted. Such a question, however, is not important. What is important is that as

96   *WILLIAM R. CHARLESWORTH*

long as the fact of selection is ignored, the melioristic tendencies of developmental psychologists will never be satisfactorily implemented. Obviously, the whole world has to act as one group for these tendencies to become effective.

Those worried about ideological agendas that are based on studies showing that genetic and natural selection factors (the two powers in evolutionary theory) indeed influence current human behavior should be just as worried about agendas that are based on programs that espouse a nature–nurture dichotomy and only view cultural factors as the most critical in controlling human behavior. Cultural change mechanisms are far easier to put into operation for inhumane social, political, or economic purposes than genetic–selection mechanisms. Actually, those worried about ideological programs built on scientific theory in general and evolutionary theorizing in particular have plenty of worries cut out for them. As history has shown, Darwin's ideas were enthusiastically (and usually incorrectly) employed as justifications for the whole political spectrum—from the far right to the far left.

The vision granted by the knowledge of human evolution and our kinship with other species, however, should hardly compel us to feel reduced to other species and all the laws that govern them. Unless one can succeed in putting an authoritarian hammerlock on our approach to empirical reality, biology cannot be transformed into psychology or psychology into biology. It is not a question of deciding disciplinary boundaries but a question of the very nature of human nature.

There are too many obvious differences between humans and other species to assume we are in all respects fundamentally similar. In certain respects, humans are unique as all species are unique. To ignore the exceptionality of a species' particular set of adaptations is to violate a basic methodological tenet of evolutionary biology, namely, to be open to the nature and function of all of a species' adaptations, no matter how singular or unusual. A good example of a unique human adaptation is the excitement that scientists feel at recognizing an interesting scientific problem. This excitement and the efforts that it motivates cannot be matched by any other species. The reductionistic claim that chimpanzees also recognize and solve problems is much too crude to qualify as a valid scientific claim that chimpanzee cognition is fundamentally no different from humans.

In all this, we can ask the general question of why reductionism must attend every phase (especially the explanatory phase) of the scientific process. It is true that the specialization required of good empirical research requires a reductionistic attitude. But specialization, like other aspects of science, is always in the service of a wider picture of understanding. Such a picture requires expanding interdisciplinary collaboration rather than contracting it. Why should the three branches of genetics—phylo-genetics, gene-genetics, and onto-genetics—attempt to reduce each other to their own definitions? Why can they not operate within the same conceptual mansion? Their special concentrations of research energy are not alternatives but complements that reinforce each other in the pursuit of comprehensive and coherent knowledge.

Our best tool in all this is the scientific method, no matter what theory is used to employ it. And our best attitude is openness to all theories. If Darwin did anything revolutionary as a scientist, it was surely his success in producing a more comprehensive and coherent picture of life than anyone up to his time. He could do this only because he chose freely across disciplines and methods to create this picture.

Darwin's potential impact on the science of human behavior and development has scarcely been recognized. Today, only a few of Darwin's contributions (along with more recent elaborations of his ideas) are being used to help unravel the complexities of human development. Hopefully, more of them will be used in the future and used more intensely, for this appears to be a valuable way to expand the range of developmental research. This range has to be expanded because it deals with the most complex phenomenon in the universe—the developing human.

Expanding developmental research in this manner is also a way to put Darwin's grand ideas to hard empirical tests. Darwin's theorizing has already been subject to revision, and there is no reason why further revision is not possible. As in all science, we move between the authority of general ideas and the authority of particular empirical observations. It is the latter, though, when in numerically large and comprehensive aggregates, that have the most decisive word.

However, a break on our enthusiasm for evolutionary theory is also in order. Although a good number of evolutionary concepts are relevant for the work of developmentalists, a purely evolutionary approach will most likely not attend the final unraveling of developmental secrets. Darwin's contribution has its limits. There are too many proximate ontogenetic secrets—genetic, neurophysiological, social, and cognitive—that Darwin could not anticipate. Such unraveling will have to be done by developmentalists themselves, as Darwin the scientist would surely appreciate.

Notwithstanding this limitation on Darwin's contribution, his efforts toward understanding what happened during human evolution, the historical factors that shaped human ontogeny, and the informational residue they have deposited in our genes will be very helpful in expanding developmental psychology. As Darwin said, and as developmentalists well know, "If we look to first origin there must be progress."

REFERENCES

Alexander, R. D. (1979). *Darwinism and human affairs*. Seattle: University of Washington Press.

Alexander, R. D. (1987). *The biology of moral systems.* Chicago: Aldine.

Baldwin, A. L. (1967). *Theories of child development.* New York: Wiley.

Barrett, P. H., Weinshank, D. J., Ruhlen, P., & Ozminski, S. J. (Eds.). (1987). *A concordance to Darwin's The descent of man and selection in relation to sex.* Ithaca, NY: Cornell University Press.

Beer, G. (1985). Darwin's reading and the fictions of development. In D. Kohn (Ed.), *The Darwin heritage* (pp. 543–588). Princeton, NJ: Princeton University Press.

Belsky, J., Steinberg, L., & Draper, P. (1991). Childhood experience, interpersonal development, and reproduction strategy: An evolutionary theory of socialization. *Child Development, 67,* 647–670.

Boring, E. G. (1950). *A history of experimental psychology.* New York: Appleton-Century-Crofts.

Burgess, R. L., Kurland, J. A., & Pensky, E. E. (1988). Ultimate and proximate determinants of child maltreatment: Natural selection, ecological instability, and coercive interpersonal contingencies. In K. B. MacDonald (Ed.), *Sociobiological perspectives on human development* (pp. 293–319). New York: Springer-Verlag.

Burghardt, G. M., & Bekoff, M. (1978). *The development of behavior: Comparative and evolutionary aspects.* New York: Garland STPM Press.

Burkhardt, R. W. (1983). The development of an evolutionary ethology. In D. S. Bendall (Ed.), *Evolution from molecules to men* (pp. 429–444). Cambridge, England: Cambridge University Press.

Buss, D. N. (1991). Evolutionary personality psychology. *Annual Review of Psychology, 42,* 459–491.

Cairns, R. (1983). The emergence of developmental psychology. In P. Mussen (Ed.), *Handbook of child psychology* (formerly Carmichael's *Manual of child psychology*) (4th ed., pp. 41–102). New York: Wiley.

Carmichael, L. (Ed.). (1946). *Manual of child psychology* (1st ed.). New York: Wiley.

Carmichael, L. (Ed.). (1954). *Handbook of child psychology* (2nd ed.). New York: Wiley.

Charlesworth, W. R. (1979). Ethology: Understanding the other half of intelligence. In M. von Cranach, K. Foppa, W. Lepenies, & D. Ploogs (Eds.), *Human ethology: Claims and limits of a new discipline* (pp. 491–529). Cambridge, England: Cambridge University Press.

Charlesworth, W. R. (1986). Darwin and developmental psychology: 100 years later. *Human Development, 29,* 1–35.

Charlesworth, W. R. (1987). Resources and resource acquisition during ontogeny. In K. B. MacDonald (Ed.), *Sociobiological perspectives on human development* (pp. 24–77). New York: Springer-Verlag.

Charlesworth, W. R. (1991). The development of the sense of justice. *American Behavioral Scientist, 34,* 350–370.

Charlesworth, W. R., & Kreutzer, M. A. (1973). Facial expressions of infants and children. In P. Ekman (Ed.), *Darwin and facial expressions: A century in review* (pp. 91–168). San Diego: Academic Press.

Chisholm, J. S. (1988). Toward a developmental evolutionary ecology of humans. In K. B. MacDonald (Ed.), *Sociobiological perspectives on human development* (pp. 78–102). New York: Springer-Verlag.

Costall, A. (1986). Evolutionary gradualism and the study of development. *Human Development, 29,* 4–11.

Crawford, C. B., & Anderson, J. L. (1989). Sociobiology: An environmentalist discipline? *American Psychologist, 44*(12), 1449–1459.

Daly, M., & Wilson, M. (1978). *Sex, evolution and behavior: Adaptation for reproduction.* North Scituate, MA: Duxbury Press.

Darwin, C. (1936). *The origin of species by means of natural selection.* London: John Murray. (Original work published 1859)

Darwin, C. (1936). *The descent of man and selection in relation to sex.* New York: Appleton-Century-Crofts. (Original work published 1871)

Darwin, C. (1965). *The expression of the emotions in man and animals.* Chicago: University of Chicago Press. (Original work published 1872)

Darwin, C. (1890). *The formation of vegetable mold through the action of worms, with observations on their habits.* New York: Appleton-Century-Crofts.

Dennis, W. (1972). (Ed.). *Historical readings in developmental psychology.* New York: Appleton-Century-Crofts.

Dobzhansky, T., Ayala, F. J., Stebbins, G. L., & Valentine, J. W. (1977). *Evolution.* San Francisco: Freeman.

Draper, P., & Harpending, H. (1988). A sociobiological perspective on the development of human reproductive strategies. In K. B. MacDonald (Ed.), *Sociobiological perspectives on human development* (pp. 340–372). New York: Springer-Verlag.

Eaves, L. J., Martin, N. G., Heath, A. C., Hewitt, J. K., & Neale, M. C. (1990). Personality and reproductive fitness. *Behavior Genetics, 20*(5), 563–568.

Ekman, P. (1973). (Ed.). *Darwin and facial expressions: A century in review.* San Diego: Academic Press.

Ghiselin, M. (1969). *The triumph of the Darwinian method.* Berkeley, CA: University of California Press.

Ghiselin, M. T. (1986). The assimilation of Darwinism in developmental psychology. *Human Development, 29,* 12–21.

Gottlieb, G. (1991). Experiential canalization of behavioral development: Theory. *Developmental Psychology, 27,* 4–13.

Gould, S. J. (1977). *Ontogeny and phylogeny.* Cambridge, MA: Belknap/Harvard University Press.

Gruber, H. E. (1974). *Darwin on man: A psychological study of scientific creativity* (together with Darwin's early and unpublished notebooks). London: Wildwood House.

Hardin, G., & Bajema, C. (1978). *Biology: Its principles and implications* (3rd ed.). San Francisco: Freeman.

Herrnstein, R. J., & Boring, E. G. (Eds.). (1965). *A source book in the history of psychology*. Cambridge, MA: Harvard University Press.

Hess, E. H. (1970). Ethology and developmental psychology. In P. H. Mussen (Ed.), *Manual of child psychology* (3rd ed., pp. 1–38). New York: Wiley.

Kessen, W. (1965). *The child*. New York: Wiley.

Kohn, D. (Ed.). (1985). *The Darwinian heritage*. Princeton, NJ: Princeton University Press.

Konner, M. J. (1981). Evolution of human behavior development. In R. H. Monroe, R. L. Monroe, & B. B. Whiting (Eds.), *Handbook of cross-cultural human development* (pp. 3–51). New York: Garland STPM Press.

Krebs, D., Denton, K., & Higgins, N. C. (1988). On the evolution of self-knowledge and self-deception. In K. B. MacDonald (Ed.), *Sociobiological perspectives on human development* (pp. 103–139). New York: Springer-Verlag.

Langer, J. (1969). *Theories of development*. New York: Holt, Rinehart & Winston.

Lerner, R. M. (1983). *Developmental psychology: Historical and philosophical perspectives*. Hillsdale, NJ: Erlbaum.

Lewontin, R. C. (1983). Gene, organism, and environment. In D. S. Bendall (Ed.), *Evolution from molecules to men* (pp. 273–285). Cambridge, England: Cambridge University Press.

MacDonald, K. B. (Ed.). (1987). *Sociobiological perspectives on human development*. New York: Springer-Verlag.

MacDonald, K. B. (1988). *Social and personality development: An evolutionary synthesis*. New York: Plenum Press.

Mayr, E. (1982). *The growth of biological thought: Diversity, evolution, and inheritance*. Cambridge, MA: Harvard University Press.

Mayr, E., & Provine, W. B. (Eds.). (1980). *The evolutionary synthesis: Perspectives on the unification of biology*. Cambridge, MA: Harvard University Press.

McGraw, M. (1935). *Growth: A study of Johnny and Jimmy*. New York: Appleton-Century-Crofts.

Morss, J. R. (1990). *The biologising of childhood: Developmental psychology and the Darwinian myth*. Hillsdale, NJ: Erlbaum.

Mussen, P. H. (Ed.). (1970). *Carmichael's manual of child psychology* (3rd ed.). New York: Wiley.

Odling-Smee, F. J. (1988). Niche-constructing phenotypes. In H. C. Plotkin (Ed.), *The role of behavior in evolution* (pp. 73–132). Cambridge, MA: MIT Press.

Oyama, S. (1985). *The ontogeny of information: Developmental systems and evolution*. Cambridge, England: Cambridge University Press.

Patterson, C. (1983). How does phylogeny differ from ontogeny. In B. C. Goodwin, N. Holder, & C. C. Wylie (Eds.), *Development and evolution* (pp. 1–31). Cambridge, England: Cambridge University Press.

Plotkin, H. C. (1988). Learning in evolution. In H. C. Plotkin (Ed.), *The role of behavior in evolution* (pp. 133–164). Cambridge, MA: MIT Press.

Preyer, W. (1909). *The mind of the child.* New York: Appleton-Century-Crofts. (Original work published 1895.)

Reinert, G. (1979). Prolegomena to a history of life-span developmental psychology. In P. B. Baltes & D. G. Brian, Jr. (Eds.), *Life-span development and behavior* (pp. 205–254). San Diego: Academic Press.

Roe, A., & Simpson, G. G. (1958). *Behavior and evolution.* New Haven, CT: Yale University Press.

Schulz, D. (1981). *A history of modern psychology* (3rd ed.). San Diego: Academic Press.

Shinn, M. W. (1909). *Notes on the development of a child* (Vol. 1). University of California Publications in Education. (Original work published 1893)

Shipley, T. (Ed.). (1961). *Classics in psychology.* New York: Philosophical Library.

Spencer, H. (1870). *Principles of psychology.* (2nd ed.). London: Williams & Norgate.

Stearns, S. C. (1976). Life-history tactics: A review of ideas. *Quarterly Review of Biology, 51,* 3–47.

Tooby, J., & Cosmides, L. (1990). On the universality of human nature uniqueness of the individual: The role of genetics and adaptation. *Journal of Personality, 58,* 17–67.

Trivers, R. (1985). *Social evolution.* Menlo Park, CA: Benjamin/Cummings.

Waddington, C. H. (1957). *The strategy of genes.* Winchester, MA: Allen & Unwin.

Weismann, A. (1889). Concept of germ plasm. In E. Poulton et al. (Trans.), *Essays upon heredity* (1st ed.). Oxford, England: Clarendon Press.

Wilson, E. O. (1975). *Sociobiology: The new synthesis.* Cambridge, MA: Harvard University Press.

Wohlwill, J. F. (1973). *The study of behavioral development.* San Diego: Academic Press.

World Resources Institute. (1990). *World Resources, 1990–91: A report by the World Resources Institute.* New York: Oxford University Press.

3

G. STANLEY HALL:
FROM PHILOSOPHY TO
DEVELOPMENTAL PSYCHOLOGY

SHELDON H. WHITE

In 1884, G. Stanley Hall was appointed professor of psychology and pedagogics at Johns Hopkins University. Today, when we have come to see psychology as distinct from philosophy, the appointment is generally referred to as the first professorship in psychology in the United States. Hall and Daniel Coit Gilman, president of Johns Hopkins, saw the appointment as a strategic new professorship in philosophy (O'Donnell, 1985; D. J. Wilson, 1990).

Hall (1876, 1879) had examined the teaching of philosophy in 300 American colleges, and he saw psychology as vital to the regeneration of that teaching. Gilman was building the first successful graduate university in America and wanted a reconstructed philosophy, but he had to be careful. Johns Hopkins had been criticized when opening-day ceremonies opened and closed without prayer and Thomas Huxley, the notorious Darwinian, had been brought in to give an invited address. Many people in Baltimore

Reprinted from *Developmental Psychology*, 28, 25–34. Copyright 1992 by the American Psychological Association.

considered Johns Hopkins to be a center of godless materialism. The new philosophy professor had to be "safe." Three potential philosophy professors held half-time lectureships. Charles Sanders Peirce held a lectureship in logic. What he taught was not controversial, but his name came to be linked with divorce and scandal. George Sylvester Morris was a brilliant lecturer and a man who had been a mentor to G. Stanley Hall and would be one to John Dewey, but Morris had once turned down a chair at Bowdoin rather than give assurances about his orthodoxy. Hall was the third half-time lecturer. There was evidence that he was a fine teacher, and William James had told Gilman that Hall was the only man in America other than himself qualified to teach the new physiological psychology. Hall had reassured Gilman that he was a Christian believer:

> I am as far as *possible* from materialism in every form. My physiological studies of the nervous system bring me incessantly before the question of the identity of thought and matter, and I can only say that my deepest private feeling . . . is that materialism is simply want of education. As to my religious sentiments. I am a graduate of divinity, and without agreeing entirely with all that I hear, am in the habit of church going, and indeed am still a nominal church member I believe. (Quoted in Albrecht, 1960, p. 112)

In 1884, Hall was given the Johns Hopkins chair. In an introductory lecture on October 6 of that year, he mapped out the new psychology he would teach. It had three branches—comparative, experimental, and historical—and it was fundamentally and profoundly religious:

> This whole field of psychology is connected in the most vital way with the future of religious belief in our land. . . . The new psychology, which brings simply a new method and a new standpoint to philosophy, is, I believe, Christian to its root and center; and its final mission in the world is . . . to flood and transfuse the new and vaster conceptions of the universe and of man's place in it . . . with the old Scriptural sense of unity, rationality, and love. . . . The Bible is being slowly re-revealed as man's great text book in psychology—dealing with him as a whole, his body, mind, and will, in all the larger relations to nature, society,—which has been misappreciated simply because it is so deeply divine. That something may be done here to aid this development is my strongest hope and belief. (Hall, 1885, pp. 247–248)

Hall would hold true to his religious conception of psychology until the end of his life (Hall, 1917; Rodkin, 1990).

Beginning with his new position in Johns Hopkins, Hall would become a leader in the building of the modern research university, the establishment of psychology in that university, and diverse outreach efforts to create philosophies of social practice for individuals reconstructing American institutions for education, welfare, and health. Hall was one of a new class of Americans in the late 19th century—people whose work stitched thousands of localities and "island communities" together into a national political order (Wiebe, 1967).

THE OLD PSYCHOLOGY IN AN OLDER COLLEGE SYSTEM

What was G. Stanley Hall like as a person? Various shorter or longer, warmer or cooler, literary snapshots of him exist. In Hall's (1923) *Life and Confessions*, he talks about himself in his own voice. There are warm accounts of him by colleagues and former students (Burnham, 1925; Pruett, 1926; Sanford, 1924; Starbuck, 1925; L. N. Wilson, 1914); a mixed estimation offered in a superb full-length biography (Ross, 1972); and an unfriendly sketch in a recent book by Karier (1986).

Hall was born in 1844 in Ashfield, a village in western Massachusetts. His father farmed, but his father and his mother had some education and had once been schoolteachers. Both parents were pious Congregationalists, with ambitions for their son to become a minister. When G. Stanley Hall got older, he would look back on his country boyhood with warmth and nostalgia (e.g., Hall, 1907), although his student, Pruett (1926, p. 35), saw that early life as hard:

> There is a bareness, a lack of softness, about his early life, a sense of angles and harsh lines, which is a little painful to contemplate, although in his last years Hall himself declared that he would not have had it otherwise.

Hall went to Williston Seminary in 1862 for 1 year and then to Williams College, where he took the classical curriculum of the old-time American college. For the first 2 years, there was an obligatory sequence of Greek, Latin, and intermediate mathematics, with recitations in each subject every day. There were no electives. As a junior, Hall got a little leeway, but not much. Almost no science was taught, but then there was almost no literature, modern languages, or philosophy, as we now teach those subjects. In his senior year, Hall took moral philosophy with Mark Hopkins, president of the college, and in that course he met an older, theistic developmental psychology.

MARK HOPKINS AND WILLIAMS COLLEGE

Mark Hopkins had studied a little law and had completed medical training, but he presented himself to his undergraduates as an ordained minister full of the dignity and authority of an old-time college president. He was not learned nor did he aspire to be. "It is now long since I have read anything but newspaper," he wrote in 1862. He had never read Kant or Hume. He attacked Darwin and Huxley but had not read them (Rudolph, 1956, p. 28). He saw himself as an inspirational teacher whose goal was to make men.

Hopkins is remembered today largely because of a flight of oratory by President James Garfield, who once said, "Give me a log hut with only a simple bench, Mark Hopkins on one end and I on the other, and you may have all the buildings, apparatus and libraries without him." Four years before Garfield's speech, young Hall experienced the reality of Hopkins's teaching. Fifty-eight years later, he would recollect it in four pages of his *Life and Confessions.* The moral philosophy Hall studied was written out in Hopkins's *Lectures on Moral Science* in 1865 and elaborated 20 years later (Hopkins, 1885). We have a reasonably good picture of Hopkins's course.

Mark Hopkins's teaching was designed to turn the minds of Williams seniors towards contemporary human affairs, to help them grasp the ways of people and politics, and to explain the moral basis of civil society. The course was part of an older tradition of college education. Other presidents in other American colleges taught senior-year courses in which an older psychology that listed the faculties, powers, and motives of the human mind was put together with other precursors of the behavioral and social sciences to offer spiritual and moral guidance (Hall, 1879; Wetmore, 1991).

Moral Science of Conditionality

Hopkins's declared goal was to treat morality scientifically: Moral science has usually been studied as isolated. My wish is to connect it with the laws of that physical system which not only supports man, but has its culmination in him. I wish to show that there runs through both one principle of gradation and one law for the limitation of forces and activities, and so of the forms of good resulting from them. (Hopkins, 1865, p. 63)

Psychology was fundamental for Hopkins's moral science but subordinate to it. Because psychology is conditional for moral philosophy, the moral philosopher stands above the psychologist:

The moral philosopher is, therefore, not excluded from the domain of the psychologist. It is *his* domain. It is the soil into which his science strikes its roots . . . and if the psychologist does not do his work in those portions as he thinks it ought to be done, he has a right to revise it, and do it for himself. It is not to be allowed that the mere psychologist may lay down such doctrines as he pleases regarding the moral nature. (Hopkins, 1865, p. 80)

Conditionality was an important tool of Hopkins's analysis. It is a relationship between entities that allows them to be ordered. Hopkins analyzed physical objects, people, mental faculties, and social institutions to determine which are conditional for, and therefore subordinate to, others:

> The forces that are at work around us and the faculties within us, from the lowest to the highest, may be ranked as higher and lower as they are or are not a condition for one another. That which is a condition for another is always the lower. (Hopkins, 1865, pp. 63–64).

Orders of Physical Matter

All physical things are ordered in a pyramid of six planes of organization. At the bottom there is rudimentary matter massed by gravitation. Matter aggregated by cohesion or crystallization stands on a second plane. Chemically bound molecules stand on a third plane, vegetable life on a fourth, animal life on a fifth, and humankind on the sixth and topmost plane. Higher order entities are built from lower level entities by the method of addition. At each higher plane we meet more complex forms of matter that link with others of their kind in more complex ways. Man stands at the top of the pyramid of creation, incorporating all its levels:

> Hence, the plan of the creation may be compared to a pyramid, growing narrower by successive platforms. It is to be noticed, however, that while the field of each added and superior force is narrowed, yet nothing is dropped. Each lower force shoots through and combines itself with all that is higher. Because he is rational, man is not the less subject to gravitation, and cohesion, and chemical affinity. He has also the organic life that belongs to the plant, and the sensitive and instinctive life that belongs to the animal. In him none of these are dropped; but the rational life is united with and superinduced upon all these, so that man is not only a microcosm, but is the natural head and ruler of the world. (Hopkins, 1865, p. 67)

Hopkins's moral reasoning linked formal properties of conditionality with human relations of authority and submission. Ultimately, such linkages enabled him to find sermons in nature.

Law of Limitation

Because the human body embodies lower levels of physical organization, it has lower level needs that the individual should meet but in a measured way respecting the law of limitation:

> Hence the law of limitation will be, that every activity may be put forth, and so every good be enjoyed, up to the point when it is most perfectly conditional for a higher good. Anything beyond that will be excess and evil. . . . Here, then, is our model and law. Have we a lower sensitive and animal nature? Let that nature be cherished and expanded for all its innocent and legitimate enjoyments, for it is an end. But—and here we find the limit,—let it be cherished only as

subservient to the higher intellectual life, for it is also a means. (Hopkins, 1865, pp. 72–73)

Man must satisfy his natural desires, but to give the lower levels of his being more than they need is excess and evil. Hopkins (1865) gave his law of limitation wide application. We should care for a child's bodily development to set the stage for the higher planes of the child's development (p. 76). We should care for the body while aiming for the mind, care for people while aiming to elevate and educate them, cherish woman and give her "her true place" while aiming for perfect social organization. Similarly, we should care for children, servants, slaves, and criminals (p. 76). In politics, the law of limitation teaches us that we should give the lower sectors of government their due and try to harmonize their requirements with those of higher sectors (p. 253).

Orders of Psychological Faculties

Turning to mind, Hopkins discerned a second pyramid of psychological faculties. The intellect and the cognitive faculties are conditional for the feelings and the emotions; these in turn are conditional for the faculties of desire and of will. Now, however, we leave the material world and entities built by the method of addition. Psychological faculties are built stratum on stratum by a method of development. Hopkins said that development is the uniquely human principle. There were other 19th-century writers who said development is a unique principle of living things. Robert Chambers (1853) made the same argument in his book *Vestiges of the Natural History of Creation*, a widely read popular precursor of Darwinian theory.

Powers of the Mind

Hopkins's psychology set forth a hierarchical analysis of human goalfulness and purposefulness. The lower strata of the mind are spontaneous, and the higher are voluntary. Arising spontaneously are the instrumental powers in thought—mechanical, unconscious, and unwilled (the instincts, appetites, desires, and affections). The higher, voluntary powers of the mind are directive. With them, the human declares ends to himself and becomes self-motivated, autonomous, and responsible. Three classes of these higher powers complete the second pyramid: reason, the rational will or will in freedom, and finally, man's knowledge of his own ends (Hopkins, 1865, p. 166).

Two Orders of Governance

In the end, Hopkins moved to declarations of what is ethical and right. A former student, writing to Hopkins in 1859, recalled a moment of academic dramaturgy:

After you had . . . given us somewhat in detail the great principles that underlie all reasoning . . . you laid aside your glasses, passed your hand slowly over your forehead, bowed your head amid the reigning silence for a few seconds, then slowly uttered the words 'But—Nature . . . [is] moral' and the class dismissed. (Rudolph, 1956, p. 52)

Hopkins defined the rights of authority—the parent, guardian, teacher, magistrate, and government—as the ability to declare motives or ends to subordinates. The authority of the governing over the governed is legitimately directed toward certain ends and is not unlimited. It imposes duties on the governing and the governed. Hopkins wrote, "Government has no right *to be*, except as it is necessary to secure the ends of the individual in his social capacity; and it must, therefore, be found *so to be* as to secure these ends in the best manner." (Hopkins, 1865, p. 266)

In the physical world, lower forms are independent of and unmodified by the higher forms that they constitute. In the living world, lower forms and higher forms act on one another. There are two orders of governance:

At first, and in mere organizations, the lower builds up the higher, and sustains it, and is wholly for that. Any action from the higher to the lower is simply to sustain the lower in its own place and function as tributary, but never to elevate it out of that sphere. But when we reach the sphere of intelligence the object of the action from above is to elevate the lower. (Hopkins, 1865, p. 264)

The higher sphere brings forth growth and righteousness. The highest form of governance is that which leads to development in which the high help the low to become higher.

CHANGES AT WILLIAMS COLLEGE

The Williams College that Hall attended was a country college slowly becoming more citified and sophisticated. Nathaniel Hawthorne attended the Williams commencement in 1838 and described the students as "great unpolished bumpkins . . . rough, brown-featured, schoolmaster looking, half-bumpkin, half scholar figures, in black ill-cut broadcloth;— their manners quite spoilt by what little of the gentleman there was in them." (Rudolph, 1956, p. 65). But Williams's undergraduates were changing. Fewer were going into the ministry—28% between 1836 and 1845, 22% between 1846 and 1865, 13% between 1866 and 1872— and more were turning towards law, business, and medicine. (Bledstein, 1976, p. 198, has noted a similar trend away from the ministry among the graduates of Yale, Bowdoin, Brown, and Dartmouth at that time.)

Hall studied with Mark Hopkins when the older man was nearing the end of a 36-year presidency. Hopkins was a stalwart of an older tradition, standing his ground against winds of change that in a few years would begin to transform small old-time colleges into large modern universities. Twenty-five years later, G. Stanley Hall—now himself a college president—would call the year 1870 "almost the Anno Domini of educational history" (Veysey, 1965, p. 1). The winds of change could be felt in Hall's time; Williams's students supplemented their official course work with a substantial amount of student-run education.

Students' Curriculum

Students at Williams had established two literary societies, one of them the one the young Hall attended that by 1861 owned over 8,000 books to supplement the Williams College collection (Rudolph, 1956, pp. 74–76). (Williams's library, like its courses, was classical and religious; it was open one afternoon a week for juniors and seniors and one afternoon a week for freshmen and sophomores.) Hall met with a Saturday night club to talk about Emerson, Carlyle, Coleridge, Lamb, Wordsworth, the Lake Poets, Tennyson, Shakespeare, Dante, Goethe, Schiller, and Lessing. These authors were presumably too frivolous to be represented in the regular curriculum. Other philosophical and scientific writers were held to be harmful because they "taught men to hold no opinions." It would take the young Hall years after Williams to read Darwin, Spencer, Tyndall, Renan, Strauss, Emerson, Feuerbach, Comte, Tom Paine, Charles Kingsley, Canon Farrar, Matthew Arnold, G. H. Lewes, John Stuart Mill, and John Smith (Hall, 1923, pp. 184–185).

A Lyceum of Natural History, founded by eight Williams students in 1835, was the scientific counterpart of the student literary societies. Lyceum members studied flying machines, the dyes used in the manufacture of cotton cloth, the usefulness of spiders in the manufacture of raw silk, cotton culture and industry, artesian wells, the mechanics of nest building, natural resources, coal beds, whale fisheries, oil wells, iron ores, gold mining, volcanoes, giraffes, condor hunting, icebergs, entrances to the Sphinx, etc. The Lyceum offered courses in botany in 1836. It laid the foundation for a science library in 1839, raised money and constructed a building of its own in 1855, and hired an assistant of Louis Agassiz to aid in the classification of its fishes in 1863. The Lyceum was in communication with leading scientists of the United States. It sent expeditions to Nova Scotia in 1835, Florida in 1857, Greenland in 1860, South America in 1867, and Honduras in 1871. Finally, between 1868 and 1871, Williams College absorbed the Lyceum and in effect made the Lyceum's mission its own. The second scientific curriculum that Hall found available to him at Williams could be found in other old-time colleges. Kohlstedt (1988) notes that student natural history societies providing courses in science and putting together study collections were established between 1822 and 1848 at Amherst, Brown, Williams, Rutgers, Yale, Wesleyan, Harvard, Geneva, Pennsylvania, Marshall, and Haverford.

Hall did not turn towards science at Williams; he was a romantic at this stage of his life. Ross (1972) remarks:

> His classmates said that "when Stan gets to thinking clearly, he will think greatly," and they considered him "the smartest man" in their class. Hall's persistent effort to give intellectual form to the full range of his emotional experience was the chief source of both the insight and confusion he would display in his intellectual career. (pp. 28–29)

Hall was class poet. He graduated Phi Beta Kappa in 1867 and went on to Union Theological Seminary to become a divinity student. He took a time-out and went to Europe to study philosophy and theology but came back reluctantly because his parents would support him no further in Europe. He became an ordained minister, and for a short time he preached and might have gotten stuck in a country parish for life, "out of place, a misfit, restless and unhappy" (Hall, 1923, p. 183). Fate helped him take a doctorate at Harvard with James and Bowditch and then to go to Europe again, this time for scientific training.

In the introduction to his *Founders of Modern Psychology*, Hall (1912) would later summarize all his German education. Between 1870 and 1882 he spent nearly 6 years as a student in Germany. In his first 3-year visit, ending in 1873, he concentrated on philosophy and attended lectures on theology, Aristotle, biblical psychology, logic, recent psychology, comparative religions, Hegel, and Herbart. In his second 3-year stay, he took courses in chemistry, biology, physiology, anatomy, neurology, psychopathology, and anthropology. Hall returned from his studies in Germany equipped to work in a new kind of college that, in a sense, he had no choice but to help to establish.

NEW PSYCHOLOGY IN A NEW UNIVERSITY

Hall's professorship at Johns Hopkins placed him in the vanguard of what Jencks & Riesman (1968) call an academic revolution—when the American college "ceased to be a marginal, backward-looking enterprise shunned by the bulk of the citizenry" and became instead a "major growth industry." The new American college was larger, was governed by a faculty of arts and sciences, and offered electives and lectures rather than textbooks and recitations. Jencks & Riesman (1968, p. 13) say, "Perhaps the most important breakthroughs were the founding of Johns Hopkins and Clark as primarily graduate universities." After establishing the new psychology at Hopkins, Hall would carry the torch from Hopkins to Clark.

The new psychology Hall taught at Hopkins took 3 years to deliver.

He gave 1 year to sensation, half of the second year to perception and psychophysics, and half to association, memory, habit, attention, and the will. His third year was spent on "the topics of instinct in animals, psychogenesis in children, the psychological parts of anthropology (including animism, the chief mythic cycles, traditions, rites, and ceremonies), and morbid psychology (especially aphasia, hypnotic and allied states, paranoia, epilepsy, hysteria, paralysis, etc.) . . ." (Evans, 1984, p. 54).

Hall established a brass-instruments laboratory at Johns Hopkins. He had done his thesis research in Henry Pickering Bowditch's physiology laboratory at Harvard Medical School (Hall, 1878), and he cared about physiology, but he was not completely committed to experimental psychology, and he would do only a limited amount of work in it (Miles & Miles, 1929; Ross, 1972, pp. 155–157). His major research program would be the questionnaire studies of child development he would undertake with his students at Clark University.

FIRST "NORMAL SCIENCE" OF DEVELOPMENTAL PSYCHOLOGY

In the spring of 1888, Hall left Johns Hopkins and moved to Worcester, Massachusetts, to live as a guest in Jonas Clark's home while Clark built the university that Hall would take over as president. Hall planned to build a set of graduate departments—psychology, biology, chemistry, physics, and mathematics—to create first a graduate school and then in time an undergraduate college. Hall toured Europe gathering ideas. He put together a faculty that was by all accounts distinguished. Clark University opened in 1889 with 18 faculty and 34 students. Hall had a special vision of what a university ought to be like, and for 2 or 3 years the vision lived. Then there were personal and professional tragedies. Hall's wife and daughter were accidentally killed in 1890. There were town–gown problems in Worcester, and Jonas Clark, sole financial supporter of the university, began to withdraw his support. In one of the famous raids of academic history, William Rainey Harper, president of the new University of Chicago, swooped down on Clark and made off with two thirds of the faculty and 70% of the students.

In 1891, Hall turned towards child study, at first probably because he needed an activity at Clark that would win some popular support in the city of Worcester and later because he saw it as an activity that might help him sustain his university. He founded the *Pedagogical Seminary* (now the *Journal of Genetic Psychology*), and he began a program of questionnaire studies of child development that had to be for a time a prominent force in psychology. It must be remembered that as late as 1898, 30 of the 54 doctorates in psychology awarded in the United States had been awarded by Hall. A science has to have some form of cooperative empirical inquiry, and Hall's "Clark method" is one of the three forms of psychological research identified by Danziger (1985, 1990) in his content analyses of the early psychological journals.

Hall had done some preliminary questionnaire studies of children in the 1880s, extending prior German work. He could find scientific precedents for questionnaire inquiries in antecedent work of Darwin, Fechner, and Calton (White, 1990). On the one side, questionnaire studies of childhood seemed feasible and reasonable; on the other, a grass roots movement called for scientific child study. The movement reflected the rise of the "whole child professions" and the turn-of-the-century renegotiation of American social contracts distributing responsibilities for the socialization of children among families, professionals, and governmental institutions (Siegel & White, 1982).

Hall's (1923) autobiography lists the titles, dates, and authors of 194 topical syllabi (questionnaires) published at Clark between October 1894 and February 1915. He was personally most involved in the questionnaire work between 1894 and 1903, and this is when the work of the program looked most like early developmental psychology. Students and associates have left us descriptions of the child study work (Monroe, 1899; Sheldon, 1946; Smith, 1905; Wiltse, 1895, 1896–97). Near the end of his active period, Hall (1903) offered a summary of what in his estimation the contribution of the research program had been. Wilson's (1975) bibliographies list over 4,000 entries and give a useful sense of the larger social movement toward child study.

Hall's questionnaire studies were rather vigorously denounced within a few years after they were begun. Some of the denunciation was probably politically motivated. Hall had been a powerful figure, but he had been high-handed in his dealings, and now personal and political troubles made him vulnerable. Opponents happily pointed out scientific shortcomings of the questionnaire studies. There were real problems, but, nonetheless, those studies sketched a picture of child development not dissimilar to the picture we hold today (White, 1990).

The questionnaire inquiries dealt with (a) simple automatisms, instincts, and attitudes, (b) the small child's activities and feelings, (c) control of emotions and will, (d) development of the higher faculties, (e) individual differences, (f) school processes and practices, and (g) church processes and practices.

Simple Automatisms, Instincts, and Attitudes

Many of the questionnaires sought for the inborn predispositions of childhood (*Early Forms of Vocal Expression; Some Common Traits and Habits; Tickling, Fun, Wit, Humor, Laughing*) and beliefs and habits of the small child (*Migrations, Tramps, Truancy, Running Away, Etc.*, vs. *Love of Home; Affection and its Opposite States in Children.*). Such questionnaires generally tried to trace the movement of the developing child from the spontaneous to the voluntary, from instinct to reason, and from simple sociality to the development of scientific and ethical reasoning.

Nowadays, much research on infancy and toddlerhood tends to be upward seeking, looking for early signs of reason, language, numerical understanding, morality, self-awareness, altruism, etc. Hall, because of his great concern about the dangers of precocity, looked for the simplest and crudest organizations of children's behavior, the unique and the non-adult-like characteristics of children. It has taken us much serious effort to come to terms with the fact that the playful in children is serious. Hall's questionnaires again and again sought out mannered, stylized, playful, theatrical facets of children's behavior, taking for granted that these were important organizers of childhood behavior. A questionnaire on *Early Forms of Vocal Expression* in January 1895 asks the following:

> Describe any expressive gesture or attitude, whether of hands, body or face, and note rhythm, stress, inflection and especially spontaneous singing. Describe every trace of pantomime, special gesture with a speech value, buffoonery, mimicry, love of acting.

In February 1895, *Some Common Traits and Habits* invited respondents to write about teasing, bullying, showing off, mimicry and imitation, bashfulness, awkwardness and boldness, and curiosity:

> SHOWING OFF . . . Describe mincing, acting a part, putting on airs, acts or words thought to show superfine manners or breeding, playing the role of another self. How far is this due to vivid imagination, how long kept up, is it sustained or practiced when alone, or only before others, and are the traits assumed systematized or incoherent.

Small Child's Activities and Feelings

A second group of questionnaires asked about the objects children care about and like to deal with—*Dolls, Toys and Playthings*—and the rhythmic, ritualistic, or superstitious aspects of children's behavior. For Hall, mind is built on feelings, and many of the questionnaires tried to get at children's feelings about themselves and things about them—*The Early Sense of Self, Feelings for Objects of Inanimate Nature, Feelings for Objects of Animate Nature, Children's Thoughts, Reactions, and Feelings to Animals*—and to pursue the idea that such feelings are the foundation for later, more rational understandings.

Control of Emotions and Will

There were questionnaire inquiries into children's outbursts of emotionality. Generally, the questions on these moved towards questions about when and by whom the emotions were eventually controlled. Question sequences like this are found in *Anger, Crying and Laughing, Fears in Childhood and Youth,* and *Affection and Its Opposite States in Children.* It was assumed that at first parents and other adults regulated and controlled a child's outbursts, but later the child gradually came to exert self-control and self-regulation. Very important for the latter were the growth of higher faculties.

Development of the Higher Faculties

Hall and his students were keenly interested in the development of moral and religious sentiments in children—through growth and through moral education. There were early questionnaires entitled *Moral and Religious Experiences, Moral Education,* and *Confession.* Increases in cognitive capacity were thought to be essential for participation in complex forms of human society, and so there was a questionnaire on *Memory,* and numerous inquiries into children's capacities to think in symbolic and ideal terms. The questionnaires asked about more humane and altruistic sentiments: *Pity, The Sense of Honor Among Children, Unselfishness in Children.*

Individual Differences

The four groups of questionnaires so far described explored general processes of child development. A fifth group explored dysfunction. A 1901 questionnaire entitled *Sub-normal Normal Children and Youth* by Arthur R. T. Wylie opens with the following text:

> It is desired by means of this syllabus to gain material for the study of the bad and troublesome children of school and family life, those who have reached their limit in only one line, the runaways, the vagrants, spendthrifts, dudes, hoboes, hoodlums, religious fanatics, sensualists, sentimentalists, vicious and impulsive characters, impulsive masturbators, the ne'er-do-wells, the gilded youth and those who gave early promise but dropped into a humble station which they just managed to fill.

Nowadays, inquiries into individual differences are usually directed towards continuous, normally distributed individual differences in cognition or personality. Hall's inquiries into individual differences explored the boundaries of psychopathology and sociopathology. Many in the late 19th century were concerned about degeneracy as a source of crime, anarchism, vagrancy, social disorder, mental disease, and various human dysfunctions.

Clark questionnaires such as *Peculiar and Exceptional Children, Moral Defects and Perversions, Signs of Nervousness,* and *Precocity and Tardiness of Development* were directed towards exploring early signs of such characteristics in children.

School Processes and Practices

Many of the Clark questionnaires, particularly in the later years of the program, were directly oriented to problems of schools and professional educators. These questionnaires were one point of beginning of an applied child study. Some were directed at curriculum, some at methods, some at professional and political issues in teaching (e.g., *The Beginnings of Reading and Writing, Kindergarten, Number and Mathematics, Examinations and Recitations, Local Voluntary Association Among Teachers, Examinations, Differences Between Old and Young Teachers*).

Church Processes and Practices

As in the case of schools, there were Clark questionnaires directed toward a mixture of psychological and service-oriented issues confronting members of the ministry. Psychological questionnaires were directed toward *Religious Experiences, Immortality, Questionnaire on the Soul,* and *Questionnaire on Children's Prayers.* More institutional questionnaires were directed towards *Sabbath and Worship in General, Questions for the Essential Features of Public Worship,* and *Hymns and Sacred Music,* or *The Sermon.*

G. STANLEY HALL'S SCHEME OF CHILD AND ADOLESCENT DEVELOPMENT

Hall's developmental psychology was spelled out in his two-volume *Adolescence: Its Psychology and its Relations to Physiology, Anthropology, Sociology, Sex, Crime, Religion, and Education* (Hall, 1904). The volumes are unread today. They are mentioned from time to time as (a) an argument for recapitulationism, (b) a source of the Sturm und Drang view of adolescence, or (c) occasionally, a source for what some claim is 20th-century society's invention of adolescence. There is more to the volumes than their condensation into a few slogans would suggest.

The first volume of *Adolescence* gives extended reviews of (a) anthropometric and body-organ studies of growth in size and weight, (b) studies of the growth of motor power and functional abilities and of various training schemes designed to foster that growth, (c) physical and mental diseases associated with adolescence; (d) sociological, criminological, and cross-cultural studies of adolescent crimes and antisocial behavior; (e) physical and psychological phenomena of sexual development; (f) phenomena of animal and human sexual periodicity; and (g) literary, biographical, and historical writings about adolescence.

The second volume discusses (a) sensory and voice changes in adolescents; (b) evolution of the feelings and instincts; (c) adolescent feelings about nature and their response to science; (d) cross-cultural and cross-religious practices in the initiation and education of adolescents; (12) phenomena of adolescent religious conversion; (e) social instincts and institutions among adolescents; (f) intellectual development and education; (g) adolescent girls and their capabilities for and response to education; and (h) the possibility of an ethnic psychology and of a pedagogy missionaries might use for "adolescent races."

Some Suggested Patterns of Human Development

The two *Adolescence* volumes are huge, and Hall is prodigious in the scholarly detail that he presents and the variety of practical issues that he takes up for discussion. It seems worthwhile to present here a very rudimentary sketch of Hall's scheme of human development. The following are some of his principal theses:

1. People, human faculties, social institutions, or societies may be ordered on an evolutionary line, with the order reflecting not only the historic time at which they came into existence but their relative state of perfection.

2. Child development recapitulates human evolution:

> Holding that the child and the race are each keys to the other, I have constantly suggested phyletic explanations of all degrees of probability. . . . Realizing the limitations and qualifications of the recapitulation theory in the biologic field, I am now convinced that its psychogenetic applications can have a method of their own, and although the time has not yet come when any formulation of these can have much value I have done the best I could with each instance as it arose. Along with the sense of the extreme importance of further coordinating childhood and youth with the development of their race, has grown the conviction that only here can we hope to find true norms against the tendency to precocity in home, school, church, and civilization generally, and also to establish criteria by which to both diagnose and measure arrest and retardation in the individual and in the race. (Hall, 1904, Vol. 1, p. viii)

3. What mediates this recapitulation is biology—the fact that evolutionarily older areas of the brain mature before evolutionarily newer areas. Work of John Hughlings Jackson, Flechsig, Kaes, Vulpius, and others has shown that the central nervous system "is made up of three superposed

levels closely correlated" (Hall, 1904, Vol. 1, p. 110) and that the lower levels mature before the higher ones:

> Certain types of insanity are rare before puberty, because the child can not reason according to adult standards until fourteen, the age at which Aristotle would begin the education of reason. Before this comes the age of the spinal reflex and automatic nascency of the late prenatal life and the early months of infancy. Then comes the stage of controlled muscular actions—walking, plays—when drill, habituation, memory, and instinct culminate, which is associated with the mid-level regions of the brain. Lastly comes the age of rational thought, higher logical correlation, personal opinion and conviction, higher esthetic enjoyments, deliberate choice, and willed action. . . . Each lower level, however, must have its full development, for it is a necessary condition for the unfoldment of the higher. Logical methods, on the other hand, if too early, tend to stultify and violate the law that fundamental must always precede accessory structures and functions. (Hall, 1904, Vol. 1, p. 111)

4. There are "nascent stages." The child grows towards not one but a series of perfections. The stages do not center on feelings and motives as in Freud's theory, nor on cognition as in Piaget's theory. Each stage is the attainment of a mode of social existence or a way of life. As children get older, feelings, sentiments, attitudes, motives, and abilities change so that they become capable of participating in ever more complex and sophisticated societies.

5. In very small children you find many automatisms, fidgets, non-volitional movements, "motor odds and ends." They increase in the kindergarten years, diminishing in the primary years. They are associated with fatigue, task difficulty, and the need to maintain fixed attention. They are mostly in the accessory muscles; those in the fundamental muscles disappear rapidly with age. The automatisms diminish as the will grows in force. They are (Hall, 1904, Vol. 1, p. 160) "paleopsychic."

6. Ages 6 or 7 represent an old time of human maturity, the "shores of an ancient pubic sea":

> After the critical transition age of six or seven, when the brain has achieved its adult size and weight and teething has reduced the chewing surface to its least extent, begins an unique stage of life marked by reduced growth and increased activity and power to resist both disease and fatigue which . . . suggests what was, in some just post-simian age of our race, its period of maturity. Here belong discipline in writing, reading, spelling, verbal memory, manual training, practice of instrumental technique, proper names, drawing, drill in arithmetic, foreign languages by oral methods, the correct pronunciation of which is far harder if acquired later, etc. The hand is never so near the brain. Most of the content of the mind has entered it through the senses, and the

eye- and ear-gates should be open at their widest. Authority should now take precedence of reason. Children comprehend much and very rapidly if we can only refrain from explaining, but this slows down intuition, tends to make casuists and prigs and to enfeeble the ultimate vigor of reason. It is the age of little method and much matter . . .

[By the end of this preadolescent era] Morally he should have been through many if not most forms of what parents and teachers commonly call badness and Professor Yoder even calls meanness. He should have fought, whipped and been whipped, used language offensive to the prude and to the prim precisian, been in some scrapes, had something to do with bad, if more with good associates, and been exposed to and already recovering from . . . many forms of ethical mumps and measles. . . . Something is amiss with the lad of ten who is very good, studious, industrious, thoughtful, altruistic, quiet, polite, respectful, obedient, gentlemanly, orderly, always in good toilet, docile to reason, who turns away from stories that reek with gore, prefers adult companionship to that of his mates, refuses all low associates, speaks standard English, or is pious and deeply in love with religious services . . . (Hall, 1904, Vol. 2, pp. 451–453)

7. Motor activity and education are essential for child development, Hall says, and he gives extended arguments for industrial education, manual training, gymnastics, and sports. "Motor specialties requiring exactness and grace like piano-playing, drawing, writing, pronunciation of a foreign tongue, dancing, acting, singing, and a host of virtuosities" should be begun before adolescence (Hall, 1904, Vol. 1, p. 164). However, from ages 4 to age 8, overexercising the accessory muscles may "sow the seeds of chorea." From age 8 to age 12, overprecision, especially if fundamental activities are neglected, will bring nervous strain and stunting precocity.

8. Adolescence is a second point of initiation for socialization and education. Early adolescence, age 8 to age 12, constitutes a "unique period in human life." The child develops a life of its own outside the home; it is "never so independent of adult influence"; it has acute perception, immunity to exposure, danger, and accident, as well as temptation. In short, the child is independently viable but capable of participating in a very simple sort of society. "Reason, true morality, religion, sympathy, love, and esthetic enjoyment are but slightly developed" (Hall, 1904, Vol. 1, p. ix). Hall conveys an image of the early adolescent prepared for a *Lord of the Flies* kind of social life, and somewhere in his writings he regrets the fact that we have to coop youths of that age in middle schools, when they would be happiest in simple self-run societies. The tendency of adolescents to form a great number and variety of clubs reflects this natural development.

9. Adolescence is a time of oscillations and oppositions, between inertness and excitement, pleasure and pain, self-confidence and humility, selfishness and altruism, society and solitude, sensitiveness and dullness, knowing and doing, conservatism and iconoclasm, and sense and intellect.

10. One can introduce science at adolescence, slowly. A need to explain the world arises at the very beginning as a feeling that the mysteries of nature must be looked at and addressed. The youth responds to nature sentimentally and is drawn towards mythic or poetic formulations or the religions of nature. Next in the genetic order comes an interest in popular science:

> Here . . . belongs every contact which science can suggest with the daily life of the pupil at home or school, at play or resting, in dress and regimen, and here, too begins the need of abundant apparatus, models, diagrams, collections, and all aids that eye or hand can give the mind. A science building or course without these is a soulless corpse.

Then comes an interest in the practical, technological side of science. Last and highest comes an interest in pure science freed from all alloy of myth, genetic stage, or utility, and cultivated for its own sake, with no motive but love of truth (Hall, 1904, Vol. 2, pp. 153–154).

11. At adolescence, one can begin to teach a higher morality. Hall (1904, Vol. 2, pp. 433–448) proposes a radical change in the pedagogy of the vernacular language, literature, and history. The prime purpose would be moral—so to determine intelligence and will to secure the largest increase of social service, advance altruism, and reduce selfishness through (a) oratory and debates; (b) drama; (c) reading, particularly myths; (d) the Bible; and (e) history and literature.

From the very beginning of his child study work, Hall had challenged the American kindergarten movement and had a very substantial impact on it (Shapiro, 1983; White & Buka, 1987). The *Adolescence* volumes represented for Hall the culmination of his child study interests. There are many and various practical suggestions scattered through the volumes; both the suggestions and the question of their possible impacts on American social practices deserve more serious examination than they have so far had. It seems most likely that Hall, along with Edward L. Thorndike and John Dewey, had a very substantial impact on American educational and social institutions at a historic time of great flux and change (White, 1991).

Echoes of Mark Hopkins's Developmental Psychology

Buried beneath the wealth of new scientific work and scholarly detail, Hall's developmental analysis in *Adolescence* carried forward some of the developmental themes presented to him out of an older philosophy by Mark Hopkins. In Hall's concern about the dangers of precocity, a concern about bringing children too rapidly into adulthood that he would express again and again in *Adolescence*, Hall echoed Hopkins's law of limitation, a principle that he appealed to again and again in his moral philosophy. Like Hopkins, Hall argued the following:

1. The human mind and human nature may be understood by a developmental analysis.
2. People, human faculties, social institutions, and societies may be ordered genetically, with the order reflecting not only the historic time at which they came into existence but their relative state of perfection.
3. Lower order mental faculties are mechanical, unwilled and animal-like; higher order faculties are self-motivated, autonomous, and responsible.
4. Human relationships of authority and subordination may be derived from the developmental analysis as well as some human responsibilities.
5. Ultimately, the mental science that gives the developmental analysis forms the ground on which a moral philosophy—a set of ethical prescriptions—may be built.
6. Recall Mark Hopkins's pyramid of ever more complex and perfect entities, each aggregating with its kind in ever more complex and perfect ways. As Hall's children get older, they become capable of participating in ever more complex and sophisticated societies.

LATER INTERESTS: HALL'S RETURN TO RELIGION—THE CHILDREN'S INSTITUTE

With the completion of his *Adolescence*, Hall's personal interests turned away from child study. He said in his *Life and Confessions:*

> In 1904, when I printed my two volumes on adolescence, that subject became thereafter more or less of a closed one to me. As usual, having printed, I never read it again and avoided the subject in my courses of instruction, and in 1911 I closed my account with child study as applied to education by publishing my two volumes, *Educational Problems*, and thereafter ceased to lecture on education. (Hall, 1923, p. 405)

In his last years, Hall turned back to religion. The last chapter of *Adolescence* proposes that genetic psychology be made the basis for a "science of missions." In the same year in which he published *Adolescence*, Hall founded the *American Journal of Religious Psychology and Education*. He had largely drafted his two-volume *Jesus, the Christ, in the Light of Psychology* in 1900, but he held off publication until 1917 (Hall, 1917; Ross, 1972, p. 418). Hall was not completely finished with genetic psychology, however. He turned toward the exploration of old age and what we call life-span development, writing a book on *Senescence* (Hall, 1922).

Hall tried to give Clark University a continuing position in child study. Suddenly, the children's cause was beginning to win ground in American politics. The first White House Conference was convened in 1909, and the Children's Bureau was established in 1912. In 1910, Hall persuaded the Clark trustees to appropriate $5,000—no small sum in those days—to establish a Children's Institute to serve as a center for research on childhood (Burnham & Fitzsimmons, 1912; Hall, 1910; L. N. Wilson, 1910). Hall hoped that Clark would become the partner and research arm of the forthcoming Children's Bureau. Hall's vision of the future was accurate, but he could not consolidate Clark's place in that future. A few years later, in 1917, Cora Bussey Hillis succeeded in establishing the Iowa Child Welfare Research Station, and it was at Iowa that the second growth wave of developmental psychology began.

G. STANLEY HALL'S CONTRIBUTION: A REAPPRAISAL

G. Stanley Hall's psychological work deserves more direct examination than it has recently received. Because Hall was active and influential at just the right time, he compiled many firsts and foundings—as Wundt's first American student, first American professor of psychology, founder of what some say was the first American psychology laboratory, founder of the *American Journal of Psychology*, first president of Clark University, founder and first president of the American Psychological Association, leader of the child study movement, founder of the *Pedagogical Seminary*, and so on. Hall invited Freud to Clark University in 1909 and thus helped psychoanalysis get international recognition. Recent writings usually picture Hall as a functionary and figurehead, condense his ideas into a few slogans, quote criticisms of his work by his often rivalrous peers, and effectively concede Hall his administrative trophies while ignoring most of what he had to say. What Hall had to say about developmental psychology is worth some contemporary examination:

1. Through his questionnaire program, Hall set up a first cooperative "normal science" of child development. The findings obtained through that work suggested local patterns and orderlinesses and a larger movement that is quite consistent with our view of child development today. The questionnaire work was methodologically weak, to be sure, but the methodological regulations psychology subsequently put into place have probably been excessively restrictive. Hall's questionnaires asked people to give narrative accounts of children's behaviors in everyday situations, and this kind of approach is becoming more popular nowadays.

2. Hall elaborated a social–biological conception of childhood. As children grow, they develop capacities that enable them to participate in more and more complex kinds of social organization. Growth brings changes in cognition, memory, feelings, emotions, symbolization, and social be-

haviors, but what orchestrates all the changes and brings them toward a unity is the movement of the child toward different forms of social participation. Contemporary research and theory are reviving Hall's vision and moving away from the view that cognitive development should be taken as synonymous with child development, the faster the better (e.g., Elkind, 1981).

3. Hall wrote a massive account of adolescence, looking across the work of different disciplines, examining social practices, and trying to arrive at scientific syntheses on the one side and practical recommendations on the other. We need to trace the influence of Hall's ideas and recommendations as they entered the complex infrastructure of American professional and social services for children. By looking at such influences, we may better understand when and how and to what extent the work of developmental psychology can be meaningful and useful for society.

REFERENCES

Albrecht, F. M., Jr. (1960). The new psychology in America: 1880–1895. Unpublished doctoral dissertation, Johns Hopkins University, Baltimore.

Bledstein, B. J. (1976). *The culture of professionalism: The middle class and the development of higher education in America.* New York: Norton.

Burnham, W. H. (1925). The man, G. Stanley Hall. *Psychological Review, 32,* 89–102.

Burnham, W. H., & Fitzsimmons, M. E. (1912). The educational museum at Clark University: Catalogue of the department of school hygiene. *Pedagogical Seminary, 19,* 526–552.

Chambers, R. (1853). *Vestiges of the natural history of creation* (10th ed.). London: John Churchill.

Danziger, K. (1985). The origins of the psychological experiment as a social institution. *American Psychologist, 40,* 133–140.

Danziger, K. (1990). *Constructing the subject: Historical origins of psychological research.* Cambridge, England: Cambridge University Press.

Elkind, D. (1981). *The hurried child: Growing up too fast too soon.* Reading, MA: Addison-Wesley.

Evans, R. B. (1984). The origins of American academic psychology. In J. Brozek (Ed.), *Explorations in the history of psychology in the United States* (pp. 17–60). Lewisburg, PA: Bucknell University Press.

Hall, G. S. (1876). College instruction in philosophy. *Nation, 23,* 180.

Hall, G. S. (1878). The muscular perception of space. *Mind, 3,* 433–450.

Hall, G. S. (1879). Philosophy in the United States. *Mind, 4,* 89–105.

Hall, G. S. (1885). The new psychology. *Andover Review, III,* 120–135, 239–248.

Hall, G. S. (1903). Child study at Clark University: An impending new step. *American Journal of Psychology, XIV*, 96–106.

Hall, G. S. (1904). *Adolescence: Its psychology and its relations to physiology, anthropology, sociology, sex, crime, religion, and education* (2 vols.). New York: Appleton-Century-Crofts.

Hall, G. S. (1907). Boy life in a Massachusetts country town forty years ago. In T. L. Smith (Ed.), *Aspects of child life and education* (pp. 300–322). Lexington, MA: Ginn Press.

Hall, G. S. (1910). General outline of the new child study work at Clark University. *Pedagogical Seminary, 17*, 160–165.

Hall, G. S. (1912). *Founders of modern psychology.* New York: Appleton-Century-Crofts.

Hall, G. S. (1917). *Jesus, the Christ, in the light of psychology* (2 vols.). Garden City, NY: Doubleday.

Hall, G. S. (1922). *Senescence: The last half of life.* New York: Appleton.

Hall, G. S. (1923). *Life and confessions of a psychologist.* New York: Appleton-Century-Crofts.

Hopkins, M. (1865). *Lectures on moral science.* Boston: Gould and Lincoln.

Hopkins, M. (1885). *The law of love and love as a law: Or, Christian ethics* (rev. ed.). New York: Scribner.

Jencks, C., & Riesman, D. (1968). *The academic revolution.* Garden City, NY: Doubleday.

Karier, C. J. (1986). *Scientists of the mind: Intellectual founders of modern psychology.* Urbana: University of Illinois Press.

Kohlstedt, S. C. (1988). Curiosities and cabinets: Natural history museums and education on the antebellum campus. *Isis, 79*, 405–426.

Miles, W., & Miles, C. (1929). Eight letters from G. Stanley Hall to Henry Pickering Bowditch, with introduction and notes. *American Journal of Psychology, 41*, 326–336.

Monroe, W. S. (1899). Status of child study in Europe. *Pedagogical Seminary, 6*, 372–381.

O'Donnell, J. M. (1985). *The origins of behaviorism: American psychology, 1870–1920.* New York: New York University Press.

Pruett, L. (1926). *G. Stanley Hall: A biography of a mind.* New York: Appleton-Century-Crofts.

Rodkin, P. C. (1990, June). Blasphemers of method: How G. Stanley Hall and William James undertook to reconcile their psychology and their religion. Paper presented at the annual meeting of the Cherion Society, Westfield, MA.

Ross, D. (1972). *G. Stanley Hall: The psychologist as prophet.* Chicago: University of Chicago Press.

Rudolph, F. (1956). *Mark Hopkins and the log: Williams College, 1836–1872.* New Haven, CT: Yale University Press.

Sanford, E. C. (1924). Granville Stanley Hall, 1846–1924. *American Journal of Psychology, 35,* 313–321.

Shapiro, M. S. (1983). *Child's garden: The kindergarten movement from Proebel to Dewey.* University Park, PA: Pennsylvania State University Press.

Sheldon, H. D. (1946). Clark University, 1897–1900. *Journal of Social Psychology, 24,* 227–247.

Siegel, A. W., & White, S. H. (1982). The child study movement: Early growth and development of the symbolized child. *Advances in Child Development and Behavior, 17,* 233–285.

Smith, T. L. (1905). Child study at Clark University. *Pedagogical Seminary, 12,* 93–96.

Starbuck, E. D. (1925). G. Stanley Hall as a psychologist. *Psychological Review, 32,* 89–102.

Veysey, L. R. (1965). *The emergence of the American university.* Chicago: University of Chicago Press.

Wetmore, K. E. (1991). The evolution of psychology from moral philosophy in the nineteenth century American college curriculum. Unpublished doctoral dissertation, University of Chicago.

White, S. H. (1990). Child study at Clark University: 1894–1904. *Journal of the History of the Behavioral Sciences, 26,* 131–150.

White, S. H. (1991). Three visions of educational psychology. In L. Tolchinsky-Landsmann (Ed.), *Culture, schooling, and psychological development* (pp. 1–38). Norwood, NJ: Ablex.

White, S. H., & Buka, S. (1987). Early education: Programs, traditions, and policies. *Review of Research in Education, 14,* 43–91.

Wiebe, R. H. (1967). *The search for order: 1877–1920.* Westport, CT: Greenwood Press.

Wilson, D. J. (1990). *Science, community, and the transformation of American philosophy, 1860–1930.* Chicago: University of Chicago Press.

Wilson, L. N. (1910). Library facilities for the work of the Children's Institute and the new building for this work. *Pedagogical Seminary, 17,* 166–175.

Wilson, L. N. (1914). *G. Stanley Hall: A sketch.* New York: Stechart & Co.

Wilson, L. N. (1975). *Bibliography of child study: 1898–1912.* New York: Arno Press.

Wiltse, S. E. (1895). A preliminary sketch of the history of child study in America. *Pedagogical Seminary, 3,* 189–212.

Wiltse, S. E. (1896–97). A preliminary sketch of the history of child study, for the year ending September, 1896. *Pedagogical Seminary, 4,* 111–125.

4

THE MAKING OF A DEVELOPMENTAL SCIENCE: THE CONTRIBUTIONS AND INTELLECTUAL HERITAGE OF JAMES MARK BALDWIN

ROBERT B. CAIRNS

> I then determined—under the inspiration, also, of a small group of writers lately treating the subject—to work out a theory of mental development in the child . . .
>
> James Mark Baldwin (1895, p. vii)

> Baldwin proposed a biosocial, genetic theory of intelligence, a theory of mind in the broadest sense, which was conceptually far ahead of its time. This theory contained within it, en germe, many of the most important concepts of the biological theory of intelligence and of the genetic epistemology which Piaget was to develop.
>
> Robert Wozniak (1982, p. 42)

Any account of the scientific study of cognitive and social development in the United States must take note of the contributions of James Mark Baldwin. His primacy as an intellectual leader of the emergent discipline is now well established. Baldwin's *Mental Development in the Child and the Race* (1895) was one of the first attempts to construct a genetic epistemology

This research was supported in part by a grant of the Spencer Foundation to Robert B. Cairns. I thank Donald T. Campbell and Jaan Valsiner for their generosity in providing me with their materials on Baldwin and his contemporaries and Beverley Cairns for her suggestions on how to clarify several issues raised in this article.

Reprinted from *Developmental Psychology*, 28, 17–24. Copyright 1992 by the American Psychological Association.

within the framework of the "new psychology" (Broughton & Freeman-Moir, 1982; Cairns & Ornstein, 1979; Mueller, 1976). The companion volume, *Social and Ethical Interpretations of Mental Development* (Baldwin, 1897), was the first systematic effort by a psychologist to use developmental ideas to bridge the gap between the study of social institutions (i.e., sociology) and the study of individual functioning (i.e., psychology).

Recent scholarship has compared Baldwin's proposals and those of Jean Piaget, on the one hand, with Lev Vygotsky's, on the other. This work shows the direct lines of common descent for several key terms and ideas (Broughton, 1981; Cahan, 1984; Valsiner & Van der Veer, 1988; Wozniak, 1982). But it would be a mistake to view Baldwin's thinking only through a Piagetian or Vygotskian lens. Baldwin's distinctive ideas on evolutionary epistemology, cross-generational transmission of developmental accommodations, the dynamics and social embeddedness of personality, and the dual genesis of cognition are sufficiently provocative to demand study in their own right.

Baldwin is less of a shadowy figure nowadays than he was just 10 years ago (Broughton & Freeman-Moir, 1982, p. 2).[1] Baldwin was born in 1861 in Columbia, South Carolina, and died in 1934 in Paris. Following undergraduate training in philosophy and psychology and a year of advanced study in Europe (including a semester in Leipzig with Wilhelm Wundt), Baldwin completed a doctorate at Princeton University in 1888. In the 4 years that he was on the faculty at the University of Toronto, he founded an experimental laboratory and began a research program in infant psychology. The results of this work, which were published in the journal *Science* 100 years ago, dealt with the ontogeny of movement patterns, handedness, color vision, suggestibility, and research methodology (Baldwin, 1890, 1891, 1892, 1893). These findings provided the empirical basis for his first major work on mental development.

From the beginning, Baldwin was more a theoretical psychologist than an experimental one. He employed research findings to illustrate theoretical principles rather than to systematize empirical phenomena. Primary in Baldwin's thinking was the "conviction that no consistent view of mental development in the individual could possibly be reached without a doctrine of the race development of consciousness, — i.e., the great problem of the evolution of mind"[2] (Baldwin, 1895, vii). In this conviction, he followed the theoretical lead of Herbert Spencer in philosophy and George Jean

---

[1] This is due in large measure to an increased awareness among developmental psychologists of their past. That the present series of articles on historical figures was initiated by the editors of *Developmental Psychology* is a case in point. Similarly, chapters on the intellectual history of the discipline were included for the first time in the fourth edition of the *Handbook of Child Psychology* (Mussen & Kessen, 1983).

[2] *Race development* is one of the unconventional expressions employed by Baldwin. Race in this context refers to variations across the human species. In effect, cross-cultural studies of the development of cognition are required to complement studies of individual development in humans.

Romanes in biology, and the empirical lead of Wilhelm Preyer and Alfred Binet.[3] After this intensive but brief involvement with the laboratory investigation of infants, Baldwin returned to issues of psychological and evolutionary theory, historical commentary, editorial activities, and philosophical construction and systemization. The study of development was no longer an empirical activity for him, but questions of psychological genesis remained at the core of his theoretical and philosophical speculations.

He was a key figure in the organization of psychology as a science, including the establishment of three of its basic journals (*Psychological Review, Psychological Bulletin, and Psychological Abstracts*), and the founding of two major departments of psychology (the University of Toronto and Princeton University) and the reestablishment of a third (Johns Hopkins University). He served as one of the first presidents of the American Psychological Association when he was only 36 years old. He won the highest honors available to psychologists in his day, including the Gold Medal of the Royal Academy of Denmark and one of the first honorary doctorate of science degrees awarded by Oxford University. It is now generally acknowledged by those who have reviewed the record that Baldwin stands alongside William James, John Dewey, and C. S. Peirce as one of the primary intellectual forces involved in the founding of American psychology as a science.

This chapter has two aims. One is to summarize and update recent critical evaluations of Baldwin's genetic perspective. The other is to examine the intellectual and scientific heritage that Baldwin provided and to determine what went wrong. More broadly, the goal of this historical review is to clarify some of the scientific antecedents and prospects of a developmental science.

TWO CENTRAL ISSUES: METAPHYSICS AND DEVELOPMENT

In an excellent analysis of the structure of Baldwin's thought, Wozniak (1982) writes, "Baldwin had deep intellectual roots in the 'mental philosophy' tradition which dominated American higher education during the nineteenth century" (p. 13). Yet he early gained a respect for the emerging biological and behavioral science and the possibility that there might be a scientific explanation for the origin of knowledge and the perception of reality. Accordingly, at the outset of his career, Baldwin explicitly oriented his empirical and theoretical work toward a synthesis of metaphysics and psychological science (Wozniak, 1982, p. 14). In the early 1890s, he became

---

[3] Preyer expanded developmental science by investigations of behavioral embryology (see Gottlieb, 1979), and Binet established the foundations of experimental child psychology and cognitive development (Cairns & Ornstein, 1979).

convinced that genetic study must be the central theme for the synthesis of reason and reality.

Throughout the remainder of his career, "the great topic of development itself" (Baldwin, 1895, p. x) dominated his work and thinking. In his day, Baldwin expanded the application of genetic concepts in three emergent disciplines—psychology, evolutionary biology, and sociology—and in one established discipline—philosophy. Baldwin's own scientific life illustrates his view that cognitive development is not limited to childhood. As Wozniak (1982) observes:

> Baldwin was himself subject of a series of intellectual transformations. So great, in fact, are the differences in conceptual structure and content among his major books . . . that one wonders if perhaps there might not have been three Baldwins at work: a mental philosopher (roughly to 1889), an evolutionary psychologist (approximately 1889–1903), and an evolutionary epistemologist (1903–1915) (p. 14).[4]

Given the scope and complexity of Baldwin's work, any brief summary is likely to be misleading. Shortcomings in the following account may be corrected by consulting more complete analyses that have recently become available, including Wozniak (1982) on the intellectual origins of genetic epistemology, Mueller (1976) and Valsiner and Van der Veer (1988) on the relations between psychology and sociology, and Cahan (1984) on the comparison of the genetic psychologies of Baldwin and Piaget. The edited volume of Broughton and Freeman-Moir (1982) has several informative chapters. In addition, various chapters in the fourth edition of the *Handbook of Child Psychology* attempt to place Baldwin's contributions into contemporary and historical context (Cairns, 1983; Harter, 1983; Sameroff, 1983). Then there are the voluminous writings of Baldwin himself, including 21 books and more than 100 articles. Baldwin's own thoughtful summary of his life's work is perhaps the best place to begin (Baldwin, 1930).

MENTAL DEVELOPMENT AND SOCIAL ONTOGENY

The two works of Baldwin that have proved most stimulating to modern developmental psychologists are *Mental Development in the Child and the Race* (Baldwin, 1895) and *Social and Ethical Interpretations of Mental Development* (Baldwin, 1897). The first book presented Baldwin's attempt to formulate a genetic epistemology. In individual development, a key mechanism for bringing about growth in the cognitive scheme is the circular reaction. This invention of Baldwin's is linked to concepts of learning that

---

[4]Although Wozniak's characterization of the marked intellectual transitions in Baldwin's career seems accurate, Baldwin appears to have moved beyond scientific psychology even before the turn of the century, coincident with his work on the *Dictionary of Philosophy and Psychology*.

appeared later and explained how experience could become internalized into habit through recurrent self-stimulation or imitation. A consideration of ontogenesis challenged the then-dominant idea that consciousness was "a fixed substance, with fixed attributes" (Baldwin, 1895, p. 2). He writes with respect to the static conceptions of traditional approaches:

> The genetic idea reverses all this. Instead of a fixed substance, we have the conception of a growing, developing activity. Functional psychology succeeds faculty psychology. Instead of beginning with the most elaborate exhibition of this growth and development, we shall find most instruction in the simplest activity that is at the same time the same activity. Development is a process of involution as well as of evolution, and the elements come to be hidden under the forms of complexity which they build up. . . . Now that this genetic conception has arrived, it is astonishing that it did not arrive sooner, and it is astonishing that the "new" psychology has hitherto made so little of it. (Baldwin, 1895, p. 3).

In Baldwin's eyes, development proceeds from infancy to adulthood through stages, beginning with a reflexive or physiological stage, continuing through sensorimotor and ideomotor stages, and progressing to a stage of symbolic transformations (Baldwin, 1895). Only in the most advanced stage do "syllogistic forms come to have an independent or a priori force, and pure thought emerges—thought, that is, which thinks of anything or nothing. The subject of thought has fallen out, leaving the shell of form" (Baldwin, 1930, p. 23). From its earliest formulation, Baldwin's stage theory of mental development focused attention on process as much as on structure. Many of the terms that he employed—*accommodation, assimilation, imitation, circular reaction*—are commonplace in today's textbooks, although it cannot be assumed that Piagetian meanings are necessarily the same as Baldwinian ones.

Social and Ethical Interpretations in Mental Development: A Study in Social Psychology (Baldwin, 1897) appeared only 2 years later. This book is the first work by an American psychologist on social–cognitive development in childhood; it is also the first volume in English that includes social psychology in its title (Mueller, 1976). In this work, the cognitive-stage model is extended to issues of social development, social organization, and the origins of the self. Baldwin felt that the essential issues of social psychology had been neglected because of the void that existed between the concepts of psychology and sociology:

> And it is equally true, though it has never been adequately realized, that it is in genetic theory that social or collective psychology must find both its root and its ripe fruitage. We have no social psychology, because we have had no doctrine of the *socius*. We have had theories of the ego and the alter; but that they did not reveal the socius is just their condemnation. So the theorist of society and institutions has

floundered in seas of metaphysics and biology, and no psychologist has brought him a life-preserver, nor even heard his cry for help. (Baldwin, 1895, p. ix).

In social development, there is a dialectic of personal growth that progresses from an egocentric receptive stage to a subjective one and, eventually, an empathic social stage. In Baldwin's scheme:

> The development of the child's personality could not go on at all without the modification of his sense of himself by suggestions from others. So he himself, at every stage, is really in part some one else, even in his own thought of himself. (Baldwin, 1897, p. 30).

Consistent with his emphasis on developmental processes of the self rather than static structures, personality is not fixed, neither by early experience nor by genes. Accordingly, "Personality remains after all a progressive, developing, never-to-be-exhausted thing" (Baldwin, 1897, p. 338). Actions are fluid, dynamic, and responsive to the immediate setting. In his view, the child's

> . . . wants are a function of the social situation as a whole. . . . His wants are not consistent. They are in every case the outcome of the social situation; and it is absurd to endeavor to express the entire body of his wants as a fixed quantity under such a term of description as "selfish," or "generous," or other, which has reference to one class only of the varied situations of his life. (Baldwin, 1897, p. 31).

The self becomes progressively and inevitably accommodated to others and to the traditions of society. This social heredity is mediated through imitation and the operation of an internal circular reaction. From each relationship, there emerges a refined sense of oneself and of others. "The only thing that remains more or less stable is a growing sense of self which include both terms, the ego and the alter" (Baldwin, 1897, p. 30).

SOCIOGENESIS

One other primary developmental concern of Baldwin involves the relations between nature and nurture and the cross-generational transmission of modifications in individual development. In light of the metaphysical synthesis that guided Baldwin's thinking, it was entirely fitting for him to argue that the nature–nurture dichotomy falsely "supposes that these two agencies are opposed forces" and that it fails to entertain the possibility that "most of man's equipment is due to both causes working together" (Baldwin, 1895, p. 77). Evolutionary adaptations and developmental accommodations operate toward the same goals, although they are established over vastly different time intervals.[5] Extending this analysis to the problem of how this synchrony is established and maintained, Baldwin wrote:

> It is clear that we are led to relatively distinct questions: questions which are now familiar to us when put in the terms covered by the words, "phylogenesis" and "ontogenesis." First, how has the development of organic life proceeded, showing constantly, as it does, forms of greater complexity and higher adaptation? This is the phylogenetic question. . . . But the second question, the ontogenetic question, is of equal importance: the question, How does the individual organism manage to adjust itself better and better to its environment? . . . This latter problem is the most urgent, difficult, and neglected question of the new genetic psychology (Baldwin, 1895, pp. 180–181).

Beginning in his first developmental volume (Baldwin, 1895) and continuing through *Development and Evolution* (Baldwin, 1902), Baldwin expanded on his view of the cross-generational transmission of behavior tendencies through organic selection. Accordingly, he proposed that accommodations that occur in the lifetime of the individual could be transmitted to the next generation in the form of adaptations of the species by means of the process that he labeled "organic selection" (Baldwin, 1895, p. 174).[6] The essence of the idea was that ontogenetic accommodations can serve to direct the course of evolutionary change. How was it accomplished? On this matter, debate continues on exactly what processes were implicated (e.g., Gottlieb, 1979, 1987; Piaget, 1978; Vonèche, 1982). Baldwin was clearly reaching for a developmental mechanism of directed selection that would supplement the Darwinian concept of natural selection, without invoking the Lamarckian factor (i.e., the inheritance of acquired characteristics). This proposal became known in biology as the *Baldwin effect* (Cairns, 1983; Gottlieb, 1979).

TOWARD A CRITICAL EVALUATION

Since the modernity of Baldwin's theory became acknowledged, it has seemed reasonable to evaluate its adequacy by modern standards. Certain

---

[5]Elsewhere we employed the term *sociogenesis* to refer to this general collaboration of internal and external events in social adaptation (i.e., *genesis* referred to the joint operation of both ontogenetic and phylogenetic variations; Cairns & Cairns, 1988). Sociogenesis was intended to reflect the ongoing synthesis of individual experience and the preparedness of the species in the regulation of social patterns, consistent with the proposals of Morgan (1902) and Baldwin (1902). The same term has been employed to describe Vygotsky's position on the social origins of cognition and personality (Valsiner & Van der Veer, 1988). It is of interest to observe that both meanings are related to Baldwin's concepts, but they are linked to quite different features.

[6]Partly because Baldwin (1902) made so much of it, there has been some debate about who deserves priority for proposing that there could be a non-Lamarckian account for the linkage between ontogenetic accommodations and phylogenetic adaptations. See, for example, Vonèche (1982) and Wozniak (1982) on the dates offered for Baldwin's first mention of organic selection.

shortcomings in coherence and expression appear in a cursory examination of his books; other problems demand the examination of the work of Baldwin's contemporaries. Doubtless the most important measure of his theory has to do with its effects on subsequent investigators, including those in our generation.

NOVELTY AND INCONSISTENCY

Perhaps because of his openness to novel conceptions, Baldwin sometimes evolved the meaning of basic concepts in the theoretical models that he proposed. The relativity of his ideas to time and context renders any static description of his theory misleading. It also confounds comparisons that may be made with his contemporaries and apparent intellectual heirs, including Piaget and Vygotsky.

Baldwin's work illustrated another premise of his theoretical perspective, namely, that an individual undergoes the "constant modification of his sense of himself by suggestions from others" (1897, p. 30). On this score, his early work in mental philosophy was heavily influenced by the metaphysical view of Scottish commonsense philosophy in general and the intuitional realism of James McCosh, his mentor at Princeton (Mueller, 1976; Wozniak, 1982). During the second period, his research laboratory owed much to the prior work of Preyer, Binet, and Shinn. Similarly, his conceptions of organic selection seemed to have drawn much from the work of Morgan (1896) and Osborn (1896). In the work on genetic logic and precision of philosophical definition, Baldwin drew on the work of contemporaries William James and C. S. Peirce in his conception of the task and its execution. Baldwin typically was generous in acknowledging these influences, and thereby highlighted his own distinctive insights and creativity.

Baldwin's writing style and organization were unfortunately uneven. On some issues, as is illustrated by some quotes in this article, he was incisive, powerful, and challenging. He could also, however, be obtuse. William James, one of the few American psychologists who remained friendly with Baldwin, gently remarked, "His article (like much of its author's [Baldwin's] writing) is in places deficit in perspicuity" (James, 1894, p. 210). Other critics were less generous. James Sully, an important British experimentalist and contemporary of Baldwin, began and ended a review of *Mental Development in the Child and the Race* with the following comments:

> This is a book which presents special difficulties to the reviewer. One looks on a biological work—for such Professor Baldwin's work seems to be quite as much as a psychological one—for arrangement, structure, organic form: in the present case one is struck almost at first glance by

the apparent absence of these attributes. And the first impression is by no means dispelled as one begins to read. (Sully, 1896, p. 97)

To sum up my impression of Prof. Baldwin's book. It seems to me in many respects fresh and stimulating. On the other hand in what looks like an over-straining after originality apparent newness of conception often turns on closer examination to be but newness of phrasing. *When new ideas are put forward one misses for the most part an impartial and thorough-going confronting of theory with fact.* (Sully, 1896, p. 102, my italics)

Unclarity was not limited to this first volume. In comparing Baldwin's discussions of social development with those of C. H. Cooley (1902), Sewney (1945, p. 84) indicated that "Cooley presented his views in a language that is lucid and readable, and free of the confusing and jumbled terminology that fills the writings of Baldwin." In an unpublished journal located by Mueller (1976, p. 250), Cooley himself allowed the following comments on Baldwin's style and motivation:

A great fault with strenuous writers like Baldwin is that in their eagerness to produce they do not allow time enough for their imaginations to grow naturally and thoroughly into the mastery of a subject. They force it, and so impair its spontaneity, its sanity and humanness. What they write may be stimulating, consecutive, attractive for a time, but it is not food to live on. A style like this Goethe calls mannerism or "das Manirierte." If you wish to produce anything of lasting value, you see to it that the subject matter, the truth, is the first interest of your mind, not your books, your essay, yourself as discoverer and communicator of truth.

A modern reviewer, otherwise sympathetic to Baldwin, indicated that "there is much in Baldwin's work that is unfinished and confusing" (Broughton, 1981, p. 402). Examples of the unfinished business that was cited included theoretical discontinuities in Baldwin's social theory and internal inconsistencies in the description of stages.

Baldwin's abstruse style may have been more than an inconvenience for readers. It was also functional in that it permitted him, perhaps without awareness, to reform explanations and concepts so that one and the same term could take on fresh nuances or alternative meanings, depending on its context. Imprecision in presentation thereby promotes projection in interpretation. Perhaps this is why there is considerable dispute as to what exactly was meant by Baldwin in his use of such terms as *organic selection, imitation,* and *genetic method.*

Baldwin tended to incorporate new ideas into his own developmental view and did not always appear to be sensitive to possible contradictions between the new and the old. Baldwin seems to have benefited greatly from Josiah Royce and William James in his concepts of the social self (Valsiner & Van der Veer, 1988). He also introduced some of the ideas of Osborn

(1896) and Morgan (1896) in his revision of the concept of organic selection. It was a process of assimilation, however, not imitation. Most of the ideas were transformed when they became incorporated into a genetic framework. This long-term pattern of intellectual reformulation and reconstruction may account for why Baldwin invented new terms for old ideas and was particularly sensitive to the issue of intellectual priority and ownership. In his eyes, the concepts were new inventions. Priority and recognition were especially important for Baldwin, and this concern may help explain his haste in publication.

To illustrate, consider the key concept of organic selection. The aim of the concept was clear from the beginning, namely, to link the accommodations that occurred in the life history of the individual to the adaptations that occurred in the life history of the species. But the identification of the precise mechanisms has proved to be something of a projective test. This is due in part to the assimilation by Baldwin of the terms and logical argument outlined by C. Lloyd Morgan (1896). In a brief but brilliant supplementary essay on this matter published as an appendix in Baldwin's volume on *Development and Evolution,* Morgan (1902) refers to the collaboration of individual modification in development and adaptive variation in phylogenesis as *coincident variations.* The kernel argument offered by Morgan was embodied in three propositions, namely:

> So far there is no direct relation between specific modifications and specific variations. Individual accommodation, as a factor in survival, affords time. . . for the occurrence of *any* variations of an adaptive nature.
>
> My own modest contribution to the further elucidation of the subject is the suggestion (1) that where adaptive variation v is simiar in direction to individual modification m, the organism has an added chance of survival from the coincidence $m + v$; (2) that where the variation is antagonistic in direction to the modification, there is a diminished chance of survival from the opposition $m - v$; and hence (3) that coincident variations will be fostered while opposing variations will be eliminated.
>
> If this be so, many of the facts adduced by Lamarckians may be interpreted in terms of the survival and gradual establishment of coincident variations by natural selection under the favourable environing conditions of somatic modifications. (Morgan, 1902, p. 348).

The concept of coincident variation was incorporated into Baldwin's account of organic selection, but it was unclear when he accepted the important corollary that there were no direct connections between specific individual experiences in ontogeny and specific variations in phylogeny.

All this is to say that the contributions of Baldwin did not arise independently of the rich intellectual context in which he lived and drew inspiration from. But he also inspired his colleagues. Consistent with his model of social–cognitive development, the influences were bidirectional. There is now ample evidence that a large number of investigators in four disciplines were challenged by Baldwin's proposals and conceptions on development. In his commitment to the concept of development and its systematic application, Baldwin was more persuasive, thoughtful, and persistent than any of his peers, including G. Stanley Hall.[7] He envisioned a new "genetic science" (Baldwin, 1930).

HERITAGE AND INFLUENCE

Lawrence Kohlberg deserves credit—more than any other psychologist of our generation—for having brought attention to the theoretical contributions of Baldwin. Before Kohlberg's (1969) classic article on social cognition, there was scant recognition among modern developmental psychologists of the extent to which Baldwinian insights have persisted in the discipline. Kohlberg himself studied Baldwin's work independently in graduate school to establish a theoretical framework for his investigation of ethical and moral development. It is therefore fitting that the primary book on Baldwin's theory should be edited by two of Kohlberg's former students (Broughton & Freeman-Moir, 1982) and that Kohlberg's chapter in that volume contained some of its most noteworthy passages. His essay provides a succinct answer to the question, What are the real differences between Baldwin's and Piaget's theories? Kohlberg writes:

> In the end, the fundamental distinction between Baldwin's moral psychology and Piaget's is that Piaget's psychology has no self. Piaget starts with an ego knowing objects, but knowing them first egocentrically. Development is a progressive movement toward objectivity. In contrast, for Baldwin all experience is experience of a self, not just of a bodily and cognitive ego. This means first that central to the self is not cognition but will. Second, it means that from the start experience is *social* and reflective. The child's sense of self is a sense of will and capacity in the relation of self to others. The individual is fundamentally a potentially moral being, not because of social authority and rules (as Durkheim and Piaget thought) but because his ends, his will, his self is that of a shared social self (Kohlberg, 1982, pp. 311–312).

It is also an integrative self. Baldwin (1897) himself indicated that "In spite of the large place which I assign to Imitation in the social life, I should prefer to have my theory known as the 'Self' or the 'Self Thought' theory of social organization" (p. xviii).

Baldwin's theoretical work anticipated much of Piaget's theory of cog-

---

[7]He did, however, have support in this activity. Beyond psychology, one has the remarkable developmental insights of Canadian zoologist Wesley Mills (1899), and beyond North America, there were several key developmentalists, including Preyer, Binet, and Freud.

nitive and moral development.[8] Piaget's use of Baldwin's distinctive terms—from circular reaction and cognitive scheme to accommodation, assimilation, and sensori-motor—point to a direct line of intellectual descent. More importantly, as Cahan (1984, p. 128) has observed, "The goals, genetic approach, and epistemological assumptions underlying Piaget's inquiry into cognitive development found explicit statement around the turn of the century in Baldwin's work." The mediational linkages from Baldwin are readily identified. From 1912 to his death in 1934, Baldwin's primary residence was in Paris. His work was well regarded in French intellectual circles in general and by Pierre Janet in particular. As Piaget wrote to Mueller (1976, p. 244),

> Unfortunately I did not know Baldwin personally, but his works had a great influence on me. Furthermore, Pierre Janet, whose courses I took in Paris, cited him constantly and had been equally very influenced by him. . . .

There is also a pattern in Piaget's citations of Baldwin. Curiously, these references appeared in works that were published very early (1926) or very late (1978) in his career.

It would be a mistake to infer that Piaget's theory was simply a revision of Baldwin's original. As Broughton (1981) and Cahan (1984) have observed, the differences are as great as the similarities. In addition to the insightful distinction made by Kohlberg, there is a large difference in the scientific styles of the two investigators that in turn gave rise to marked differences in the content of their approaches. Baldwin used the methods and analyses of experimental psychology to illustrate developmental theory. He learned early that the methods of experimental psychology were inadequate for evaluating the developmental theory that he was constructing. Given this dilemma, he chose to abandon the scientific issues and address the philosophical ones.

Piaget, on the other hand, was trained in biology rather than philosophy. As an empirical scientist, he employed observations to understand phenomena rather than merely demonstrate principles. Piaget was challenged to invent methods appropriate to the empirical issues he sought to comprehend. The clinical method of direct observation and the creation of developmentally appropriate tasks provided him with the tools for revising, extending, and evaluating his proposals. They also permitted others to assess the replicability of the phenomena and determine the adequacy of the theory. More important, the objective tracking of phenomena over time permitted Piaget and those who followed his lead to arrive at insights

---

[8] An informal interview was conducted with Piaget (1982) on his relations with Baldwin. The publication is posthumous, and possibly it should not have been published at all. Piaget's brief written response to Mueller's question (1976) on his relationship with Baldwin seemed to be more informative than the oral history.

that were not self-evident to experimentalists or armchair observers. The insights, in turn, contributed to the vitality of Piaget's developmental model.

Despite the weaknesses in Baldwin's theoretical system and empirical work, his proposals have nonetheless exercised a large direct and indirect influence on developmental theorists in the 20th century. As Valsiner and Van der Veer (1988) document, a straight line can be drawn between Baldwin's (1897) concepts of the development of the self in social context and George H. Mead's symbolic interactionism (1934), on the one hand, and Lev Vygotsky's (1962) propositions on the social–contextual origins of personality, on the other. Baldwin's work was the common denominator because neither Mead nor Vygotsky referred to each other directly. The Valsiner and Van der Veer (1988) analysis is consistent with independent evidence that (a) Baldwin's work had a significant influence on C. H. Cooley as well as Mead in formulations of symbolic interactionism; and (b) Baldwin's influence on Vygotsky was mediated primarily through Janet's writings. Finally, Valsiner and Van der Veer (1988) point out that the assimilation of Baldwin's influence was selective. On the one hand, Cooley (1902) and Mead (1934) tended to discard the developmental features of Baldwin's self theory. On the other hand, Vygotsky (1962) preserved both the developmental focus and the social dynamics of Baldwin's system.

Of at least equal importance are those contemporary investigators who have been directly inspired to invent methods that were not accessible to Baldwin but who found his developmental ideas useful in their own theoretical formulations. Examples include investigations of interpersonal development (e.g., Selman, 1980; Youniss, 1980), the development of the self (e.g., Harter, 1983; Lewis & Brooks-Gunn, 1979), ontogeny and evolution (e.g., Cairns, Gariépy, & Hood, 1990; Gottlieb, 1987, 1991), and the development of social networks.

IMPLICATIONS FOR DEVELOPMENTAL SCIENCE

In addressing the issue of what lasting significance Baldwin's developmental concepts may have for the science, we first must ask why they vanished from psychology in the first place. Only speculations may be offered at this juncture. The explanations that have been proposed by Mueller (1976), Broughton (1981), Cahan (1984), and Wozniak (1982) include (a) Baldwin's theoretical formulations were out of line with empirical trends that dominated the new psychology of the early 20th century; (b) his abstruse writing style failed to inspire confidence in the validity of his ideas; (c) his failure to produce students who might continue his work (i.e., in the 5 years that he was at Johns Hopkins, no students completed the doctoral program in psychology); and (d) his severe embarrassment in a personal scandal and abrupt termination from his academic position at Johns Hopkins in 1909. After that incident, he spent little time in the United States, and his name seems to have been virtually blacklisted by the next generation of psychologists. Each of these events may have contributed to the regression and extended latency of Baldwin's concepts in American psychology.[9]

There are two other explanations that could be important for the future of developmental science. One is simply that the developmental concepts Baldwin proposed were too vague and imprecise to qualify as scientific propositions. His psychological–biological–sociological–philosophical integration, though "stimulating and attractive for a time," may simply not be capable of supporting an empirical science.

The second explanation is related to the first, except the burden is shifted from the perspective to the methods. It is true that the further Baldwin went beyond the study of infancy, the more speculative and removed from data he became. But the fulfillment of his aim—the building of a science of development—demanded a continuing tension between a drive for system and a drive for evidence. As Quine (1981, p. 31) has observed, "If either of these drives were unchecked by the other, it would issue in something unworthy of the name of scientific theory: in the one case a mere record of observations, and in the other a myth without foundation." Baldwin seems to have lacked the talent or the patience to translate his ideas into an empirical science. Without empirical checks, he became caught up in some myths of his own invention.

Of the two explanations, the second leaves the door open for the creation of a developmental science. The root problem is to establish methods, techniques, and analyses that are appropriate for developmental study. Recent methodological critiques have suggested that the systematic study of developmental processes requires not only different statistics, but also different research designs and different ways to organize empirical observations. Furthermore, it was explicit in Baldwin's proposals that the task of disentangling development in context was necessarily an interdisciplinary activity that extends beyond the traditional boundaries of psychology. Sully (1896) was probably correct when he observed that Baldwin's *Mental Development in the Child and the Race* was as relevant to biology as it was to psychology. And Mueller (1976) was likely accurate when he noted that Baldwin's *Social and Ethical Interpretation of Mental Development* book was as relevant to sociology as to psychology.

The broader point is that Baldwin may have failed in his larger goal even if he had written more precisely, recruited more students, and died of old age in Baltimore rather than Paris. He would have failed because he had envisioned a science different from any that could be accommodated

---

[9]Ironically, Baldwin's forced move to Paris may have facilitated the acceptance of his concepts. European psychologists have been more receptive to developmental concepts and methods (e.g., longitudinal study, person-oriented statistics, developmental novelty, and irreversibility) than their American counterparts.

by the new psychology. It appears that many of the obstacles that precluded the adoption of developmental concepts into the psychology of the 1890s remain in place today.

So what might we conclude about James Mark Baldwin? Beyond whatever shortcomings that may have existed in his writing and teaching, and beyond whatever honors he coveted and disappointments he endured, he ultimately succeeded in reaching the part of the goal that was within his grasp. He had insight and vision to describe developmental ideas that continue to inspire and challenge 100 years after they were formulated.

REFERENCES

Baldwin, J. M. (1890). Origin of right or left-handedness. *Science, 16,* 302–303.

Baldwin, J. M. (1891). Suggestion in infancy. *Science, 17,* 113–117.

Baldwin, J. M. (1892). Infants' movements. *Science, 19,* 15–16.

Baldwin, J. M. (1893). New method in child psychology. *Science, 21,* 213–214.

Baldwin, J. M. (1895). *Mental development in the child and the race: Methods and processes.* New York: Macmillan.

Baldwin, J. M. (1897). *Social and ethical interpretations in mental development: A study in social psychology.* New York: Macmillan.

Baldwin, J. M. (1902). *Development and evolution.* New York: Macmillan.

Baldwin, J. M. (1930). James Mark Baldwin. In C. Murchison (Ed.), *The history of psychology in autobiography* (Vol. 1, pp. 1–30). Worcester, MA: Clark University Press.

Broughton, J. M. (1981). The genetic psychology of James Mark Baldwin. *American Psychologist, 36,* 396–407.

Broughton, J. M., & Freeman-Moir, D. J. (1982). Introduction. In J. M. Broughton & D. J. Freeman-Moir (Eds.), *The cognitive developmental psychology of James Mark Baldwin: Current theory and research in genetic epistemology* (pp. 1–12). Norwood, NJ: Ablex.

Cahan, E. D. (1984). The genetic psychologies of James Mark Baldwin and Jean Piaget. *Developmental Psychology, 20,* 128–135.

Cairns, R. B. (1983). The emergence of developmental psychology. In P. H. Mussen (Gen. ed.) & W. Kessen (Vol. ed.), *Handbook of child psychology* (Vol. 1, pp. 41–102, 4th ed.). New York: Wiley.

Cairns, R. B., & Cairns, B. D. (1988). The sociogenesis of self concepts. In N. Bolger, A. Caspi, G. Downey, & M. Moorehouse (Eds.), *Persons in social context: Developmental processes* (pp. 181–202). Cambridge, England: Cambridge University Press.

Cairns, R. B., Gariépy, J.-L., & Hood, K. E. (1990). Development, microevolution, and social behavior. *Psychological Review, 97,* 49–65.

Cairns, R. B., & Ornstein, P. A. (1979). Developmental psychology. In E. Hearst

(Ed.), *The first century of experimental psychology* (pp. 459–510). Hillsdale, NJ: Erlbaum.

Cooley, C. H. (1902). *Human nature and the social order.* New York: Free Press of Glencoe.

Gottlieb, G. (1979). Comparative psychology and ethology. In E. Hearst (Ed.), *The first century of experimental psychology* (pp. 147–176). Hillsdale, NJ: Erlbaum.

Gottlieb, G. (1987). The developmental basis for evolutionary change. *Journal of Comparative Psychology, 101,* 262–272.

Gottlieb, G. (1991). Experiential canalization of behavioral development: Theory. *Developmental Psychology, 27,* 4–13.

Harter, S. (1983). Developmental perspectives on the self-system. In P. H. Mussen (Series ed.) & M. Hetherington (Vol. ed.), *Handbook of child psychology* (Vol. 4, pp. 275–386, 4th ed.). New York: Wiley.

James, W. (1894). Review of "Internal speech and song." *Psychological Review, 1,* 209–210.

Kohlberg, L. (1969). Stage and sequence: The cognitive-developmental approach to socialization. In D. A. Goslin (Ed.), *Handbook of socialization theory and research* (pp. 347–480). Chicago: Rand McNally.

Kohlberg, L. (1982). Moral development. In J. M. Broughton & D. J. Freeman-Moir (Eds.), *The cognitive developmental psychology of James Mark Baldwin: Current theory and research in genetic epistemology* (pp. 277–325). Norwood, NJ: Ablex.

Lewis, M., & Brooks-Gunn, J. (1979). *Social cognition and the acquisition of self.* New York: Plenum Press.

Mead, G. H. (1934). *Mind, self, and society.* Chicago: University of Chicago Press.

Mills, W. (1899). The nature of animal intelligence and the methods of investigating it. *Psychological Review, 6,* 262–274.

Morgan, C. L. (1896). On modification and variation. *Science, 4,* 733–740.

Morgan, C. L. (1902). "New statement" from Professor Lloyd Morgan. In J. M. Baldwin, *Development and evolution* (pp. 347–348). New York: Macmillan.

Mueller, R. H. (1976). A chapter in the history of the relationship between psychology and sociology in America: James Mark Baldwin. *Journal of the History of Behavioral Sciences, 12,* 240–253.

Mussen, P. H., & Kessen W. (Vol. Ed.) (Series Ed.). (1983). *Handbook of child psychology: History, theory, and methods* (Vol. 1, 4th ed.). New York: Wiley.

Osborn, H. F. (1896). Ontogenetic and phylogenetic variation. *Science, 4,* 786–789.

Piaget, J. (1926). *The language and thought of the child.* New York: Harcourt Brace.

Piaget, J. (1978). *Behavior and evolution.* New York: Pantheon Books.

Piaget, J. (1982). Reflections on Baldwin. In J. M. Broughton & D. J. Freeman-Moir (Eds.), *The cognitive developmental psychology of James Mark Baldwin:*

Current theory and research in genetic epistemology (pp. 80–86). Norwood, NJ: Ablex.

Quine, W. V. (1981). *Theories and things.* Cambridge, MA: Belknap Press.

Sameroff, A. J. (1983). Developmental systems: Contexts and evolution. In P. H. Mussen (Gen. ed.) & W. Kessen (Vol. ed.), *Handbook of child psychology: Vol. 1. History, theory, and methods* (pp. 237–294). New York: Wiley.

Selman, R. L. (1980). *The growth of interpersonal understanding: Developmental and clinical analyses.* San Diego: Academic Press.

Sewney, V. D. (1945). *The social theory of James Mark Baldwin.* New York: King's Crown Press.

Sully, J. (1896). Review of "Mental development in the child and the race: Methods and processes." *Mind, 5,* 97–103.

Valsiner, J., & Van der Veer, R. (1988). On the social nature of human cognition: An analysis of the shared intellectual roots of George Herbert Mead and Lev Vygotsky. *Journal for the Theory of Social Behaviour, 18,* 117–136.

Vonèche, J. J. (1982). Evolution, development, and the growth of knowledge. In J. M. Broughton & D. J. Freeman-Moir (Eds.), *The cognitive developmental psychology of James Mark Baldwin: Current theory and research in genetic epistemology* (pp. 51–79). Norwood, NJ: Ablex.

Vygotsky, L. (1962). *Thought and language.* Cambridge, MA: M.I.T. Press.

Wozniak, R. (1982). Metaphysics and science, reason and reality: The intellectual origins of genetic epistemology. In J. M. Broughton & D. J. Freeman-Moir (Eds.), *The cognitive developmental psychology of James Mark Baldwin: Current theory and research in genetic epistemology* (pp. 13–45). Norwood, NJ: Ablex.

Youniss, J. (1980). *Parents and peers in social development.* Chicago: University of Chicago Press.

5

JOHN DEWEY AND HUMAN DEVELOPMENT

EMILY D. CAHAN

John Dewey was born on October 20, 1859, in Burlington, Vermont, the third of four sons born to a merchant father and a devout mother. Charles Darwin had just published *The Origin of Species*, and James Buchanan was president. Dewey died in his apartment on Fifth Avenue in New York City in June 1952, when Dwight David Eisenhower was securing the presidency. Dewey grew up amidst Burlington's traditional democratic community, surrounded by the Green Mountains. He spent most of his mature years in the impersonal urban complexities of Chicago and New York.

Dewey's steady stream of major works began with the 1887 publication *Psychology* and ended with the 1949 publication with Arthur Bentley of *Knowing and the Known*. During his long life, the United States transformed itself from a country of small farms to a nation of sprawling cities and factories. The changes that Dewey witnessed in his journeys from Vermont

Emily D. Cahan is grateful to William Kessen and Sheldon White for our many conversations about John Dewey and related matters.

Reprinted from *Developmental Psychology*, 28, 205–214. Copyright 1992 by the American Psychological Association.

through the Midwest and to New York reflected a wider set of changes in American life, and Dewey devoted much of his life to insisting that philosophy, psychology, and education should respond in kind. Dewey took especially seriously the cultural change in the role of science in American life. During Dewey's life, scientific inquiry had emerged from a study engaged in by a small elite to a requirement of all educated persons. For 50 years Dewey "persistently worked to transform the scientific method of knowledge into an instrument of individual moral guidance and enlightened social planning" (Rockefeller, 1991, p. 3). In science lay the possibility of rationally reconstructing our social institutions. In such reconstructions lay the promise of a fuller and freer life. Dewey's ideal society bears a close relationship to his psychology. Dewey felt that a society governed jointly by the epistemological norms of science (taken broadly to mean rational inquiry, not a technical set of procedures) and the political norms of democracy held the most promise for individual growth and freedom. Optimal human development required a society ordered on the basis of rationality and democracy. Dewey wrestled most explicitly with the question of development in children in his pedagogical writings. Education was Dewey's most enduring, comprehensive, and synthetic philosophical problem and the one for which he became best known. His interest in education "fused with and brought together what might otherwise have been separate interests—that in psychology and that in social institutions and social life" (Dewey, 1930, p. 156).

In 1875, just short of 16 years of age, Dewey entered the University of Vermont, New England's fifth oldest college, and acquired a taste for philosophy from Professor H. A. P. Torrey. After graduating, Dewey taught high school, first in Oil City, Pennsylvania, and then back in Vermont. While in Oil City, Dewey submitted an article entitled "The Metaphysical Assumptions of Materialism" to W. T. Harris, the editor of the *Journal of Speculative Philosophy* and a prominent American Hegelian. Harris accepted for publication the article from this shy young man who felt uncertain of his abilities and commitments. Encouraged by Morris and Torrey, and having obtained a loan from an aunt, Dewey attended graduate school at Johns Hopkins University. There he "listened to Charles Peirce but did not come under his direct influence" (Hook, 1939, p. 12), took courses on the new experimental psychology from G. Stanley Hall, and deepened his interest in and early inclination toward idealist philosophy. Hall warned his students of the dangers of excessive idealism, and "from his studies with Hall and such admonitions" (Rockefeller, 1991, p. 90), Dewey became more conscious of his own "inclination toward the schematic and formally logical" (Dewey, 1930, p. 150) and his tendency to "give way to the dialectical development of a theme" (Dewey, 1930, p. 150). Hall helped him to recognize the need to "balance" (Rockefeller, 1991, p. 90) this "formal, theoretic interest" with careful attention to "the concrete, empirical, and 'practical'" (Dewey, 1930, p. 151). In the short turn, however, the idealistic lessons of George S. Morris captivated Dewey more than the warnings of Hall.

Neo-Hegelianism seemed, at least in his early years as a budding philosopher, to satisfy Dewey's personal craving for a philosophical system in which parts related to a whole in a manner consistent with the new evolutionary biology with its emphasis on the organism in interaction with the environment. Slowly, unevenly, and over the course of many decades, Dewey turned from a philosophy based on objective Mind to a philosophy based on experience. Dewey admitted that Hegel "left a permanent deposit in my thinking" (Dewey, 1930, p. 154) but claimed that in his later years, he found that "the form, the schematicism of Hegel's system" seemed "artificial to the last degree" (Dewey, 1930, p. 154). Professionally, Dewey developed his philosophy at the Universities of Michigan, Minnesota, and Chicago and brought his thought to "rounded completion" (Hook, 1939, p. 5) at Columbia University. Always an activist though never an agitator, Dewey's pen never "ceased its flow of comment on public issues of the day" (Scheffler, 1974, p. 187). At the height of his career in the early decades of this century, Dewey exerted a major influence on American culture as well as having an impact overseas (Rockefeller, 1991). He was a man of affairs, and his most enduring influences were to be in education and philosophy. He wrote quietly but wisely about the "new psychology" that was so quickly taking form.

This chapter will abstract from Dewey's enormous corpus his views on the meaning and nature of a psychology of human development. The article begins with Dewey's early commitment to idealistic philosophy, makes a turn with his discovery of social psychology, and proceeds to Dewey's "consummate" interest in education. Dewey's educational writings reveal a theory of development that leans less on nature than do the writings of many of his contemporary developmentalists and more on culture in ways we now associate with the later discovered writings of Lev S. Vygotsky. In essence, Dewey's idea of development is one of noninevitable progress toward ends that depend deeply and essentially on social practices and values. Psychology provides a means for realizing those values and in so doing promoting human growth and social progress. Finally, Dewey's commitment to empirical inquiry informs his ideas of development no less than it permeates his entire pragmatic philosophy.

FROM PHILOSOPHY TO SOCIAL PSYCHOLOGY

In the 1880s and 1890s, the new psychology began to establish itself in American universities. The sine qua non of this new psychology lay in laboratory-based investigations of elementary problems of sensation and perception. Dewey had a much broader vision for the new psychology. For

Dewey, this new psychology was made possible by two great intellectual achievements: one in biology, the other in the social and historical sciences. In his eloquent 1884 article entitled "The New Psychology," Dewey reviews these influences. From biology and Darwin comes the concept of organism in environment; from the human sciences comes a method of observing active minds in cultural settings. Together, these influences constitute the basis of a social psychology from which developmental psychology cannot be separated. There are casualties along the way from the old to the new, including the method of introspection and the psychology of ready-made faculties. But there are new promises and possibilities as well, including a truly social psychology that would consider people in relationship to their social circumstances:

> To biology is due the conception of organism. . . . In psychology this conception has led to the recognition of mental life as an organic unitary process developing according to the laws of all life, and not a theatre for the exhibition of independent autonomous faculties, or a *rendezvous* in which isolated, atomic sensations and ideas may gather, hold external converse, and then forever part. Along with this recognition of the solidarity of mental life has come that of the relation in which it stands to other lives organized in society. The idea of environment is a necessity to the idea of organism, and with the conception of environment comes the impossibility of considering psychic life as an individual, isolated thing developing in a vacuum. (Dewey, 1884, p. 56)

The individual is born into an "organized social life . . . from which he draws his mental and spiritual substance" and in which he must "perform his proper function or become a mental and moral wreck" (Dewey, 1884, p. 57). We need new methods, however, for studying people in relation to organized social life—for studying mind in culture. Dewey here turns to the social and historical sciences:

> I refer to the growth of those vast and as yet undefined topics of inquiry which may be vaguely designated as the social and historical sciences— the sciences of the origin and development of the various spheres of man's activity. (Dewey, 1884, p. 57)

These sciences provide a method—objective observation—and thus contain the promise of widening the scope of existing experimental psychology:

> With the development of these sciences has come the general feeling that the scope of psychology has been cabined and cramped till it has lost all real vitality, and there is now the recognition of the fact that all these sciences possess their psychological sides, present psychological material, and demand treatment and explanation at the hands of psychology. Thus the material for the latter, as well as its scope, have been indefinitely extended. (Dewey, 1884, p. 57)

In an era when psychology was becoming narrowly defined as a laboratory-based enterprise, Dewey claimed that "folk-lore and primitive culture, ethnology and anthropology, all render their contributions of matter and press upon us the necessity of explanation" (Dewey, 1884, p. 57). Dewey concludes that he "could go through the various spheres of human activity, and point out how thoroughly they are permeated with psychological questions and materials" (Dewey, 1884, p. 57).

The young Dewey believed in an identity of method in philosophy and psychology, and he wrote his 1887 textbook with the dual purpose of presenting the findings of the new scientific psychology and of providing an introduction to philosophy. His *Psychology* reviewed an extraordinary amount of the normal science that had accumulated in the new psychology and assimilated it to a Hegelian scheme. Because the fundamental characteristic of the self is consciousness, psychology may also be called *the science of consciousness*. The person is a self-determining will. He or she explores self-realization by studying the way in which knowing, feeling, and willing contribute to the unification of the self with the ideal self and to an overcoming of the separation of subject and object, individual and universal (Rockefeller, 1991, p. 100). "In other words, the *Psychology* is a study of the way in which the self finds its true self and union with the divine in and through science, philosophy, art, social relations, and religion" (Rockefeller, 1991, p. 101). The book is "young Dewey's major defense of the world view of ethical idealism" (Rockefeller, 1991, p. 101). The text earned praise from some (e.g., Morris) and drew criticism from others (e.g., G. Stanley Hall and William James).

For present purposes it is important to understand that the "resultant advice" of Dewey's text "for the psychologist who wishes to understand the human mind is to go out and watch its results in a cultural setting" (White, 1943/1964, p. 58). Dewey was beginning his call for a social psychology of mind in experience. It would be wrong, Dewey articulated some years later, for psychology to model its methods after the methods of the natural sciences. The most interesting aspects of social science are just those aspects of experience that get stripped away in the traditional natural sciences laboratory setting:

> It would require a technical survey . . . to prove that the existing limitations of 'social science' are due mainly to unreasoning devotion to physical science as a model, and to a misconception of physical science at that. Without making any such survey, attention may be directly called to one outstanding difference between physical and social facts. The ideal of the knowledge dealing with the former is the elimination of all factors dependent upon distinctively human response. 'Fact,' physically speaking, is the ultimate residue after human purposes, desires, emotions, and ideas and ideals have been systematically excluded. A social 'fact,' on the other hand, is a concretion in external form of precisely these human factors. (Dewey, 1931b, p. 64)

THE NEED FOR A SOCIAL PSYCHOLOGY

In a 1917 address before the American Psychological Association, Dewey called for two psychologies—one biological and the other social. Dewey credits the French sociologist Gabriel Tarde for a most fruitful psychological conception that was "ahead of his time and went almost unnoticed" (Dewey, 1917, p. 54). Tarde's notion

> was that all psychological phenomena can be divided into the physiological and the social, and that when we have relegated elementary sensation and appetite to the former head, then all that is left of our mental life, our beliefs, ideas and desires, falls within the scope of social psychology. (Dewey, 1917, p. 54)

Now Dewey poses the fundamental problem of social psychology of which child development is a part. The problem is to understand the relation between universal aspects of human nature and its different forms of expression in different social circumstances or arrangements. In so stating the problem, Dewey raises the further problems of education and social reform. Dewey credits his colleague from the University of Chicago, W. I. Thomas, for suggesting the approach:

> On the one hand our problem is to know the modifications wrought in the native constitution of man by the fact that the elements of his endowment operate in this or that social medium; on the other hand, we want to know how control of the environment may be better secured by means of the operation of this or that native capacity. Under these general heads are summed up the infinity of special and difficult problems relating to education on the one hand and to constructive modification of our social institutions on the other. To form a mind out of certain native instincts by selecting an environment which evokes them and directs their course; to re-form social institutions by breaking up habits and giving peculiar intensity and scope to some impulse is the problem of social control in its two phases. To describe how such changes take place is the task of social psychology stated in generalized terms. (Dewey, 1917, p. 56)

Neither Dewey nor Tarde nor Thomas was alone or first to propose two psychologies (Cahan & White, 1992). Like John Stuart Mill in England, Auguste Comte in France, Hugo Münsterberg in the United States, Lev S. Vygotsky in Russia, and others elsewhere, Dewey called for a social psychology of people in relation to circumstances to stand beside and complement the first, experimental psychology. Each version of the second psychology would serve a strategic purpose in the design of society (Gay, 1969). Dewey's emerging social and developmental psychology was indeed a strategic inquiry. The purpose of social psychology is to aid in the reconstruction of the institutions of social life by understanding individuals in relation to their social settings. The place, therefore, to study the psychology of the child is in the social circumstances of the child. In complex societies such as our own, that place is school. To consider schools as proper places for understanding child development, however, one must modify or extend the traditional definition of a laboratory.

SCHOOLS AS LABORATORIES OF HUMAN DEVELOPMENT

While boasting of the methodological promises of an empirical psychology, Dewey warned against the excesses and indicated the limits to the knowledge gathered in those laboratories. In contemporary terms, Dewey warned of the threats to ecological validity of a psychology that was limited to the traditional laboratory experiment:

> The great advantage of the psychological laboratory is paid for by certain obvious defects. The completer the control of conditions, with resulting greater accuracy of determination, demands an isolation, a ruling out of the usual media of thought and action, which leads to a certain remoteness, and easily to a certain artificiality. . . . Unless our laboratory results are to give us artificialities, mere scientific curiosities, they must be subjected to interpretation by gradual approximation to conditions of life. . . . The laboratory, in a word, affords no final refuge that enables us to avoid the ordinary scientific difficulties of forming hypotheses, interpreting results, etc. In some sense (from the very accuracy and limitations of its results) it adds to our responsibilities in this direction. (Dewey, 1899a, p. 145)

More recently, Dewey's critique of a psychology limited to the empiricism of a traditional laboratory has surfaced perhaps most forcefully in Urie Bronfenbrenner's proposals for an ecology of human development (e.g., Bronfenbrenner, 1979).

In 1896, Dewey began a small primary school under the auspices of the University of Chicago Department of Pedagogy. He called the school a "laboratory school" and used it as the source for his normal science. The time was growing ripe, Dewey felt, for scientific experimentation in education. Dewey called for a more

> coherent philosophy of experience and a philosophy of the relation of school studies to that experience; that we can accordingly take up steadily and wisely the effort of changing school conditions so as to make real the aims that command the assent of our intelligence and the support of our moral enthusiasm. (Dewey, 1901, p. 282)

The time was ripe, Dewey thought, to control aspects of the school environment in such a way as to make real the ends that we wish to foster in children. Dewey's new school was to be a genuine laboratory where hypotheses could be tested under reasonably controlled conditions, a place where inquiry or experience could be directed. In ways that most certainly echo Dewey, Donald T. Campbell has argued that psychologists should consider social reforms as experiments (Campbell, 1969). For Dewey, the laboratory school "bears the same relation to the work in pedagogy that a laboratory bears to biology, physics, or chemistry" (Dewey, 1896c, p. 437):

> Now the school, for psychological purposes, stands in many respects midway between the extreme simplifications of the laboratory and the confused complexities of ordinary life. Its conditions are those of life at large; they are social and practical. But it approaches the laboratory in so far as the ends aimed at are reduced in number, are definite, and thus simplify the conditions; and their psychological phase is upper-most — the formation of habits of attention, observation, memory, etc. — while in ordinary life these are secondary and swallowed up. (Dewey, 1899a, p. 145)

The school, he said, serves educators as

> a focus to keep the theoretical work in touch with the demands of practice, and also makes an experimental station for the testing and development of methods which, when elaborated, may be safely and strongly recommended to other schools. (Dewey, 1896a, p. 244)

By such means, "psychology becomes a working hypothesis, instruction is the experimental test and demonstration of the hypothesis; the result is both greater practical control and continued growth in theory" (Dewey, 1899a, p. 146).

The school was an experiment — an experiment in the possibilities of human development in arranged environments. If we vary aspects of this simplified social environment, we can better understand and direct child development toward desired ends. The school thus served Dewey as a laboratory for exploring the possibilities among children, teachers, and curricula. An analysis of the "Deweyan" classroom becomes relevant to an understanding of child development because it is conceived and constructed to simulate the conditions under which the epistemological and political ideals of a democratic society are best learned and practiced. In this analysis, the classroom becomes the context in which Dewey's ideals for society are expressed as desirable norms of growth for the individual child. The work of Dewey's school proceeded on the basis of a set of ideas about the nature of experience, inquiry, and child development that are well worth exploring.

EXPERIENCE, INQUIRY, AND THE DEVELOPMENT OF REASON

Dewey's 1896 article, "The Reflex Arc Concept in Psychology," is widely recognized as an early and important expression of his functional psychology. The article begins with a critique of the way in which the idea of the reflex arc had become "an organizing principle to hold together the multiplicity of fact" in psychology (Dewey, 1896b, p. 96). Dewey rejects the notion that stimulus and response represent separate, unrelated entities and insists instead that they are functionally related to each other through purposeful activity. Dewey wants to see sensory stimulus, central connections, and motor responses not as "separate and complete entities in themselves, but as divisions of labor, functioning facts, within the single concrete whole" (Dewey, 1896b, p. 97).

The real beginning of this sequence for Dewey is with the act of seeing, not the bare sensation of light as a stimulus to grasp as a response. Instead of a simple reflex arc in which light acts as a stimulus to grasp, we have a circuit because "the motor response determines the stimulus, just as truly as sensory stimulus determines movement" (Dewey, 1896b, p. 102). Both the stimulus of light and the response of grasping must be defined by the context of child seeing a burning candle. Stimulus and response define each other and are therefore not "distinctions of existence, but teleological distinctions, that is, distinctions of function, or part played, with reference to reaching or maintaining an end" (Dewey, 1896b, p. 104). Distinctions of stimulus and response are functional phases of a circuit of purposeful activity.

Dewey's analysis of the reflex arc concept proved to be pivotal to his emerging experimental logic and theory of inquiry. It foreshadows his philosophy of experience and his eventual "explicit identification of the stimulus with the problematic situation" (Smith, 1983, p. 121). For Dewey, thought "is not self-contained but has a function to perform in relation to the environment, and that function is the clue to its nature" (Smith, 1983, p. 124). Specifically, the function of thought is to resolve the relationship between doubt and inquiry to attain a state of assuredness or certainty (Dewey, 1900, 1903, 1909). And a theory of thinking demands for Dewey "a statement in which all the distinctions and terms of thought . . . shall be interpreted simply and entirely as distinctive functions or divisions of labor within the doubt–inquiry process" (Dewey, 1900, p. 174.).

Thinking is thus synonymous with inquiry. Thought is a process through which doubt is subjected to inquiry and, if successful, eventually gives way to assurance—a kind of temporary equilibrium known as knowledge. This relationship between doubt and inquiry passes through distinctive stages. Dewey's discussion of these stages is rough and unsystematic. In ways that differ only subtly, Dewey discusses stages in inquiry in several works, including his early (1903) *Studies in Logical Theory*, as well as his more mature statement in *Logic: A Theory of Inquiry* (1938a); his synthetic work on the philosophy of education, *Democracy and Education* (1916); his psychological treatise written for teachers, *How We Think* (1909); and some smaller pieces more directly addressed to the development of reasoning in children (1900, 1913).

Dewey is interested in discerning the ways in which one learns to relate facts and ideas, to consider facts as evidence in relation to ideas. Roughly, the stages represent a progression from a period in which ideas are fixed, when "facts and relations are taken for granted" (Dewey, 1903, p. 307); to a recognition of a problem accompanied by an unsystematic "period of occupation with relatively crude and unorganized facts" (Dewey, 1903, p. 307); to a speculative stage of guessing and making hypotheses; to, finally, a period that we may identify with scientific rationality. The end in the development of inquiry is

> a period when observation is determined by experimental conditions depending upon the use of certain guiding conceptions; when reflection is directed and checked at every point by the use of experimental data, and by the necessity of finding such a form for itself as will enable it to serve in a deduction leading to evolution of new meanings, and ultimately to experimental inquiry which brings to light new facts. (Dewey, 1903, p. 307)

Clearly, the end of this process for Dewey as "a period of fruitful interaction between ideas and facts" (Baker, 1955, p. 39) is that which we associate with scientific method. The process, however, does not result in any kind of stable truth. Rather, the course of inquiry leads only to new problems:

> There is no such thing as a final settlement, because every settlement introduces the conditions of some degree of a new unsettling. In the stage of development marked by the emergence of science, deliberate institution of problems becomes an objective inquiry. (Dewey, 1938a, p. 42)

The world is no longer shot through with logic. Instead, Dewey sees life as "precarious and uncertain, full of doubt and conflict" (Baker, 1955, p. 36). Dewey is rejecting his earlier Hegelianism and is "setting forth a naturalism that excludes any transcendental element in the explanation of man's experience" (Rucker, 1969, p. 60). Thought has no final objective of reaching Truth; its only objective is to attain a state of equilibrium— plausible truths, warranted assertions—that solve current dilemmas while posing further inquiries.

With respect to the application of this developmental scheme to children, Dewey remains essentially and persistently ambiguous. On the one hand, Dewey attributes a certain degree of natural scientific rationality to the child. For example, in *How We Think*, Dewey wrote that

> this book represents the conviction . . . that the native and unspoiled attitude of childhood, marked by ardent curiosity, fertile imagination, and love of experimental inquiry, is near, very near, to the attitude of the scientific mind. (Dewey, 1909, p. 179)

"Tendencies," Dewey claims,

toward a reflective and truly logical activity are native to the mind, and . . . they show themselves at an early period, since they are demanded by outer conditions and stimulated by native curiosity. There is an innate disposition to draw inferences, and an inherent desire to experiment and test. (Dewey, 1933a, p. 181)

On the other hand, and of critical importance to understanding the meaning of development, Dewey insists that a truly cultivated scientific frame of mind depends on education for its development. The child is a natural problem solver while, at the same time, true or disciplined scientific procedures and reasoning must be learned:

> Science is a name for knowledge in its most characteristic form. It represents in its degree, the perfected outcome of learning, — its consummation. . . . It consists of the special appliances and methods which the race has slowly worked out in order to conduct reflection under conditions whereby its procedures and results are tested. *It is artificial (an acquired art), not spontaneous; learned, not native.* To this fact is due the unique, the invaluable place of science in education . . . (Dewey, 1916, pp. 196–197; emphasis added)

Scientific logic is an ideal that can only be attained under proper conditions of education. "*Effective* intelligence is not an original, innate endowment. . . . The actuality of mind is dependent upon the education which social conditions effect" (Dewey, 1927), and "the real problem of intellectual education is the *transformation* of more or less casual curiosity and sporadic suggestion into attitudes of alert, cautious, and thorough inquiry" (Dewey, 1933a, p. 181).

DEWEY'S CRITIQUE OF DEVELOPMENT IN EDUCATION

Dewey's emphases on the social context of development also reflected his dissatisfactions with the idea of development as it had come to be used in educational circles and, more broadly, with his commitment to a social psychology. Dewey criticized educational doctrines in which "development is conceived not as continuous growing, but as the unfolding of latent powers toward a definite goal" (Dewey, 1916, p. 61). Rousseau likened the development of a child to "the development of a seed into the full-grown plant" (Dewey, 1934, p. 195). Dewey felt that Rousseau used this analogy to "draw the conclusion that in human beings there are latent capacities which, if they are only left to themselves, will ultimately flower and bear fruit" (Dewey, 1934, p. 195). Consequently, proponents of development in education "framed the notion of *natural* development . . . as opposed to directed growth which they regarded as artificial" (Dewey, 1934, p. 195). The metaphor of a seed is limited because the seed's future is "largely prescribed by its antecedent nature" (Dewey, 1934, p. 195). The seed

. . . has not got the capacities for growth in different directions towards different outcomes that are characteristic of the more flexible and richly endowed human young. The latter is also, if you please, a seed, a collection of germinal powers, but he may become a sturdy oak, a willow that bends with every wind, a thorny cactus, or a poisonous weed. (Dewey, 1934, p. 195; with emendations)

Unlike the seed, the child is plastic, and in that plasticity lies the possibility of many different ends being realized—some good and desirable, others bad and undesirable.

Through the influence of Rousseau on Pestalozzi, Froebel, and other educational theorists, Dewey felt that education "in accordance with nature" had come to mean "that there were certain intrinsic laws of development or unfolding, physical, mental, and moral in children, and that these inherent principles of growth should furnish the norms of all educational procedure" (Dewey, 1912–1913, p. 289):

The child is expected to "develop" this or that fact out of his own mind. He is told to think things out, or work things out for himself, without being supplied any of the environing conditions which are requisite to start and guide thought. Nothing can be developed from nothing; nothing but the crude can be developed out of the crude— and this is what surely happens when we throw the child back upon his achieved self as a finality, and invite him to spin new truths of nature or of conduct out of that. (Dewey, 1902, p. 282)

In the case of reasoning, Dewey rejects a predetermined end and substitutes growth as directed by classroom practices. Again, we find that Dewey rejects the notion that the development of thought represents the unfolding of a latent ability:

There is no ground for assuming that "thinking" is a special, isolated natural tendency that will bloom inevitably in due season simply because various sense and motor activities have been freely manifested before; or because observation, memory, imagination, and manual skill have been previously exercised without thought. (Dewey, 1909, p. 231)

In thinking, the possibilities of multidirectionality, the potential for negative as well as positive, are present. The absence of any kind of inevitability to the process points to the need for systematic training with particular ends in mind:

Thinking may develop in positively wrong ways and lead to false and harmful beliefs. The need of systematic training would be less than it is if the only danger to be feared were lack of any development; the evil of the wrong kind of development is greater. (Dewey, 1933b, p. 129)

Just because . . . it [thinking] is an operation of drawing inferences, of basing conclusions upon evidence, of reaching belief *indirectly*, it is an operation that may be wrong as well as right, and hence is one that needs safeguarding and training. The greater its importance the greater are the evils when it is ill-exercised. (Dewey, 1909, p. 195)

For Dewey, then, education is responsible for directing inquiry toward desired social and intellectual ends.

REASONING IN CHILDREN AND ADULTS

Unlike many of his contemporaries (cf. Baldwin, 1906–1915; Hall, 1904), Dewey made no special claims for qualitative shifts in reasoning in development. Dewey insists that "the power of reasoning in little children does not differ fundamentally from that of adults" (Dewey, 1913, p. 370) and that the apparent differences between childish and adult mentality are functional rather than structural. Because of differences in the materials with which thinking is done and the "ends or objects for the sake of which it is carried on, the impression is easily created that the thinking itself is of a radically different order" (Dewey, 1913, p. 370). Thinking involves three elements for Dewey: (a) an end to be reached or purpose to be achieved; (b) a method, or the selection of means by which to arrive at such purpose; and (c) the possibility of new discoveries that lead to further inquiry in working toward the end (Dewey, 1913, p. 370). Children and adults appear to reason differently because they simply have "different objects to think about and different purposes for which to think" (Dewey, 1913, p. 370). The difference between reasoning in children and adults lies in variations around the purpose and means of solving problems and can be reduced to two categories. "There are different objects to think about, and different purposes for which to think, because children and grownups have different kinds of acts to perform—different lines of occupation" (Dewey, 1913, p. 370). Consistent again with Dewey's naturalism with its commitment to functional analyses, differences in childish and adult thought reveal to Dewey differences not so much in process as in the purpose of thought—the active ends to which thought is applied:

> The ends which a young child has are different from those of the grownup and the materials, means, and habits which he is able to fall back upon are different, but the process—one involving these three factors—*is exactly the same*. (Dewey, 1913, p. 372)

In contrast with the relatively unfocused nature of childish thought, the objects and ends of adult thinking have a "definitely established character, have a more specialized organization" (Dewey, 1913, p. 370). The difference then, between childish and adult thought is a "difference in the psychological landscape . . . rather than a difference in the actual process of thinking itself" (Dewey, 1913, p. 372). Development for Dewey is associated then with an increase in the range of environments in which the child is capable of conducting inquiry—reconstructing experience. "Inquiry develops" for Dewey "as the cognitively emergent way in which organisms, already functioning pre-cognitively at least in terms of survival, enlarge the range of interactions with the environing world" (Margolis, 1977, p. 140). The development of reason for Dewey is associated not with general structural reorganization(s) of thought, but with an increase in the range and complexity of situations to which the child is capable of applying reasoned inquiry. More recently, Sheldon White and Alexander Siegel (1984) as well as Barbara Rogoff (1990) have proposed similar approaches to cognitive development.

Rousseau further marred his assertion that education must be a natural development and not something forced on or grafted on individuals from without "by the notion that social conditions are not natural" (Dewey, 1916, p. 65). Social conditions are not only natural in the course of the child's development; the child's development is absolutely dependent on such influences.

Dewey contrasts what he calls the contemporary notion of develop-ment with the older notion of development in two respects. First, Dewey suggests that the contemporary idea of development "insists that devel-opment must be measured from the standpoints of specific ends to be attained. There is no development at large going on" (Dewey, 1911, p. 422). Second, the contemporary notion of development recognizes "the positive necessity of a favorable environment to secure development" (Dewey, 1911, p. 422). "It is not enough," Dewey argues, "to eliminate arbitrary and perverting conditions; growth cannot go on in a vacuum. As the body requires air and food, so mind and character require a culture medium in order to develop" (Dewey, 1911, p. 422). Specifically, the cultural medium is responsible for determining the very direction of development, or, as Dewey most consistently expressed it, growth. In complex societies such as our own, the particular social institution responsible for directing growth is education.

For Dewey, the notion of development or growth is anchored at one end by native interests, at the other end by social values, and mediated by social institutions and practices:

> Development, in short, has become a notion which, on one side em-phasizes the native and spontaneous existence, in the one educated, of the fundamental and initial factors of education, while, on the other, it emphasizes the social nature of growth as aim and the necessity of social conditions in order that growth may be in the right direction. (Dewey, 1911, p. 422)

Dewey searched, in his doctrine of growth in the child, for a middle course between the notion that development is a matter of the inevitable unfolding of latent powers from within and the notion that development is externally imposed from without. He claimed that the alternative of growth "is not just a middle course or compromise between the two procedures. It is something radically different from either" (Dewey, 1934, p. 198; with emendations).

In contrast to the idea of development as the unfolding of latent powers from within toward a remote end, growth has all the time "an immediate end—the direct transformation of the quality of experience" (Dewey, 1916, p. 82). Development then "does not mean just getting something out of the mind. It is a development of experience and into experience that is really wanted" (Dewey, 1902, p. 282). The immediate goals and objectives of education are set by the interests and capabilities of the child and are not imposed by adults as fixed ends. The subject matter of education should be drawn from the child's present environment and from the child's current interests. It is then up to the educator to guide the child's interests in relation to the ideals of growth:

> Existing likes and powers are to be treated as possibilities, as starting points, that are absolutely necessary for any healthy development. . . .
> The great problems of the adult who has to deal with the young is to see, and to feel deeply as well as merely to see intellectually, the forces that are moving in the young; but it is to see them as possibilities, as signs and promises; to interpret them; in short, in the light of what they may come to be. (Dewey, 1934, pp. 198–199)

Therefore,

> The fundamental factors in the educative process are in an immature, undeveloped being; and certain social aims, meanings, values incarnate in the matured experience of the adult. The educative process is due to the interaction of these forces. (Dewey, 1902, p. 273)

Dewey's experience in the laboratory school at Chicago helped him to synthesize the doctrine of growth with educational theory and practice. Reaching what he considered to be a technical definition of education, Dewey declared that education "is that reconstruction or reorganization of experience which adds to the meaning of experience, and which increases ability to direct the course of subsequent experience" (Dewey, 1916, p. 82). Education "means supplying the conditions which foster growth" (Dewey, 1916, p. 56). Thus growth is a process in which the organism enhances its ability to participate with its environment.

Dewey's doctrine of growth can be summarized by three central propositions: (a) Education and growth are synonymous with each other, (b) growth has ends neither external nor beyond itself, and (c) the value of schooling depends on the extent to which schooling creates a desire for and provides the means for continued growth (Dewey, 1916, pp. 82–86). In its baldest form, growth constitutes the only end—the only moral end— of education—growth conceived as the capacity for more growth. Education, growth, and inquiry thus become synonymous; the ideals for each hold good for the others; each is identified with "a constant reorganizing or restructuring of experience" (Dewey, 1916, p. 82).

IDEALS OF GROWTH

Dewey wisely recognized that "when it is said that education is development, everything depends upon *how* development is conceived" (Dewey, 1916, p. 54). Specifically, "unless growth has a direction, there is no genuine development. Unless we have antecedent knowledge of what is good, we do not know if the development is desirable" (Hook, 1959, p. 12). Education, although falling back on "the prior and independent existence of natural powers," is nonetheless concerned with "their proper direction" (Dewey, 1909, p. 204). Education thus sets the direction of development "in order that growth may be in the right direction." It is the "business of the school to set up an environment in which play and work shall be conducted with reference to facilitating desirable mental and moral growth" (Dewey, 1916, p. 196). A declaration of desired direction demands the articulation of an ideal:

> Unless we set up some definite criterion representing the ideal by which to judge whether a given attitude or act is approximating or moving away, our sole alternative is to withdraw all influences of the environment lest they interfere with proper development. (Dewey, 1916, p. 62)

Dewey leans hard on the ideals of democracy and science for individuals and society. Classroom activities are designed to bring about a fuller realization of these ideals. Specifically, it is the transformation of experience toward the systematic application of rational, empirical methods to shared problems that emerge from a classroom atmosphere of cooperative inquiry and activity that constitute the desired direction to the child's growth— the ideal of development—not as a static end but as the ideal context for self-development. Experience is intrinsically social; intellectual and moral ideals develop in the child through systematic, guided transformations of classroom experiences. These ideals are themselves built up from experience and, for Dewey, reflect the best and most appropriate ideals for social life in a democratic society. In short, "the experimental method is the only one compatible with the democratic way of life, as we understand it" (Dewey, in Mayhew & Edwards, 1936, p. 439). Dewey strives to articulate a necessary conjunction of science with democracy as a social philosophy. This conjunction is first learned by experience as a pupil in a classroom and later lived in adult life as a participating citizen in a democratic society.

On the intellectual side of growth, Dewey is most concerned with the development of a critical mind, a mind attuned to observation and experiment rather than individual bias or acceptance of a prejudice that might be imposed from some outside or arbitrary authority. In short, Dewey is concerned with the development of objectivity in the broadest sense of the word, a mode of reasoning mindful of the impartial authority of evidence rather than the bias of either personal authority or sentiment. On the moral side, Dewey is concerned with facilitating the political conditions in which this ideal of objectivity will best flourish. Knowledge and politics become one as science in the public forum becomes democracy in action. The demand in the classroom

> is for social intelligence, social power, and social interests. Our resources are (1) the life of the school as a social institution in itself; (2) methods of learning and of doing work; and (3) the school studies or curriculum. In so far as the school represents, in its own spirit, a genuine community life; in so far as the methods used are those which appeal to the active and constructive powers, permitting the child to give out; and thus to serve; in so far as the curriculum is so selected and organized as to provide the material for affording the child a consciousness of the world in which he has to play a part, and the relations he has to meet; in so far as these ends are met, the school is organized on an ethical base. (Dewey, 1897a, p. 75)

Thus, the "school must be itself made into a vital social institution," and the school "cannot be a preparation for a social life excepting as it reproduces, within itself, the typical conditions of social life" (Dewey, 1897a, p. 61). A curriculum, Dewey insists,

> which acknowledges the social responsibilities of education must present situations where problems are relevant to the problems of living together, and where observation and information are calculated to develop social insight and interest. (Dewey, 1916, p. 200)

The educator's task then becomes one of helping children to systematize and direct those native tendencies toward socially productive ends, ends that serve to enhance the child's participation in the community:

> It thus becomes the office of the educator to select those things within the range of existing experience that have the promise and potentiality of presenting new problems which by stimulating new ways of observation and judgement will expand the area of further experience. (Dewey, 1938b, p. 50)

In back of Dewey's emphasis on growth through the reconstruction of experience is his Hegelian conviction that reason itself most fully realizes itself in action. Hence, the pupil in the classroom must

> have a genuine situation of experience—that there be a continuous activity in which he is interested for its own sake; secondly, that a genuine problem develop within this situation as a stimulus to thought; third, that he possess the information and make the observations needed

to deal with it; fourth, that suggested solutions occur to him which he shall be responsible for developing in an orderly way; fifth, that he have the opportunity and occasion to test his ideas by application, to make their meaning clear and to discover for himself their validity. (Dewey, 1916, p. 170)

The problem of education for Dewey is to discover the means for making scientific thought more widespread in society and giving it a deepening hold among people—for extending his ideals for individual growth in the classroom into society:

> . . . if scientific thought is not something esoteric but is a realization of the most effective operation of intelligence, it should be axiomatic that the development of scientific attitudes of thought, observation, and inquiry is the chief business of study and learning. (Dewey, 1931a, p. 60)

In schools, "we want that type of education which will discover and form the kind of individual who is the intelligent carrier of a social democracy" (Dewey, 1918, p. 57). "[S]ince democracy stands in principle for free interchange, for social continuity, it must develop a theory of knowledge which sees in knowledge the method by which one experience is made available in giving direction and meaning to another" (Dewey, 1916, p. 354).

GROWTH AND THE RECONSTRUCTION OF SOCIETY

By the turn of the century, Dewey had clearly expressed his faith in the school as the most effective means for social progress. In 1897, Dewey wrote an essay for teachers entitled "My Pedagogic Creed" and declared that "education is the fundamental method of social progress and reform" (Dewey, 1897b, p. 93). In his 1922 treatise on social psychology entitled *Human Nature and Social Conduct*, Dewey asserted that

> a future new society may be created by a deliberate humane treatment of the impulses of youth. This is the meaning of education; for a truly humane education consists in an intelligent direction of native activities in the light of the possibilities and necessities of the social situation. (Dewey, 1922c, p. 69)

Faith in education as a source of progress "signifies nothing less than belief in the possibility of deliberate direction of the formation of human disposition and intelligence" (Dewey, 1922b, p. 318). And "in directing the activities of the young, society determines its own future in determining that of the young" (Dewey, 1916, p. 46).

When the school is structured as a small society unto itself, the child may "directly experience and develop the intellectual and moral virtues to enable him to develop a better society" (Bernstein, 1966, p. 41). In schools, we must create the type of community that will foster the development of this scientific intelligence. The school's cultivation of science led Dewey to conclude that "ultimately and philosophically, science is the organ of general social progress" (Dewey, 1916, p. 239).

The teacher in this view is "a social servant set apart for the maintenance of proper social order and the securing of the right social growth" (Dewey, 1897b, p. 95). And the community's duty to education is therefore its "paramount moral duty" because it is through education that "society can reformulate its own purposes, can organize its own means and resources, and thus shape itself with definiteness and economy in the direction in which it wishes to move" (Dewey, 1897b, p. 95). When teachers become "sufficiently courageous and emancipated" to insist on an education that teaches discrimination, skepticism, the suspension of judgment, an appeal to observation rather than sentiment, and inquiry rather than conventional idealizations, then schools will "begin to be supremely interesting places." Schools will become interesting places because they will have become part of a larger social and political process. "For it will have come about that education and politics are one and the same thing because politics will have to be in fact what it now pretends to be, the intelligent management of social affairs" (Dewey, 1922a, p. 334). Thus, the school "is recalled from isolation to the center of the struggle for a better life" (Cremin, 1961/1964, p. 119). The school is cast as a lever of social change; educational theory "becomes political theory and the educator is inevitably cast into the struggle for social reform" (Cremin, 1961/1964, p. 118). In short, growth considered as the end of education is a political proposition:

> [W]hen the school introduces and trains each child of society into membership within such a little community, saturating him with the spirit of service, and providing him with the instruments of effective self-direction, we shall have the deepest and best guaranty of a larger society which is worthy, lovely, and harmonious. (Dewey, 1899b, pp. 19–20)

And education for Dewey becomes "the supreme human interest in which . . . problems cosmological, moral, logical, come to a head" (Dewey, 1930, p. 160). Education thus provides Dewey with the means for extending his ideals for individual development to the social fabric as a whole because in schools "we may produce . . . a projection in type of the society we should like to realize" (Dewey, in Hofstadter, 1963, p. 378). The real value of science and democracy lies in the kind of social conditions they create for further individual growth and fulfillment. In the process, psychology provides a tool for realizing values.

PSYCHOLOGY AND VALUES

In his 1899 presidential address before the American Psychological Association entitled *Psychology and Social Practice*, Dewey began to work through the social place and meaning of psychology in culture. Psychology was for Dewey a tool through which values can be both explored and realized—a tool for understanding the means through which desired ends in human affairs may be achieved. It cannot tell us what to do; it cannot define what is good; but it can tell us how to achieve that which we deem as good:

> Psychology, after all, simply states the mechanism through which conscious value and meaning are introduced into human experience. . . . Psychology will never provide ready-made materials and prescriptions for the ethical life. . . . But science . . . makes known the conditions upon which certain results depend, and therefore puts at the disposal of life a method for controlling them. Psychology will never tell us just what to do ethically, nor just how to do it. But it will afford insight into the conditions which control the formation and execution of aims, and thus enable human effort to expend itself sanely, rationally and with assurance. We are not called upon to be either boasters or sentimentalists regarding the possibilities of our science. . . . But we are entitled in our daily work to be sustained by the conviction that we are not working in indifference to or at cross-purposes with the practical strivings of a common humanity. The psychologist in his most remote and technical occupation with mechanism may be contributing his bit to that ordered knowledge which alone enables mankind to secure a larger and to direct a more equal flow of the values of life. (Dewey, 1899a, p. 150)

Psychology becomes a tool in the reconstruction of values. And to make declarations about good and bad development is to make political proclamations. Development thus becomes a political and moral idea. Dewey recognized this when he wrote:

> To say that the welfare of others, like our own, consists in a widening and deepening of the perceptions that give activity its meaning, in an educative growth, is to set forth a proposition of political import. (Dewey, 1922c, p. 202)

Of the many connections between Dewey's psychology and contemporary attempts to situate child development in culture and history, perhaps this is the most important. As Kaplan (1967, 1986) and Kessen (1990) have reminded us, once we renounce natural ends to development, we become politically, morally, and scientifically engaged in determining both that which will be considered good development and how we might best achieve it.

A FINAL WORD

Vygotsky and his commentators have taught us much about the social bases of development by calling our attention to the important ways in which culturally constituted tools mediate thought. Dewey focuses our attention on the socially constituted values and social practices that stand beside or perhaps even behind such tools. Dewey is not well known to contemporary psychologists, nor did he exert a strong influence on the emergence of a disciplinary psychology; there are many reasons for such a state of affairs. To appreciate fully the cogency of Dewey's writings, one must, to some extent, immerse oneself in Dewey's own words and exercise the kind of patience implied by such immersion. In his own day, Dewey's proposals for a psychology based on social values and practices reached beyond the limits of available methods and empirical tools of the time. Dewey's conviction that psychology was a tool for the realization of value had no place in a field that self-consciously eschewed questions of value in its search for facts. But in these days of centennial reflection, with the return to history, culture, and value that such moments entail, perhaps we can learn about the place of facts, values, and social practices in psychology from a renewed acquaintance with the wisdom of John Dewey.

REFERENCES

Baker, M. C. (1955). *Foundations of John Dewey's educational theory*. New York: Columbia University Press.

Baldwin, J. M. (1906–1915). *Thought and things: A study in the development and meaning of thought, or, genetic logic* (4 vols.). New York: Putnam. (reprinted 1974 by Arno Press)

Bernstein, R. J. (1966). *John Dewey*. New York: Washington Square Press.

Bronfenbrenner, U. (1979). *The ecology of human development: Experiments by nature and design*. Cambridge, MA: Harvard University Press.

Cahan, E. D., & White, S. H. (1992). Proposals for a second psychology. *American Psychologist, 47*, 224–235.

Campbell, D. T. (1969). Reforms as experiments. *American Psychologist, 24*, 409–429.

Cremin, L. (1964). *The transformation of the school*. New York: Random House. (Original work published 1961)

Dewey, J. (1884). The new psychology. *EW* (Vol. 1, pp. 48–60).[1]

---

[1]*Note.* The references for the cited works by Dewey are taken from the 37 volumes of *The Early Works of John Dewey, 1882–1897* (1967–1972; abbreviated *EW*); *The Middle Works of John Dewey, 1899–1924* (1976–1983; abbreviated *MW*); and *The Later Works of John Dewey, 1925–1953* (1981–1990; abbreviated *LW*). All volumes are published by the Southern Illinois University Press (Carbondale, IL) under the editorship of Jo Anne Boydston.

Dewey, J. (1887). *Psychology. EW* (Vol. 2).

Dewey, J. (1896a). A pedagogical experiment. *EW* (Vol. 5, pp. 244–246).

Dewey, J. (1896b). The reflex arc concept in psychology. *EW* (Vol. 5, pp. 96–109).

Dewey, J. (1896c). The university school. *EW* (Vol. 5, pp. 437–441).

Dewey, J. (1897a). Ethical principles underlying education. *EW* (Vol. 5, pp. 54–83).

Dewey, J. (1897b). My pedagogic creed. *EW* (Vol. 5, pp. 84–95).

Dewey, J. (1899a). Psychology and social practice. *MW* (Vol. 1, pp. 131–150).

Dewey, J. (1899b). *The school and society. MW* (Vol. 1, pp. 1–110).[1]

Dewey, J. (1900). Some stages of logical thought. *MW* (Vol. 1, pp. 151–174).

Dewey, J. (1901). The educational situation. *MW* (Vol. 1, pp. 257–314).

Dewey, J. (1902). The child and the curriculum. *MW* (Vol. 2, pp. 271–292).

Dewey, J. (1903). Studies in logical theory. *MW* (Vol. 2, pp. 293–378).

Dewey, J. (1909). How we think. *MW* (Vol. 6, pp. 177–356).

Dewey, J. (1911). Development. *MW* (Vol. 6, pp. 420–422).

Dewey, J. (1912–1913). Nature. *MW* (Vol. 7, pp. 287–291).

Dewey, J. (1913). Reasoning in early childhood. *MW* (Vol. 7, pp. 369–376).

Dewey, J. (1916). *Democracy and education: An introduction to the philosophy of education. MW* (Vol. 9).

Dewey, J. (1917). The need for social psychology. *MW* (Vol. 10, pp. 53–63).

Dewey, J. (1918). Education and social direction. *MW* (Vol. 11, pp. 54–57).

Dewey, J. (1922a). Education as politics. *MW* (Vol. 13, pp. 329–334).

Dewey, J. (1922b). Education as religion. *MW* (Vol. 13, pp. 317–322).

Dewey, J. (1922c). Human nature and social conduct. *MW* (Vol. 14, pp. 1–230).

Dewey, J. (1927). The public and its problems. *LW* (Vol. 2, pp. 235–372).[1]

Dewey, J. (1930). From absolutism to empiricism. *LW* (Vol. 5, pp. 147–160).

Dewey, J. (1931a). Science and society. *LW* (Vol. 6, pp. 49–63).

Dewey, J. (1931b). Social science and social control. *LW* (Vol. 6, pp. 64–68).

Dewey, J. (1933a). The process and product of reflective activity: Psychological process and logical forms. *LW* (Vol. 8, pp. 171–186).

Dewey, J. (1933b). Why reflective thinking must be an educational aim. *LW* (Vol. 8, pp. 125–139).

Dewey, J. (1934). The need for a philosophy of education. *LW* (Vol. 9, pp. 194–204).

Dewey, J. (1938a). *Logic: A theory of inquiry. LW* (Vol. 12).

Dewey, J. (1938b). Progressive organization of subject matter. *LW* (Vol. 13, pp. 48–60).

Gay, P. (1969). *The enlightenment: An interpretation: The science of freedom* (vol. 2). New York: Norton.

Hall, G. S. (1904). *Adolescence: Its psychology and its relations to physiology, anthropology, sociology, sex, crime, religion, and education* (Vols. 1 & 2). New York: Appleton-Century-Crofts.

Hofstadter, R. (1963). *Anti-intellectualism in American life.* New York: Vintage.

Hook, S. (1939). John Dewey: An intellectual portrait. New York: John Day.

Hook, S. (1959). John Dewey: Philosopher of growth. In S. Morgenbesser (Ed.), *Dewey and his critics: Essays from the Journal of Philosophy.* New York: Journal of Philosophy, Inc. 9–17.

Kaplan, B. (1967). Meditations on genesis. *Human Development, 10,* 65–87.

Kaplan, B. (1986). Value presuppositions in theories of human development. In R. Lerner (Ed.), *Developmental psychology: Historical and philosophical perspectives* (pp. 185–228). Hillsdale, NJ: Erlbaum.

Kessen, W. (1990). *The rise and fall of development.* Worcester, MA: Clark University Press.

Margolis, J. (1977). The relevance of Dewey's epistemology. In S. Cahn (Ed.), *New studies in the philosophy of John Dewey* (pp. 117–148). Hanover, NH: University of New England Press.

Mayhew, K., & Edwards, A. (1936). *The Dewey school: The laboratory school at the University of Chicago, 1896–1903.* New York: Appleton-Century-Crofts.

Rockefeller, S. (1991). *John Dewey: Religious faith and democratic humanism.* New York: Columbia University Press.

Rogoff, B. (1990). *Apprenticeship in thinking: Cognitive development in social context.* New York: Oxford University Press.

Rucker, D. (1969). *The Chicago pragmatists.* Minneapolis: University of Minnesota Press.

Scheffler, I. (1974). *Four pragmatists: A critical introduction to Peirce, James, Mead, and Dewey.* Atlantic Highlands, NJ: Humanities Press.

Smith, J. (1983). *The spirit of American philosophy.* New York: SUNY Press.

White, M. (1964). *The origins of Dewey's instrumentalism.* New York: Octagon Books, Inc. (Original work published 1943)

White, S. H., & Siegel, A. (1984). Cognitive development in time and space. In B. Rogoff & J. Lave (Eds.), *Everyday cognition: Its development in social context* (pp. 238–277). Cambridge, MA: Harvard University Press.

II

THE CONSOLIDATION OF A SEPARATE SCIENCE OF DEVELOPMENT

INTRODUCTION

THE CONSOLIDATION OF A SEPARATE SCIENCE OF DEVELOPMENT

With psychology no longer a stepchild of philosophy, a period of consolidation (1900–1925) began, characterized by the identification of issues and of methods unique to the newly emerged discipline of psychology in general and to developmental psychology in particular. In this section, we consider three of the major consolidators: Binet, Freud, and Watson. Each offered a unique vision of the possibilities for the new science of development.

In considering Binet, the most underappreciated of this developmental trio, Siegler (chapter 6), in his aptly titled essay, introduces an Alfred Binet seldom encountered in intellectual journeys. Binet has long been recognized for his monumental contributions to the standardized assessment of intelligence and to the implicit recognition of the value of developmental psychology for addressing applied social and educational problems. In fact, Binet is in a direct lineage with Hall and Dewey in his commitment to the use of science for the improvement of human functioning and for the solution of social problems. Although Siegler does not minimize this seminal contribution, he underscores the wide array of largely unheralded but substantive and methological contributions that Binet made to the new developmental science. Although Darwin and Watson are often credited with demonstrating both the feasibility and potential of an empirical, experimentally based study of human development, Binet clearly belongs in this same elite intellectual company. As Siegler documents, Binet's investigations ranged from studies of constructive memory and eyewitness testimony to work on group conformity and cognitive style—a thoroughly modern list of topics. Methodologically, he clearly preceded Piaget in his skilled use of interviews to probe childrens' underlying cognitive and problem-solving strategies. A major contribution of Siegler's chapter is his clear call for a fuller appreciation of Binet's role in our early intellectual heritage.

Few theorists can lay claim to so many themes and trajectories that are central to developmental inquiry as Freud. Freudian theory has clearly passed its zenith of influence on developmental psychology, especially in terms of the use of Freudian stage-based theory as an explicit framework for the guidance of developmental research. However, as Emde (chapter 7) argues, Freudian influence on modern developmental theory and research is revealed in more subtle and less obvious ways. Emde uses Freud's work on play, his views on developmental processes, and his innovative approach to nonconscious mental activity as vehicles for illustrating the highly contemporary relevance of Freudian theory. Linking Freud's work in new ways to contemporary issues in developmental theory and research, this chapter serves as a reminder of how much the form and substance of modern developmental inquiry has been shaped by Freudian thought. The current revitalized interest in the affective aspects of social and cognitive life, as well as the renewed focus on unconscious processes and repressed memories, makes the continuing importance of psychoanalytic theory evident. Less well known are the contributions of René Spitz, a psychoanalytic researcher who, unlike Freud, worked directly with infants and children in both his research and practice. Spitz is familiar to developmentalists for his pioneering studies of the effects of institutionalization on the development of infants. His less well-known work on observational assessments of infants, a clear precursor to both Bayley and Brazelton's later efforts, is highlighted, as is his work on affective dialogue in caregiving relationships. Again, the contemporary relevance of Spitz's theory and research is clearly evident, as exemplified in the writings of Bruner, D. Stern, Osofsky, and Emde himself. Part II of this book represents a clear lineage from Darwin through Freud and Spitz to the present.

The contrasts and controversies that characterize the early days of developmental psychology are evident in the juxtaposition of Freud and Watson. Whereas the European-born Freud focused on unconscious processes, clinical contexts, and subjective methods, while espousing a discontinuous stage and critical period view of development, the American pioneer John Watson took a decidely different approach. In a radical break with the European import, introspectionism, Watson initiated a new psychology based on objective and observable principles. Moreover, consistent with a Darwinian heritage, Watson argued that the new behaviorism could generate laws that apply equally to the behavior of all species and, by implication, to all points across development as well. Steeped in the American values of opportunity, optimism, equality, and modifiability, Watson's developmental vision clearly illustrated how social and cultural contexts shape our theoretical views. As Horowitz (chapter 8) observes, Watson's denial of biological influence has been roundly rejected, but his search for principles of learning remains a thoroughly modern endeavor. Similarly, his conviction that these laws can be harnessed to aid in interventive and applied efforts remains part of the Watsonian legacy, even though Watson does not often receive his due. His methological breakthroughs were highly influential in illustrating that objective scientific strategies could be used in studying infants and children. Some (Kessen, 1965) credit Watson with signaling the true beginning of a modern science of development, in spite of the earlier demonstrations of Darwin and Binet.

By the mid 1920s, developmental psychology was a well-established field, although as our review of Binet, Freud, and Watson reveals, there was little consensus about either an agenda for the new field or the methods that should guide it.

REFERENCE

Kessen, W. (1965). *The child*. New York: Wiley.

6

THE OTHER ALFRED BINET

ROBERT S. SIEGLER

Their act of memory is accompanied by an act of translation. They impose on the passage, which they force into their minds, the mark of their personality, they make it their own, they give it their perspective of thinking, they make it the passage of a child. This is a phenomenon one might give the name, comparable to that which occurs in nutrition, of *verbal assimilation*.

The above statement seems unremarkable until one considers its source: Binet and Henri (1894, p. 52). Binet's use of the concept, the nutritional analogy, and even the term *assimilation* all predated Piaget's by more than three decades. And the example is not an isolated one. Binet's findings on prose memory, eyewitness testimony, group pressure toward conformity, intrinsic motivation, and expertise in chess and mental calculation all long preceded better known recent studies that have rediscovered the same phenomena. As Cairns (1983) commented, "It has taken experimental child psychology 70 years to catch up with some of Binet's insights on cognition and the organization of memory" (p. 47).

This research was supported by a grant from the Mellon Foundation, by a grant from the Spencer Foundation, and by Grant HD19011 from the National Institutes of Health. I thank Ken Kotovsky, Rich Schulz, and Jim Staszewski for helpful comments on the article.

Reprinted from *Developmental Psychology, 28*, 179–190. Copyright 1992 by the American Psychological Association.

Almost every introductory psychology student learns that Alfred Binet was the father of the IQ test. Not ordinarily included in the lesson, then or later, is the remarkable depth and diversity of Binet's contributions to our understanding of cognition and cognitive development. The contributions have been recognized in a handful of relatively recent books and articles (Cairns, 1983; Pollack & Brenner, 1969; Sarason, 1976; Tuddenham, 1962; Wesley, 1989; Wolf, 1973) but do not seem to have become common knowledge. Few realize that the large majority of Binet's research had little to do with the intelligence test; instead, it involved detailed investigations of a broad variety of cognitive phenomena. The findings and many of the interpretations in these studies remain fresh and contemporary even after the passage of almost a century. Moreover, the vividness and clarity of the descriptions of children's thinking are unsurpassed, as might be expected from a man who—in addition to authoring almost 300 published books, articles, and reviews—wrote four plays that were produced on the Paris stage.

It is ironic that Binet's contribution should be so strongly associated with reducing intelligence to a single number, the IQ score, when the recurring theme of his research was the remarkable diversity of intelligence. This orientation led him to examine the most varied populations: typical children and adults; children and adults with varying degrees of mental retardation; residents of mental hospitals; experts at chess and mental calculation; and professional actors, directors, authors, and artists. It also led him to study any area that he thought might shed light on individual differences in mental functioning: consciousness, will, attention, sensation, perception, esthetics, creativity, suggestibility, hypnotism, cognitive styles, love fetishes, pain thresholds, mental fatigue, language development, memory development, conceptual development, and many other topics. Just as his intelligence test gained much of its power through sampling diverse aspects of mental functioning, so did his overall research program.

A further irony of the strong association between Binet and the concepts of mental age and IQ was that throughout his career he emphasized qualitative differences over quantitative ones. He actively resisted equating the mental activity of people of differing ages who performed comparably on test questions. Thus, he frequently noted that although a mentally retarded adult and a typical child might obtain the same score on the intelligence scale, their thinking still differed profoundly. Even in arguing for the importance of developing standardized tests of intellect, he contended that "there are, in any group of individuals, qualitative differences which are at least as important to know as are the quantitative differences" (Binet & Henri, 1895, cited in Wolf, 1973, p. 122). Consistent with this argument, much of Binet's research was devoted to identifying stylistic differences in thinking, such as those captured within the modern construct of impulsivity–reflectivity.

This chapter includes four main sections. The first surveys the major events of Binet's life and career. The second describes in greater depth his contributions to the understanding of intelligence, development, and memory. The third focuses on why his intelligence test garnered so much recognition and his other contributions so little. The fourth highlights issues that his observations raise for current efforts to understand individual differences and to formulate unified theories of cognition. A central goal throughout the article is to underscore the importance of Binet's fundamental objective: to understand both the variability and the commonalities in human cognition.

BIOGRAPHICAL SKETCH

Varon (1935) and Wolf (1973) have provided interesting and comprehensive accounts of Binet's intellectual achievements; Wolf's book also provides considerable biographical information. Alfred Binet was born in 1857 in Nice, France, the only child of a father who was a physician (as were both his grandfathers) and a mother who was an artist. His parents separated when he was quite young; thereafter, he lived with his mother. When he was 15, his mother and he moved to Paris, where he could attend a well-regarded lycée. After a successful though unexceptional period as a student there, he enrolled in law school in 1872. He received his licence in 1878 but apparently was not particularly taken with the profession. He did not attempt to establish a practice and later commented, "As for the law, that is the career of men who have not yet chosen a vocation" (Binet, 1904, cited in Wolf, 1973, p. 3).

Binet's pursuit of what was to become his vocation began not with attendance at a graduate school—he never did receive graduate training in psychology—but with his reading psychology at the Bibliothèque Nationale. Beginning in 1879 or 1880, he read on his own the books and articles of major thinkers of the time, especially English associationists such as John Stuart Mill, Herbert Spencer, and Alexander Bain. His first article (Binet, 1880), his first book (Binet, 1886), and most of his other early efforts were devoted to extending the associationist principles espoused in these books to account for aspects of perception, reasoning, and other psychological phenomena.

After several years as a "library psychologist," Binet began to work in Charcot's laboratory at the Salpetrière, a well-known hospital in Paris. During his time there (1883–1890), he was an aggressive proponent of Charcot's positions that there were three distinct types of hypnotic states and that people with deteriorated or unstable nervous systems were uniquely susceptible to hypnosis. He further argued, together with Fère, that hypnotic states could be influenced in a variety of ways by the use of magnets. These positions aroused considerable criticism, and the findings reported by Binet and Fère eventually were discredited as attributable to suggestion effects (Delboeuf, 1889).

After this embarrassing exchange, Binet severed his connections with Charcot and his group at the Salpetrière. After seeking an institutional affiliation for more than a year, he became a member of the staff of the Laboratory of Physiological Psychology at the Sorbonne. Three years later, he became director of the laboratory, a position he held until his death in 1911. Despite the prestigious-sounding title, the position, like the prior one at the Salpetrière, was unpaid; throughout his career, only Binet's independent income allowed him to conduct his research.

Neither Binet's early armchair efforts to use associationist principles to explain cognitive and perceptual phenomena nor his initial foray into hypnotism research foretold great later achievement. However, from 1890 to the year of his death, 1911, Binet produced a series of investigations remarkable for both quality and quantity. In those 21 years, he published more than 200 books, articles, and reviews in what now would be called experimental, developmental, educational, social, and differential psychology. The diversity of topics addressed by these studies can be seen by considering his publications from just one typically productive year, 1894. They included two books (one an introduction to experimental psychology methods and one on the psychology of expert calculators and chess masters); four articles on children (three involving their memory for words, prose, and visual information and one on their suggestibility); two studies of professional dramatists; one article on spatial orientation (published in volume 1 of the new American journal *Psychological Review*); and a description of a graphical method for recording piano-playing techniques. He also found time to be cofounder and editor of the first French psychological journal, *L'Année Psychologique*, which he continued to edit for the next 17 years and which is still in existence.

Even more striking than the quantity of research was its high quality. Again, consider just the research programs represented in Binet's books and articles of 1894. Thieman and Brewer (1978) translated and analyzed an 1894 Binet and Henri article on memory and commented, "This study was the first major experimental investigation of memory for prose material, and yet is remarkably similar to recent research on sentence memory, both in terms of empirical findings and theoretical interpretations" (p. 245). Regarding Binet's work on suggestibility, Cunningham (1988) commented, "These conclusions made 90 years ago are mirrored in modern conceptualizations of the nature of children's suggestibility" (p. 271). Similar sentiments have been expressed by Simmel and Barron (1966) about the work on chess expertise, by Pollack and Brenner (1969) about the work on visual memory, and by Cairns (1983) about the methodological principles. A number of the findings and interpretations that have elicited such high regard are discussed later in this article.

As the 1890s progressed, Binet focused increasingly on the goal of understanding and measuring individual differences in intelligence. His prior experience in studying intellectual functioning in a wide variety of domains led him to take quite a different approach to studying the subject than such prominent contemporaries as Galton, Spearman, and Cattell. Whereas their work focused on simple, easy-to-measure capacities such as sensory discrimination and simple reaction time, Binet emphasized complex mental processes as the main locus of individual differences in intellect. This key insight appeared in Binet's first major article on the subject (Binet & Henri, 1895) in the context of a critique of other investigators' approaches to assessing individual differences:

> If one looks at the series of experiments made—the *mental tests* as the English say—one is astonished by the considerable place reserved to the sensations and the simple processes, and by the little attention lent to the superior processes. . . . The objection will be made that the elementary processes can be determined with much more precision than the superior processes. This is certain, but people differ in these elementary ones much more feebly than in the complex ones; there is no need, therefore, for as precise a method for determining the latter as for the former. . . . Anyway, it is only by applying one's self to this point that one can approach the study of individual differences. (pp. 426, 429)

This initial article also described in surprising detail Binet and Henri's plan to develop an easy-to-use test of individual differences in mental functioning. The test would include measures of multiple competencies (memory, comprehension, etc.), with each subtest including multiple items to allow reliable assessment. All of the items were to be "appropriate to the milieu to which the individual belongs" (cited in Wolf, 1973, p. 243); their completion was to take no longer than 1½ hr, to avoid tiring the children.

The story of the immediate stimulus that led to the realization of this plan in 1905 is well known. Writing in 1907 (in an article published in 1909), Binet recalled:

> There is nothing like necessity to generate new ideas. We undoubtedly would have retained the status quo, using fragmentary tests, if a matter of true social interest three years ago, had not made it mandatory for us to measure intelligence by the psychological method. It had been decided to try to organize some special classes for abnormal children. Before these children could be educated, they had to be selected. How could this be done? . . . It was under these circumstances that our devoted collaborator, Dr. Simon, and I formulated a plan for measuring

intelligence which we called "a metric scale of intelligence." (Binet, 1909/1975, pp. 104–105)

The scale developed by Binet and Simon had much in common with current versions of the Stanford-Binet Scale. It included many of the same subtests: digit span, vocabulary, reproduction of block designs, paper folding, comprehension, and similarities. A number of specific items within the subtests have also endured through the many subsequent revisions of the test. Other familiar features present in the 1905 scale were the arrangement of test questions in order of ascending difficulty, instructions that warned against the experimenter inadvertently playing the role of teacher, and a recommendation to test children alone except for the reassuring presence of someone familiar to the child.

Another irony of Binet's life, given the subsequent emphasis in the field of psychometrics on huge and representative samples, was the small and unrepresentative sample on which he validated this most famous test. The sample reported by Binet and Simon (1905b) included only 50 children, 10 each of ages 3, 5, 7, 9, and 11 years, all chosen by their teachers for being of average ability. Rather than representing the culmination of a massive, systematic, statistical analysis, selection of items for the Binet-Simon test was largely impressionistic. The selection reflected Binet and coworkers' senses of which items best discriminated among children of varying degrees of intelligence. These were not uneducated guesses; they reflected the experience of at least 10 years of observation, with the goal of selecting such items in mind. Nonetheless, selection of items for the test was grounded primarily in implicit rather than explicit statistics.

Binet and Simon revised the test in 1908 and again in 1911. The samples for these subsequent versions were much larger and more intellectually and socioeconomically diverse. They also included a wider range of ages. Some items were dropped from the original test, others were modified, yet others were added. These revised versions, like the original, were quickly put to use in much of the Western world. In Binet's native France, however, the scale was ignored until the 1930s; even when it came into use, it was generally known as the Terman-Merrill rather than the Binet-Simon or Stanford-Binet.

Between 1905 and 1911, Binet spent substantial amounts of time on test revision. It was far from his only professional activity, however. In the same period, he wrote books on the relation of mind and brain, on children's ideas, on retarded children, and on the theater. He also published more than 100 articles. Only a few focused on the test; many others examined psychotic patients, courtroom testimony, the relation between language and thought, the psychology of famous artists, the effects of mental fatigue on intellectual performance, and a host of other loosely related topics. These diverse activities are consistent with Wolf's (1961) judgment that "the scale, which has made Binet famous, was only an important incident in a much wider goal. His quest . . . was to understand the nature of man" (p. 248).

During these years, Binet also spent considerable time pursuing educational reform and the creation of a scientifically based "mental orthopedics." Toward this end, he joined La société libre pour l'étude psychologique de l'enfant in its first year (1899) and thereafter played a leading role in the organization. He became its president in 1902. During his 9-year presidency, membership grew from 350 to 750. The organization acted in part as an advocate for the interests of children, and was an important stimulus for the 1904 creation of the Commission on the Education of Retarded Children, for which he developed the 1905 Binet-Simon Scale. The organization also served to involve educators in psychological research on children, and its members provided research assistants and access to subject populations for Binet's experiments.

Another way Binet pursued his educational goals was by founding an experimental laboratory school. It seems to have been the first such school in Europe (Wolf, 1973). A number of the experiments he conducted at the school produced interesting and useful findings. For example, Binet (1907) found that approximately 5% of the children had difficulty in school simply because they could not see the blackboard. He and Simon, who was a physician, produced a simple-to-administer vision test that teachers could use without waiting for the occasional visit of a physician to the school. At first, medical doctors criticized the scale; Binet responded by giving the scale to ophthalmologists, who tested and subsequently endorsed it. The scale came into wide use in the schools of Paris and Bordeaux.

What was the man like who made so many and varied contributions? Wolf (1973) characterized him as a very energetic man who spent most of his time working. He told a friend, "One of my greatest pleasures is to have a piece of white paper to fill up. I take to work as naturally as a hen lays eggs" (Wolf, 1973, p. 134). He was also a shy but critical person who had little patience for activities that he judged unworthy of his time. Such activities clearly included scientific conferences. Binet never left France to attend an international conference, and it is unclear whether he attended any of those held within France. Even the intelligence scale was first announced by Simon at the 1905 International Congress of Psychology in Rome; Binet did not attend.

Although descriptions of Binet's personality are varied, they have a core similarity. His collaborator Simon (1954b, p. 347) wrote that "to examine patients with him was always an extreme pleasure, for he brought to the situation so much imagination" and recalled "What afternoons we passed with these subjects. What delicious conversations we had with them. And what laughs too" (Simon, 1954a, p. 412). A less sympathetic coworker (Pieron, 1960) described him as being "difficult, dominant, perhaps even domineering" (cited in Wolf, 1973, p. 31) and claimed that he alienated many collaborators. The comments of Binet's daughter Madeleine, written two decades after her father's death, provide an interesting perspective on the qualities that elicited these different views:

> My father was above all a lively man, smiling, often very ironical, gentle in manner, wise in his judgments, a little skeptical of course. . . . Without affectation, straightforward, very good-natured, he was scornful of mediocrity in all its forms. Amiable and cordial to people of science, pitiless toward bothersome people who wasted his time and interrupted his work. . . . He always seemed to be deep in thought. (cited in Wolf, 1973, p. 36)

Outside of his family and his work, Binet's great interest was the theater. He frequently attended plays; staged little vaudeville shows with his family at home; studied the psychology of playwrights, directors, and actors; and wrote four plays that were performed in Paris theaters. The common theme of these plays was the horrifying consequences of the mistakes of stupid bureaucrats, pompous physicians, and greedy businessmen (Wolf, 1982). For example, in *L'Homme Mysterieux*, which was performed 25–30 times in 1910 at the Sarah Bernhardt Theatre, the financially motivated insistence of a businessman that his brother be released from an insane asylum is soon followed by the former patient turning on his brother and murdering him. Binet's fascination with the macabre, evident in these plays, is also apparent in some of the distinctive items he chose for the intelligence scale (e.g., What is wrong with these statements, (1) An unfortunate bicycle rider smashed his head and died instantly; he was taken to the hospital and it is feared he may not recover; (2) A railroad accident took place yesterday. It was not a serious one; only 48 people died; (3) Yesterday the body of an unfortunate young woman, cut into eight pieces, was found on the fortifications. It is believed she killed herself [Binet, 1909/1975, p. 100]). Such examples notwithstanding, it seems likely that writing plays provided Binet with greater opportunity to explore his Hitchcockian interests than did developing the intelligence scale.

THREE MAJOR CONTRIBUTIONS

Reviewing all of Binet's interesting findings and discoveries is well beyond the scope of a single article. Here, I discuss three sets of contributions that seem among the most important: contributions to understanding intelligence, development, and memory.

Contributions to Understanding Intelligence

Binet's insights in this area can be found in the intelligence scale itself, in his discussions of the scale's virtues and limitations, and in his ideas about the nature of intelligence. The scale itself embodied a number of ideas that still appear valid: that the best way to understand unusual performance is with regard to typical performance, that the largest individual differences in intellect reside in complex rather than simple processes, that intelligence has no single essence but rather incorporates a large number of specific processes, that it is therefore necessary for any reasonable assessment of intelligence to sample this variety of processes, and that a useful composite estimate of intellectual development can be created by summing across diverse specific processes. Some of these insights have been so well accepted that they appear matters of common sense today, but they differed greatly from the prevailing wisdom when they were formulated and for some years thereafter (Tuddenham, 1962; Wolf, 1973).

Binet developed the test in large part because of his profound skepticism regarding the alternative to objective tests—subjective assessments of ability by teachers, parents, principals, and physicians. He noted that teachers in standard schools might denigrate troublesome students' competence to have them removed from the classroom; conversely, teachers in special schools might exaggerate their students' achievements to boost their own success as instructors. Parents might overstate the accomplishments of their children to avoid the embarrassment of special school placements or understate them if they wished to escape responsibility for the child (Binet & Simon, 1905b). Evaluators using classification criteria inconsistently was also a problem. Binet found that evaluators used the same diagnostic terms in strikingly different ways. For example, he observed, "while one principal claimed he didn't have a single abnormal child in his school, the principal of another school nearby counted 50 of them in his" (Binet & Simon, 1909, p. 37). The Binet-Simon Scale was formulated to provide a more consistent, less biased means of evaluation.

Though viewing the test as preferable to subjective evaluations, Binet readily admitted its shortcomings. One limit noted by Binet and Simon (1905b) was that it did not yield an absolute measure of intelligence. To cite their analogy, the measure of intelligence that it yielded was not like the measure of length yielded by a ruler; instead, it yielded an ordinal classification in which the measure of intelligence was entirely relative to that of other individuals of the same age.

A second caveat Binet offered involved the multitude of factors other than intellectual ability that could influence performance on the test. Some involved the testing circumstances; for example, he noted that performance on the test frequently understated children's intelligence because of the unnaturalness of the testing situation and its potential for intimidating young children (Binet & Simon, 1905a). Longer term influences, such as family and school background, health, and past effort in school, were also seen as affecting test performance. For these reasons, the only reasonable comparisons of test results were among children from comparable backgrounds (Binet, 1909/1975).

Binet also called for frequent retesting of children's intelligence. This was necessary not only because the tests were fallible but also because intellectual development progressed within individuals at variable rates (Binet, 1909/1975). This uneven intellectual development reflected both different rates of maturation and different educational experiences. Consistent with this perspective, Binet often emphasized the potential of education for increasing intelligence. To quote one argument,

> A few modern philosophers seem to lend their moral support to these deplorable verdicts when they assert that an individual's intelligence is a fixed quantity which cannot be increased. We must protest and react against this brutal pessimism. . . . With practice, training, and above all method, we manage to increase our attention, our memory, our judgment, and literally to become more intelligent than we were before. (Binet, 1909/1975, pp. 106–107)

What conception of intelligence underlay these views? Some aspects of Binet's conception are evident in his comments on the scale: that intelligence is malleable (within limits) rather than fixed, that the social environment exercises a pervasive influence on it, and that the development of intelligence proceeds at variable rates within as well as between individuals.

Binet also attempted to characterize explicitly what intelligence was. At least from 1890 on, he consistently adopted a constructivist perspective. This perspective is evident in Binet's (1909/1975) statement that intelligence" is above all a faculty directed toward the external world and striving to reconstruct that world by means of the small fragments of it which we perceive" (p. 91). It is similarly evident in Binet's (1894) statement, "behind the sensation, there is always the intelligence, as behind the movement, there is always the will" (p. 25).

Binet's efforts to become more specific were hampered by his understanding of the complexity of intelligence. He specifically eschewed advancing a definition of intelligence, noting that "intelligence is not a single function, indivisible and of a particular essence" (Binet, 1909/1975, p. 107). The closest he came to a definition was probably the following characterization in which he argued for the central role of judgment:

> In intelligence there is a fundamental faculty, the alteration or the lack of which is of the utmost importance for practical life. This faculty is judgment, otherwise called good sense, practical sense, initiative, the faculty of adapting one's self to circumstances. To judge well, to comprehend well, to reason well, these are the essential activities of intelligence. A person may be a moron or an imbecile if he is lacking in judgment; but with good judgment he can never be either. (Binet & Simon, 1905b, pp. 42–43)

Binet distinguished among three aspects of judgment—direction, adaptation, and criticism. Direction involved strength of concentration on the task and on the requirements of the solution strategy. It was reflected both in the complexity of ideas generated as possible solutions and in their persistence in the face of distractions. Adaptation involved the appropriateness of choices among alternative ideas and their progressive refinement to fit task constraints. Criticism referred to internally generated feedback used for evaluating potential solutions to a problem and culling out inadequate ideas. The framework closely resembles current ideas about the role of metacognition in intelligence, a view reinforced by Binet's emphasis on learning to learn as a central determinant of adaptation (Campione, Brown, & Ferrara, 1982).

Recognition of qualitative differences in thinking, like those involved in current research on cognitive styles (Kogan, 1983), played a ubiquitous role in Binet's thinking about intelligence. He appears to have been especially impressed with these in his research on his daughters, Madeleine and Alice. Binet's descriptions of Madeleine resemble the modern category "reflective," whereas his descriptions of Alice fit the "impulsive" prototype (Wesley, 1989). He observed differences from early in their lives. When Madeleine learned to walk, she would only go to objects a short distance away; Binet noted that "these movements were executed with great seriousness in perfect silence." In contrast, with Alice, "it was evident that she never anticipated which object could furnish support, because she advanced without the least hesitation to the middle of an empty part of the room" (both quotations from Binet, 1890b). Even after developing the quantitatively based intelligence scale, Binet continued to emphasize the importance of qualitative differences in intelligence. He wrote often on the importance of analyzing and interpreting properly a child's specific errors on the intelligence scale and also often contrasted the different patterns of strengths and weaknesses yielded by alternative cognitive styles such as scientific versus literary, objective versus subjective, and conscious versus unconscious.

These and Binet's other descriptions of intelligence were more impressionistic than scientifically rigorous. Nonetheless, the impressions were often so compelling as to merit close consideration. Consider one such impression, that people of different mental levels differ in their rate of production of ideas as well as in the quality of the ideas they produce:

> A normal child shows an abundance of ideas. . . . His intelligence meeting an obstacle makes an effort against it. With an imbecile, the slow production of ideas is indeed striking, and the number of attempts to solve (the game) is extremely small. It is no longer living water that flows, but rather a rivulet of wax that congeals. . . . It is indeed this paucity of ideas that makes a conversation with an imbecile so insipid. Recall our friend Albert who, when we asked him . . . after a week's

absence: "Well friend Albert, it's been a long time since we met. What have you been doing all this time?" replied simply "I have been sweeping." . . . Briefly, the imbecile tries only one or two keys to open a lock, and even these fit badly. (Binet & Simon, 1909, pp. 137–139)

Such ideas and observations seem to be getting at something central to the nature of intelligence. Capturing them within a coherent scientific theory remains a challenge for current theories of intelligence, as it did for Binet himself.

Contributions to Understanding Development

A substantial percentage of Binet's experiments and theorizing was devoted to children. Much of this work is summarized in Binet's (1909/ 1975) excellent book *Modern Ideas About Children*, probably the most intriguing and directly relevant of all his writings for those interested in development. As is evident throughout this book, although Binet did not believe in discrete stages of development, his general perspective on cognitive development, his methodological approach, and a number of the particular tasks and findings that he described resemble surprisingly closely those of Piaget.

Several of Binet's general ideas about cognitive development that foreshadowed Piaget's have already been described—the views that cognitive development is a constructive process; that the purpose of cognitive development is adaptation to the physical and social worlds; that children assimilate new experience to existing ways of thinking; and that intelligence pervades all activities, simple as well as complex.

Another shared belief was that children's high levels of physical activity, particularly their play, is essential to the developmental process:

The third, final characteristic is the child's ceaseless experimenting with all sorts of things to become familiar with external objects or to exercise his faculties. As a baby, he takes objects, manipulates them, strikes them, sucks them, and later he spends hours involved in play. . . . All beings in the process of development are distinguished by and characterized by their involvement in play. (Binet, 1909/1975, p. 94)

Binet's characterization of differences between the thinking of young children and adults also resembled Piaget's. For example, Binet (1909/1975) noted that a young child "might be struck by a detail which we adults will not have noticed, but he will not see a whole, a panorama of things, and especially is he incapable of distinguishing between the essential and the accessory" (p. 94). He also noted distinctive characteristics in young children's language that he thought indicative of the nature of their thinking:

Rarely used are conjunctions (for, because, if, when), those small words which are perhaps the noblest part of language, the most logical, since they express the subtle relationships between ideas. He uses concrete words mainly, abstract words much less often. All this points to the same thing: a comprehension which is of a sensory nature and which remains superficial. (Binet, 1909/1975, p. 95)

The resemblances to the findings and interpretations in *The Language and Thought of the Child* (Piaget, 1926) and *Judgment and Reasoning in the Child* (Piaget, 1928) are striking.

Binet's methodological stances also resembled Piaget's. He was harshly critical of what he considered false objectivity, preferring revealing over precise measures when a choice was necessary. Consider his characterization of the experimental procedures of most of his contemporaries:

Subjects go into a little room, respond by electrical signals, and leave without so much as a word to the experimenters. The experimenters' aim is simplicity, but it is only a factitious one, artificial, produced by the suppression of all troublesome complications. . . . The responses of the experimental subject should not be limited and simplified; on the contrary, he should be left the full freedom of expressing what he feels. . . . In this way, one can many times find some new and unexpected facts that often permit an understanding of the mechanism that produced a certain state of consciousness. (Binet, 1894, pp. 28–30)

Binet, like Piaget, also emphasized the revealing nature of particular errors, especially those of children. One example came from Binet's (1890a) study of children's word definitions. Binet found that young children often defined words exclusively in terms of their functions, especially as these affected the child. For example, he cited a child answering the question "What is a knife?" by saying "It can cut little children." Similarly, Binet and Henri (1894) discussed in detail the intrusion errors that children made in recalling stories; they argued that the errors were indicative of the children's underlying way of thinking.

The similarity extended beyond general perspective and methodological attitudes to a number of shared tasks and empirical findings. Consider Binet's (1890c) report of a first cousin of Piaget's (1952b) number conservation task and findings. Binet first presented to his 4-year-old daughter two sets of counters, with the individual counters in each set being the same size. The girl accurately indicated which collection had more objects, even when the numbers of objects in the two collections were large and similar (e.g., 18 vs. 17). Binet then presented her sets with similar numbers of counters in which the counters in the more numerous set were smaller and occupied a smaller area. Now she consistently chose the set that was less numerous but that occupied a larger area. Anticipating the yet later results of Gelman (1972) and Siegler (1981), this finding was obtained only when large numbers of counters were used. When each set included five or fewer objects, the child judged correctly even when the objects' sizes differed. The task was not a true conservation problem because it did not involve transformations, but the phenomenon of a misleading visual difference overwhelming judgments based on relative number seems essential to both.

Was there a direct link between these ideas and observations and Piaget's subsequent investigations? Circumstantial evidence suggests so. In 1920, Piaget began working with Simon, Binet's former collaborator and one of his closest friends, at the Binet Laboratory in Paris (Flavell, 1963). According to Wolf (1961), who interviewed Simon weekly over a 3-month period, Simon's attitude toward Binet "was a mixture of admiration and hero worship" (p. 246). It is hard to imagine how Piaget could have worked in such an environment without becoming familiar with Binet's thinking and findings. Further, in 1921, Claparède, the head of the Jean-Jacques Rousseau Institute in Geneva, hired Piaget to be director of research. Claparède was also a good friend of Binet's. Again, it seems likely that Claparède would have brought Binet's work to Piaget's attention if he did not already know about it, especially given the similarity of their interests.

The main argument against this view is that Piaget did not acknowledge any influence of Binet, either in his autobiographical chapter (Piaget, 1952a) or in citations within his books. The autobiographical chapter does not mention Binet. Citations of Binet in his other writings are few and almost always brief. For example, the name index of Gruber and Voneche's (1977) compendium *The Essential Piaget* indicates that Binet's name appears on only 4 of the 866 pages. An additional sampling of name indexes revealed that Binet was mentioned on average less than once per book in the 12 books written by Piaget that I examined. Almost all of these citations were criticisms of the quantitative measure yielded by the Binet-Simon Scale or brief allusions to findings from the scale regarding children's performance on seriation and word definition items.

Still, the circumstantial evidence seems too strong to ignore. It seems reasonable at minimum to conclude with Wolf (1973, p. 331) that Binet's work probably "was an inspiration to Piaget's own ingenious investigations on constructive operations."

Contributions to Understanding Memory

Some of Binet's most insightful experiments involved investigations of memory. These include his examinations of children's memory for prose, their eyewitness testimony, and the role of memory in mental calculation expertise.

Thieman and Brewer (1978) published an annotated translation of Binet and Henri's (1894) article on prose memory. They pursued this task because of the many parallels between Binet's perspective on memory and the perspective that came to prevail in the 1970s. In the particular experiment, Binet and Henri presented 9- to 12-year-olds with paragraphs of between 11 and 86 words and then had them write what they recalled. They found that the children's recall focused not on isolated words but rather on what Binet and Henri termed "memory for ideas." As was rediscovered in many studies in the 1970s, this focus on ideas or gist became more pronounced with increases in the delay period prior to recall. Another critical finding was that the more important an idea within the overall paragraph, the more likely it was to be retained. Both the particular words and the syntactic forms that were used in recall included numerous intrusion errors in which the child's knowledge and typical mode of expression influenced the content and form of what was remembered. The amount of material recalled was far superior to the number of isolated words that children of these ages remembered in another Binet and Henri study published in the same year. The findings led the investigators to conclude that memory for isolated words and memory for connected discourse were qualitatively different. As they wrote, "The meaning of a sentence is quite distinct from the meaning of the words; it does not result from the simple addition of the meanings of the words" (Binet & Henri, 1894, cited in Wolf, 1973, p. 252). The concordance between these findings and interpretations and those acclaimed as revolutionary 75 years later led Thieman and Brewer (1978) to conclude, "Overall it is clear that the Binet and Henri paper translated here is one of the most impressive and original experiments in the development of experimental psychology" (p. 262).

A similar appraisal led Cunningham (1988) to devote an article to Binet's research on how suggestibility influences children's memory. Binet (1900) presented 7- to 14-year-olds a poster with a number of objects and a depiction of a scene on it. Exposure to the poster was quite brief (12 s). As in recent investigations of eyewitness testimony, children who were just asked to describe what they had seen made fewer but more accurate observations than students who were asked specific questions about the display. Binet's investigation also revealed strong effects of the particular wording of the question; it appears to have been the first study to indicate this influence (Cunningham, 1988). Similarly in accord with recent findings, the relation between age and suggestibility was quite weak.

Binet's (1900) suggestibility research also yielded a result that foreshadowed later findings within the Asch conformity paradigm. Four children were shown a first card with a group of lines and then a second card with a single line. The task was to indicate which of the lines on the original card matched the one on the new card. On the first few trials, there was always a match. During this time, the pattern within most groups of children was that a single child emerged as the "leader" and called out the answer on each trial. On the test trial, the same procedure was followed, but none of the lines on the first card matched the line on the second. Although the particular answer advanced by the leader varied among the groups, few children challenged whatever answer the leader advanced, even when it was plainly wrong. Binet's comment on the implications of this finding: "Woe betide him who is alone" (Cunningham, 1988).

Another contribution to the understanding of memory came from Binet and Henneguy's (1894) study of mental calculation expertise. This research involved intense examination of two expert calculators, Inaudi and Diamandi. Memory limits prevent most people from approaching the mental calculation feats of these experts (e.g., subtracting one 21-digit number from another without any external record of the initial numbers or of intermediate results). Much of Binet's study of these calculators focused on what allowed them to overcome such limits. He found, as have others subsequently (e.g., Chase & Simon, 1973), that the feats could not be attributed to generally superior background or intelligence. Inaudi, the more skillful of the two calculators, was a simple shepherd of otherwise modest intellect. Nor were the feats attributable to generally superior memory skills; Inaudi's span for arbitrarily chosen letters was a very average 5 or 6. Instead, the key factor that Binet identified was the way that the experts represented the numerical information, a finding that has since been replicated for other calculation experts (Staszewski, 1988) and extended to experts in other domains, such as chess (Chase & Simon, 1973). Binet also found that both experts used a left-to-right calculation strategy, a finding again consistent with contemporary analyses of expert calculation strategies. An additional, quite surprising discovery was the ability of at least one of the expert calculators to repeat back perfectly the approximately 200 numbers that had been presented in a 2-hour session; again, this finding has reemerged in recent findings on expert memory (Staszewski, 1988). In summary, Binet's findings and ideas about memory, like those regarding intelligence and development, continue to be timely and informative almost a century after they were put forth.

REASONS FOR BINET'S SUCCESSES AND FAILURES

The foregoing discussion raises two questions: Why was the impact of the Binet-Simon Scale so powerful and lasting? Why was the impact of Binet's other contributions so limited and short lived? Ideas, individuals, and historical circumstances all played important roles.

Why Was the Binet-Simon Scale So Successful?

The Binet-Simon Scale was a remarkable achievement. It met Binet and Henri's (1895) goal of a test that was inexpensive, easy to administer, objectively scorable, and predictive of classroom performance. It combined numerous insights to go far beyond what was available previously. It was also useful for the practical goal of allowing school systems to identify students who were likely to learn less rapidly than most of their peers and who, therefore, were candidates for special educations. Thus, part of the scale's success is attributable to its accomplishing the difficult and important tasks for which it was designed.

The acclaim that quickly followed the test's introduction also reflected the historical circumstances. Binet's shift in focus in the mid-1890s toward the goal of accurately measuring individual differences did not take place in a vacuum. In the late 19th century, in a number of Western European and North American countries, business and civic leaders joined in promoting universal public education. Once such systems were adopted, the challenge of educating the new, diverse population of children stimulated efforts to develop easy-to-use tests of ability to benefit from instruction. Advocacy groups for retarded children, teachers' organizations, and many educational researchers lobbied for special schools that would meet the needs of retarded children, as well as easing the teachers' task by creating classes of children with relatively homogeneous abilities. Binet and many of his contemporaries, including members of groups devoted to helping retarded people, saw a test that classified the learning abilities of different children as a necessary first step toward providing appropriate education for each child.

More generally, the late 19th- and early 20th-century enthusiasm for ability testing can be seen as a predictable by-product of the ongoing movement toward a meritocratic society. Progress toward a society in which people's occupations were determined by individual talents, rather than inherited position, demanded some means of determining who the talented individuals were. Galton's success in measuring and statistically characterizing individual status on a wide variety of other dimensions suggested that intelligence also could be measured accurately. The enthusiasm of the times is evident in the American Psychological Association in 1895, and the American Association for the Advancement of Science in 1896, chartering committees to coordinate different laboratories' collection of data on individual differences in mental and physical abilities. Thus, it was not entirely coincidental that 1895 was also the year in which Binet and Henri announced their plan for developing an intelligence test.

The test's success reflected not only the general interests and attitudes of the time but also the efforts of several vigorous advocates. H. H. Goddard, director of the Vineland School for the Retarded, was among the first to translate Binet's scale into English, try it, and find it useful. Thereafter, he worked tirelessly toward the scale's widespread adoption; Tuddenham (1962) wrote, "Probably no one had so much to do with launching the Binet method in the United States" (p. 490). Lewis Terman found the test helpful for studying gifted students, and in 1916 he published a revised and improved version, the Stanford-Binet, based on a standardization sample of 2,300 children in the United States. This revision was the first to use the IQ construct, suggested by Stern in 1912, that allowed examination of stability in individual test performance across age. Subsequent findings of relatively high stability of IQ scores over age lent further momentum to the scale's dissemination and widespread adoption.

Many of the early advocates of the test, Goddard among them, championed it in part for reasons quite antithetical to Binet's own thinking. They promoted it as a pure measure of a genetically determined general intelligence, corresponding to Spearman's g. Binet's own lack of a rigorous theory of intelligence, the ease of mapping the IQ score that emerged from the test onto the construct of "general intelligence," and the early 20th-century faith in genetic explanations of individual differences all contributed to their success in promulgating this view. A number of previous reviewers of Binet's contribution (Cairns, 1983; Sarason, 1976; Tuddenham, 1962; Wolf, 1973) have noted the irony. Binet, who explicitly indicated that intelligence was greatly influenced by the environment, subject to improvement through mental orthopedics, variable over time, and unlike Spearman's g, came to be associated with the opposite of each of these views.

Why Did Binet's Other Contributions Have So Little Impact?

Binet published well over 200 books, articles, and reviews that had nothing to do with the intelligence test. Many of them remain interesting and informative almost a century later. Yet these contributions to developmental, experimental, educational, and social psychology received only limited and fleeting recognition. In one more irony, the same types of personal, historical, and intellectual influences that led to the great success of the intelligence scale also contributed to the limited impact of Binet's other contributions.

As noted earlier, Binet never received formal training in psychology. Being self-taught may have contributed to the originality of his views, but it reduced his opportunities for establishing alliances with more senior investigators who might have promoted his contributions and helped him win a professorial position. Binet's perception of his own situation is evident in a letter he wrote to a friend in 1901: "I educated myself all alone, without any teachers; I have arrived at my present scientific situation by the sole force of my fists; *no one*, you understand, no one, has ever helped me" (cited in Wolf, 1973, p. 23). Wolf indicated that this outburst overstated the case, that some older scholars such as Ribot did lend some help. However, Wolf also indicated that lack of a powerful mentor (and competition from others who were sponsored by such mentors) was important in Binet's failure to obtain any of the three professorships for which he applied (two at the Sorbonne, the third at the College de France). In this context,

Binet's previously quoted comment, "Woe betide him who is alone," takes on special poignance.

Binet's personality exacerbated the problem. Claparède (1939) described him as a reserved man who "approached every unknown person with a sort of timidity that was basically an instinctive distrust of charlatans and bluffers, but who was most amiable upon further acquaintance" (cited in Wolf, 1973, pp. 34–35). Simon (1954b) implied a similar view when he described Binet as "lively when he was in a sympathetic environment" (cited in Wolf, 1973, p. 28). Both indicated that many of Binet's contemporaries, working on related problems, knew him only slightly or not at all. Wolf (1973) speculated that such shyness, together with the lack of a professorship or other prestigious position, contributed to Binet's avoidance of scientific meetings at which he and his experimental research might have become better known and accepted. In economics terms, Binet's product was strong, but his marketing was weak.

The lack of a professorship did not prevent Binet from pursuing his investigations. It did, however, prevent him from attracting many students. He was not part of any program that could grant advanced degrees. This would have discouraged all but the most determined (or heedless) students from doing graduate work with him. More generally, Binet suffered the dual handicap of not being accorded a highly valued position within French experimental psychology and of French experimental psychology not being accorded a highly valued position within the international psychological community. These factors conspired against his training potentially eminent young scholars who might have carried on and popularized his experimental and developmental research in the same way as Goddard, Terman, and others did his intelligence scale.

Reinforcing these obstacles were general intellectual trends within the field of psychology. Neither of the two great movements of the time, structuralism and behaviorism, was compatible with the functionalist perspective that Binet's work embodied. Functionalism was fairly influential in North American psychology but never attained similar stature in France or elsewhere on the European continent; thus, Binet was isolated from investigators who shared his basic approach. From a contemporary cognitive perspective, Binet's ideas seem much more congenial than those of either Wundt or Watson. They must have seemed different to their contemporaries, though.

An additional factor that limited the impact of Binet's experimental and developmental research is that it never fit neatly into the mainstream of any one subarea of psychology. Instead, it sat astride two great intellectual fault lines, one separating experimental and differential psychology, the other separating developmental and educational psychology. Cronbach (1957) described the first of these divisions in his famous article, "The Two Disciplines of Scientific Psychology." His characterization of attitudes within the two disciplines highlights factors that have worked against acceptance of Binet's goal of simultaneously studying typical human characteristics and individual differences:

> Individual differences have been an annoyance rather than a challenge to the experimenter. His goal is to control behavior, and variation within treatments is proof that he has not succeeded. Individual variation is cast into that outer darkness known as "error variance." For reasons both statistical and philosophical, error variance is to be reduced by any possible device. (p. 674)

Ironically, the widespread acceptance of one of Binet's guiding ideas, which he wrote about repeatedly, may also have guaranteed the long eclipse of his overall research agenda. This idea was that unusual behaviors can be understood only in terms of their relation to typical ones. The inference that most researchers drew from this belief was that understanding of typical behavior must come first; only then would a deep understanding of atypical behavior be possible. Binet tried to unite the two by studying in close temporal proximity general trends and individual differences. However, most experimental and developmental researchers have implicitly or explicitly adopted the position that much better understanding of typical activity was needed before penetrating analyses of individual differences (especially within "normal" populations) were possible. The spate of recent books analyzing the sources of individual differences in both adult cognition (Ackerman, Sternberg, & Glaser, 1989; Just & Carpenter, 1987; Sternberg, 1985) and cognitive development (Bjorklund, 1989; Ceci, 1990; Plomin, 1986) suggests that understanding of typical behavior may have progressed sufficiently now to encourage large numbers of investigators to try to bridge the gap. It just has taken awhile.

The fault line between psychology and education, at least within North American psychology, also seems to have contributed to the eclipse of Binet's research agenda. Binet was interested in developmental psychology in part because he believed that only an understanding of children's natures at different ages would make effective instruction possible. He concluded that, in general, the most effective instruction was that which (a) began with the concrete and moved to the abstract, (b) was somewhat, but not greatly, beyond the child's existing ability to understand and reason, (c) matched children's high activity levels with numerous opportunities for active participation, and (d) emphasized discovery (Binet, 1909/1975). He singled out Dewey, Rousseau, and Froebel as philosophers of education whose views agreed with his own. As noted earlier, Binet's involvement in education extended beyond his theoretical research and the intelligence scale. He was president for 9 years of a society whose main goal was to involve educators in research, spent considerable time establishing an experimental school, and wrote a particularly compelling book (Binet, 1909/

1975) that discussed at length how psychological findings could be used to inform education. Many subsequent developmental psychologists have agreed in the abstract with Binet's goal of bringing together psychology and education. However, few have followed him in making it a central focus of their work. As was the case with individual differences research, this gap seems to be shrinking, as evident in the instructionally oriented work of such current developmental psychologists as Ann Brown (e.g., Palincsar & Brown, 1984), Robbie Case (e.g., Case & Griffin, 1990), and Carl Bereiter and Marlene Scardamalia (e.g., Bereiter & Scardamalia, 1987). Again, however, it has taken awhile.

BINET AND THE FUTURE

The issues raised by Binet not only are timely; they set an agenda for the future. Two goals suggested by his research were alluded to in the previous section: to integrate the study of individual differences with the study of typical cognition and cognitive development and to integrate developmental psychology and education. In this concluding section, I discuss two additional goals that his research suggests: to identify characteristic tendencies in children's thinking and to create unified theories of cognition and cognitive development.

Characteristic Tendencies in Children's Thinking

An enduring goal of developmental psychology has been to provide accurate depictions of what children of particular ages are like. Part of the appeal of Piaget's stage descriptions has been that they provide a depiction of this type that is clear, concise, and memorable. By taking the position that stage limits are absolute and unyielding, Piaget increased the elegance and testability of the theory. Adopting such a position had a high cost in terms of accuracy, however. One after another, the many claims that "children of age N cannot understand X" have been disconfirmed.

The disconfirmations have left the field of cognitive development in a strange state. On the one hand, results of many experiments have demonstrated that infants and young children have a much wider range of competencies than envisioned in Piaget's theory. On the other, the fact remains that in a great many situations, these competencies fail to manifest themselves. Infants possess some form of object permanence (Baillargeon, 1987) but often do not act as if they do, young children can acquire the transformational reasoning underlying the conservation concept (Field, 1987) but rarely do so unless they participate in a training experiment, and so on. The tasks that cause infants and young children such difficulty are not inherently problematic; somewhat older infants and children generally solve the same problems with ease. Yet developmentalists may too often have been satisfied with the demonstrations that infants and young children really do have the competence in question, without explaining precisely why they failed in the other situations.

The problem can be made concrete in the context of the standard Piagetian liquid quantity conservation problem. Many studies have shown that 5-year-olds can learn to solve such problems through referring to the type of transformation. Yet 5-year-olds rarely adopt this approach without receiving training specifically aimed at getting them to do so. Few 8-year-olds are limited in this way; they succeed without any special training. But what experience or change allows 8-year-olds outside the laboratory to succeed at this task on which 5-year-olds so regularly fail? Children of both ages have seen and conducted many pouring operations involving water, milk, sand, and other materials; children of neither age receive direct instruction in the concept outside the laboratory. Thus, the demonstrations that 5-year-olds can be trained to reason in terms of transformations only rule out the extreme view that such reasoning is impossible for them; such demonstrations do not explain the differences in typical reasoning.

Although the inadequacies of Piaget's theory are well known, it would be hard to find an introductory textbook in developmental psychology that did not present the stage descriptions at length. Much of the reason is that the descriptions communicate characteristic tendencies in children's thinking, even if they do not provide invariant laws. They point to distinctive qualities of children's thinking, even if they do not explain them.

This value is also present in the writings of Binet and other gifted observers of children from previous eras. Their work seems to provide numerous accurate depictions of characteristic tendencies in children's thinking. In many cases, the phenomena they describe still have not been integrated into modern developmental theories or even been the subject of subsequent empirical research. Consider Binet's (1909/1975) description of the young child:

> He is apt to forget what he was engaged in doing, to become disgusted with his occupations, or to become distracted by a fantasy, a caprice, an idea which crosses his mind. In a conversation or in telling a story, he skips and hops from one subject to another in response to idea association. Observe his lack of direction as he goes to school. He does not go straight to the goal as an adult would, but zigzags along, forever stopping or making unnecessary detours to view some spectacle which interests him, distracting him from his goal and attracting him to the opposite sidewalk. When absorbed by some occupation, he loses sight of others, and often needs to be told "Pay attention." (p. 92)

To me at least, this description feels right, in the same way that many of Piaget's descriptions do. Unburdened by a stage theory, Binet did not need to claim that it was impossible for young children to focus on what they are doing. Instead, he could simply observe that they tended not to do so. Binet's observation raises two questions that are as relevant today as when he made them: Is it true that young children more often wander from goals they are pursuing than do adults, and if so, what processes generate the difference? Similar questions could be asked about many of Piaget's constructs (e.g., egocentrism). Young children clearly are not invariably egocentric, but the question remains: Do they behave egocentrically more often than adults, and if so, what processes lead them to do so? As these examples suggest, it may be possible to recycle the observations of Binet, Piaget, and other insightful observers of children as a source of ideas about characteristic tendencies, rather than of absolute constraints on cognitive development.

Unified Theories of Intelligence

Today, as 100 years ago, a primary goal of our discipline is to generate unified theories of cognition. The goal is being approached in far different ways now than then, however. Contrasting Binet's research with the most advanced current efforts to realize similar goals sheds light both on what has been gained and on what still needs to be done.

Binet's research can be viewed as an early effort to generate a unified theory of cognition. His central theoretical goal was to account for individual differences in thought processes. Before the goal could be attacked directly, however, it was essential to obtain a substantial data base on the thinking of diverse individuals on diverse tasks and to relate the thinking of members of atypical groups to that of those in more typical ones. Establishing methods for documenting the differences was also assigned a high priority. As the relevant data and measures became available, increasingly precise hypotheses about the mechanisms that generated the individual differences could be advanced and tested.

The results of Binet's efforts reflected these priorities as well as the relative difficulty of achieving the goals. He unambiguously succeeded in generating an immensely varied and informative data base. He also established useful methods for measuring individual differences, not just the standardized test that bears his name but also the more general emphasis on error patterns as a means for revealing qualitative aspects of thinking. His efforts to describe the mechanisms that produced the differences in thinking, however, were less successful. Naming processes believed to play important roles in intelligence—such as judgment, direction, adaptation, and criticism—was simply no substitute for describing exactly how each process operated and how they worked together to produce cognitive functioning. The amorphous descriptions of mechanisms that resulted limited the degree of unification that Binet's theory could attain.

The subsequent histories of cognitive psychology in general and cognitive development in particular could be described similarly. Efforts to obtain a substantial data base and to develop effective methods for studying cognition have been both more numerous and more successful than efforts to characterize the underlying mechanisms. As a result, the field has become data rich but theory poor.

This problem, elegantly posed in Newell's (1973) article "You Can't Play 20 Questions with Nature and Win," has been brought into special currency with the publication of Newell's (1990) book, *Unified Theories of Cognition*. Newell's proposed solution to the problem is to begin by positing a small set of fundamental mechanisms and to build the theory around them. The mechanisms must be sufficiently specified so that their operation can be described in terms of mathematical equations or computer simulations. Thus, "a unified theory of cognition does not mean a high-level theory that gains its unifications because it backs off to vagueness and platitudes. Calculations and simulations count" (Newell, 1990, p. 16).

Newell argued that two current systems, his own SOAR model and Anderson's (1983) ACT* model, have reached a sufficient point in specification of mechanisms and breadth of coverage to merit the appellation "unified theories." Connectionist models now also appear to qualify for the designation, since they are similarly well specified and have been applied to a similarly broad range of areas. All three of these systems have the clear virtues of pointing to mechanisms that could plausibly explain a wide range of cognitive activity, of specifying these mechanisms mathematically so that some of their properties can be proven, of demonstrating the sufficiency of these mechanisms to provide good quantitative fits to many experimental findings, and of inspiring a great deal of interesting experimentation aimed at testing predictions from the models. Thus, they seem to define the state of the art in general theories of cognition.

Newell's approach suggests a challenge for current developmentalists: how to generate unified theories of development. Developmental psychology seems to have a sufficient body of well-established phenomena to support such theories; what seems lacking is precisely specified mechanisms that explain how the phenomena arise. A number of investigators have decried this deficiency (e.g., Klahr, in press; Siegler, 1989; Sternberg, 1984), and they, as well as others (e.g., Gentner, 1989; Halford, 1990; Kail, 1991), have made specific efforts to remedy it. Nonetheless, unified theories of development require much more progress in explicating developmental mechanisms.

Thinking about the role of mechanisms provides an additional perspective on why Binet's intelligence test lasted and on why so much of his "other" research fell by the wayside. The intelligence test did not demand well-worked-out mechanisms; it was useful in practical settings and therefore could stand alone. In contrast, Binet's scientific research on development, cognition, personality, and education demanded a supportive theory, complete with mechanisms, to explain what the findings meant and why they were important. Without such theory and mechanisms, the findings lacked the internal coherence that would have worked against their vanishing into the ocean of empirical findings about psychology.

The example sounds a cautionary note for all of us. Well-specified mechanisms are the glue that holds together scientific findings. If not tied together by such mechanisms, findings become increasingly difficult to integrate. Ultimately, the vast majority are forgotten. Many factors contribute to which findings endure and which are lost, but one way we can help our findings endure is to identify the mechanisms that generate them.

REFERENCES

Ackerman, P. L., Sternberg, R. J., & Glaser, R. (1989). *Learning and individual differences*. San Francisco: Freeman.

Anderson, J. R. (1983). *The architecture of cognition*. Cambridge, MA: Harvard University Press.

Baillargeon, R. (1987). Object permanence in $3\frac{1}{2}$- and $4\frac{1}{2}$-month-old infants. *Developmental Psychology, 23*, 655–664.

Bereiter, C., & Scardamalia, M. (1987). *The psychology of written composition*. Hillsdale, NJ: Erlbaum.

Binet, A. (1880). De la fusion des sensations semblables. *Revue philosophique, 10*, 284–294.

Binet, A. (1886). *La psychologie du raisonnement*. Paris: Alcan.

Binet, A. (1890a). Children's perception. *Revue philosophique, 30*, 582–611.

Binet, A. (1890b). Studies on movements in some young children. *Revue philosophique, 29*, 297–309.

Binet, A. (1890c). The perception of lengths and numbers in some small children. *Revue philosophique, 30*, 68–81.

Binet, A. (1894). *Introduction à la psychologie expérimentale*. Paris: Alcan.

Binet, A. (1900). *La suggestibilité*. Paris: Schleicher Frères.

Binet, A. (1907). La valeur médicale de l'examen de la vision par les instituteurs. *Bulletin de la Société libre pour l'étude psychologique de l'enfant, 40*, 146–163.

Binet, A. (1975). *Modern ideas about children*. (S. Heisler, Trans.). (Original work published 1909).

Binet, A., & Henneguy, L. (1894). *La psychologie des grands calculateurs et joueurs d'échecs*. Paris: Hachette.

Binet, A., & Henri, V. (1894). La mémoire des phrases (mémoire des idées). *L'année psychologique, 1*, 24–59.

Binet, A., & Henri, V. (1895). Psychologie individuelle. *L'année psychologique, 2*, 411–465.

Binet, A., & Simon, T. (1905a). Application of the new methods to the diagnosis of the intellectual level among normal and subnormal children in institutions and in the primary schools. *L'année psychologique, 12,* 245–336.

Binet, A., & Simon, T. (1905b). New methods for the diagnosis of the intellectual level of subnormals. *L'année psychologique, 12,* 191–244.

Binet, A., & Simon, T. (1909). L'intelligence des imbeciles. *L'année psychologique, 15,* 1–147.

Bjorklund, D. F. (1989). *Children's thinking: Developmental function and individual differences.* Pacific Grove, CA: Brooks/Cole.

Cairns, R. B. (1983). The emergence of developmental psychology. In W. Kessen (Ed.), *Handbook of child psychology: History, theory, and methods* (pp. 41–102). New York: Wiley.

Campione, J. C., Brown, A. L., & Ferrara, R. A. (1982). Mental retardation and intelligence. In R. J. Sternberg (Ed.), *Handbook of human intelligence* (pp. 392–490). Cambridge, MA: Cambridge University Press.

Case, R., & Griffin, S. (1990). Child cognitive development: The role of central conceptual structures in the development of scientific and social thought. In C.-A. Hauert (Ed.), *Developmental psychology: Cognitive, perceptuo-motor, and neuropsychological perspectives.* The Netherlands: Elsevier Science Publishers.

Ceci, S. J. (1990). *On intelligence . . . more or less: A bio-ecological treatise on intellectual development.* Englewood Cliffs, NJ: Prentice-Hall.

Chase, W. G., & Simon, H. A. (1973). The mind's eye in chess. In W. G. Chase (Ed.), *Visual information processing* (pp. 215–281). San Diego: Academic Press.

Claparède, E. (1939). *Centenaire de Th. Ribot, 1839–1939: Jubilé de la psychologie scientifique française.* Paris: Agen.

Cronbach, L. J. (1957). The two disciplines of scientific psychology. *American Psychologist, 12,* 671–684.

Cunningham, J. L. (1988). Contributions to the history of psychology: XLVI. The pioneer work of Alfred Binet on children as eyewitnesses. *Psychological Reports, 62,* 271–277.

Delboeuf, J. L. R. (1889). *Le magnétisme animal à propos d'une visite a l'école de Nancy.* Paris: Alcan.

Field, D. (1987). A review of preschool conservation training: An analysis of analyses. *Developmental Review, 7,* 210–251.

Flavell, J. H. (1963). *The developmental psychology of Jean Piaget.* Princeton, NJ: Van Nostrand.

Gelman, R. (1972). The nature and development of early number concepts. In H. Reese & L. P. Lipsitt (Eds.), *Advances in child development and behavior.* San Diego: Academic Press.

Gentner, D. (1989). The mechanisms of analogical transfer. In S. Vosniadou & A. Ortony (Eds.), *Similarity and analogical reasoning.* London: Cambridge University Press.

Gruber, H. E., & Voneche, J. J. (1977). *The essential Piaget.* New York: Basic Books.

Halford, G. S. (1990). *Children's understanding: The development of mental models.* Hillsdale, NJ: Erlbaum.

Just, M. A., & Carpenter, P. A. (1987). *The psychology of reading and language comprehension.* Boston: Allyn and Bacon.

Kail, R. (1991). Developmental change in speed of processing during childhood and adolescence. *Psychological Bulletin, 109,* 490–501.

Klahr, D. (in press). Information-processing approaches to cognitive development. In M. H. Bornstein & M. E. Lamb (Eds.), *Developmental psychology: An advanced textbook* (3rd ed.). Hillsdale, NJ: Erlbaum.

Kogan, N. (1983). Stylistic variation in childhood and adolescence: Creativity, metaphor, and cognitive styles. In J. H. Flavell & E. M. Markham (Eds.), *Handbook of child psychology: Vol. III. Cognitive development* (pp. 630–706). New York: Wiley.

Newell, A. (1973). You can't play 20 questions with nature and win: Projective comments on the papers of this symposium. In W. G. Chase (Ed.), *Visual information processing* (pp. 283–308). San Diego: Academic Press.

Newell, A. (1990). *Unified theories of cognition.* Cambridge, MA: Harvard University Press.

Palincsar, A. S., & Brown, A. L. (1984). Reciprocal teaching of comprehension-monitoring activities. *Cognition and Instruction, 1,* 117–175.

Piaget, J. (1926). *The language and thought of the child.* New York: World Book.

Piaget, J. (1928). *Judgment and reasoning in the child.* New York: World Book.

Piaget, J. (1952a). Jean Piaget. In E. G. Borg, H. Werner, R. M. Yerkes, & H. S. Langfeld (Eds.), *History of psychology in autobiography* (Vol. 4, pp. 237–256). Worcester, MA: Clark University Press.

Piaget, J. (1952b). *The child's concept of number.* New York: W. W. Norton.

Plomin, R. (1986). *Development, genetics, and psychology.* Hillsdale, NJ: Erlbaum.

Pollack, R. H., & Brenner, M. W. (1969). *The experimental psychology of Alfred Binet.* New York: Springer.

Sarason, S. B. (1976). The unfortunate fate of Alfred Binet and school psychology. *Teachers' College Record, 77,* 579–592.

Siegler, R. S. (1981). Developmental sequences within and between concepts. *Monographs of the Society for Research in Child Development, 46* (Whole No. 189).

Siegler, R. S. (1989). Mechanisms of cognitive development. *Annual Review of Psychology, 40,* 353–379.

Simmel, M. L., & Barron, S. B. (1966). Mnemonic virtuosity: A study of chess players. *Genetic Psychology Monographs, 74,* 127–162.

Simon, T. (1954a). L'échelle Binet-Simon et l'intelligence. *Bulletin de la Société libre pour l'étude psychologique de l'enfant, 418,* 409–420.

Simon, T. (1954b). Souvenirs sur Alfred Binet. *Bulletin de la Société libre pour l'étude psychologique de l'enfant, 415,* 342–360.

Staszewski, J. J. (1988). Skilled memory and expert mental calculation. In M. T. H. Chi, R. Glaser, & M. J. Farr (Eds.), *The nature of expertise* (pp. 71–128). Hillsdale, NJ: Erlbaum.

Sternberg, R. S. (1984). Mechanisms of cognitive development: A componential approach. In R. J. Sternberg (Ed.), *Mechanisms of cognitive development.* San Francisco: Freeman.

Sternberg, R. J. (1985). *Beyond IQ: A triarchic theory of human intelligence.* New York: Cambridge University Press.

Thieman, T. J., & Brewer, W. F. (1978). Alfred Binet on memory for ideas. *Genetic Psychology Monographs, 97,* 243–264.

Tuddenham, R. D. (1962). The nature and measurement of intelligence. In L. Postman (Ed.), *Psychology in the making: Histories of selected research problems* (pp. 469–525). New York: Knopf.

Varon, E. J. (1935). The development of Alfred Binet's psychology. *Psychological Monographs, 46* (Whole No. 207).

Wesley, F. (1989). Review: Developmental cognition before Piaget: Alfred Binet's pioneering experiments. *Developmental Review, 9,* 58–63.

Wolf, T. H. (1961). An individual who made a difference. *American Psychologist, 16,* 245–248.

Wolf, T. H. (1973). *Alfred Binet.* Chicago: University of Chicago Press.

Wolf, T. H. (1982). A new perspective on Alfred Binet: Dramatist of *Le théâtre de l'horreur. The Psychological Record, 32,* 397–407.

7

INDIVIDUAL MEANING AND INCREASING COMPLEXITY: CONTRIBUTIONS OF SIGMUND FREUD AND RENÉ SPITZ TO DEVELOPMENTAL PSYCHOLOGY

ROBERT N. EMDE

This chapter highlights contributions of two psychoanalytic pioneers—Sigmund Freud (1856–1939) and René Spitz (1887–1974)—to developmental psychology. Although more than a generation apart, their lives crossed in a way that left the younger man feeling a deep sense of intellectual continuity with the investigative spirit of his predecessor. Freud is known as the founder of psychoanalysis, but today's reader may find surprise in the extent to which his contributions frame a good deal of our contemporary developmental thinking. Spitz, closer to our time, applied Freud's approaches to observations and on-the-spot experiments with infants. His contributions are more accessible to us, and, because they are more recent, they may be more difficult to evaluate in historical perspective.

Reprinted from *Developmental Psychology*, 28, 347–359. Copyright 1992 by the American Psychological Association.

We concentrate mostly on Freud, therefore, and the contributions of Spitz are discussed in the concluding part of the article.

Freudian insights having to do with play, a Darwinian approach to individual ontogeny, nonconscious mental activity, and constructivism are highlighted. Spitzian insights having to do with the importance of infant observation and assessment, developmental transitions, and processes of affective communication will be highlighted. A theme of the article is that both contributors gave central importance to understanding individual meaning. Both also addressed the challenges of understanding increasing developmental complexity, although neither acknowledged the challenge in these terms. The latter consideration frames a portrayal of the limitations of the ideas of each from our contemporary perspective. A final section of the chapter looks to the future, invoking the creative spirit of these scientific ancestors as part of today's living history. We ask what the approaches of Freud and Spitz offer us as we address the challenges of increasing complexity and seek new developmental advances in the 21st century.

CONTRIBUTIONS OF FREUD TO CURRENT THINKING

In the discussion that follows, we emphasize Freud's influence on some key trends in today's developmental psychology, giving only brief mention to the history of child development between Freud's time and ours. The choices of contributions made in this chapter are necessarily limited. It is hoped, however, that engaging in this kind of "back-to-the-future" journey will provide us with both pleasure and some fresh insights.

Freud's living contributions draw our attention to the meaning of individual experience. They tell us that much about the course of human development and its vicissitudes can be described in terms of lawful principles; priority, however, must be given to investigating individuality. Freud was a practicing clinician who learned early that variations in private meaning cannot be taken for granted. Related to this point is another straightforward one, which, like the first, continues to permeate our developmental dialectics even today. This concerns the reality of psychic life and the assertion that understanding an individual's unique life and living perspective is worthy of both study and therapeutic attention. Strong contemporary statements of both points for developmental psychology can be seen in Bruner (1990) and in Stern (1985).

Play

Play offers a good way to begin taking a fresh look at Freud. We can envision Freud attending to the meaning of individual experience and theorizing in ways that are both simple and profound. Writing in 1920, Freud described observations of his 1½-year-old grandson who lived with him for some weeks. He commented that the child was not at all precocious in language development and frequently threw things away from himself— for example, in a corner or under a bed. On these occasions, the child often pronounced a long, drawn-out "Oooo"—an utterance that the child's mother and Freud agreed seemed to represent the German word *fort* (i.e., gone):

> One day I made an observation. . . . The child had a wooden reel with a piece of string tied round it . . . what he did was to hold the reel by the string and very skillfully throw it over the edge of his curtained cot, so that it disappeared into it, at the same time uttering his expressive "Oooo." He then pulled the reel out of the cot again by the string and hailed its reappearance with a joyful "Da" (there). This, then, was the complete game—disappearance and return. As a rule, one only witnessed its first act, which was repeated untiringly as the game in itself, for there is no doubt that the greater pleasure was attached to the second act. (Freud, 1920/1955a, p. 15)

Freud added a footnote to this work in which he documents a subsequent observation that seemed to confirm his inference:

> One day the child's mother had been away for several hours and on her return was met with the words "Baby Oooo!" which was at first incomprehensible. It soon turned out, however, that during this long period of solitude the child had found a method of making *himself* disappear. He had discovered his reflection in a full-length mirror which did not quite reach to the ground, so that by crouching down he could make his mirror image "gone." (Freud, 1920/1955a, p. 15)

Most of Freud's developmental contributions were derived from reconstructions of adults in analysis. Here, however, we find one of Freud's rare recorded observations of children used to formulate a theory of play that has persisted as a cogent one to the present time. The origins of play in early childhood have to do with the child's actively repeating the experience of separation and return so as to master the tension of helplessness when mother is not present. In today's terms we can appreciate that what Freud did was to generate the basis for a motivation to master (see Morgan & Harmon, 1984; White, 1963; Yarrow et al., 1983). In addition, he even came close, in the above-cited mirror observation, to providing a basis for what is later taken up in our psychology as the onset of reflective self-awareness at this age (see Amsterdam, 1972; Lewis & Brooks-Gunn, 1979; Schulman & Kaplowitz, 1977).

Returning to play, however, he discovered something more (Freud, 1926/1959). Peek-a-boo was an infancy game that seemed prototypic, with a particular aspect of this game being especially important. Freud noted that the mother encouraged the infant's becoming aware of return after her disappearance "by playing the familiar game of hiding her face from it with her hands and then, to its joy, uncovering it again" (Freud, 1926/1959, pp. 169–170). Again, in today's terms we can see a basis for what is referred to in Vygotskian theory as *maternal scaffolding* in early infant communications (Bruner, 1982; Kaye, 1982), and, even more remarkable, we can see a basis for emotional scaffolding, something that is just beginning to command research attention (Biringen & Robinson, 1991).

It is interesting to note that the child's response to separation became a Freudian prototype not just for mastery and play but for ego development in general. Mourning, he postulated, is a reaction to loss that is possible when the child develops a separate sense of self and can come to grips with another's no longer existing. Moreover, a transformation in internal mental structuring was seen to take place through identification, a process Freud also linked to the psychological awareness of separation from loved objects (i.e., from caregiving parents).[1]

Although we are not assuming the task of tracing the intervening lines between Freud's time and ours, it is important to point out that the ideas cited above formed a basis for the line of thinking that led to the so-called British Object Relations School that became so influential in clinical work with mothers and children (Balint, 1948; Fairbairn, 1963; Guntrip, 1971; Winnicott, 1965). It also led to the thinking of Spitz (1965) and of Bowlby (1969), who made direct contributions to research in child development. The contributions of John Bowlby and his attachment theory to our contemporary thinking are the subject of the chapter by Bretherton in this volume. Still, we often lose sight of the fact that today's attachment research, launched so productively by Ainsworth and her students (Ainsworth, Blehar, Waters, & Wall, 1978), and based on observations of separations and reunions in early childhood, has its clear origins in these contributions of Freud.

Darwinian Approach to Individual Ontogeny

That Freud took Darwin's evolutionary approach and applied it to the individual ontogeny of psychological functioning is widely appreciated (see Ritvo, 1990; Sulloway, 1979). Early in his clinical career, Freud came to appreciate, citing Darwin, that an individual's behavior could be better understood if functions were taken into account not just in terms of a present situation but also in terms of a past history and "as Darwin has taught us . . . of actions which originally had a meaning and served a purpose" (Freud, 1893–1895/1955b, p. 181). What subsequently came to

---

[1]Freud's terminology had it that the ego was a "precipitate of abandoned object cathexes" (Freud, 1923/1961, p. 29).

be known as the *genetic point of view* (really an ontogenetic view) then occupied a central place in psychoanalytic psychology. Priority was assigned to early experience, with Freud emphasizing the successive, orderly nature of developmental phases. Moreover, in analogy to Darwin's evolutionary principles of competition and natural selection (as well as his emotion expression principles of thesis and antithesis; see Ritvo, 1990), Freud identified conflict, along with its dynamic resolution and synthesis, as central in both mental development and symptom formation.

Freud's theorizing about successive phases of childhood conflict (i.e., the psychosexual stages of development) is well known. Less widely appreciated, however, are two other aspects of Freud's theorizing that stem from the genetic point of view. These have to do with what we would today consider an early version of a developmental systems approach and a developmental progression for mastering helplessness. The latter contributions can be highlighted by considering the two major developmental books of Freud. Once more, we will be selective, picking features that are influential today and putting matters in contemporary terms insofar as possible.

Freud wrote *Three Essays on the Theory of Sexuality* in 1905/1953b, and in spite of its voice that addressed a sexually suppressed audience of the time, it is full of accessible insights for today's reader. The first essay discussed sexual aberrations. Two formulations emerge. First, such aberrations were seen as exaggerations of component processes of healthy sexual life. Second, what was seen as pathological about these exaggerations were their exclusiveness and fixation (or rigidity). In other words, pathology occurs when the components of what is usually organized in normal sexuality are exaggerated or come apart and are not under the organizing influence of a biologically adaptive overall sexual aim.

The neuroses (e.g., hysteria) are characterized by an excessive aversion to sexuality as well as an excessive craving. A conflict between the two cravings results in symptom formation. The neuroses also illustrate a lack of the usual organization of sexual functioning in that symptoms reflect exaggerations of components that have both active and passive features. Normal sexual life, on the other hand, contrasts with this situation. There is some activity (or discharge) and some inhibition; neither is there a fixed exaggerated discharge of sexuality (as in sexual deviation), nor is there a massive inhibition of sexuality (as in the neuroses).

The second essay addressed infantile sexuality. In his theory of erotogenic zones, Freud came to the idea that early forms of infantile sexuality revolve around self-preservative adaptive functions. Thus thumb sucking gives sensual pleasure in relation to nourishment; anality provides sexual pleasure in relation to defecation, and genital pleasure occurs in relation to micturition. Although the erotogenic zones have predominance in developmental phases according to a lawful and ordered sequence, they do not come preformed. Instead, as Freud discussed, they are codetermined (using our terms of today) by biological preparedness and by particular experience with a caregiving environment. Today we can see this as an early precursor of a developmental theory that enlists a progression of modes of functioning, as well as a progression of zones of predominance (Erikson, 1950), and of broader stage-related theories of cognitive development (Piaget, 1952). Freud's ideas can also be seen as an early version of today's dialogues about epigenesis (for example, Gottlieb, 1991).

Freud's third essay addressed transformations of puberty and placed his psychosexual theory in what we today could call a *developmental systems framework*. Earlier sexuality is characterized by component aspects that are not yet connected and are relatively independent in their pleasure aims. Later in development, at puberty, these components become coordinated such that all aspects are directed toward another person and give pleasure under the sway of age-appropriate adaptive, reproductive functioning. What was organized previously as component sexual activity now generates pleasure, but it also yields increasing tension in forepleasure that builds toward the genital end pleasure connected with orgasm. Other features of this developmental progression of sexuality are also emphasized. The successive activation and inhibition of sexual phases in early childhood is a normal developmental process; if there is not such a progression, genital reorganization at puberty may not result. The order in which early childhood components of sexual activity occur and their duration seems determined by heredity. Moreover, the long period of sexual maturation in the child before puberty allows for socialization of moral precepts, in particular, according to Freud, for inculcation of the barrier against incest.

In a section of this essay that was added later, Freud introduced the model of a complemental series across development, one that expresses the influences between constitutional and environmental (or what Freud calls "accidental") factors. Both interact in determining developmental outcomes with respect to sexuality. Influences stemming from the environment in early childhood, however, have a place of preference. Thus, in early childhood the interaction of constitutional and environmental influences becomes dispositional, such that the later age complemental series involves the earlier age disposition interacting with later environmental (e.g., traumatic) influences. This discussion reminds us of contemporary views of temperament that conceptualize early dispositions as arising in similar ways, from innate tendencies interacting with environmental matches (Chess & Thomas, 1984).

A remarkably modern-sounding section of the essay concerned a discussion of the influences from early childhood in the form of prototypes. There is an infantile prototype of every relation of love, and Freud draws special attention to sucking at mother's breast, a mode that he describes persisting as "anaclitic" and as an "attachment one" (Freud, 1905/1953b, p. 222). This mode becomes influential in that later choices for love are based on earlier prototypes of loving people who are caring. Freud also postulates that infantile anxiety is a reaction to feeling the loss of the caregiver's love. The latter is a basis for the infant's fear of strangers and also the young child's fear of the dark. To illustrate, Freud adds a vivid observation of a 3-year-old boy. The boy called out from the dark, "Auntie, speak to me! I'm frightened because it's so dark." His aunt answered him: "What good would that do? You can't see me." "That doesn't matter," replied the child. "If anyone speaks, it gets light" (Freud, 1905/1953b, p. 224).

Inhibitions, Symptoms, and Anxiety, which Freud wrote in 1926, continued ideas about early experiential prototypes and linked them in a developmental series. The focus was now on the affective realm—on helplessness, anticipatory anxiety, and symptom formation. Freud distinguished automatic anxiety (a more biologically based form that dominated his very early theories of psychopathology) from anxiety as a mental signal that anticipates the experience of helplessness.

Anxiety arises as a reaction to an actual state of danger, and later in development it gets reproduced as a signal. The prototypes of original reactions in infancy include observed anxiety to being alone, being in the dark, and being with a stranger—all three instances have a basis in "missing someone who is loved and longed for" (Freud, 1926/1959, p. 136). In these situations, anxiety is a reaction to a felt loss and increasing tension from needs and resultant helplessness. The idea is that the absence of mother then comes to signal the danger of helplessness before it occurs. Freud referred to this as "an intentional reproduction of anxiety as a signal of danger" (Freud, 1926/1959, p. 138).

A developmental anxiety series beyond infancy was then portrayed. In the phallic phase of the preschooler, there is anxiety from the fear of being separated from one's genitals—that is, castration anxiety—now a more specific fear than the helplessness of infancy. Next is moral anxiety, when an anxiety signal results from an internalized scenario in which one seeks to avoid a helpless state in which one's conscience (or superego) is overcondemnatory; in other words, one seeks to avoid a loss of self-esteem resulting from an inner voice that makes one feel unloved. Freud also speculates on a later existential anxiety in which one develops anxiety about "the powers of destiny" and about death (Freud, 1926/1959, p. 140).

Two case histories illustrate the childhood formation of symptoms. In one, now known in the psychoanalytic literature as Little Hans, the child had a symptom of phobia of horses, but Freud inferred that he was really afraid of his father, with whom he had earlier played with horses. Freud stated that mental displacement had occurred that made use of a primitive mode that children use at an early age in which ". . . the grown man, the object of their fear and admiration, still belongs to the same category as the big animal who has so many enviable attributes but against whom they have been warned because he may become dangerous" (Freud, 1926/1959, p. 103). In another case, known in psychoanalytic literature today as Wolf Man, the patient had a fear of being eaten by a wolf, and Freud traced the fear to early play with father pretending to be a wolf who could eat him. Freud's formulation is that in both of these cases there is a warding off of fears related to being castrated by father as part of the Oedipus complex. Symptoms, such as fear of being bitten by horses or eaten by wolves, are unconsciously constructed by the individual to avoid a danger situation whose presence has been signaled by the anticipatory anxiety linked to the childhood memory.

In today's terms, we would see Freud relating the above anxieties to different levels of cognition and social competence. Each situation of danger corresponds to a particular developmental phase of understanding. When such anxieties are involved in symptom formation, unintegrated earlier levels of organization and understanding are confronted. The individual "behaves as though the old danger situations still existed, and keeps hold of all the earlier determinants of anxiety" (Freud, 1926/1959, p. 147). We would also see influences of varying developmental levels of categorization abilities, person schemas, and role-taking perspectives (Horowitz, 1988).

Interestingly, in an addendum to this work, Freud returned to the prototypical phenomenon of infantile stranger anxiety in a way that again seems like speculation from today's discussions in social cognition. The infant feels pain in stranger anxiety, as can be inferred from the expression on its face and the crying. This is because, early on, the infant cannot distinguish between a temporary absence and a permanent loss and therefore experiences the missing of its mother not as a danger situation but as a traumatic one. Pain is the actual reaction to a loss, whereas anxiety is the reaction to the danger that the loss entails.

Nonconscious Mental Activity and Constructivism

The above discussion illustrates Freud's application of a Darwinian approach to understanding meaning according to the individual's biologically driven sequence of development in interactions with the caring environment. Sequences of development concerning sexuality and anxiety are seen to be based on struggle, conflict, and competition with processes of compromise symptom formation and syntheses. Early prototypes in experience become a basis for more complex forms of experience that can be reinvoked. Evolutionary theory also laid stress on the dynamic, instinctual, and nonrational in human behavior, and, as Sulloway (1979) points out, Freud's emphasis on the role of the dynamic unconscious in human ontogeny carried forward this line of Darwin's thinking.

Writing in 1915 on *Instincts and Their Vicissitudes*, Freud put forth a number of formulations about transformations in ontogeny with respect to intrinsic inclinations. Instincts in his view not only had a source but were organized according to their aims and their objects, or the persons at whom they were targeted. The active aim precedes the passive aim in development (e.g., looking precedes the desire to be looked at), but the two sides of a tendency can be seen to coexist. Moreover, there is ambivalence of an instinctual aim at each developmental stage, with attraction and repulsion tendencies linked to pleasurable feelings, on the one hand, and to unpleasurable feelings in connection with a person, on the other hand. There is also a corresponding ambivalence in a tendency to come closer versus a tendency to avoid, flee, or destroy. Today's reader will note the precursor to attachment theory, with its stated inborn tendencies of caregiver proximity and exploration (Bowlby, 1969), and also to separation–individuation theory, with its concept of ambi-tendency (Mahler, Pine, & Bergman, 1975).

The same 1915 essay also enumerated "the three great polarities that dominate mental life" (Freud, 1915/1957), namely, pleasure–unpleasure, active–passive, and internal–external. How is this a contribution? Freud's polarities fit very well with contemporary psychological views of polarities that organize the dimensionality of emotions throughout the life span (Abelson & Sermat, 1962; Emde, 1980; Frijda & Phillipszoon, 1963; Gladstone, 1962; Osgood, 1966; Russell & Ridgeway, 1983; Woodworth & Schlosberg, 1954). This contribution becomes more cogent for today's psychoanalytic views, as well with some theorists reinterpreting Freud's instinct theory so that the developmental organization of affects are central (Emde, 1988; Kernberg, 1976; Lichtenberg, 1989).

The above tendencies are not conscious. Many readers probably associate Freud's name primarily with his ideas about unconscious mental activity. I believe that his developmental contributions in this realm can best be seen by discussing transference. In an essay entitled *Remembering, Repeating, and Working Through*, Freud (1914/1958) showed that discoveries of psychoanalysis have revealed that patients do not remember what has been forgotten or repressed; instead, patients reproduce painful memories in action without the patient knowing that he or she is repeating it. A patient, for example, does not say that he remembers that he was once quite critical of his parents' authority but instead acts in a critical manner toward his doctor. Freud states, "As long as the patient is in the treatment, he cannot escape from this compulsion to repeat; and, in the end, we understand that this is his way of remembering" (Freud, 1914/1958, p. 150). Freud referred to transference as a "playground" within the psychoanalytic situation in which there is freedom to display such enactments that can be interpreted, understood, and made conscious. Transference repetitions, however, also occur more widely in intimate life relationships that are important. In today's parlance, we would say that early painful enacted schemata are once more activated in a way that can be contrasted with current circumstances within the context of new relationships, and, in the therapeutic situation, there is often an opportunity to reintegrate painful affects with the help of another. Transference phenomena are being investigated today in psychotherapy and development from the point of view of schema theory and social cognition (Horowitz, 1988). Freud also wrote compellingly about the process of repeating in psychoanalysis compared with remembering, noting that the former involves enactments with more pieces of real life. Today's reader is reminded of autobiographical or episodic memory compared with semantic or schematic memory and of distinctions we make between procedural knowledge and declarative knowledge (Clyman, in press). According to today's thinking, Freud even may have underestimated the extent to which human mental activity is nonconscious.

In passing, we should also take note of another contribution of Freud in the cognitive realm, namely, his contribution to Piaget's method of inquiry. Piaget learned from Freud the value of open-ended inquiry and, above all, the value of attending to an individual's errors even more than an individual's successes when struggling with problems. We can also see that origin of a constructivist approach to the world in Freud's emphasis on the child's active fantasy making. One cannot take the child's experience for granted, and one must discover what the child makes of reality and what is apt to be significant from the child's perspective at any given age.

Two essays written at the end of his life review aspects of his developmental thinking and show Freud struggling with what he still could not understand. In *An Outline of Psycho-Analysis*, written in 1938, he reviewed his developmental theory of anxiety. The individual's developing ego is "governed by considerations of safety" and by "the task of self preservation," and it "makes uses of the sensations of anxiety as a signal to give a warning of dangers that threaten its integrity" (Freud, 1938/1964a, p. 199). Freud added that children are at first protected against threatening dangers by the care of their parents, but "they pay for this security by a fear of loss of love" (Freud, 1938/1964a, p. 200). Freud thus built on his developmental model of security and helplessness, linking the concept of security to early mother–infant interactions. Emphasis, however, was put on the relationship of security to minimizing fearfulness in the context of libidinal drive discharge. Bowlby (1973), of course, brought this theory into a different balance when he postulated a new motivational structure with the attachment/security-exploration system.

In *Analysis Terminable and Interminable* (Freud, 1937/1964b), Freud wrote about the prospects for psychoanalysis as a treatment and its major limitations in achieving favorable outcomes. But Freud was concerned with a developmental issue as well. In considering issues of individual differences in what he terms "adhesiveness of the libido," "cyclical inertia," and "revisions of old repressions and developmental transformations wherein earlier organizations persist alongside of newer ones," Freud was thinking of adults coursing through life. He is preoccupied with how to minimize neurotic repetitions so that development can continue in a more adaptive way. Although he did not make it explicit, Freud was considering individual differences in development as much as he was considering individual differences in psychoanalytic treatment. Perhaps because he was unaware of the limitations caused by a child-only oriented view of development and of the fact that psychoanalysis with an adult was a form of enhancing adult development as much as revising aspects of child development, Freud remained pessimistic. This seems a time, therefore, to move to a consideration of the limitations of Freudian contributions as we see them today.

LIMITATIONS OF FREUDIAN IDEAS

Paradoxically, a major strength of Freud frames a major scientific limitation from today's science. This strength resides in his style and language. Freud's narrative style was cogent and persuasive, and, although he never won a major scientific prize in his lifetime, he won the Goethe Prize in recognition of the literary and humanistic qualities of his writings (Jones, 1955). Freud used metaphor, dramatic illustration, and anthropomorphic constructs to great advantage in his theorizing in a way that some have traced to his love of 19th-century German Romantic philosophy (Ackerknecht, 1959). Although this style led to devoted readers over the years, it also had adverse consequences. Constructs such as ego, superego, and id were envisioned as battling entities that competed for consciousness and action, a reification that was not helped by the official translation by Strachey of Freud's rather straightforward German *das ich* (the I) into English as *the ego*, which sounds more thinglike. Freud's metaphors also provide us with a view of his limitations stemming from the scientific zeitgeist of his time, which drew more on models of late 19th-century physics than those of the 20th century. Earlier in the article, we portrayed Freud's thinking as a forerunner of our developmental systems way of thinking, but Freud was unaware of the major perspectives of that approach. His model was constrained by what we would today call a *closed systems view* of development in which all mental functioning obeyed the law of entropy (i.e., drive discharge) and ran downward to a lower level of organization. Today's view of development, in contrast, is centered around the recognition of negentropy (i.e., increasingly organized complexity as a basic premise of development).

A related limitation from today's perspective stems from Freud's mechanistic and reductionistic proclivities. Mechanistic formulations pervade his theory in terms of modeling the mind as a linear processing machine with components arrayed along the way (Freud, 1900/1953a) and with memories seen in terms of fixed traces, stored according to veridical units

(Paul, 1967; Wolff, 1960). Contrast this with today's view of memory seen in terms of dynamic schemata that are open to the world, participating in and coconstructing a reality that may or may not be conflictual. Freud's reductionism is both psychological and historical. Psychological reductionism kept his mental theory operating according to a trend in which all affects, action, and thoughts were seen as derivatives of instinctual drive stimuli. Historical reductionism kept his theory operating according to a tendency in which most later behaviors of significance were seen as derivatives of childhood conflicts.

Another limitation from our current perspective stems, ironically, from Freud's correction of what he considered a grand mistake. The early years of his medical practice convinced him of the importance of early childhood trauma in the causation of neurosis, particularly because parental abuse and especially childhood seduction was a common factor in the histories of his patients (Freud, 1896/1962). A childhood seduction theory of hysteria therefore guided his early clinical work. But a dramatic correction then occurred. Freud pondered the high incidence of hysterical neuroses and doubted that childhood abuse and seduction could be so prevalent. Moreover, he discovered through his own self-analysis that he had similar thoughts involving his own parents when he was a child, and he came to his corrected view: Early childhood seduction by the parent of the opposite sex and punishing abuse (usually by the parent of the same sex) are not actual memories; instead they represent universal wishes and their variations. The childhood wishes in turn reflect the maturation of instinctual drives according to a timetable wherein the child experienced desires to sexually possess the opposite sex parent, on the one hand, and to eliminate or kill the same sex parent, on the other hand.

Today we recognize the striking limitations of the above formulations that became the core of Freud's theory of the Oedipus complex. We now can appreciate (after decades of professional denial) that parental abuse and seduction of children are devastatingly widespread and that childhood sexual trauma is a significant cause of pain and disorder among young women. Freud's correction of what he thought was his mistake led to productive aspects of his drive theory, repression, and to dynamic psychiatry. But his initial view of developmental psychopathology that gave a central importance to trauma resulting from child abuse seems to have been more correct than not.

The theory of the Oedipus complex became, for many, a centerpiece for psychoanalysis. Because this developmental theory illustrates a good deal about the historical context with regard to Freud's inferences about normal development, as well as its limitations, we will review it in more detail.

Freud's Oedipal theory has three basic postulates. The first is that the preschool child normally experiences sexual desires toward the parent of the opposite sex (at the extreme, a desire for sexual possession). The second postulate is that the child naturally has feelings of competitive rivalry with the parent of the same sex (at the extreme, a murderous rage). A third postulate is that the child encounters fear of retaliation from the parent of the same sex for such wishes. Fears of this kind involved fantasies of bodily harm and castration.

What initiates the Oedipus complex is a maturation of naturally occurring psychosexual urges, along with other aspects of mental development and the child's increasing curiosity. The usual outcome of the Oedipus complex is thought to include an identification with a parent of the same sex and the formation of the basic structure for morality, the superego. Both outcomes are expected between 5 and 7 years of age.

Other features of Freud's basic Oedipus complex were implicit. These included its universality and its role in the child's normal motivations. Although many features of the Oedipus complex in the young child would be seen in manifest behavioral enactments, increasingly the forces of repression occasioned by fear and guilt would make Oedipal wishes unconscious.

Freud and the early psychoanalysts soon found it necessary to make additions to the childhood Oedipus complex. Originally modeled for boys, it then became elaborated for girls. Boys could preserve their original heterosexual orientation to mother, but girls found the complex more difficult because the object of love had to be changed from mother to father. Because of this, Freud believed girls had a more complex moral development than boys. Without adding more details of his Oedipal theory, let us consider its limitations from the perspective of today's knowledge.

First, the child's superego, or conscience formation, is not an outcome of the resolved Oedipus complex. The clinical literature of child analysis and of psychoanalytically informed observation provides many examples of superego formation without the resolution of Oedipal conflicts (Sandler, 1960). Moreover, there is considerable moral development before age 3, with both moral conflict and some capacity for its resolution manifest well before age 7 (Emde, Johnson, & Easterbrooks, 1988; Radke-Yarrow, Zahn-Waxler, & Chapman, 1983). Both moral conflict and the capacity for its resolution are manifest at an early age.

Second, research has shown that gender identity is not an outcome of the Oedipus complex. Core gender identity is established earlier, usually in the second and third years of life (Stoller, 1980).

Third, female development is not secondary or less powerful than male development during the age period of the Oedipus conflict. Freud was a product of his time and culture and focused on male development as prototypic, with female development somehow secondary and more complex. If, however, one wants to invoke a biological bias, then the opposite is the case. Research has shown that femininity is primary; the fetal brain must be androgenized for masculinity to occur; otherwise, femininity will be phenotypic. Research has also shown that the female superego is not weaker.

Instead, females may have a greater propensity for empathy and a greater concern with maintaining reciprocity and relationships in their moral development. It is the case that male children are more aggressive, a fact that seems linked to testosterone as well as to socialization of gender differences that begin to become manifest during the child's third and fourth years (Maccoby, 1990; Maccoby & Martin, 1983).

Fourth, psychoanalysts have come to see variations in the family environment as playing a major role in the course of the child's Oedipal complex. Fenichel (1945), in his midcentury review of psychoanalytic experience, pointed to the decisive influence of many of these factors. Only in the past two decades, however, have we come to appreciate the horrific and the widespread existence of child maltreatment by parents (Cicchetti & Carlson, 1989). We have also come to appreciate the conditions under which there are grim repetitions of maladaptive Oedipal conflicts across two and three generations (Cramer et al., 1990; Fraiberg, Adelson, & Shapiro, 1975; Zeanah & Barton, 1989). Correspondingly, recent schools of thinking in psychoanalysis have become more outward oriented rather than inward or drive oriented in their views of early childhood conflicts. Kohut (1971, 1977) found the origins of narcissism in empathic deficits in parenting. Bowlby (1973), following Winnicott (1965), theorized about a splitting of self-experience during early childhood on the basis of the harsh realities presented by many abusing families. At the same time, research on childhood observations of traumas, violence, and sexual activity has indicated that the Oedipal age child of 3 to 7 can be a credible witness (Goodman & Hahn, 1987). All of this recent evidence contrasts with earlier theories of the unreliability of child observations caused by imaginative fantasy and of the child's experience being dominated by internally driven wishes.

Finally, Freud's portrayal of the child's experience during the family Oedipal drama is oversimplified. We know today that fathers do not appear later on the stage to interrupt an earlier affectionate relationship with mother when the child becomes 3 or 4. Research has shown that fathers, under normative conditions, develop early and qualitatively separate affectionate relationships with both young boys and girls. Such relationships are measurable at the end of the first year and continue to develop (Grossmann, Grossmann, Huber, & Wartner, 1981; Lamb, 1977; Main & Weston, 1981).

Taken together, the story of Freud's Oedipal theory shows a concatenation of limitations. Recent research indicates that there are normal developmental phenomena that deserve a fresh look (Buchsbaum & Emde, 1990; Cohen, Marans, Dahl, Marans, & Lewis, 1987; Watson & Getz, 1990). We await a new theory that takes into account the increasing complexity as seen from our contemporary knowledge of social cognition, psycholinguistics, and the dynamics of family systems in different ecologies.

The challenge, as with Freud, will be to understand the child's individual experience in such a way so as not to be dominated by our own styles and stories.

CONTRIBUTIONS OF SPITZ TO CURRENT THINKING

In reviewing Freud's contribution to today's developmental thinking, we highlighted his observations of play, his schematic perspectives on developmental processes, and his pioneering theoretical approaches involving nonconscious mental activity in the context of constructivism. In reviewing Spitz's contributions to today's thinking, we will move through a similar order. We will begin with his contributions to infant observation and assessment, then take up his schematic perspectives on developmental processes, and conclude with his pioneering theoretical approaches involving affective communications in the context of caregiving.

Spitz's links with Freud were direct. In 1911, he consulted Freud in Vienna and began with him what became known as the first *didactic analysis*, that is, a psychoanalysis conducted primarily for training rather than therapeutic purposes. Afterward, Spitz considered Freud his mentor, and he continued to learn from his written contributions while identifying with his investigative spirit. In contrast to Freud, however, Spitz based most of his thinking on empirical investigations on infancy rather than on psychoanalytic investigations into adulthood.

Infant Observations and Assessment

Perhaps the greatest contributions of Spitz came from his innovations with respect to strategies of investigation. Spitz pioneered in showing the value of infant observation. Understanding normal development in the early years was important, not only for psychology, but also for psychiatry and the medical sciences. He also showed the value of observing infants developing in different contexts, including those involving maternal and emotional deprivation. He demonstrated the value of the use of regular developmental assessments, not just for research on intellectual development, but for research and intervention with respect to socioemotional development. Spitz also pioneered in the use of filmed observations. He routinely used 16-mm movies for documentation and study of nonverbal interactions. Since the advent of video technology, the research usefulness of a visual record tends to be taken for granted. But in the 1940s and 1950s, this was not the case, and Spitz's film libraries, as well as his published films, became invaluable sources of information. If it were not for his published films documenting the devastating effects of grief and deprivation

in infancy and documenting the importance of socioemotional development, his work would not have had nearly the same impact.

Spitz was also unusual for his time in integrating thinking from a
variety of multidisciplinary approaches, including ethology, embryology,
experimental psychology, psychiatry, and pediatrics. Among those who
have acknowledged his influence on child development are Bowlby (1951),
Brazelton (1983), Campos (1983), and Fraiberg (1982).

Spitz's best known empirical and theoretical contributions concern
his studies involving the deprivation of mothering. It may seem strange to
us today, but it used to be considered best for a baby awaiting adoption to
be in an institution for a prolonged period. A waiting period was thought
necessary to provide time for the developmental unfolding of the baby's
intellectual and personality features; this would in turn allow for an appropriate match with adoptive parents. When many institutionalized infants
were unable to meet the standards of adoptive parents for intellect and
sociability, it was thought to be a reflection of the morally inferior nature
of women conceiving out of wedlock. Indeed, many of these unwed mothers
were labeled as *constitutional psychopathic inferiors*, a diagnosis that crystal-
lized a prevailing attitude that such a condition was to a large extent
constitutional, fixed, and not deserving of attempts at amelioration. Indeed,
the fact that the offspring of these women were typically sickly in spite of
good institutional hygienic care fit in with a Protestant ethic regarding the
products of sinfulness and also with a social Darwinism, which maintained
that humanity was naturally evolving toward a state of social betterment.
In other words, sickly infants, constitutionally less equipped for adaptation
and survival, were confirmation of an evolutionary process at work. Spitz's
findings presented an alternative explanation. The experience of institutionalized infants led to developmental and physical retardation, and much
of that experience had to do with deficits in mothering, separation, and
depression. In a series of classic papers (Spitz, 1946a, 1946b, 1983a, 1983c),
Spitz recorded his findings, which included repeated developmental testing,
prolonged observations, social interaction experiments, and health outcomes. The effects of socioemotional deprivation could be devastating in
terms of developmental competence, health, and survival. Moreover, the
consequences of maternal separation after the middle of the first postnatal
year were different than at an earlier age because the nature of the caregiving
love relationships became specific at that time. After the middle of the first
year, a caregiving relationship was internalized so that no one else would
do. Developmentalists of the time did not believe that infants could suffer
grief syndromes; Spitz, however, not only documented these in the latter
part of infancy but also showed their connection with the quality of a
preexisting caregiving relationship.

Spitz's observations ultimately became compelling, and, as a result of
Bowlby's (1951) report reviewing them and adding more evidence, adoption

procedures were changed around the world. Waiting for adoption ceased to be valued, and the goal instead became to adopt early wherever possible. This work also contributed to a more hopeful view that developmental improvement through environmental change was possible. In rereading these articles today, one becomes impressed that Spitz was not just writing about babies deprived of their mothers; he was also writing about understanding the mothering process. This leads us to Spitz's contributions concerning affective reciprocity and other concepts of ego development.

Developmental Processes: The Role of Affect and Transformations

René Spitz was aware of his contributions being made in the course of a living history that connected him with continuing the work of others. Like Freud, Spitz had a continuity-in-the-midst-of-change view of human history. In many ways, his intellectual connections with Darwin were even more direct than Freud's, with his borrowing concepts from animal behavior and his preoccupations about the ontogeny of emotion and evolutionary adaptiveness. My links with Spitz were personal because Spitz provided research supervision from 1961 to 1963 and because Spitz was again present as a colleague in Denver during his final 6 years (1969–1974). During his final days, he talked a good deal about Darwinian ideas. He wanted his final words to be remembered as "survival, adaptation, and evolution" (personal communication).

"The Smiling Response: A Contribution to the Ontogenesis of Social Relations" is the title of a monograph that Spitz and Wolf wrote in 1946. Observations were presented in support of a theory that the smiling response is a maturationally driven universal milestone in development appearing at around 3 months of age. Social experiments were conducted that made use of concepts borrowed from Gestalt psychology, and these led to a specification of the most potent stimulus configurations for eliciting early smiling that were found in the human face. Additionally, the onset of social smiling was seen to represent a major transformation in social reciprocity and in the organization of pleasure for the child and for those around the child. Many of Spitz's formulations and observations about early smiling stand up quite well today, although we appreciate that there are a variety of forms of early endogenously, as well as exogenously, elicited smiles (for a review, see Emde & Harmon, 1972.)

Spitz made other empirical contributions to the development of affect in infancy. These included his descriptions of stranger anxiety and separation responses, as well as his descriptions of the developmental onset of the child's expressions of the *no* in gesture and word. In a major theoretical work, *A Genetic Field Theory of Ego Formation*, written in 1959, he borrowed models from embryology to propose a series of psychic organizers in infancy and related these to affect. Development was uneven; periods of stability or steady incremental change were interspersed with periods of developmental transformation. Affective changes were indicators of these periods of transformation: They included the onset of the smiling response, "eight months' anxiety," and the developmental onset of the semantic no. In later articles (Spitz, Emde, & Metcalf, 1970; Spitz, 1972), Spitz again took up the notion of these times of transformation, stating that they were equivalent to the development of a new modus operandi, introducing a better way of adaptation on a higher level of complexity. Such a way of adaptation would persist until increasing complexity resulted in the need for another modus operandi and regulation at a higher level; at that time there would be another reorganization.

Contemporary developmental psychology is now beginning to confront the mysteries of developmental transformation with methods that include multivariate approaches, behavioral genetic approaches, and approaches that track individuals' development over time. Spitz's theory of organizers provides a background for today's interest in developmental transformation. Empirical support for the times of transformation that Spitz pointed to was summarized more than a decade ago with the suggestion of another transformation time at 12 to 13 months (Emde, Gaensbauer, & Harmon, 1976; Kagan, Kearsley, & Zelaso, 1978; McCall, 1979). More recent discoveries in the neurosciences have generated renewed interest in the brain bases for such transitions, especially during the 7- to 9-month shift for language comprehension (Bates, Thal, & Janowsky, in press) and for cognitive functioning (Welsh & Pennington, 1988).

Another area of Spitz's contributions has to do with his formulations concerning early psychobiological prototypes of mental functioning and the early development of self. In several key articles, Spitz discussed his ideas about prototypes of defenses and coping behavior that enlarge on the prototype model conceived by Freud (Spitz, 1961, 1983e; Spitz et al., 1970). Early innate modes of functioning require repeated interaction with the social environment before they become transformed into psychological structures. Spitz also expanded his theory of social–affective development into a theory of the emergence of self during the first 2 years. His constructs about self are best formulated in two books (Spitz, 1957, 1965) and two articles (Spitz, 1958, 1966). The period between 15 and 18 months is a time of developmental transformation with increasing self-regulation in which the acquisition of the semantic no is a milestone that marks a shift from the passivity involved in obeying a prohibition to the activity involved in constructing a negative. From now on the child has possibilities for discussion in addition to possibilities for discharge of aggression in fight or flight, a developmental turning point that Spitz dramatized by referring to it from a phylogenetic point of view as marking the "humanization of man." Spitz also wrote of the mushrooming of imitation and identification at this age. These formulations provide a background for today's renewed interest in the early development of self in both psychology and psychoanalysis. (For example, see Brownell & Kopp, 1991; Emde, 1983; Kohut, 1977; Lewis & Brooks-Gunn, 1979.)

Affective Communications

As Spitz considered the mothering process in infancy, he turned his attention to the condition of affective reciprocity, and he came to his concept of the dialogue. Although the concept did not appear until 1963, one can see its origins in the monograph on the smiling response of 1946. It became elaborated in key articles entitled "Life and the Dialogue" (1983e), "The Derailment of the Dialogue" (1983b), and "The Evolution of Dialogue" (1983d). Spitz chose the word *dialogue* to emphasize that a basic communication process exists in infancy, even before speech. Although communications are not verbal, they are complex, emotional, and two way, providing adaptive information for both parent and infant. Spitz not only extended the psychoanalytic static concepts of object relations in the social sphere but also legitimized the study of the ways in which the infant sends and receives signals and influences his or her own experience of being cared for. Such approaches have since come to the forefront of research both with interactional work (for example, Bell & Harper, 1977; Brazelton, Koslowski, & Main, 1974; Osofsky, 1979; Stern, 1977) and in thinking more broadly about intersubjectivity and shared meaning in infancy (Bruner, 1982, 1990; Stern, 1985; Wertsch, 1991).

Limitations of Spitz's Contributions

In continuing Freudian thinking, Spitz used some of the language and metaphors of his predecessor, thus taking on their limitations. Were it not for the abstract language of Freud's psychoanalytic metapsychology, the contemporary readings of Spitz's theoretical works might be considered more widely relevant. Spitz also adhered, more or less, to Freud's drive-reduction orientation. The modification of metapsychology provided by Hartmann's (1939) adaptive point of view allowed for a conflict-free sphere of development. But Spitz's incorporation of the additional abstract language of Hartmann made for more difficulty in understanding, and it did not liberate his theory from its entropic, mechanistic orientation. Ironically, Spitz, who introduced the importance of the smiling response in early infancy, was also not able to see fully the implications of a separately organized positive emotion system. His theory of self-formation, following Freud, was largely one of negative emotions and of the infant's renunciation of need-satisfying wishes related to mother. Ironically, Spitz, who introduced a theory of developmental transformations and of the successive levels of organized mental functioning in infancy, was not able to see fully the implications of increasing complexity (or negentropy) beyond drive reductionism, nor was he able to see the child's increasing autonomy in these terms. Similarly, Spitz, who introduced a theory of dialogic development from earliest infancy, was not able to see fully the implications of the open-systems dynamisms of early affective communication that he was describing, implications that frame much of today's thinking about intersubjectivity.

Spitz was an empiricist and later in life was fond of quoting his friend, Konrad Lorenz, to the effect that any scientist worth his salt would discard a favorite hypothesis before breakfast. Other limitations, however, as seen from today's vantage point stem from the manner of presentation of his empirical method and results. The Pinneau–Spitz controversy surfaced in the *Psychological Bulletin* in 1955 and illustrates the point. This controversy is not only of historical interest but is also of contemporary interest in forcing us to think about how Spitz was able to rise beyond his limitations and avoid the pitfalls of a Type II (as well as a Type I) inference error. Pinneau criticized the articles on maternal emotional deprivation that became so influential in clinical and social welfare circles. In succeeding issues of the *Psychological Bulletin*, Spitz replied to Pinneau and Pinneau then to Spitz.

The major thrust of Pinneau's criticism was aimed at Spitz's inadequate descriptions of background, sample, and observational methods. There was no description of interobserver reliability nor of the conditions under which observations were made, and it was difficult to determine how many cases were observed longitudinally and how many cross sectionally. Specification of the initial health conditions of infants was lacking, and it was difficult to reconstruct statistical relationships between the decline of infants and the times of separation from mothers. Pinneau also attacked the validity of the developmental testing instrument (the Hetzer-Wolf Test), citing its inadequate standardization and the lack of established predictive validity.

Subsequent evidence has confirmed the correctness of Spitz's inferences regarding links between maternal separation and infant sadness, depression, and apathy (Bowlby, 1951; Robertson & Robertson, 1971). Evidence has also confirmed Spitz's discovery regarding the differential effects of acute separation before and after 6 months of age (Bowlby, 1969; Schaffer & Callender, 1959). This raises a provocative question. Given Pinneau's valid criticisms about method and the developmental instrument, how could Spitz's discoveries stand up? The crux of the matter appears to be something that Spitz did not enumerate in his replies. I believe that it has to do, from today's perspective, with the nature of longitudinal inference in individual infants. Spitz followed a number of infants and noticed that after separation from their mothers they became weepy, had sad faces, and were immobile; some had dazed looks and engaged in autoerotic activities. Spitz felt saddened and was reminded of depression in adults. Even though the infants could not tell him how they felt, he felt that they were depressed and related their plight to the loss of the loved one. A feeling was communicated by the infants, and Spitz made use of that feeling to broaden his perceptions. He was able to envision a clinical syndrome, one that included a pattern of behavior, affective communication, and events occurring over time. The developmental tests were used not so much as a predictor of retardation but as a standard protocol for assessing an individual infant's level of functioning in the context of current interactive exchanges and then using that instrument again to document change.

Today we are aware of other limitations of Spitz's deprivation findings. We now appreciate that the effects of early caretaking on subsequent development are complex and bidirectional, with influences going from infant to parent, as well as from parent to infant (Bell & Harper, 1977). We understand that the typical caregiving experience is not limited to one caregiver (Clarke-Stewart, 1977; Lamb, 1978). We also know that the young child who has experienced early deprivation can be remarkably resilient, provided that there is a major salutary and enduring change in the caregiving environment and that major cognitive deficits can be made up (see Clarke & Clarke, 1976; Kagan et al., 1978).

In concluding, we return to a new horizon envisioned by Spitz but left to others to explore. In his response to Pinneau, Spitz became less concerned with the loss of mother per se and more concerned with affective reciprocity as the key ingredient missing in those deprived infants who did not recover. Spitz did not reply to many of Pinneau's criticisms, but he restated his conclusions in terms that looked beyond. To quote:

> Affective interchange is paramount, not only for the development of emotion itself in infants, but also for the maturation and the development of the child . . . this affective interchange is provided by the reciprocity between the mother (or her substitute) and the child . . . depriving the child of this interchange is a serious, and in the extreme case, a dangerous handicap for its development in every sector of the personality. (Spitz, 1955, p. 454)

CONCLUSION: FREUD AND SPITZ LOOKING TO THE FUTURE

Our historical review has highlighted those contributions of Freud and Spitz to developmental psychology that are influential today. In concluding, we ask a further question: Do the approaches of these clinicians point us to future directions? We can well imagine that they do. The two overall dimensions of their contributions we have discussed, namely, understanding individual meaning and understanding increasing complexity, will present greater challenges for us in the future than ever before. Let us consider, in the tradition of a living history, what directions the Freudian and Spitzian approaches would urge us to explore in the midst of our continuing changes in scientific technology and social—ecological circumstances.

The Freudian approach has particular relevance for modern developmental biology. As we map the human genome and as we investigate the genetic determination of brain development while tracing neural pathways with the technology of tomorrow, the Freudian approach urges us toward understanding the influences of experience. We need to investigate the individuality of that experience and to incorporate our findings in thinking about genetically influenced syndromes of personality and of pathology. If we do this, the study of individuality can then be pursued in terms of the dynamisms of gene—environment interactions through the course of life.

The creative spirit of Freud also beckons us to rethink old ideas about consciousness in the light of today's cognitive sciences. Traditional ideas about dimensions of nonconscious activity need to be expanded, for example, with more investigations in areas that today are referred to as *procedural, implicit, skill based*, and *distributed*.

The creative approaches of Freud also urge us to investigate factors concerning variability and the meaning of individual experience in social context. A wider array of family configurations and real experiences need to be introduced into our emerging individualized dynamic life-span psychology. By the same token, the humanistic approaches of Freud urge us to study creativity itself. In the future, such study need not be limited by a historical reductionism that seeks to explain creativity in terms of childhood experiences; instead, new formulations need to be made that encompass developmental transformations across life and that recognize the influence of new social relationships involving fresh patterns of experience.

The Spitzian tradition urges us to investigate communicative processes. Individuality in the context of a variety of interactive circumstances and in the context of a variety of intimate relationships of increasing complexity require study in both child and adult development. The Spitzian approach urges us to do cross-cultural and ethnographic research. In particular, it points to increasing investigations in developmental psycholinguistics and emotional signaling where we can mine such notions as interintentionality and intersubjectivity. In a sense, the Spitzian tradition prepares us for the new trend in cultural psychology, but it cautions us to avoid the extremes of cultural relativism and to keep in mind our common biology with its species-wide evolutionary origins. Finally, the Spitzian tradition urges us to investigate those developmental processes that regulate affective memories in individuals and in relationships. It urges us to accumulate knowledge that can be articulated in a general theory of self-transformations throughout development. Such a theory would give special attention to intrinsic variations in affect organization throughout life, as well as to reciprocal changes that occur with significant others.

However else we regard these prospects, we can acknowledge that history lives on in individual, dynamic ways in each of us. The contributions of Freud and Spitz, whether implicit or explicit, are part of that history, and, as such, they influence the way we as developmentalists come to regard our increasingly complex world.

REFERENCES

Abelson, R. P., & Sermat, V. (1962). Multidimensional scaling of facial expressions. *Journal of Experimental Psychology, 63,* 546–554.

Ackerknecht, E. H. (1959). *A short history of psychiatry* (S. Wolff, Trans.). New York: Hafner Publishing Company. (Original work published 1957.)

Ainsworth, M. D., Blehar, M., Waters, E., & Wall, S. (1978). *Patterns of attachment.* Hillsdale, NJ: Erlbaum.

Amsterdam, B. K. (1972). Mirror self-image reactions before age 2. *Developmental Psychology, 5,* 297–305.

Balint, M. (1948). Individual differences of behavior in early infancy and an objective way of recording them. *Journal of Genetic Psychology, 73,* 57–110.

Bates, E., Thal, D., & Janowsky, J. (in press). Early language development and its neural correlates. In I. Rapin & S. Segalowitz (Eds.), *Handbook of neuropsychology: Vol. 6. Child Neurology.* Amsterdam: Elsevier.

Bell, R. Q., & Harper, L. V. (1977). *Child effects on adults.* Hillsdale, NJ: Erlbaum.

Biringen, Z., & Robinson, J. (1991). Emotional availability in mother–child interactions: A reconcept for research. *American Journal of Orthopsychiatry, 6,* 258–271.

Bowlby, J. (1951). *Maternal care and mental health.* World Health Organization Monograph No. 2. Geneva, Switzerland: World Health Organization.

Bowlby, J. (1969). *Attachment and loss: Vol. 1. Attachment.* New York: Basic Books.

Bowlby, J. (1973). *Attachment and loss: Vol. 2. Separation, anxiety and anger.* New York: Basic Books.

Brazelton, T. B. (1983). Pediatrics. In R. N. Emde (Ed.), *René A. Spitz: Dialogues from infancy* (pp. 439–441). Madison, CT: International Universities Press.

Brazelton, T. B., Koslowski, B., & Main, M. (1974). The origins of reciprocity: The early mother-infant interaction. In M. Lewis & L. Rosenblum (Eds.), *The effect of the infant on its caregiver (Vol. 1).* New York: Wiley.

Brownell, C. A., & Kopp, C. B. (1991). Common threads, diverse solutions: Concluding commentary. *Developmental Review, 11,* 288–303.

Bruner, J. (1982). *Child's talk: Learning to use language.* New York: Norton.

Bruner, J. (1990). *Acts of meaning.* Cambridge, MA: Harvard University Press.

Buchsbaum, H. K., & Emde, R. N. (1990). Play narratives in thirty-six-month-old children: Early moral development and family relationships. *The Psychoanalytic Study of the Child, 40,* 129–155.

Campos, J. J. (1983). Psychology. In R. N. Emde (Ed.), *René A. Spitz: Dialogues from infancy* (pp. 445–447). Madison, CT: International Universities Press.

Chess, S., & Thomas, A. (1984). *Origins & evolution of behavior disorders—from infancy to early adult life.* New York: Brunner/Mazel.

Cicchetti, D., & Carlson, V. (1989). *Child maltreatment.* Cambridge, England: Cambridge University Press.

Clarke, A. M., & Clarke, A. D. B. (1976). *Early experience: Myth and evidence.* London: Open Books.

Clarke-Stewart, A. (1977). *Child care in the family.* San Diego: Academic Press.

Clyman, R. B. (in press). The procedural organization of emotions: A contribution from cognitive science to the psychoanalytic theory of therapeutic action. *Journal of the American Psychoanalytic Association* (Suppl.).

Cohen, D. J., Marans, S., Dahl, K., Marans, W., & Lewis, M. (1987). Analytic discussions with oedipal children. In A. J. Solnit & P. B. Neubauer (Eds.), *The psychoanalytic study of the child, 42,* 59–83. New Haven, CT: Yale University Press.

Cramer, B., Robert-Tissot, C., Stern, D. N., Serpa-Rusconi, S., DeMuralt, M., Besson, G., Palacio-Espapa, F., Bachmann, J., Knauer, D., Berney, C., & D'Arcis, U. (1990). Outcome evaluation in brief mother–infant psychotherapy: A preliminary report. *Infant Mental Health Journal, 11*(3), 278–300.

Emde, R. N. (1980). Levels of meaning for infant emotions: A biosocial view. In W. A. Collins (Ed.), *Development of cognition, affect and social relations. Minnesota Symposia on Child Psychology, Vol. 13* (pp. 1–37). Hillsdale, NJ: Erlbaum.

Emde, R. N. (1983). The prerepresentational self and its affective core. *The Psychoanalytic Study of the Child, 38,* 165–192.

Emde, R. N. (1988). Development terminable and interminable: I. Innate and motivational factors from infancy. *International Journal of Psycho-Analysis, 69,* 23–42.

Emde, R. N., Gaensbauer, T. J., & Harmon, R. J. (1976). Emotional expression in infancy: A biobehavioral study. *Psychological Issues: A Monograph Series, 10*(37, No. 1). Madison, CT: International Universities Press.

Emde, R. N., & Harmon, R. J. (1972). Endogenous and exogenous smiling systems in early infancy. *Journal of the American Academy of Child Psychiatry, 11,* 177–200.

Emde, R. N., Johnson, W. F., & Easterbrooks, M. A. (1988). The dos and don'ts of early moral development: Psychoanalytic tradition and current research. In J. Kagan & S. Lamb (Eds.), *The emergence of morality* (pp. 245–277). Chicago: University of Chicago Press.

Erikson, E. (1950). *Childhood and society.* New York: Norton.

Fairbairn, W. R. D. (1963). Synopsis of an object-relations theory of the personality. *International Journal of Psychoanalysis, 44,* 224–225.

Fenichel, O. (1945). *The psychoanalytic theory of neurosis.* New York: Norton.

Fraiberg, S. (1982). Pathological defenses in infancy. *Psychoanalytic Quarterly, 51*, 612–635.

Fraiberg, S., Adelson, E., & Shapiro, V. (1975). Ghosts in the nursery. *Journal of Child Psychiatry, 14*(3), 387–421.

Freud, S. (1953a). The interpretation of dreams. In J. Strachey (Ed. and Trans.), *The standard edition of the complete psychological works of Sigmund Freud* (Vol. 5, pp. 509–621). London: Hogarth Press. (Original work published 1900)

Freud, S. (1953b). Three essays on the theory of sexuality. In J. Strachey (Ed. and Trans.), *The standard edition of the complete psychological works of Sigmund Freud* (Vol. 7, pp. 125–245). London: Hogarth Press. (Original work published 1905)

Freud, S. (1955a). Beyond the pleasure principle. In J. Strachey (Ed. and Trans.), *The standard edition of the complete psychological works of Sigmund Freud* (Vol. 18, pp. 7–64). London: Hogarth Press. (Original work published 1920)

Freud, S. (1955b). Studies on hysteria. In J. Strachey (Ed. and Trans.), *The standard edition of the complete psychological works of Sigmund Freud* (Vol. 2). London: Hogarth Press. (Original work published 1893–1895)

Freud, S. (1957). Instincts and their vicissitudes. In J. Strachey (Ed. and Trans.), *The standard edition of the complete psychological works of Sigmund Freud* (Vol. 14, pp. 109–140). London: Hogarth Press. (Original work published 1915)

Freud, S. (1958). Remembering, repeating, and working through. In J. Strachey (Ed. and Trans.), *The standard edition of the complete psychological works of Sigmund Freud* (Vol. 12, pp. 145–156). London: Hogarth Press. (Original work published 1914)

Freud, S. (1959). Inhibitions, symptoms and anxiety. In J. Strachey (Ed. and Trans.), *The standard edition of the complete psychological works of Sigmund Freud* (Vol. 20, pp. 87–175). London: Hogarth Press. (Original work published 1926)

Freud, S. (1961). The ego and the id. In J. Strachey (Ed. and Trans.), *The standard edition of the complete psychological works of Sigmund Freud* (Vol. 19, pp. 19–29). London: Hogarth Press. (Original work published 1923)

Freud, S. (1962). Aetiology of hysteria. In J. Strachey (Ed. and Trans.), *The standard edition of the complete psychological works of Sigmund Freud* (Vol. 3, pp. 189–221). London: Hogarth Press. (Original work published 1896)

Freud, S. (1964a). An outline of psycho-analysis. In J. Strachey (Ed. and Trans.), *The standard edition of the complete psychological works of Sigmund Freud* (Vol. 23, pp. 141–207). London: Hogarth Press. (Original work published 1938)

Freud, S. (1964b). Analysis terminable and interminable. In J. Strachey (Ed. and Trans.), *The standard edition of the complete psychological works of Sigmund Freud* (Vol. 23, pp. 209–253). London: Hogarth Press. (Original work published 1937)

Frijda, N., & Phillipszoon, E. (1963). Dimensions of recognition of expression. *Journal of Abnormal and Social Psychology, 66*, 45–51.

Gladstone, W. H. (1962). A multidimensional study of facial expressions of emotion. *Australian Journal of Psychiatry, 14*, 95–100.

Goodman, G. S., & Hahn, A. (1987). Evaluating eyewitness testimony. In I. Weiner & A. Hess (Eds.), *Handbook of forensic psychology* (pp. 258–292). New York: Wiley.

Gottlieb, G. (1991). Experiential canalization of behavioral development: Theory. *Developmental Psychology, 27*(1), 4–13.

Grossmann, K. E., Grossmann, K., Huber, F., & Wartner, U. (1981). German children's behavior toward their mothers at 12 months and their fathers at 18 months in Ainsworth's strange situation. *International Journal of Behavioral Development, 4*, 157–181.

Guntrip, H. (1971). *Psychoanalytic theory, therapy, and the self.* New York: Norton.

Hartmann, H. (1939). *Psychoanalysis and the problem of adaptation.* Madison, CT: International Universities Press. (Original work published 1939)

Horowitz, M. J. (1988). *Psychodynamics and cognition.* Chicago: University of Chicago Press.

Jones, E. (1955). *The life and work of Sigmund Freud* (Vol. 2). New York: Basic Books.

Kagan, J., Kearsley, R., & Zelaso, P. (1978). *Infancy: Its place in human development.* Cambridge, MA: Harvard University Press.

Kaye, K. (1982). *The mental and social life of babies: How parents create persons.* Chicago: University of Chicago Press.

Kernberg, O. F. (1976). *Object relations theory and clinical psychoanalysis.* Northvale, NJ: Jason Aronson.

Kohut, H. (1971). *The analysis of the self.* Madison, CT: International Universities Press.

Kohut, H. (1977). *The restoration of the self.* Madison, CT: International Universities Press.

Lamb, M. E. (1977). Father–infant and mother–infant interaction in the first year of life. *Child Development, 48*, 167–181.

Lamb, M. E. (1978). Qualitative aspects of mother– and father–infant attachments. *Infant Behavior and Development, 1*, 265–275.

Lewis, M., & Brooks-Gunn, J. (1979). *Social cognition and the acquisition of self.* New York: Plenum Press.

Lichtenberg, J. D. (1989). *Psychoanalysis and motivation.* Hillsdale, NJ: Analytic Press.

Maccoby, E. E. (1990). Gender and relationships: A developmental account. *American Psychologist, 45*, 513–520.

Maccoby, E. E., & Martin, J. A. (1983). Socialization in the context of the family: Parent–child interaction. In P. H. Mussen (Series Ed.) & E. M. Hetherington (Vol. Ed.), *Handbook of child psychology: Vol. 4. Socialization, personality, and social development* (4th ed., pp. 1–101). New York: Wiley.

Mahler, M. S., Pine, F., & Bergman, A. (1975). *The psychological birth of the human infant: Symbiosis and individuation.* New York: Basic Books.

Main, M., & Weston, D. R. (1981). The quality of the toddler's relationship to mother and to father: Related to conflict behavior and the readiness to establish new relationships. *Child Development, 52,* 932–940.

McCall, R. B. (1979). The development of intellectual functioning in infancy and the prediction of later I.Q. In J. Osofsky (Ed.), *Handbook of infant development* (pp. 707–741). New York: Wiley.

Morgan, G. A., & Harmon, R. J. (1984). Developmental transformations and mastery motivation: Measurement and validation. In R. N. Emde & R. J. Harmon (Eds.), *Continuities and discontinuities in development* (pp. 263–291). New York: Plenum Press.

Osgood, C. (1966). Dimensionality of the semantic space for communication via facial expression. *Scandinavian Journal of Psychology, 7,* 1–30.

Osofsky, J. (Ed). (1979). *Handbook of infant development.* New York: Wiley.

Paul, H. (1967). The concept of scheme in memory theory [Monograph 18–19]. *Psychological Issues, 5*(23), 219–258.

Piaget, J. (1952). *The origins of intelligence in children* (2nd ed.). Madison, CT: International Universities Press.

Radke-Yarrow, M., Zahn-Waxler, C., & Chapman, M. (1983). Children's prosocial dispositions and behavior. In P. H. Mussen (Series Ed.) & E. M. Hetherington (Vol. Ed.), *Handbook of child psychology: Vol. 4. Socialization, personality, and social development* (4th ed., pp. 470–545). New York: Wiley.

Ritvo, L. B. (1990). *Darwin's influence on Freud: A tail of two sciences.* New Haven, CT: Yale University Press.

Robertson, J., & Robertson, J. (1971). Young children in brief separation: A fresh look. *Psychoanalytic Study of the Child, 26,* 264–315.

Russell, J. A., & Ridgeway, D. (1983). Dimensions underlying children's emotion concepts. *Developmental Psychology, 19,* 795–804.

Sandler, J. (1960). On the concept of superego. *Psychoanalytic Study of the Child, 15,* 128–162.

Schaffer, H., & Callender, W. (1959). Psychological effects of hospitalization in infancy. *Pediatrician, 24,* 528–539.

Schulman, A. H., & Kaplowitz, C. (1977). Mirror-image response during the first two years of life. *Developmental Psychobiology, 10,* 133–142.

Spitz, R. A. (1946a). Anaclitic depression. *Psychoanalytic Study of the Child, 2,* 313–342.

Spitz, R. A. (1946b). Hospitalism: A follow-up report on investigation described in Volume I, 1945. *Psychoanalytic Study of the Child, 2,* 113–117.

Spitz, R. A. (1955). Reply to Dr. Pinneau. *Psychological Bulletin, 7*(5), 453–549.

Spitz, R. A. (1957). *No and yes: On the genesis of human communication.* Madison, CT: International Universities Press.

Spitz, R. A. (1958). On the genesis of superego components. *The Psychoanalytic Study of the Child, 13,* 375–404.

Spitz, R. A. (1959). *A genetic field theory of ego formation.* Madison, CT: International Universities Press.

Spitz, R. A. (1961). Some early prototypes of ego defenses. *Journal of the American Psychoanalytic Association, 9,* 626–651.

Spitz, R. A. (1965). *The first year of life.* Madison, CT: International Universities Press.

Spitz, R. A. (1966). Metapsychology and direct infant observation. In R. Loewenstein, L. Newman, M. Schur, & A. Solnit (Eds.), *Psychoanalysis—a general psychology* (pp. 123–151). Madison, CT: International Universities Press.

Spitz, R. A. (1972). Bridges: On anticipation, duration, and meaning. *Journal of the American Psychoanalytic Association, 20,* 721–735.

Spitz, R. A. (1983a). Autoerotism: Some empirical findings and hypotheses on three of its manifestations in the first year of life. In R. N. Emde (Ed.), *René A. Spitz: Dialogues from infancy* (pp. 53–83). Madison, CT: International Universities Press. (Reprinted from *The psychoanalytic study of the child, Vol. 3/4* [pp. 85–118], 1949, Madison, CT: International Universities Press)

Spitz, R. A. (1983b). The derailment of the dialogue: Stimulus overload, action cycles and the completion gradient. In R. N. Emde (Ed.), *René A. Spitz: Dialogues from infancy* (pp. 161–178). Madison, CT: International Universities Press. (Reprinted from the *Journal of the American Psychoanalytic Association,* 1964, *12,* 752–775)

Spitz, R. A. (1983c). Diacritic and coenesthetic organizations: The psychiatric significance of a functional division of the nervous system into a sensory and emotive part. In R. N. Emde (Ed.), *René A. Spitz: Dialogues from infancy* (pp. 202–214). Madison, CT: International Universities Press. (Reprinted from *The Psychoanalytic Review,* 1945, *32,* 146–160)

Spitz, R. A. (1983d). The evolution of dialogue. In R. N. Emde (Ed.), *René A. Spitz: Dialogues from infancy* (pp. 179–195). Madison, CT: International Universities Press. (Reprinted from *Drives, affects, behavior, Vol. 2* [pp. 170–190] edited by M. Schur, 1965, Madison, CT: International Universities Press)

Spitz, R. A. (1983e). Life and the dialogue. In R. N. Emde (Ed.), *René A. Spitz: Dialogues from infancy* (pp. 147–160). Madison, CT: International Universities Press. (Reprinted from *Counterpoint: Libidinal object and subject,* edited by H. S. Gaskill, 1963, Madison, CT: International Universities Press)

Spitz, R. A., Emde, R. N., & Metcalf, D. R. (1970). Further prototypes of ego formation: A working paper from a research project on early development. *The Psychoanalytic Study of the Child, 25,* 417–441.

Spitz, R. A., & Wolf, K. M. (1946). The smiling response: A contribution to the ontogenesis of social relations. *Genetic Psychology Monographs, 34,* 57–125.

Stern, D. N. (1977). *The first relationship: Mother and infant.* Cambridge, MA: Harvard University Press.

Stern, D. N. (1985). *The interpersonal world of the infant.* New York: Basic Books.

Stoller, R. J. (1980). A different view of oedipal conflict. In S. I. Greenspan & G. H. Pollock (Eds.), *The course of life, Vol. I. Infancy and early childhood* (pp. 589–602). Adelphi, MD: Mental Health Study Center.

Sulloway, F. J. (1979). *Freud: Biologist of the mind.* New York: Basic Books.

Watson, M. W., & Getz, K. (1990). The relationship between oedipal behaviors and children's family role concepts. *Merrill-Palmer Quarterly, 36*(4), 487–505.

Welsh, M., & Pennington, B. (1988). Assessing frontal lobe functioning in children: Fuse from developmental psychology. *Developmental Neuropsychology, 4,* 199–230.

Wertsch, J. V. (1991). *Voices of the mind: A sociocultural approach to mediated action.* London: Harvester Wheatsheaf.

White, R. W. (1963). Ego and reality in psychoanalytic theory. *Psychological Issues, Monograph No. 11.* Madison, CT: International Universities Press.

Winnicott, D. W. (1965). Ego distortion in terms of true and false self. In *The maturational processes and the facilitating environment.* Madison, CT: International Universities Press.

Wolff, P. (1960). The developmental psychologies of Jean Piaget and psychoanalysis. [Monograph 5]. *Psychological Issues, II*(1). Madison, CT: International Universities Press.

Woodworth, R. S., & Schlosberg, H. S. (1954). *Experimental psychology.* New York: Holt.

Yarrow, L. J., McQuiston, S., MacTurk, R. H., McCarthy, M. E., Klein, R. P., & Vietze, P. M. (1983). Assessment of mastery motivation during the first year of life: Contemporaneous and cross-age relationships. *Developmental Psychology, 19,* 159–171.

Zeanah, C. H., & Barton, M. L. (1989). Introduction: Internal representations and parent–infant relationships [Special issue]. *Infant Mental Health Journal, 10*(3), 135–141.

8

JOHN B. WATSON'S LEGACY: LEARNING AND ENVIRONMENT

FRANCES DEGEN HOROWITZ

In his time, John Broadus Watson (1878–1958) was controversial. So he remains. In preparation for this reflective essay on his legacy to developmental psychology, I sent a questionnaire to a nonrandom sample of mostly senior developmental psychologists.[1] The 45 respondents ranged widely in their perceptions of Watson's contributions and in their evaluations. Watson's name, it appears, can still elicit strongly negative reactions. For example, in relation to his contribution to developmental psychology and psychology in general, Watson was described as "an embarrassment," "harmful," and "very important, but mostly a negative influence." One

The original draft of this article was written while the author was at the University of Kansas.

Reprinted from *Developmental Psychology*, 28, 360–367. Copyright 1992 by the American Psychological Association.

[1] I wish to acknowledge the following people, who responded to the survey: Donald Baer, Harry Beilin, Sidney Bijou, Andy Collins, John Colombo, Cynthia Deutsch, John Flavell, Norman Garmezy, Roberta Golinkoff, Charlie Greenbaum, John Hagen, Willard Hartup, Aletha Huston, Dick Jessor, Jerome Kagen, William Kessen, Claire Kopp, Michael Lamb, Jonas Langer, Lewis Lipsitt, Bob McCall, Neal Miller, Edward Morris, David Palermo, Anne Pick, Herb Pick, Robert Siegler, Hayne Reese, Carolyn Rovee-Collier, Arnold Sameroff, Irving Sigel, Charles Spiker, Joe Spradlin, Harold Stevenson, Sheldon White, Mont Wolf, and John Wright, plus eight other respondents who chose not to provide their name.

respondent said his "main contribution was obfuscation," another that "he had little lasting effect," and yet another that the "long-term effect of Watson was harmful."

Other comments were more positively valenced, such as that his "biggest contribution was balancing the scales between nature and nurture by overstating the case," his "major contribution was to establish behavior as an important phenomenon in its own right," his "thoroughgoing empirical orientation was of the greatest import," and his "methodological behaviorism is to be found in neobehaviorism, behavior analysis and much of cognitive psychology." One person wrote, "Contemporary developmental psychology would not be the same had not Watson contributed to this field."

John B. Watson died more than 35 years ago. His active contributions to the field of psychology ceased more than 50 years ago, and an evaluation of him and his work still evokes strong reactions and little consensus about his legacy. About half of the respondents rated Watson on the positive side in agreeing that his main contribution was in the area of methodology; the other half shaded to the disagreeing side. A few more than half felt he had ignored biological variables, but the remainder tended to disagree with that characterization.

Diversity of opinion is rife in developmental psychology today, but when asked to evaluate the theoretical and methodological contributions of Baldwin, Binet, Darwin, Freud, Gesell, Hall, Lewin, Piaget, and Vygotsky, this same group of respondents showed much more consensus. This was true even for the figures in the list whose active careers had ceased around the same time as or before Watson's. For example, the theoretical contributions were strongly and positively acknowledged for Darwin, Freud, Lewin, Piaget, and Vygotsky. There was also a general consensus about the methodological contributions of Binet, Lewin, and Piaget.

Evaluating John B. Watson's legacy to developmental psychology thus appears to involve a considerably more complex set of considerations than is the case for other major figures. Indeed, some of the respondents objected to identifying Watson as a developmentalist, claiming that he was, at best, a psychologist concerned only with defining psychology as a natural science and, at worst, a dogmatist who went far beyond his data to popularize his beliefs about development. If there was any consensus to be found, it was that Watson's tireless championing of behaviorism as the only acceptable way of looking at behavior succeeded in making his point of view the dominant one for many years.

To be sure, there were balanced evaluations: Some of them were thoughtful and lengthy, pointing out that Watson had to be evaluated in the context of his time, that his extreme views were necessary to establish behaviorism, and that the field was the better for it in the long run even as less dogmatic perspectives came to pass. There was also consensus, among those who chose to comment on it, that the extreme nature of his environmentalism as it was translated into popular child-rearing advice was regrettable.

It will be useful, in examining Watson's legacy to developmental psychology, to consider his contributions in his own time, his influence in the years after he ceased to be a contributor, and his current and perhaps future impact.

IN HIS OWN TIME

The opening sentences of Watson's (1913) manifesto, "Psychology as the Behaviorist Views It," declare clearly and unequivocally that "psychology as a behaviorist views it is a purely objective experimental branch of natural science. Its theoretical goal is the prediction and control of behavior" (Watson, 1913, p. 158). He was, as everyone notes, sounding the charge against introspection, establishing a purely American position in the field, and, interestingly enough, in a somewhat anti-Darwinian spirit, suggesting there was no necessary relationship between the laws governing animal behavior and those describing human behavior.

Seven years later Watson was deeply embroiled in the nature–nurture controversy. He had claimed the principles of learning as the central and practically only variable controlling the acquisition of human behavior. He had come to focus his attention largely on the application of behaviorism to the study of the behavior of infants and young children. And he was soon to leave his academic position at Johns Hopkins University and take up employment in the field of advertising even though he would continue to write about behaviorism and to engage in the popularization of his ideas in magazines and on the radio for almost 20 years (Buckley, 1989; Nance, 1970).

It is not easy to separate the impact of Watson's ideas about behavior and development in his own time from Watson's persona. By all accounts he was a man given to opportunism, to making extreme statements, to evincing strong ego needs for visibility and notoriety, and to displaying a cold and imperious style. He did not have many personal supporters when he was ousted from Johns Hopkins University in the wake of what was then considered public scandal in relation to his divorce and remarriage (Buckley, 1989). It is not clear whether any university would hire him after that, and he went, quite profitably, into the field of advertising, where his application of behavioristic principles was very successful.

Although the 1913 statement defining the behavioristic view of psychology was not about development, Watson's major focus, ultimately, was on the development of behavior. Even so, many developmentalists today do not count him as a developmentalist. In his time, neither Watson nor most of his contemporary developmentalists distinguished between behavioral development and the acquisition of specific responses. Gesellians saw behavioral acquisition and development as an unfolding of largely inherited behaviors. Watson—taking an opposing, environmental point of view—credited learning, namely conditioning, as the sole process responsible for development.

By the time Watson published the first edition of his text, *Psychology From the Standpoint of a Behaviorist*, in 1919 (which had second and third revised editions in 1924 and 1929, respectively), he was applying behavioristic analyses to development and using the analyses to explain the acquisition of behavior. The basic principles he asserted in the 1919 publication were repeated in his 1924 publication, *Behaviorism* (Watson, 1924/1970), and are relevant to my discussion. First, Watson exhibited a healthy respect for the biological functions of the human organism, discussing at length what was then known about genes, the nervous system, and the human muscular system. He recognized the human body as an extremely complex organismic system that was highly integrated with the behavioral system. He was wont to stress, again and again, that the body acts as a whole and that behavior is rooted in and roots the organism.

The second observation is that Watson clearly believed that learning was almost entirely responsible for behavioral development but also acknowledged the role of structural change. In fact, in discussing the motor behaviors that develop in the infant and young child, he used italics to stress the point:

> *In the great majority of these later activities* [i.e., crawling, standing, sitting up, walking, running, jumping] *it is difficult to say how much of the act as a whole is due to training or conditioning. A considerable part is unquestionably due to the growth changes in structure, and the remainder is due, we believe, to training or conditioning.* (Watson, 1924/1970, p. 135–136)

A third observation involves the strategies and program Watson advocated for developmental research. He stressed the need to study infants, he focused heavily on the central role of emotions, and most obviously, he was relentless in his insistence on learning as the major mechanism for explaining behavior and development. He had already used the experimental method to show learning as the basis for the acquisition of emotional responses in the young infant. The particular experiment for which Watson is most known purported to demonstrate how emotional reactions in a young child could be conditioned and to suggest, by implication, that this was the model for the acquisition of most emotional responses (Watson & Rayner, 1920). This experimental effort, involving the use of infants to study emotional behavior, was considered a breakthrough, though there had been earlier reports of the conditioning of motor responses using infants

(Krasnogorski, 1909; Mateer, 1918). Its findings and advocacy for the experimental strategy were strengthened in subsequent reports by Jones of experiments designed to show the conditioning and the unconditioning of the fear response in the very young child (Jones, 1924a, 1924b).

Watson's developmental model was exceedingly simple, containing no discussion of stages and little of sequences; there was no consideration that learning principles were in any way influenced by the age of the child. Furthermore, the developmental progression, despite the nod to structural change as a variable, was linear and cumulative.

Finally, *Behaviorism* (Watson, 1924/1970) reflects the major thrust of Watson's position, the aspect that served as the main lightning rod for his critics and caricaturists then and now: a practically unqualified belief in the role of experience and environment in shaping the human behavioral repertoire:

> Give me a dozen healthy infants, well-formed, and my own specified world to bring them up in and I'll guarantee to take any one at random and train him to become any type of specialist I might select—doctor, lawyer, artist, merchant-chief and, yes, even beggar-man and thief, regardless of his talents, penchants, tendencies, abilities, vocations and race of his ancestors. (Watson, 1924/1970, p. 104)

This passage is widely quoted and often ridiculed, but it is generally provided without the two sentences that follow it:

> I am going beyond my facts and I admit it, but so have the advocates of the contrary and they have been doing it for many thousands of years. Please note that when this experiment is made I am to be allowed to specify the way the children are to be brought up and the type of world they have to live in. (Watson, 1924/1970, p. 104)

Throughout the book, Watson the scientist took care to indicate the limitations of the data and the need for more research. After presenting a strong argument for the pervasiveness of conditioning of emotional reactions, he concluded with a cautionary note drawing the reader's attention to the fact that all his conclusions "are based now upon too few cases and too few experiments" (Watson, 1924/1970, p. 195), but he was optimistic that those already at work on the problems would rectify the situation.

Watson was not only scientist but advocate, in this book and elsewhere. The aspect of Watson's career that elicits the strongest negative reactions was his willing and unqualified popularization of his belief in the efficacy of extreme measures of environmental control in the form of advice to parents and teachers about the rearing of children. For example, he took the position that physical affection and expressions of love impeded good development. His judgments about what was good and bad for children rested on a model in which he advised that it was good to limit the influence of emotion on behavior and to train children so as to maximize independence and skill acquisition. Interestingly, he appeared to accept Freud's observations, made reference to Freudian concepts, and believed them entirely amenable to a learning analysis.

By any standard, his environmentalism was unbridled. He saw no role for inherited characteristics as ultimately having any determining role in developmental outcome. He did not deny genetic influences, but he believed that what the environment provided in the way of experience and training could override organismic variables and ultimately determine developmental outcome. Watson's view about human potential was egalitarian in the extreme, and he plied the perspective in every arena.

Watson did not shy away from admitting that there are inherited differences, but he made a distinction between the inheritance of structures and the inheritance of function. The former was clearly heritable, the latter not. Function was the result of how the environment shaped the hereditary structure, such shaping beginning in the prenatal environment. He rejected behavioral differences as being due to racial or other hereditary variables, claiming that environmental experience alone would account for observed differences (Watson, 1924/1970). Watson, on every issue, took the extreme environmental position in the nature–nurture controversy.

A tireless advocate for the relevance of psychology, Watson believed strongly in the application of psychological principles to the solution of practical problems. He plumped for the importance of applied research; his view of its potential for doing good in society was optimistic in the extreme. In some of this he was not unlike Gesell. Perhaps it was part of the American zeitgeist that Gesell and Watson both believed that the application of the principles of development (in Watson's case the principles of learning) to the rearing of children would result in happier children, despite Gesell's not buying any of Watson's environmental determination of developmental outcome.

The America of Watson and of Gesell was coming to value science more and more, to see science as a panacea for social ills. Industrialization had taken hold. Science applied to making an industrialized society efficient and socially progressive was the desideratum. Watson's ideas about social engineering were a positive fit for the times.

WATSON DIFFUSED

By the end of the 1930s, John B. Watson had been separated from academic psychology and laboratory science for almost 15 years. His expression of his own point of view remained static, unperturbed by new data or theoretical advance. His active participation in psychology had begun to decline, but his methodological behavioristic credo that insisted on the necessity for objectively collected, independently verifiable data gained wide acceptance and became the standard for doing psychological science.

Though Watson's persona was beginning to fade from the field, his influence spread to experimental psychology, to social psychology, and to developmental psychology. Clark Hull and his Yale colleagues and students took up the interest in conditioning. They elaborated on Watson and Pavlov and explored the parameters of classical and instrumental conditioning. They embellished the philosophical rationale for behaviorism by adopting the point of view of the logical positivists; they made formal theory drive experimental research in a manner exceedingly more sophisticated than Watson's efforts (Hull, 1943). One difference between the Hullians and Watson was that the Hullians were more inclined than Watson to see animal behavior as an analogue for simple human behavior.

A Watsonian emphasis on stimulus–response (S–R) relations and the primacy of learning in the context of a Hullian approach found outlets in work on imitation (Miller & Dollard, 1941), frustration and aggression (Miller, 1941), and personality and psychopathology (Dollard & Miller, 1950). Watson's belief in the efficacy of studying the young, relatively naive organism to understand how the principles of learning operated was reflected in the flourishing field of experimental child psychology (McCandless & Spiker, 1956).

The explicit developmental emphasis in all of these efforts was mainly muted. There was not much developmental theory per se guiding the research. A linear, cumulative model was generally accepted, if not articulated, though an early study by Kuenne (1946) introduced something of a counterweight. Kuenne's work on transposition suggested that the level of a child's language development modified how learning occurred, thus introducing a quite modest developmental caveat into the learning literature. A stronger developmental focus was eventually to find expression in the work of the Kendlers (H. H. Kendler & T. S. Kendler, 1961, 1969; T. S. Kendler & H. H. Kendler, 1959, 1966; T. S. Kendler, H. H. Kendler, & Learnard, 1962).

The translation of Freudian theory into behavioristic terms and an emphasis on dyadic interactions stimulated what eventually was to become social learning theory (Sears, 1951). A stimulus–response analysis married to Freudian developmental stages provided for a strong behavioristically oriented developmental approach with ties back to Watson through the Miller-Dollard work. During the 1950s Watson's methodological influence was unquestioned. His methodological influence on developmental and child psychology research was pervasive. So, to a lesser degree, was his environmentalism.

Watson's most direct descendent is generally identified as B. F. Skinner. Skinner published *The Behavior of Organisms* in 1938, focusing on operant learning as the basic mechanism controlling behavioral acquisition.

The influence of this book may have been restricted by the subsequent onset of World War II and by the diversion of the efforts of most psychologists, Skinner included, to the war effort. An alternate view is that Skinner's effort would, in any event, have been eclipsed by the intensity of the debate between Hull and Tolman and the advocates for their positions.[2]

Skinner's (1953) publication of *Science and Human Behavior* restated many of the basic views of the 1938 book, though it was less theoretical and had a more applied focus. A reading of *Science and Human Behavior* gives one a strong sense of being in contact with "Watson updated" and "Watson sophisticated," although Skinner's emphasis on the overriding importance of contingent reinforcement in the shaping of human behavior might well have been deemed too teleological by Watson. The empirical work stimulated by Skinner was fully in the Watsonian methodological tradition and revived the labeling of these efforts as *radical behaviorism*, with *radical* suggesting extremism.

Watson and Skinner shared an unyielding commitment to environmentalism, though Skinner's analysis was placed in a larger evolutionary context than Watson ever entertained (Skinner, 1974). Skinner advocated an almost singular focus on operant conditioning; Watson recognized both instrumental and classical conditioning. Watson's interest in classical conditioning stemmed, in part, from his conviction about the centrality of emotional behavior. He felt, from an applied point of view, that it was important to be very careful about how the emotions were conditioned early in life so as to shape an independent, self-reliant, and unemotional personality that would thus result in the most functional and happy of people.

The application of the Skinnerian approach to study the basic principles of learning in children was taken up by Bijou (1955, 1957, 1958) and Bijou and Baer (1961, 1963). The basic research on children's learning continued, but it was the growth of applied research under the rubric of *behavior modification* or *behavior analysis* that came to characterize the Skinnerians. Watson's vision for an applied psychological science driven by experimental results was to find its fullest realization in the work inspired by Skinnerian principles. Skinner, himself, had served the theoretical vision in writing *Walden Two* (1948).

Watson would have cheered the outpouring of research designed to apply behaviorism to the real world, research conducted first by Skinnerians and subsequently in fields such as behavioral medicine, industrial and organizational psychology, and community psychology. Particularly, Watson would have applauded the testing and application of the principles of learning to improve the functioning of persons with mental and physical hand-

---

[2] I am indebted to the anonymous reviewer for this alternative perspective.

icaps, to improve classroom deportment and learning, and to modify the behavior of delinquent youths.

In 1970 the *Journal of Applied Behavioral Analysis* was founded. It lent the field of applied behaviorism a professional stamp. A year before, in his essay on "Behaviorism at Fifty," Skinner declared, "In the fifty years since a behavioristic philosophy was first stated, facts and principles bearing on the basic issues have steadily accumulated" (1969, p. 228). Watson would have, with gratification, agreed.

WATSON'S INFLUENCE NOW AND IN THE FUTURE

Gustav Bergmann (1956) considered that John Broadus Watson was, with the exception of Freud, "the most important figure in the history of psychological thought during the first half of the century" (p. 265). Skinner's obituary for Watson, appearing in *Science*, likened Watson's stature to that of Darwin and Lloyd Morgan (Skinner, 1959). Bergmann's estimate rested solely on Watson's methodological contribution of wresting psychology from introspection and mentalisms. He deemed Watson's social philosophy and what he called Watson's metaphysical outlook as "silly" (Bergmann, 1956). Today Skinner is widely—and somewhat erroneously—regarded as being as arch an environmentalist as Watson was; Skinner's estimate of Watson, however, was that his extreme environmentalism and his inclination for being polemical undermined both his impact and his effectiveness.

One does not know, of course, how and to what degree Watson's ideas would have changed had he lived the rest of his life as an active empirical psychologist or, consequently, what impact he might have had on the field of developmental psychology. It is something of a paradox that in the 1950s Bergmann and Skinner placed Watson in the same league as Darwin and Freud, whereas some psychologists today regard Watson as an embarrassment and as having done harm to the field. Some today make the quite harsh judgment that Watson cost psychology in general, and developmental psychology in particular, 50 years of floundering, using a wrong and unproductive paradigm. Others still see, on balance, Watson's legacy as positive and enduring. Some of the distinctions that he insisted on making with respect to definitional and methodological practices, for example, have remained cornerstones in psychology. Definitional standards for stimuli and responses and criteria for making objective and reliable observations can be traced back to Watson and continue to characterize acceptable investigatory practices today.

To weigh these contradictory estimates of Watson's contribution, it is necessary to consider the current condition of developmental psychology, particularly as practiced in the United States. The present state of affairs in the field can be traced to the late 1960s and early 1970s. At that time, by many accounts, S-R psychology and behaviorism and its strong environmentalist orientation were, with the exception of the Skinnerian brand, eclipsed (overthrown?) by the organismic/cognitive revolution (Horowitz, 1987; Stevenson, 1983). At first this was fueled by American developmentalists' having discovered Piaget. There followed an almost "gee whiz" response as it was shown that infants and young children were capable of much more complex behavior than had been previously supposed (Kessen, Haith, & Salapatek, 1970; Stone, Smith, & Murphy, 1973).

At the same time, the development of some new methodologies involving techniques to study habituation in infants (Berlyne, 1958; Fantz, 1964) and assessments of neonatal behavior produced an explosion of information on infant capabilities. As a result of many demonstrations, it became obvious that there was a much more well developed behavioral repertoire in the newborn and young infant human organism than anyone had previously described (Brazelton, 1973; Kessen et al., 1970; Stone et al., 1973).

This growing body of evidence about the abilities of the infant and young child served to challenge the behaviorist assumption that learning accounted for the acquisition of early behavior. This evidence, coupled with the demonstration of the Piagetian phenomena, particularly in the realm of cognitive development through adolescence, called into question the entire behavioristic enterprise. If Gesell's name did not surface in the discussion of these matters, it was certainly a return, albeit in a more sophisticated framework, to some of Gesell's basic tenets.

Even as Piagetian theory was being modified, the discussions of systems theory and transactional theory applied to developmental theory offered attractive theoretical alternatives to behaviorism (Sameroff & Chandler, 1975; Sameroff, 1983). The infant was not a tabula rasa; experience could not write anything it wished. No one denied some role to learning, but it certainly was not considered a central mechanism. Basic research on learning in children declined precipitously. Studies of children's learning were increasingly confined to research inspired by Skinnerian principles.

At the same time, the 1960s bloom of optimism about the power of early intervention programs to change developmental outcome began to fade (A. M. Clarke & A. B. D. Clarke, 1976). Though many of these programs were not behavioristic in their programmatic orientation, the rationale for mounting them was strongly influenced by the environmentalism that had predominated since the 1930s. However, the fledgling intervention efforts had failed to demonstrate dramatic changes in developmental outcome, school achievement, or IQ (Horowitz & Paden, 1973; Jensen, 1969). Advances in genetics identifying genetic contributions to behavior strengthened further the growing belief in organismically determined behavioral development and developmental outcome. No one was suggesting that experience and the environment were irrelevant to behavioral development, but the pendulum had clearly swung away from environmental determinism and toward genetic and organismic determinism.

The inclination to cognitivism in developmental psychology and to organismic and genetic determinism is, however, just that: an inclination rather than a reflection of consensus. In fact, clear theoretical labels are hard to come by among today's developmentalists. When the 45 respondents to the survey used in preparation for writing this essay were asked to identify how they classified themselves theoretically, a total of 26 different labels were used. The two most frequent classifications were *eclectic* and *constructivist*, each typifying four persons. Eight persons used some variation of *cognitive*: *cognitive developmental, cognitive social learning, sociocognitive*. Adding the one who used *cognitive behaviorism, cognitive* was by far the most frequently used theoretical term. Seven persons, however, used some form of *behaviorist*: *descriptive behaviorist, behavior analyst, liberalized S-R*, or *social interactive behaviorist*. One person proposed *social evolutionary cognitive behaviorism* as a preferred label.

The respondents also did not agree about whether most current psychologists are, from a methodological point of view, functionally Watsonian behaviorists. A little over 60% disagreed or tended to disagree with such a claim. Thus, in this sample, there was a lack of agreement even about what many have felt was the methodological standard for the field. In response to a question asking whether the emphasis on learning and environment will reassert itself in the field, the respondents split almost evenly in their tending to agree or disagree that this was a likely possibility.

Although those responding to the questionnaire were not a random sample, almost all of the respondents were relatively senior developmentalists (see footnote 1), and they obviously represented a wide spectrum of opinion. The dispersion of self-describing theoretical labels and the ambivalence with respect to the likelihood of a return of emphasis on environment and learning suggest that developmental psychology is currently in a rather fluid theoretical period. In trying to identify Watson's legacy and the possibility of a Watsonian presence in the field in the coming years, one is struck by a number of contradictory possibilities.

Putting methodology aside, Watson's basic position was that the principles of learning would account for the largest share of behavioral development and developmental outcome and that these principles are exercised almost exclusively through environmental opportunities for children to learn. Though the theoretical interest in children's learning has waned, in fact, there is a great deal of research on learning in the field of education, as well as among those who identify themselves as Skinnerians. Though the belief that environment and experience are the main shapers of human behavioral development no longer exists in its extreme form, there is, in fact, widespread acceptance of the idea that experience is important to development. Intervention programs continue to be mounted, albeit often without any recourse to an explicit use of learning principles even as the intervention appears to rest on the assumption that experience will make a difference. Environment and experience are given importance in recent discussions of cultural diversity and how cultural experience contributes to the shaping of the behavioral repertoire. However, the mechanisms by which this occurs are often not addressed (Horowitz, 1987).

Transactional theory (Sameroff & Chandler, 1975) and dynamical systems theory (Thelen, 1990; Thelen, Kelso, & Fogel, 1987), as well as Vygotsky's theory (Brown, 1982; Rogoff, 1990), are heavily referenced these days and arrayed with the organismic approach. Yet an analysis of Vygotsky and of transactional theory, and even of systems theory, reveals that these approaches give a healthy role both to the environment and to learning in an interaction with the organism. No developmentalists totally exclude experience and the environment as variables contributing to developmental outcome, so one wonders whether the negative reactions to Watson and behaviorism are focused still on Watson's persona, or on what some have perceived as extreme Skinnerian claims for the power of the environment, or just on the simplistic nature of Watson's developmental approach.

One survey respondent stated that the misguided theoretical position of Watson and behaviorism was responsible for a loss of some 50 years of productive developmental research. Is it possible to ask whether the retreat from basic research on learning in a developmental context, the dismissal of Watson and behaviorism, and the isolation of much of applied Skinnerian research has not had *its* costs?

Is the current quite fluid state of developmental theory related to the lack of a clear vision about how to parse into the developmental equation a functional role for learning and environment in development? Is there now a sufficient body of new data that makes this a possibility?

There are a number of signs that the pendulum is swinging back to a middle position. The proposal for a structural/behavioral model to account for development outcome (Horowitz, 1987) suggests, among other things, a possible rapprochement between the behavioral and organismic emphases. It does this by focusing on the idea that a productive approach to under-standing behavioral development is to consider that there are two groups of behaviors that develop: those that are universal behaviors and those that are nonuniversal behaviors.

In the structural/behavioral model, the universally acquired behaviors are defined as species typical. They have an evolutionary base, and they occur with almost 100% probability in all normal human organisms. Although some environmental transactions—perhaps learning—are necessary for their acquisition, these behaviors are rooted in organismic characteristics. The nonuniversal behaviors are acquired only as learned behaviors and are dependent on environmental opportunity, though they may have a base in the universal behavioral repertoire. In the adult repertoire, the larger share of the repertoire probably is made up of nonuniversal behaviors. Furthermore, many of these define whether a person will be able to function productively and successfully in a society or culture.

From the perspective of the structural/behavioral model, a full understanding of development will not be achieved unless ways are found to account for the acquisition of both the universal and nonuniversal behaviors. This means psychologists must include in their scientific agenda basic research on all the mechanisms involved in learning.

Terms like *contextualism*, *transaction*, and *transcontextual*, as well as discussions of a developmental contextual model (Lerner, 1991), are broadening the perspective of developmental psychology. Thus behavior and development are placed in a dynamic systems perspective in which the organism is in constant transaction with the environment, particularly with the social environment (Cairns, 1991). Environment, experience, and the mechanisms that describe the organism–environmental relationships must, ultimately, include some understanding of how learning operates in dynamic systems.

The strongest case currently being made for the role of experience and environment in a systems context involves the recognition of the mutually influential gene–environment relationships. Here it is acknowledged that genetic expression requires an environmental context and is affected by variations in environment (Oyama, 1985). Expanding on Waddington's (1966) notions of the canalization of development, Gottlieb (1991) has proposed that normally occurring experience can also serve the canalization process. These ideas bring us full circle back to Watson.

Watson believed that environmental shaping of behavior began prenatally. His ideas stimulated Z-Y. Kuo, a skeptical Chinese scientist, to undertake in the 1930s and 1940s a series of experiments in which Kuo systematically altered the prenatal embryonic environments of chicks and other species to see if he could produce different behavioral repertoires. He found evidence for Watson's speculations. Due to the vagaries of life in China during those and subsequent years, Kuo's work did not become widely known in the United States until the 1960s and 1970s (Kuo, 1976).

Numerous studies supporting Kuo's data (and, indirectly, a number of Watson's ideas) have appeared. All of them demonstrate the same basic principle: Manipulations of prenatal and postnatal environments in a variety of animal species produce different patterns of behavior and affect behaviors once thought to be innate, genetically controlled, and unalterable (e.g., Gottlieb, 1978; Marler, 1977).

Watson's legacy to developmental psychology, aside from methodology, is the emphasis he placed on the importance of learning and experience in development and on the need to understand the principles by which learning and experience function. He insisted that learning and experience could be the sole elements determining development and took the position to its extremes. As soon as other data were seen as challenging Watson's assertions, dislike for both his dogmatism and his persona appears to have given critics broad license for dismissing and caricaturing him and all of behaviorism. His point of view has been labeled *mechanistic*, which is seen as synonymous with simplistic. Yet, mechanisms need not be simple, and complex systems are understandable only in terms of the mechanisms that account for their functioning. Is this likely to be less true for behavior?

What has flourished in the name of behaviorism has been largely associated with Skinner and with applied psychology, though not necessarily applied developmental psychology. Applied behaviorism has been relatively isolated from the mainstream of developmental psychology. In the broadening view of contexts and transactions and dynamic interchange that appears to be gaining in developmental psychology, will there be a return to some meaningful inclusion of the processes of learning in the developmental research agenda?

Prognostication about the direction in which a scientific field will move is risky business. The strength of Watson and behaviorism in focusing on learning is that it is a focus on process. To understand behavior, development, contexts, and systems, we must ultimately understand the processes that account for the phenomena of interest. It is difficult to think that much progress will be made on understanding processes in development without understanding how the principles of learning operate across the life span.

Today's discussions of developmental theory and developmental psychology refer to an exceedingly more complex enterprise than existed in Watson's time. We now have many more facts about both behavioral and biological events. The ability to relate behavioral and biological functioning and social context as interacting or transacting with one another and to think of doing this developmentally has put us on the threshold of a much more powerful developmental science than we might have envisioned even 10 years ago. If Watson has any enduring legacy to the field of developmental psychology beyond his methodological manifesto, it is currently to be found in his active descendants. Among these is a small group of experimental child psychologists working still with Hull-Spence theory (e.g., Cantor & Spiker, 1989) or actively studying learning in young children using experimental techniques (e.g., Rovee-Collier, 1986; Rovee-Collier, Earley, & Stafford, 1989). A larger group works within the Skinnerian tradition (e.g., Poulson, Nunes, & Warren, 1989; Riegler & Baer, 1989). Watson's influence may continue in the future among those who elect to bring back into mainstream developmental psychology an emphasis on understanding the principles of learning and how they operate in developmental processes.

Watson's methodological position has been widely regarded as his most enduring influence. Yet, many psychologists today deny that they are methodological behaviorists. It is not clear whether this is a rejection of the label or of the methodological tenets themselves. A scan of the basic psychological journals reveals, still, a general use of the standards of independently verifiable observations in ways obviously Watsonian, though not necessarily involving only experimental paradigms. Watson's point of view on experience and environment has been moderated by most contemporary psychologists and some times dismissed. Yet there is considerable evidence that the influence of experience and the environment on development are acknowledged even as the mechanisms by which they operate are not articulated or a focus of much theoretically sophisticated research. Watson's S-R psychology is clearly of the past. Yet, even in complex systems, there are relationships of stimuli and responses for which psychologists need to account.

John Broadus Watson was a controversial man. His theory was controversial. His advocacy for an uncompromising position on the role of the environment was extreme. It will be to the benefit of developmental psychology if we can finally overcome his persona, his ill-advised extremism, and the unproductive caricaturing of both in favor of a greater understanding and appreciation of the roles that learning and experience play in behavioral development. The data, if not human tolerance, ought to push us in that direction.

REFERENCES

Bergmann, G. (1956). The contribution of John B. Watson. *Psychological Review*, 63, 265–276.

Berlyne, D. E. (1958). The influence of the albedo and complexity of stimuli on the visual fixation in the human infant. *British Journal of Psychology*, 49, 315–318.

Bijou, S. W. (1955). A systematic approach to an experimental analysis of young children. *Child Development*, 26, 161–169.

Bijou, S. W. (1957). Patterns of reinforcement and resistance to extinction in young children. *Child Development*, 28, 47–54.

Bijou, S. W. (1958). Operant extinction after fixed interval schedules with young children. *Journal of Experimental Analysis of Behavior*, 1, 25–49.

Bijou, S. W., & Baer, D. M. (1961). *Child development* (Vol. 1). New York: Appleton-Century-Crofts.

Bijou, S. W., & Baer, D. M. (1963). Some methodological contributions from a functional analysis of child development. In L. P. Lipsitt & C. C. Spiker (Eds.), *Advances in child development and behavior* (Vol. 1, pp. 147–196). San Diego: Academic Press.

Brazelton, T. B. (1973). *Neonatal Behavioral Assessment Scale*. Philadelphia: Lippincott.

Brown, A. L. (1982). Learning and development: The problems of compatibility, access and induction. *Human Development, 25,* 89–115.

Buckley, K. W. (1989). *Mechanical man: John Broadus Watson and the beginnings of behaviorism.* New York: Guilford Press.

Cairns, R. B. (1991). Multiple metaphors for a singular idea. *Developmental Psychology, 27,* 23–26.

Cantor, J. H., & Spiker, C. C. (1989). Children's learning revisited: The contemporary scope of modified Spence discrimination theory. In H. W. Reese (Ed.), *Advances in child behavior and development* (Vol. 21, pp. 121–151). San Diego: Academic Press.

Clarke, A. M., & Clarke, A. B. D. (1976). *Early experience: Myth & evidence.* New York: Free Press.

Dollard, J., & Miller, N. E. (1950). *Personality and psychotherapy.* New York: McGraw-Hill.

Fantz, R. L. (1964). Visual experience in infants: Decreased attention to familiar patterns relative to novel ones. *Science, 146,* 688–690.

Gottlieb, G. (1978). Development of species identification in ducklings. Change in species-specific perception caused by auditory deprivation. *Journal of Comparative & Physiological Psychology, 92,* 375–387.

Gottlieb, G. (1991). Experiential canalization of behavioral development: Theory. *Developmental Psychology, 27,* 413.

Horowitz, F. D. (1987). *Exploring developmental theories: Toward a structural/behavioral model of development.* Hillsdale, NJ: Erlbaum.

Horowitz, F. D., & Paden, L. Y. (1973). The effectiveness of environmental intervention programs. In B. M. Caldwell & H. N. Ricciuti (Eds.), *Review of child development research* (Vol. 3, pp. 331–401). Chicago: University of Chicago Press.

Hull, C. L. (1943). *Principles of behavior.* New York: Appleton-Century-Crofts.

Jensen, A. R. (1969). How much can we boost IQ and scholastic achievement? *Harvard Educational Review, 39,* 11–23.

Jones, M. C. (1924a). The elimination of children's fears. *Journal of Experimental Psychology, 7,* 382–390.

Jones, M. C. (1924b). A laboratory study of fear: The case of Peter. *Pedagogical Seminary, 31,* 308–315.

Kendler, H. H., & Kendler, T. S. (1961). Effect of verbalization on discrimination rehearsal shifts in children. *Science, 134,* 1619–1620.

Kendler, H. H., & Kendler, T. S. (1969). Reversal-shift behavior: Some basic issues. *Psychological Bulletin, 72,* 229–232.

Kendler, T. S., & Kendler, H. H. (1959). Reversal and nonreversal shifts among kindergarten children. *Journal of Experimental Psychology, 58,* 56–60.

Kendler, T. S., & Kendler, H. H. (1966). Optional shifts of children as a function of number of training trials on the initial discrimination. *Journal of Experimental Child Psychology, 3,* 216–224.

Kendler, T. S., Kendler, H. H., & Learnard, B. (1962). Mediated responses to size and brightness as a function of age. *American Journal of Psychology, 75,* 571–586.

Kessen, W., Haith, M., & Salapatek, P. (1970). Human infancy: A bibliography and guide. In P. H. Mussen (Ed.), *Carmichael's manual of child psychology* (Vol. 1, 3rd ed., pp. 287–447). New York: Wiley.

Krasnogorski, N. (1909). Ueber die Bedingungsreflexe im Kindesalter [Conditioned reflexes in childhood]. *Jahrbuch für Kinderheitkunde und Physische Erziehung, 19,* 1–24.

Kuenne, M. R. (1946). Experimental investigation of the relation of language to transposition behavior in young children. *Journal of Experimental Psychology, 36,* 471–490.

Kuo, Z-Y. (1976). *The dynamics of development* (rev. ed.). New York: Plenum Press.

Lerner, R. M. (1991). Changing organism–context relations as the basic process of development: A developmental contextual perspective. *Developmental Psychology, 27,* 27–32.

Mateer, F. (1918). *Child behavior: A critical and experimental study of young children by the method of conditioned reflexes.* Boston: Badger.

Marler, P. (1977). Development and learning of recognition systems. In T. H. Bullock (Ed.), *Recognition of complex acoustic signals.* Berlin, Germany: Dahlem Konferenzen.

McCandless, B. R., & Spiker, C. C. (1956). Experimental research in child psychology. *Child Development, 27,* 75–80.

Miller, N. E. (1941). The frustration–aggression hypothesis. *Psychological Review, 48,* 337–342.

Miller, N. E., & Dollard, J. (1941). *Social learning and imitation.* New Haven, CT: Yale University Press.

Nance, R. D. (1970). G. Stanley Hall & John B. Watson as child psychologists. *Journal of the History of the Behavioral Sciences, 6,* 303–316.

Oyama, S. (1985). *The ontogeny of information.* Cambridge, England: Cambridge University Press.

Poulson, C. L., Nunes, L. R. de Paula, & Warren, S. F. (1989). Imitation in infancy: A critical review. In H. W. Reese (Ed.), *Advances in child development and behavior* (Vol. 21, pp. 271–298). San Diego: Academic Press.

Riegler, H. D., & Baer, D. M. (1989). A developmental analysis of rule-following. In H. W. Reese (Ed.), *Advances in child development and behavior* (Vol. 21, pp. 191–219). San Diego: Academic Press.

Rogoff, B. (1990). *Apprenticeship in thinking.* Oxford, England: Oxford University Press.

Rovee-Collier, C. (1986). The rise and fall of infant classical conditioning research: Its promise for the study of early development. In L. P. Lipsitt and C. Rovee-Collier (Eds.), *Advances in infancy research* (Vol. 4, pp. 139–159). Norwood, NJ: Ablex.

Rovee-Collier, C., Earley, L., & Stafford, S. (1989). Ontogeny of early event memory: III. Attentional determinants of retrieval at 2 and 3 months. *Infant Behavior and Development, 12,* 147–162.

Sameroff, A. J. (1983). Developmental systems: Contexts and evolution. In P. H. Mussen (Ed.) & W. Kessen (Vol. ed.), *Handbook of child psychology: Vol. 1. History, theory and methods* (pp. 273–294). New York: Wiley.

Sameroff, A. J., & Chandler, M. (1975). Reproductive risk and the continuum of caretaking casualty. In F. D. Horowitz (Ed.), *Review of child development research* (Vol. 4, pp. 187–244). Chicago: University of Chicago Press.

Sears, R. R. (1951). A theoretical framework for personality and social behavior. *American Psychologist, 6,* 476–483.

Skinner, B. F. (1938). *The behavior of organisms: An experimental analysis.* New York: Appleton-Century-Crofts.

Skinner, B. F. (1948). *Walden two.* New York: Macmillan.

Skinner, B. F. (1953). *Science and human behavior.* New York: Macmillan.

Skinner, B. F. (1959). John Broadus Watson, behaviorist. *Science, 129,* 197–198.

Skinner, B. F. (1969). Behaviorism at fifty. In B. F. Skinner (Ed.), *Contingencies of reinforcement: A theoretical analysis* (pp. 221–268). New York: Appleton-Century-Crofts.

Skinner, B. F. (1974). *About behaviorism.* New York: Knopf.

Stevenson, H. (1983). How children learn—the quest for a theory. In P. H. Mussen (Ed.) & W. Kessen (Vol. ed.), *Handbook of child psychology: Vol. 1. History, theory and methods* (pp. 213–236). New York: Wiley.

Stone, J., Smith, H., & Murphy, L. (Eds.). (1973). *The competent infant.* New York: Basic Books.

Thelen, E. (1990). Dynamical systems and the generation of individual differences. In J. Colombo & J. Fagen (Eds.), *Individual differences in infancy: Reliability, stability, prediction* (pp. 19–43). Hillsdale, NJ: Erlbaum.

Thelen, E., Kelso, J. A. S., & Fogel, A. (1987). Self-organizing systems and infant motor development. *Developmental Review, 7,* 39–65.

Waddington, C. H. (1966). *Principles of development and differentiation.* New York: Macmillan.

Watson, J. B. (1913). Psychology as the behaviorist views it. *Psychological Review, 20,* 158–177.

Watson, J. B. (1919). *Psychology from the standpoint of a behaviorist.* Philadelphia: Lippincott.

Watson, J. B. (1970). *Behaviorism* (rev. ed.). New York: Norton. (Original work published 1924)

Watson, J. B., & Rayner, R. (1920). Conditioned emotional reactions. *Journal of Experimental Psychology, 3,* 1–14.

III

THE MIDDLE YEARS: STAGES, NORMS, AND CULTURE

INTRODUCTION

THE MIDDLE YEARS: STAGES, NORMS, AND CULTURE

In this section, we explore the continuing legacies encountered in the earlier eras, but see how the promises of these beginnings reached fruition in the 1920–1940 era. The first four chapters of part 3 consider different manifestations of the continential intellectual tradition, as exemplified in the work of Piaget, Stern, Vygotsky, and Werner. All were influenced by this tradition to greater or lesser degrees, and all share a direct linkage to early philosophical traditions, as well as to the earlier writings of Baldwin and Hall.

In chapter 9, Beilin shows how the conceptual insights of Baldwin and the methodological innovations of Binet led Piaget to his monumental theory of cognitive growth. Piaget accomplished for cognitive development what Freud achieved for social and affective development. Together, these two theorists revolutionized the shape of developmental theory and research for a large part of this century. Although we tend to focus on only a small and early corpus of Piaget's work (largely his work in the 1920s and 1930s), Beilin provides a guide to the often neglected later works. Beilin argues that Piaget's influence on both past and current formulations of issues of cognitive development are without peer in the history of the field. A depth, breadth, and richness characterize the effort in a way that previously has not often been fully appreciated—a reminder of how little we really know about this major 20th-century thinker.

Some theorists stand apart from the mainstream movements of developmental psychology, while others provide clear and easily identifiable links with the past. Glick (chapter 10) focuses on Heinz Werner, who represents the Clark University tradition in developmental psychology started by G. Stanley Hall. Glick usefully locates Werner in the continental intellectual tradition that influenced Piaget, Stern, and to a lesser extent, Vygotsky. However, "in comparison to his rough contemporaries, Vygotsky or Piaget, Werner seems to have precipitously faded from view" (p. 292). Glick traces the reasons for the current relative obscurity of this original developmental theorist. Theories have their time and place, and views that are out of sync with current practice and tradition often fail to affect the field, although these same ideas, in another era, may have altered profoundly the theoretical course of our field. Glick argues that this, in part, accounts for the fate and fading of Werner's theory and influence. By his focus on processes rather than on achievements and on his dismissal of the legitimacy of separate categories (e.g., language, cognition, or affect) as convenient organizers that could guide empirical work, Werner's theory was viewed as difficult to assimilate into current theoretical schemes and, therefore, largely ignored. However, revived interest in dynamic systems theory (Smith & Thelen, 1993), as well as rekindled recognition of the value of Werner's microgenetic methodology (e.g., Siegler & Crowley, 1991) and the heightened appreciation of the interconnectedness of seemingly separate domains of development (e.g., interplay between language and cognition or affect and social behavior), suggests that Werner's theory may have more relevance to several contemporary trends than previously thought. Glick's invitation to reconsider the relevance of Werner's theorizing for our current developmental accounts may, in fact, be a timely one.

William Stern, another German developmentalist who preceded and influenced Werner, suffered the same fate of being largely unrecognized by subsequent developmental scholars. Most of us know Stern as the originator of the IQ score, which places him in a direct lineage with Binet. Few of us, however, appreciate the depth and range of Stern's contributions to developmental psychology. Kreppner (chapter 11) calls for a reevaluation of Stern's ideas and notes the similarities between Stern's early notions and many contemporary issues in developmental psychology. As an early contextualist, Stern was a fervent advocate of recognizing the interplay between *endowment*, or dispositions, and environmental conditions and offered a pioneering but decidely modern model of person–context relationships (e.g., Lerner, Magnusson). Kreppner places Stern squarely in the mainstream of historical figures in developmental psychology by noting his intellectual ties to both Baldwin and Piaget. Moreover, his work foreshadowed the later theorizing of Lewin, Werner, and Vygotsky. Kreppner's call for a ressurection of Stern is clearly well founded if we are to appreciate fully our own historical and theoretical roots.

Perhaps the most contemporary of our early theorists is Lev Vygotsky, whose writings have experienced a dramatic revival in the 1980s and 1990s. Wertsch and Tulviste (chapter 12) trace the reasons for the resurgence of interest in Vygotsky and the relevance of his ideas for contemporary developmental thought. Just as Baldwin recognized at the turn of the century, and Vygotsky agreed, cognition and social activity are closely linked. However, Vygotsky went beyond Baldwin not only by recognizing that all mental processes are embedded in social contexts but also by empirically demonstrating ways in which the social settings and relationships influence cognitive development. Of particular relevance for a modern developmental psychology that exists both within multicultural societies and in international cultural settings is Vygotsky's emphasis on the influential role of culture in human mental functioning. Moreover, Vygotsky's appreciation of history is also highlighted, an idea that is beginning to be recognized by contemporary life course theorists and by historically minded developmentalists as well (Baltes, 1987; Elder, Modell, & Parke, 1993). Finally, some of the misuses of Vygotsky are underscored as well, with an invitation to move beyond a crude caricature of Vygotsky to a more sophisticated understanding of his theoretical ideas.

While Piaget was busily watching the myriad of ways in which children of different ages fail to solve common problems relating to their physical world, Arnold Gesell and Myrtle McGraw were busy observing how human and nonhuman infants develop physically and in motor skills. These American pioneers provided a rich descriptive base and provocative theories of how children learn to crawl and walk, an accomplishment in its own domain that rivals Piaget's and Freud's contributions to their areas of cognition and affect.

Gesell was a maturationist, a strong advocate of biological destiny and a practitioner who recognized the value of norms for aiding in the detection of abnormalities. Just as Binet had provided a strategy for generating norms of intelligence, Gesell performed a similar service for the motor and growth arenas. Thelen and Adolph (chapter 13) challenge our field's simplistic views of Gesell as a strict maturation theorist. Instead, as is characteristic of the chapters in this book, the authors provide an argument and an example that illustrate the complexity of the theorist's views. For instance, Gesell paid more attention to environmental influences than was generally thought and pioneered the use of dynamic systems approaches to development, especially motor development. The relevance of Gesell's thinking for contemporary theory, especially dynamic systems theories, is highlighted in Thelen and Adolph's revisionist view of this early maturationalist. As with Binet, there are parts of Gesell that have largely remained obscure and underappreciated.

Myrtle McGraw was another early pioneer infant watcher and chronicler of infant growth and motor development. Although McGraw addressed many issues in common with Gesell, Bergenn and his colleagues (chapter 14) clearly differentiate the views and contributions of these two individuals. In contrast to Gesell, McGraw was much more balanced in her views about the interplay between biology and environment and offered an original and contemporary neuromuscular theory of development. She is very contemporary in her recognition of the importance of interdisciplinary collaboration in the investigation of developmental issues. The authors of this chapter highlight her seldom recognized contribution to our understanding of how attitudes shape our problem solving. Again, the chapter calls for a reevaluation of our views of McGraw that confronts the uniqueness and complexity of her theoretical positions. Clearly, there are many more reasons to remember McGraw than simply her famous twin study of Johnny and Jimmy. Finally, the chapter serves as a reminder that many women were important contributors to our early developmental science, although as McGraw's own career illustrates, barriers to recognition of their work and to regular academic and research positions were clearly evident for women scientists in these early years—barriers that still exist in the 1990s.

REFERENCES

Baltes, P. B. (1987). Theoretical propositions of life span developmental psychology: On the dynamics of growth and decline. *Developmental Psychology*, 23, 611–626.

Elder, G., Modell, J., & Parke, R. D. (Eds.). (1993). *Children in time and place.* Cambridge, England: Cambridge University Press.

Siegler, R. S., & Crowley, K. (1991). The microgenetic method: A direct means of studying cognitive development. *American Psychologist*, 46, 606–620.

Smith, L. B., & Thelen, E. (Eds.). (1993). *A dynamic systems approach to development.* Cambridge, MA: MIT Press.

9

JEAN PIAGET'S ENDURING CONTRIBUTION TO DEVELOPMENTAL PSYCHOLOGY

HARRY BEILIN

No one affected developmental psychology more than Jean Piaget (1896–1980).[1] From his earliest publications in the 1920s to the time of his death, the influence he exercised was extraordinary. His theory, which has no rival in developmental psychology in scope and depth, underwent change from beginning to end. With one posthumous publication appearing after another, it is still undergoing change. Nevertheless, the theory has maintained continuity in most of its core assumptions, despite one or another of its features being transformed by additions, deletions, or changes in emphasis and interpretation. In the end, it is more than a theory: It is a research program on a vast scale (Beilin, 1985). The number of experiments conducted by Piaget and his colleagues has never been tabulated,

Reprinted from *Developmental Psychology, 28*, 191–204. Copyright by the American Psychological Association.

[1] An anonymous reviewer of a draft of this article, to whom I am grateful for a number of valuable suggestions, observed that "assessing the impact of Piaget on developmental psychology is like assessing the impact of Shakespeare on English literature or Aristotle on philosophy—impossible. The impact is too monumental to embrace and at the same time too omnipresent to detect." I agree. This article, then, is a modest and limited attempt to do the impossible.

but it is unrivaled in the history of developmental psychology. At the same time, it is difficult to identify a theory that has been more debated and attacked than Piaget's. The curve of the theory's popularity looks more like a business cycle with peaks and troughs than a classical growth curve, with eventual decline. Although the theory appears to have passed its peak in popularity, it is difficult to imagine its disappearance.

After the Second World War, when Piaget's theory appeared in a new guise to the English-speaking community, it created a near sensation with its striking counterintuitive experimental data and bold theoretical claims that struck at the heart of the then-dominant neobehaviorism. The reaction at first was to attempt to replicate his findings or to attack the research on methodological or theoretical grounds. Investigators, for the most part, took the path of least resistance and focused on the most counterintuitive findings (e.g., the conservations) and on those phenomena that seemed to embody the clearest theoretical claims (e.g., the counterempiricist training claims). The strategy was to strike at Achilles's heel, and Achilles (Piaget's theory) would fall flat on his face. Thus, there were countless (ad nauseam) studies of conservation, the object concept, formal operational reasoning, training, and more, some of which continues. The negative consequence of this strategy has been a generally distorted picture of Piaget's theory that has hindered a full appreciation of the theory's potential contribution.

Why and how Piaget's theory has gone into a decline provides a prototypic case in the history and sociology of science that cannot be pursued in this limited space. Suffice it to say that it took place at a time when other structuralist theories of commanding presence, such as Levi-Strauss's sociological theory and Chomsky's linguistic theory, experienced the same loss of authority and interest. Piaget's theory, like the others, however, still exercises considerable influence and will continue to do so.

There are a number of reasons for this. To start, Piaget's theory represents a constructivist view of development so fundamental that it will always find a place among theories of development. Piaget's version of constructivism, for the present at least, is its prototypic representative. Second, it is a developmental theory to its core. It presupposes developmental mechanisms in a theory of equilibration, which even if it is not satisfactory to everyone, requires by its very presence that other theories offer alternative explanations of developmental change. Furthermore, the theory is built on two forms of explanation that cognitive accounts of development, by their very nature, cannot do without, namely, structural explanation and functional explanation. Although which of these forms of explanation is emphasized changes, as they did in Piaget's own theory building, a theory that emphasizes either form or function to the exclusion of the other is bound to be incomplete. Piaget's theory is still the best example of a developmental theory that integrates both. Again, the research program is of such scope and the empirical data it produced so prodigious and of such significance to numerous issues that it behooves investigators of cognitive development, if they aspire at all to scholarly standards, to locate Piaget's data and interpretations as a reference point for their own studies. Furthermore, the extent of the unexplored yet astonishingly productive, simple, and straightforward experiments he reported can keep generations of investigators yet unknown busy for their own lifetimes. Last, although these do not exhaust the reasons for Piaget's theory's continued influence, he was concerned with epistemological issues of an enduring nature to which, he argued, psychological research, particularly development research, provides important insights. His own theory was an example of this and in the 1960s was one of the first to gain the attention of philosophers of mind (Mischel, 1971), who up to then were wary of psychological theories for fear of contaminating their analyses and arguments with psychologisms.

Thus, Piaget is more than a historical figure, large as he looms in the historical landscape of developmental psychology. His theory is still very much a contending presence in the free-for-all that defines current psychological theorizing. What makes that presence more salient is that we have not heard the last from Piaget. As later books are translated and published, what is abundantly clear is that they represent a new era in the evolution of his theory. The emphases and the interpretations of developmental phenomena are sufficiently changed from his "standard" theory that I believe they require us to see it as a "new" theory (Beilin, 1989).

FOUR PHASES IN PIAGET'S PROGRAM

Piaget had a different effect on developmental psychology with each phase in his research program, which can be divided into four such periods (Montangero, 1985). His first books, in the 1920s and 1930s, provided a view of children's thought that was very much in keeping with the scientific mood in continental Europe. The first research reports were nonetheless sufficiently revolutionary to draw immediate attention. Then followed a period, different in both method and content, in which Piaget embarked on detailed observation and interpretation of his own three children's early cognitive development. The reports of these studies extended Piaget's theory (and his reputation) to global proportions. Before the Second World War, Piaget's research took off in yet another direction, and, in the safety provided by Swiss neutrality, it continued through the war years. When the war ended and communication was resumed among the previously warring and occupied countries, Piaget's theory came on the scene in a new guise, with a structuralist and cognitivist framework that electrified the psychological community, already oversaturated and disaffected with behaviorism and other functionalisms. Here was Piaget's "grand" theory laid out in a series of books that soon provided the standard interpretation of the theory. The structuralist-oriented theory initiated an era in developmental psychology that it almost completely dominated until the end of the 1970s. Piaget's influence, however, experienced a gradual decline in the 1980s.

It is interesting that from the 1970s on, in the last 10 years of Piaget's life, his research and theory took a turn in yet another direction. In part, it was a return to functionalism—not the functionalism of the 1920s and 1930s but a new version, influenced to a degree by the structuralism of the standard theory.

Each phase in the research program added something new and important to the theory, in addition to whole bodies of empirical data. I would like to detail what some, if not all, of these additions were.

Phase 1: On the Child's Conception of Reality Mediated Through Language and Social Interaction

On Language and Thought

The first book-length report of his research, in 1923, on children's language and thought brought Piaget immediate worldwide attention as the work was translated into many languages (Piaget, 1923/1926). The ideas expressed are still controversial and bear on fundamental issues that will continue to be debated. The research addressed the question of the functions served and the needs satisfied by the use of language. Piaget's approach to children's speech was descriptive and classificatory but not without a functional explanation that was very much in the spirit of Claparède, who at the time was director of the Institut Jean-Jacques Rousseau and Piaget's predecessor in that post. Piaget made the point that descriptive categories are of little utility in themselves without knowledge of the functional origins of the behaviors classified. He applied this methodological dictum to the two principal categories that he identified in young children's speech, the egocentric and the socialized. *Egocentrism*, a term Piaget later rejected because of, among other things, its misleading connotations of emotional self-centeredness, was applied to various specific categories of speech (e.g., echolalia and monologue). These uses reflected the child's reference of all events to his or her own point of view. Thus, much of children's speech was said to be for themselves, not their audience, and did not take into account others' points of view. Socialized speech, which comes as a later development, was said to be for the purpose of communication and social engagement. Piaget detailed three stages in this development, reporting that at the age of 6 years, about 45% of speech is egocentric. (Not all the speech is egocentric, a point often overlooked.) However, egocentric thought is not purely asocial. When children retold a story told by Piaget, they were well aware that they were trying to communicate. The difficulty was that young children did not differentiate their own from the other's point of view. Piaget's interest in the study of language was to provide a window into the child's processes of thought. His concern was only secondarily with the nature of language itself; language, in fact, never became a serious focus of study for Piaget (Beilin, 1975).[2]

Piaget's first major work, aside from its attempt to discern and differentiate form and function in the child's thought principally through language, delineated the stages in this development. Describing the stages, first through a scheme of descriptive classification and then largely as a functional explanation of the changes in the properties of these different forms of speech, set a pattern for Piaget's later research. He continued to use stage description to the very end of his career.[3] What also characterized the first and second phases of Piaget's theory and research was their emphasis on functional description and explanation that were typical of both Continental and American psychology at the time. The significance of this theoretical and methodological commitment is made more evident by the radical shift in another direction that took place in the third phase of his research.[4]

The work on language and thought led to further insights that were to lay the groundwork for later theory. A study of children's spontaneous questions provided the basis for attributing a form of precausal thinking to the child, characterized by lack of differentiation between causal explanation and intentional explanation. In the developmental course described by Piaget, children at 3 years of age become concerned (in their first *whys*) with intentionality, although there is said to be no discrimination between causality and agency, as is evident by their projection of intention onto physical objects. This precausal type of thinking yields to the differentiation of subject and object and, by way of an explicatory function, leads to the differentiated categories of causality, reality, time, and space in the child's thought. In this differentiation from precausal syncretism (i.e., the fusion of elements), there emerges the parallel implicatory function. Again, as subject and object are differentiated, the regulatory function leads to clas-

---

[2] Piaget's notion of egocentricity and its decline with development has been considerably battered over the years. When Piaget learned that Vygotsky was among those critical of the linguistic version of this notion, he wrote (Piaget, 1962a) that, had Vygotsky been aware of the later version that substitutes the concept of decentration for egocentricity, he would likely have approved. Vygotsky's English-speaking followers, at least, appear to have been anything but sanguine about the change.

[3] Some influential former colleagues of Piaget's have tried to diminish the role that stages play in Piaget's theorizing. I frankly don't buy it. Whereas many aspects of the interest and interpretation of Piaget's stage theory are misleading (e.g., the age norms and structure-of-the-whole concept), the stage notion is critical for the theory. The evidence of this is that the stage concept was used by him to the end; it is essential for understanding a number of important claims made by the theory, and in the later theory, he revised the stage idea he held previously.

[4] Implicit in the work just described, and in other research of this period, is the claim that the young child's thought is syncretic and undifferentiated in its understanding of reality and its own mind. This implies that the child has no coherent "theory" of reality. This conception has been vigorously contested in the child's-theory-of-mind literature (cf. Astington, Harris, & Olson, 1988; Wellman, 1990).

sification, naming, number, and logical relations. A mixed function of explication and implication leads to the motivation for action and rule justification. The distinction between explicatory and implicatory functions reverberates through Piaget's later theory in a variety of distinctions, such as those between causal and logical thought, between physical and logico-mathematical knowledge, and between physical abstraction and reflective abstraction.

On Relations

Language and Thought of the Child (Piaget, 1923/1926) was intended to be the first of a set of two. The other, *Judgment and Reasoning in the Child* (Piaget, 1924/1928), concerned issues raised in the former, in some cases in greater detail and more systematically. For example, the study of why questions of the earlier book was followed now by a study of logical and causal connectives such as *because, therefore,* and *although.* In addition to expressing logical and causal relations, these terms also can express motivational (psychological) connections; their use by children appears at between 3 and 7 years, with logical uses appearing at about 7 years, paralleling the decline in egocentric speech. Many of the early uses attributed to the connectives reflected what Piaget referred to as *juxtaposition,* the tendency to link one thought to another successively when there was a causal or logical relation between them. This concept is the opposite of syncretism, the tendency to blend two thoughts together. Piaget saw the separation of juxtaposition and syncretism as representing the incomplete ability to understand part–whole relations. Piaget tied these notions into a model of equilibrium that was to play an increasingly important role in the theory. Juxtaposition and syncretism were seen as complementary aspects of an unstable equilibrium: In juxtaposition, the parts predominate over the whole; in syncretism, the whole dominates over the parts.

In *Judgment and Reasoning in the Child* (1924/1928), Piaget also pursued the study of relations within a verbal context, a study that he would pursue extensively later in largely nonlinguistic forms. For this purpose, he used Simon-Binet's absurdities text, in which the typical assertion and question are, "I have three brothers: Paul, Ernest and myself. What is wrong with that sentence?" Together with a variation of this, children were studied from 4 to 12 years of age. Young children typically were unable to differentiate between two points of view, that is, between their own and others', a problem of relations as opposed to class, with which young children had less difficulty.

In a study of simple arithmetic reasoning, Piaget discovered that even when it appeared evident, for example, from their mutterings, how young children were solving a problem, when asked how they solved it, they were unable to explain how they had done so or provided an ordering opposite to how they had actually solved the problem. This was the case even when they gave correct answers to the arithmetic questions. Chapman (1988) pointed out that this was an early defense by Piaget of his use of linguistic justification criteria for the attainment of a concept. Inasmuch as providing a correct answer can be achieved in a variety of ways, the child's verbal justification is required to determine whether the child in fact grasps the concept. The issue of whether to accept correct answers alone as a criterion for achievement of a concept was to become a contested issue in later research, as in the well-known conservation studies. This early insight into children's inabilities to indicate how they solved a problem was taken up in one of Piaget's last books, *The Grasp of Consciousness* (1974/1976), and was shown to have relevance to an understanding of the nature of consciousness itself.

The study of verbal definitions led to a consideration of the nature of contradiction because of young children's difficulties in handling a general term and particular features simultaneously. Beyond describing how children handle contradiction (by "amnesia," forgetting one judgement as they pass to the next, or "condensing" and assimilating the content to contrary categories), Piaget considered the differences between logical and psychological contradiction. Whereas logic asserts the impossibility of holding contradictory propositions, in logical thinking, contradictory propositions are handled psychologically. To address this issue, Piaget again invoked the notion of equilibrium. Noting that logical noncontradiction is a state of equilibrium, the normal state of mind is one of disequilibrium—or, rather, a state of "moving equilibrium." He claimed that the psychological equivalent of the logical principle of noncontradiction is *operational reversibility*, that is, the simultaneous holding of relations that are the inverse or the reciprocal of one another (as he was to define operational reversibility later). Operational reversibility refers to processes or logical relations that take place simultaneously rather than successively. This notion played a critical role in all of Piaget's later theories. At this point in the theory's development, he introduced two other notions that he adopted from biological theory, the *assimilation of reality to the mind* and the *imitation of reality*. Although the assimilation of current to prior events and the imitation of occurring events can occur independently, operational reversibility is achieved only in the balance of assimilation and imitation. Furthermore, as though to emphasize the systematic aspects of his theorizing by integrating the critical concepts of the theory into a coherent totality, Piaget asserted that assimilation by itself is the predominance of the whole (in the form of existing schemes) over the parts (the elements assimilated); imitation alone is the predominance of the elements themselves (the parts) over the relations among the elements (the whole). In parallel, syncretism and juxtaposition express these general functions specifically in children's thought (Chapman, 1988, p. 46). Later development of the theory led to the substitution of the more general concept of accommodation for the notion of imitation.

Piaget proposed two stages in an attempt to tie together the research covered in these first two books. In the first, three "global" stages were described in the development of children up to the ages of 7–8 years during which their thinking is nonreversible and transductive (transductive thinking being reasoning from one particular to another, in contrast to deductive thinking, going from the universal to the particular, and inductive reasoning, going from the particular to the universal). In the second stage, from 7–8 to 11–12 years, there is partial reversibility in thought, limited however to actual observations. From ages 11–12 onward, children's reasoning is not limited by observed reality but is capable of dealing with the hypothetical. In this progression are the seeds of the later distinction between preoperational, concrete operational, and formal operational thought.

Early critics reacted vigorously to a number of Piaget's striking claims. One criticism that Piaget felt needed an unequivocal response was the impression that his stage characterizations were confined to particular age norms. Although Piaget made clear in *Judgment and Reasoning in the Child* (1924/1928) that the ages delineated were a function of the methods he used, the disclaimer did not still the controversy or the misinterpretation of his intent.

A second criticism was directed at the description of early egocentric thought and language, both their reality and the explanation given for them. It was clear that the theory had to account for why earlier egocentrism gives way to socialized speech and thought. The mechanism for the transition, according to Piaget at the time, was social interaction, in particular interaction with peers. Conflicts and arguments were said to force on children the need to examine their own views of the world relative to the views of others (Flavell, 1963). Piaget would again invoke social interaction as an explanation of cognitive change in his research on moral reasoning, but this type of social explanation was limited to the theory of the earliest period.[5]

On Realism

Of the books that followed, the next two, which dealt with reality and causality, *The Child's Conception of the World* (Piaget, 1923/1929) and *The Child's Conception of Physical Causality* (Piaget, 1927/1930) were a pair. The next book on moral judgment, *The Moral Judgment of the Child* (Piaget 1927/1932), although concerned with a different context, nevertheless re-

---

[5]There have been a number of recent attempts to introduce social causation into some version of Piagetian theory (e.g., Chapman, 1992; Youniss & Damon, 1992). It is well to remember why Piaget abandoned his earlier reliance on that form of explanation (Piaget, 1947/1950). As he put it, he came to see that instead of the effects of social influence being the basis of an explanation, they were a phenomenon to be explained.

flected the same theoretical framework as the preceding four in its characterization of development proceeding from egocentricity to social reasoning.

Piaget's research on realism is another example of a topic that interests current investigators, albeit as an area in which Piaget's findings and explanations are largely contradicted. Piaget's claims concerned three concepts that he introduced. The first, *childhood realism*, results from the lack of differentiation between self and the world such that psychological and physical events are not clearly differentiated. The second, *animism*, refers to the reverse process of attributing to physical objects and events the properties of biological and psychological phenomena; that is, young children endow physical objects with life and consciousness. The third, *artificialism*, treats physical phenomena as the consequences of human invention.

With regard to realism, for example, Piaget claimed that young children identified thought with the voice as a material event rather than as a mental process (intellectual realism). Names were said to be located in their referents, so that the name *dog* is part of the properties of the animal itself and known from looking at the object (nominal realism). Dreams for the young child were said to be material entities existing external to the child, as in a room. Piaget saw in these instances a stagelike progression that pointed to a "general direction of thought, not a comprehensive and coherent system of beliefs" (Flavell, 1963, p. 283). This development, as with the others characterized in this period, was related to early egocentrism (seeing the world from one's own perspective). As has been pointed out by more than one sympathetic observer, although Piaget reported these developments as stagelike achievements, he did not claim that they were uniform or unitary. Levels of realism, animism, and artificialism could be achieved at quite different paces, not necessarily in synchrony.

The current attacks on Piaget's notions of realism have come from the growing group of investigators studying the "child's theory of mind" (e.g., Astington, Harris, & Olson, 1988; Wellman, 1990), who claim that even young children (3 years) do not mistake the contents of mind (thoughts, feelings, and dreams) for material objects outside the head. Second, the young child is on the way to a coherent set of beliefs about mind that can be considered a theory of mind. Theory-of-mind counterclaims concerning childhood realism, for example, are not without controversy themselves (Beilin & Pearlman, in press), although the principal empirical counterclaims appear to have support.

Piaget's study of physical causality concentrated on the study of movement (of clouds, water, etc.) by predicting the outcome of an action or event and then questioning the cause after the event occurred (e.g., predicting the water level after dropping various objects into a glass vessel). In the process, Piaget identified 17 types of causal explanations, again within a developmental framework in which there is a gradual decrease in egocentricity and increase in socialization of thought, incorporating greater objectification and reciprocity of viewpoints.

On Method

In *The Child's Conception of the World* (Piaget, 1923/1929), there was extensive discussion of one of the most controversial aspects of Piaget's work, his so-called clinical method (later referred to as *the method of critical inquiry*) based on questioning and counterquestioning. He contrasted his method with traditional methods in use at the time, noting the disadvantages of others and the advantages of his own. He was also very clear on the dangers in the use of the clinical method (e.g., spontaneous fantasy, suggestion, and chance) and the safeguards that are needed to avoid false conclusions. Piaget's clinical method has been faulted for many reasons. Experimentalists, working within an essentially logical empiricist framework, identified the method as more in the tradition of the "logic of discovery" than in that of the "logic of justification" or truth testing. Others faulted the method for allowing the introduction of theoretical biases, even into what appear like methodological safeguards. The status of Piaget's methods will be discussed again later, but there can be little doubt that the clinical method was extremely fruitful in the first phase and later in generating a wide variety of data that contributed to provocative interpretation and theory building.

Another aspect of methodological epistemology concerned Piaget in the early work, *The Child's Conception of Physical Causality* (Piaget, 1927/ 1930). It was the distinction between reality as conceived by the child and reality as conceived by the scientist. Piaget was quite conscious that the scientist's frame of reference for interpreting the nature of reality, against which one relates the child's conception of reality, was a convention that was deliberately chosen yet was to be guarded against so as not to allow it to lead to "epistemological realism" (i.e., reification; Chapman, 1988, p. 54). Piaget declared that through psychology it would be possible to address significant problems in the theory of knowledge by the very contrast between the scientist's (and society's) and the child's conceptions of reality.

On Moral Judgment

The final work of this first period was Piaget's *The Moral Judgment of the Child* (1932). In this work, he considered children's knowledge of "rules of the game" (in playing marbles), notions of lying, and conceptions of justice. He described a general course of development, although again, he was aware of considerable variability among children and even among social classes (inasmuch as his sample consisted of poor children in Geneva). The developmental course was from what he termed a *morality of constraint* (based on conformity to "superior" adult norms) to a *morality of cooperation and reciprocity* (based on mutual respect among equals). This developmental course was manifest in different ways in each domain (rules, lies, and justice).

Again, the mechanism for the development from nonrational to rational morality, which underlies the development of rationality in general, was the give-and-take of peer interaction in the context of peers who try to cooperate: "This kind of interindividual exchange provokes a social decentration as well as cognitive decentration. Norms stem from the grasp of consciousness of the results of this decentration" (Montangero, 1985, p. 24).

After completing his work on moral judgment, Piaget never returned to it. Kohlberg (1969), however, undertook its study in the 1950s with a theory, modeled on Piaget's, that created a considerable and controversial literature of its own.

Summary

The first period in Piaget's research, spanning the years (in publication) from 1923 to 1932, was characterized by a theory of development based on the transition from egocentrism to socialized thought, along with a theory of social causation in which the retreat from egocentrism is propelled by the consequences of peer interaction and the exchange between thought and action. It was a highly fecund period in which Piaget's study of language and conceptions of reality, causality, and moral judgment affected the course of much developmental research worldwide and introduced a theoretical orientation to be reckoned with that resulted in considerable controversy. It was a period, also, for the introduction of a definitively cognitive orientation to work on child development, with a discovery procedure (the clinical method) of considerable utility in detailing the course of cognitive development. It also offered the beginnings of a theory of knowledge that was to have lasting significance for developmental psychology.

Phase 2: Stages in Sensorimotor Development. The Theory of Adaptation

In the 1930s, there was a decided shift in Piaget's research and theory. It was an era marked by Piaget's close observation of the early development of his own three children (born in 1925, 1927, and 1931). There were changes as well in the explanatory model for development. These were not the only changes, however.

Whereas the earlier research was based almost exclusively on verbal exchanges between experimenter and child or between children themselves, the studies of this period entailed to a greater extent observation of the child's action on objects. In fact, in a significant epistemological move from that period on, Piaget characterized his principal concern as the (dialectic) relation between subject and object.

On Action

The six stages he delineated in sensorimotor development during this period are well known. They led to the distinctly Piagetian conclusion that both language and thought are preceded and prepared for by a "logic of action" represented in the development of the schemes of sensorimotor action and coordination. The child's action was seen as the fundamental source of knowledge, rather than the traditionally defined sources of perception and language. It is here, too, that Piaget's theory established itself with a distinctive point of view that only later would be widely accepted in psychological theory, namely, that the child is active in the creation of knowledge through constructive processes with which he or she is naturally endowed. Piaget adopted from biological theory the processes of assimilation and accommodation as functional invariants. In assimilation, existing structures (schemes) in mind incorporate the abstract properties of actions on objects; in accommodation, mind modifies existing structures to the varying proper ties of objects. Whereas assimilation stresses the functional identity of actions on objects, accommodation stresses the functional differences among objects. Organization provides a self-regulatory mechanism for the relations among the resulting structures. The compensatory balance between assimilation and accommodation through organization makes possible the organism's adaptation to the physical and social world. Thus, the theory of adaptation that Piaget adopted at this point depended largely on endogenous processes such that the effect of socialization relied on for explanation in the prior period was no longer invoked or seen as relevant. In fact, social interaction and the effects of social exchange were themselves now explained by the theory of adaptation.

Theory of Adaptation

The functional theory of adaptation explained the origin of the categories of thought. Assimilation was identified with what Piaget called the *implicative function*, which included the logic of classes (based broadly on functional equivalence) and the logic of relations (based on functional differences). Accommodation, in turn, corresponded to the *explicative function*, the categories of reality entailing objects and their causal relations in time and space. Organization functions to create totalities (relations of part-whole or reciprocities) and has a regulative function in adaptation.

The model of adaptation, with its shift away from a model of social to biological explanation, has not to be everyone's satisfaction to this day

(Chapman, 1992; Youniss & Damon, 1992). Furthermore, despite Piaget's emphasis on the necessary role of the object in the dialectic of the subject–object relation, the theory rests primarily, although not exclusively, on endogenous processes and on the subject's own action and reflection. Contemporary contextualist theorists, from the mildest to the most radical, have not been happy with what they have seen as Piaget's exclusion or dismissal of social, historical, and interpersonal factors in the construction of knowledge (e.g., Dixon, 1987). Neo-nativist theorists, in turn, have been unhappy with Piaget's constructivism, being more inclined themselves either to differentiation theories or to (local) learning theories, as well as to the assumption of greater naturally given mental structures and processes than Piaget was willing to warrant (e.g., Carey & Gelman, 1991). In Piaget's later theory, the adaptation model itself was modified away from implied biological adaptation to a more dialectic model in the theory of equilibration.

Structure d'ensemble: *Theory of Representation*

In delineating the six stages of sensorimotor development, Piaget's theory emphasized the important role of the repetition of actions (in the "circular reaction," a notion he openly adopted from J. M. Baldwin) (Broughton & Freeman-Moir, 1982), the increasing role of intentionality, and the varieties of assimilation and accommodation evident in the child's developing repertoire. With respect to organization, he introduced the notion of *structure d' ensemble* (structure-of-the-whole) that was to be an important, if highly debated, aspect of the theory. A further feature of the exposition of sensorimotor development was the delineation of a developmental theory of signs. This was essentially a theory of representation leading from identification of the function of signals (i.e., conditioned responses) to the index function (further distancing of the representation from the stimulus), and then to the symbolic (later identified as the semiotic) function in which the representation need have no similarity to the referent. This representational development was to be later adapted and altered by Bruner (Bruner, Olver, & Greenfield, 1966) in his theory of representational development from the enactive to iconic to symbolic functions. Again, the theory of signs that Piaget (1962b) proposed, following in part on Saussure's model, anticipated many later theories of representation, although some still questioned the need for a developmental component of representational theories of mind (Fodor, 1975; see also Perner, 1991).

The Object Concept and Space

Piaget's description of particular developments in this period also elicited extraordinary interest, research, and debate, as in the case of the development of the object concept (i.e., the concept of a permanent object). As in many later experiments, Piaget's reports of his observations were initially so counterintuitive (especially the so-called stage IV A, not B, phenomenon, in which the child looks to where an object was originally hidden rather than to the place to which it was seen to be displaced) that countless studies were undertaken to test (and contest) Piaget's findings. Piaget's report of the phenomenon has withstood extensive experimentation, although controversy still exists over the theoretical interpretation that he applied to its developmental course (Harris, 1983). (For a different view, see Wellman, Cross, & Bartsch, 1986. Representative of more recent experimental work are Baillargeon, DeVos, & Graber, 1989, and Diamond, 1988.) The same was true of Piaget's characterization of the sensorimotor development of spatial concepts, although not to the same degree. In this case, Piaget applied Poincaré's concept of the mathematical group to space (Piaget & Inhelder, 1948/1956), a notion on which he was to expand considerably in his later theory. In this early proposal, Piaget already claimed that every closed system of operations had the properties of a group (Chapman, 1988, p. 112).

Causality

Piaget's study of causal thinking in the sensorimotor phase laid the groundwork for two later studies in causality. The explanation of causal thought was to concern Piaget throughout his later work. His first intent was to account for scientific and prescientific theories of causality, which had troubled philosophers for centuries. His further interest was in the relation of causal thought to operational thought within his own system.

In this second phase of the theory, Piaget recognized in a new way the importance of language in development and tried to account for its developmental course. His account showed its relation to the evolution of concepts, arguing that the child's first words represent preconcepts. His analysis of early language was clearly influenced by Saussure's semiotics; from which Piaget adopted the idea that the referents of words are concepts, rather than objects or events, as usually conceived. Piaget's own studies of language were limited to observations of development in the sensorimotor period. A basic tenet of his position, which was to be more clearly enunciated in his later debates with Chomsky (Piatelli-Palmarini, 1980), was that a long period of nonlinguistic cognitive development precedes and makes possible the acquisition of linguistic forms. Sinclair, in the 1960s, was to undertake a comprehensive study of language within the Piagetian framework (see Sinclair, 1992, for a history of this research).

Method and Explanation

Much criticism in this period was directed at Piaget's extensive generalizations and claims for the universality of functions and structures made on the basis of observations and experiments on his own three children. Almost forgotten was the fact that the studies of the earlier period were based in some cases on hundreds of children.

Piaget's methodological approach in the 1930s' studies of his own children was to detail the children's behavior toward objects in their natural surroundings, as well as toward objects that he introduced. The observation protocols reported, although clearly selected from countless hours of observation and experiment, were essentially factual descriptions of the children's behavior, with further interpretations by Piaget of their functional significance. At another level of explanation, Piaget mapped his biological model of adaptation onto the data and, more particularly, various other theories (such as Saussure's, Poincaré's, and Baldwin's) to explain more local phenomena. The model throughout was basically functional. In the next period of the theory's development, a marked shift occurred wherein the implicit and subtly explicit structural elements of the theory were made the central focus of explanation.

Phase 3: The Structuralist Period. Logico-Mathematical Models, Concrete and Formal Operations, and the Standard Theory

In the late 1930s and early 1940s, Piaget's books on numerical and physical quantities signaled a new turn in the theory. These initiated the structuralist period that was to last until the 1960s and 1970s and was marked by the use of structural analysis and explanation, as well as the introduction of models adapted from logic and mathematics.

The transition to this phase was easily enough accomplished inasmuch as it built on an approach implicitly in place. Starting with an intensive examination of a particular domain of knowledge, such as number, a variety of experiments were undertaken that exposed the child's ways of dealing with the conceptual elements and complexities of the domain, as well as their limitations.

Studying children at different ages yielded information on the functional characteristics of the child's thought, but in studying younger children in the formative stages of development, Piaget also emphasized constructive elements in the process of formation. Piaget has often been criticized by one group of critics (among them Bruner, Flavell, and Gelman) who claim that his approach in characterizing development was negative; that is, in describing a particular stage, he detailed what the child lacked in relation to the stages that follow. This type of criticism fails to recognize Piaget's usually extensive description of the achievements of the stage over that of the prior one. It also fails to recognize that in detailing what was missing in a stage, Piaget wished to emphasize the ways in which the developmental history of the phenomenon studied was not complete.

Armed with a functional description of natural logic in the ages of operational thought (from 6 or 7 years on), what was missing from Piaget's theory up to that time was an adequate explanation for these more powerful forms of thought. Piaget was aware before this time of Poincaré's mathematical models applied to space (Piaget & Inhelder, 1956) and later of the work of the Bourbaki (the group of French mathematicians), which led to his adapting their models and mapping them onto the description of natural logic emerging from his current empirical work (Beth & Piaget, 1966). In this third phase of his work, he had a sophisticated group of collaborators, the principal among them being Bärbel Inhelder, who undertook an extraordinarily wide range of experiments on logical, mathematical, and scientific thinking.

Out of this research, Piaget defined the developmental periods of concrete operations and formal operations, the first starting at around the age of 6–7 years, the second at around 11–12 years. A large number of claims were made in relation to the developments of these periods that were consolidated into a view of the theory and that were strikingly different from the character of the theory prior to that time. When this work, which was carried out shortly before and during the years of the Second World War, became known after the war, it created a revolution in thinking about cognitive development. The constituents of the theory developed at this time became what many consider to be the standard version of the theory. The central concept on which the logical architecture of the standard theory was built was the logical operation, interpreted as the mental internalization of a physical action, with the property of (simultaneous or concurrent) reversibility. In the period after World War II, with the progressive demise of behaviorism and its strictures against mentalistic constructs, there was greater acceptability of Piaget's cognitivism and its lexicon of mentalisms only indirectly tied to observable behavior. Piaget, however, very carefully distanced himself from an idealist position, consistently claiming that the cognitive elements of the theory were always tied to some observed behavior, usually in the form of repeated patterns of a particular kind that would imply the existence of a mental structure.

Groupings and Groups

Thus, the (mental) action of combining classes of objects or object properties into a larger class was said to be indicative of logical addition, whereas other mental actions were involved in logical subtraction, multiplication, and negation. Paralleling the system of logical operations was a system of logic very much like the formal systems of traditional logic. There was, however, one difference that some critics either did not see or did not appreciate. In adapting these logical theories to a psychological system, they were no longer the axiomatic of logic itself or of the operational structures of natural logical processing; they constituted a "psychologic," as Piaget called it, a formal psychological model for the underlying structures of rational thought. The psychological reality of these structures was to be supported by their ultimate tie to the evidence of thought in actual problem solving and reasoning.

The central concept of this psychologic was group structure, the model of which came from the (closed) mathematical group, with its properties of composition, associativity, identity, and inversion. However, inasmuch as these were not mathematical but psychological groups, they had other properties (special identities) such as tautology and resorption. The logical structures first constituted in the period of concrete operations were said to lack the properties of group structures in part because these logical systems were tied to the actual manipulation of objects. Instead, Piaget differentiated and identified what he called *groupings* (*groupement*), which had some but not all the properties of a group. The groupings were said to underlie (or map onto) the logic of classes and the logic of relations, which, together with the reversibility operations of the conservations of quantity, charac-terized the structural underpinnings of rational thought of the concrete operational period. The groupings were defined by the logical addition of symmetrical and asymmetrical classes, as well as (ordering) relations, and by the logical multiplication of one-to-one and one-to-many relations be-tween classes and (ordering) relations. The groupings were said to be man-ifest in classification thinking in such instances as the class-inclusion task, which became a classic among Piagetian methods. When two classes, such as x roses and y violets, are combined into single (superordinate) class, $^\cap$owers $(x + y)$, and children are asked which there are more of, flowers or roses, proper understanding of the relation of inclusion is said to be the critical test of understanding part–whole organization, the most funda-mental structures of which are the groupings. The logic of classes and the logic of relations were said to become integrated in the understanding of the nature of number, which integrates these logics into a single system (reflected in the cardinal and ordinal numbers). Whereas almost everyone at the time thought that Russell and Whitehead, following Peano and Frege, had succeeded in reducing number to logic (the logicist program; Benacceraf & Putnam, 1964), Piaget instead believed he had succeeded in reducing the logic of number to a psychological phenomenon that reflected the (mental) internalization of action and, by doing so, had established that number was not reducible, by virtue of the definitions of set or class logic alone, but had to entail an integration of class and order (seriation) logics.

Conservations of Quantity: Décalage *and Structures-of-the-Whole*

Piaget's study of the conservation of quantity (number, mass, weight, length, area, etc.) turned out to be among the most visible, engaging, and provocative of his many experiments. The reports of young children's failures at conservation were so counterintuitive that they led to a veritable avalanche of studies to verify the phenomenon. When the child's developmental course in achieving conservation was tied by Piaget, in his equilibration theory, to the limitations of assimilation, because the child was said to lack the structures to permit acquiring conservation, a large number of training studies were undertaken to challenge this claim. The training studies, in the main, represented an attack on the very foundations of the equilibration theory. Piaget trivialized these studies at first as merely designed to show that development could be accelerated, reflecting a controversy that had plagued discussion of Piaget's theory from the 1930s onward. The training studies (principally of conservation), however, brought a number of features of the theory to general attention, many of which are still controversial (Beilin, 1971, 1978, provide extensive reviews of this literature).

Two of these are intimately related: the problem of (principally horizontal) *décalages* and the issue of the *structure d' ensemble* (structure-of-the-whole), which bears on the constitution of stages. It was almost immediately apparent in the replication of Piaget's experiments that the achievement of the many conservations of quantity were not concurrent. That is, children did not achieve number, length, liquid quantity, weight, and such at the same time. It was assumed by most investigators that this was at variance with Piaget's theory in that the logical structures of the concrete operational period, the groupings, would be achieved on an all-or-none basis and that the structures-of-the-whole represented by the groupings would require concurrent achievement not only of the conservations but of the elements of class and seriation logics. Piaget's early writing on this score may have led to this view inasmuch as he often reported concurrent achievements, as in the achievement of length, area, and volume measurement. But as Chapman (1988) made clear in a painstaking analysis of Piaget's writings on these issues (particularly those of 1941), Piaget never intended that a structure-of-the-whole should encompass the whole of the contents, or the domains of knowledge, in a stage. Rather, each of the eight or nine groupings functioning in a given content area is a structure-of-the-whole unto itself and is functionally distinct (Chapman, 1988, p. 149). Thus, synchrony was to be more the exception than the rule in development. Knowledge was dependent not only on the grouping structure in question but also on its domain of application, that is, the content and form of the domain (e.g., weight would offer different properties to be conserved from mass, even though both are quantities). Consequently, the domains of application would represent different levels of difficulty for a child. Montangero (1985) held that Piaget's early account of *décalage* assumed priority of one concept over another such that the concept of mass, involving the retrieval of matter, would precede weight, which would involve the weighing of matter. Piaget's later explanation had more to do with the varying resistances of objects to being acted on and with the figurative aspects of the situation, such as the location of an object, and the physical laws applying to objects (Piaget, 1975/1985, p. 41). Inhelder, Sinclair, and Bovet (1974) developed further the idea that achieving a concept such as a conservation is a function of the basic logical structure of the system (e.g., the groupings) and the special physical properties of the domain (weight, number, etc.). Nevertheless, Piaget did hold that in some cases various groupings did appear to develop at the same time, but this was not necessarily a consequence of the structure-of-the-whole of a given stage (Chapman, 1988, p. 151). Horizontal *décalages* are to be expected (but not of necessity) when formally equivalent groupings are applied to qualitatively different areas of content, as in the conservations. Synchrony is to be expected when the same grouping is applied to different objects in the same content domain (Chapman, 1988, p. 152).

The manner of Piaget's description of the relations between logical structure and domain contents argues against the often-cited view that Piaget believed that logical structures are acquired and function in a content-free manner. To the contrary, even in this very structuralist of periods in his theory, he maintained that there is no structure without function and no function without structure. Nor is a structure achieved at once in an all-or-none fashion and then applied to specific contents. Rather, structures are the logical organizing properties of operations, and operations are, by definition, contentful. Again, contrary to the prevailing view held of Piaget's standard theory, he did not maintain that a child passes from one stage to the next in an all-or-none fashion. Instead, the child is at different stages for different content domains at the same time. Owing to the association of the notion of "global" stage progressions to the stage concept, there has been a retreat among a number of investigators from the stage concept to concepts of domain specificity, except among some neo-Piagetians such as Case (1985; Case, Marini, McKeough, Dennis, & Goldberg, 1986). The domain-specificity argument is that if structures of organizations in mind exist, they do so within domains and not within structures that cut across a stage (e.g., language, areas within language, classification, weight). There is, however, no necessary incompatibility between the stage concept and domain specificity, as Piaget's own later conception of stage development as spiral suggests. (See Levin, 1986, for a discussion of the issues.)

The nature of developments in concrete operational thought was delineated in considerable detail in books devoted to the study of time, space, movement and speed, and geometry. Less well known, although published during the same period, was a series of essays on sociology (see Chapman, 1988) in which Piaget elaborated a theory of social exchange, although again, within a structuralist framework.

Genetic Epistemology

The work of the structuralist period continued into the 1950s as Piaget's group or "school" began to identify itself as established in a new discipline, genetic epistemology (for the study of which they established the International Centre for Genetic Epistemology). The aims of this program have led a number of people to characterize Piaget as a philosopher in that his intent was to illuminate traditional questions in epistemology on the basis of the study of cognitive development, principally. The essential plan was to study the history of ideas relating to knowledge and its forms in each of the sciences, although his analyses were confined in large measure to the physical sciences and mathematics. (In Piaget's 1968/1970 *Structuralism*, his analysis also concerned the biological and social sciences.) Piaget was interested in showing that there was a parallel development in the history of ideas in a science and the development of concepts in children relative to concepts in that science. More importantly, Piaget (later with Garcia) claimed that the mechanisms underlying evolutionary developments in the science and child cognitive development are analogous. Aside from this long-term project in genetic epistemology, which did not reach fruition until the end of Piaget's life (in *Psychogenesis and the History of Science*, Piaget & Garcia, 1989), the structuralist period was rounded out with a characterization of the nature of formal operations.

Equilibration, Causality, and Formal Operations

Of considerable general significance was Piaget's continued elaboration of the theory of equilibration. To this end, the generation and generalization of structures had to be more precisely accounted for than "merely" detailing the functions of assimilation, accommodation, and self-regulating and self-organizing processes. In accord with the distinction between physical knowledge and logico-mathematical knowledge, on which the studies of the concrete operational period focused, Piaget proposed two forms of mental activity or mental processes that augmented the prior equilibration account. In this instance, physical abstraction was said to be the source of physical knowledge, the knowledge that comes from experience with objects, the properties of which (such as size or shape) are abstracted, generalized, and organized into classes. This process was said to lead to the physical knowledge of objects and events. This knowledge-generating process, however, does not account for logico-mathematical knowledge of the kind manifest in the concrete operational period. Instead, Piaget proposed that another process, reflective abstraction, results in the construction of newer and higher forms of knowledge from those at lower levels (e.g., operations at the level of thought as opposed to schemes at the level of action), with a reflective aspect involving another level that integrates new and old knowledge to yield novel forms and structures. The reflective abstraction concept was developed further in the last phase of Piaget's thought and was to become one of the cornerstones of the theory of constructivism by accounting for transitions in cognitive development and in the construction of new knowledge structures.

A continuing puzzle for Piaget that emerged in this phase of his work was the understanding of causality: how causal relations come to be seen in the actions of objects on one another in the real world, how the conception of causality undergoes change in development, and how, finally, causal relations relate to operational thought. It took Piaget two books (Piaget, 1927/1930; Piaget & Garcia, 1974) to arrive at a reasonably satisfactory solution. In essence, Piaget argued that the focus of the child's own actions on objects is projected onto or attributed to the objects themselves, such that an object becomes the surrogate agent in its action on another object. In the later works, Piaget more formally contrasted causality and operations in thought.

One of the most contested aspects of Piaget's theory is the characterization of the formal operational period and the logical operations of that level of thought. Piaget brought the full armament of his logical theory to bear on the thought of this period, ostensibly because the theory was capable of accounting for the generation of advanced thought of a physical, mathematical, and logical nature in the adult.

To this end, Piaget sought to merge the groupings of concrete operational thought and integrate them into a now-closed logical system, the logico-mathematical groups proper. The logical system adopted was to carry all the weight of explanation variously described by logicians as propositional logic, first-order logic, extensional logic, and truth-table logic. As already indicated, although Piaget adopted this formal logic, he adapted it for the purpose of constructing his psychologic, particularly in the explanation of formal operations. The later logics that he used were intrapropositional relations and interpropositional relations. The former are involved in concrete operations (in the groupings), and the latter, more elegant in their functions, apply to hypothetical and combinatorial thinking in the period from adolescence onward and reflect the operation of group structures.

Piaget's claim was that taking single propositions (e.g., the book is on the table) and relating them to other single propositions by way of the basic logical connectives (e.g., conjunction and disjunction and their linguistic counterparts, *and* and *or*, respectively) leads to a system of 16 binary operations, the truth values of which can be tested in a systematic way. Whereas concrete operational child's thought is characterized by the associations between classes and relations so that binary propositions can be solved only on a trial-and-error basis, formal operational adolescent's thought, armed with group structure competence, can conceive of these associations in advance of facing a problem-solving task and treat them as hypotheses to be tested. The adolescent is now said to have a technique (the implicit truth table) for testing all possible combinations of such propositions as he or she enters into logical and scientific problem-solving situations. The full power of adolescent and adult thought comes from the interpropositional operations in which a given propositional operation, such as p or q (disjunction), is transformed in logical ways into other propositions. Thus, the negation of the disjunctive proposition changes everything in the propositional pair. Consequently, the negation of p or q results in *not p and not q*. There are four such transformations in Piaget's so-called "4 group": identity (I), negation (N), reciprocal (R), and correlative (C). Applying the transformations successively leads back to the original propositional disjunction; hence, the group is referred to as a closed system. The 4-group structure was used by Inhelder and Piaget (1955/1958) to explain problem solving with verbal logic problems and the experimental application of logical relations to physical operations.

Piaget's logical claims for group structures—in particular, the combinatorial system, the INRC group, and Genevan empirical claims—generated considerable controversy among logicians and psychologists. (For one of the most critical and detailed analyses of Piaget's early logic, see Ennis, 1982.) In addition, a different sort of argument has arisen as to whether Piaget's proposals for formal operational thought, and its attendant psychologic, represent the final form of thought in adolescent and adult cognition (see, e.g., Alexander & Langer, 1990). With regard to adult cognition, various sources claim that they are not. One type of claim misses the point of Piaget's argument, which is that with respect to rational, scientific, and mathematical types of thought and problem solving, no other logical systems or forms of thought are likely beyond formal operations, not on principle but on the basis of what is evident in human development. On this score, no counterclaims have been forthcoming from Piaget's critics as to the existence of other logical systems of thought. Other criticisms, based on the assumption that adult thought forms in domains other than the scientific (e.g., the aesthetic) entail other kinds of thinking, have been quite reasonable, although Piaget always made clear that he was not studying all forms of thought and their development. Furthermore, although Piaget's theory was designed to account for novelty and generativity in cognitive development, he did not deal with intellectual creativity as such. Some of the alternative proposals do, and they may account for some of the creative features of adult production with which Piaget did not deal.

The structuralist period was rounded out by studies of mental imagery, perception, and memory, collectively characterized as the figurative aspects of thought. These components offer structures that are complementary to those of operative thought and on which operative structures act.

The structuralist period did not end abruptly. Gradual dissatisfaction with various important aspects of the theory accumulated, which resulted in changes both in the body of Piaget's ideas and in the direction the theory was taking. The resulting work, beginning in the late 1960s and 1970s, led to further radical changes in the theory, which were of such a nature that it is fair to say that the work of the 1970s leading up to Piaget's death in 1980 constituted a new theory (Beilin, 1989, 1992).

Phase 4: Return to Functionalism. Preoperational Thought, Strategies, Intentional Logic, and the Theory of Meaning

Functions and Correspondences

In Piaget's description of the progression from sensorimotor intelligence to formal operations, the preoperational period from 2 years to 7 years of age was relatively neglected. If any aspect of Piaget's work could have been said to be deformed by default, this period was it. For the most part, preoperational thought, for example, was described by the lack of the properties of reversibility typical of operational and other types of thought. If there was a case in which it could be said that Piaget dealt with a period in a somewhat negative fashion, this was it, although, at the same time, it was also characterized as the period of representational thought, and many concepts developed in this stage were detailed. In the 1960s, Piaget returned to this stage in development and, with a continuation of structural analysis, defined the underlying nature of thought in the form of functions and correspondences. In the process, Piaget changed and augmented one of the fundamental assumptions to which the theory up to that time adhered, namely, that thought entails transformations and the construction of invariants in the face of such transformations. In the new work, Piaget discerned that childrens' thought also reflected the construction of invariants through establishing correspondences by acts of comparison. The other product of these studies was the description of functions that are intermediate between simply having concepts and relating concepts in reversible operations. The intermediate step, now described, included one-way functions, or semilogics, in which the child was said to be capable of understanding an asymmetrical logical relation (e.g., *Joan is taller than Ann* but not concurrently *Ann is shorter than Joan*). The logical model from which Piaget drew to explain the results of studies with correspondences was the newly developed mathematical category theory of MacLane (1972). In addition to describing correspondences, Piaget saw two types of functions that also defined preoperational thought: the preparatory or *constitutive functions* and the later quantified *constituted functions* of operational thought.

The importance of functional thought, Piaget claimed, is that the functional relations, of which actions consist, are the source of both logico-mathematical operations and causality; they develop in parallel in some contexts and in interaction in others. The study of functions, besides filling a significant gap in Piaget's stage theory, marked a shift in emphasis of the work in Geneva toward functionalism, despite the structuralist character of the introduction of category theory into the logical architecture of Piaget's theory.

Strategies and Procedures

The shift in emphasis was first evident in the training studies reported by Inhelder et al. (1974). In the new work, the emphasis shifted to the study of strategies in children's actions and thought and to the procedures that are used in problem solution. Two components define children's problem solving and reasoning: structural knowledge and procedural knowledge. Piaget and Inhelder argued for a dialectical process involved in the progressive development of structures into more advanced, integrated, and coherent forms, in contrast with procedures that progressed only by diversification and accretion. Nonetheless, they claimed, "Every structure is the result of a procedural construction, and every procedure makes use of some aspects of structure" (Inhelder & Piaget, 1980, p. 26).

The last period of Piaget's research, from the end of the 1960s to 1980, was rich in its productivity and in the significance of its empirical content and theory. Any other investigator would be renowned on the basis of the works of this period alone. Unfortunately, Piaget's writing of this period is not generally known, and not all the major works of the period are available in English. I have detailed the nature of much of this later work (Beilin, 1989, 1992; see also Chapman, 1988) and so will give only the briefest account of it here.

Causality and Consciousness

As already indicated, Piaget was dissatisfied with his early explanations of causality and therefore, along with Garcia, a philosopher of science and a physical scientist, returned to its study in the late 1960s. The general result of the new research (Piaget & Garcia, 1974) was the claim that causality entails the attribution of operational structures to the object but is more than a system of transformations reduced to relations of cause and effect. Going further, they claimed that operations are causal structures applicable to extratemporal forms and are distinguishable from physical causality, which is a system of operations brought about by natural objects. This correspondence between operations and causality works because an operation (a mental action) is itself a "physical" object subject to causality, as are all other objects. The study of causality was to have even broader consequences, however, to be described later.

Two closely related books of research were completed in this period: *The Grasp of Consciousness* (Piaget, 1976) and *Success and Understanding* (Piaget, 1978). Piaget proposed that cognizance of an action transforms the action scheme into a concept so that cognizance is in essence an act of conceptualization. This process only provides the "knowing how" aspect of cognizance. The "knowing why" requires seeking functional reasons for it. Some strikingly simple studies were reported that at first are counterintuitive (e.g., the inability of many adults to recount what they did when walking "on all fours"; an experiment in hitting a target with a ball in a sling, which after being successfully done without cognizance results in failure when the process is conceptualized by the child). The results of these studies, although important in themselves, led to further development of the theory of equilibration and in particular the refinement of reflective abstraction. The studies of success and understanding involved the effects of "resistances" of objects on the development of reasoning. They led to a theoretical description of how action that is initially autonomous progresses to a form of conscious conceptualization that becomes a central mechanism in thought and then has the reverse effect of influencing the action itself. The experiments showed that at first, conceptualization lags behind action, but later, by virtue of reflective abstraction, conceptualization can totally predate and anticipate actions. These studies led to theoretical progress in the proposal that the most general characteristic of conscious states is the expression of "significations," which are connected by what Piaget called *signifying implications*. In essence, he redefined mental operations as *signifying actions*. That is, connections in mind are implicative and are unlike causal actions; hence, Piaget's reference to operations as internalized actions. The significance of this theoretical move is that the system of signifying implications provides for understanding in thought that extracts the reasons for things and events, in contrast with mental processes that reflect effective application or use.

Other studies explored why young children have more difficulty with negations than with affirmations and why the neglect of negative elements in reasoning produces all sorts of conflicts and contradictions. In the spirit of the new theory, the studies of contradiction (Piaget, 1974/1980a) redirected attention from logical and formal aspects of contradiction and their structural properties to their functions alone. In the new view, functions precede and prepare for structures through disequilibrium inherent in contradictions. Also new was the view that the oppositions that result from disequilibria are dependent on the contents of thought and action alone.

Possibility and Necessity

One of the most important redirections of Piaget's theory, as I see it, was the new emphasis on possibility (Piaget, 1981/1987a, 1981/1987b). In this view, the development of knowledge results from previously created possibilities. That is, each creation of a structure in cognitive development, by its very nature, embodies new possibilities for how the structure functions in thought. The new functions in turn lead to new structures with their own new possibilities. The reverse side of the coin is that each set of possibilities does not engender unlimited flexibility; rather, there are inherent constraints that lead necessarily to some outcomes and not others. Thus, there is a dialectic relation between possibility provided by procedural freedom (flexibility) and necessity, which is provided by the self-regulating aspects of the equilibration process and system-binding organization. Strikingly, in the new theory, operations are the product of possibilities, not of their source, and with the differentiation of possibility, necessity, and reality, operations are now integrated and subordinated by a new type of equilibrium between differentiation and integration. Revision of the theory of equilibration, which the new studies of possibility and necessity led to, resulted from considering each new possibility as a simultaneous construction and a new "opening." Possibility generates innovation at the same time that it fills a gap, a limitation, or a disturbance that has to be compensated for.

Equilibration

The theory of equilibration (Piaget, 1975/1985), which is at the heart of the functional and processing aspects of Piaget's theory, underwent considerable refinement in the last phase. The new theory rests on the distinction between observable and nonobservable coordinations between objects and actions. Empirical abstraction is applied to observable features and reflective abstraction to the coordination of internalized (nonobservable) actions. Action, however, gives rise to both forms of abstraction. There are said to be two levels of reflective abstraction: One, unconscious, is the source of inferential coordinations; the other is conscious and involves reasoning. Equilibration is the key element in the constructive process of thought, but because constructions invariably entail contradictions (and disequilibrium), they necessarily involve regulations of various kinds. The notion of regulations was thus revised from an earlier version of the theory. Regulations serve to avoid incoherence and consequently move thought processes in the direction of equilibration—with equilibriums, however, that are always temporary. Even logico-mathematical structures are only local and temporarily stable inasmuch as new structures reopen and create new problems. Consequently, the central problem becomes one of accounting for successive improvement in forms of equilibration. In essence, improvement is the result of new regulations that act on new forms that are richer than earlier ones by virtue of being constituted of greater and more complex component elements; as each new structure is created, it opens up new possibilities.

The new theory of equilibration augmented the earlier theory principally in fleshing out its functional components and further differentiating its properties. It was essentially a conservative move. A radical move in the research program came in the last year of Piaget's life, although the events leading up to it started in the late 1960s in Piaget's work on causality. The new work that followed on correspondences, functions, possibility and necessity, and contradiction and consciousness, among others, increasingly exposed the limitations of truth-table logics (essentially propositional logic) on which the standard theory of the structuralist period rested. These limitations within the theory itself, as well as knowledge of debates among logicians over these logics, led to a new direction in thinking about the logical models that informed Piaget's views of how to explain and account for rational thought.

Theory of Meaning

Piaget and Garcia (1991) emphasized that the new direction that developed in Genevan thinking "converged" with Anderson and Belnap's (1975) development of relevance-entailment logic. The result was that in 1980 Piaget (Piaget, 1980b) declared that he had been in error in placing primary emphasis on truth-table or extensional logic and proposed that a new theory of meaning was necessary that would integrate a "decanted" version of his earlier extensional logic with a new component that paralleled the intensional logic of Anderson and Belnap. The description of the new theory of meaning, however, did not deliver on the decanted version of extensional logic; instead, it offered a programmatic statement of what such a theory should look like. Piaget's death prematurely ended this project, although a body of studies remains with some striking claims. Piaget's central thesis was that at all levels, starting from the most elementary, knowledge always involves inference. In addition, the first evidence of (proto-) logical thought is in the period of sensorimotor development when the child anticipates an action and understands the relations among actions, well before language and later developing forms of propositional thought. Anticipation of action entails inference that denotes a logical relation, namely, implication. Thus, a relation between actions is already a logical implication but not in the extensional sense of requiring a truth-value determination. Rather, it is a meaning implication, an intension. Meaning exists from the start in objects, that is, in their description and in what can be thought of them (e.g., classifying and relating them). The meaning found in actions is in what they lead to, in the transformations they produce in objects or situations. In this, Piaget was proposing a new theoretical model for understanding sensorimotor development, a model that I have called a *logical hermeneutics of action* (Beilin, 1992). The model, as applied to the sensorimotor and preoperational periods, requires a functional analysis of how subjects approach a task, such as pushing or pulling blocks, and details the actions of the child, the objects acted on, and above all an interpretation of the inferences that the child makes in carrying out the task (e.g., "If I push the block, it will hit the car in its path").

In this last work, Piaget provided a final (if uncompleted) integration of the theory. He took the classical division between meaning and truth (or sense and reference) in the philosophy of mind (following Frege) and integrated them into a single dialectical system. In this system, developing cognitive competencies are constituted of the rational features of mind that enable logical thought to pursue truth by increasingly sophisticated means and concurrently to give meaning to objects and events by the progressive elaboration of concepts and implications.

CONCLUSION

At the most general level, Piaget, more than anyone before him, changed our conception and understanding of the cognitive resources of children. Piaget showed that from birth onward, intellectual competencies undergo continuous development until they attain their adult forms. And, as his later work emphasized, that development never ends. It is therefore highly ironic that a number of otherwise astute investigators, in a short-sighted view of our history, have faulted Piaget for underestimating the cognitive competencies of young children.

What Piaget did most directly for the philosophy of mind was to show that perennial questions in epistemology can be better understood from an empirical demonstration of how mind works and develops than from analysis alone. Furthermore, his own work did much to break the behaviorists' long stranglehold on the study of cognition.

To developmental psychology, he bequeathed a powerful conception of mind, through a constructivist perspective, as active in the construction of knowledge that swept away a variety of views of the subject as passive in the process of knowledge acquisition. At the heart of his theory was the dialectic relation between subject and object that a number of social determinist critics faulted as not taking the object (i.e., social influences) seriously, and nativists faulted for not taking the subject (i.e., natively given influences) seriously. He stood his ground firmly against both types of assault, although not always for the best of reasons.

In the spirit of Darwinism, and the earlier influences of J. M. Baldwin and G. S. Hall, he offered a distinctly biological model for developmental change in cognitive functions. Although that model, the theory of equilibration, has often been attacked as vague and untestable, no more convincing models of developmental change engage the loyalties of developmental psychologists. In the present debates between computational theories and biologically based connectionist theories, my own view is that despite the likelihood that some form of computational models will survive, the day will be won by the biological theories, although not of the associationist kind. Recent dynamic system theories of the Prigogine type (Prigogine & Stengers, 1984), to which Piaget was sympathetic, also buttress the Piagetian biological model of development. On one score, Piaget expended much effort in the attempt to convince biologists and developmentalists of his neo-Lamarkian theory of evolution. Not many, including myself, were convinced.

Piaget's research program was itself a model for the integration of functionalist and structuralist forms of explanation, although at various times the emphasis was on one or the other form. As Piaget liked to put it, there is no form without function and no function without form. Theories that use one form of explanation to the exclusion of the other are bound to fail in providing an adequate account of development.

Piaget's mappings of logico-mathematical models onto cognitive development, in his structuralist period in particular, were a bold attempt to account for diverse kinds of rational and scientific thought. As I have previously argued (Beilin, 1985), Piaget was not committed to any one of these models and substituted others or added and modified them when their mappings onto the child's thought or activity were found to be wanting. Others can do no less.

Methodologically, Piaget made respectable his so-called clinical method, despite much criticism from behaviorists, neobehaviorists, and others and his own disposition to use classical experimental methods when needed (as in his experiments on perception). Although he did not rely on traditional forms of causal explanation, his analyses intended to serve the same purpose. Whether his essential discovery procedure adequately served this way or not, his studies yielded insights into development that were singularly important and better served science, as he often pointed out, than did scores of controlled experiments.

Piaget has left a monumental body of ingenious, provocative, and theory-rich research. The many, as yet, unexplored treasures in that trove, which are anything but hidden, will serve as resources for generations of investigators to come. From this body of experiments and findings, it is nearly impossible to predict what will capture the interest and imagination of future investigators, as the recent child's-theory-of-mind research illustrates with respect to the realism and animism work of the 1920s.

Some veins are nearly, if not thoroughly, exhausted, as in the case of the conservations and training studies. Piagetian-type studies of language acquisition are few and will probably remain so, although the Piagetian claim of cognitive precursors to language is not likely to die. Nevertheless, research on sensorimotor development, classification, and concept, and logic-based research, will probably continue unabated, with Piaget's research and theory acting as a reference point, at the very least. If, in the future, Piaget's theory and research are to compete actively in the marketplace of ideas, it will be, I believe, with respect to the new theory and the attendant experimental work.

But Piaget's theory has formidable competition and adversaries, despite the widespread diffusion of Piagetian concepts and assumptions in other frameworks. The competition (Beilin, 1983) comes principally from neo-nativists, neo-computationalists (information processors and those influenced by them), contextualists, "theory" theorists, and neo-pragmatists (a diffuse group of investigators with no clear theoretical allegiances). One needs no crystal ball to know that no one of these positions will survive intact by the end of the next century. Nevertheless, if present trends continue, some form of biologically oriented theory will have a greater role in developmental theory and research as neuroscience expands into the field. It is difficult to see how contextualism, in one form or another but without radical relativism, will not have a significant place in its debates with modularity theory and nativism. In other words, everything will change, but some things will remain the same. Piaget's theory, as at present, in some form should mediate in staking out a vigorous middle ground between nativism and environmentalism.

It cannot be ignored that Piaget was a product of the Enlightenment, which manifested itself most cogently in his interest in describing and explaining the development of rational thought. We live at present in an intellectual climate in which radical relativism undermines claims to truth and in which nonrational and irrational aspects of mind are the focus of much attention. Utopian post-Enlightenment dreams of a world made up of rational minds and institutions organized on rational principles are now seen for what they always were, utopian. But life in this world cannot do without rationality any more than it can do without Piaget.

REFERENCES

Alexander, C. N., & Langer, E. J. (Eds.). (1990). *Higher stages of human development: Perspectives of adult growth.* New York: Oxford University Press.

Anderson, A. R., & Belnap, N. D., Jr. (1975). *Entailment: The logic of relevance and necessity.* Princeton, NJ: Princeton University Press.

Astington, J. W., Harris, P. L., & Olson, D. R. (Eds.). (1988). *Developing theories of mind.* Cambridge, England: Cambridge University Press.

Baillargeon, R., DeVos, J., & Graber, M. (1989). Location memory in 8-month-old infants in a non-search A–B task: Further evidence. *Cognitive Development, 4,* 345–367.

Beilin, H. (1971). The training and acquisition of logical operations. In M. F. Rosskopf, L. P. Steffe, & S. Toback (Eds.), *Piagetian cognitive-developmental research and mathematical education* (pp. 81–124). Washington, DC: National Council of Teachers of Mathematics.

Beilin, H. (1975). *Studies in the cognitive basis of language development.* San Diego: Academic Press.

Beilin, H. (1978). Inducing conservation through training. In G. Steiner (Ed.), *Psychology of the 20th century: Vol. 7. Piaget and beyond* (pp. 260–289). Zurich, Switzerland: Kindler.

Beilin, H. (1983). The new functionalism and Piaget's program. In E. K. Scholnick (Ed.), *New trends in conceptual representation: Challenges to Piaget's theory?* (pp. 3–40). Hillsdale, NJ: Erlbaum.

Beilin, H. (1985). Dispensable and core elements in Piaget's theory. *The Genetic Epistemologist, 13,* 1–16.

Beilin, H. (1989). Piagetian theory. In R. Vasta (Ed.), Six theories of child development: Revised formulations and current issues. *Annals of Child Development, 6,* 85–132.

Beilin, H. (1992). Piaget's new theory. In H. Beilin & P. B. Pufall (Eds.), *Piaget's theory: Prospects and possibilities* (pp. 1–17). Hillsdale, NJ: Erlbaum.

Beilin, H., & Pearlman, E. G. (in press). Children's iconic realism: Object vs. property realism. In H. W. Reese (Ed.), *Advances in child development and behavior* (Vol. 23). San Diego: Academic Press.

Benacerraf, P., & Putnam, H. (1964). *Philosophy of mathematics.* Englewood Cliffs, NJ: Prentice Hall.

Beth, E. W., & Piaget, J. (1966). *Mathematical epistemology and psychology.* Dordrecht, The Netherlands: Reidel.

Broughton, J. M., & Freeman-Moir, D. J. (Eds.). (1982). *The cognitive-developmental psychology of James Mark Baldwin: Current research in genetic epistemology.* Norwood, NJ: Ablex.

Bruner, J. S., Olver, R. R., & Greenfield, P. M. (1966). *Studies in cognitive growth.* New York: Wiley.

Carey, S., & Gelman, R. (Eds.). (1991). *The epigenesis of mind: Essays on biology and cognition.* Hillsdale, NJ: Erlbaum.

Case, R. (1985). *Intellectual development: Birth to adulthood.* San Diego: Academic Press.

Case, R., Marini, Z., McKeough, A., Dennis, S., & Goldberg, J. (1986). Horizontal structure in middle childhood. Cross domain parallels in the course of cognitive growth. In I. Levin (Ed.), *Stage and structure: Reopening the debate* (pp. 1–39). Norwood, NJ: Ablex.

Chapman, M. (1988). *Constructive evolution: Origins and development of Piaget's thought.* Cambridge, England: Cambridge University Press.

Chapman, M. (1992). Equilibration and the dialectics of organization. In H. Beilin & P. B. Pufall (Eds.), *Piaget's theory: Prospects and possibilities* (pp. 39–59). Hillsdale, NJ: Erlbaum.

Diamond, A. (1988). The abilities and neural mechanisms underlying A–B performance. *Child Development, 59,* 523–527.

Dixon, R. A. (1987). Wittgenstein, contextualism, and developmental psychology. In M. Chapman & R. A. Dixon (Eds.), *Meaning and the growth of understanding: Wittgenstein's significance for developmental psychology* (pp. 49–67). Berlin: Springer-Verlag.

Ennis, R. (1982). Children's ability to handle Piaget's propositional logic: A conceptual critique. In S. Modgil & C. Modgil (Eds.), *Jean Piaget: Consensus and controversy* (pp. 101–130). New York: Praeger.

Flavell, J. H. (1963). *The developmental psychology of Jean Piaget.* Princeton, NJ: Van Nostrand.

Fodor, J. A. (1975). *The language of thought.* Cambridge, MA: Harvard University Press.

Harris, P. H. (1983). Infant cognition. In P. H. Mussen (Series Ed.) and H. H. Haith & J. J. Campos (Vol. Eds.), *Handbook of child psychology: Vol. 2. Infancy and developmental psychobiology* (4th ed., pp. 689–782). New York: Wiley.

Inhelder, B., & Piaget, J. (1958). *The growth of logical thinking from childhood to adolescence.* New York: Basic Books. (Original work published in French in 1955)

Inhelder, B., & Piaget, J. (1980). Procedures and structures. In D. R. Olson (Ed.), *The social foundations of language and thought: Essays in honor of Jerome S. Bruner* (pp. 19–27). New York: Norton.

Inhelder, B., Sinclair, H., & Bovet, M. (1974). *Learning and the development of cognition.* Cambridge, MA: Harvard University Press.

Kohlberg, L. (1969). Stage and sequence: The cognitive developmental approach to socialization. In D. A. Goslin (Ed.), *Handbook of socialization theory and research* (pp. 347–480). Chicago: Rand McNally.

Levin, I. (1986). *Stage and structure: Reopening the debate.* Norwood, NJ: Ablex.

MacLane, S. (1972). *Categories for the working mathematician.* New York: Springer-Verlag.

Mischel, T. (Ed.). (1971). *Cognitive development and epistemology.* San Diego: Academic Press.

Montangero, J. (1985). *Genetic epistemology: Yesterday and today.* New York: CUNY, Graduate School and University Center.

Perner, J. (1991). *Understanding the representational mind.* Cambridge, MA: MIT Press.

Piaget, J. (1926). *Language and thought of the child.* London: Kegan Paul, Trench, & Trubner. (Original work published in French in 1923)

Piaget, J. (1928). *Judgment and reasoning in the child.* London: Kegan Paul, Trench, & Trubner. (Original work published in French in 1924)

Piaget, J. (1929). *The child's conception of the world.* London: Kegan Paul, Trench, & Trubner. (Original work published in French in 1923)

Piaget, J. (1930). *The child's conception of physical causality.* London: Kegan Paul, Trench, & Trubner. (Original work published in French in 1927)

Piaget, J. (1932). *The moral judgment of the child*. London: Kegan Paul, Trench, & Trubner. (Original work published in French in 1932)

Piaget, J. (1950). *The psychology of intelligence*. London: Kegan Paul, Trench, & Trubner. (Original work published in French in 1947)

Piaget, J. (1962a). *Comments concerning Vygotsky's critical remarks concerning* The language and thought of the child *and* Judgment and reasoning in the child. Cambridge, MA: MIT Press.

Piaget, J. (1962b). *Play, dreams, and imitation in childhood*. New York: Norton.

Piaget, J. (1970). *Structuralism*. New York: Basic Books. (Original work published in French in 1968)

Piaget, J. (1976). *The grasp of consciousness*. Cambridge, MA: Harvard University Press. (Original work published in French in 1974)

Piaget, J. (1978). *Success and understanding*. London: Routledge & Kegan Paul. (Original work published in French in 1974)

Piaget, J. (1980a). *Experiments in contradiction*. Chicago: University of Chicago Press. (Original work published in French in 1974)

Piaget, J. (1980b). The constructivist approach: Recent studies in genetic epistemology. *Cahiers de la Fondation Archives Jean Piaget*. No. 1., 1–7.

Piaget, J. (1985). *The equilibration of cognitive structures*. Chicago: University of Chicago Press. (Original work published in French in 1975)

Piaget, J. (1987a). *Possibility and necessity: Vol. 1. The role of possibility in cognitive development*. Minneapolis: University of Minnesota Press. (Original work published in French in 1981)

Piaget, J. (1987b). *Possibility and necessity: Vol. 2. The role of necessity in cognitive development*. Minneapolis: University of Minnesota Press. (Original work published in French in 1981)

Piaget, J., & Garcia, R. (1974). *Understanding causality*. New York: Norton.

Piaget, J., & Garcia, R. (1989). *Psychogenesis and the history of science*. New York: Columbia University Press.

Piaget, J., & Garcia, R. (1991). *Toward a logic of meaning*. Hillsdale, NJ: Erlbaum.

Piaget, J., & Inhelder, B. (1956). *The child's conception of space*. London: Routledge & Kegan Paul. (Original work published in French in 1948)

Piatelli-Palmarini, M. (Ed.). (1980). *Language and learning: The debate between Jean Piaget and Noam Chomsky*. Cambridge, MA: Harvard University Press.

Prigogine, I., & Stengers, I. (1984). *Order out of chaos*. New York: Bantam Books.

Sinclair, H. J. (1992). Changing perspectives in child language acquisition. In H. Beilin & P. B. Pufall (Eds.), *Piaget's theory: Prospects and possibilities* (pp. 211–228). Hillsdale, NJ: Erlbaum.

Wellman, H. M. (1990). *Children's theories of mind*. Cambridge, MA: Bradford Books/MIT Press.

Wellman, H. M., Cross, D., & Bartsch, K. (1986). Infant search and object permanence: A meta-analysis of the A not B error. *Monographs of the Society for Research in Child Development, 51*(3, Serial No. 214).

Youniss, J., & Damon, W. (1992). Social construction in Piaget's theory. In H. Beilin & P. B. Pufall (Eds.), *Piaget's theory: Prospects and possibilities* (pp. 267–286). Hillsdale, NJ: Erlbaum.

10

HEINZ WERNER'S RELEVANCE FOR CONTEMPORARY DEVELOPMENTAL PSYCHOLOGY

JOSEPH A. GLICK

When a field formally undertakes an examination of its past, it is often a way of finding its present. The search for history accomplishes, intentionally or not, two related goals. On the one hand, the past is constructed so as to legitimize the present by giving it a history, grounding some current practices and understandings in a tradition, leading from the past, that seems to point to the present. The present is then seen as an extension of the fundamental insights of that past. On the other hand, finding a history can be a way of relegating figures of potentially contemporary relevance to "history" and, hence, outside of the domain of current interests. In both of these senses, finding one's history is really a way of constructing oneself in the present. These processes are particularly apparent in the '80s and '90s, during which this process of selective construction is seen at an accelerated pace, with figures at temporal distance treated as

Reprinted from *Developmental Psychology*, 28, 558–565. Copyright by the American Psychological Association.

contemporaries and some more historically proximal thinkers put in the past as historical relics.

At the outset, then, I must confess a certain tension in presenting Heinz Werner as part of a historical series of articles. I am not sure that he belongs there. In many senses, although he is currently mostly forgotten, those of us who trained with him or who occupied the same departmental space cannot treat him as part of history. In some respects, Werner was a very modern thinker whose theoretical views were so at variance with normal professional practices that his message is yet to be heard.

Werner died in 1964, approximately 30 years after Vygotsky and 16 years before Piaget. If you attempt to judge Werner's impact on the field from the volume of citations in current references in journals, books, or book chapters, it would seem that his psychology has had little impact. In cases in which he is cited, it appears that his views have been transcended by better information or more modern conceptualizations. Many of the remaining citations of Werner put him even more firmly in the past by putting his work on the wrong side of areas of contemporary consensus, particularly with respect to what are presented as his views about psychological functioning in non-Western societies (e.g., LCHC [Laboratory of Comparative Human Cognition], 1983).

Particularly in comparison to his rough contemporaries, Vygotsky and Piaget, Werner seems to have precipitously faded from view. The volume of references to Vygotsky has been increasing, markedly it seems, in recent years. New volumes on Vygotsky continue to appear (Moll, 1990; Wertsch, 1985, among many others), and new translations of his works are forthcoming. Volume 1 of the Plenum Press translation of the Russian edition of Vygotsky's collected works appeared in 1987, with four more volumes forthcoming. Piaget is still an obligatory comparison point to frame, at the least, a systematic alternative to current positions. New volumes of Piaget's work have appeared in French as late as 1990—*Morphismes et categories: Comparer et transformer* [Morphisms and Categories: Comparison and Transformation] and in English as late as 1987—*Possibility and Necessity: Vol. 2. The Role of Necessity in Cognitive Development.*

In contrast, Werner's last publication, *Symbol Formation*, coauthored with Bernard Kaplan, appeared in 1963. Werner is seldom cited in mainstream literature, and there is very little in the way of secondary scholarship devoted to working out, clarifying, or otherwise integrating his views within the context of contemporary debate. A chapter dedicated to Werner's theoretical ideas was dropped somewhere between the third and fourth editions of the *Manual of Child Psychology*.

All of this could be understandable as the inevitable result of the passage of time since Werner's last publication. As publications become more and more historically remote, they come to be cited less and less. Interestingly, thanks to the historical factors and the vagaries of posthumous editing and translation, developmental psychology in the United States is, at this moment, currently witnessing a reversal of normal historical process. Some very old manuscripts are seeing the light of day for the first time and appearing with current publication dates. There are good reasons for this. Vygotsky, for example, had published in the (then) Soviet Union and was sufficiently controversial that much of his writing did not go public, in English or in Russian. Therefore, the discovery of Vygotsky is, in part, truly a contemporary discovery. But people are not simply discovering Vygotsky because he is there for the discovery; his discovery makes sense with respect to current interests and practices. I suspect that if there were to be found an undiscovered portion of Werner's work—unpublished manuscripts in great profusion—a discovery and secondary scholarship industry would not develop.

The thesis of this chapter is that Werner has faded from view in large part because his core message is perceived to be out of sync with the contemporary construction of the interests and, particularly, the practices of developmental psychologists. Indeed, in some areas, Werner's fading from view is related to his being too close to some contemporary concerns but seeming to be at too great a variance from contemporary consensus.

Because some of the judgment of the irrelevance of Werner to contemporary issues is based on a misunderstanding of his views, the body of this chapter restates some of the core elements of Werner's approach in a more contemporary idiom. It is my suspicion that this journey to the dustbin of history may well yield some precious finds that the field is at peril to ignore.

REFERENCE POINTS: KEY PUBLICATIONS

Although Heinz Werner published profusely in areas as diverse as mental retardation (e.g., Werner, 1945; Werner & Strauss, 1942) and visual and auditory form perception (Werner, 1935, 1940), his core works are represented in three books, each of which represents a different body of work and scholarship, differing not only in topic but also in method. *Comparative Psychology of Mental Development* was initially published in German in 1926 and was continuously updated thereafter (the last edition was in 1957). This book is largely literature oriented, with numerous citations to other people's studies in psychology, biology, anthropology, and other related fields. Werner's contribution was an attempt to see large general themes that underlay an astoundingly diverse literature and to conceptualize all of these themes within a comprehensive developmental framework. This work is most often treated as representative of Werner's theoretical thinking, and it has drawn contemporary fire when cited at all. *Perceptual Development* (coauthored with Seymour Wapner) presents the results of extensive experimental work on perceptual processes, bundled under the general heading of sensori-tonic field theory (Wapner & Werner, 1957). *Symbol Formation* (coauthored with Bernard Kaplan) also presents extensive work, both experimental and descriptive, on language development and the relation of language activity to other developing functions (Werner & Kaplan, 1963).

Although seemingly diverse, these core publications relate to one another. Although researchers in the field seem to understand Werner in terms set out in *Comparative Psychology of Mental Development* (Werner, 1926/1957), those who worked with him understood his work in terms of a larger enterprise, encompassed by the three key works.

BACKGROUND

In many respects, Werner was preoccupied with some of the same sorts of problems that preoccupied Piaget. His roots lay in a continental intellectual tradition heavily influenced by Kant and neo-Kantian philosophers such as Cassirer. Kant had identified a rich presuppositional structure of human thinking and experiences. These conditions of the possibility of thinking were posed as logically prior to experience, because they were the necessary forms within which experience took place. Hence they were posited as the a priori or necessary substrate of experience. Put succinctly, the Kantian assertion of the a priori seemed to leave no room for development. The problem that both Piaget and Werner attempted to solve was how to provide an account of development while at the same time recognizing the fundamental insight provided by Kant.

Werner's search was not unlike Piaget's in many respects. Both were concerned with the attempt to reconcile the fundamental insight of the Kantian position—that experience presupposed an underlying level that made for the conditions of the possibility of having that experience—with the need to account for developmental transformation without a simple appeal to biological preformation. Piaget's answer was to focus on the growth of logic and to develop a systematic alternative account, which saw the Kantian forms as resulting from a process of construction over the early years of life. Piaget's interest was in the constructive mechanisms, whether those be called assimilation, accommodation, organization, or, later, equilibration and reflective abstraction, which could be used to account for the constructive moments in the development of cognitive functions.

Werner's most proximate influence was Gestalt psychology, not the Berlin School (Kohler, Koffka, or Goldstein), but the Leipzig gestalt group (e.g., Felix Sanders). The Berlin gestalt group followed an essentially Kantian quest, seeing a priori structures as the ground for perceptual organization. The gestalt laws posed by this group were timeless or autochthonous and hence were seen as a perceptual equivalent to Kantian categories. In contrast, the Leipsig gestalt school saw the laws of perceptual organization as stemming from a developmental process of formation. What to the Berlin gestalt group were such elementary forms as the segregation of a perceptual field into figure and ground were taken by the Leipzig gestalt group as results of a developmental process. In one of his most prescient studies, Werner (1935) anticipated the technique of backward masking by showing that the development of a contour (which separates a figure from a ground) took microdevelopmental time to be accomplished and that if the temporal process was interrupted, the contour would never be seen (and was therefore backwardly masked).

However, beyond the mere assertion that things take time to develop, Werner was early on struck by the directionality and ubiquity of developmental changes. Not only did things take time to develop—whether in phylogenesis, ontogenesis, or microgenesis—but the direction of those changes displayed an orderly progression, unfolding a succession of organizational forms that succeeded one another in a lawlike fashion.

Although sharing with Piaget an interest in providing a developmental account of the a priori, Werner conceptualized the problem of development more radically. Whereas Piaget methodologically isolated a set of functions—the cognitive functions—and sought the principles of their development, Werner took as his unit of analysis the concept of development itself and sought to trace developmental changes in a wider field and in broader terms.

This search led Werner in two directions, which seem, on the surface, to be contradictory. On the one hand, Werner adopted an *organismic* perspective, by which he sought answers to the problem of the development of the a priori in the way in which organismic functions related to one another. On the other hand, Werner adopted a *comparative* perspective, casting his search for developmental principles more widely into cultural areas.

In this regard, elements of Werner's project shared some features in common with Vygotsky's approach. Development does not proceed unaided or without context. For Werner, it is half an answer to talk of the organismic without at the same time talking about the context within which the organism functions. And, because organisms grow in different cultures, some of the story of the development of the a priori had to be told by coreference to the story of cultural development. For this aspect of his approach, Werner borrowed heavily from the parallel work of Ernst Cassirer (1953, 1955, 1957) in philosophy.

However, Werner differed from Vygotsky, too. As much as it is half an answer to talk about the organismic without the cultural, so also is it half an answer to talk of the cultural without the organismic. The problem, as Werner posed it, was to find a way of talking about development within which these two perspectives could be seen in relation to each other.

CORE THEMES

Werner's developmental psychology is not just older; it is fundamentally different from current conceptions of the problem of accounting for development. Indeed, some of the construction of Werner as relic involves a lack of understanding of some of his most basic ideas. This misunderstanding is itself understandable, because the words that Werner used seem to be familiar. However, as understood within Werner's enterprise, these familiar words referred to unfamiliar concepts, grounded in intellectual traditions that are outside of the traditions shared by most American developmental psychologists. Indeed, if the core messages were fully assimilated, Werner's developmental psychology would likely prove too radical for contemporary tastes.

Werner's conceptual system is distinguished by several sets of core ideas, each of which stands at some variance with current theory and practice. In this article, I focus on three of the core ideas that serve to distance Werner most clearly from contemporary conceptualizations within developmental psychology but that, ironically, serve to ally him quite closely with modern developments in other fields.

Development as Heuristic, Not as Phenomenon

Perhaps the greatest mismatch between contemporary practice and the core of Werner's approach concerns the relation of the concept of "development" as defined by Werner to the topics studied by contemporary developmental psychologists and the way in which such knowledge is constructed with respect to a topic.

For Werner, development was not a substantive topic area. Rather, it was a way of studying things. Developmental theory was, from his perspective, not an explanation of changes that might be observed with age; it did not really have particularly much to do with age changes at all. It was rather a standpoint for interrogating phenomena. It was a set of questions that investigators posed to themselves about the nature of the phenomena they were studying.

This method was grounded in Werner's wide-ranging investigations of development presented in his synoptic book, *Comparative Psychology of Mental Development* (Werner, 1926/1957), in which development was seen as a two-aspect process: differentiation of organismic functions from a primordial global and undifferentiated state to a state of hierarchic integration of the differentiated parts. This "orthogenetic" principle of development had radical implications that served to make Wernerian psychology fundamentally different from other developmental views. The most radical implication was that the topic of developmental study was by no means clear.

Werner's question was of the form, "given an organism and its development, how do the various functions of that organism's development emerge as studyable entities?" Thus, rather than being able to start with language, cognition, logic, or whatever, Werner started with the notion of an organism, which would eventually develop into an organism with differentiated functions, each of which could then be studied. The study of their development would necessarily, within this view, take account of the current level of differentiation of a specific function from the others. Development could then be seen, not as the historical story of a given function at different levels of organization, but rather as a set of qualitatively distinct states marked by varying levels of intrafunctional organization at varying levels of interfunctional organization.

Seen in this way, the problem of the study of development doubled. Traditional conceptualizations of the problem were well geared to examine intrafunctional developmental changes. Research designs or observational paradigms are, in fact, particularly well suited to look at various levels of a common target function. Where they run into difficulty is when the function that is methodologically segregated for study is not segregated within the organism. Werner always questioned the level of independence of a function, as well as its history. And when this question is raised, the study of development becomes complex in ways that challenge available experimental techniques. Rather than looking, for example, at cognitive development in infants, one would look at infants with an eye toward whether there was such a thing as a separable and differentiated cognitive function within them.

This view of the problem makes the study of development far more complex than traditional approaches that take the entities to be studied for granted and trace their history. Although this aspect of Werner's thinking puts him at variance with ordinary practices within professionalized developmental psychology, it simultaneously allies him more closely with various postmodernist approaches in other disciplines. The postmodernist perspective sees the entities that are studied as products of particular practices that "form" them for study. It doubles the enquiry so that one must not only account for the laws of the entity as they are proposed within theories, but one must also account for the processes of "entification" that form the entities into the things that are then studied.

This fact alone makes Werner easily fated for extinction, because this way of theorizing, while perhaps suitable for philosophical and literary journals, is at variance with the normal practices of developmental psychologists. In normal practice, researchers address themselves to a literature by following some topic and then aligning various theories and research findings with respect to that topic. Theoretical ideas must be ideas of sufficient concreteness that they can themselves be treated as the kind of higher order topics that can allow a literature to be organized around them. For example, the *zone of proximal development* (Vygotsky, 1978) and *operations* (Piaget, 1983) are the kinds of topics around which one can organize one's thinking. When topics begin to exceed a searchable range of concreteness, they fall off into the unclassifiable, and hence they have their place only in books and articles devoted to "theories." Such is Werner's sometimes home now (Crain, 1992).

Processes Versus Achievements

The interest in the "entification" processes of development and developmental analysis was coupled with an analytic stance that was typical of the Wernerian approach. There was a sharp distinction made between the surface structure of phenomena (the level at which one measures and identifies them) and the deep structure of phenomena, which was something that had to be unearthed by clever experimental means. This matter goes deeply to the heart of the methodological construction of developmental psychological practices.

To study the development of "an X" over some stretch of time, one has to take into account a prior operation that one can call the "construction of the X to be studied." To the extent that developmental analysis requires the repeated measurement of "an X" at various points in time, one must be confident that it is the same "X." Thus, if one wants to study the development of logic, one must be able to posit a class of measurements laid out over a time series as all being measures that somehow reflect the underlying topic, that is, logic. If this assumption of methodological continuity is questioned, then the possibility of developmental analysis is threatened.

The manner in which this methodological continuity is constructed and examined was of critical concern to Werner. In a ground-breaking article on "Process and Achievement" published in 1937, Werner demonstrated that underneath a supposedly continuous function such as brightness constancy, there was a succession of differential organizations of behavior that made the supposedly continuous phenomenon a product of a series of discontinuities that related to one another only on the plane of psychologists' measurements. However, these were not necessarily related in terms of a series of structures that build on one another. On one level, brightness constancy might be achieved by a reflexive organization at the pupillary level (where reflexive dilation and constriction of the pupil allowed for differential amounts of light to reach the retina), hence suggesting a sensorimotor form of constancy. This level of organization of the process might then be succeeded by other levels involving higher levels of processing that involve a computational relation between figure and ground to be calculated. Finally, there was a level of constancy that depended on a knowledge base that specified how the object was supposed to look (e.g., coal in bright light). Therefore, although a common set of measures (achievements) might be applied, and data laid out in the form of connected points that traced the development of the constancy function, the underlying conception of process suggests that there is no warrant for connecting the points, because they represent very different behavioral organizations. Werner saw, presciently, that one of the greatest dangers for developmental analysis was the posing of false continuities that mask fundamental process discontinuities.

There are a number of modern echoes of this Wernerian insight, but characteristically, they are echoes without citation. For example, a series of studies by Sroufe and his colleagues (Sroufe, 1979) has been able to show that the standard practice of seeking cross-age correlations between behaviors that look alike often seeks measurement continuity at the wrong level. The correlations between look-alike behaviors are often low, whereas the correlations between behaviors that are dissimilar on the surface but that are similar on the process level are much stronger. Similarly, some fundamental insights of dynamical systems theory (Thelen, 1989) and the older levels-of-organization view of Schneirla (e.g., 1972) share a common stance with a Wernerian developmental perspective. All of these positions draw a sharp distinction between the way things look when they are the topic of psychological measurement and the way they are when analyzed at the level of process.

Development of a Process Analysis

Although the distinction between process and achievement that Werner posed may seem noncontroversial in a seemingly postbehaviorist world of practice, the somewhat radical methodological and theoretical implications of that view are neither easily grasped nor easily practiced. For Werner, as well as for those who follow in his footsteps, the production of a process description is not something that is easily achieved, because a somewhat atypical stance toward the study of phenomena is demanded. From the Wernerian point of view, the process will not simply reveal itself either by close examination or by a sensitive approach to data analysis. The process can only be revealed by a planned structure of investigatory activity that constantly seeks to find differentiating measurement operations that can expose to view process differences that might otherwise be hidden. The organization of data and evidence in terms of achievements is almost second nature to normal practitioners of normal developmental science, who organize data topically, and the topics are provided by the achievement level of organization. The "titling" practices stress an achievement continuity. A title such as "Logical Thinking in 6-, 8-, and 11-Year-Olds" posits an underlying entity—logic—which is then measured at different points on a time–age continuum.

Yet, if the implied continuity is or may be somehow "illusory," the question remains whether it is a real continuity or only a measurement continuity. Because the practice of the field predisposes it to seek continuities, the burden of proof lies on those who would question that seemingly self-evident continuity. Such is the burden of all levels-of-organization points of view, which seek differential organizations underlying a supposedly continuous function.

Werner's fundamental insight was that an alternative practice was necessary, one that was guided by a strong theory of development that would exert theoretical pressure on normal measurement and titling practices. Werner pursued a solution to this problem along three different dimensions.

First, to look for possible differential underlying organizations, one must find a theoretical guidepost that tells one where to look and how to look for it. Second, one needs to identify an interactive plane within which the proposed process phenomena occur and in terms of which relations between successive organizations can be found. Third, one needs to find a sufficiently enriched description of both phenomena and influences on phenomena so that variables can be identified, the manipulation of which will be instructive to process-oriented experiments.

Theoretical Guideposts to a Process Analysis

Although Werner's theory is talked about as if it were "a theory"—an interrelated set of propositions about development—either it was a theory of such general scope so as to be not usable, or it was not a theory at all. If Werner's theory is to be thought of as a theory, it must be understood as a theory on the "grand scale," as a theory about organisms and their development that did not hinge on or come to rest on a delimited set of phenomena. Such grand theories are currently out of fashion, perhaps justifiably. The test of theories is whether they help to produce phenomena that are interesting and studyable (the heuristic value of theory), as well as to simultaneously provide an explanation of those phenomena. An additional modern demand is that the theory have pragmatic value, that is, that it relate to practice in identifiable ways.

Although Werner's theory has great heuristic value, it does not really provide explanations that count as explanations, and although it has pragmatic and practical implications, those are not its focus. I have found it useful to think of Werner's theory as a methodological guidepost telling one where to look to identify the operations that serve to distinguish levels of functioning and, hence, to allow for layered process descriptions.

The fundamental theoretical–methodological stance is that processes are likely to be organized at one of three different levels: the sensorimotor, the perceptual, or the symbolic. These different levels of organization will be reflected in methodological terms by different classes of stimulus variation influencing variation of functioning within the organizational level. One must, then, painstakingly examine the level of structural–functional organization by being sensitive to the various classes of variation that might apply. The work of Lewkowitz and Turkewitz (1980) with infants and the work of Pollack (1983) on the influence of lower level stimulus features determining processing that is often taken as indicative of higher level functioning are cases in point of the use of these methodological tactics to illuminate a field of inquiry by differentiating various levels of organization of processes.

The methodological constraint of finding classes of variation that will serve to differentiate similar-looking achievements leads inevitably in another direction as well. There is a commitment to an enriched representation of the kinds of stimulus fields that are the actual surround of a behavior in question. Within a Wernerian world view, the stimulus world as defined and definable by an experimenter involves both a specific point of focus and a specific point of blindness to things that might have been focused on but were not.

Although this is a recognized feature of any treatment of method taken at some level of analytic depth, it is a centrally constitutive feature of the Wernerian approach. The evaluation of the looked-at against the backdrop of the not-looked-at was a matter of central theoretical concern. Moreover, and more deeply, the evaluation of how the looked-at was looked at was also at the core of the issue. In this respect, Wernerian psychology shared some deep assumptions with Vygotskian thinking. Both schools drew a sharp distinction between *fossilized* behaviors and *nascent* behaviors, in which development could be more clearly seen. It became a matter of concern for both schools to peel away the fossilized levels in order to make development seeable. In Vygotsky's work, this tactical move led to the use of a method of double stimulation, in which normal access routes to functioning were systematically deprived and alternative means offered in their place. In Werner's work on language development, presented in *Symbol Formation* (Werner & Kaplan, 1963), similar techniques were used. A variety of alternative media for expression—for example, line drawings or gestures— were used in order to experimentally "primitivize" language use so that more dynamic, nascent, and unfossilized features of language use could be observed.

The upshot of many of these experiments was an attempt to show that the development of word meaning was not simply a matter of the extension of reference; rather, the language function was seen as undergoing a differentiation process from deeper sensorimotor roots. It was not until later stages of development and in fossilized usages that language could be seen to function as an autonomous medium.

Search for a Process Language

One of the characteristic features of a Wernerian view of process was that a means must be found to represent processes and the relation among functions in a set of terms that could allow for an understanding of how seemingly different functions could interrelate. In this sense, Werner demanded an organismic theory that could account for the way in which the psychological functions could interact with one another at various levels of differentiation.

Wapner and Werner's *Perceptual Development*, published in 1957, summarized nearly a decade of experimental work devoted to working out elements of such an organismic theory, called sensori-tonic field theory. The original formulations of sensori-tonic field theory were in reaction to many of the "new look" studies in perception that demonstrated the interrelation among affective, cognitive, and perceptual functions. For Werner, it was not enough to assert, or even to experimentally demonstrate, that knowledge states or affective states were variables that influenced such seemingly remote processes as perceptual recognition. Rather, Werner took it as incumbent on those who would talk of these interrelations to develop notions of organismic representation of process that could account for how the effects could be achieved.

This way of dealing with the problem has a somewhat modern ring to it, because problems of representation have taken on an increasingly central role in attempts to describe processes (Mandler, 1983). However, whereas modern attempts to deal with representational structure focus on the organization of functioning within a domain, Werner was seeking the kind of representation that could be understood as applying to organisms and, in particular, that would allow for a representation suitable for interfunctional relations. Werner's notion of an organismic representational system, pursued in the context of perceptual work and through the study of language development, was not fully worked out at the time of his death. However, it was sufficiently different in kind from current notions of representation so as to be scarcely recognizable to them.

The reason for this is clear and characteristic. Many attempts at developing a representational language do so within the segregated domain of an area of functioning. Some function is isolated, some problem within that area of function is defined, and possible psychological representations are fitted with and tested against the performance of various age groups.

However, for Werner, the topic was the organism and the way in which the various functions within the organism relate to one another. Therefore, his basic intuition was that a fundamentally organismic form of representation was needed, one that did not necessarily link an organism's function to a problem structure but that linked an organism's functions to each other.

For this purpose, Werner pursued the usefulness of a vectorial or dynamic treatment of organismic representation. The basic idea was that although each of the separate functions may use its own representations, the possibility of their interrelation presupposed a more basic level of representation that could provide a common language by means of which the various functions could communicate. Thus, in perceptual studies, Werner (Wapner & Werner, 1957) pursued the usefulness of a theoretical language that could describe intersensory relations in terms of dynamic tendencies, counteractive forces, and the like.

Similarly, in their language studies, Werner and Kaplan (1963) pursued an analytic attempt to decompose word meanings into a dynamic-vectorial language that could be used to account for the connotational structure of concepts and relations between concepts as they are represented in language. Their basic position was that although one could attempt to represent the denotational structure of concepts by traditional (componential) means, one could not understand language use, which is in essence connotational, without recourse to deeper levels of representation.

Organism and Environment as Multiple Moments

Both Piaget's and Vygotsky's theories are taken as dealing with an understanding of the relation between a developing organism and its environment. For Piaget, the standpoint of analysis was, at least in part, an issue of the transactional cycles that link behavior to the environment, considered largely as a physical environment. For Vygotsky, the issue was, at least in part, the relation between developing organisms and their sociohistorical environment. Thus, both of these theories have profound educational implications and accord well with a field of developmental psychology that fundamentally looks for the mechanisms by which capacities come into the competence of organisms as they develop. These conceptualizations leave room for environmental input and point toward the kinds of things that interest and that can allow developmentalists to talk to various constituencies that may be looking for help (e.g., parents, teachers, or educational systems).

Werner's focus on the organism seems to leave the organism cut off from the environment in a way that could lead one to believe that his theory had little relation to environments, considered either physically or sociohistorically. Such is not the case, and it is the conceptualized relation between organism and environment that has led to the deepest misconstruals of the Wernerian enterprise.

We have already seen how the topics that developmentalists study and the theoretical apparatus of Wernerian developmental psychology are somewhat mismatched. This mismatch has been pursued so far in the context of the conception of topic. The mismatch is deeper than that.

For Werner, the analysis of development required an understanding of a system that necessarily included a designation of the interrelation of organismic functions (process analysis) but that also included an environment with respect to which and within which these functions were organized. Psychological functions were seen as being organized within such moments of functioning, in which a given level of interfunctional organization was mobilized with respect to an environment.

Perhaps this mode of thinking is best exemplified by the work pursued by Werner and Kaplan (1963) with respect to the relation of linguistic organization to various mediational forms. Their work focused, in particular, on the way in which concept and medium shaped each other. The basic theoretical idea was that language use involves a process of dual schematization. On the one hand, a concept was underpinned by a particular connotational structure that led to a particular "shaping" of a symbolic vehicle (e.g., the intonation of speech or the way in which one could represent the concept by a line drawing). At the same time, the nature of the symbolic medium itself could be seen as supporting a particular means of expression (e.g., a concept could take on a different connotational structure, depending on the available means for its expression). This principle underlay the analysis of symbol development. Thus, Werner and Kaplan were talking neither about symbolic development in children of different ages nor about the nature of symbolic media. They were talking about the meeting point, or moment of interaction, between a symbolic medium and an organism. The result of these two inputs would yield a particular level of developmental organization of the symbolic function. The process of "double schematization" described earlier was considered to be illustrative of the general problem of development.

Development was seen as a series of such moments linking an organism at a given level of development with a medium within which that development would be expressed. The resultant development level would be a joint function of the two sets of determinants. In this way, Werner reconciled his organismic and comparative viewpoints.

If one pursues the line of thinking opened up by the dual schematization notion, there are a number of radical consequences for understanding the relation between Wernerian thinking and the normal interests of developmental psychologists. Some of the more obvious consequences are highlighted here.

Reconceptualization of the Unit of Analysis

The most obvious consequence of this analytic approach is to break up one of the most fundamental units that child psychologists use. If the notion of developmental analysis is defined by moments of linkage between organismic functions and environments that support or call out different levels of functioning (dual schematization), the fundamental analytic unit cannot be conceptualized in terms of age or even function at an age (e.g., concrete operations in 5-, 7-, and 9-year-olds). The fundamental unit becomes the moment that is codefined by an existing organismic level of interfunctional development and by an environmental medium within which, and with respect to which, the organism is organized.

The immediate consequence is to regard the child as being composed of multiple and nonfixed functional systems. The multiplicity of functional systems stems from the notion that behavior is always organized with respect to some environment that is itself organized. Variation can stem from either source. Because variation can stem from either source, it is quite possible to change the measured level of performance by changing the environmental organization within which that performance is called on.

Within this conceptual framework, people would be seen to be at simultaneously multiple developmental levels. The matter of which level is expressed is a matter of the way in which the moment of measurement was constructed. Thus, Wernerian developmental theory is not a theory about people either at various ages or in various cultures. It is rather a theory about "moments" of people by environment interactions. This point is critical for an understanding of the enterprise.

Werner has often been construed as talking about developmental issues at the level of "people." Thus, his identifications of certain phenomena within certain non-Western groups have been called into question. He is criticized as failing to understand that the non-Western people he described are not primitive, that they are fully capable of developing more advanced functions and that certain of their practices are, in fact, more advanced than Werner described. Indeed, casual reading of some of Werner's (and Cassirer's) descriptions of anthropological evidence supports this discomfort. It is, however, a reading without a context. Concepts such as "primitivity" are, in context, concepts that apply on the level of moments of organization and not on the level of people. Werner did not have a primitive in mind (if that primitive is taken to be a person); rather, he had a picture of development in mind, in which some levels of organization were more primitive than others (Werner & Kaplan, 1956).

Although Werner himself never developed an experimental approach to the issue, the approach embedded in the concept of the moment (a term, by the way, which Werner never used) is quite in sympathy with Vygotsky's notions of the mediation of psychological functions, in particular with respect to the possibility of extending the range of an organism's functioning by providing appropriate mediational tools (the "zone of proximal development"). Whether the external mediator was another person or a different symbolic medium was not a key issue for Werner; nor, in retrospect, does it seem a key issue for Vygotsky. The key issue for both of them was that a given, measured level of functioning was not fully determined by in-the-person factors; rather, the analytic unit must take into account the mediational surround.

Conceptualization of Processes of Development

A second main consequence of the analysis by moment was to broaden the range of phenomena to which the concept of development could be applied. Werner's notions extended the concept of development to apply to *microgenesis*, or the time that it takes to assemble a functional system at the moment of its being called into play. Thus, development not only extended laterally—across ages, across functions, and across environments—it applied vertically as well. This thoroughly developmental view followed directly on his notion of the moment of functioning. If one is not dealing with fixed patterns within organisms, then it follows that each occasion of behaving would require some "assembly time" and, hence, would undergo some period of formation that could be analyzed in terms of developmental theory.

Werner devised several means for seeing these microdevelopmental phenomena and describing them. Although I do not dwell on the results of the microgenetic studies, it is important to show how they serve to further complicate the developmentalist's task. If a thoroughly developmental approach requires the consideration of assembly time, then it becomes critical to determine the point in the assembly process when a measurement has been taken. Any given measure would therefore have a different significance for indicating developmental level, depending on the point in an assembly process that the measure tapped into.

As much as this concept adds to the difficulty, it also offers promise for some new directions for study. If measured functions have undergone a period of assembly through a microdevelopmental process, one might expect that some portion of the lower levels are brought along to the higher levels. Thus, a presumably autonomous function would be expected to have, as part of its connotational structure, some elements that bind it, potentially, to other functions. This notion opens the way not only for studying the display of higher level functions but also for finding a way of locating them in broader areas of the personality.

RADICAL CHALLENGES OF WERNERIAN THEORY

Far from comfortably fitting within current developmental conceptualizations, Werner's concept of development poses a number of radical challenges to them. Therefore it is not surprising that Werner has somehow faded from view. Moreover, it should not be particularly surprising to search in vain for Werner's legacy in terms of his students' contributions to the developmental psychology literature. Although some important figures in the field have emerged from Werner's school (e.g., John Flavell and Eugene Gollin), they typically identify themselves outside of the domain of Wernerian psychology.

The thesis of this review of Werner's thinking is that his conceptualization of the problem of development is so radically at odds with the ordinary practices by means of which developmental psychologists practice their craft that the discipline of developmental psychology and its current close ties with child psychology make the field seem alien and unreceptive.

Werner's psychology, at its deepest levels, challenges the ordinary topics that developmentalists address. In place of functions, in which development can be studied, there are levels of organization, which bear a variable and somewhat uncertain relation to the functions that are topicalized for study. In place of an ability to address a literature in terms of statements about the state of a function at a given age or developmental era, there are statements that talk of the moment of functional organization as it is expressed in a particular environment and at a particular level of functional assembly. In place of a representational language that can link elements of problems to elements of psychological functions, there is a representational language whose main purpose is to recompose these representations to deeper dynamic levels.

Indeed, as I have argued elsewhere (Glick, 1983), Werner suffers from the fact that he does not have a topic that accords well with the topical organization of the field. Yet, his theoretical apparatus is one that could break down some of the artificial separations (e.g., between affect and cognition) that are produced, in part, because of the current topicalization practices.

Werner's theory is perhaps best understood outside the domain of developmental psychology as developmentalists know it. His was one of the earliest attempts at a critical theory of development. It is a critical theory that comes from a completely unexpected place—not from an attempt to question the reifications of some social or economic system but rather from an attempt to find universal laws of development and to relate those laws to the lives of organisms and to the environments within which those lives are lived and, from that perspective, to challenge the research practices of developmental psychologists.

Werner's historic position has suffered from this. Perhaps an article such as this one may serve to relink Werner's thinking to the field. His thinking has much to teach us yet, and although his theoretical ideas are linked to emerging ideas in a somewhat subterranean way, a more careful conceptualization of his contemporary relevance may open up some issues that have remained buried under decades of disciplinary practice.

REFERENCES

Cassirer, E. (1953). *Philosophy of symbolic forms. Vol. I.* New Haven, CT: Yale University Press.

Cassirer, E. (1955). *Philosophy of symbolic forms. Vol. II.* New Haven, CT: Yale University Press.

Cassirer, E. (1957). *Philosophy of symbolic forms. Vol. III.* New Haven, CT: Yale University Press.

Crain, W. (1992). *Theories of development: Concepts and applications.* (3rd ed.). Englewood Cliffs, NJ: Prentice-Hall.

Glick, J. (1983). Piaget, Vygotsky and Werner. In S. Wapner & B. Kaplan (Eds.), *Toward a holistic developmental psychology* (pp. 35–52). Hillsdale, NJ: Erlbaum.

Laboratory of Comparative Human Cognition. (1983). Culture and cognitive development. In P. Mussen (Series Ed.) & W. Kessen (Vol. Ed.), *Handbook of child psychology: Vol I. History, theory and methods* (pp. 295–356). New York: Wiley.

Lewkowitz, D. J., & Turkewitz, G. (1980). Cross-modal equivalence in early infancy: Auditory–visual intensity matching. *Developmental Psychology, 16,* 597–607.

Mandler, J. M. (1983). Representation. In P. Mussen (Series Ed.) & J. H. Flavell & E. M. Markman (Vol. Eds.), *Handbook of child psychology: Vol. III. Cognitive development* (pp. 420–494). New York: Wiley.

Moll, L. C. (Ed.) (1990). *Vygotsky and education: Instructional implications and applications of sociohistorical psychology.* New York: Cambridge University Press.

Piaget, J. (1983). Piaget's theory. In P. Mussen (Series Ed.) & W. Kessen (Vol. Ed.), *Handbook of child psychology: Vol. I. History, theory and methods* (pp. 103–128). New York: Wiley.

Piaget, J. (1987). (H. Feider, Trans.) *Possibility and necessity: Vol. 2. The role of necessity in cognitive development.* Minneapolis: University of Minnesota Press. (Original work published 1983)

Piaget, J. (1990). *Morphismes et categories: Comparer et transformer* [Morphisms and categories: Comparison and transformation]. Neuchâtel, Switzerland: Delachaux et Nièstle.

Pollack, R. H. (1983). Regression revisited: Perceptuo-cognitive performance in the aged. In S. Wapner & B. Kaplan (Eds.), *Toward a holistic developmental psychology* (pp. 133–142). Hillsdale, NJ: Erlbaum.

Schneirla, T. C. (1972). Levels in the psychological capacities of animals. In L. A. Aronson, E. Tobach, J. S. Rosenblatt, & D. S. Lehrman (Eds.), *Selected writings of T. C. Schneirla* (pp. 199–237). San Francisco: Freeman. (Reprinted from R. W. Sellars, V. J. McGill, & M. Farber [Eds.]. [1949]. *Philosophy for the future: The quest for modern materialism*. New York: McMillan)

Sroufe, L. A. (1979). The coherence of individual development. *American Psychologist, 34*, 834–841.

Thelen, E. (1989). Self-organization in developmental processes: Can systems approaches work? In M. Gunnar & E. Thelen (Eds.), *Systems and development: The Minnesota symposium on child psychology* (Vol. 22, pp. 77–117). Hillsdale, NJ: Erlbaum.

Vygotsky, L. S. (1978). *Mind in society: The development of higher psychological processes*. Cambridge, MA: Harvard University Press.

Vygotsky, L. S. (1987). *The collected works of L. S. Vygotsky: Vol. 1. Problems of general psychology*. New York: Plenum Press.

Wapner, S., & Werner, H. (1957). *Perceptual development*. Worcester, MA: Clark University Press.

Werner, H. (1935). Studies on contour. *American Journal of Psychology, 47*, 40–64.

Werner, H. (1937). Process and achievement. *Harvard Educational Review, 7*, 353–368.

Werner, H. (1940). Musical "microscales" and "micromelodies." *The Journal of Psychology, 10*, 149–156.

Werner, H. (1945). Perceptual behavior of brain-injured children. *Genetic Psychology Monographs, 31*, 51–111.

Werner, H. (1957). *Comparative psychology of mental development* (rev. ed.). New York: International Universities Press. (Original work published 1926)

Werner, H., & Kaplan, B. (1956). The developmental approach to cognition: Its relevance to the psychological interpretation of anthropological and ethnolinguistic data. *American Anthropologist, 58*, 866–880.

Werner, H., & Kaplan, B. (1963). *Symbol formation*. New York: Wiley; and Hillsdale, NJ: Erlbaum.

Werner, H., & Strauss, A. (1942). Disorders of conceptual thinking in brain-injured children. *Journal of Nervous Mental Disease, 96*, 153–171.

Wertsch, J. V. (1985). *Vygotsky and the social formation of mind*. Cambridge, MA: Harvard University Press.

11

WILLIAM L. STERN:
A NEGLECTED FOUNDER OF
DEVELOPMENTAL PSYCHOLOGY

KURT KREPPNER

William Stern is practically unknown in modern American psychology. No school of thinking is associated with his name, and his works are not cited in today's textbooks. Yet I will argue that this largely unknown person ought to be considered one of the founders of modern developmental psychology.

William Stern will be remembered by some students of psychology as the inventor of the IQ (presented in a paper delivered in 1912 at the Fifth Conference of the Society of Experimental Psychology in Berlin), the index of an individual's degree of intelligence. Fewer may recall that Stern introduced the notion of "differential psychology" (Stern, 1900, 1911) and did exciting experiments on the perception of pitch and tone (Stern, 1896, 1898, 1903). Among students of language development, William Stern and his wife Clara are known as authors of a comprehensive description of

I am grateful for the many helpful suggestions made by the two reviewers.

Reprinted from *Developmental Psychology, 28,* 539–547. Copyright by the American Psychological Association.

language use in infancy and childhood (C. Stern & W. Stern, 1907). However, unlike other early practitioners of our discipline, such as Baldwin, Piaget, Lewin, and Karl and Charlotte Bühler, William Stern has not found a place in American psychology's "hall of fame."

Although his main opus, *General Psychology From the Personalistic Standpoint*, which was published in its German version in Holland in 1935, also appeared in an English version in the United States in February 1938, about 1 month before his death, his pioneering ideas never attained a high level of visibility outside of European academic circles. In 1938, one of his former students, Gordon W. Allport, wrote Stern's obituary in the *American Journal of Psychology*. During the following years and decades, however, the person as well his work were forgotten not only in the United States but also in Germany.

In this chapter, I first trace the major outlines of Stern's career and depict the forces that might have contributed to his pioneering creative thinking. Second, I introduce basic concepts of his that have relevance to developmental psychology, some of which appear to have been "rediscovered" during the 1970s and 1980s. Third, I elaborate on some crucial concepts of his that I believe were revolutionary for their time but were poorly understood by most of his colleagues and were subsequently forgotten.

Bound to diverse contemporary philosophical traditions located in opposite camps (such as empiristic vs. nativistic or elementaristic–experimental vs. understanding–wholistic positions), Stern put much effort into explicating his vision of a new psychology and into overcoming common templates of either-or thinking. Aside from being a formative figure as a great initiator in the field of applied psychology and as an organizer of creative research in various domains of our science, Stern should also be considered one of the persons who gave the discipline of psychology momentum by opening new windows on innovative perspectives. His intention was to transform psychology by giving it a new foundation. For Stern, this new psychology had its focus in a new unit, the person as the "unitas multiplex." In addition, Stern was also active in the field of experimental psychology. Finally, he was an active disseminator of knowledge from different branches of psychology to other fields, including industry, psychiatry, law, and education.[1]

---

[1] I would like to add a technical note here concerning Stern's writings. Stern's works in their original German versions are difficult to read for today's students of psychology; Stern's German comes from an earlier time in which different words and terms were "alive." Thus, for a contemporary reader, the language may appear somewhat dusty and bound to discussions referring to forgotten concepts or authors. Because this article is written for an American readership, I decided not to quote the original German texts themselves but tried to translate them into English. However, a problem emerged: To capture Stern's German would require a psychological vocabulary similar to that of his contemporaries such as William James or James Mark Baldwin. By using modern terminology, rather than the terms used by his contemporaries, I hope to better illuminate Stern's ideas. Furthermore, I also decided not to use Spoerl's translation of Stern's (1938) last book, *General Psychology From the Personalistic Standpoint*, but rather attempted to translate from the German original (Stern, 1935).

THE PERSON AND HIS CAREER

William Stern was a rising star in European psychology during the early years of this century, between 1900 and 1915. From 1916 to 1933, he institutionalized research programs as the director of the Hamburg Institute. He was at the zenith of his career during the late 1920s and the early 1930s, when he initiated intense collaborations with those in other disciplines such as biology, law, and education. However, he was abruptly barred from his institute by the Nazis in April of 1933 and expelled from Germany in the same year. After a year's stay in The Netherlands, he moved to the United States in 1934. He died on March 27, 1938.

Born in Berlin on April 29, 1871, he was the only child of the retailer Sigismund Stern and his wife Rosa. He began to study philosophy and psychology at the university in his native city in 1888. At that time, a department of psychology did not exist at Berlin University, and two different schools in psychology were fighting each other: a mechanistic, elementaristic psychology oriented toward the natural sciences, on the one hand, and a wholistic, explanatorily oriented psychology on the other. This conflict was later vividly documented in Dilthey's (1894/1924) essay, "Ideas About a Descriptive and Dissecting Psychology." It also reverberated in the discussion between Dilthey, the "understanding" philosopher and wholistic psychologist, and Ebbinghaus, the experiment-guided associationist and elementarist.

This fundamental division between elementaristic and wholistic viewpoints characterized the first academic years of William Stern. His teachers included Friedrich Paulsen, the wholist; Moritz Lazarus, a somewhat moderate, nonexperimental associationist and elementarist; and Hermann Ebbinghaus, a hard-core elementarist who conducted mnemonic experiments by letting subjects memorize endless strings of meaningless syllables. It was here that Stern developed his intention to reconcile what seemed to be irreconcilable. In 1893 he finished his dissertation under Ebbinghaus on *The Analogy in Folk Thinking*. He followed Ebbinghaus to the University of Breslau in 1897, where he completed his habilitation on the *Psychology of the Perception of Change* in the same year (however, it was published in 1898). He became a *Privatdozent* (outside lecturer) for psychology. What followed was perhaps the most creative and fruitful period in Stern's career, from 1897 until 1907 (Eckardt, 1989). These were the years in which he worked on a new foundation of psychology that emphasized a personalistic perspective and invented the IQ and differential psychology. In 1904 ("Psychology of the Child as a Theoretical Science") and 1907 ("Basic Questions of Psychogenesis"), he published two articles in which he presented his ideas about developmental psychology and emphasized the role of both biological and environmental components in human ontogeny. Most of Stern's work from this phase, which encompassed developmental, intelligence, and differential aspects, as well as his foundation of a new, person-oriented psychology, was published later in a series of articles and books between 1908 and 1918. These publications included "Facts and Causes of Psychological Development" (1908), *Differential Psychology in its Methodological Principles* (1911), "Methods for Testing Intelligence" (1912), *Psychology of Early Childhood* (1914), *Psychology and Personalism* (1917), and *Person and Thing* (1918b). It is interesting (for the family researcher) that the creative period between 1897 and 1907 is also the time when Stern founded his family: His three children were born in 1900 (Hilde), 1902 (Günter), and 1904 (Eva). During this period, he and his wife Clara conducted intense observations of their children, focusing on both cognitive and language development. An outcome of this joint venture was the publication of *Children's Speech* (C. Stern & W. Stern, 1907).

In 1906, together with Otto Lipmann, Stern founded the Institute for Applied Psychology in Berlin, a center for applied research, and coedited the journal *Zeitschrift für angewandte Psychologie* [Journal for Applied Psychology]. Although he lamented a bit over his philosophical isolation in Breslau (Stern, 1927, p. 140), these years seem to have been crucial for his career. In 1907, he became an associate professor at the University of Breslau and the director of the psychology department. In 1909, he was honored by Clark University with a doctoral degree. At this time, Stern was 38 years old. The following quote (which appeared in *The Worcester Telegram* of September 11, 1909) may illuminate the reputation Stern had at that time:

> William Stern, *ausserordentlicher* professor of philosophy in the University of Breslau; pioneer in the study of individual psychology; a leader among European students of child life; known and honored wherever psychology itself is honored, doctor of laws. (cited by Hardesty, 1976, p. 31)

Moreover, Stern was also strongly committed to promoting the dissemination of psychological knowledge in the established worlds of industry, law, and education. During these years, for example, he created the "Projekt Jugendkunde" (Dudeck, 1989), a project to foster a new and culture-oriented mode of instruction and a new knowledge about adolescence, which was aimed, in part, at helping teachers better understand their students. In order to pursue his idea, Stern fought against conservatism, psychoanalysis, and wholism, three different schools in education, to clear the ground for his vision of a new psychology.

After Meumann's death in 1915, Stern applied for a position at the Hamburg Kolonialinstitut und Allgemeines Vorlesungswesen [Institute for Colonial Studies], an institution that combined a mainly municipal program of general lectures offering various subjects in social and political sciences and the humanities with an institution founded in 1908 that dealt with colonial matters. There were plans to transform this institution into a new university. The position was attractive for Stern because Meumann, when he had accepted the position in Hamburg in 1911, had established a new department of philosophy, including a psychological laboratory. In Hamburg, teachers had a traditional right to participate in making appointments to this institution. One of the effects of Stern's involvement in the Projekt Jugendkunde was that the Hamburg teachers all voted for him when the vacancy for a professor of philosophy had to be filled. Thus, he was appointed in 1916. After the end of the First World War, in 1918, Stern pressed the faculty council to resurrect the old plans to form a university to meet the needs of the returning veterans. From January 1, 1919, private university courses were offered. During the first years, two assistants, Heinz Werner and Martha Muchow, contributed considerably to the forming of what became the Psychological Institute in Hamburg. In this institute, many divergent branches and practical applications of psychology were fostered under Stern's directorship. The diversity and openness to new approaches created a climate for which the institute was famous. As a result, psychology acquired a new status and high visibility among other disciplines and in the many public sectors such as law, industry, and, last but not least, education.

New windows were opened with challenging empirical research such as Stern's studies dealing with adolescence (Stern, 1922, 1923, 1924, 1925) and Martha Muchow's pioneering efforts in the field of environmental psychology (see Schoggen, 1985; Siegel, 1985; Wapner, 1985; Wohlwill, 1985). Stern initiated and supported the series of environmental studies, which mark a turning point in developmental psychology. These were the first investigations that systematically took into account the objective environmental structures in which children grow up; for example, studies examined the effects of urban areas with certain subcultural characteristics (Muchow, 1935) and the influences of ecological change such as summer camp at the seaside on children's development (Muchow, 1926). Another representative of new directions in developmental psychology was Heinz Werner, who came as a young postdoctoral research associate from Vienna and did his habilitation in 1920, the very first in Hamburg, to become a *Privatdozent*. He was one of Stern's closest colleagues and helped effectively to push forward the organismic view. For 3 years, Fritz Heider, who later became a famous social psychologist, worked at the Hamburg Institute. Though not working at the Hamburg Institute, another young scientist who was strongly influenced by Stern's thinking and associated with Stern's and Lippmann's Institute for Applied Psychology was Kurt Lewin. Stern supported him, for example, by publishing his very first article, "Kriegslandschaft" ("War landscape") in a journal he edited (Lewin, 1917) and by presenting his studies of expressive movements in children in the 1927 edition of Stern's famous *Psychology of Early Childhood*.

Furthermore, Stern organized a well-equipped, full-fledged laboratory for conducting experiments, helped establish a teachers' college, and promoted extensive collaboration with industry. His ability to convey to the public theoretical and empirical knowledge that had accumulated in the discipline helped the Hamburg Institute gain a strong reputation in Germany. During the 1920s, the reputation of the Hamburg Institute was comparable to that of the well-known Vienna Institute associated with the names of Charlotte and Karl Bühler and Hildegard Hetzer. In its years of "full swing" (Hardesty, 1976), 1929 through 1933, the environmental approach of the Hamburg Institute was supported by courses that were cosponsored by von Uexkuell's Institute for Environmental Research (Umweltforschung) and by departments of the university's schools of medicine and law, which made the Hamburg Institute famous as a hub for divergent lines of thought in theoretical, methodological, and practical developments in psychology.

This ended abruptly when Stern, at the age of 62, was barred from his own institute in April of 1933 by the Nazis and had to leave Germany later in the same year. After a year of waiting in Holland, where Kohnstamm unsuccessfully tried to get a position for him, Stern arrived in 1934 in the United States, where he finally got a position with the help of William McDougall at Duke University in Durham (Hardesty, 1976). In addition to his permanent position at Duke, Stern gave lectures at various American universities such as Brown, Columbia, and Harvard. He died on March 27, 1938, at the age of nearly 67.

MAJOR CONCEPTS IN STERN'S THINKING

Stern's interest in reconciling divergent theoretical positions may also account for his roles as an instigator of interdisciplinary research and as a promoter of applications of psychological knowledge in public areas. He recognized the detrimental effects on the entire discipline of the many public fights between opposite camps in psychology. His political and enlightenment-driven impetus to serve the public may help explain his search for a synthetic view that would keep the two diverging psychologies together (Eckardt, 1989): On the one hand, Stern sought to overcome the schism between the empirical approach of natural science and the philosophical approach. On the other hand, he aimed to create a unified mainstream psychology that would have multiple branches and be of practical value in solving the problems of his time. He was convinced that only a unified psychology could consolidate the new discipline among the other well-established disciplines in academia and gain public recognition as a science. The elementarists' fruitless and frustrating attempts under Ebbinghaus, as well as the exaggerated claims of Dilthey's school of "understanding" psychology, were negative examples that led him to conceptualize a theory that could reconcile both viewpoints.

However, Stern's personalistic psychology was interpreted by many of his contemporaries as being too idealistic (e.g., his concept of society as a hierarchy of personalities). Stern clearly dissociated himself from the elementarists, whom he saw as adding elements mechanically to form a sum. He also criticized their theorizing that psychological elements are carriers of psychological forces. He was convinced that this model deviated too far from reality, and he offered an alternative in which he underlined his belief that, for example, a person's actions are defined not by single elements but by the entire structure of environment, person, and person–environment interaction. Thus, a wholistic view was one of the fundamental bases from which Stern constructed his person-oriented theoretical framework. However, Stern's conception was not identical with what later became the core of wholistic psychology, or *Ganzheitspsychologie*. Instead, the central idea is the "embeddedness" of a person's actions in the environment.

Although one could elaborate on many areas in which Stern offered new concepts or experimental designs, the following samples of his contributions are selected from the domain of developmental psychology. They are examples of his basic person- and environment-oriented approach manifest in the theory of convergence and in the model of the active–reactive personality. Some of the concepts he created to grasp the *process* of development are presented in more detail, such as his ideas about activity–passivity, proximal space, and egocentrism.

Theory of Convergence

The idea of conflict and convergence grew out of Stern's intention to create an overarching concept in which both nativism and environmentalism could be accepted as two aspects of the same process—namely, individuation. Thus Stern focused on the interplay between the individual's endowment, or "dispositions," on the one hand and the environmental conditions influencing individual development on the other. Although Stern's approach may appear somewhat similar to Piaget's concepts of assimilation and accommodation, it places more emphasis on the process of exchange between the individual's evolving propensities and talents and the environment's hindering or supporting conditions. The two aspects, endowment and environment, *converge* in the process of development. While explicating the theory of convergence, Stern also highlighted the goal-directedness of the individual's actions: The active person is striving to achieve his or her goals and vital needs, and social values and norms provide guidelines for the realization of development.

Within this framework, Stern's concept of the individual's endowment, *disposition*, is to be understood as always linked to the environment;

it is viewed as a goal-directed but flexible entity. Disposition, according to Stern, is a "causality with a leeway." Within this scope, the same disposition may have quite different outcomes, depending on the specific environmental conditions. Thus, very early, Stern developed the idea of *plasticity* and *malleability* as essential characteristics of the person:

> This is the fact of personal plasticity or malleability, a domain of intentional education or unintentional influences of the milieu. This domain is narrower than many empiricists might be aware of. For the person is not only a passive recipient of the environmental forces impinging on him, but he is also reacting to these forces. The way he shapes and keeps a kind of plasticity is not only a symptom of the conflict between activity and passivity, it is also a tool for overcoming it: It is a mirror which is a weapon at the same time. (W. Stern, 1918a, pp. 50–51, translated by K. K.)

Unitas Multiplex

The linking of genetic disposition and environment in the theory of convergence leads to the rich conceptualization of *personality*, of the individual as a complex unit, a *unitas multiplex*, which is neither entirely determined by disposition nor entirely determined by environment. This key concept is essential for the understanding of Stern's idea of a person as an active, gestalt-shaping individual whose behavior is dependent both on the diversity of dispositions and on the conditions of the environment. From this perspective, not only are a person's actions defined by a multitude of personal and contextual factors but they also possess a high degree of freedom. Thus the sorting out of single behaviors or functions within the person seems to be of only limited value.

The philosophy of personalism and the key construct of *unitas multiplex* as an overarching concept grew out of Stern's intention to lay ground for a new psychology that could overcome the old controversy between mind and matter or, as William James called it, between mind and stuff. Stern introduced a new dualism, person versus matter. Reintroducing the person as a fundamental unit, he turned against the mainstream elementaristic psychology dominant at the end of the 19th century in which concepts such as self, ego, and volition were given up in favor of the search for "elements" of the mind (Cassirer, 1950). However, by underlining the role of context and the dynamics resulting from tensions between environmental conditions and a person's intentions and goals, Stern provided a rather modern model of the person–context relationship.

STERN'S PROCESS-ORIENTED UNDERSTANDING OF DEVELOPMENT

The two concepts just presented illustrate highlights of Stern's more general theoretical groundwork; they indicate his transactional and contextual orientation, which, after 70 years, appears amazingly modern (Bronfenbrenner, 1979; Sameroff, 1975). In the following section, three developmental concepts are presented to illustrate Stern's process orientation: active development, proximal space, and egocentrism.

Stern's Dialectic View and His Theory of Active Development

The individual's course of development is regulated by two different features: the tendency to maintain an extant state and to avoid changes, that is, preservation of the self, versus the tendency to reach out for new goals to promote development, that is, the unfolding of the self. By introducing this dialectical approach to understanding continuity and change, Stern stressed the importance of the process character. These concepts show certain parallels to Baldwin's and Piaget's ideas of assimilation and accommodation. The individual is seen, as in Piaget's theory, not only as a subject of cognitive development but also as a person with an active self who shapes his or her own developmental course. However, whereas Piaget's main interests lay more in the evolution of cognitive functions, Stern's concern was more directed toward the interplay between the active person and his or her environment. Stern seemed to pursue a line of thought that was later reactivated at the beginning of the 1980s (Lerner, 1982), one in which development was interpreted as a process of integrating the individual's activities resulting from growing abilities with selective effects generated by environmental conditions. The merging of the two tendencies of preservation and unfolding creates a state of tension in the developing individual that Stern described in the following statement:

> All organismic events are constituted by the tendency of self-preservation and self-unfolding. Self-preservation strives to affirm one's own existence and to maintain the characteristics that have been acquired. Self-unfolding strives to increase one's own existence, it attempts to go beyond the achieved characteristics and reaches out for new contents, tasks, and achievements, thus increasingly opening the access to the objective world of values. . . . All living manifests its inner goal orientation by the merging of self-preservation and self-unfolding in the process of development. (Stern, 1927, pp. 28–29, translated by K. K.)

Many reflections that are presented by Stern in his *Psychology of Early Childhood* point both implicitly and explicitly to Werner's ideas about the parallels between phylogenetic and ontogenetic developmental processes. The well-known orthogenetic principle—that is, the processes of differentiation, specification, and hierarchical organization—elaborated later by Werner (1957) is evident in Stern's theory describing the developing personality. The following citation may give an impression:

Increasing structuring and also "exclusion or destructuration" is the transition from a diffuse, unclarified general condition to a more and more structured condition in which boundaries, parts, separations and connections are manifest more and more. Every separation is at the same time an increased differentiation and centrification: What is blurred and contourless in the beginning is separated. However, at the same time a misty unshapedness is substituted by a higher super- or subordination of the single parts in an encompassing whole which contains center and subparts. (Stern, 1927, p. 31, translated by K. K.)

Stern also discussed the role of conflicts and crises in progressions during development and emphasized the possibility of different functions being asynchronous in developmental speed, an issue that was elaborated on later by Riegel (1975). Although explicitly referring to Piaget's concept of stages during development, Stern elaborated more than Piaget on the aspect of tensions and on the sequences of metamorphoses during the process of development. Tensions were seen as starting points for increased activities that push the individual through a sequence of metamorphoses that may occur in synchrony or asynchrony with other developmental processes.

The Role of Context: The Concept of Proximal Space

Stern defined a person's proximal space as the place of realization, as where the person was affected by his or her environment and where the person was shaping this environment according to his or her needs and abilities. In his time, Stern was one of the few who tried to further differentiate the environment–individual duality, which consisted of subjective experience inside the individual on the one hand and of objective events in the environment on the other. Stern created a location where the mutual exchange between individual and environment could take place. It could be neither the larger "environment" nor the "inner" subject. The larger environment was too far from and not accessible to the individual, whereas the inner subject was too far away from the objective world. Thus, the concept of the proximal space of the person, as Stern called it ("personaler Nahraum"), was introduced. It was here that the interplay between individual and environment was to be studied. Stern not only emphasized the constructive aspect of this exchange process (similarly to Piaget) but also underlined the individual's receptivity to external conditions, the selection of environmental bids, and the generation of meaning from the specifics of environmental living conditions:

Experiencing is partial, but this partiality is neither incidental nor meaningless, it rather fits into the means–end embeddedness of the personal life . . . one finds an effective selection which directs the assessment of life events according to *personal relevance* [italics added], tensions and pathologies. (W. Stern, 1935, pp. 106–107, translated by K. K.)

Moreover, Stern also took into account the relativity of the environmental influence on individual development; he was convinced that a general and unspecified concept of environment could not capture what he assumed to be the essential site of exchange, the location where an action of the individual does affect the environment and where, conversely, a change in the environment really modifies the individual's behavior. The mutuality between person and environment and the interactive perspective in the person's proximal space seem well documented in the following citation:

> By the permanent exchange between person and world not only the person is being shaped, but also her or his world. The "environment" of an individual does not consist just of that part of the objective world which is accidentally surrounding this individual and therefore affects him or her. Environment is rather that portion of the world that the individual actively brings close to him or her as he or she is both receptive and sensitive to this portion. At the same time, the individual tries to shape this piece of world which is fitting his personality. (Stern, 1935, p. 125, translated by K. K.)

By creating an arena for exchange, Stern defined what in more modern terminology is called the *ecological niche* of a person and what he called "biosphere" or "personal world." This arena of exchange was taken by Stern as essentially influencing a person's formation of cognitions about the world, such as the generation of beliefs about being able or unable to exert control. A person's biosphere or arena of exchange is exactly that part of the wider environment that is relevant for him or her; it is identical neither to the person's set of experiences and inner representations nor to the "objective" environment. For Stern, a third location between experiencing (subjective side) and a physical description of environmental conditions (objective side) was the necessary condition for characterizing the person's activities in an environment. He introduced the concept of "gelebte Welt" (the world a person is living in), which is different from both "erlebte Welt" (experience) and "objektive Welt" (the objective world) and is a new facet of the environment. Thus, Stern challenged the ongoing nature–nurture discussion by this three-pronged approach. He put the focus on the process of "interaction" between person and environment, in which the person, by his or her actions in the proximal space, reconciles the incongruities between expectancy sets and the results of actions, which, in turn, create new experience and new sets of expectancies:

> The personal world is not identical to that set of experiences we call "world view." This experienced "world" is but a segment of the world in which the individual really exists or "lives" (gelebte Welt). Objective

events can only become part of an individual's experience by the fact that they fit into the world in which he or she exists. The relationship we have to explore, therefore, is not two-pronged (objective world, subjective experience) but three-pronged (transpersonal objective world, world of individual's existence, experienced subjective world). Between the physical stimulus and the experience of perception lies the integral situation of stimulation in which the individual exists. Between the sociological unit "family" and the experience of one's family lies the individual's vital and introceptive connectedness with the family. (Stern, 1935, p. 124, translated by K. K.)

Applying his person-oriented approach, Stern also developed ideas about the processes leading to the person's inner representation of cultural norms, values, and rules. They are encountered in the "Erlebnisraum" (experiential space) and then represented in the individual's own cultural, social, moral, or religious values that he or she carries along and passes on to the next generation; they are transmitted from the environment to the person by the process of *introception*, a process described by Stern as a permanent fight between the individual's own vital needs and wishes and the culture's and society's formats. For Stern, the process of introception causes tensions and frictions and promotes developmental shifts as it contributes to the awakening and differentiation of conscience. In turn, the values and norms are incorporated into the person's action system. In this sense, introception appears to be a process akin to Freud's idea about the development of the superego, but for Stern, the process was more cognitive and transactional than that of Freud.

The Concept of Egocentrism

Stern (1927) criticized Piaget's concept of egocentrism, particularly his opinion concerning the timing of the emergence of social competence in small children. In reading Stern's references to observations he conducted with his own three children, one is sometimes reminded of statements made by human ethologists during the 1970s when they reported about their observational studies of interactions in mother–child dyads (Shaffer & Dunn, 1979; Trevarthen & Hubley, 1978). Stern claimed that the development of sociocentric thinking in the child starts earlier than Piaget suggested and, furthermore, that the development of social competence depends also on the social conditions of children's life conditions:

> The social structure of the child's environment plays an important role. Martha Muchow (1926) found out in her study with five-year-old kindergarteners from Hamburg that only one third of their speech was egocentric. She concludes that these kids in the kindergarten are living in closer, family-like units which cause a stronger social attitude. This may be rather different from the Geneva daycare home of Piaget (similar

to Montessori daycare homes), where children exhibit only looser ties to one another when handled individually. (Stern, 1927, p. 147, footnote 2, translated by K. K.)

Moreover, Stern was sensitive to situation-specific variations: He stated that strong forms of egocentrism as described by Piaget predominantly occur when children are together with peers, whereas children reach mutual understanding much earlier when together with adults. By the same token, he also claimed that mutuality is attained much earlier than the 3rd year:

> This thesis of a late beginning (of mutual understanding) may come from the fact that Piaget focuses on children's behavior when dealing with one another. When talking to adults, particularly with the mother, this stage is reached by intelligent children much earlier. (Stern, 1927, p. 148, footnote 1, translated by K. K.)

Discussing the onset of language use and communication, Stern asked how children who do not use language properly can communicate with each other. Again he referred to Piaget, who tried to explain mutual understanding by pointing to the fact that language is only one aspect of understanding. Stern elaborated on this interpretation by embedding it into his and Werner's conception of development. He defined children's communication as a period of transition in which more global and nonverbal tools are applied for the exchange of messages. Under a differential developmental perspective, communication instruments other than language, such as gestures or actions, are judged to possess a status equivalent to language during this period, but they become less important later:

> Gestures, mimics, actions are the main instruments that mediate mutuality among playing children; expressive movements are immediately understood, actions are mirrored or even continued, the spoken words have more the character of accompanying decoration than that of the core medium of communication.
>
> We find here a very illustrative example for the slowly moving differentiation or separation of children's functions: Originally, spoken language (for adults identical with language in general) does not exist as a separate reality; it is rather differentiated slowly, step by step, from the diffuse *body language* [italics added] to become later the isolated medium for thinking and transmission of thoughts. (Stern, 1927, p. 148, translated by K. K.)

These reflections not only suggest that Stern was an excellent and precise observer of his children but also show him as a scientist who, as early as 1927, had developed a concept of children's social competence and language development that took into account contextual relativity; it was, at least in some points, more differentiated than Piaget's egocentristic approach and closer to an interactionistic position. Moreover, by placing language use and language development into the framework of differentiation, specification, and hierarchical organization, Stern's concept exhibits amazing similarities with the theoretical approaches proposed much later by Bruner (1977) and Bates (1979) that finally opened the windows to a broader understanding of infant speech. However, these approaches are normally traced back not to Stern but to Vygotsky (1962) and his context-oriented "inner speech" concept.

CONCLUSION

Without doubt, had Stern's work on developmental psychology been present during the late 1960s and early 1970s in British and American textbooks, he and his ideas would have had a major revival in current discussions. Though still acknowledged as late as 1960 by a very few, such as Wolman in his *Contemporary Theories and Systems in Psychology*, Stern's very modern blueprint of the person was largely forgotten. Wolman described Stern's vision of a person as "a living whole, individual, unique, striving toward goals, self-contained and yet open to the world around him; he is capable of having experience" (Wolman, 1960, p. 413). At a time when mechanistic elementarism still stood against vague wholism in psychology, Stern's idea of the unity of the person went far beyond the common models and descriptions of his contemporaries; he courageously explored new roads to find a comprehensive framework in which both a differentiated perspective on the environment and a humanistic view on the individual could dwell under one theoretical roof. By creating personalism as a new focus in psychology, he drew the elementarists' attention to the human (and perhaps humanistic) aspects of behaviors in their subjects, which they had ignored. At the same time, he tried to attract the wholists' attention to the situational flexibility and plasticity of individuals' behaviors. Stern never stopped in his attempts to convince the antagonists. He emphasized not only his new, unifying personalistic psychology but also his openness to nomothetic and idiographic approaches on the one hand and to experimental and hermeneutic methodology on the other. Stern is viewed by many of those looking back at the history of psychology as a practitioner whose major merits lay in the dissemination of psychology to the public. Furthermore, he is characterized as a person who, like G. Stanley Hall in American psychology, advanced psychology as a science by restlessly expanding laboratories and founding new journals. This is true, but it is not his only claim to a permanent place in the history of psychology. His theoretical framework was evident in most of his publications, and his last work, *General Psychology From the Personalistic Standpoint* (Stern, 1938), is a fine example of his continuing quest for a more integrated approach to psychology.

The concepts selected for presentation in this article are samples of

Stern's pioneering thinking in the area of developmental psychology; they may help us to acknowledge his role and stature in the light of contemporary paradigms such as contextualism and transactionalism. One is tempted to speculate on why Stern, who pioneered these modern conceptions, did not play a more prominent role in our history and on why his thinking did not become established as a school or provide guidelines for research. Perhaps Stern's death came too suddenly and his stay in the United States was too short after his expulsion from Germany to gain wide recognition on the American academic scene. His way of thinking did not fit into the mainstream philosophy of American psychology during the 1930s. For example, one of his closest colleagues, Heinz Werner, who also was forced to emigrate to America during the 1930s, was not recognized for many years for his views on development (e.g., comparative psychology, Werner, 1948; a general theory of perception, Werner & Wapner, 1952; or the orthogenetic principle, Werner, 1957).

For Stern, however, aside from the time factor, there could be deeper reasons: Perhaps it was his fate to belong to those of a first generation who try to break down barriers in extant world views and build new frameworks but who still lack a new terminology to convey their message. Those in the generation who came after him—for example, Lewin (1931, 1936, 1939)—could successfully transform some of Stern's basic ideas into a new terminology, such as field theory or topological psychology, and find new ways to explore both context and persons under the perspective of dynamic exchange. The new paradigm, Lewin's dynamic field, presented the concept of the person's proximal space in a purified and, in a way, depersonalized version that won attention and acceptance during the 1940s and 1950s. Another version of Stern's concept of proximal space that achieved considerable recognition was Vygotsky's (1978) conception of the "zone of proximal development." As can be concluded, for example, from citations in his *Foundations of Pedology* (1935), Vygotsky referred explicitly to Stern's three-pronged approach to describe the arena of exchange between the individual and the environment; and he stressed the importance of the concrete situation in relation to the passivity or activity of the person, pointing to the "right moment" when shaping the child's environment to initiate learning processes, particularly with regard to the development of ability and skills. In short, Vygotsky recognized the relevance of a person's proximal space. The interplay between cultural values and norms on the one hand and the child's own activity on the other, which creates tensions that thus promote development, well known in Stern's framework, is one of the essential concepts in Vygotsky's "zone of proximal development."

It is a matter of speculation why Vygotsky's version of the child–context exchange, and not Stern's, won such attention in the United States during the 1960s and 1970s, when Vygotsky's work was extensively translated and cited. As Valsiner (1988, pp. 120–123) suggested, Vygotsky had his roots in the European tradition and was influenced, aside from Stern, by Bühler, Hetzer, Werner, and Ach. His ideas, which stood against the Russian school of reflexological reductionism, fostered the idea of an actively developing individual who was either encouraged or restricted by the context. Vygotsky developed an extension of the stimulus–response theory by pointing to the active child on the one hand but maintaining a pragmatic and empiristic view of the individual's learning process within a given context on the other. During the late 1960s and the early 1970s, when language development and cognition became major issues in American developmental psychology, Vygotsky was perhaps the more appropriate person to be cited, for example, by Bruner (Bruner, Olver, & Greenfield, 1966) or Berlyne (1965) in reference to the ongoing Piaget–Vygotsky controversy concerning language and thought development. The complexity of Stern's three-level approach and his intended universalism concerning the individual–context exchange possibly limited his reception by American scholars, whereas the more pragmatic and teaching-oriented approach of Vygotsky fit better with contemporary thinking.

Stern influenced the work of his contemporaries in other ways as well. With his pioneering studies in child development, he most likely had an impact on Piaget. This claim is supported by numerous citations of Stern in Piaget's early works, such as *La construction du réel chez l'enfant* (Piaget, 1937), in which Stern's *Psychology of Early Childhood* alone is mentioned six times, mostly when space perception and subject–object groupings are discussed. It seems as if Stern's meticulous observations of his own children at 4 to 9 months of age had stimulated Piaget to focus on phenomena (space *bucale*) that Stern brought to his attention. As to language development, Piaget (1962) discussed extensively Stern's alternative concept of egocentrism in his *Le langage et la pensée chez l'enfant*. The work of Stern's colleague Martha Muchow with Hamburg kindergarten children is reviewed in this book in great length as well.

Stern's dynamic and process-oriented approach to development was also acknowledged by Charlotte Bühler. When she argued against Watson's behavioristic position by pointing to the spontaneous emergence of behaviors during development, she referred explicitly to Stern and his conceptual framework describing endowment–environment tensions as a factor in promoting developmental shifts (Bühler, 1927).

The obviously high stature Stern had in European psychology was neither recognized nor acknowledged in American psychology. For example, one of Stern's most impressive creations, the contextual and transactional view for understanding developmental processes, could not be transferred to American psychology during the 1930s. It was nearly four decades before a dialectical and transactional view of human development was presented to American developmental audiences (Riegel, 1975; Sameroff, 1975). It is noteworthy that Klaus Riegel, who formulated an explicit dialectical perspective on developmental processes, was influenced not only by Vygotsky but also indirectly by Stern, because Riegel was a student of Curt Bondy in Hamburg, who was in turn an earlier student of William Stern (see Stern, 1921).

By comparing Stern's ideas with current theories about the endowment–environment relationship, one can find fascinating parallels between, for example, the conceptions of convergence and proximal space and the concept of ecological niches (Plomin, 1986; Scarr & McCartney, 1983) or the conception of siblings in the same family actively developing in different directions (Dunn & Plomin, 1990; Plomin & Daniels, 1987).

In sum, Stern presented a modern, process-oriented description of the child's growing abilities and competences during development; he developed and promoted concepts across the entire area of psychology that were in part more innovative than many others that were produced during the 1940s, 1950s, and even 1960s. I would like to close this homage to the philosopher, humanist, and psychologist William Stern with a citation of Frank Hardesty's (1976) description of the Hamburg years:

> Stern emerges as a totally committed individual—in today's terms a humanist—who, with a mode of synthesis characteristic of him throughout his career, sought a fusion of theory and practice, attempting to apply the best to both. His work, especially that associated with his years in Hamburg, attests not only to his belief that a basic unity underlies all facets of the field in psychology but to his complete faith in psychology as essentially a tool for the enlightenment of man and for providing a basis for social reform. For Stern, psychology as an institution existed not as a unit in the fraternity of sciences but as an instrument for confronting and contributing to the solution of the social problems of his day (p. 40).

REFERENCES

Allport, G. W. (1938). William Stern: 1871–1938. *The American Journal of Psychology, 51*, 770–773.

Bates, E. (1979). *The emergence of symbols: Cognition and communication in infancy.* San Diego: Academic Press.

Berlyne, D. E. (1965). *Structure and direction in thinking.* New York: Wiley.

Bronfenbrenner, U. (1979). *The ecology of human development.* Cambridge, MA: Harvard University Press.

Bruner, J. S. (1977). Early social interaction and language acquisition. In H. R. Schaffer (Ed.), *Studies in mother–infant interaction* (pp. 271–289). San Diego: Academic Press.

Bruner, J. S., Olver, R. R., & Greenfield, P. M. (1966). *Studies in cognitive growth.* New York: Wiley.

Bühler, C. (1927). Die ersten sozialen Verhaltungsweisen des Kindes [The first social behaviors of the child]. *Quellen und Studien zur Jugendkunde, 5,* 1–102.

Cassirer, E. (1950). William Stern. Zur Wiederkehr seines Todestages [William Stern. For the anniversary of his death]. In W. Stern, *Allgemeine Psychologie auf personalistischer Grundlage* (2nd. ed., pp. XXXIII–XLX). Dordrecht, The Netherlands: Martinus Nijhoff.

Dilthey, W. (1924). Ideen über eine beschreibende und zergliedernde Psychologie [Ideas about a descriptive and dissecting psychology]. In W. Dilthey (Ed.), *Gesammelte Schriften* (Vol. 5, pp. 139–240). Leipzig, Germany: Teubner. (Original work published 1894)

Dudeck, P. (1989). William Stern und das Projekt "Jugendkunde" [William Stern and the project "adolescence"]. *Zeitschrift für Pädagogik, 35,* 153–174.

Dunn, J., & Plomin, R. (1990). *Separate lives: Why siblings are so different.* New York: Basic Books.

Eckardt, G. (1989). William Stern—Aspekte seines wissenschaftlichen Lebenswerkes. Zum 50. Todestag am 27. März 1988 [William Stern—Aspects of his scientific work. For the 50th anniversary of his death, March 27, 1988]. *Psychologie für die Praxis, 7,* 3–27.

Hardesty, F. P. (1976). Louis William Stern: A new view of the Hamburg years. *Annals of the New York Academy of Sciences, 270,* 31–44.

Lerner, R. M. (1982). Children and adolescents as producers of their own development. *Developmental Review, 2,* 342–370.

Lewin, K. (1917). Kriegslandschaft [War landscape]. *Zeitschrift für angewandte Psychologie, 12,* 440–447.

Lewin, K. (1927). Kindliche Ausdrucksbewegungen [Expressive movements of the child]. In W. Stern (Ed.), *Psychologie der frühen Kindheit* (4th ed., pp. 503–511). Leipzig, Germany: Quelle & Meyer.

Lewin, K. (1931). Environmental forces in child behavior and development. In C. Murchison (Ed.), *Handbook of child psychology* (pp. 94–127). Worcester, MA: Clark University Press.

Lewin, K. (1936). *Principles of topological psychology.* New York: McGraw Hill.

Lewin, K. (1939). Field theory and experiment in social psychology: Concepts and methods. *American Journal of Sociology, 44,* 868–897.

Muchow, M. (1926). Psychologische Untersuchungen über die Wirkung des Seeklimas auf Schulkinder [Psychological studies on the effect of sea climate on schoolchildren]. *Zeitschrift für pädagogische Psychologie, 27,* 18–31.

Muchow, M. (1935). *Der Lebensraum des Großstadtkindes* [The ecology of the urban child]. Hamburg, Germany: Riegel. (Reprinted 1978 in *Päd Extra,* Bensheim, Germany)

Piaget, J. (1937). *La construction du réel chez l'enfant* [The construction of reality in the child]. Neuchâtel, Switzerland: Delachaux et Niestle.

Piaget, J. (1962). *Le langage et la pensée chez l'enfant* [Language and thought of the child]. Neuchâtel, Switzerland: Delachaux et Niestle.

Plomin, R. (1986). *Development, genetics, and psychology.* Hillsdale, NJ: Erlbaum.

Plomin, R., & Daniels, D. (1987). Why are children in the same family so different from one another? *Behavioral and Brain Sciences, 10,* 1–60.

Riegel, K. F. (1975). Toward a dialectical theory of development. *Human Development, 18,* 50–64.

Sameroff, A. J. (1975). Transactional models in early social relations. *Human Development, 18,* 65–79.

Scarr, S., & McCartney, K. (1983). How people make their own environments: A theory of genotype–environment effects. *Child Development, 54,* 424–435.

Schoggen, P. (1985). Martha Muchow: Precursor to ecological psychology. *Human Development, 28,* 213–216.

Shaffer, D., & Dunn, J. (Eds.). (1979). *The first year of life.* New York: Wiley.

Siegel, A. W. (1985). Martha Muchow: Anticipations of current issues in developmental psychology. *Human Development, 28,* 217–224.

Stern, C., & Stern, W. (1907). *Die Kindersprache: Eine psychologische und sprachtheoretische Untersuchung* [Children's speech: A psychological and linguistic study]. Leipzig, Germany: Barth.

Stern, W. (1893). *Die Analogie im volkstümlichen Denken* [The analogy in folk thinking]. Doctoral dissertation in philosophy, Berlin University, Berlin, Germany.

Stern, W. (1896). Die Wahrnehmungen von Tonveränderungen [The perceptions of changes in sound]. *Zeitschrift für Psychologie, 11,* 1–30, 449–459.

Stern, W. (1898). *Psychologie der Veränderungsauffassung* [Psychology of the perception of change]. Habilitationsschrift, Breslau, Germany (today Poland): Preuss & Jünger.

Stern, W. (1900). *Über Psychologie der individuellen Differenzen* [On the psychology of individual differences]. Leipzig, Germany: Barth.

Stern, W. (1903). Der Tonvariator [The sound variator]. *Zeitschrift für Psychologie, 30,* 422–432.

Stern, W. (1904). Die Psychologie des Kindes als theoretische Wissenschaft: Genetische Psychologie [Psychology of the child as a theoretical science: Genetic psychology]. *Zeitschrift für Pädagogische Psychologie, 5,* 391–394.

Stern, W. (1907). Grundfragen der Psychogenesis [Basic questions of psychogenesis]. *Zeitschrift für Pädagogische Psychologie, Pathologie und Hygiene, 9,* 77–80.

Stern, W. (1908). Tatsachen und Ursachen der seelischen Entwicklung [Facts and causes of psychological development]. *Zeitschrift für Angewandte Psychologie, 1,* 1–43.

Stern, W. (1911). *Die differentielle Psychologie in ihren methodischen Grundlagen* [Differential psychology in its methodological principles]. Leipzig, Germany: Barth.

Stern, W. (1912). Die psychologischen Methoden der Intelligenzprüfung [Methods for testing intelligence]. In F. Schulmann (Ed.), *Bericht über den V. Kongreß für experimentelle Psychologie* (pp. 1–102). Leipzig, Germany: Barth.

Stern, W. (1914). *Psychologie der frühen Kindheit* [Psychology of early childhood]. Leipzig, Germany: Quelle & Meyer.

Stern, W. (1917). *Die Psychologie und der Personalismus* [Psychology and personalism]. Leipzig, Germany: Barth.

Stern, W. (1918a). *Grundgedanken der personalistischen Philosophie* [Basic concepts of the personalistic philosophy]. Berlin, Germany: Reuther & Reichard.

Stern, W. (1918b). *Person und Sache: System des kritischen Personalismus* [Person and thing: System of the critical personalism] (2 volumes). Leipzig, Germany: Barth.

Stern, W. (1921). Zur Psychographie der proletarischen Arbeiterbewegung (auf Grund von Untersuchungen von Curt Bondy) [On the psychography of the proletarian workers' movement (based on studies conducted by Curt Bondy)]. *Zeitschrift für Pädagogische Psychologie, 22,* 376–379.

Stern, W. (1922). Vom Ich-Bewußtsein des Jugendlichen [On the ego-awareness of the adolescent]. *Zeitschrift für Pädagogische Psychologie, 23,* 8–16.

Stern, W. (1923). Über die Entwicklung der Idealbildung in der reifenden Jugend [On the development of the formation of ideals during adolescence]. *Zeitschrift für Pädagogische Psychologie, 24,* 34–45.

Stern, W. (1924). Das "Ernstspiel" der Jugendzeit [The "serious game" of adolescence]. *Zeitschrift für Pädagogische Psychologie, 25,* 241–252.

Stern, W. (1925). *Die Anfänge der Reifezeit. Ein Knabentagebuch in psychologischer Bearbeitung* [The onset of maturation: A boy's diary revised under psychological perspectives]. Leipzig, Germany: Barth.

Stern, W. (1927). *Psychologie der frühen Kindheit* [Psychology of early childhood] (4th. ed.). Leipzig, Germany: Quelle & Meyer.

Stern, W. (1935). *Allgemeine Psychologie auf personalistischer Grundlage* [General psychology from the personalistic standpoint]. Dordrecht, The Netherlands: Martinus Nijhoff.

Stern, W. (1938). *General psychology from the personalistic standpoint.* (H. D. Spoerl, Trans.). New York: MacMillan.

Trevarthen, C., & Hubley, P. (1978). Secondary intersubjectivity: Confidence, confiding and acts of meaning in the first year. In A. Lock (Ed.), *Action, gesture and symbol* (pp. 183–229). San Diego: Academic Press.

Valsiner, J. (1988). *Developmental psychology in the Soviet Union.* Bloomington, IN: Indiana University Press.

Vygotsky, L. (1935). *Osnovy pedologii* [Foundations of pedology]. Leningrad: Gosudarstvennyi Pedagogicheskii Institut imeni A. I. Gerzena.

Vygotsky, L. (1962). *Thought and language.* Cambridge, MA: MIT Press.

Vygotsky, L. (1978). *Mind in society: The development of higher psychological processes.* Cambridge, MA: Harvard University Press.

Wapner, S. (1985). Martha Muchow and organismic–developmental theory. *Human Development, 28*, 209–213.

Werner, H. (1948). *Comparative psychology of mental development*. New York: International Universities Press.

Werner, H. (1957). The concept of development from a comparative and organismic point of view. In D. B. Harris (Ed.), *The concept of development* (pp. 125–148). Minneapolis: University of Minnesota Press.

Werner, H., & Wapner, S. (1952). Toward a general theory of perception. *Psychological Review, 59*, 324–338.

Wohlwill, J. F. (1985). Martha Muchow, 1892–1933: Her life, work, and contribution to developmental and ecological psychology. *Human Development, 28*, 198–224.

Wolman, B. B. (1960). *Contemporary theories and systems in psychology*. New York: Harper.

12

LEV SEMYONOVICH VYGOTSKY AND CONTEMPORARY DEVELOPMENTAL PSYCHOLOGY

JAMES V. WERTSCH AND PEETER TULVISTE

Over the past decade there has been a major upsurge of interest in the ideas of Lev Semyonovich Vygotsky (1896–1934). This is reflected in the dramatic rise in citations of Vygotsky's publications (Belmont, 1988), in the spate of new translations of his writings (Vygotsky, 1978, 1981a, 1981b, 1981c, 1986, 1987, in press), and in several new volumes about his life and work (Kozulin, 1990; A. A. Leont'ev, 1990; Minick, Forman, & Stone, in press; Moll, 1990; Puzerei, 1986; Ratner, 1991; van der Veer & Valsiner, in press; Wertsch, 1985a, 1985b, 1991; Yaroshevskii, 1989).

The reasons for the new interest in Vygotsky in the United States are not altogether clear, but several factors seem to have played a role. One of them is the recent publication or republication of most of his writings in Russian (Vygotsky, 1982a, 1982b, 1983a, 1983b, 1984a, 1984b) and

The writing of this chapter was assisted by grants from the Spencer Foundation to James V. Wertsch and Peeter Tulviste. The statements made and the views expressed are solely the responsibility of the authors.

Reprinted from *Developmental Psychology*, 28, 548–557. Copyright by the American Psychological Association.

the subsequent translation of these items into English (Vygotsky, 1987, in press). Another is that increased scholarly exchanges between the United States and the former Soviet Union and the emigration of several Soviet psychologists to the West have provided a coterie of experts who can deal authoritatively with these writings. Yet a third is the fact that many of Vygotsky's ideas seem directly relevant to issues in education and other applied fields (Moll, 1990). And perhaps the most important factor is that Western scholars, especially those in the United States, have been actively searching for new theoretical frameworks, and Vygotsky's ideas seem to address many of the issues that have motivated their quest.

Our goal in this chapter is not to provide a general review of the origins and fate of Vygotsky's ideas. This task has been carried out admirably by authors such as Kozulin (1990) and van der Veer and Valsiner (in press). Instead, our intent is to review a few of Vygotsky's ideas that have particular relevance for contemporary developmental psychology and to see how these ideas can be extended in light of recent theoretical advances in the social sciences and humanities. Our discussion focuses primarily on two points in Vygotsky's theoretical approach: his claims about the social origins and social nature of higher (i.e., uniquely human) mental functioning and his uses of culture. In examining these points, we also touch on his use of a developmental method and on his distinction between elementary and higher mental functioning.

SOCIAL ORIGINS OF INDIVIDUAL MENTAL FUNCTIONING

Perhaps the major reason for Vygotsky's current appeal in the West is his analysis of the social origins of mental processes. This is a theme that has reemerged with considerable force in Western developmental psychology over the past 20 years or so, and Vygotsky's ideas have come to play an important role in this movement.

In Vygotsky's view, mental functioning in the individual can be understood only by examining the social and cultural processes from which it derives. This involves an analytic strategy that may appear to some to be paradoxical at first glance—namely, it calls on the investigator to begin the analysis of mental functioning in the individual by going outside the individual. As one of Vygotsky's students and colleagues, A. R. Luria (1981), put it,

> In order to explain the highly complex forms of human consciousness one must go beyond the human organism. One must seek the origins of conscious activity . . . in the external processes of social life, in the social and historical forms of human existence. (p. 25)

This view stands in marked contrast to the strong individualistic assumptions that underlie the bulk of contemporary Western research in psychology (see Sarason, 1981, for a critique of these assumptions).

Vygotsky's claims about the analytic priority to be given to social processes were in evidence throughout his career as a psychologist (basically the decade before his death of tuberculosis in 1934). For example, in one of his first articles from this period, he asserted that "the social dimension of consciousness is primary in time and in fact. The individual dimension of consciousness is derivative and secondary" (Vygotsky, 1979, p. 30). As Bruner (1962) noted, this aspect of Vygotsky's approach bears a striking resemblance to the ideas of George Herbert Mead. Its actual origins in Vygotsky's writings, however, seem to have been in the writings of Marx (Wertsch, 1985b) and in the ideas of the French psychiatrist and psychologist Pierre Janet (1928; also see Van der Veer & Valsiner, 1988), who was in turn strongly influenced by the French sociological school of Emile Durkheim.

Perhaps the most useful general formulation of Vygotsky's claims about the social origins of individual mental functioning can be found in his "general genetic law of cultural development":

> Any function in the child's cultural development appears twice, or on two planes. First it appears on the social plane, and then on the psychological plane. First it appears between people as an interpsychological category, and then within the child as an intrapsychological category. This is equally true with regard to voluntary attention, logical memory, the formation of concepts, and the development of volition . . . [I]t goes without saying that internalization transforms the process itself and changes its structure and functions. Social relations or relations among people genetically underlie all higher functions and their relationships. (Vygotsky, 1981b, p. 163)

There are several aspects of this statement worth noting. The first is that the notion of mental functioning it presupposes differs from that which is typically assumed in contemporary Western psychology. Instead of beginning with the assumption that mental functioning occurs first and foremost, if not only, within the individual, it assumes that one can speak equally appropriately of mental processes as occurring *between* people on the intermental[1] plane. Indeed, it gives analytic priority to such intermental functioning in that intramental functioning is viewed as being derivative, as emerging through the mastery and internalization of social processes.

This fundamental difference in orientation is clearly manifested in how terms are used. In contemporary usage, terms such as *cognition, memory,*

---

[1]In this chapter, we shall use the terms *intermental* and *intramental* rather than *interpsychological* and *intrapsychological*, respectively. This follows the translation practices established in Vygotsky (1987) and contrasts with those found in earlier translated texts (Vygotsky, 1978, 1981b). *Intermental* and *intramental* are translations of the Russian terms *interpsikhicheskii* and *intrapsikhicheskii*, respectively.

and *attention* are automatically assumed to apply exclusively to the individual. In order to use these terms when speaking of processes carried out on the social plane, some modifier must be attached. This is the source of recent terms such as *socially shared cognition* (Resnick, Levine, & Behrend, 1991), *socially distributed cognition* (Hutchins, 1991), and *collective memory* (Middleton, 1987). The need to use modifiers such as "socially shared" reflects the derivative, or nonbasic, status that mental functioning carried out on the social plane is assumed to have in contemporary paradigms.

In contrast to traditions in which individualistic assumptions are built into the very terms used to discuss psychological phenomena, Vygotsky's view was based in his claims about the social origins and "quasi-social nature" (Vygotsky, 1981b, p. 164) of intramental functioning. This orientation reflects an implicit rejection of the primacy given to individual functioning and to the seemingly neat distinction between social and individual processes that characterize many contemporary approaches in psychology. In contrast to such approaches, Vygotsky viewed mental functioning as a kind of action (Wertsch, 1991) that may be carried out by individuals or by dyads and larger groups. Much like that of authors such as Bateson (1972) and Geertz (1973), therefore, his view is one in which mind is understood as "extending beyond the skin." Mind, cognition, memory, and so forth are understood not as attributes or properties of the individual, but as functions that may be carried out intermentally or intramentally.

Vygotsky's claims about the social origins of individual mental functioning surface in many ways throughout his writings. Two issues that have taken on particular importance in contemporary developmental psychology in the West are the "zone of proximal development" (Vygotsky, 1978, 1987) and "egocentric" and "inner speech" (Vygotsky, 1987). Each of these phenomena has taken on a sort of life of its own in the contemporary developmental literature, but from a Vygotskian perspective it is essential to remember how they are situated in an overall theoretical framework. In particular, it is important to remember that they are specific instances of more general claims about the social origins of individual mental functioning.

The zone of proximal development has recently received a great deal of attention in the West (e.g., Brown & Ferrara, 1985; Brown & French, 1979; Cole, 1985; Rogoff, 1990; Rogoff & Wertsch, 1984; Tharp & Gallimore, 1988). This zone is defined as the distance between a child's "actual developmental level as determined by independent problem solving" and the higher level of "potential development as determined through problem solving under adult guidance or in collaboration with more capable peers" (Vygotsky, 1978, p. 86).

Vygotsky examined the implications of the zone of proximal development for the organization of instruction and for the assessment of intelligence. With regard to the former, he argued that instruction should be tied more closely to the level of potential development than to the level of actual development; with regard to the latter, he argued that measuring the level of potential development is just as important as measuring the actual developmental level. He used the following example to illustrate his ideas about assessment:

> Imagine that we have examined two children and have determined that the mental age of both is seven years. This means that both children solve tasks accessible to seven-year-olds. However, when we attempt to push these children further in carrying out the tests, there turns out to be an essential difference between them. With the help of leading questions, examples, and demonstrations, one of them easily solves test items taken from two years above the child's level of [actual] development. The other solves test items that are only a half-year above his or her level of [actual] development. (Vygotsky, 1956, pp. 446–447)

Given this set of circumstances, Vygotsky (1956, p. 447) went on to pose the question, "Is the mental development of these two children the same?" In his view, it was not:

> From the point of view of their independent activity they are equivalent, but from the point of view of their immediate potential development they are sharply different. That which the child turns out to be able to do with the help of an adult points us toward the zone of the child's proximal development. This means that with the help of this method, we can take stock not only of today's completed process of development, not only the cycles that are already concluded and done, not only the processes of maturation that are completed; we can also take stock of processes that are now in the state of coming into being, that are only ripening, or only developing. (Vygotsky, 1956, pp. 447–448)

In such analyses, it is essential to keep in mind that the actual and potential levels of development correspond with intramental and intermental functioning, respectively. By doing so, one can avoid the temptation to view the zone of proximal development simply as a formulation for improving the assessment of individual mental functioning. Instead, it can be seen as having powerful implications for how one can *change* intermental, and hence intramental, functioning. This has been the key to intervention programs such as the "reciprocal teaching" outlined by Palincsar and Brown (1984, 1988).

As in the case of the zone of proximal development, Vygotsky's account of egocentric and inner speech reflects his more general concern with the sociocultural origins of individual mental functioning and has given rise to a spate of recent research (e.g., Berk, 1986; Berk & Garvin, 1984; Bivens & Berk, 1990; Bivens & Hagstrom, in press; Diaz & Berk, in press;

Emerson, 1983; Goudena, 1987; Kohlberg, Yaeger, & Hjertholm, 1968; Wertsch, 1979a, 1979b, 1985b). Vygotsky claimed that inner speech enables humans to plan and regulate their action and derives from previous participation in verbal social interaction. Egocentric speech is "a [speech] form found in the transition from external to inner speech" (Vygotsky, 1934, p. 46). The appearance of egocentric speech, roughly at the age of 3, reflects the emergence of a new self-regulative function similar to that of inner speech. Its external form reflects the fact that the child has not fully differentiated this new speech function from the function of social contact and social interaction.

As was the case in his account of the zone of proximal development, Vygotsky's treatment of egocentric and inner speech is grounded in the assumptions spelled out in his general genetic law of cultural development. This is reflected at several points in his treatment. For example, let us turn once again to the terminology involved. Why did Vygotsky formulate his claims in terms of inner *speech* rather than in terms of *thinking, mental processes*, or some other commonly used label? The answer to this question lies in his assumptions about the social origins and quasi-social nature of intramental functioning. As was the case for other theorists in his milieu (e.g., Potebnya, 1922), Vygotsky's use of the term *speech* here reflects the fact that he viewed individual mental functioning as deriving essentially from the mastery and internalization of social processes.

Vygotsky's emphasis on the social origins of individual mental processes in this case emerges quite clearly in his analysis of the functions of language. He argued that "a sign is always originally a means used for social purposes, a means of influencing others, and only later becomes a means of influencing oneself" (Vygotsky, 1981b, p. 157). And focusing more specifically on the sign system of language, he argued that "the primary function of speech, both for the adult and for the child, is the function of communication, social contact, influencing surrounding individuals" (Vygotsky, 1934, p. 45). With regard to egocentric and inner speech, Vygotsky argued that because these forms derive from "communication, social contact, influencing surrounding individuals," it follows that they should reflect certain properties of their intermental precursors, properties such as a dialogic structure. This is precisely what he seems to have had in mind when he asserted that "egocentric speech . . . grows out of its social foundations by means of transferring social, collaborative forms of behavior to the sphere of the individual's psychological functioning" (Vygotsky, 1934, p. 45). Explications and extensions of this basic argument of how social, dialogic properties of speech characterize inner speech have been made by scholars such as Bibler (1975, 1981), Emerson (1983), and Wertsch (1980, 1985b, 1991).

THE ROLE OF A DEVELOPMENTAL METHOD

A second theme in Vygotsky's work that has made it attractive to contemporary Western psychology is his use of a developmental, or genetic, method. His reliance on this method is reflected in the very title of his "general genetic law of cultural development." The fact that the law is formulated in terms of developmental transitions reflects his assumption that the most adequate way to understand human mental functioning is to trace it back through the developmental changes it has undergone. In his view,

> We need to concentrate not on the *product* of development but on the very *process* by which higher forms are established. . . . To encompass in research the process of a given thing's development in all its phases and changes—from birth to death—fundamentally means to discover its nature, its essence, for "it is only in movement that a body shows what it is." Thus, the historical [that is, in the broadest sense of "history"] study of behavior is not an auxiliary aspect of theoretical study, but rather forms its very base. (Vygotsky, 1978, pp. 64–65)

Vygotsky's account of a genetic method derived from several theoretical sources. For example, his debt to his contemporaries in psychology is reflected in the distinction he drew between description and explanation in psychology:

> Following Lewin, we can apply [the] distinction between the phenotypic (descriptive) and genotypic (explanatory) viewpoints to psychology. By a developmental study of a problem, I mean the disclosure of its genesis, its causal dynamic basis. By phenotypic I mean the analysis that begins directly with an object's current features and manifestations. It is possible to furnish many examples from psychology where serious errors have been committed because these viewpoints have been confused. (Vygotsky, 1978, p. 62)

Unlike many contemporary developmental psychologists, Vygotsky did not limit the application of his genetic analysis to ontogenesis. Instead, he viewed ontogenesis as one of several "genetic domains" (Wertsch, 1985b) that must eventually be taken into consideration in order to provide an adequate account of human mental processes. In addition, he was concerned with phylogenesis, sociocultural history, and microgenesis (Wertsch, 1985b). In his view, an adequate account of human mental functioning could be derived only through understanding how these various genetic domains operate within an integrated system.

Vygotsky posited that change in each genetic domain is associated with a distinct set of explanatory principles:

> The use and "invention" of tools in humanlike apes crowns the organic

development of behavior in evolution and paves the way for the transition of all development to take place along new paths. It creates *the basic psychological prerequisites for the historical development of behavior.* Labor and the associated development of human speech and other psychological signs with which primitives attempt to master their behavior, signify the beginning of the genuine cultural or historical development of behavior. Finally, in child development, along with processes of organic growth and maturation, a second line of development is clearly distinguished—the cultural growth of behavior. It is based on the mastery of devices and means of cultural behavior and thinking. (Vygotsky & Luria, 1930, pp. 3–4)

In this view, it is misguided to reduce the account of change in one genetic domain to the principles invoked in connection with another, a point associated with Vygotsky's basic antirecapitulationist orientation (Wertsch, 1991).

Vygotsky was particularly interested in "revolutionary," as opposed to evolutionary, shifts in development. For example, in outlining his account of the form of genetic transition involved in phylogenesis, sociocultural history, and ontogenesis, he argued,

All three of these moments are symptoms of new epochs in the evolution of behavior and indications of *a change in the type of development itself.* In all three instances we have thereby selected turning points or critical steps in the development of behavior. We think that the turning point or critical moment in the behavior of apes is the use of tools; in the behavior of primitives it is labor and the use of psychological signs; in the behavior of the child it is the bifurcation of lines of development into natural-psychological and cultural-psychological development. (Vygotsky & Luria, 1930, p. 4)

The tenets of Vygotsky's developmental approach provided the basic methodological framework within which all other aspects of his analyses were formulated.

VYGOTSKY'S USES OF CULTURE

Up to this point, our comments on the social origins and social nature of individual mental functioning have focused on a particular kind of social process. Specifically, we have concentrated on intermental functioning in the form of dyadic or small-group processes and how it fits into Vygotsky's genetic analysis. This was a major focus of Vygotsky's thinking and certainly constitutes one of the ways in which mind may be said to extend beyond the skin in his approach. It has also been the concern of a great deal of Vygotsky-inspired research in contemporary Western psychology (e.g., Rogoff, 1990; Rogoff & Wertsch, 1984; Wertsch, 1979a).

There is a second, equally important sense, however, in which mental functioning may be said to extend beyond the skin in Vygotsky's writings, a sense that draws on his notion of culture. Mind extends beyond the skin in this second sense because human mental functioning, on the intramental as well as intermental plane, involves cultural tools, or mediational means. In contrast to the "unencumbered image of the self" that is presupposed by so much of contemporary psychology (Taylor, 1985; Wertsch, 1991), Vygotsky's account of culture suggests that humans are never as autonomous and as free of outside interference as it might at first appear. Instead, human mental functioning, even when carried out by an individual acting in isolation, is inherently social, or sociocultural, in that it incorporates socially evolved and socially organized cultural tools.

The two senses in which mental functioning may be said to extend beyond the skin are analytically distinct and hence require the use of different theoretical and methodological categories. However, in concrete human action they are inextricably linked, a point that surfaces in many forms throughout Vygotsky's writings. For example, the relationship between intermental functioning and culture is outlined in his statement that

> the word "social" when applied to our subject has great significance. Above all, in the widest sense of the word, it means that everything that is cultural is social. Culture is the product of social life and human social activity. That is why just by raising the question of the cultural development of behavior we are directly introducing the social plane of development. (Vygotsky, 1981b, p. 164)

From this statement, one can see that Vygotsky understood culture as something that comes into concrete existence in social processes, and he viewed these social processes as providing the foundation for the emergence of individual mental processes. However, he did not assume that it is possible to reduce an account of culture to a set of principles that apply to intermental or intramental processes.

Despite the clear role that cultural tools played in Vygotsky's approach, his account of the more general category of culture is by no means well developed. Furthermore, the difficulties that arise in understanding his notion of culture are not primarily difficulties that can be resolved by correcting translations or by making more texts available. The fact is that even though the school of psychology he founded came to be called the cultural-historical school in the Soviet Union in the 1930s, neither Vygotsky nor his followers provided extensive accounts of the notion of culture.[2]

An explication of Vygotsky's notion of culture must be based on an

---

[2]The second part of the term *cultural-historical* has had better luck, notably in Scribner's (1985) analysis of "Vygotsky's Uses of History," from which we borrowed to formulate the title of the present section.

analysis of the role that culture played in his overall theoretical system. In this system, Vygotsky gave the idea of mediation analytic priority over the notion of culture (as well as other themes; see Wertsch, 1985b). Indeed, his analysis of culture is part of his attempt to elaborate the notion of mediation. In his view, a criterial feature of human action is that it is mediated by tools ("technical tools") and signs ("psychological tools"). His primary concern was with the latter (what we are here calling "cultural tools"), and for that reason we shall focus primarily on "semiotic mediation."

Basic to this perspective is Vygotsky's insight that the inclusion of psychological, or cultural, tools into human functioning fundamentally transforms this functioning. The incorporation of mediational means does not simply facilitate processes that would otherwise have occurred. Instead,

> by being included in the process of behavior, the psychological tool alters the entire flow and structure of mental functions. It does this by determining the structure of a new instrumental act, just as a technical tool alters the process of a natural adaptation by determining the form of labor operations. (Vygotsky, 1981c, p. 137)

According to Vygotsky (1981c),

> The following can serve as examples of psychological tools and their complex systems: language; various systems for counting; mnemonic techniques; algebraic symbol systems; works of art; writing; schemes, diagrams, maps, and mechanical drawings; all sorts of conventional signs; and so on. (p. 137)

In all cases, these are mediational means that are the products of socio-cultural evolution and are appropriated by groups or individuals as they carry out mental functioning.

Vygotsky's tendency to approach the notion of culture via his account of mediation reflects the fact that he understood culture in terms of sign systems, an understanding that has been considerably elaborated in more recent Soviet cultural analyses (e.g., Lotman, 1973; Lotman & Uspensky, 1978). Vygotsky's semiotic view of culture probably derives from the work of Saussure, which was very influential among Russian linguists in the 1920s (see Matejka, 1973; Voloshinov, 1973). As was the case for Saussure, Vygotsky was primarily interested in one sign system, language. In his studies, he focused on psychological processes that make use of natural language and on systems built on natural language—above all, prose and poetry (cf. Vygotsky, 1971). At the same time, he showed a continuing interest in the use of nonverbal signs. For example, he often drew on examples having to do with the use of sign systems from traditional societies, such as tying knots to organize memory, and he was involved in A. N. Leont'ev's (1931) early research on children's and adults' use of pictures to assist performance in memory tasks (see Vygotsky, 1978).

Vygotsky was quite familiar with the general theories of culture that were being developed in his time by scholars in sociology, anthropology, and other disciplines. However, he chose not to incorporate them into his writings in any major way. Indeed, he firmly rejected the basic assumptions of the British evolutionary anthropologists that laws of individual mental functioning (i.e., laws of association) were adequate for explaining the historical development of culture, human behavior, and human thinking. Instead of assuming that human mental functioning remains basically the same across historical epochs, he argued that

> culture creates special forms of behavior, changes the functioning of mind, constructs new stories in the developing system of human behavior. . . . In the course of historical development, social humans change the ways and means of their behavior, transform their natural premises and functions, elaborate and create new, specifically cultural forms of behavior. (Vygotsky, 1983a, pp. 29–30)

On the issue of the relation between culture and language, Vygotsky's views are quite close to those of the French sociological school of Durkheim (but see Tulviste, 1991, on their differences), and on the issue of the qualitative changes in thinking that occur in the course of historical development, he had much in common with the views of Levy-Bruhl (1923; also see Tulviste, 1987). Furthermore, he often turned to the work of Thurnwald, but this was mainly to find examples of how signs are used in "primitive" cultures or to find support for his claim that changes in humans during sociocultural history are attributable not to changes in brain structure but to changes in other aspects of higher mental processes. Throughout all of his work, however, there is little evidence of any major interest on Vygotsky's part in the general theories of culture being elaborated by evolutionists, French sociologists, or cultural relativists. To the extent that he drew on them, he did so in connection with his interest in the cultural tools used to mediate intermental and intramental functioning.

A first major fact about Vygotsky's notion of culture, then, is that it was motivated primarily by a concern with semiotic mediation and its role in human mental functioning. A second fact is that he held strongly to an evolutionist account of culture (one that was heavily influenced by figures such as Marx, Spencer [1900], and Tylor [1888]). In line with his mediation-based approach to culture, this fact was manifested in his comments on mediational means. These means were viewed as being capable of supporting more "rudimentary" and advanced levels of intermental and intramental functioning. A correlate of this was Vygotsky's concern with more and less developed cultures, primitive and modern cultures, people, minds, and so forth.

This evolutionist approach to culture, which contrasts with approaches being outlined at the time by Boas (1966) and Sapir (1921), carries with it some intellectual baggage that is not widely accepted today. For example, as Van der Veer and Valsiner (in press) have noted, it reflects a kind of ethnocentric perspective, namely a Eurocentrism, that makes it difficult to interpret some of the most interesting findings generated by cross-cultural studies.

The issue here is not so much the terminology, which was commonplace in his time (Tulviste, 1991; Van der Veer & Valsiner, in press), but rather the fact that Vygotsky clearly regarded some cultures as inferior to others. It must be recognized that he believed people in all cultures to be capable of, and indeed in need of, developing. For instance, he argued that education in Soviet Russia should aim at turning all children into "supermen" or "new [Soviet] men." The notion of a superman was of course borrowed from Nietzsche, but in Vygotsky's view, cultural, rather than biological, factors were capable of creating this new kind of human (Vygotsky, 1930).

In addition to their role in the ideological framework within which Vygotsky was operating, his evolutionist ideas were manifested in concrete ways in his empirical research. This is most apparent in his account of conceptual development. As Wertsch (1985b) noted, the "decontextualization of mediational means" (p. 33) serves as a kind of developmental metric in Vygotsky's analysis of sociocultural history and of ontogenesis. While he argued that all humans share a capacity to use language in a variety of ways, Vygotsky's assumption was that only more advanced groups had taken the evolutionary step necessary to use words in abstract, decontextualized ways. This assumption underlay several studies conducted by Luria (1976) in the 1930s in Soviet Central Asia that compared the performance of various cultural groups.

Vygotsky and Luria tended to interpret the results of these studies in terms of whether subjects were from primitive or advanced societies. They proceeded on the assumption that it is possible to characterize individuals and groups generally in terms of whether they use "scientific" versus "everyday" concepts (Vygotsky, 1987), rely on "abstract" versus "situational" thinking (Luria, 1976), and so forth. This is entirely consistent with Vygotsky's evolutionist approach to culture, according to which it is possible to rank cultures on some kind of scale from lower to higher.

In reanalyzing and extending the studies by Luria, authors such as Scribner and Cole (1981) and Tulviste (1986, 1991) argued that it is more accurate to interpret subjects' performance in these studies in terms of the demands of particular task settings than in terms of the general level of subjects' mental functioning or of a culture. Specifically, they demonstrated that the kinds of differences documented in subjects' performances are primarily attributable to differences in experience with the activity of a particular institutional setting, formal schooling. This is the crux of Scribner and Cole's (1981) "practice account of literacy" (p. 235). According to this account, subjects' exposure to the patterns of speaking and reasoning in formal instructional settings gives rise to a particular set of discourse and cognitive skills. Instead of assuming that these skills represent a general measure by which one can classify individuals and groups, Scribner and Cole emphasized that they are a particular form of skill associated with a particular form of literacy practice. The form of activity here contrasts, for example, with literacy practices, such as memorizing religious texts, that were found to be associated with other cognitive skills.

Tulviste (1986, 1991) developed a related set of claims in his analysis of the "heterogeneity" of activities in which humans participate. Drawing on the ideas of Vygotsky and Vygotsky's student A. N. Leont'ev (1959, 1981), Tulviste outlined an analysis of "activity relativity" that parallels the ideas about linguistic relativity proposed by the American linguistic anthropologist Whorf (1956). As with Scribner and Cole (1981), a major point of Tulviste's account is that rather than viewing forms and levels of human mental functioning as some kind of general, immutable property of individuals or groups, the key to understanding their mental processes lies in the activity settings in which they are required to function. Furthermore, given the heterogeneity of such settings, we should anticipate a heterogeneity of forms of situationally specific mental processes.

The roots of this explication and extension of Vygotsky's ideas are to be found in the writings of Vygotsky himself. His claims about the situational specificity of mental functioning began to emerge only in the last years of his career, but they are clearly manifested in the differences between chapters 5 and 6 of *Thinking and Speech* (Vygotsky, 1987). Both chapters deal with the ontogenetic transition from "complexes" to "genuine," or "scientific," concepts. They differ, however, in what Vygotsky sees as relevant developmental forces. In chapter 5 (based on research with Shif [1935] and written in the early 1930s), concept development is treated primarily in terms of intramental processes, that is, children's conceptual development as they move from "unorganized heaps" to "complexes" to "concepts."

In chapter 6 (written in 1934) there is an essential shift in the way Vygotsky approached these issues. He clearly continued to be interested in intramental functioning, but he shifted to approaching concept development from the perspective of how it emerges in particular spheres of socioculturally situated activity. Specifically, he was concerned with how the forms of teacher–student intermental functioning encountered in the institutional setting of formal schooling provide a framework for the development of conceptual thinking.

This shift in Vygotsky's focus is an essential shift for two reasons. First, it was a move toward analyzing conceptual thinking in terms of its intermental precursors. This of course is in line with the argument he had used all along in connection with issues such as inner speech, and it follows naturally from his general genetic law of cultural development. Second, and more important for our purposes, it was a move toward recognizing that an account of the social origins of intramental functioning cannot stop with the intermental plane. Instead, the point is that the forms of mediated intermental functioning involved must themselves be recognized as being socioculturally situated with respect to activity settings and associated mediational means.

This transition in Vygotsky's thinking is important because it indicates a direction he was beginning to consider which, among other things, suggests a way out of the quandary of Eurocentrism. It suggests that instead of viewing particular forms of mental functioning as characterizing individuals or groups in a general way, these forms can be viewed as being characteristic of specific settings. As Tulviste (1991) noted, then, it follows that because individuals and groups are exposed to varieties of activity settings, we can expect them to master a heterogeneous set of mediational means and hence a heterogeneous set of mental processes.

PROBLEMS AND PROSPECTS

There is little doubt that the renewed interest in Vygotsky's writings has had a powerful and positive influence on contemporary studies in developmental psychology. However, this by no means should be taken to indicate that there are no weaknesses in his approach or that revision and extension are not in order. In this final section, we touch on a few of these weaknesses and outline some ways in which they can be addressed.

The first of these concerns Vygotsky's Eurocentrism. In our opinion, Vygotsky made some major contributions to the discussion of historical differences in mental functioning, an issue that has seldom been addressed satisfactorily in psychology since his time. However, we believe that he tended to use the notion of a developmental hierarchy too broadly when trying to interpret differences in mental functioning. The result was a view in which modern European cultural tools and forms of mental functioning were assumed to be generally superior to the tools and functioning of other peoples. In many instances, we believe it is more appropriate to view differences in terms of coexisting but qualitatively distinct ways of approaching a problem, rather than as more or less advanced general levels of mental functioning.

As we noted in the preceding section, there are indications that Vygotsky was moving away from a view in which forms of mental functioning are viewed as properties that characterize the general level of individuals' and groups' functioning. In its place he seems to have been suggesting that particular forms of mental functioning are associated with particular institutionally situated activities. An implication of this is that it is more appropriate to characterize the mental functioning of individuals in terms of heterogeneity (Tulviste, 1986, 1991) or a "cultural tool kit"

(Wertsch, 1991) of mental processes, rather than in terms of a single, general level. This has been the focus of research directly motivated by Vygotsky's writings (e.g., Laboratory of Comparative Human Cognition, 1983; Tulviste, 1991; Wertsch, 1991), as well as of research only indirectly motivated by Vygotsky's ideas (Gardner, 1983).

Reformulating mental functioning in terms of heterogeneity and cultural tool kits helps avoid the often ungrounded assumption that various individuals or groups can generally be ranked as inferior or superior to others. However, it still leaves unresolved the issue of what role developmental progression plays in mental processes. There is little doubt in most people's minds that there has been historical progress in at least certain forms of activities and the mental processes (e.g., reasoning) associated with them. For example, if one considers scientific knowledge about electricity, there is little doubt that the past two centuries have witnessed significant progress. It follows that *within specific domains of knowledge*, certain activities, cultural tools, and forms of reasoning may be more advanced than others. One of the major challenges of a Vygotskian approach, then, is how to capture such facts about developmental progression without falling prey to ungrounded assumptions about the general superiority or inferiority of individuals or groups.

A second major issue in Vygotsky's approach that will require further attention emerges in his account of the ontogenetic domain. In formulating his notion of this domain, he argued that two lines of development—the cultural line and the natural line—come into contact and transform one another:

> The growth of the normal child into civilization usually involves a fusion with the processes of organic maturation. Both planes of development—the natural and the cultural—coincide and mingle with one another. The two lines of change interpenetrate one another and essentially form a single line of sociobiological formation of the child's personality. (Vygotsky, 1960, p. 47)

Although this general formulation continues to make a great deal of sense, the fact is that Vygotsky said very little and was quite unclear about the natural line of development. At some points he spoke of "organic growth and maturation" (Vygotsky & Luria, 1930, p. 4) when dealing with this line of development. This could refer to everything from the emergence of sensory abilities to motor skills to neurological development, but he did not specify which. In other places he seems to have been concerned with developmental changes that are not attributable directly to organic maturation on the one hand but are not cultural by his definition on the other. For example, he sometimes referred to changes in young children's abilities to use primitive tools, such as those outlined by Piaget (1952) in his account of the sensorimotor development having to do with new means to old ends.

Furthermore, Vygotsky said almost nothing about how the "elementary mental functioning" that grows out of the natural line of development might influence the "higher mental functioning" that derives from the mastery of cultural tools. Instead, he focused almost exclusively on ways in which cultural forces transform the natural line of development. In accordance with such a view, the natural line provides a kind of raw material whose fate is to be transformed by cultural forces.

A further problem with Vygotsky's account of the natural and cultural lines in ontogenesis is that he viewed these lines as operating quite independently of one another during early phases of life. Since the time he made these claims, investigators such as Piaget (1952), Bower (1974), and Bruner (1976) have made major research advances that bring this assumption into question, and some of Vygotsky's own followers have taken a critical stance toward it. In reviewing Vygotsky's theoretical approach, A. N. Leont'ev and Luria noted that "after all, even in children at the very earliest ages mental processes are being formed under the influence of verbal social interaction with adults who surround them" (1956, p. 7).

Vygotsky's relatively unsophisticated view of the natural line of development can be traced largely to the dearth of theoretical and empirical research on infants available in the early decades of the 20th century. However, it also reflects another problematic assumption that underlay his work. This is the assumption that the primary force of development comes from outside the individual. Whereas one of the reasons for Vygotsky's renewed influence in contemporary psychology is that his ideas provide a corrective to the tendency to isolate individuals from their sociocultural milieu, passages such as the following might seem to suggest that ontogenesis is solely a function of the environment and leaves little room to consider the role of the active individual:

> The environment appears in child development, namely in the development of personality and specific human qualities, in the role of the source of development. Hence the environment here plays the role not of the situation of development, but of its source. (Vygotsky, 1934, p. 113)

Such passages in Vygotsky's writings seem to suggest that social and cultural processes almost mechanistically determine individual processes. This view minimizes the contributions made by the active individual. Among other things, it raises the question of how individuals are capable of introducing innovation and creativity into the system.

It is clear that Vygotsky has often been read in ways that make this a major problem. However, we believe that several points in his theoretical approach contradict such a reading. For the most part, these points do not emerge in the form of explicit counterstatements; instead, they surface in the assumptions about human action that underlie the entire framework of

Vygotsky's approach. As we have stressed throughout this article, the notion of mediation by cultural tools plays a central role in his approach. This applies nowhere more forcefully than in his account of action. The basic form of action that Vygotsky envisioned was *mediated action* (Wertsch, 1991; Zinchenko, 1985). Such action inherently involves cultural tools, and these tools fundamentally shape it. However, this does not mean that such action can be reduced to or mechanistically determined by these tools and hence by the more general sociocultural setting. Instead, such action always involves an inherent tension between the mediational means and the individual or individuals using them in unique, concrete instances.

In such an approach, one cannot derive an adequate account of mediated action by focusing either on the mediational means or on the individual or individuals initiating and carrying out action in isolation. Instead, both components are inherently involved in such a way that agency is defined as "individual(s)-operating-with-mediational-means" (Wertsch, 1991; Wertsch, Tulviste, & Hagstrom, in press). This account allows for innovation because each concrete use of mediational means by individuals involves some differences from other uses. Indeed, the individual use may vary quite radically from previous uses. On the other hand, mediated action is always constrained in certain fundamental ways by the fact that existing cultural tools are used. As a result, any creativity that occurs involves the transformation of an existing pattern of action, a new use for an old tool.

It is possible to trace the implications of this claim more concretely as they relate to semiotic mediation by considering the ideas of some of Vygotsky's contemporaries. In particular, the ideas of the Soviet philosopher, semiotician, and literary scholar M. M. Bakhtin (1981, 1984, 1986) on "voice" and "dialogicality" complement those of Vygotsky in many important respects. In Bakhtin's view, speaking always involves a concrete individual in a unique setting using language tools provided by others to create utterances. As outlined by Wertsch (1991), such ideas provide concrete ways for exploring the Vygotskian account of agency as individual(s)-operating-with-mediational-means.

Such analyses should not be taken to suggest, however, that the issue of mediated action has been adequately addressed in the Vygotskian literature. Major attention has been given to the issue of action in Soviet theories of activity (e.g., A. N. Leont'ev, 1959, 1975; Rubinshtein, 1957), and there are complementary ideas to be found in the writings of authors such as Bakhtin. In general, however, it is only recently that the notion of mediated action has been explored in detail in connection with Vygotsky's writings (Wertsch, 1991; Zinchenko, 1985).

The presentation and critique of Vygotsky we have outlined in this article should by no means be assumed to be exhaustive. Much more in the way of background and interpretation can be obtained by consulting the publications we listed in the first section of our article. Furthermore, one should not assume that our interpretation and critique of Vygotsky's ideas are uncontested. Although there is widespread agreement that Vygotsky's ideas are extremely rich and have major implications for contemporary research in developmental psychology, there are also major differences among authors over how these ideas should be understood and applied. Perhaps the one thing that is clear to all, however, is that Vygotsky's writings are of more than historical concern. They are capable of providing the basis for major reformulations in developmental psychology today and hence are again proving their merit as classic texts.

REFERENCES

Bakhtin, M. M. (1981). *The dialogic imagination: Four essays by M. M. Bakhtin* (M. Holquist, Ed.; C. Emerson & M. Holquist, Trans.). Austin, TX: University of Texas Press.

Bakhtin, M. M. (1984). *Problems of Dostoevsky's poetics* (C. Emerson, Ed. and Trans.). Minneapolis: University of Minnesota Press.

Bakhtin, M. M. (1986). *Speech genres and other late essays.* (C. Emerson & M. Holquist, Eds.; V. W. McGee, Trans.). Austin, TX: University of Texas Press.

Bateson, G. (1972). *Steps to an ecology of mind: A revolutionary approach to man's understanding of himself.* New York: Ballantine.

Belmont, J. M. (1988). Cognitive strategies and strategic learning: The socio-instructional approach. *American Psychologist, 44,* 142–148.

Berk, L. E. (1986). Relationship of elementary school children's private speech in behavioral accompaniment to task, attention, and task performance. *Developmental Psychology, 22,* 671–680.

Berk, L. E., & Garvin, R. A. (1984). Development of private speech among low-income Appalachian children. *Developmental Psychology, 20,* 271–286.

Bibler, V. S. (1975). *Myshlenie kak tvorchestvo* [Thinking as creation]. Moscow: Izdatel'stvo Politicheskoi Literatury.

Bibler, V. S. (1981). Vnutrennyaya rech' v ponimanii L. S. Vygotsogo (Eshche raz o predmete psikhologii) [Inner speech in L. S. Vygotsky's conceptualization (once again on the object of psychology)]. In *Nauchnoe tvorchestvo L. S. Vygotskogo i sovremennaya psikhologiya.* Tezisy dokladov vsesoyuznoi konferentsii, Moskva, 23–25 iyunya 1981 [The scientific work of L. S. Vygotsky and contemporary psychology. Papers presented at the all-union conference, Moscow, June 23–25, 1981]. Moscow: Akademiya Pedagogicheskikh Nauk SSSR.

Bivens, J. A., & Berk, L. E. (1990). A longitudinal study of the development of elementary school children's private speech. *Merrill-Palmer Quarterly, 36,* 443–463.

Bivens, J. A., & Hagstrom, F. (1991). The representation of private speech in children's literature. In R. M. Diaz & L. E. Berk (Eds.), *Private speech: From social interaction to self-regulation.* Hillsdale, NJ: Erlbaum.

Boas, F. (1966). Introduction. In F. Boas (Ed.), *Handbook of American Indian Languages.* Lincoln, NE: University of Nebraska Press.

Bower, T. G. R. (1974). *Development in infancy.* San Francisco: Freeman.

Brown, A. L., & Ferrara, R. (1985). Diagnosing zones of proximal development. In J. V. Wertsch (Ed.), *Culture, communication, and cognition: Vygotskian perspectives* (pp. 273–305). New York: Cambridge University Press.

Brown, A. L., & French, L. A. (1979). The zone of potential development: Implications for intelligence testing in the year 2000. *Intelligence, 3,* 255–277.

Bruner, J. S. (1962). Introduction to L. S. Vygotsky. In *Thought and language.* Cambridge, MA: MIT Press.

Bruner, J. S. (1976). Early social interaction and language acquisition. In H. R. Schaffer (Ed.), *Studies in mother–infant interaction* (pp. 56–78). San Diego: Academic Press.

Cole, M. (1985). The zone of proximal development: Where culture and cognition create each other. In J. V. Wertsch (Ed.), *Culture, communication, and cognition: Vygotskian perspectives* (pp. 146–161). New York: Cambridge University Press.

Diaz, R. M., & Berk, L. E. (Eds.). (1991). *Private speech: From social interaction to self-regulation.* Hillsdale, NJ: Erlbaum.

Emerson, C. (1983). The outer word and inner speech: Bakhtin, Vygotsky, and the internalization of language. *Critical Inquiry, 10,* 245–264.

Gardner, H. (1983). *Frames of mind: The theory of multiple intelligences.* New York: Basic Books.

Geertz, C. (1973). *The interpretation of cultures.* New York: Basic Books.

Goudena, P. (1987). The social nature of private speech of preschoolers during problem solving. *International Journal of Behavioral Development, 10,* 187–206.

Hutchins, E. (1991). The social organization of distributed cognition. In L. B. Resnick, J. M. Levine, & S. D. Teasley (Eds.), *Perspectives on socially shared cognition* (pp. 283–307). Washington, DC: American Psychological Association.

Janet, P. (1928). *De l'angoisse à l'extase: Etudes sur les croyances et les sentiments. Vol. 2: Les sentiments fondamentaux* [From anguish to ecstasy: Studies on beliefs and emotions. Vol. 2: The basic emotions]. Paris: Librairie Félix Alcan.

Kohlberg, L., Yaeger, J., & Hjertholm, E. (1968). Private speech: Four studies and a review of theories. *Child Development, 39,* 691–736.

Kozulin, A. (1990). *L. S. Vygotsky.* Brighton, England: Harvestor Press.

Laboratory of Comparative Human Cognition, University of California, San Diego. (1983). Culture and cognitive development. In W. Kessen (Ed.), *Mussen's handbook of child psychology* (4th ed., Vol. 1). New York: Wiley.

Leont'ev, A. A. (1990). *L. S. Vygotsky.* Moscow: Prosveshchenie.

Leont'ev, A. N. (1931). *Razvitie pamyati: Eksperimental'noe issledovanie vysshikh psikhologicheskikh funktsii* [The development of memory: Experimental research on higher psychological functions]. Moscow–Leningrad: Uchpedgiz.

Leont'ev, A. N. (1959). *Problemy razvitiya psikhiki* [Problems in the development of mind]. Moscow: Izdatel'stvo Moskovskogo Universiteta.

Leont'ev, A. N. (1975). *Deyatel'nost', soznanie, lichnost'* [Activity, consciousness, personality]. Leningrad: Izdatel'stvo Politicheskoi Literaturi.

Leont'ev, A. N. (1981). The problem of activity in psychology. In J. V. Wertsch (Ed.), *The concept of activity in Soviet psychology* (pp. 37–71). Armonk, NY: Sharpe.

Leont'ev, A. N., & Luria, A. R. (1956). Mirovozrenie psikhologii L. S. Vygotskogo [L. S. Vygotsky's outlook on psychology]. In L. S. Vygotsky, *Izbrannye psikhologicheskie issledovaniya* [Selected psychological investigations] (pp. 3–22). Moscow: Izdatel'stvo Akademii Pedagogicheskikh Nauk.

Levy-Bruhl, L. (1923). *Primitive mentality* (L. A. Clare, Trans.). London: Allen & Unwin.

Lotman, Yu. M. (1973, October 12). Different cultures, different codes. *Times Literary Supplement*, pp. 1213–1215.

Lotman, Yu. M., & Uspensky, B. A. (1978). On the semiotic mechanism of culture. *New Literary History, 9*, 211–232.

Luria, A. R. (1976). *Cognitive development: Its cultural and social foundations.* Cambridge, MA: Harvard University Press.

Luria, A. R. (1981). *Language and cognition* (J. V. Wertsch, Ed.). New York: Wiley Intersciences.

Matejka, L. (1973). On the first Russian prolegomena to semiotics. In V. N. Voloshinov, *Marxism and the philosophy of language* (pp. 161–174). New York: Seminar Press.

Middleton, D. (1987). Collective memory and remembering: Some issues and approaches. *Quarterly Newsletter of the Laboratory of Comparative Human Cognition, 9*, 2–5.

Minick, N. J., Forman, E., & Stone, C. A. (in press). *Education and mind: The integration of institutional, social, and developmental processes.* New York: Oxford University Press.

Moll, L. C. (Ed.). (1990). *Vygotsky and education: Instructional implications and applications of sociohistorical psychology.* Cambridge, England: Cambridge University Press.

Palincsar, A. S., & Brown, A. L. (1984). Reciprocal teaching of comprehension-fostering and comprehension-monitoring activities. *Cognition and Instruction, 1*, 117–175.

Palincsar, A. S., & Brown, A. L. (1988). Teaching and practicing thinking skills to promote comprehension in the context of group problem solving. *RASE, 9*, 53–59.

Piaget, J. (1952). *The origins of intelligence in children.* New York: International Universities Press.

Potebnya, A. A. (1922). *Mysl' i yazyk* [Thought and language]. Odessa, Ukraine: Gosudarstvennoe Izdatel'stvo Ukrainy.

Puzerei, A. A. (1986). *Kul'turno-istoricheskaya teoriya L. S. Vygotskogo i sovremennaya psikhologiya* [L. S. Vygotsky's cultural-historical theory and contemporary psychology]. Moscow: Izadetel'stvo Moskovskogo Universiteta.

Ratner, C. (1991). *Vygotsky's sociocultural psychology and its contemporary applications.* New York: Plenum.

Resnick, L. A., Levine, R., & Behrend, A. (1991). *Perspectives on socially shared cognition.* Washington, DC: American Psychological Association.

Rogoff, B. (1990). *Apprenticeship in thinking: Cognitive development in social context.* New York: Oxford University Press.

Rogoff, B., & Wertsch, J. V. (Eds.). (1984). Children's learning in the "zone of proximal development" (no. 23). In *New directions for child development.* San Francisco: Jossey-Bass.

Rubinshtein, S. L. (1957). *Bytie i soznanie* [Being and consciousness]. Moscow: Izdatel'stvo Akademii Nauk, SSSR.

Sapir, E. (1921). *Language: An introduction to the study of speech.* New York: Harcourt, Brace, & World.

Sarason, S. B. (1981). An asocial psychology and a misdirected clinical psychology. *American Psychologist, 36,* 827–836.

Scribner, S. (1985). Vygotsky's uses of history. In J. V. Wertsch (Ed.), *Culture, communication, and cognition: Vygotskian perspectives* (pp. 119–145). New York: Cambridge University Press.

Scribner, S., & Cole, M. (1981). *The psychological consequences of literacy.* Cambridge, MA: Harvard University Press.

Shif, Zh. I. (1935). *Razvitie nauchnykh ponyatii u shkol'nika: Issledovanie k voprosu umstvennogo razvitiya shkol'nika pri obuchenii obshchestvovedeniyu* [The development of scientific concepts in the schoolchild: The investigation of intellectual development of the schoolchild in social science instruction]. Moscow–Leningrad: Gosudarstvennoe Uchebno-Pedagogicheskoe Izdatel'stvo.

Spencer, H. (1900). *The principles of sociology.* New York: Appleton.

Taylor, C. (1985). *Human agency and language. Philosophical papers 1.* Cambridge, England: Cambridge University Press.

Tharp, R. G., & Gallimore, R. (1988). *Rousing minds to life.* New York: Cambridge University Press.

Tulviste, P. (1986). Ob istoricheskoi geterogennosti verbal'nogo myshleniya [The historical heterogeneity of verbal thinking]. In Ya. A. Ponomarev (Ed.), *Myshlenie, obshchenie, praktika: Sbornik nauchnykh trudov* [Thinking, society, practice: A collection of scientific works] (pp. 19–29). Yaroslavl, USSR: Yaroslavskii Gosudarstvennyi Pedagogicheskii Institut im. K. D. Ushinskogo.

Tulviste, P. (1987). L. Levy-Bruhl and problems of the historical development of thought. *Soviet Psychology, 25,* 3–21.

Tulviste, P. (1991). *Cultural-historical development of verbal thinking: A psychological study.* Commack, NY: Nova Science Publishers.

Tylor, E. B. (1888). *Primitive culture: Researches into the development of mythology, philosophy, religion, language, art, and custom.* New York: Holt.

van der Veer, R., & Valsiner, J. (1988). Lev Vygotsky and Pierre Janet: On the origin of the concept of sociogenesis. *Developmental Review, 8,* 52–65.

van der Veer, R., & Valsiner, J. (in press). *A quest for synthesis: Life and work of Lev Vygotsky.* London: Routledge.

Voloshinov, V. N. (1973). *Marxism and the philosophy of language* (L. Matejka & I. R. Titunik, Trans.) New York: Seminar Press.

Vygotsky, L. S. (1930). Sotsialisticheskaya peredelka cheloveka [The socialist transformation of man]. *VARNITSO, 9–10,* 36–44.

Vygotsky, L. S. (1934). *Myshlenie i rech': Psikhologicheskie issledovaniya* [Thinking and speech: Psychological investigations]. Moscow and Leningrad: Gosudarstvennoe Sotsial'no-Ekonomicheskoe Izdatel'stvo.

Vygotsky, L. S. (1956). *Izbrannye psikhologicheskie issledovaniya* [Selected psychological investigations]. Moscow: Izdatel'stvo Akademii Pedagogicheskikh Nauk.

Vygotsky, L. S. (1960). *Razvitie vysshykh psikhicheskikh funktsii* [The development of higher mental functions]. Moscow: Izdatel'stvo Akademii Pedagogicheskikh Nauk.

Vygotsky, L. S. (1971). *The psychology of art.* Cambridge, MA: MIT Press.

Vygotsky, L. S. (1978). *Mind in society: The development of higher psychological processes* (M. Cole, V. John-Steiner, S. Scribner, & E. Souberman, Eds.). Cambridge, MA: Harvard University Press.

Vygotsky, L. S. (1979). Consciousness as a problem in the psychology of behavior. *Soviet Psychology, 17,* 3–35.

Vygotsky, L. S. (1981a). The development of higher forms of attention in childhood. In J. V. Wertsch (Ed.), *The concept of activity in Soviet psychology* (pp. 189–240). Armonk, NY: Sharpe.

Vygotsky, L. S. (1981b). The genesis of higher mental functions. In J. V. Wertsch (Ed.), *The concept of activity in Soviet psychology* (pp. 144–188). Armonk, NY: Sharpe.

Vygotsky, L. S. (1981c). The instrumental method in psychology. In J. V. Wertsch (Ed.), *The concept of activity in Soviet psychology* (pp. 134–143). Armonk, NY: Sharpe.

Vygotsky, L. S. (1982a). *Sobranie sochinenii, Tom pervyi: Voprosy teorii i istorii psikhologii* [Collected works, Vol. 1: Problems in the theory and history of psychology]. Moscow: Izdatel'stvo Pedagogika.

Vygotsky, L. S. (1982b). *Sobranie sochinenii, Tom vtoroi, Problemy obshchei psikhologii* [Collected works, Vol. 2: Problems of general psychology]. Moscow: Izdatel'stvo Pedagogika.

Vygotsky, L. S. (1983a). *Sobranie sochinenii, Tom tretii. Problemy razvitiya psikhiki* [Collected works, Vol. 3: Problems in the development of mind]. Moscow: Izdatel'stvo Pedagogika.

Vygotsky, L. S. (1983b). *Sobranie sochinenii, Tom pyati: Osnovy defektologii* [Collected works, Vol. 5: Foundations of defectology]. Moscow: Izdatel'stvo Pedagogika.

Vygotsky, L. S. (1984a). *Sobranie sochinenii, Tom chetvertyi: Detskaya psikhologii* [Collected works, Vol. 4: Child psychology]. Moscow: Izdatel'stvo Pedagogika.

Vygotsky, L. S. (1984b). *Sobranie sochinenii, Tom shestoi: Nauchnoe nasledstvo* [Collected works, Vol. 6: Scientific legacy]. Moscow: Izdatel'stvo Pedagogika.

Vygotsky, L. S. (1986). *Thought and language* (Abridged from 1934; A. Kozulin, Trans.). Cambridge, MA: MIT Press.

Vygotsky, L. S. (1987). *Thinking and speech* (N. Minick, Ed. and Trans.). New York: Plenum. (translation of Vygotsky, 1982b)

Vygotsky, L. S. (in press). *Foundations of defectology* (J. Knox, Ed. and Trans.). New York: Plenum. (translation of Vygotsky, 1983b)

Vygotsky, L. S., & Luria, A. R. (1930). *Etyudy po istorii povedeniya: Obez'yana, primitiv, rebenok* [Essays on the history of behavior: Ape, primitive, child]. Moscow and Leningrad: Gosudarstvennoe Izdatel'stvo.

Wertsch, J. V. (1979a). From social interaction to higher psychological processes: A clarification and application of Vygotsky's theory. *Human Development, 22,* 1–22.

Wertsch, J. V. (1979b). The regulation of human action and the given-new organization of private speech. In G. Zivin (Ed.), *The development of self-regulation through private speech* (pp. 79–98). New York: Wiley.

Wertsch, J. V. (1980). The significance of dialogue in Vygotsky's account of social, egocentric, and inner speech. *Contemporary Educational Psychology, 5,* 150–162.

Wertsch, J. V. (Ed.). (1985a). *Culture, communication, and cognition: Vygotskian perspectives.* New York: Cambridge University Press.

Wertsch, J. V. (1985b). *Vygotsky and the social formation of mind.* Cambridge, MA: Harvard University Press.

Wertsch, J. V. (1991). *Voices of the mind: A sociocultural approach to mediated action.* Cambridge, MA: Harvard University Press.

Wertsch, J. V., Tulviste, P., & Hagstrom, F. (in press). A sociocultural approach to agency. In E. Forman, N. Minick, & C. A. Stone (Eds.), *Knowledge construction and social practice: Institutional and interpersonal contexts of human development.* New York: Oxford University Press.

Whorf, B. L. (1956). *Language, thought, and reality.* Cambridge, MA: MIT Press.

Yaroshevskii, M. (1989). *Lev Vygotsky.* Moscow: Progress.

Zinchenko, V. P. (1985). Vygotsky's ideas about units of analysis of mind. In J. V. Wertsch (Ed.), *Culture, communication, and cognition: Vygotskian perspectives* (pp. 94–118). New York: Cambridge University Press.

13

ARNOLD L. GESELL: THE PARADOX OF NATURE AND NURTURE

ESTHER THELEN AND KAREN E. ADOLPH

Arnold Lucius Gesell (1880–1961) stands as a giant in the field of developmental psychology. He pioneered the scientific observation of infants and children through innovative and technically sophisticated methods for collecting a vast archive of behavioral data. He published prodigiously over four decades to an enormous audience of psychologists, educators, physicians, policymakers, and other social scientists. His works have been translated into more than 20 languages and continue to be widely cited in scholarly books and journals. Through his popular books and columns, his name became a household word. He introduced a wide public to the science of child rearing and allowed for his successors, Benjamin Spock and Berry Brazelton, to become cultural icons. Gesell popularized the practice of developmental testing, with reverberations to this day in pediatricians'

This work was supported by a Research Scientist Development Award from the National Institute of Mental Health (NIMH) to Esther Thelen and a National Research Service Award from NIMH to Karen E. Adolph.

We thank Louise Bates Ames for her helpful discussion and David Thelen and Herbert A. Thelen for their insightful comments.

Reprinted from *Developmental Psychology*, 28, 368–380. Copyright by the American Psychological Association.

offices and school clinics. He was an active crusader for child welfare and for humane and child-centered educational practices, especially for developmentally handicapped children. And from his earliest writings, Gesell was a consummate developmental theorist. In its own terms, his theory was comprehensive, coherent, and informed by the best biological science of his day. Although he remained a steadfast maturationist, he had a sophisticated understanding of developmental processes and prefigured many dominant themes of modern developmental theory.

Yet a survey of contemporary developmentalists in academia or clinical practice would reveal few acknowledged Gesellians, in contrast to many who might claim an intellectual heritage from Piaget, Vygotsky, Erikson, Lewin, or E. J. Gibson. There is no chapter on Gesell in a recent textbook on developmental theories and scant mention in the text (Miller, 1989). Are the man and his work forgotten? Or has he been relegated, like Watson and the behaviorists, to extreme positions of the past, straw men in our introductory lectures on the nature-versus-nurture theme?

In this chapter, we argue that Gesell is very much a part of contemporary developmental study but that his influence is both subtle and largely unrecognized. To make our point, we critically evaluate Gesell's developmental theory and his contribution to the scientific study of the child, emphasizing the social and intellectual climate in which he worked. We speculate on why even before his death his direct influence waned, leaving few disciples. Finally, we show that there are strong neo-Gesellian themes recurrent in many streams of contemporary developmental study, and we suggest a reevaluation of the enduring nature of his influence. We begin with a brief summary of Gesell's career.

ARNOLD GESELL'S PROFESSIONAL CAREER

Gesell's professional experience was uniquely rich and broad. He was trained as an educator, as a developmental psychologist, and as a physician at some of the foremost institutions of his day, and he practiced actively in these fields of child development throughout his career. In each professional capacity, he maintained his commitment to normative description and child welfare.

After receiving a teaching degree in 1899 from Teachers College at Columbia University, Gesell taught high school courses and then served as a high school principal. In 1915, he became the first official school psychologist for the State Board of Education of Connecticut, traveling from one rural school to another to identify handicapped students and organize special classes for them. From 1911 until 1948, Gesell served as director of the Yale Clinic of Child Development, where he maintained daily contact with teachers and children at the clinic's nursery school. The clinic recruited "well babies" and deviant children for normative observation and served the New Haven community by providing clinical interventions and advice to parents and adoption agencies.

Gesell and his fellow graduate student and friend Louis Terman received psychological training at Clark University under the tutelage of G. Stanley Hall. Both were trained in Hall's questionnaire method for describing "the contents of children's minds" (Kessen, 1965, p. 149), but Gesell especially admired Hall's commitment to Darwinian theory and his exuberant, wide-ranging inquiry into developmental process (Gesell, 1952a). Terman (1906) wrote a dissertation entitled *Genius and Stupidity*, whereas Gesell (1906) investigated normal and abnormal manifestations of jealousy in animals and humans at ascending age periods beginning with infancy. Both received doctoral degrees in 1906. The following year, Gesell joined Terman as professor of psychology at the Los Angeles State Normal School. Whereas Terman contributed to our knowledge of gifted children and the technical and statistical problems of intelligence testing, it was Gesell's use of developmental tests as a theoretical device that promulgated the traditions of Darwin, Galton, and Hall (Kessen, 1965).

In 1911, Gesell was appointed assistant professor of education at Yale, where he taught courses in the graduate school and began his medical studies. This third area of professional training was tackled to gain a "realistic familiarity with the physical basis and the physiological processes of life and growth" (Gesell, 1952a). In 1915, Gesell received his medical degree from Yale and was promoted to professor of child hygiene in the graduate school. In 1935, largely because of Gesell's influence, the American Board of Pediatrics established the field of growth and development as a basic requirement for specialty certification, formally acknowledging the importance of developmental principles for preventive medicine (Gesell, 1952a). Gesell continued his clinical practice as counseling psychologist–pediatrician even after his mandatory retirement from Yale in 1948.

From the early 1930s to the later 1940s, Gesell was at the height of his career. The Yale psychoclinic grew from one room with a table and desk into a world-renowned center for testing, clinical intervention, and graduate and medical training, occupying five floors of the Yale Human Relations Institute, with a staff of 31. Associates such as Halverson, Castner, Thompson, Washburn, Ames, Ilg, Amatruda, Bullis, and Learned amassed enormous amounts of normative data and published prodigously with Gesell on a range of topics from infant development to adolescent development, both normal and deviant. The clinic's research program had a large endowment during these years, primarily from the Rockefeller Foundation, and impressive facilities for photographic and cinematic recordings were constructed. In the last 2 years before Gesell's retirement, more than 2,000 visitors came to the clinic to use the voluminous film library and learn Gesell's diagnostic techniques (Ames, 1989).

Shortly after Gesell's mandatory retirement in 1948, the Human Relations Institute was dismantled. The clinic survived with a grant from the American Optical Company, which allowed collection of normative data on the development of vision (Gesell, Ilg, & Bullis, 1949). In 1950, Yale University refused to continue to sponsor Gesell's clinic. Given the enormous success of the clinic, its worldwide reputation, and Gesell's renown, Yale's actions seem nearly inexplicable. Louise Ames (personal communication, August 1991) attributes their removal to several factors, including the ascendancy of Freudians in the Department of Psychiatry, the dominance of learning theorists in experimental psychology, and the general distrust that academics feel toward colleagues who are widely popular and who write for general audiences. Nonetheless, with the swing of the intellectual pendulum to more biological psychology, Yale has had a change of heart and recently even established an Arnold L. Gesell professorship in the Yale Child Study Center.

After leaving Yale, several of Gesell's colleagues purchased a modest building that they renamed the Gesell Institute, at which normative and clinical research continued despite scarce funding. Daily newspaper columns in 65 papers throughout the country and a television program provided advice to parents and raised funds for the new clinic, which allowed the group to follow their remaining subjects through adolescence and which culminated in their final major book, *Youth: The Years From 10 to 16* (Gesell, Ilg, & Ames, 1956), in 1956 (Ames, 1989). The Gesell Institute continues today.

GESELL'S THEORY

More than many theorists, Arnold Gesell maintained an internally coherent, steadfast, and clearly articulated theory of development throughout his nearly 40 years of active research and writing. To understand his unwavering commitment to his principles of growth despite the comings and goings of contemporaries such as Anna Freud, Watson, Piaget, Lewin, and Margaret Mead, it is useful to consider Gesell's own intellectual heritage, which he often explicitly acknowledged.

Like Piaget, Gesell claimed deep roots in the science of biology. Also like Piaget, he saw all behavior and mental activity as continuous with and inseparable from other biological processes, including those that engender the physical form of the organism. (Gesell differed from Piaget, however, in his account of the nature of those processes.) Gesell's vision was of a unitary science of development, encompassing evolution, comparative psychology, embryology, neurophysiology, and anthropology, and he continually wove these perspectives into his accounts of human infants and children (cf. Gesell, 1928, 1945, 1948). Two influences were particularly powerful:

Charles Darwin, as the father of the scientific study of the child, and G. E. Coghill, who, along with other early embryologists, was the first to detail processes of behavioral growth experimentally.

Gesell's Darwinian Legacy

Gesell's debt to Darwin was twofold. First, Gesell venerated Darwin for rescuing human infants from the speculations of philosophy and theology and admitting them into the domain of respectable scientific inquiry. Before Darwin, infants and children were understood primarily in theological terms—as possessed by original sin and to be saved by baptism. According to Gesell (1948, p. 44), these "gloomier beliefs of fixity and fate" trammeled the spirit and stifled any scientific inquiry into human nature. Because Darwin established the gradual origins of all living things, including the human mind, Gesell (1948, p. 44) credited Darwin with giving scientists "absolute freedom in the study of laws of nature. . . . Without that freedom it would be impossible to penetrate into the meaning of human infancy and into the nature of child development."

Just as Gesell paid tribute to Darwin's seminal role in the intellectual heritage of child study, he also greatly admired Darwin's methods of investigation. Gesell saw Darwin, perhaps as he saw himself, as a naturalist, "tirelessly" seeking "ideological order" (Gesell, 1948, p. 36). This order was gained through relentless observation and comparison. Gesell (1948, p. 37) remarked that Darwin "left no stone unturned in his search for data." For example, in his investigations on the origins of human emotions, Darwin closely observed his own children and studied emotional expressions in other animals and in children and adults of other cultures. He was interested in the physiology of emotions as well. According to Gesell (1948, p. 43), contemporary child development study also needed "the naturalist's breadth of vision." Gesell (1948, p. 57) followed Darwin in thinking that "the understanding of the human mind . . . will be attained not through the researches of a single discipline, but through the conjunctive results of a great interlocking system of sciences."

This discussion of Gesell and Darwin raises a recurrent tension, which is the central enigma of Gesell's legacy: the resolution of Gesell's clearly articulated beliefs in ultimate biological causality with his equally firmly held ideals of human freedom. Gesell clearly owes to Darwin his core assumption that the growth of mental life is continuous with and impelled by the same processes that drive all organic growth. The assumption that the forces of natural selection work with equal power over all aspects of function led Gesell from descriptions of the orderly progression of motor development in infancy to equally detailed and orderly accounts of intellectual, personality, and social stages during all of childhood and adolescence. Once he demonstrated order in development, however, Gesell ascribed this order to biological destiny. Critics might detect a certain irony in Gesell replacing the fixity and fate of the Calvinist view of childhood with a biological determinism that is in many ways as rigid. We see variations of this paradox repeated in all aspects of Gesell's work and career. How does Gesell reconcile a genetically driven maturational program with his beliefs in children's individuality and active exploration of the environment and in the importance of the nursery, preschool, and school environment and with his concern for child welfare both in the home and in society at large? How can he be so aware of the dynamic interplay of multiple influences in development and yet ignore these processes in favor of biological causation? Gesell's decline as a major developmental theorist is due at least in part to these unresolved tensions in his work.

Coghill and the Influence of Embryology

Gesell's contemporary, embryologist G. E. Coghill (1969), stood second only to Darwin as an inspiration to Gesell. (Myrtle McGraw, e.g., 1935, also drew heavily on Coghill for her maturationist–organismic approach to development.) Gesell believed that Coghill, in his studies of the embryo of the salamander *Amblystoma*, had unearthed the very essence of vertebrate development, and Gesell used Coghill's work as an explicit model for his research on human infants. According to Gesell (1946, p. 295), in the hands of Coghill, "this primitive vertebrate . . . has become a touchstone for elucidating problems of human behavior."

Coghill's major contribution was to show a correlation between behavioral development and corresponding changes in the nervous system. In the work that so captivated Gesell, Coghill first described the ontogeny of locomotion in *Amblystoma* in exquisite detail and then traced the neurological and muscular basis of those movements. Most exciting to Gesell was Coghill's demonstration that the onset of particular behavioral configurations was coincident with the growth of specific neural connections. Because Coghill found that these early motor patterns emerged before the animal developed the corresponding sensory tracts, he concluded that swimming was the result of these neural connections and not their cause.

Coghill's Enduring Legacies

A number of Coghill's legacies dominate Gesell's work. First is the idea that behavior has form and that development can be understood by changes in shape or morphology of the organism's behavior. It is instructive to compare Coghill's tracings from motion pictures of the swimming patterns of *Amblystoma*, for instance, with Gesell's films of the postures and movements of infants. It was surely this preoccupation with documenting changing form that compelled Gesell's monumental labors in photographing in-

362   ESTHER THELEN AND KAREN E. ADOLPH

fants and children in all aspects of their lives. Indeed, throughout his career, Gesell was to claim that "posture is behavior. Postural patterns are behavioral patterns" (Gesell & Thompson, 1934; see also Gesell, 1952b, p. 65). Only within the last few years, with the rediscovery of Bernstein (1967) and renewed interest in motor development, would this statement be viewed with any seriousness. Where Gesell may have gone beyond Coghill, however, was in his extension of the principles of morphology and growth to all facets of mental life. This led Gesell to a descriptive classification of children's expected behavior almost absurd in its detailed caricatures of age-related changes (cf. Gesell & Ilg, 1943).

Second, Gesell derived from Coghill that behavioral morphology is a direct readout of the neural structures that underlie it. "How does the mind grow?" asks Gesell. He answers, "It grows like the nervous system; it grows with the nervous system. Growth is a patterning process. It produces patterned changes in the nerve cells; it produces corresponding changes in patterns of behavior" (Gesell & Ilg, 1943, p. 18). Gesell repeats this principle continually, and it stands as the justification for his dominant enterprise: developmental norms. That is, the behavior of the child in relation to his or her expected maturational stage reflects the integrity of the nervous system. This is perhaps Gesell's most enduring legacy, as we discuss further.

Third, and perhaps most important theoretically, is that these neural changes are autonomous products of growth, inherent and lawful and not subject to the influence of function. "Patterns of behavior in all species tend to follow an orderly genetic sequence in their emergence," Gesell wrote. "This genetic sequence is itself an expression of elaborate pattern — a pattern whose basic outline is the product of evolution and is under the influence of maturational factors" (Gesell, 1933, p. 217). Throughout his career, Gesell remained unwavering in his conviction that maturation was the ontogenetic source of all behavior. He was abundantly aware of the questions raised about his view. What and how do children learn? What is the role of the environment? How does one account for individual differences? Gesell addressed these questions frankly if not entirely consistently within his theoretical view.

For example, Gesell's descriptions of the experiential world of the infant would do justice to Piaget or E. J. Gibson and is consistent with contemporary neuroembryological theories of the origins of mind (e.g., Edelman, 1987). On the acquisition of the infant's sense of self, Gesell and Ilg (1943, p. 33) wrote:

> He spends many moments looking at his hands, fingering his hands, mouthing his hands. These sensory experiences, — visual, tactile, wet, dry, still, moving, stop–go, oral, palmar, touching and being touched, provide him with a medley of data. By gradual degrees he comes to realize that he has a hand which feels when it contacts (active touch), which feels when it is contacted (passive touch), which feels when it

is moved (sense of motion, or kinesthetic sense mediated by sensory end organs in muscles, joints and tendons). His ceaseless manipulation, therefore, acquaints him not only with the physical universe and the physical presence of other persons, but with the physical presence of himself. . . . His manipulation of objects also gives him an increasing sense of mastery of his environment.

Gesell (1933, p. 214) noted that even the salamander's behavior was not fixed and rigid, so experience must have "much to do in determining when and to what extent performance will take place." How then can patterns of behavior—their timing as well as their form—be ultimately configured by the genes? Again, Gesell referred to Coghill: The neural structures for the mechanisms of learning must also mature, like the motor mechanisms, to anticipate their function.

Gesell and the Growth of Individuality

The domination of structure is the genesis of Gesell's beliefs about individual differences, which posed a formidable challenge to his views and which he met with less than full success. Gesell devotes chapters (e.g., Gesell, 1928; Gesell & Ilg, 1943) and indeed entire books (Gesell, Amatruda, Castner, & Thompson, 1939) extolling infants as individuals and describing the individuality of their growth patterns in relation to his developmental norms in short vignettes. Where does this individuality come from? In his earlier works, Gesell seemed puzzled and ambivalent. In describing children who on developmental tests "frequently" have equivalent scores but "differ chronologically by two, three, five, or ten years," he wistfully wrote, "Their very equivalence emphasizes their contrasts and calls for an interpretation of these contrasts in terms of habituation, inheritance, environment" (Gesell, 1925, p. 291). What to make of these "developmental peers of incongruent age" (Gesell, 1925, p. 291)? Gesell viewed both retardation and precocity as potentially unbalancing the harmonious progression of normal development, especially when parents or others induced children to perform beyond their naturally unfolding patterns of growth.

In his later works, Gesell was more direct and explicit in explaining behavioral individuality. Infants are individuals from before birth, and their individuality manifests itself not only in characteristic pathways of physical growth but also in stable and enduring personality traits and in the maturation of mental styles and capabilities. Individual differences in behavior are as much a part of the organism as patterns of physical growth, and all are traits inherited both from the family and from the race as a whole. Although infants are plastic and learn from the culture, the limits of this plasticity are themselves genetically determined. Children's constitutions determine "how, what, and to some extent even when" they will learn (Gesell & Ilg, 1946, p. 40).

Gesell viewed individuality in another important way. At the same time children have innate and prefigured individual developmental pathways, they also have biological individuality as a function of their age. This individuality is reflected in physical skills, cognitive abilities, and temperament. Only Gesell's own language can convey the strength of the stage imperative (Gesell & Ilg, 1943, p. 224):

> THREE has a conforming mind. FOUR has a lively mind. THREE is assentive; FOUR, assertive. Indeed, FOUR tends to go out of bounds both with muscle and mind. And why should he not? If he remained a delightful, docile THREE, he would not grow up. So he surges ahead with bursts of movement and of imagination. His activity curve again takes on the hither and thither pattern typical of TWO YEARS. . . .
> If at times he seems somewhat voluble, dogmatic, boastful and bossy, it is because he is a blithe amateur swinging into fresh fields of self expression.

Poetic language aside, there is a sense throughout Gesell's voluminous descriptions of the lives of children from newborn through adolescent of a relentless inevitability, of an organism neither in control of itself nor impelled by forces surrounding it. Rather, the child seems possessed by a resident homunculus, capricious but wise, whose wild mood swings serve in the end the developmental dialectic. Gesell never resolves these dual aspects of individuality: how a child maintains individuality, whatever its source, while at the same time marching through an inexorable series of prescribed stages.

Given his views on individual differences, what did Gesell see as the importance of the family, the school, and the culture? In both his writing and his clinical and policy work, Gesell was clear. Society and the family must provide children with an environment that allows the inherent growth potential of each child to be fully and optimally realized. The whole purpose of developmental norms was to identify the individual status of each child so as to guide children more suitably to optimal growth. The environment must be precisely tailored to fit the child's capabilities. Children who are delayed must be provided with a supportive and humane environment; those who are accelerated must be watched for balanced growth. No child should be given tasks beyond his or her state of maturational readiness. In a guidance nursery, the guidance teacher must continually channel the natural tendencies of the children into constructive and appropriate activities.

Thus, Gesell's enterprise for the scientific study of the child led him from the naturalist's belief in description and categorization to the physiologist's need for understanding mechanism to the physician's consideration for diagnosis and diagnostic categories and ultimately to the educator's concern for the welfare of children. As we will discuss, Gesell had many blind spots, and his theory is by any account both incomplete and stifling. He also had many brilliant insights, he was motivated by a lifelong devotion to the well-being of children, and he remains a pervasive if not fully acknowledged influence on the field.

Embryology and the Process of Development

Before leaving the topic of Coghill and his legacy, it is important to mention another common thread, one that we see as a continuing influence on contemporary developmentalists. Coghill was well known for his principle of behavior differentiation: that mature behavior evolves through a process of increasing specificity from an integrated substrate rather than being constructed from isolated reflexes. The developing organism is a gestalt, not a collection of incomplete pieces; specific functions are carved out and not glued together. Coghill and Gesell after him saw no distinction between the processes of differentiation and growth of the earliest embryo and those of later neurological and behavioral development and indeed, for Gesell, all aspects of mental activity.

Gesell's embryology was most directly reflected in his *principles of behavior development*, which he articulated in his later works (Gesell, 1946, 1952b). The *principle of developmental direction*—that behavior proceeded from head to toe and from proximal to distal structures—echoed the embryological concept of polarity and gradients. His dialectic *principle of reciprocal interweaving* reflects the cyclic ebb and flow of organic life, the essential excitation and inhibition or "duplexity . . . reflected in life processes at every level of functioning" (Gesell, 1952b, p. 67). Not only is reciprocal interweaving characteristic of the changing dominance of flexor and extensor muscles in infancy, but it is also characteristic of the development of the senses and the emotions. Reciprocal interweaving does not produce complete symmetry, however, as "nature evidently did not intend" (Gesell, 1952b, p. 67) humans to be completely balanced. According to the *principle of functional asymmetry*, the infant must break free from symmetry to accomplish functional ends such as lateral handedness, much as even the organ systems in the embryo cannot be perfectly symmetrical. Embryological themes are again dominant in Gesell's *principle of self-regulation*. As all organisms store and distribute energy, "the maturing organism oscillates between self-limiting poles as it advances" (Gesell, 1952b, p. 68). But the thrusts and retreats of the developmental process must be kept within bounds. This inherent self-regulation also protects the developing organism from too many or irrelevant or dangerous stimuli. Likewise, organic integrity is preserved through the *principle of optimal realization*, which buffers the organism and maintains its integrity even when resources for growth are threatened.

The embryological themes became closely woven with a distinct sys-

tems approach by the mid- to late 1940s. At that point, Gesell was citing
von Bertanlannfy (Gesell, 1946), and it is likely that the developmental
principles reflect this influence. As we elaborate further, Gesell's systems
principles are incorporated in many aspects of contemporary dynamic systems theory in development.

The Coghill assumptions were critical to every aspect of Gesell's theory. They guided nearly a half century of descriptive research. We continue
our evaluation of Gesell's impact by discussing his research.

Gesell's Contribution to the Scientific Study of the Child

Most of the research conducted at the Yale psychoclinic was devoted
to compiling a comprehensive schedule of developmental norms. These
norms were presented in nearly every published work either quantitatively
in percentages and averages or qualitatively in the form of developmental
vignettes or age caricatures. Postural, prehensory, adaptive, social, and
linguistic abilities were observed from infancy (including preterm "fetal
infants") to adolescence at specified intervals. Some children were observed
cross-sectionally and others longitudinally at either monthly or yearly intervals. More than 500 children, 50 at each of 10 age levels, contributed
to the original developmental norms (Gesell & Thompson, 1934). Interestingly, children were carefully sampled from the New Haven community
to provide a homogeneous, white, middle-class group of British or German
extraction from intact two-parent families (e.g., Gesell & Thompson, 1938).
This sample, however, was meant to generalize to any infant, regardless of
upbringing, environmental opportunities, and racial heritage, and was presented to clinicians as the yardstick from which to diagnose abnormality
in development (see especially Gesell et al., 1939; Gesell & Amatruda,
1941).

In particular, Gesell and colleagues concentrated on documenting age-
related change in behavior patterns during children's first year of life. Observations were scheduled at monthly rather than yearly intervals during
this period, and more data were collected at each testing session. For these
first months of the infant's life, Gesell looked for preformations of later
behavior patterns. In fact, the battery of test items and behavioral situations
was organized according to the assumption that mature forms of a behavior
(e.g., "plucks pellet with precise pincer prehension") are presaged in early
forms (in this case, "visual prehension" at 4 weeks prefigures pincer grasp
at 40 weeks). At each stage, Gesell described involvement of the total
organism and the holistic behavioral pattern, rather than its piecemeal
construction. Today, protobehaviors are well-accepted concepts, as witnessed in Trevarthen's (1977) protocommunication, von Hofsten's (1984)
prereaching, or Meltzoff and Moore's (1983) neonatal imitation.

Adequate procedures for collecting normative data in infancy required a keen appreciation for these small and taciturn subjects. After the flurry of motor development research by Gesell and his contemporaries such as Mary Shirley and Myrtle McGraw, developmental psychologists and pediatricians nearly uniformly emphasized young infants' reflexive behavior or their incompetence in relation to older children and adults. From the beginning, Gesell focused on young infants' perceptual—motor and social competence and their ability to purposefully exploit aspects of the environment, rather than focusing on their inadequacies.

PROCEDURAL AND METHODOLOGICAL INNOVATIONS

Gesell's behavioral interview, the centerpiece of his normative research, was exceedingly clever. Simple materials such as an enamel cup, a small bell, a red wooden block, or a sugar pellet were presented straightforwardly to the infant in the hope that these homely objects "carried their own enticement" and that "the infant has an ingrained propensity to exploit his physical environment" (Gesell & Thompson, 1934, p. 35). Most test materials were presented repeatedly to children at different ages on the assumption that infants would attend to the stimulus values appropriate to their developmental level. For example, infants first used the performance box, a 20-cm × 20-cm × 40-cm construction with slots for the insertion of various rods and shapes to pull themselves to the erect position. Weeks later, the box was used primarily for its intended purpose, inserting rods into the holes (see Gesell & Thompson, 1934, p. 34). Years before E. J. Gibson and colleagues began investigating infants' exploration of the affordances of objects and events, with the belief that shifts in attention to environmental properties are driven by the development of new action systems (e.g., E. J. Gibson, 1988), Gesell and Thompson (1934, p. 293) wrote that "development is a process in which the mutual fitness of organism and environment is brought to progressive realization. This process . . . is a series of biochemical, morphogenetic events: a process of continuous differentiation, 'coordinated in time and place, leading to specific ends'."

The behavioral interview was designed to promote active responses that reflect infants' competencies, even during the first month of life when the behavioral repertoire is limited. Long before young infants' active looking, listening, mouthing, and manipulative behaviors were exploited experimentally in preferential looking or habituation tasks (e.g., Cohen, 1972; Fantz, 1958), long before infants' spontaneous arm, leg, or head movements were harnessed for contingent reinforcement paradigms by American psychologists (Rovee & Rovee, 1969; Siqueland & Lipsitt, 1966), and long before the era of "the competent infant" (e.g., Stone, Smith, & Murphy, 1973), Gesell had used infants' manifold abilities to formulate his developmental norms.

The apparatus used to conduct the behavioral interviews were equally innovative and clever in a homespun and simple way. Gesell expends many pages describing in words and photographs the specially built multiuse crib (which transformed from sleeper to test table to playpen to fort), the many-pocketed materials bag, the support chair (adjustable for different levels of postural control and with washable canvas inserts), the examination play-house in the nursery room (with gabled roof, built-in "reaction screens," and "secret" basement passage to entice reluctant preschoolers to enter), and so on (e.g., Gesell, 1928; Gesell & Thompson, 1938). Perhaps drawing on his background as a teacher or his clinical experience with young children, Gesell considered each aspect of his testing procedure in minute detail. Explanations are given of how to make friends with babies, precautions against frightening them, and exhortations to gain mothers' trust before the interview (e.g., see Gesell & Thompson, 1938, pp. 65–68). In fact, the infant is often discussed in the context of the mother–infant dyad, prefiguring many modern research topics (e.g., Gesell, 1928).

In addition to the behavioral interview, Gesell compiled normative data on the infant's behavioral day primarily from parental reports but also collected in the institute's research "hotel," in which mother and infant spent a few days under continuous observation (Gesell, 1928; Gesell & Ilg, 1937; Gesell & Thompson, 1938). These data were used to justify more relaxed feeding and sleeping schedules than advised by Gesell's predecessor, J. B. Watson (1928), who had prescribed rigid schedules and minimal physical contact with young infants. The comparative behavioral interview examined two babies of different chronological ages simultaneously in the same task, mostly for demonstration purposes. The experimental method of co-twin control (appropriate only for identical twins) was used to test the effects of specific training versus maturation on development (e.g., Gesell & Thompson, 1929). As in McGraw's (1935) classic study of Jimmy and Johnny, Gesell gave one twin several weeks of training in a task such as stair climbing and then compared behavioral patterns with those of the control twin tested at the same chronological age before and after the training regimen. These studies provided further support to the matura-tionist perspective because the control twin usually achieved a similar de-velopmental level without special training.

ACTION PHOTOGRAPHY AND CINEMATOGRAPHY

From his earliest writings, Gesell was fascinated by the research op-portunities afforded by photographic technology. He saw the camera's eye as impartial, precise, and permanent. A generous endowment from the

Figure 1. Gesell's photographic dome. (From *Infancy and Human Growth* by A. Gesell, 1928, p. 67, Fig. 25, New York: Macmillan. Copyright 1928 by Macmillan. Reprinted by permission.)

Laura Spelman Rockefeller Foundation in 1926 provided funding for the construction of elaborate photographic recording studios, apparatus for developing and analyzing film, and a voluminous archival film library.

Every aspect of the cinematic procedure, from recording to analysis, was designed and described in minute detail (e.g., Gesell, 1928): appropriate ambient lighting, innovative one-way vision screens, the famous photographic dome (Figure 1), film development, coding procedures, and "cinemanalyses." Several major publications were devoted solely to the presentation of action photography and cinematic data (e.g., Gesell, Thompson, & Amatruda, 1934), and numerous films were edited for educational and public viewing.

In his many publications, Gesell rarely mentioned the early work of Muybridge and never credited the innovative film techniques of his own contemporary, Myrtle McGraw. Ironically, the vast film library so carefully catalogued and compiled from more than 20 years of cinematic recordings was abandoned after Gesell's clinic was separated from Yale University. Many films were lost because of poor storage facilities, and the remaining recordings are currently housed at the University of Akron.

What is the lasting legacy of Gesell's methodological and technical innovations? The photographic records presented throughout Gesell's books are astonishingly clear and elucidating. Gesell's verbal pictures of infants and children are less illuminating, however, often cartoonlike caricatures of behavior. Compared with those of his contemporaries Piaget, Shirley, or McGraw, Gesell's verbal descriptions have less import, and they are rarely cited today.

FROM DESCRIPTION TO PRESCRIPTION

The thrust of Gesell's empirical legacy was a catalogue of infant and child behavior. Like the naturalists whom he admired, he described to classify. From the range of variability he saw—however truncated his sampling and selective his vision—he distilled the essence of both what the child was like and what the child was doing. The typical 1-year-old spends a typical day eating, sleeping, eliminating, and being social in neat progression (Gesell & Ilg, 1943). Just as biological species have morphology and exist in time and place, so does the behavior of the child, and the latter can be classified and labeled just as confidently as the skulls and skins of the natural history collection. Indeed, Gesell claimed that the ossification of the wrist bones was more variable than normal infant behavior (Gesell, 1928).

The sleight-of-hand here was Gesell's leap from description—what is—to prescription—what ought to be—and thus his lifelong preoccupation with developmental norms. Developmental norms for infants and children were a direct heritage from Gesell's association with Terman, as well as the influence of Galton, Hall, and Binet. Like Binet, Gesell was motivated by his concern for providing education that was appropriate for the child's capabilities and for diagnosing delayed development for the purposes of intervention. But somehow within these laudable clinical goals, there was a transformation from the typical into the desirable. Gesell elevated the typical child, who of course was no child, into a biological reality, with profound consequences for both theory and practice.

The Legacy of Developmental Norms

Norms of development are without question Arnold Gesell's most enduring legacy. Many items in his test battery have been imported virtually unchanged into the two most widely used infant developmental tests: the Denver Developmental Screening Test and the Bayley Scales of Infant Development. According to Louise Bates Ames, Gesell's long-time associate and the director of the Gesell Institute after his death, the so-called Denver developmental test is a "flagrant unacknowledged use of Gesell test items," with only the substitution of raisins for pellets (Ames, 1989, p. 116). These tests are widely accepted and frequently used all over the world for both research and clinical purposes. The vast bulk of scholarly citations to Gesell over the last 25 years have been to his developmental norms (Table 1),

TABLE 1
Gesell's Most Cited Publications

Publication	Years of citations[a]					Total citations	Mean citations per year	SD
	1966–1970	1971–1975	1976–1980	1981–1985	1986–1990			
Developmental diagnosis (1941)	86	80	111	71	55	403	16.12	6.42
First 5 years of life (1940)	46	61	58	57	38	260	10.40	4.16
Child from 5 to 10 (1946)	29	30	31	27	10	127	5.08	2.93
Journal of Genetic Psychology (1947)	9	10	41	37	23	120	4.80	3.50
Embryology of behavior (1945)	24	13	28	22	7	94	3.76	2.24
Infant and child in culture today (1943)	17	13	25	17	9	81	3.24	2.11
Youth: Years 10 to 16 (1956)	12	18	26	11	8	75	3.00	2.02
Vision: Its development (1949)	25	15	15	7	5	67	2.68	1.95
Infant behavior (1934)	6	10	25	15	9	65	2.60	2.00
Manual of child psychology (1946)	16	8	11	12	7	54	2.16	1.37

[a]Data taken from Social Science Citation Index, 1966 to 1990.

referenced in an astounding range of fields, including developmental psychology, education, medical and clinical sciences of every type, anthropology, and other social sciences. Nearly every developmental textbook contains the obligatory inclusion of a table of motor milestones in the chapter on infancy. Indeed, it is probably hard to overestimate how thoroughly we have internalized the idea of age-appropriate activities as an index of intrinsic biological functioning.

In addition to the patent and undeniable value of developmental norms for diagnosis, other aspects of the heritage were more subtle and perhaps less clearly beneficial. First was the elevation of empirical data into statements of eternal values. Parents reading Gesell's popular books such as *Infant and Child in the Culture of Today* (Gesell & Ilg, 1943) saw descriptions of "typical" infants and children drawn in such detail and with such confidence that even minor deviations might be viewed with alarm. And because the typical child was a quasi-statistical amalgam, every parent's child would naturally deviate.

Gesell's motive for developing norms was to promote the "mental hygiene" of the child, and he meant it to inform and reassure parents and teachers. "We must not lose faith if at the age of 2½ years the child grabs a toy from his playmate; if at 4 years he calls names and brags and boasts and tells tall tales . . . we must recognize the nature of his immaturity" (Gesell, 1948, p. 9). Nonetheless, as Kessen (1965, p. 210) later wrote, "the detail and volume of his descriptive works (together with the avid reception given his books by mothers keen on quantifying the hitherto imprecise business of comparing babies) block an appreciation of his intentions."

The typical child living his typical day was clearly male, white, native born, middle class, and in an intact family, with a virtually invisible father and a devoted but strangely passive mother who acted without agency in an intermittently compliant culture. An extended quotation (Gesell & Ilg, 1943, p. 135) conveys the subtle force of the language. At 15 months old, for example:

> At about 12:30 he is toileted and may have his first or second bowel movement, after which he is returned to his crib. The effects of acculturation now become evident. Typically he makes no protest against the impending nap. He snuggles under his covers. He likes to watch the shades go down. . . . He is likely to wake wet. He is changed and toileted. He usually wakes in high mettle, eager to get out of his crib to continue with his behavior day. . . . Having arrived in the park or in a neighbor's play yard, he likes to be set free on the wide expanse of a lawn or a sidewalk. . . . He returns home at about 4:30 and continues his characteristic play activities, utilizing the apparatus of the living room, with a special interest in all containers, particularly waste-baskets.

Did Gesell and his typical child really influence how a generation of parents raised their children? Were parents beset with worry and guilt if their child wasn't completely toilet trained by 2 or did not manifest interest in containers at 15 months? We cannot answer these questions in this essay, but we do know that many thousands read Gesell and took him seriously. Especially in social classes and cultures in which the mechanics of child-rearing were not universally learned through the extended family and in which experts and scientific advice permeated even the economics of the home, Gesell clearly filled a need. Is my child all right? Am I raising him or her correctly? The paradox of Gesell's answer remains: Yes, your child is an individual, but let me tell you what he or she should be like. Yes, a nurturing environment is important, but gender, class, race, ethnicity, geography, personal values, and style were subservient to the biological imperative embodied in the behavioral norms. At the same time, that very biological imperative could give parents a sense of enormous relief. Parenting might not engender later neuroses or more severe emotional illnesses, as a generation raised with Freud and his followers might believe. (Recall that as late as 1967, Bettelheim was blaming childhood autism on mothers' emotional coldness.) Nor could parents, by their scheduling or conditioning routines, infinitely mold their children's personalities, as suggested by other Gesell contemporaries. Gesell therefore delivered a double message, one that could be both reassuring and alarming.

The second, more subtle, and more lasting legacy of Gesell for the profession was the elevation of developmental stages not only into desirable way stations on the way to middle-class maturity but into real neurological structures generated by genetic design. So inexorable was the unfolding of the ontogenetic pattern from the embryo to the adult that stages became reified, with age the only explanatory variable. In an early account of his normative sample, in which he admitted to leaving out the very bright, the very dull, the very poor, and children from homes where languages other than English were spoken, Gesell reassured readers that they examined children only within 2 weeks of their chronological age: "Whatever imperfections our method of selection may have in other directions, with respect to this factor of central importance it is reliable" (Gesell, 1925, p. 42).

Gesell and the Behaviorists

Gesell's tenacious biological determinism seems all the more remarkable considering that his work precisely paralleled that of the great learning theorists: Tolman, Hull, Skinner, and especially John B. Watson. It is crucial to note here that Gesell was not writing in ignorance of learning theory but in direct and conscious opposition to it. "The extreme versions of environmentalism and conditioning theories," wrote Gesell (1933, p.

230), "suffer because they explain too much." Most contemporary developmentalists would agree. He continues:

> They suggest that the individual is fabricated out of the conditioning patterns. They do not give due recognition to the inner checks which set metes and bounds to the area of conditioning and which happily prevent abnormal and grotesque consequences.

Although environment channels and modifies development, it cannot generate growth. It lacks the structure to produce the regularity of outcome Gesell documented. The inherent and destined individuality of children protected them from random and perhaps evil influences of the physical, social, and political millieu. Writing in an age that saw the rise of racial hatred, genocide, war, and mass manipulation of never-imagined proportions, Gesell retained a steadfast belief in the ultimate outcome of optimal growth. The role of the scientist in bettering human nature, Gesell believed, was not to manipulate and predict human behavior, but to watch it, understand it, and optimize its natural self-righting course. By taking care of our children, we would set the world right (Gesell, 1948).

Again, we come up against the central paradox of Gesell. He was impelled throughout his career by a deep and abiding concern for providing nurturant family and school environments. He witnessed the turbulence of two world wars and the rise of Nazism and the nuclear age. He recognized the unity of child and environment. Yet neither in his theory nor in his research was he explicitly concerned with the mechanisms that integrated growth with the environment that sustained and guided it.

Gesell and Contemporary Developmental Psychology

Gesell's legacy, like his career, is dualistic and somewhat paradoxical. On the one hand, Gesell's developmental norms continue to be a visible and lasting influence. On the other hand, his theoretical contribution is pervasive but less direct. In distinct contrast to Piaget, Gesell left no army of disciples in virtually every psychology and education program in the Western world. He did not spawn tens of thousands of studies to expand, support, or contradict his research. He inspired few revisionists or neo-Gesellian defenders. No annual conferences are held in his name.

It is not difficult, given Gesell and his times, to speculate why this is so. First and foremost, Gesellian developmental psychology leaves experimental psychologists with nothing to do. The child unfolds; understanding is through observation. The only formal experiments Gesell did were his studies with twins, which were hardly models of experimental science. Gesell thought it worthwhile to use genetics as the independent variable, but because the environment did not engender differences or change, in his system experimentally manipulating the environment would not test basic developmental processes. Thus, there was nothing in Gesell to generate the rigorous hypothesis testing to which the science of behavior aspired. At the same time, Gesell was not modest in proclaiming that he and his colleagues preempted the field of observation and description. For example, Gesell never mentions or cites his contemporary Myrtle McGraw, whose documentation of early motor development was equal and in many ways superior to Gesell's in technical and descriptive elegance. One would not know from reading Gesell that other large longitudinal growth studies were being conducted in Iowa, Berkeley, or Yellow Springs. In short, the theory squelched experimentation while leaving the impression that the necessary observational studies were conducted in Gesell's laboratory alone.

Second, Gesell fell from grace because his theory simply was insufficiently mentalistic to accommodate the domains of mainstream psychology. Gesell was disinterested in the content and workings of the mind. He thought of Piaget, for example, as "too mentalistic to be readily brought into a biological discussion" (Gesell, 1933, p. 226). Gesell's theory was just as "black box" as the most strict stimulus–response psychology, but he substituted biological destiny for the equally unspecified mechanisms of association. Gesell was additionally unpalatable, however, because he was nonexperimental. So in a climate dominated by learning theory but also seeing the rising influence of Piaget and a growing interest in memory and cognition and in information-processing metaphors, Gesell must have appeared to be a musty cataloguer in the same way that natural history curators would be viewed by modern molecular biologists—interesting, perhaps, but irrelevant.

The most fundamental reason that Gesell has not inspired succeeding generations is that his theory itself is incomplete, is deterministic, and leaves little room for the study of developmental processes. Here Gesell might argue that growth is a process; we have discovered lawful principles and showed that they apply for many species and over many domains of change. Gesell's great logical error here was to assume that lawfulness and pattern can have their genesis only in lower level laws and prescriptions, that is, the genes. Gesell understood as well as any the dynamics of development: the totality of the organism, the cyclic phases of equilibrium and disequilibrium, the participation of infants in their own change, and the self-righting tendencies of the organism. Yet he doggedly assigned the intricacies of development to a single cause. By explaining everything, he, like the behaviorists he criticized, explained nothing.

The most tangible legacy of Gesell was the virtual disappearance of the study of early motor development from the mainstream of developmental psychology from the mid-1950s until the last decade. Perhaps because of the growing mentalistic bias of psychology as a whole, developmentalists were content to relegate motor development to biology, and Gesell's accounts were accepted without criticism. Stages of motor development were and still are used as examples of a pure maturational timetable. Because these stages had been described fully by Gesell and his contemporaries, motor development warranted little further study. One turning point may have been Philip Zelazo's experiment that demonstrated a training effect on an infant reflex (P. R. Zelazo, N. A. Zelazo, & Kolb, 1972). So ingrained was the belief that although mental structures evolve through interaction, motor patterns represented the march of the genes, that this experiment captured wide attention. Only in the last decade, however, are process accounts of infant motor development supplanting the legacy of Gesell, and as we argue, maturationist assumptions still prevail in much contemporary developmental thinking.

Gesell as a Stage Theorist

Although the heritage of Gesell's developmental norms is clear, direct, and easy to document, his influence as a stage theorist is less obvious. Gesell raised stage theory to an unparalleled degree of refinement. Who before or since has had the tenacity to describe 58 stages of pellet behavior, 53 stages of rattle behavior, and so on for 40 different behavioral series (Gesell & Thompson, 1938)? Although such fine-grained descriptions of stages are absent in contemporary studies, it is likely that Gesell had a hand in the widespread acceptance of the stage theory of Piaget and his followers. Recall that Piaget, like Gesell, viewed stages as biological necessities, part of the very architecture of growth, with its destined directionality and dialectic cycles of change. Today, there is ongoing debate over whether developmental stages represent neurological realities or convenient categories of the developmental theorist (cf. Brainerd, 1978). Nonetheless, stage theory continues to be a dominant theme, especially in the study of cognition. There are strong maturationist currents in contemporary stage theory as well. For example, in Case's (1985) neo-Piagetian approach, the overarching horizontal structures that determine children's functioning at any particular age are ultimately determined by working memory, a maturational function. Mounoud is more explicitly Gesellian. In describing the origin of developmental stages common to all areas of knowledge, he claimed (1986, p. 55),

> This conception ascribes a more important role to the process of neural maturation and the biological substrates of behavior which determine the origin of steps in this developmental sequence. The maturation of the neural system itself depends on the nature of the interactions of the organism with the environment, but in a nonspecific way these interactions at the most being able to accelerate or slow down the process.

Even removed from a Piagetian framework, there is widespread acceptance of maturationally based reorganizations of the brain occurring at regular intervals during infancy, for example, 2 months (Prechtl, 1982), 6 months (Diamond, 1990c; Mounoud, 1986), and 8–12 months (Diamond, 1990b; Goldman-Rakic, 1987; P. R. Zelazo, 1982).

Maturationist Themes in Contemporary Developmental Psychology

The search for behavioral change in neural maturation is a direct Coghill–Gesell legacy that continues with great vigor in contemporary developmental study (e.g., Diamond, 1990a; Gibson & Peterson, 1991). A number of structural changes have been hypothesized to account for performance changes. Some authors attribute the direction and pace of early development to rates and cycles of myelination (K. R. Gibson, 1991; Konner, 1991). Goldman-Rakic (1987) proposed that the explosion of cognitive skills seen in human infants from 8 months to 2 years of age could be attributed to the exuberant growth of cortical synapses during that period, which are later pared down, and Fisher (1987) has tried to relate cycles of synaptogenesis to sensorimotor levels in infancy. According to the extensive work of Diamond (1990c), the maturation of the hippocampus is necessary for recognition memory, and the prefrontal cortex is essential for tasks that require representational memory and the inhibition of predominant response tendencies (Diamond, 1990b).

A full understanding of behavioral development must include knowledge of its underlying neural structures and functions. Nonetheless, note that themes in the current work can lead to the same ultimate nativism as did Gesell's. If behavior emerges as the brain matures, what causes the brain to mature? The answer—if the question is addressed, which it frequently is not—is that the form and sequence of brain development and its behavioral manifestations are genetically encoded. In a recent article, Konner (1991, p. 199), explicitly citing Gesell, concluded, "motor development sequences are largely genetically programmed." Despite some cultural variability, consistency of motor milestones among populations "suggests a species-specific and species-wide timing of events in motor and sensorimotor development" (Konner, 1991, p. 200), presumably paced by myelin deposition.

Just as Gesell assumed that his stages reified the race's biological destiny, accounts such as Konner's assign the global similarity of developmental pathways to an executive agent—in other words, to a prescription in the genes for, say, the pattern of prehension, the timetable for the onset of locomotion, the inevitable stages toward acquiring Piagetian conservation, or the mechanism of parent–infant attachment. Although few today would assign the environment as little power as Gesell did, many believe in autonomous maturation, with structures whose final form is known by the genes and where time is meted out by a genetic clock.

Another common Gesellian theme in contemporary developmental studies is that of innate knowledge. "The human mind has an appreciable amount of innately specified knowledge about persons, objects, space, cause–effect relations, number, language, and so forth," concluded Karmiloff-Smith (1991, p. 174). Innate knowledge means that the core knowledge structures of specific domains are genetically wired into the brain, as are the constraints on subsequent learning (e.g., Carey & Gelman, 1991). The infant is rational from birth (Bower, 1989). Evidence for innate knowledge structures comes from several directions. Surprisingly, young infants appear to understand some properties of physical objects and their actions (e.g., Baillargeon, 1987; Spelke, 1988). Numerous experiments have demonstrated early perceptual biases for voices, faces, shapes, and other features that have been interpreted as innately adaptive (e.g., Alegria & Noirot, 1978; Fantz, 1963; Slater, Morrison, & Rose, 1983). In addition, many theorists believe that complex abilities such as language could not be acquired so rapidly without help from the genes in the form of built-in linguistically relevant principles (e.g., Pinker & Bloom, 1990). Finally, many find it compelling that other species have innate knowledge of biologically important skills and that biological continuity would deem that humans are no different. "All the neonate and infancy data that are accumulating serve to suggest that the nativists have won the battle in accounting for the *initial structure* of the human mind" (Karmiloff-Smith, 1991, p. 173), but the debate continues over whether this innate knowledge is merely enriched during development (Spelke, 1991) or whether new forms are actually constructed through experience (Karmiloff-Smith, 1991).

A further important way in which the maturationist principles of Gesell recur in current developmental work is through the search for genetic continuity in individual differences. Recall that one of Gesell's unwavering beliefs was in the deterministic nature of individual growth profiles from birth and what he called the "prophetic characteristics of the behavior traits displayed in the first year of life" (Gesell, 1939, p. 307). Many today continue to look for measurable variables in infants that will foreshadow their later cognitive, social, and temperamental qualities. For example, certain aspects of attention, detected in the first months of life, are believed to predict later intelligence (e.g., Bornstein & Sigman, 1986; Thompson, Fagan, & Fulker, 1991). Even more prevalent in the current literature are studies looking for continuity in personality or temperament. "Personality may be regarded as a pervasive superpattern which expresses the unity and the behavioral characteristicness of the individual," Gesell wrote (1939, p. 304). Many contemporary developmentalists would agree, and they have produced vast numbers of studies tracing the behavioral indexes of stable temperament and its physiological and genetic underpinnings (for review, see Bates, 1987; Kagan, Resnick, & Snidman, 1987). An important goal of Gesell's monumental efforts to describe infant development was early diagnosis, and this effort continues with great vigor, especially with populations at medical or social risk.

Finally, Gesell's influence continues today in behavior-genetic research. The goal of behavioral genetics is to partition that part of the developing child that is biologically prescribed—contained in the genes—from that part that is acquired from the world. Again, the assumption here is that there is something fixed within the organism that mixes to various degrees with the information outside the organism. Sophisticated longitudinal studies have measured cognitive, temperamental, and social characteristics in twins, nontwin siblings, and adopted children to determine the heritability of particular traits (e.g., Plomin & DeFries, 1985; Scarr, 1981). These efforts have led to somewhat murky conclusions, for example, that a large proportion of the variance in behavior cannot be so neatly partitioned (Plomin & Daniels, 1987).

Maturationism and alternative theories

Critics of Gesellian nativism in its pure form and contemporary guises do not dispute the incontrovertable evidence that newborns show organized behavior. What is at issue, however, is the sufficiency of genetic determinism as a developmental explanation. When developmentalists assign causality to autonomous change (maturation), to mental structures that are there from the beginning (innate knowledge), or to factors inherited from parents (genetics), they often stop looking for process, that is, mechanisms of change. As happened to Gesell, this leads to descriptions of what is— what immature organisms can and cannot do, and most important, when they can and cannot do it—and to correlations between typical anatomy and typical behavior and between performance and various degrees of genetic similarity.

Nativism in any form thus leads to a static science, with no principles for understanding change or for confronting the ultimate challenge of development, the source of new forms in structure and function. Process-oriented research has shown that developmental phenonema that were long believed to be phylogenetically determined, such as imprinting and the onset of locomotion, emerge instead from complex, contingent, dynamic, and multidetermined processes (Gottlieb, 1991; Thelen, 1984). Developmental changes are sometimes engendered from hidden and nonobvious sources or from nonspecific but universal properties of the physical and social environments (Thelen & Fisher, 1982; West & King, 1987).

Second, nativism devalues the active role of animals in their own development. Experiments have shown that from early infancy children begin to behave adaptively through self-initiated, active exploration of their environments (Adolph, Eppler, & E. J. Gibson, 1992; E. J. Gibson, 1988). Current neurophysiological research emphasizes the remarkable plasticity of the developing brain and the role of experience in determining brain structure, even in adults (Edelman, 1987; Greenough, Black, & Wallace, 1987; Kaas, 1991). Yet we know very little about how infants' everyday encounters with the world shape and mold what has been assumed to be innate. One alternative to innate structures is that the neuroanatomy provides only a rough outline and that the details of brain mappings are etched in through function (Edelman, 1987; Jenkins, Merzenich, & Recanzone, 1990). For instance, there is compelling evidence that even a basic activity such as walking develops as an outside-in process, that is, that stable pathways are discovered by function rather than by autonomous, time-dependent neural changes (Thelen & Ulrich, 1991; Thelen, Ulrich, & Jensen, 1989).

Neonativism also ignores variability and *décalage*, which must be accounted for in a principled way and cannot be dismissed either as noise, measurement error, or genetic in origin. Just as Gesell's infants often assumed cartoonlike characteristics, the search for genetic universals can make development seem abstract and impoverished. In reality, children have goals, and they move, explore, discover, test limits, develop strategies, practice, find alternatives, rely on social partners, and actively engage the world from early infancy. Static descriptions of what children have in their genes or nervous systems cannot capture these various and complex pathways.

Candidates for a process-oriented developmental theory must account for Gesell's observations that behavioral development can appear to be both stagelike and sequential and must have species-typical characteristics yet avoid the pitfalls and sterility of ultimate nativism (Thelen, 1989). Such alternative accounts may thus invoke (a) the child's active perceptual exploration of the environment (E. J. Gibson, 1988), (b) the convergent influence of both the universals of the niche of the developing organism (West & King, 1987) and specific task requirements (Newell, 1986), (c) the plasticity of the developing brain (Thelen, 1990), and (d) the dynamic, self-organizing properties of biological systems to form stable adaptive patterns without preexisting codes (Thelen, Kelso, & Fogel, 1987; Thelen & Ulrich, 1991).

GESELL'S LEGACY

It is fitting to conclude with a Gesellian paradox. Gesell himself foreshadowed many of these nonprescriptive accounts of the developmental process, although he emphasized his maturational themes so strongly and frequently that these other currents have been largely lost and forgotten. Sections of his book on vision (Gesell, 1946), for example, are positively Gibsonian in their recognition of the preeminenence of vision in organizing the world of the infant, and Gesell wrote about the integration of vision and movement in a way not dissimilar from contemporary perception–action theorists (von Hofsten, 1985). He emphasized the totality of the organism and the unity of development in all domains. His descriptions of reciprocal interweaving and the cycles of equilibrium and disequilibrium long predate the current interest in dynamic systems, with their energy flows and oscillatory processes. He likewise recognized the self-righting capabilities of such systems and the processes by which the "organism 'seeks' a maximum in the sphere of behavior" (Gesell, 1933, p. 231), which is again reminiscent of current dynamic systems concepts and vocabulary (e.g., Thelen, 1989).

We see Gesell and his influence as full of contrasts and contradictions. His devotion to maturation as the final cause was unwavering, yet he acted as though the environment mattered, and his work contains threads of real process. He believed in the individuality of the child but chose the dictates of the genes over the whims of the environment. He wanted to liberate and reassure parents but may only have added to the arsenal of parental guilt. He was committed to the welfare of children, but in his zeal to classify by age, children often come across as passive and lifeless. He left few acknowledged disciples, yet many today are working within his assumptions. What is not at issue, however, are Gesell's lasting contributions to the field of developmental psychology.

REFERENCES

Adolph, K. E., Eppler, M. A., & Gibson, E. J. (1992). *Crawling versus walking: Infants' perception of affordances for locomotion over sloping surfaces.* Manuscript submitted for publication.

Alegria, J., & Noirot, E. (1978). Neonate orientation behaviour towards the human voice. *International Journal of Behavioral Development, 1,* 291–312.

Ames, L. B. (1989). *Arnold Gesell: Themes of his work.* New York: Human Sciences Library.

Baillargeon, R. (1987). Object permanence in 3½- and 4½-month old infants. *Developmental Psychology, 23,* 655–664.

Bates, J. E. (1987). Temperament in infancy. In J. D. Osofsky (Ed.), *Handbook of infant development, second edition* (pp. 1101–1149). New York: Wiley.

Bernstein, N. (1967). *Coordination and regulation of movements.* Elmsford, NY: Pergamon Press.

Bornstein, M. H., & Sigman, M. D. (1986). Continuity in mental development from infancy. *Child Development, 57,* 251–274.

Bower, T. G. R. (1989). *The rational infant: Learning in infancy.* San Francisco: Freeman.

Brainerd, C. J. (1978). The stage question in cognitive-developmental theory. *The Behavioral and Brain Sciences, 1,* 173–182.

Carey, S., & Gelman, R. (1991). *The epigenesis of mind: Essays on biology and cognition.* Hillsdale, NJ: Erlbaum.

Case, R. (1985). *Intellectual development: Birth to adulthood.* San Diego: Academic Press.

Coghill, G. E. (1969). *Anatomy and the problem of behavior.* New York: Macmillan. (Original work published 1929)

Cohen, L. B. (1972). Attention-getting and attention-holding processes of infant visual preferences. *Child Development, 43,* 869–879.

Diamond, A. (Ed.). (1990a). *The development and neural bases of higher cognitive functions.* New York: New York Academy of Sciences.

Diamond, A. (1990b). Developmental time course in human infants and infant monkeys and the neural bases of inhibitory control in reaching. In A. Diamond (Ed.), *The development and neural bases of higher cognitive functions* (pp. 637–669). New York: New York Academy of Sciences.

Diamond, A. (1990c). Rate of maturation of the hippocampus and the developmental progression of children's performance on the delayed non-matching to sample and visual paired comparison tasks. In A. Diamond (Ed.), *The development and neural bases of higher cognitive functions* (pp. 394–426). New York: New York Academy of Sciences.

Edelman, G. M. (1987). *Neural Darwinism.* New York: Basic Books.

Fantz, R. L. (1958). Pattern vision in young infants. *Psychological Record, 8,* 43–47.

Fantz, R. L. (1963). Pattern vision in newborn infants. *Science, 140,* 296–297.

Fisher, K. W. (1987). Relations between brain and cognitive development. *Child Development, 58,* 623–632.

Gesell, A. (1906). Jealousy. *American Journal of Psychology, 17,* 437–496.

Gesell, A. (1925). *The mental growth of the pre-school child.* New York: Macmillan.

Gesell, A. (1928). *Infancy and human growth.* New York: Macmillan.

Gesell, A. (1933). *Maturation and the patterning of behavior.* In C. Murchison (Ed.), *A handbook of child psychology, Second edition revised* (pp. 209–235). Worcester, MA: Clark University Press.

Gesell, A. (1939). *Biographies of child development.* New York: Paul B. Hoeber.

Gesell, A. (1940). *The first five years of life.* New York: Harper.

Gesell, A. (1945). *The embryology of behavior: The beginnings of the human mind.* Westport, CT: Greenwood Press.

Gesell, A. (1946). The ontogenesis of infant behavior. In L. Carmichael (Ed.), *Manual of child psychology* (pp. 295–331). New York: Wiley.

Gesell, A. (1948). *Studies in child development.* Westport, CT: Greenwood Press.

Gesell, A. (1952a). Arnold Gesell. In E. G. Boring, H. S. Langfield, H. Werner, & R. M. Yerkes (Eds.), *A history of psychology in autobiography,* Vol. 4. (pp. 123–142). Worcester, MA: Clark University Press.

Gesell, A. (1952b). *Infant development: The embryology of early human behavior.* New York: Harper.

Gesell, A., & Amatruda, C. S. (1941). *Developmental diagnosis: Normal and abnormal child development.* New York: Paul B. Hoeber.

Gesell, A., Amatruda, C. S., Castner, B. M., & Thompson, H. (1939). *Biographies of child development: The mental growth careers of eighty-four infants and children.* New York: Paul B. Hoeber.

Gesell, A., & Ilg, F. L. (1937). *Feeding behavior of infants: A pediatric approach to the mental hygiene of early life.* Philadelphia: Lippincott.

Gesell, A., & Ilg, F. L. (1943). *Infant and child in the culture of today.* New York: Harper.

Gesell, A., & Ilg, F. L. (1946). *The child from five to ten.* New York: Harper.

Gesell, A., Ilg, F. L., & Ames, L. B. (1956). *Youth: The years from ten to sixteen.* New York: Harper.

Gesell, A., Ilg, F. L., & Bullis, G. (1949). *Vision: Its development in infant and child.* New York: Paul B. Hoeber.

Gesell, A., & Thompson, H. (1929). Learning and growth in identical infant twins: An experimental study by the method of co-twin control. *Genetic Psychology Monographs, 6,* 11–124.

Gesell, A., & Thompson, H. (1934). *Infant behavior: Its genesis and growth.* New York: McGraw-Hill.

Gesell, A., & Thompson, H. (1938). *The psychology of early growth including norms of infant behavior and a method of genetic analysis.* New York: Macmillan.

Gesell, A., Thompson, H., & Amatruda, C. S. (1934). *An atlas of infant behavior: A systematic delineation of the forms and early growth of human behavior patterns.* New Haven, CT: Yale University Press.

Gibson, E. J. (1988). Exploratory behavior in the development of perceiving, acting, and the acquisition of knowledge. *Annual Review of Psychology, 39,* 1–41.

Gibson, K. R. (1991). Myelination and behavioral development: A comparative perspective on questions of neoteny, altriciality, and intelligence. In K. R. Gibson & A. C. Peterson (Eds.), *Brain maturation and cognitive development: Comparative and cross-cultural perspectives* (pp. 29–63). New York: Aldine De Gruyter.

Gibson, K. R., & Peterson, A. C. (Eds.) (1991). *Brain maturation and cognitive development: Comparative and cross-cultural perspectives.* New York: Aldine De Gruyter.

Goldman-Rakic, P. S. (1987). Development of cortical circuitry and cognitive function. *Child Development, 58,* 601–622.

Gottlieb, G. (1991). Experiential canalization of behavioral development: Theory. *Developmental Psychology, 27,* 4–13.

Greenough, W. T., Black, J. E., & Wallace, C. S. (1987). Experience and brain development. *Child Development, 58,* 539–559.

Hofsten, C. von (1984). Developmental changes in the organization of prereaching movements. *Developmental Psychology, 20,* 378–388.

Hofsten, C. von (1985). Perception and action. In M. Frese & J. Sabini (Eds.), *The concept of action in psychology* (pp. 80–96). Hillsdale, NJ: Erlbaum.

Jenkins, W. M., Merzenich, M. M., & Recanzone, G. (1990). Neocortical representational dynamics in adult primates: Implications for neuropsychology. *Neuropsychologia, 28,* 573–584.

Kaas, J. H. (1991). Plasticity of sensory and motor maps in adult mammals. *Annual Review of Neurosciences, 14,* 137–167.

Kagan, J., Resnick, S. J., & Snidman, N. (1987). The physiology and psychology of behavioral inhibition in children. *Child Development, 58,* 1459–1473.

Karmiloff-Smith, A. (1991). Beyond modularity: Innate constraints and developmental change. In S. Carey & R. Gelman (Eds.), *The epigenesis of mind: Essays on biology and cognition* (pp. 171–197). Hillsdale, NJ: Erlbaum.

Kessen, W. (1965). *The child.* New York: Wiley.

Konner, M. (1991). Universals in behavioral development in relation to brain development. In K. R. Gibson & A. C. Peterson (Eds.), *Brain maturation and cognitive development: Comparative and cross-cultural perspectives* (pp. 181–223). New York: Aldine De Gruyter.

McGraw, M. B. (1935). *Growth: A study of Johnny and Jimmy.* New York: Appleton-Century-Crofts.

Meltzoff, A. N., & Moore, M. K. (1983). The origins of imitation in infancy: Paradigm, phenomena, and theories. In L. P. Lipsitt (Ed.), *Advances in infancy research, Vol. 2* (pp. 265–301). Norwood, NJ: Ablex.

Miller, P. H. (1989). *Theories of developmental psychology* (2nd ed.). San Francisco: Freeman.

Mounoud, P. (1986). Similarities between developmental sequences at different age periods. In I. Levin (Ed.), *Stage and structure: Reopening the debate* (pp. 40–58). Norwood, NJ: Ablex.

Newell, K. M. (1986). Constraints on the development of coordination. In M. G. Wade & H. T. A. Whiting (Eds.), *Motor development in children: Aspects of coordination and control* (pp. 341–360). Dordrecht, The Netherlands: Martinus Nijhoff.

Pinker, S., & Bloom, P. (1990). Natural language and natural selection. *Behavioral and Brain Sciences, 13,* 707–784.

Plomin, R., & Daniels, D. (1987). Why are children in the same family so different from one another? *Behavioral and Brain Sciences, 10,* 1–60.

Plomin, R., & DeFries, J. C. (1985). *Origins of individual differences in infancy: The Colorado Adoption Project.* San Diego: Academic Press.

Prechtl, H. F. R. (1982). Regressions and transformations during neurological development. In T. G. Bever (Ed.), *Regressions in mental development: Basic phenomena and theories* (pp. 103–115). Hillsdale, NJ: Erlbaum.

Rovee, C. K., & Rovee, D. T. (1969). Conjugate reinforcement of infant exploratory behavior. *Journal of Experimental Child Psychology, 8,* 33–39.

Scarr, S. (1981). *Race, social class, and individual differences in I.Q.* Hillsdale, NJ: Erlbaum.

Siqueland, E. R., & Lipsitt, L. P. (1966). Conditioned head-turning in human newborns. *Journal of Experimental Child Psychology, 3*, 356–376.

Slater, A., Morrison, V., & Rose, D. (1983). Perception of shape by the newborn baby. *British Journal of Developmental Psychology, 1*, 135–142.

Spelke, E. S. (1988). Where perceiving ends and thinking begins: The apprehension of objects in infancy. In A. Yonas (Ed.), *Perceptual development in infancy: Minnesota Symposia on Child Psychology* (Vol. 20, pp. 197–234). Hillsdale, NJ: Erlbaum.

Spelke, E. S. (1991). Physical knowledge in infancy: Reflections on Piaget's theory. In S. Carey & R. Gelman, *The epigenesis of mind: Essays on biology and cognition* (pp. 133–169). Hillsdale, NJ: Erlbaum.

Stone, J. L., Smith, H. T., & Murphy, L. B. (1973). *The competent infant: Research and commentary.* New York: Basic Books.

Terman, L. M. (1906). Genius and stupidity: A study of some of the intellectual processes of seven "bright" and seven "stupid" boys. *Pedagogical Seminary, 13*, 307–373.

Thelen, E. (1984). Learning to walk: Ecological demands and phylogenetic constraints. In L. P. Lipsitt (Ed.), *Advances in infancy research*, Vol. 3 (pp. 213–250). Norwood, NJ: Ablex.

Thelen, E. (1989). Self-organization in developmental processes: Can systems approaches work? In M. Gunnar & E. Thelen (Eds.), *Systems in development: The Minnesota Symposia in Child Psychology* (Vol. 22, pp. 77–117). Hillsdale, NJ: Erlbaum.

Thelen, E. (1990). Dynamical systems and the generation of individual differences. In J. Colombo & J. W. Fagen (Eds.), *Individual differences in infancy: Reliability, stability, and prediction* (pp. 19–43). Hillsdale, NJ: Erlbaum.

Thelen, E., & Fisher, D. M. (1982). Newborn stepping: An explanation for a "disappearing" reflex. *Developmental Psychology, 18*, 760–775.

Thelen, E., Kelso, J. A. S., & Fogel, A. (1987). Self-organizing systems and infant motor development. *Developmental Review, 7*, 39–65.

Thelen, E., & Ulrich, B. D. (1991). *Hidden skills: A dynamic systems analysis of treadmill stepping during the first year. Monographs of the Society for Research in Child Development, 56* (1, Serial No. 223).

Thelen, E., Ulrich, B. D., & Jensen, J. L. (1989). The developmental origins of locomotion. In M. Woollacott & A. Shumway-Cook (Eds.), *The development of posture and gait across the lifespan.* Columbia, SC: University of South Carolina Press.

Thompson, L. A., Fagan, J. F., & Fulker, D. (1991). Longitudinal prediction of specific cognitive abilities from infant novelty preference. *Child Development, 62*, 530–538.

Trevarthen, C. (1977). Descriptive analyses of infant communication behaviour. In H. R. Schaffer (Ed.), *Studies in mother–infant interaction* (pp. 227–270). San Diego: Academic Press.

Watson, J. B. (1928). *Psychological care of infant and child.* New York: Norton.

West, M. J., & King, A. P. (1987). Settling nature and nurture into an ontogenetic niche. *Developmental Psychobiology, 20,* 549–562.

Zelazo, P. R. (1982). The year-old infant: A period of major cognitive change. In T. G. Bever (Ed.), *Regressions in mental development: Basic phenomena and theories* (pp. 47–79). Hillsdale, NJ: Erlbaum.

Zelazo, P. R., Zelazo, N. A., & Kolb, S. (1972). "Walking" in the newborn. *Science, 177,* 1058–1059.

14

MYRTLE B. McGRAW:
A GROWTH SCIENTIST

VICTOR W. BERGENN, THOMAS C. DALTON, AND LEWIS P. LIPSITT

Myrtle B. McGraw was a pioneer in the study of child growth and development during its heyday in the 1920s and 1930s. She is known best for her seminal experimental study of the Woods twins in *Growth: A Study of Johnny and Jimmy* (1935a) and her succinct summary of her research regarding learning and maturation in *The Neuromuscular Maturation of the Human Infant* (1943). McGraw's prolific career can be divided into three distinct phases spanning several decades. The first, from 1929 to 1935, included her co-twin study of the effects of stimulation on development.

We thank the following archive collections and libraries for assistance in locating documents and correspondence: the Rockefeller Archive Center, the Carnegie Corporation, the Josiah Macy Junior Foundation, the Center for Dewey Studies at Southern Illinois University, Millbank Memorial Library, Teachers College, the Butler and Low Libraries at Columbia University, the History of Science Division of the National Library of Medicine, the Museum of Natural History in New York, the Spencer Research Library at the University of Kansas, the National Library of Congress, and California Polytechnic State University, San Luis Obispo, California.

We also thank Lewis P. Rowland, Director, Neurological Institute, and Michael Katz, Chair, Department of Pediatrics, of the Columbia Presbyterian Medical Center; Ronald W. Oppenheim, Department of Neurobiology and Anatomy, Wake Forest University; J. Lawrence Pool; Theodora Abel; Katherine Heyl; Mitzi D. Wertheim; Jean Gordon; and Janice Stone.

Reprinted from *Developmental Psychology*, 28, 381–395. Copyright by the American Psychological Association.

From 1936 to 1946, McGraw completed advanced studies of the neuro-muscular dynamics of infant development. Finally, from 1947 to 1988, McGraw continued her teaching and infant research at Briarcliff College (1953–1972) and published memoirs and essays addressing issues pertinent to the science of growth and development.

As a prelude to a review of McGraw's research, we will describe her style and methods, including institutional and contextual factors that set McGraw's work apart from that of her contemporaries. These details may better illuminate the nature, scope, and significance of her research for child development. Before her death in September 1988, McGraw provided tantalizing anecdotal glimpses of her education, professional development, and collegial relationships that exemplify her character and research style (Lipsitt, 1990; McGraw, 1967, 1983b, 1985, 1990; Senn, 1972). We draw on these sources to highlight some special qualities that contributed to the distinctiveness of her methods, as well as to the scope and depth of her insights about infant growth and development.

Early in her career, McGraw was given an unusual opportunity to collaborate with an advisory committee appointed to oversee her developmental studies of normal children. The committee was composed of distinguished scientists from diverse fields, including John Dewey, a philosopher, and George Coghill, a neuroanatomist, both of whom were actively involved in all phases of her studies of normal child development. Their collaboration brings to light new evidence that her research involved a joint effort not only to use novel methods in the study of growth, but to enlarge the role of judgment in inquiry. Dewey believed that McGraw's discovery of the logic of growth not only promised to "revolutionize work in the field of child study" (Ratner & Altman, 1964, p. 54) but also enabled him to demonstrate that biological principles "foreshadowed" the pattern of inquiry (Dewey, 1938, p. 23). (A complete treatment of the facts surrounding the significance of Dewey's involvement in this collaboration is beyond the scope of this essay: See Dalton & Bergenn, 1992).

Controversy has never really subsided among psychologists and others as to how to interpret correctly McGraw's (1935a) findings in her co-twin study published in *Growth*. It is our contention that ongoing disputes as to whether McGraw should be considered a maturationist can be traced back to an incomplete understanding of her objective and methods. Not surprisingly, McGraw's conception of critical periods has been caught in the cross fire of the debate. However, it is possible to navigate between these conflicting interpretations (as McGraw urged us to do) by stepping outside the dichotomies of heredity versus environment and maturation versus learning that animate and perpetuate this debate to better comprehend McGraw's research objectives through the terms that she conceived.

The period from 1936 to 1946 marked a little reported but significant watershed period for McGraw. She embarked on an attempt to determine how structural factors and behavioral functions interact in growth to produce variations in the pattern of individual development. These studies constituted the basis for McGraw's argument for the dissolution of the maturation–learning dichotomy. Another part of this work involved the novel attempt to see if the variables influencing growth rates could be formulated in equations that integrated quantitative principles from physics and embryology.

McGraw disavowed (somewhat ruefully) ever having formulated a systematic theory of growth or development (McGraw, 1985). However, during the last 41 years of her life (1947–1988), she continued to study issues of fundamental significance to developmental psychology. Moreover, her work has contributed to the revival of the field of behavioral embryology and a psychobiological approach to the study of human behavior. McGraw, like Dewey, recognized that no new theoretical orientation could ever be expected to flourish without fundamental changes in our perceptions and methods of inquiry. Therefore, instead of proposing a systematic theory of growth, she suggested the kinds of changes that our perceptions and methods would have to undergo to develop systematic theories. In so doing, McGraw contributed a number of insights pertinent to the field of developmental psychology.

SITUATING McGRAW IN THE FIELD OF CHILD STUDY

Challenging Psychological Orthodoxy: Convention and Conviction

When McGraw began her professional career in the late 1920s, the field of psychology was already well colonized by competing theoretical perspectives. Experimental psychology was largely governed by the belief that human behavior could be explored in terms of stimulus, response, association, and conditioning. Experimental and clinical psychologists not only had to demonstrate some degree of competence in methods of testing but also had to display a modicum of familiarity with psychoanalysis and genetic theories of normal development such as those that were propounded by Sigmund Freud and Arnold Gesell.

McGraw's reaction to these dominant theoretical perspectives was governed in part by their ability to handle problems in applied settings. This is well illustrated in McGraw's dissertation, which tested theories contending that differences in intellectual and motor performance of White and Black infants were due to inherent differences in biological structure or intelligence (McGraw, 1931, p. 92). In applying the battery of developmental tests created by Charlotte Bühler (1930), McGraw found little evidence to sustain these theories. Although the White babies had slightly higher developmental quotients, Blacks scored higher on some complex tasks in which they were expected to fail (McGraw, 1931, p. 93). Also, there was considerable overlap in the distribution of the developmental quotients between groups, suggesting marked variability in the individual rates of growth and development (McGraw, 1931, p. 94). McGraw foreshadowed her later studies, challenging Gesell's theories, by concluding that developmental quotients did not adequately express the relationship between growth and maturation and that only a longitudinal study that included differences in environmental influences could support any inferences about the norms of behavior for different groups (McGraw, 1931).

While a graduate student in 1929, McGraw had the opportunity to obtain clinical experience with the Institute for Child Guidance under the direction of Lawson Lowrey and David Levy. In a particularly humorous incident, formative in her subsequent career (Senn, 1972, p. 4), McGraw relates that in one case discussion Dr. Levy once diagnosed an enuretic patient by saying that the boy did so as a symbolic act of drowning his sister because he resented having to sleep in the same bed with her. McGraw then "impudently" asked whether he could not think of some other explanation (Senn, 1972, p. 5). Indeed, several years later McGraw found another explanation for children temporarily reverting to infantile behavior, as involved in occasional loss of bladder control: They are simply exhibiting the inconsistency and confusion attendant on the demand to integrate new behavioral capacities while still attempting to perfect an existing repertoire of behavior (McGraw, 1940b, p. 587; 1940d, p. 9).

McGraw also was concerned that physicians were prone to interpret infant motion according to adult patterns, which are considerably different, and to characterize any variability as indicative of a potential pathological condition. In one of her first studies of infant reflexes, McGraw was astonished at the "surprising lack of study and analysis of the normal movements and postures of newborn infants" in the American medical literature (Chaney & McGraw, 1932, p. 9). She herself found significant quantitative and qualitative differences in newborn reflex behavior. The fact that chronological age alone did not suffice to explain these individual differences led McGraw to speculate that they might result from differences in posture and by the degree of prenatal muscle tonus but that this did not imply a more mature or complete nervous system (Chaney & McGraw, 1932, p. 50).

Innovation Through Improvisation

McGraw was adept at combining naturalistic and experimental procedures in her studies of infant development. She had reservations about experimental behaviorism because of the constraints laboratory manipulations often placed on both behavioral outcomes and the environmental conditions under study (McGraw, 1935a, pp. 300–301). She considered learning and growth to be dynamic processes requiring innovative measurement techniques that were not easy to conceive or fashion. Consequently, improvisation in techniques of observation played an important role in McGraw's attempt to capture the dynamic properties of growth processes. McGraw suggested that poor observation skills were due to a preoccupation with achievement measures of performance that privilege the technical instruments and scales (i.e., test batteries or other technologies) used to measure results, thereby limiting sensitivity to the changing context in which the behavior occurs. McGraw articulated this problem cogently when she observed:

> Because of the speed of development, the same apparatus set-up presents an entirely different problem for a child at one time than it will for the same child a month or so later. The problem has changed only because the child has changed. (McGraw, 1942a, p. 89)

McGraw's objective in the co-twin study was to see if she could stimulate Johnny to his maximum potential without artificially interfering with his natural reactions. Lures were used to elicit spontaneous responses. On other occasions, the infants were placed in situations, the extrication from which required problem solving such as that involved in climbing off a stool, roller skating, or riding a tricycle. Activities such as these are not unlike those experienced by preschoolers who are often confronted with challenges seemingly beyond their capacity to handle yet mastered without intervention.

McGraw also had occasion to discover that a technique designed to elicit behavior may in fact suppress it if introduced at an inappropriate time. Unexpectedly, Johnny learned how to skate very quickly, but he could never master a tricycle, which he was introduced to at the same time. McGraw subsequently surmised that the reason for this unexpected failure was that because the child's feet were tied to the pedals, he would have had to perform the complex action "*completely* or not at all" (McGraw, 1985, p. 167 [emphasis added]), thus depriving him of the freedom of movement necessary to permit gradual exploration and problem solving. In essence, by imposing a demand for achievement, she had failed to set up the tricycling task commensurately with Johnny's phase of development.

McGraw (1935a) candidly admitted that the amount and timing of stimulation given to a child "to expedite learning" (p. 232) was a question that needed study. This issue was investigated by one of McGraw's associates, who found that the nature, intensity, and duration of the stimulus must be altered during the course of a task-oriented test to reflect the child's scope of perception and varying level of mood (Dammann, 1941, p. 245). At one stage, the child's intrinsic interest was sufficient to prompt action without stimulation, whereas at another stage, distraction or disinterest had to be overcome with a more conspicuous lure or suggestion. McGraw's associate, Dammann, defended this practice by arguing that without it, the objective of stimulating optimum motor performance would have been defeated. McGraw probably did not consider it methodologically incorrect to change the stimulus, because response was contingent on context. It would have been useful, however, for current research had McGraw elaborated in more detail the sketchy references that she made to the technique of suggestion, especially if the suggestiveness of a situation was considered intrinsic to learning experiences.

An Unusual Professional Collaboration

The Neurological Institute, founded in 1909, was at the forefront of basic research on the brain and neurosurgery when McGraw began work there in 1930 (Merritt, 1975). The institute attracted eminent people in the field, including Tilney, who was appointed medical director in 1935 after directing research there for a number of years (Elsberg, 1944; Pool, 1975). Tilney was one of the first professors at the institute to teach courses in neuroembryology when the field was in its infancy (Pool, 1990). Tilney (1917, 1926) supported an interdisciplinary perspective toward the study of human development, making it possible for McGraw to work with a number of scientists and physicians at Babies Hospital, where her studies were conducted (Weech et al., 1961).

Tilney established an advisory committee for the Normal Child Development Study (NCDS), which included distinguished members of the faculty from Columbia University, such as philosopher John Dewey, psychologists Robert Woodworth and Edward Thorndike, and John Davenport (1937, 1938) of the Carnegie Institute, as well as the ad hoc involvement of psychologist John B. Watson and neuroanatomist George Coghill of the Wistar Institute in Philadelphia. The Advisory Committee met regularly throughout the 1930s to provide interdisciplinary expertise in formulating hypotheses and consultation on methodology. McGraw (Senn, 1972, p. 32) recalled that she consulted with Dewey, who visited the project on a daily basis throughout the decade of the 1930s (Heyl, 1989), on every facet of her research.

Aside from Dewey, Tilney, and Coghill, perhaps no other figure looms larger in McGraw's seminal research on growth than Lawrence K. Frank (1962). He came to the field of child study in the early 1920s as a former student of Dewey and soon occupied strategic positions in the Rockefeller Foundation to sponsor research in child development. Frank was instrumental in helping McGraw join this network and defended her work against the growing insistence that research of this kind yield diagnostic tools for clinicians. With Gesell's infant studies already underway at Yale University with Rockefeller Foundation support, Frank urged support of McGraw's ongoing study by stressing that she was not establishing age norms but trying to "delineate the sequence through which the child passes and to discover how far that sequence is modifiable by training" (Frank, 1933, p. 1).

Frank outlined a multiyear study of growth that would yield "dynamic norms" embedded in the "coordinations and discrepancies in secular trends" (Frank, 1935a, p. 12). Frank (1935b) sought to arrange a joint study involving both Columbia and Yale Universities but was unable to overcome the evident rivalry and diffidence that prevented Gesell and McGraw from agreeing to such a venture. Nevertheless, two of Gesell's medical staff were subsequently employed in McGraw's advanced studies. Toward that end, the Rockefeller Foundation and other foundations furnished resources in 1936 enabling McGraw to conduct advanced studies of neuromuscular development (discussed later), with an interdisciplinary group of research associates that included a pediatrician, a neurophysiologist, a biochemist, and a psychologist (McGraw, 1935b). McGraw proposed to obtain more exact quantitative data on neurological, physiological, and behavioral factors involved in the transition from infracortical to cortical control in infants. These studies, summarized by Weech (1940), will be discussed in more detail later.

George Coghill, Neuroembryology, and Motor Development

George Coghill's participation in McGraw's research deserves further comment because of the evident pervasiveness of his influence on McGraw's methods of investigation. After laboring in relative obscurity for nearly two decades studying the neuroanatomy and behavior of the salamander, Coghill attracted substantial attention of psychologists, among others, when he published a series of lectures in 1929 and a subsequent essay in 1933, presenting the theoretical implications of his work (Coghill, 1929, 1930b, 1933). His research challenged the conventional wisdom that complex behavior is constructed from simple reflexes. Instead, he argued that the "individuation of partial (i.e., reflexive) behavior patterns emerges through the progressive expansion of a perfectly integrated total pattern" (Coghill, 1929, p. 38). Significantly, Coghill found that early *local segmental responses* (a term he used instead of *reflexes*) occur not as a result of stimulation but by virtue of being released through inhibition of the total response (Coghill, 1930a, pp. 432–433). He also determined that preneural and neural processes overlap and interact throughout early growth processes, reinforcing the influence of the whole on each specific behavior pattern. In addition, he found evidence of substantial overgrowth of particular nerve fibers that seemed to have the capacity to anticipate the acquisition of functions before their development was completed. As such, they constituted attitudes or tendencies ultimately expressed in behavior. Coghill (1929, p. 109) considered this phenomenon of *forward reference*, as he called it, to constitute an example of learning.

These were controversial ideas, especially for those psychologists who believed that local reflexes must be well developed before infants could be stimulated or trained to perform complex behaviors. Many psychologists, including Arnold Gesell (1934, p. 300), interpreted Coghill's notion of forward reference to mean that neural maturation is genetically predetermined and that behavioral development cannot be hastened by stimulation or exercise. Yet Coghill (1929, pp. 93–94) used the term to call attention to the fact that the potential for complex behavior in early motor development outstrips the capacity to perform it and that neuromuscular integration requires functional stimulation. Misrepresentations such as this have had the unfortunate repercussion of further obscuring the pertinence that Coghill's conceptions of growth and learning have for contemporary studies of motor development. As Oppenheim (1978, p. 57) points out, Coghill never took an explicit position on the maturation–learning debate during the 1930s, and thus uncertainty about the psychological and developmental implications of his statements permitted different interpretations.

Other researchers—most notably, W. F. Windle (1934)—challenged Coghill's findings, arguing that reflexes emerge before integrated behavior, setting off a debate for the next decade as to the order of first appearance of local reflexes. Z. Y. Kuo joined the debate in 1939, criticizing Coghill's methodology, calling into question the applicability of the distinction between an integrated prior pattern and local response. Kuo rejected the directive role of neural growth, contending instead that the reorganization of embryonic movements into their ontogenetic forms simply reflected the continuous change in behavioral gradients involved in the organism's response to environmental stimuli. Kuo (1976), who characterized his schema as an attempt to dissolve conceptually imposed differences between physiology and behavior, defines the latter term so broadly as to virtually eliminate the role of neural structures. Apparently McGraw did not find Kuo's position persuasive. In correspondence years later, she remarked: "I never knew Kuo. My remote recollection is that he [was] regarded among psychologists in general that he was such a convinced environmentalist that he ceased to be controversial" (M. B. McGraw, personal communication, October 21, 1980).

Perhaps the most significant evidence that Coghill had an open mind on the issue of maturation and learning was his participation in the NCDS. The study offered a compelling opportunity to apply his research methods to human subjects. McGraw (1935a, p. 10) readily adapted his methods for use in her study, contending that "it is the experimental embryologists, not psychologists who deserve credit for formulating the most adequate theory of behavior development." Moreover, years later McGraw acknowledged his active involvement to Oppenheim:

Coghill visited my laboratory many, many, many times—sometimes with Tilney, sometimes not. We talked and exchanged ideas. It was he and John Dewey, and the babies that got me thinking of process, not end result, or achievement. (M. B. McGraw, personal communication, December 31, 1979)

McGraw also stressed that their collaboration was essential to the success of the project:

Had he [Tilney] lived longer, Tilney, Coghill and Dewey and I (let me say the babies) might have arrived at a synthesis of the meaning of the structure and function. (M. B. McGraw, personal communication, December 31, 1979)

The tendency to label McGraw's and Gesell's positions *maturationist* stems in part from misinterpretation of Coghill's conception of the role of neural growth in development. Thelen and Adolph (1992) argue that Coghill played a formative role in Gesell's maturational theory of human development. To demonstrate the coincidence of their views, Thelen relies heavily on Gesell's interpretations of Coghill's ideas, rather than on quoting Coghill directly. To say, for example, as Thelen and Adolph (1992, p. 370) do, that "Gesell derived from Coghill that behavioral morphology is a direct readout of neural structures that underlie it" or that "neural changes are autonomous products of growth, inherent and lawful, and not subject to the influence of function," oversimplifies Gesell's ideas while misrepresenting Coghill's position.

To be certain, Gesell (1945, pp. 173–182; 1934) acknowledged the extensive interaction of maturation and growth processes during and after the postnatal period of development. However, Gesell (1945) believed that nerve structures and gradient processes played the "dominating role in nervous integration" (p. 100). Coghill considered the belief profoundly mistaken that neural growth was either equivalent to or explained by genetic factors (Herrick, 1949). Instead, he believed that neural growth processes exhibited a high degree of plasticity and adaptability, enabling an organism to learn behaviors essential to its existence. Coghill (1936, p. 12) observed that "the hypothesis that there is growth going on in the nervous system so long as the individual can adapt its behavior to changes in the environment is not untenable." Contrary to the conventional wisdom that Coghill was a structural determinist, he held that "structure operates in function and that whether one precedes or 'causes' the other is besides the mark [because] they merge in fact into a space–time relation" (Coghill, 1933, p. 137).

Perhaps one of Coghill's (1930a) most subtle and profound insights involved in his conception of pattern development was that (contrary to what seems intuitively justified), partial patterns emerge not as a result of the expansion, but rather as "the progressive reduction of the field of adequate stimulation for the particular reflex and by progressive restriction of the motor field of action" (p. 434). McGraw grasped the essence of this idea in her studies of motor development by showing that learning entails more than simply the gradual enlargement and recombination of specific motor skills through repetitive conditioning. She demonstrated that learning involves the continuous expansion and reintegration of thought and feeling through the anticipation of problems requiring the construction of more complex and varied patterns of behavioral response.

GROWTH STUDIES I: THE EFFECTS OF STIMULATION ON DEVELOPMENT

Conceptual Foundations and Objectives of Growth

The secondary scholarship on motor development, with the exception of Thelen and Ulrich (1991) and Thelen and Adolph (1992), fails to mention the importance of neuroembryology in McGraw's work. Nevertheless, McGraw (1935a, pp. 22–23) explicitly stated that a primary objective of her study was to see whether the principles of embryonic growth applied to the growth of human behavior. Experimental embryologists generally held that cell behavior constituted the basic unit of analysis in embryogenesis. As such, it not only represented one of the first forms of biological organization but furnished McGraw (1940a) a model of how to understand growth, in that the processes of cleavage, differentiation, segmentation, and regulation applied to all life forms, no matter how complex.

In McGraw's view, timing and sequence are important factors governing growth processes. Embryonic development occurs in stages, punctuated by bursts of accelerated growth followed by periods of overlap of function, eventually giving way to consolidation and integration. Although the human species exhibits a remarkable continuity in the evolution of its form, embryological evidence indicated that changes in behavioral function are likely to occur during ontogeny. This raised two important experimental questions for McGraw: (a) When and under what conditions are changes in functional behavior likely to occur? and (b) What role do neural and anatomical structures play in either facilitating or retarding functional changes in the process of neuromuscular integration? McGraw (1935a, p. 15) introduced the term *behavior course* to describe the phases through which an activity becomes organized and *behavior pattern* to refer to the form that an action assumed when it became stabilized and fixed.

The experimental advantages of this distinction were twofold. First, variations in the sequence and quality (i.e., extent of coordination) in creeping, for example, could be used to gauge the timing and extent of differences in neural connections underpinning the behavior pattern. Consequently, small but noticeable variations involved in the transition from creeping to crawling under controlled environmental conditions could support inferences about the probable configuration of neural development. To be certain, this did not constitute a judgment about maturation but rather a descriptive statement about the range of behavior afforded by the existing degree of neuromuscular integration.

Second, unlike preformationists, McGraw did not hold that the so-called mature or fixed form of behavior was predetermined by either genetics or neural factors alone. If that were the case, then it would be difficult to explain why some phyletic traits disappear whereas others persist in residual form, to be eventually incorporated into a stable pattern of behavior. McGraw hypothesized that the likelihood that phyletic rudiments would enter into the construction of ontogenetic behavior depended on the age of the trait, the rate of anatomical growth, and the specificity of organization at the segmental level. McGraw (1940c) therefore suspected correctly, for example, that early exercise of rhythmic stepping, before the capacity for erect locomotion, could accelerate the acquisition and enhance the quality of walking (McGraw & Breeze, 1941).

McGraw's contemporaries avoided drawing distinctions between phyletic and ontogenetic behaviors despite their importance to comparative psychology (Nissen, 1951) because it was largely speculative and posed difficulties for measurement. Some researchers were convinced that insuperable problems posed by the heredity-or-environment dilemma could be bypassed by limiting maturation to the interaction between the organism and its inner environment (Marquis, 1930; Shirley, 1931). Others, like Gesell (1945, p. 194), acknowledged the primacy of archaic motor systems in prenatal life but were unable to explain why its influence persisted into the postnatal period. A common assumption underlying these reservations, as Oppenheim (1982) points out, is the belief that antecedent structures or functions must somehow be shown to be necessary (phylogenetically) to the development of subsequent forms or patterns. Yet there are many examples from neuroembryology of functionally mediated adaptations that are provisional and transient (Oppenheim, 1982, p. 271). Such adaptations seem to depend in part on the inhibition or temporary screening out of stimuli which, although contributing to development at a later time, would disrupt the equilibrium of the organism.

McGraw had some salient reasons for distinguishing phyletic and ontogenetic behavior patterns. One important reason was that human phylogeny represents the record of innumerable structural and functional changes brought about by adaptation. Without an analysis of phyletic movements, she reasoned, the researcher could never be certain whether stimulation brings about the first appearance of a behavior pattern or simply contributes to the expansion of behavior already at the threshold of maturity (McGraw, 1946, p. 344). Nor would it be possible to distinguish among those aspects of a behavior pattern that are functionally necessary from ones that are clearly inessential in the construction of the mature pattern.

McGraw also believed that the phases in which behavior alternated and overlapped between diffuse and specific forms constituted critical periods in development. At this time, neural structures are in a formative but incomplete stage of growth, cortical inhibition is incipient, and behavioral patterns oscillate between rhythmic and more specific, recognizable movements. Consequently, development entails not only reciprocal but retrospective effects whereby structural mechanisms dominant in the earliest phases of development may be supplanted or modified, suppressed, and even eliminated in subsequent stages. The effectiveness of intervention to control the direction of growth at a time when it is subject to these alternating forces depends crucially on the phyletic age of the reflex, the rate of growth, and the timing of stimulation (McGraw, 1935a, pp. 19–20, 23).

This is illustrated by McGraw's discovery that the diffuse response characteristic of the older Moro reflex disappears, to be supplanted by the more specific and abbreviated startle reaction. Other behavior patterns may be either suppressed or bypassed, such as that entailed in the transition from creeping to crawling, or temporarily inhibited (e.g., bladder control) by the emergence of competing patterns. In other instances, the rhythmic but transient stepping movements occurring in early infancy could be used, for example, to evoke their ontogenetic counterpart entailed in erect locomotion, thus facilitating the emergence and enhancing the quality of subsequent behavior. This differential effect is illustrated by the greater ease with which the infant learns to swim than to walk because the reflexes for swimming are phyletically older than those for walking (McGraw, 1935a, pp. 307–310; 1939b).

Importance of Attitude in Development

One of the findings in McGraw's co-twin study that has been consistently overlooked by researchers in motor development is the significance of attitude in explaining differences in motor performance. For example, although Johnny showed "no definite superiority which could be attributed to his earlier experience" (McGraw, 1935a, p. 280), in many instances he took more time to accomplish some tasks but in doing so showed greater comprehension of the requirements. The truly significant effect of early exercise on development, according to McGraw, involved qualitative differences in the way each child organized a task and the attitude expressed in completing it. Johnny tended to pause and gauge the demands of the situation and devise a more effective method of completion than Jimmy. He also demonstrated more persistence and self-confidence in these activities. In contrast, Jimmy was more direct, less deliberative. He encountered more difficulty in devising a scheme of action, cried frequently out of frustration, and often reverted to more rudimentary behavior when more complex patterns proved elusive. Jimmy was more fearful, resistant, hesitant, and uncertain in performing tasks that required a coordinated response.

These differences in attitude appeared to McGraw (1935a, pp. 282–284) to constitute the most variable aspect of behavior. Attitudes are subject to greater modification than motor skills and are more easily transferred from one situation to another. McGraw considered attitudes to be more inclusive than emotions, a point overlooked in most accounts of her work. Attitudes, according to McGraw, "represented structurally and functionally a pervading activity of the total organism" (1935a, p. 284). They acted as catalysts, giving force and direction to "somatic action" (McGraw, 1935a, p. 284). An attitudinal state could decisively influence an activity, depending on its intensity and timing. For example, overeagerness might actually inhibit the commencement of an activity, although facilitating its completion once underway.

McGraw's conception of attitude represented a synthesis of Dewey's and Coghill's understanding of the relationship between attitude and inhibition. Dewey (1971, p. 183) believed that primitive human activity is likely to have been undivided that coordination within it occurred essentially without any emotional arousal or conflict. Only when human physical and mental capacities and repertoire of behavior grow more complex, as McGraw discovered in her developmental experiments, does emotional tension become a constraining factor, interfering with a coordinated response to a new or unusual situation. The mechanism of inhibition was thus considered by Dewey (1971, p. 183) to be simply another product of human neurophysiological development, necessitated by the expanding scope of potential response, enabling attitudes intrinsic to conditions of uncertainty to be activated in the construction of new behaviors.

Because Dewey never specifically identified how inhibition works neurologically, Coghill provided McGraw a way to conceive of it in neuromuscular terms. Coghill (1964, pp. 108–109) defined attitudes to be structural counterparts to experience that embodied latent tendencies of the total state of the organism, capable of expression only through overt behavior. Like Dewey, he believed that because somatic attitudes could be evoked only when the organism was actively engaged (i.e., neuromuscularly) in problem solving, their overt expression could be triggered only through the inhibition of partial or segmental responses. McGraw's studies of infant growth were designed to probe the neuromuscular conditions in which attitudes facilitated or impeded integration.

The importance of attitudes in shaping behavior stands out as one of McGraw's significant findings in the study of growth processes. After Dewey's pioneering attempt to show the intrinsic role that attitudes play in experience, few American psychologists attempted to analyze them experimentally. (See Bull, 1968, for an elaboration of this conception of attitude.) Dewey contended that the importance of an attitude resided not in its ability to precipitate action but in suspending action by inhibiting impulsive behavior. The acquiescent attitude that Johnny adopted best exemplifies the point that Dewey was driving at; this attitude implied not passivity but sensitivity and openness to the suggestiveness of the situation. The quality that best distinguished the motor responses of the twins was Johnny's ability to prolong the period of inquisitiveness and judgment through the postponement of impulse and moderation of excessive eagerness.

McGraw (1935a, pp. 204–205) objected to psychological theories that held that our attitudes become fixed by the emotions (e.g., fear) aroused in association with particular objects or situations. Associations are not formed by attraction to or repulsion from some object but by the use that they serve in a particular situation. The strange and unusual uses to which objects are put by infants in exploratory situations indicate that the child is simply trying to identify his or her most effective use or *affordance*, as it is termed in contemporary studies. McGraw's associates, Welch and Long, found that this process carries over into reasoning and concept formation. Welch and Long (1940b, p. 94) determined that children could manipulate objects before correctly identifying them. In addition, they discovered that children grasped the relationship between concepts before correctly classifying them (Welch & Long, 1940a, p. 21).

Moreover, McGraw believed that anxiety and insecurity could be explained best not as a result of emotional imbalances triggered by some abnormal associations but as occurring as a result of normal growth imbalances. Anxiety and frustration are likely to be most acutely felt when the capacity of discrimination first emerges, extending the infant's power of perception well beyond his or her ability at sensorimotor control. McGraw (1935a, p. 260) did not believe that growth imbalances result in any long-term impairment of function. Unfortunately, however, the line between effective stimulation and harmful deprivation has been obscured by controversy over the phenomena of maturation and critical period.

The Controversy Over Maturation and Critical Period

As Dennis (1989, p. 357) observes, what made McGraw's co-twin study so compelling was that it "contained all the ingredients necessary for a good news story"; it was timely and dramatic and included a human interest element involving suspense about the consequences of experimentation for the children's behavior and personalities. However, one risk attending press coverage of scientific research is that the slightest misunderstanding can be magnified into major misinterpretations through the process of public dissemination. Confusion is especially likely to prevail if, as in the case of McGraw's co-twin study, controversy abounds about the relative significance of nature and nurture in child development. The *New*

402   BERGENN, DALTON, AND LIPSITT

York Times, among other newspapers, created an air of expectancy that McGraw's experiment might decisively resolve this debate when it wrote in 1935 that "the experiment is of some importance because of the controversy that rages between eugenicists, who maintain that environment counts for little or nothing and the Watson behaviorists, who insist that environment is everything" (*New York Times*, 1935, p. 19).

Unfortunately, when newspapers consistently described the purpose of the study as an experiment in conditioning, they made it appear as though her findings would support behaviorism. Consequently, when McGraw failed to find any evidence of long-term benefits (i.e., as defined by standard test scores) of early stimulation, the press incorrectly interpreted this as evidence against behaviorism (Dennis, 1989, pp. 362–363). Although there were a few thoughtful, in-depth stories and magazine articles written about the co-twin study, the general impression was that McGraw's research left the maturation hypothesis intact (e.g., see Hansl, 1935; McGraw, 1942b).

To her dismay, press misrepresentations eventually found their way into the scholarly literature (McGraw, 1983b, p. 49). In a cursory survey of recent textbooks, Razel (1985, p. 17) found that the view persists among psychologists that early motor development is primarily dictated by maturation. Even those texts that attempt a more in-depth survey tend either to present her findings in a fragmented way, as illustrated by Crowell (1967), or to use her work to support other theories of development whose premises are sometimes incompatible with McGraw's ideas about growth (Fowler, 1983). Not surprisingly, the refrain of maturationism continues to be heard from experimentalists in motor development who see little difference between Gesell and McGraw's work. (See, for example, Goldfield, 1989, and Clark, Phillips, & Petersen, 1989.)

The domination of maturationism from the 1940s until the early 1960s may explain why McGraw's concept of critical period attracted little attention among researchers. Maturationism holds that the stages of infant and child development are predetermined. Consequently, no one stage is any more likely than another to exert a decisive influence on development. However, with its revival, the concept took on new meanings, some of which unfortunately redefined her conception in maturationist terms. Controversy has never abated since then. In retrospect, McGraw (1985, p. 169) considered the use of this catchy term to have been a blunder. She admitted having picked up the term from "extensive readings in embryology" (McGraw, 1985, p. 169), where the term referred to the period of embryonic induction when the gross structural characteristics of the organism (i.e., the outcome of intercellular interactions) are determined. McGraw's notion differed from this conception in that the developmental (i.e., structural or functional) effects of stimulated growth were not limited exclusively to any one period of development.

McGraw's conception of critical period also reflected the work of Julian Huxley (1931), a pioneering growth scientist, who found that changes in the proportionality between organs brought about by differences in the rate of growth contribute to change in both form and function. This led McGraw to endorse the principle that growth proceeds differentially, with faster growing parts influencing the emergence and nature of later ones. By analogy, McGraw suspected that early stimulation of specific behavior patterns may accelerate and thus alter the time of emergence and form of subsequent behavior.

McGraw (1935a, p. 311) stressed that delaying intervention beyond a critical period does not imply that behavior could never be developed later, but only that its acquisition would be rendered more difficult because of the interference from growth of other capabilities such as perception and discrimination. McGraw (1983a) emphasized years later that a critical period simply denoted "that there are opportune times when specific activities can be most economically learned." If that time is missed, according to McGraw, then instructional techniques must be altered for learning to occur at a later date. In any event, McGraw did not limit the phenomenon to any time period. Moreover, there is also substantial evidence today that interactions taking place between neural growth and behavior during sensitive periods result in decisive changes across the spectrum of developmental processes (Bornstein, 1989; Oppenheim, 1981b).

McGraw also found that early exercise does influence the ease or grace with which a task is completed. This explains why the timing of stimulation is so important. McGraw argued that to be most effective, stimulation should be introduced at the point at which partial aspects of a total pattern were perceptible but intermittent and inchoate within a background of diffuse activity. This occurred during the second of five phases of growth, just before the onset of cortical inhibition (McGraw, 1935a, pp. 121, 307). Stimulation introduced at this time would be least subject to the cross pressures from the development of other functions that might interfere with the integration of a specific pattern.

McGraw was not unmindful of the possibility that some techniques of stimulation might actually involve restrictions or other subtle forms of conditioning. For instance, she could not be certain whether the use of special equipment such as the roller cart might have retarded Johnny's "urge to creep" (McGraw, 1935a, p. 72). Nevertheless, she concluded that daily exercise "apparently conditioned Johnny to greater exercise," rather than "hasten the developmental process" (McGraw, 1935a, p. 72). Similarly, although restriction of Jimmy's exercise did not alter the course of his development, it did curtail maximum development (McGraw, 1935a, p. 73).

The distinction between restriction and deprivation has unfortunately become obscured in the current debate about whether stimulation studies such as McGraw's violate scientific ethics by interfering with normal development in some injurious way. For example, experiments by Zelazo, Zelazo, and Kolb (1972) to stimulate early walking in infants have been criticized by Pontius (1973, pp. 238–239), who argued that placing an infant in a situation in which stereotypical reflexes must be involuntarily exercised places the infant at risk because cortical integration is not sufficient to sustain such postures. She argues that early stimulation may actually delay the onset of cortical inhibition, thus interfering with the acquisition of cognitive abilities. It is strange that Pontius (1973, pp. 238–239) should cite McGraw's work to support her argument, because McGraw believed that early stimulation has no effect on when the cortex begins functioning. Stimulation simply facilitates the integration of movements before they enter the construction of a behavior governed by the cortex. Moreover, it is not self-evident that an infant necessarily feels coerced when stimulated, as Pontius believes, for McGraw encountered a great variety of reactions from infants who were provided special stimulation.

McGraw's research cannot resolve this ongoing debate definitively. However, in a follow-up study of the twins, McGraw (1939a, p. 4) found that other factors besides timing determine the permanence of motor skill, thereby anticipating the importance of a nonshared environment studied by Plomin, DeFries, and Fulker (1988). These factors include the amount of reinforcing practice, attitudes of the child about the activity, and changing physiological conditions. In general, she found that the lack of practice appears less important than the other two factors in accounting for subsequent changes in behavior. For example, once Jimmy acquired the experience of motor integration, he appeared more relaxed and interested in completing tasks. In addition, both twins underwent substantial anatomical and physiological changes after the experiment that interfered with the completion of tasks previously mastered. These reversals are best explained by the disorganizing effects of changing body proportions and shifting centers of gravity that require behavioral adaptations.

Psychiatric profiles of the twins provided indirect evidence that certain personality traits may have persisted as a result of the timing of the intervention. For example, Johnny was quieter, more reflective, and impersonal, whereas Jimmy was more impulsive, tempestuous, talkative, and outgoing. Johnny's early experience of motor integration may have strengthened his self-esteem, patience, and self-control. In contrast, Jimmy's personality may have been formed by the need to compensate for the absence of successful experiences involving such coordination. Consequently, Jimmy had to rely more on an appealing and ingratiating style to engage others in achieving his ends (McGraw, 1939a, pp. 13–15).

Interviews with the twins' parents, however, revealed that their attempt to compensate Jimmy for the greater attention that Johnny got during the experiment by giving Jimmy more affection and favoring him at home also may have accounted for other observed personality differences. For example, Jimmy was more assertive and secure at home, whereas Johnny seemed more tense and withdrawn. This seeming reversal of personalities does not necessarily support the conclusion that the effects of early exercise are nullified by subsequent experience. Nor does it warrant the inference that the twin's real personalities were shaped by genetic factors beyond the influence of motor training. The added affection that Jimmy received simply reinforced his method of getting by, rather than encouraging self-reliance. In contrast, occasions for Johnny to demonstrate his superior creativity and judgment, which he continued to exhibit in the follow-up study, were limited and went unacknowledged. This explanation suggests that although an unshared environment strongly influences temperament, it is not evident that genetics accounts for these differences, as Plomin (1986, pp. 88–89, 180–190) contends. Moreover, differences in attention and treatment seem more likely to have encouraged instrumental and dependent behavior than to have offset the integrative effects of early stimulation.

GROWTH II: ADVANCED STUDIES OF
NEUROMUSCULAR MATURATION

The co-twin study deepened McGraw's interest in understanding more about factors affecting growth and development. McGraw was unable thus far to uncover the "definitions of these rhythms and spurts of development" and therefore, "a more detailed study of the development of particular action patterns than this investigation afforded is essential if the nature of the rhythmical fluctuations is to be ascertained" (McGraw, 1935a, p. 305).

Despite Tilney's untimely death in 1938, McGraw would, in fact, carry forward Tilney's unfulfilled legacy to discover the nature of neural processes underlying development. McGraw overcame this setback by sharing her data with Dr. Leroy Conel, a neuroanatomist at Harvard studying fetal brain development. Nevertheless, her research did not constitute a correlational study in the true experimental sense but was simply based on extrapolations from Conel's (1939) work and other texts examining brain physiology, such as that by Fulton (1938).

More specifically, McGraw wanted to determine the relationship between cortical and subcortical elements in the integration of behavior. This included a more detailed analysis of the phases of specific behavior patterns to discern precisely how phyletic and ontogenetic movements entered into the construction and sequencing of a mature pattern. McGraw also sought more details as to when postural control was first evinced in the coordination of behavior. Mechanisms of postural control were particularly crucial to the achievement of sitting and erect locomotion, activities of recent phyletic heritage only weakly organized at the segmental level. Finally, McGraw wanted to find out when attitudes (as previously described) make their first appearance, to better understand their role in the integration of behavior, including their impact on the acquisition of perceptual skills. The analysis of each of these factors required the development of novel techniques by which to measure the dynamic processes involved.

Dynamics of Integration

In the course of her co-twin study, McGraw discovered that developing patterns overlap in an interdependent and alternating fashion, oscillating forward and backward in rhythmic waves (see Touwen, 1971, for the strongest corroboration of this conception of development). This idea is often confused with Gesell's conception of development as a spiral of reciprocally interwoven behaviors. Gesell's theory did not entail regression or backward movement at any stage of development. Component traits that diverge from one another look regressive, Gesell stresses, but are actually "more mature because a product of a previous combination and will soon achieve further integrations" (Gesell, 1945, p. 176). Theodora Abel, an experimentalist and clinical psychologist who was a McGraw colleague, underscored the distinctiveness of her conception:

> McGraw objected to him [Gesell] because he said infants do this in one year and that in another. It was all stereotyped. That was her big objection. McGraw believed that there is overlapping in growth and that no two babies are the same. Each baby develops certain capabilities at different times. She thought she was doing something novel and I thought she was too. No one else studied babies in this way. She had a very good point and a lot of us agreed with her (Abel, 1990).

The unusual thing about the alternating sequence that McGraw observed was that individual variations in the timing, composition, and direction of movements could occur without altering the general pattern of progressive development. The key to understanding this seemingly paradoxical phenomenon, foreshadowed by Coghill, was that excessive or redundant elements of behavior patterns were essentially eliminated in the course of development. McGraw's advanced studies were designed to specify in more detail precisely what happened to bring about the functional reorganization of behavior.

In a series of studies undertaken from 1936 to 1947, summarized in her book, *The Neuromuscular Maturation of the Human Infant* (1943), McGraw selected several behavior patterns representing different ranges in estimated phyletic age and function for intensive analysis and comparison. The maturation of each pattern exhibited a rather complex series of stages involving the participation and coordination of neuroanatomical structures and movements. Despite these differences, McGraw found that each pattern underwent similar phases during maturation, involving the transition from diffuse to specific, integrated responses. These phases are best exemplified in crawling and creeping, in which the entire body is engaged in action (McGraw, 1941a).

McGraw concluded from this and from studies of other specific behavior patterns such as suspension grasp and erect locomotion that the variations in the form or organization could be explained best by differences in the rate of growth of neural connections and their timing. She did not mean by this that behavior development depends solely on the assumption of cortical control, as secondary accounts of her work seem to imply. For example, Getchell and Roberton (1989) incorrectly claim that McGraw's hypothesis that "cerebral inhibition cause[s] developmental sequences has now been refuted" (p. 920). Instead, McGraw found evidence of a more complex interaction of neuromuscular and behavioral factors identified in previous studies by Coghill and Tilney, among others.

The fact that the cortex does not function appreciably at birth indicates that the impetus for early development originates from and is controlled by other elements of the brain. For example, McGraw inferred from this that rhythmic movements of the lower body indicate that they are under subcortical control. In some instances, such as the Moro reflex, the rhythmic movements of the extensor muscles actually enhance the power of subsequent flexion (McGraw, 1937a, p. 250). Conversely, a period of relative inactivity of a body region is essential to the transition from nuclear to cortical control (McGraw, 1941a, p. 91). Likewise, the onset of cortical inhibition over spinal flexion "paves the way," according to McGraw (1940c, p. 1038), for the exercise and development of extensor muscles.

Significantly, McGraw (1940c) found behavioral evidence that indicated that cortical inhibition occurs "selectively" (pp. 1038, 1042), that is, it alternates between upper and lower regions of the body, slowly altering the amount and range of movement in each region. She considered this to be evidence that some behavioral functions could be exercised before complete growth and maturation of their underlying neural structures. For example, the spinal extensor phase was restricted under selective cortical inhibition to the neck and shoulder area (McGraw, 1940c, p. 1038; 1941a, pp. 90–93).

This discovery provided corroboration for Coghill's theory of neurobehavioral development. Postural control plays a functionally significant role in the order of emergence of recently acquired behaviors, especially those that lack organization at the segmental level, as in the case of sitting (McGraw, 1941c, pp. 171, 174). For example, some infants are able to master the righting aspect in attaining a sitting posture in one integrated movement, whereas others first have to learn how to turn from a dorsal to a prone position. This indicates that some babies develop a precocious ability to oppose gravity—an ability that reflects the earlier maturation of neural functions. Their movements are guided by a special body sense to adjust the body to displacement in space (McGraw, 1941c, pp. 160, 172). Coghill contended that these endogenous feelings obviate the need for a well-developed sensory apparatus including synaptic inhibition because the neuromuscular system was self-adjusting. Instead, the forces of general in-hibition were exercised through a nervous equivalent to posture (Coghill, 1930a, pp. 432–433; 1936, p. 10), controlling the flexion and abduction of the muscles.

Moreover, McGraw found that the timing of access to a special body sense seems to favorably affect the balance between muscular effort and somatic attitude involved in behavior. For example, infants first able to master the righting response to inversion displayed an acquiescent attitude (McGraw, 1940c, p. 1041). Once acquired, the attitude continued to promote effective integration throughout subsequent stages of development. Noteworthy in this regard is the fact that Johnny acquired an acquiescent attitude soon after successfully mastering the righting response and that this attitude persisted throughout his special training and beyond (McGraw, 1935a, pp. 165–166).

McGraw sought a neurological explanation of balance or equilibrium in further investigations of early postural movements involving body-right-ing reflexes. In prior research, Rudolf Magnus, a physiologist, had estab-lished in experiments with cats that this constitutes an essential element in the execution of a righting response because it orients subsequent move-ments by the trunk and legs. The fact that rolling over is eliminated as an initial movement once the righting response assumes a mature form led McGraw (1941b, p. 394) to conclude that the cortex had simply taken over integrative functions first performed by the primitive brain. This lent support to Tilney's (1923, p. 168) argument that intrabrain connections play an important role in evolutionary processes whereby structural changes contribute to functional adaptations and vice versa.

These findings also supported Dewey's speculations at the turn of the century about the importance of coordination to an integrated response. For example, Dewey (1976) considered coordination to be "the centralizing principle" (p. 191) of growth, both physiologically and psychologically. Dewey (1976) believed that coordination constitutes the cornerstone of future research and expected that scientists might "discover some single continuous function undergoing development" (p. 191) so that its principles of development would be better understood—a task that, in Dewey's view, McGraw eventually achieved (see Dewey's introduction to McGraw, 1935a, pp. xi–xiii).

McGraw's advanced studies of neuromuscular maturation uncovered obscure but essential attributes and patterns of development. Clearly, struc-ture and function interact throughout the course of behavior development and maturation. The importance of this discovery was perhaps best expressed by McGraw:

> It seems fairly evident that certain structural changes take place prior to the onset of overt function. It seems equally evident that cessation of neurostructural development does not coincide with the onset of function. There is every reason to believe that when conditions are favorable function makes some contribution to further advancement in structural development of the nervous system. An influential factor in determining the structural development of one component may be the functioning of other structures which are interrelated. (McGraw, 1946, p. 363)

Indeed, McGraw found persuasive evidence that cortical maturation is gradual and selective and that mature behavior patterns are foreshadowed by the emergence of distinctive but abbreviated precursors. The appearance of precortical forms of integrated behavior led her to infer that subcortical structures and phyletic reflexes play an important role in maturation. The reciprocal interchange between structure and function strengthened McGraw's conviction that "any rigid demarcation between structure and function as two distinct processes of development is not possible" (McGraw, 1946, p. 363).

The reason that McGraw considered the conventional wisdom mistaken that sensorimotor integration must await neural maturation was that at certain critical times, neuromuscular functions exhibit "fundamental qualities of learning" (McGraw, 1943, p. 122). Consequently, she argued against the belief that learning follows maturation or that growth is merely augmentation, as Gesell (1933, p. 210) insisted, contending instead that "the qualities of learning appear concurrently with the beginning of cortical participation" (McGraw, 1943, p. 122). This denotes convergence of neural and behavioral elements of growth, sharing common characteristics that together constitute the essence of growth processes. They involve the capacity of the human organism to react to forces that impinge on its existence, reject or assimilate them, and adapt to changing conditions by anticipating how they will affect its future existence. In essence, human intelligence consists in the degree to which these capabilities are coordinated to bring about the integration of mind and body, thought and feeling, in the course of development.

Measuring Qualitative Change

McGraw's discovery that learning occurs in the course of neuromuscular integration constitutes an important contribution to knowledge about human development. She suggested that further knowledge about development might be yielded if it were possible to measure intervals of activity undergoing continuous change (McGraw, 1937b). McGraw and Breeze

(1941) conducted an analysis of erect locomotion to see if it would yield a constant to calculate the magnitude of change in functional integration involved in the development of walking. Although suggestive, McGraw and her associates could not use the rate or velocity of growth alone as an unambiguous constant by which to measure development. Fluctuations in the velocity and direction of individual development made it difficult to select any one time period comparable for two or more individuals (Campbell & Weech, 1941, p. 219). As Touwen's (1971, p. 444) study demonstrates, the extensive variation and inconsistency between developmental patterns make a uniform standard of measurement elusive.

McGraw and Breeze (1941, p. 295) concluded in their research that antedates similar recent attempts to measure jumping by Clark et al. (1989) that the development of bilateral integration in erect locomotion furnishes the best evidence obtainable that the consistency of walking increases with age. McGraw (1943, p. 79) inferred from these studies that cortical inhibitory mechanisms controlling posture advanced more rapidly during the initial phase of erect locomotion than those governing progressive movements such as height and weight because "those mechanisms which activate movement are being interwoven with those governing antigravity and static postural control."

Clark et al. (1989, p. 929) argue that it is now possible to explain infant jumping through cross-sectional comparisons with adults, for example, without assigning a singularly directing role to the central nervous system, because the speed and accuracy with which infants acquire this ability is determined almost entirely by the relationship between internal constraints (i.e., strength, body mass, and center of gravity) and task demands. Yet the delay that they found to occur in the assumption of a correct posture preparatory to the execution of complex athletic skills, for example, surely cannot be adequately explained without reference to a collateral act of judgment as to the quality of the feeling involved or the accompanying anticipation of the subsequent sequence of movements.

McGRAW'S IMPACT ON DEVELOPMENTAL PSYCHOLOGY

McGraw continued to explore and refine the implications of her seminal research on development for the remainder of her career (1947–1988). During this period, she outlined the methods, issues, and concepts germane to a theory of growth, which remain highly pertinent to the challenges that developmental psychologists face through the end of the century and beyond. She illustrated, for example, how the signals of growth, if interpreted correctly, would change our theoretical preconceptions about normal development, which often underestimate the child's capacity to communicate and reason and the parent's ability to exercise judgment. In addition, she believed that a quantitative theory of growth and development could be constructed from embryology, psychobiology, and field theory, thus anticipating recent work by Oppenheim, Gottlieb, and others. Finally, McGraw warned that the promise of developmental psychology would not be fulfilled until research was truly interdisciplinary in method and scope. Although the prospects for interdisciplinary collaboration now seem brighter than before, theoretical cleavages continue to persist along the now familiar fault between heredity and environment.

Signals of Growth, Communication, and Learning

McGraw (1940a) believed that behavior took place within a psychobiological field somewhat like that envisioned by Kurt Lewin (1936). Actions took place in situations occurring within a biological and social space whose boundaries overlap. Consequently, the form and direction of behavior development reflected the balance of forces operating on an individual as he or she underwent each new experience. Infant gestures and vocalizations provided important signals or clues as to the specific capabilities of the child during each phase of development. McGraw (1942a; 1943) devoted considerable time studying these behavioral signs of preverbal communication to determine the conditions in which language is acquired. This became the focal point of McGraw's educational approach in the late 1960s and early 1970s at Briarcliff College in an innovative program designed to instruct future parents in how to interpret the signals of growth. McGraw (1940d, p. 31) demonstrated that observation was a skill that could be improved with training, imparting a greater self-confidence and judgment during parenthood. The goal of parent education, as McGraw conceived it, was neither professionalization of knowledge nor dominance of technique but the diffusion and democratization of intelligence in child rearing.

McGraw and her associates (see Welch & Long, 1940b) never completed their studies of the relationship among gesture, pattern recognition, and the acquisition of language and therefore were unable to complete their analysis of the transition from visual reasoning to conceptualization. Nevertheless, this line of inquiry was carried forward in the Soviet Union by Elkonin's (1971) and Lisina and Neverovich's (1971) research on orienting action in the 1950s and by Bever and Trevarthen, among others in the United States, who examined cognitive patterning foreshadowed in infant motor and communicative processes. Recent studies in infant exploratory behavior by Palmer (1989) and Rochat (1989) demonstrate that such activities exhibit rudimentary forms of reasoning through visual and tactile processes of discrimination. Research by Bever (1982) and Trevarthen (1982) complements these object-based, task-oriented studies by identifying neural growth factors that account for shifts and regressions in reasoning from one modality to another.

In this regard, Heinz Prechtl, a Dutch neurologist whose work was begun during the hiatus in motor studies in the 1940s and 1950s, demonstrated that the seemingly regressive behavior of early infant development is due to the natural transience of neural growth. Prechtl (1982) contended that neural structures are reorganized throughout childhood through processes of cell death and regrowth. Consequently, he hypothesized that the periodic reappearance of rhythmic, rudimentary motor behaviors may be due to the coexistence of neural structures until cell death leads to replacement. Oppenheim (1981a, pp. 117–118) speculated that regressive processes of cell death could have arisen phylogenetically as an epigenetic factor to compensate for either heritable or noninheritable variations in presynaptic and postsynaptic components of neural systems. Consequently, neural growth processes may indeed, as Coghill (1929, pp. 99–101; 1941, pp. 45–46) supposed, involve functional interactions between neural precursors and sensorimotor structures essential to ontogenetic development.

Lipsitt (1979, p. 976; 1982, pp. 34–35) contended that the period in early infancy (i.e., 2 to 4 months) when transient reflex functions are waning, as McGraw demonstrated, constitutes a special period of jeopardy and risk for those infants unable to make the transition because of a learning disability. For example, sudden infant death (and perhaps the failure to thrive), which involves inadequate postural control and respiratory occlusion, may be explained, according to Lipsitt, by a possible deficit in neural functioning combined with deficient environmental supports manifested in the transition from subcortical to cortical control, compromising the ability of these infants to develop adaptive reflex behavior. Lipsitt's (see also Burns & Lipsitt, 1991) work invites further research regarding the nature and timing of factors that interfere with normal development and the identification of potential ways in which learning deficits can be overcome before resulting in irreversible or fatal consequences.

Growth Theory and the Boundaries of Motor Development Research

Long before the revival of motor studies of infant development in the 1960s, precipitated in part by the discovery of Bernstein's (1967) biodynamic studies of coordination (see Pick, 1989), McGraw and her associates applied and tested biometric theories and techniques elaborated by Minot (1908), Robertson (1923), Brody (1945), Wetzel (1937), and Huxley (1931). (See Zeger & Harlow, 1987, for a historical review.) These scientists were primarily interested in equations capable of predicting and explaining variations in the pattern and rate of anatomical and behavioral attributes of growing organisms throughout the life span. It is strange that contemporary researchers in motor development show little awareness of the pioneering contributions of these growth scientists whose work antedated Bernstein yet continues to provide new insights about development. (For example, *Growth*, *Development and Aging*, *Developmental Biology*, and Falkner & Tanner's 1986 treatise are journals and books dedicated to the interdisciplinary study of growth.)

McGraw (1946, p. 353) wanted to fashion growth constants capable of yielding "techniques for comparing activities which are predominantly maturational in their processes of development with those which are the result of training." McGraw's ambition may seem naive by today's standards, but it reflected her conviction that science could advance only through comparative studies. Separate studies conducted by her associates Weinbach and Davenport reported conflicting findings. Weinbach (1941a, pp. 220–221) derived an acceleration constant that predicted that human growth over the life span would include an accelerating phase lasting until birth; a segment extending from birth to puberty involving brief periods of acceleration and deceleration, followed by accelerated growth through adolescence; and, finally, a decelerating phase continuing through maturity. In contrast, Davenport's (1938, p. 301) analysis of a small sample of babies involved in the NCDS revealed more complex individual patterns not readily reducible to a curve of uniform growth. He concluded that the anatomically differential growth rates that he found were due to factors affecting cell growth either inherent in the genes or derived from hormone production (Davenport, 1938, p. 303).

McGraw showed a keen understanding of the theoretical implications of experimental embryology for understanding behavior development. She carefully sifted through evidence supporting alternative explanations of neurogenesis. She believed that Goldschmidt (1938) offered persuasive evidence that growth rates were governed in part by biochemical processes regulated by the genes (McGraw, 1946, p. 352). Goldschmidt showed that the rate at which genetic influences are expressed could be altered to produce new characteristics in ontogeny. In this regard, Oppenheim (1981b, p. 97) observed that "selective and progressive gene inactivity [or suppression] may be the more common feature in the development of higher organisms, including brain development" (p. 97). The analysis of cellular change involved in embryonic and neural development, McGraw (1946) believed, would help "resolve the real issue of maturational theory, [which was] does function determine the neural organization or does the neural organization form the framework within which function takes place?" (p. 347).

McGraw had a continuing interest in scientific advances in neuroembryology and maintained close contact with leaders in the emerging field of psychobiology such as Ronald Oppenheim and Gilbert Gottlieb. Gottlieb (1976, p. 219) indicated that McGraw was one of the first developmental psychologists to recognize the bidirectionality of neural structures and behavioral functions in infant development. Oppenheim (1978, p. 45) specifically acknowledged his debt to McGraw in aiding his attempt to reconstruct the life and work of George Coghill while singling her out, along with Herrick, Coghill, and Gesell, as one of the pioneers in recognizing the significance of prenatal development to later psychological development (Oppenheim, 1982, p. 299; Oppenheim & Hall, 1987, p. 93).

McGraw's studies of the reciprocal interaction between neural growth processes and motor development continue to influence current research in neuroembryology. Gottlieb (1991) has advanced a theory of experiential canalization to reconcile the seemingly separate roles that genetic and nongenetic factors play in behavior development. He contends that the channeling of behavior can best be explained by the coaction or reciprocal interactions taking place at all levels (i.e., vertical and horizontal) of a developing system whereby genetic structures may be modified by behavioral and other influences. Gottlieb has produced a systems theory that shows heuristic promise for comparative experimental studies of development.

Nevertheless, as Gottlieb (1991, p. 10) acknowledged, we still know very little about cellular differentiation processes, particularly as they affect embryonic induction and neurogenesis. That is why Oppenheim, Yaginuma, Homma, and Kunzi's (1991) ongoing research on molecular and other variables involved in neuron guidance systems is so important. Such research can tell us a great deal about the source and nature of cues that neurons seek and receive from their intracellular and intercellular environment. Once properties of a neuron growth field are isolated, we then may be able to determine whether a particular configuration of neural growth is correlated with specific behavioral capacities or patterns. This would continue a line of inquiry McGraw (1940a, 1946) first initiated in her studies of neuromuscular development.

Thelen's (1990) contention that neural structures largely account for the global similarities that we find in human development downplays how neural growth processes contribute to significant variations in motor development and learning. She (1990, p. 39) correctly insists that the wide variability of behavior among infants is probably due to the multiple strategies available to them in the construction of their behavior. Yet structure cannot be effectively separated from function without seriously undermining our ability to understand how the brain contributes to the formation and selection of adaptive behavior. Thus an important challenge for developmental psychologists is to explain not only the wide differences in human capabilities and behavior, but the remarkable continuity in human form and functions despite the ever-changing contingencies encountered in the course of our evolutionary existence.

Interdisciplinary Research and Social Responsibility

McGraw believed that a science of growth could not simply be reconstituted out of prevailing psychological theories. Instead, she envisioned growth science as transcending the limits of any one discipline. This explains McGraw's insistence that the "growth scientist"

> be able to devise strategies to evaluate a multiplicity of systems constantly in flux, each system influencing another in different degrees . . . to design methods which reveal the rises and falls, the pulsations and rhythms manifest in growth of a given function. (McGraw, 1983a, pp. xix–xx)

Growth science could not, in McGraw's view, be effectively monopolized by any one field because the phenomena of development cut across the boundaries of several disciplines. Practitioners might come from fields with diverse perspectives, as was the case with the NCDS. But the common denominator linking their enterprise was the experimental study of growth in development. Teamwork offered the best prospect for scientific advance, since that would promote the convergence of judgment through the sharing of insight from different perspectives.

However, the promise of the interdisciplinary study of growth in developmental processes has yet to be fulfilled, largely because of theoretical rivalries and dogmatic disputes about genetic and environmental determinism. Yet significant scientific breakthroughs are more likely to come by focusing on those unexplained phenomena and anomalies at the boundaries between rival theories. For example, proponents of dynamic motor research could focus more on how features of neural growth or physiological changes contribute to differences and similarities in problem-solving strategies by infants and how attitudes affect the capacity for integration and retention of skills over time. Likewise, regressionists might enlarge their studies of communication and language acquisition to explain how motor development affects perceptual orientation and the capacity of infants to reason through tactile, visual, and verbal modes of communication. Similarly, behavioral geneticists might devote more attention to examining the effects of genetic and environmental factors on early motor development and training and identify how differences in affection or attention contribute to variations in learning exhibited by infants and children.

McGraw (1983a, p. xx) expressed one other concern about the conduct of research: that growth scientists assume responsibility for the application of their ideas and methods. The dissemination and use of ideas is admittedly not something easily controlled, as McGraw found in the wake of the publication of *Growth*. Moreover, McGraw (1985) regretfully forfeited an opportunity to exercise leadership in the field of motor development, perhaps unintentionally contributing to the hiatus in motor development research in the United States during the 1940s and 1950s. McGraw did call attention to the difficulty involved in the control of developmental technology. The misapplication of techniques is likely to persist in a culture that divorces the ideational processes of science and basic research from their applications. Detachment and advocacy occupy an uneasy relationship to one another when the consequences of knowledge are uncertain and controversial. McGraw's persistent efforts to close the gap between knowledge and application by advocating a change in our ways of seeing and managing development should serve as a reminder that uncertainty and the need to effect social and psychological change are inseparable elements in the scientific enterprise.

REFERENCES

Abel, T. (1990, January 11). [Telephone interview by Thomas C. Dalton. Albuquerque, NM.]

Bernstein, N. A. (1967). *The coordination and regulation of movement*. Elmsford, NY: Pergamon Press.

Bever, T. (1982). Regression in the service of development. In T. Bever (Ed), *Regression in mental development: Basic phenomena and theories* (pp. 153–190). Hillsdale, NJ: Erlbaum.

Bornstein, M. (1989). Sensitive periods of development: Structural characteristics and causal interpretations. *Psychological Bulletin, 105*, 179–197.

Brody, S. (1945). Biogenetics and growth. New York: Reinhold.

Bull, N. (1968). *The attitude theory of emotion*. New York: Johnson Reprints.

Burns, B., & Lipsitt, L. P. (1991). Behavioral factors in crib death: Toward an understanding of the sudden infant death syndrome. *Journal of Applied Developmental Psychology, 12*, 159–184.

Campbell, R. V. D., & Weech, A. A. (1941). Measures which characterize the individual during the development of behavior in early life. *Child Development, 12*, 217–236.

Chaney, B., & McGraw, M. B. (1932). Reflexes and other motor activities of the newborn infant. *Bulletin of the Neurological Institute of New York, 2*, 1–56.

Clark, J. E., Phillips, S. J., & Petersen, R. (1989). Developmental stability in jumping. *Developmental Psychology, 25*, 929–935.

Coghill, G. E. (1929). *Anatomy and the problem of behavior*. New York: Hafner.

Coghill, G. E. (1930a). Individuation versus integration in the development of behavior. *Journal of General Psychology, 3*, 431–435.

Coghill, G. E. (1930b). The structural basis of the integration of behavior. *National Academy of Science Proceedings, 16*, 637–643.

Coghill, G. E. (1933). The neuroembryonic study of behavior: Principles, perspectives and aims. *Science, 78*, 131–138.

Coghill, G. E. (1936). Integration and the motivation of behavior. *Genetic Psychology, 48*, 3–19.

Coghill, G. E. (1941). Early embryonic somatic movements in birds and mammals other than man. *Monographs of the Society for Research in Child Development, 15,* (2, Serial No. 25).

Coghill, G. E. (1964). *Anatomy and the problem of behavior.* New York: Hafner. (Original work published 1929)

Conditioned child proves superiority. (1935, January 16). *New York Times,* p. 19.

Conel, J. (1939). *The postnatal development of the human cerebral cortex: Vol I. Cortex of the newborn.* Cambridge, MA: Harvard University Press.

Crowell, D. H. (1967). Infant motor development. In Y. Brackbill (Ed.), *Infancy and early childhood* (pp. 125–206). New York: Free Press.

Dalton, T. C., & Bergenn, V. (1992). *John Dewey, Myrtle McGraw and the Logic: An uncommon collaboration in the 1930s.* Manuscript submitted for publication.

Dammann, V. T. (1941). Developmental changes in attitude as one factor determining energy output in a motor performance. *Child Development, 12,* 241–246.

Davenport, C. B. (1937). Interpretation of certain infantile growth curves. *Growth, 1,* 279–283.

Davenport, C. B. (1938). Bodily growth of babies during the first postnatal year. In *Proceedings of the Carnegie Institution: No. 169. Contributions to Embryology* (pp. 273–305). Washington, DC: Carnegie Institution.

Dennis, P. (1989). "Johnny's a gentleman but Jimmy's a mug": Press coverage during the 1930's of Myrtle McGraw's study of Johnny and Jimmy Woods. *Journal of the History of the Behavioral Sciences, 25,* 356–370.

Dewey, J. (1938). *Logic: A theory of inquiry.* New York: Holt.

Dewey, J. (1971). The theory of emotion. In J. A. Boydston (Ed.), *John Dewey: The early works: Vol 4. 1893–1894* (pp. 152–185). Carbondale, IL: Southern Illinois University Press.

Dewey, J. (1976). Principles of mental development as illustrated in early infancy. In J. Boydston (Ed.), *John Dewey: The middle works: Vol. 1. 1899–1901* (pp. 175–221). Carbondale, IL: Southern Illinois University Press.

Elkonin, D. B. (1971). Development of speech. In A. V. Zaporozhets & D. B. Elkonin (Eds.), *The psychology of pre-school children* (pp. 186–254). Cambridge, MA: MIT Press.

Elsberg, C. A. (1944). *The story of a hospital: The Neurological Institute of New York, 1909–1938.* New York: Paul F. Hoeber.

Falkner, F., & Tanner, J. M. (Ed.). (1986). *Human growth* (2nd ed.). New York: Plenum Press.

Fowler, W. (1983). *Potentials of childhood: Vol. 1. A historical view of early experience.* Lexington, MA: Lexington Books.

Frank, L. K. (1933, March 13). [Memorandum of interview with Myrtle McGraw, Babies Hospital, Columbia Medical Center, New York]. General Education Board, Record Group I, Series 1.3, Box 370, Folder 3858, Rockefeller Archive Center, Tarrytown, NY.

Frank, L. K. (1935a). The problem of child development. *Child Development, 1*, 7–18.

Frank, L. K. (1935b, May 24). [Memorandum of interview with Frederick Tilney, Myrtle McGraw, and Rustin McIntosh, Babies Hospital, Columbia Medical Center, New York]. General Education Board, Record Group I, Series 1.3, Box 370, Folder 3858, Rockefeller Archive Center, Tarrytown, NY.

Frank, L. K. (1962). The beginnings of child development and family life education in the twentieth century. *Merrill–Palmer Quarterly, 8*, 207–227.

Fulton, J. F. (1938). *Physiology of the nervous system*. New York: Oxford University Press.

Gesell, A. (1933). Maturation and the patterns of behavior. In C. Murchison (Ed.), *Handbook of child psychology* (2nd ed., rev., pp. 209–235). Worcester, MA: Clark University Press.

Gesell, A. (1934). *Infant behavior*. New York: McGraw-Hill.

Gesell, A. (1945). *The embryology of behavior*. New York: Harper.

Getchell, N., & Roberton, M. A. (1989). Whole body stiffness as a function of developmental level in children's hopping. *Developmental Psychology, 25*, 920–928.

Goldfield, E. C. (1989). Transition from rocking to crawling: Postural constraints on infant movement. *Developmental Psychology, 25*, 913–919.

Goldschmidt, R. (1938). *Physiological genetics*. New York: McGraw-Hill.

Gottlieb, G. (1976). Conceptions of pre-natal development. *Psychological Review, 83*, 215–234.

Gottlieb, G. (1991). Experiential canalization of behavioral development: Theory. *Developmental Psychology, 27*, 4–13.

Hansl, E. B. (1935, May). Incredible twins. *Parents Magazine*, pp. 24, 26, 53, 55.

Herrick, C. J. (1949). *George Ellett Coghill, a naturalist and philosopher*. Chicago: University of Chicago Press.

Heyl, K. (1989, December 23). [Telephone interview by Thomas C. Dalton. Norwich, VT.]

Huxley, J. (1931). *Problems of relative growth*. New York: Dial Press.

Kuo, Z. Y. (1939). Total pattern or local reflexes? *Psychological Review, 46*, 93–122.

Kuo, Z. Y. (1976). *The dynamics of development: An epigenetic view*. New York: Plenum Press.

Lewin, K. (1936). *Principles of topographical psychology*. New York: McGraw-Hill.

Lipsitt, L. P. (1979). Critical conditions in infancy: A psychological perspective. *American Psychologist, 14*, 973–980.

Lipsitt, L. P. (1982). Developmental jeopardy in the first year of life: Behavioral considerations. In A. Baum & J. E. Singer (Eds.), *Handbook of psychology and health: Vol. 2. Children and health* (pp. 23–37). Hillsdale, NJ: Erlbaum.

Lipsitt, L. P. (1990). Myrtle B. McGraw (1899–1988). *American Psychologist, 45*, 977.

Lisina, M. I., & Neverovich, Y. Z. (1971). Development of movements and formation of motor habits. In A. V. Zaporozhets & D. B. Elkonin (Eds.), *The psychology of pre-school children* (pp. 278–366). Cambridge, MA: MIT Press.

Marquis, D. G. (1930). The criterion of innate behavior. *Psychological Review, 37,* 334–339.

McGraw, M. B. (1931). A comparative study of a group of southern White and Negro infants. *Genetic Psychology Monographs, 10,* 1–105.

McGraw, M. B. (1935a). *Growth: A study of Johnny and Jimmy.* New York: Appleton-Century-Crofts.

McGraw, M. B. (1935b, June 11). Letter to L. K. Frank. General Education Board RGI, Series 1.3, Box 370, Folder 3858, Rockefeller Archive Center, Tarrytown, NY.

McGraw, M. B. (1937a). The Moro reflex. *American Journal of Disabled Children, 54,* 240–251.

McGraw, M. B. (1937b). Quantitative behavior data and the longitudinal method: The Moro reflex. *Human Biology, 9,* 542–548.

McGraw, M. B. (1939a). Later development of children specially trained during infancy: Johnny and Jimmy at school age. *Child Development, 10,* 1–19.

McGraw, M. B. (1939b). Swimming behavior of the human infant. *Journal of Pediatrics, 15,* 485–490.

McGraw, M. B. (1940a). Basic concepts and procedures in a study of behavior development. *Psychological Review, 47,* 79–89.

McGraw, M. B. (1940b). Neural maturation as exemplified in the achievement of bladder control. *Journal of Pediatrics, 16,* 580–590.

McGraw, M. B. (1940c). Neuromuscular mechanisms of the infant: Development reflected by postural adjustments to an inverted position. *American Journal of Diseases of Children, 60,* 1031–1042.

McGraw, M. B. (1940d). Signals of growth. *Child Study, 18,* 8–10, 31.

McGraw, M. B. (1941a). Development of neuromuscular mechanisms as reflected in the crawling and creeping behavior of the human infant. *Journal of Genetic Psychology, 58,* 83–111.

McGraw, M. B. (1941b). Neural maturation of the infant as exemplified in the righting reflex, or rolling from a dorsal to a prone position. *Journal of Pediatrics, 18,* 385–394.

McGraw, M. B. (1941c). Neuro-motor maturation of anti-gravity functions as reflected in the development of a sitting posture. *Journal of Genetic Psychology, 59,* 155–175.

McGraw, M. B. (1942a). Appraising test responses of infants and young children. *Journal of Psychology, 14,* 89–100.

McGraw, M. B. (1942b, April). Johnny and Jimmy. *New York Times Magazine, 19,* 22–25.

McGraw, M. B. (1943). *The neuromuscular maturation of the human infant.* New York: Columbia University Press.

McGraw, M. B. (1946). Maturation of behavior. In L. Carmichael (Ed.), *Manual of child psychology* (pp. 332–369). New York: Wiley.

McGraw, M. B. (1967, February 9). Interview by K. Duckworth. Center for Dewey Studies, Hastings-on-Hudson, NY.

McGraw, M. B. (1983a). Challenges for students of infancy. In L. P. Lipsitt (Ed.), *Advances in Infancy Research, 1,* xv–xxii. Norwood, NJ: Ablex.

McGraw, M. B. (1983b). Myrtle B. McGraw. In A. N. O'Connell & N. F. Russo (Eds.), *Models of achievement: Reflections of eminent women in psychology* (pp. 43–54). New York: Columbia University Press.

McGraw, M. B. (1985). Professional and personal blunders in child development research. *Psychological Record, 35,* 165–170.

McGraw, M. B. (1990). Memories, deliberate recall, and speculation. *American Psychologist, 45,* 934–937.

McGraw, M. B., & Breeze, K. W. (1941). Quantitative studies in the development of erect locomotion. *Child Development, 12,* 267–303.

Merritt, H. (1975). The development of neurology in New York City and New York State. In D. Denny-Brown, A. S. Rose, & A. L. Sachs (Eds.), *Centennial anniversary volume of the American Neurological Association, 1875–1975* (pp. 380–387). New York: Springer.

Minot, C. S. (1908). *The problem of age, growth and death: A study of cytomorphosis.* New York: Knickerbocker Press.

Nissen, H. (1951). Phylogenetic comparisons. In S. S. Stevens (Ed.), *Handbook of experimental psychology* (pp. 347–386). New York: Wiley.

Oppenheim, R. W. (1978). G. E. Coghill (1872–1941): Pioneer neuroembryologist and developmental psychobiologist. *Perspectives in Biology and Medicine, 22,* 45–64.

Oppenheim, R. W. (1981a). Neuronal cell death and some related regressive phenomena during neurogenesis: A selective historical review and progress report. In W. Maxwell Cowan (Ed.), *Studies in developmental neurobiology* (pp. 74–133). New York: Oxford University Press.

Oppenheim, R. W. (1981b). Ontogenetic adaptations and retrogressive processes in the development of the nervous system and behavior: A neuroembryological perspective. In K. J. Connolly & H. F. R. Prechtl (Eds.), *Maturation and development: Biological and psychological perspectives* (pp. 73–109). Philadelphia: Lippincott.

Oppenheim, R. W. (1982). The neuroembryological study of behavior: Progress, problems, perspectives. In R. K. Hunt (Ed.), *Current topics in developmental biology* (Vol. 17, pp. 257–309). San Diego: Academic Press.

Oppenheim, R. W., & Hall, W. G. (1987). Developmental psychobiology: Prenatal, perinatal and early postnatal aspects of behavior development. *Annual Review of Psychology, 38,* 91–128.

Oppenheim, R. W., Yaginuma, H., Homma, S., & Kunzi, R. (1991). Pathfinding by growth cones of commissural interneurons in the chick embryo spinal cord: A light and electron microscopic study. *Journal of Comparative Neurology, 304,* 78–102.

Palmer, C. F. (1989). The discriminating nature of infants' exploratory actions. *Developmental Psychology, 25,* 885–893.

Pick, H. L., Jr. (1989). Motor development: The control of action. *Developmental Psychology, 25,* 867–870.

Plomin, R. (1986). *Developmental genetics and psychology.* Hillsdale, NJ: Erlbaum.

Plomin, R., DeFries, J., & Fulker, D. (1988). *Nature and nurture during infancy and early childhood.* Cambridge, England: Cambridge University Press.

Pontius, A. A. (1973). Neuro ethics of "walking" in the newborn. *Perceptual and Motor Skills, 37,* 235–245.

Pool, L. (1975). *The Neurological Institute of New York, 1909–1974.* Lakeville, CT: Pocketknife Press.

Pool, L. (1990, March 29). [Telephone interview by T. Dalton. West Cornwall, CT.]

Prechtl, H. F. R. (1982). Regressions and transformations during neurological development. In T. Bever (Ed.), *Regression in mental development: Basic phenomena and theories* (pp. 103–116). Hillsdale, NJ: Erlbaum.

Ratner, S., & Altman, J. (1964). *John Dewey and Arthur F. Bentley: A philosophical correspondence, 1932–1951.* New Brunswick, NJ: Rutgers University Press.

Razel, M. (1985). A reanalysis of the evidence for the genetic nature of early motor development. In E. Sisel (Ed.), *Advances in applied developmental psychology* (Vol. 1, pp. 171–211). Norwood, NJ: Ablex.

Robertson, T. B. (1923). *The chemical basis of growth and senescence.* Philadelphia: Lippincott.

Rochat, P. (1989). Object manipulation and exploration in 2- to 5-month-old infants. *Developmental Psychology, 25,* 871–884.

Senn, M. (1972, May 9). Interview with Myrtle McGraw. Hastings-on-Hudson, New York. *Oral histories of child development: 1962–1983.* Milton Senn Collection at the History of Medicine Division, National Library of Medicine, National Institutes of Health, Bethesda, MD.

Shirley, M. M. (1931). The sequential method for the study of maturing behavior patterns. *Psychological Review, 38,* 507–528.

Thelen, E. (1990). Dynamical systems and the generation of individual differences. In J. Colombo & J. Fager (Eds.), *Individual differences in infancy* (pp. 19–43). Hillsdale, NJ: Erlbaum.

Thelen, E., & Adolph, K. E. (1992). Arnold L. Gesell: The paradox of nature and nurture. *Developmental Psychology, 28,* 368–380.

Thelen, E., & Ulrich, B. D. (1991). *Hidden skills* (Monographs of the Society for Research in Child Development, Vol. 56, Serial 223, No. 1). Chicago: University of Chicago Press.

Tilney, F. (1917). Opportunities in neurology. *Journal of Nervous and Mental Disease, 46,* 1–7.

Tilney, F. (1923). Genesis of cerebellar functions. *Archives of Neurology and Psychiatry, 9,* 137–169.

Tilney, F. (1926). Neurology and education. *Archives of Neurology and Psychiatry, 16,* 539–554.

Touwen, B. C. (1971). A study on the development of some motor phenomena in infancy. *Developmental Medicine and Child Neurology, 13,* 435–446.

Trevarthen, C. (1982). Basic patterns of psychogenetic change in infancy. In T. Bever (Ed.), *Regression in mental development: Basic phenomena and theories* (pp. 7–46). Hillsdale, NJ: Erlbaum.

Weech, A. A. (1940). *Report of scientific program of Normal Child Development Study.* New York: Butler Library, Columbia University.

Weech, A. A., Alexander, H. E., Damrosch, D. S., Day, R. L., Riley, C. M., & Silverman, W. A. (1961). *The McIntosh era at Babies Hospital, 1931–1960.* New York: Babies Hospital.

Weinbach, A. P. (1941a). The human growth curve: I. Prenatal. *Growth, 5,* 217–234.

Weinbach, A. P. (1941b). The human growth curve: II. Birth to puberty. *Growth, 5,* 235–255.

Welch, L., & Long, L. (1940a). A further investigation of the higher structural phases of concept formation. *Journal of Psychology, 10,* 211–220.

Welch, L., & Long, L. (1940b). The higher structural phases of concept formation of children. *Journal of Psychology, 9,* 59–95.

Wetzel, N. C. (1937). On the motion of growth: Theoretical foundations. *Growth, 1,* 6–59.

Windle, W. F. (1934). Correlation between the development of local reflexes and reflex arcs in the spinal cord of cat embryos. *Journal of Comparative Neurology, 59,* 487–505.

Zeger, S. L., & Harlow, S. D. (1987). Mathematical models from laws of growth to tools for biologic analysis: Fifty years of *Growth. Growth, 51,* 1–21.

Zelazo, P. Z., Zelazo, N. A., & Kolb, S. (1972). Newborn walking. *Science, 177,* 1058–1060.

IV

THE MODERN ERA
(1960 TO PRESENT)

INTRODUCTION

THE MODERN ERA
(1960 TO PRESENT)

In this section, we move to the modern era of developmental psychology, a period spanning the past 30 years. The Freudian tradition in developmental psychology is well represented in two theories: the Bowlby–Ainsworth ethological approach to attachment and the social learning theory tradition of Sears and, to a lesser extent, of Bandura.

Bowlby combined insights from Freud's psychoanalytic theory with the theoretical approaches of modern ethology and control systems theory. From psychoanalytic theory, Bowlby retained the focus on the importance of the nature of the early mother–infant relationship for later development. By using ethological theory, he escaped the constraint imposed by Freudian theory that the feeding context was critical for development, although he recognized that biologically based predispositions on the part of both mother and infant were sufficient to account for the development of the early attachment relationship. Ainsworth, in turn, not only helped refine the theory based on her own early work with Blatz but also provided a new research paradigm that allowed evaluation and assessment of the underlying theoretical ideas. Bretherton's (chapter 15) account provides a historical overview of the emergence of the theoretical collaboration and highlights the new research directions that have been stimulated by this theory. New work on representation and attachment, shifts in attachment relationships across the life span, cross-cultural work, and implications for developmental psychopathology is outlined. As chapter 15 demonstrates, the Bowlby–Ainsworth theory continues to have implications for the field of social and affective development well beyond the issue of attachment. Instead, the theory demonstrates the heuristic value of interdisciplinary collaborative efforts and the advances that are achieved by combining insights from several fields. Finally, it is a reminder that, in many regards, we have returned to our Darwinian beginnings, as seen in the central roles of Darwinian-influenced Freudian theory and of evolutionary-influenced ethology in the Bowlby–Ainsworth position.

Whereas Bowlby and Ainsworth combined Freudian theory with ethological concepts, Sears and the social learning theorists combined Freudian theory and Hullian theory. Grusec (chapter 16) a former Bandura protégé, traces the ways in which Freudian ideas about development were subjected finally to empirical tests by joining with the behavioral language of Hullian learning theory. For nearly 30 years, Sears and his colleagues provided a series of ingenious evaluations of Freudian-inspired notions about the development of children's social behavior as a consequence of family child-rearing practices. Grusec illustrates how Freudian theoretical influences continued to dominate our choice of topics, major sources of influence (e.g., the family), and central processes well into the 1950s and 1960s. In conjunction with Emde and Bretherton, Grusec (chapter 16) is testimony to the continuing and pervasive debt that developmental psychology owes to psychoanalytic theory. Although retaining allegiance to Freudian theory, Sears made a number of advances, both methodologically and theoretically, that are contemporary in their flavor. For example, his focus on the dyad as the unit of analysis is both contemporary as well as reminiscent of J. Mark Baldwin's turn-of-the century plea for considering dyadic-level analyses, and his use of interviews and projective doll play techniques has been adopted by current investigators.

Under the guidance of Bandura, social learning theory took a decidely different turn. While retaining the largely Freudian-inspired categories of behavior as outcome measures, Bandura (in collaboration with Richard Walters) proposed a very different set of explanatory processes. In contrast with the historically oriented theory of Sears, Bandura's emphasis was on situational control, with observational learning and Skinnerian-inspired reinforcement principles playing a central role as processes to account for the acquisition, maintenance, and modification of behavior. In subsequent writings, Bandura has emphasized the role of cognition, as well as the role of self-regulatory processes, in accounting for behavioral development and change. By the 1980s, social cognitive theory had evolved into a general theory of behavior that extended well beyond its origins in developmental work and that continues to play an influential role in clinical, social, and health psychology.

Nancy Bayley shares with her intellectual ancestor, Alfred Binet, the fate of being recognized largely for a single achievement: the Bayley Scales of Motor and Mental Development. These widely used scales for assessing infant development alone would secure Bayley's place in the history of our field, but Rosenblith (chapter 17) reminds us of the wide range of her contributions beyond this singular achievement. Her pioneering work on the continuities in IQ, as well as her ground-breaking theoretical work on the circumflex model of maternal child-rearing behavior, are noted. Even less well known is her anticipation of several themes of contemporary inquiry, including recent emphasis on nonshared environment effects in behavior genetics, the impact of timing of maturation in adolescence, and life-span approaches to cognitive development. Finally, Rosenblith underscores Bayley's life-long commitment to championing longitudinal research as an ideal and even necessary design for addressing central developmental questions.

Eleanor J. Gibson, a proponent of a novel theory of perceptual development, is the final theorist in this section. In chapter 18, Pick contrasts Gibson's emphasis on the central role of differentiation in perceptual development and learning with the alternative associationist accounts of development. This radical departure from prior theory shifts the focus from the response side in the learning process to an increased focus on the stimulus or input side of the learning equation. As Pick notes, Gibson's emphasis on "affordances" presents alternative explanations of recent work on infant cognitive and perceptual competencies. Finally, "her emphasis on activity as a crucial aspect of perceptual development and learning provides a bridge with Soviet research and theory as well as a way of bridging the gap between cognition and action" (Pick, this volume, p. 537). The implications of Gibson's theoretical formulation for contemporary work on perception, motor development, and cognition are only beginning to be realized.

15

THE ORIGINS OF ATTACHMENT THEORY: JOHN BOWLBY AND MARY AINSWORTH

INGE BRETHERTON

Attachment theory is the joint work of John Bowlby and Mary Ainsworth (Ainsworth & Bowlby, 1991). Drawing on concepts from ethology, cybernetics, information processing, developmental psychology, and psychoanalysis, John Bowlby formulated the basic tenets of the theory. He thereby revolutionized our thinking about a child's tie to the mother and its disruption through separation, deprivation, and bereavement. Mary Ainsworth's innovative methodology not only made it possible to test some of Bowlby's ideas empirically but also helped expand the theory itself and is responsible for some of the new directions it is now taking. Ainsworth contributed the concept of the attachment figure as a secure base from which an infant can explore the world. In addition, she formulated the concept of maternal sensitivity to infant signals and its role in the development of infant–mother attachment patterns.

I would like to thank Mary Ainsworth and Ursula Bowlby for helpful input to a draft of this article. I am also grateful for insightful comments by three very knowledgeable anonymous reviewers.

Reprinted from *Developmental Psychology, 28,* 759–775. Copyright by the American Psychological Association.

The ideas now guiding attachment theory have a long developmental history. Although Bowlby and Ainsworth worked independently of each other during their early careers, both were influenced by Freud and other psychoanalytic thinkers—directly in Bowlby's case, indirectly in Ainsworth's. In this chapter, I document the origins of ideas that later became central to attachment theory. I then discuss the subsequent period of theory building and consolidation. Finally, I review some of the new directions in which the theory is currently developing and speculate on its future potential. In taking this retrospective developmental approach to the origins of attachment theory, I am reminded of Freud's (1920/1955) remark:

> So long as we trace the development from its final outcome backwards, the chain of events appears continuous, and we feel we have gained an insight which is completely satisfactory or even exhaustive. But if we proceed in the reverse way, if we start from the premises inferred from the analysis and try to follow these up to the final results, then we no longer get the impression of an inevitable sequence of events which could not have otherwise been determined. (p. 167)

In elucidating how each idea and methodological advance became a stepping stone for the next, my retrospective account of the origins of attachment theory makes the process of theory building seem planful and orderly. No doubt this was the case to some extent, but it may often not have seemed so to the protagonists at the time.

ORIGINS

John Bowlby

After graduating from the University of Cambridge in 1928, where he received rigorous scientific training and some instruction in what is now called developmental psychology, Bowlby performed volunteer work at a school for maladjusted children while reconsidering his career goals. His experiences with two children at the school set his professional life on course. One was a very isolated, remote, affectionless teenager who had been expelled from his previous school for theft and had had no stable mother figure. The second child was an anxious boy of 7 or 8 who trailed Bowlby around and who was known as his shadow (Ainsworth, 1974). Persuaded by this experience of the effects of early family relationships on personality development, Bowlby decided to embark on a career as a child psychiatrist (Senn, 1977b).

Concurrently with his studies in medicine and psychiatry, Bowlby undertook training at the British Psychoanalytic Institute. During this period Melanie Klein was a major influence there (the institute had three groups: Group A sided with Freud, Group B sided with Klein, and the Middle Group sided with neither). Bowlby was exposed to Kleinian (Klein, 1932) ideas through his training analyst, Joan Riviere, a close associate of Klein, and eventually through supervision by Melanie Klein herself. Although he acknowledges Riviere and Klein for grounding him in the object-relations approach to psychoanalysis, with its emphasis on early relationships and the pathogenic potential of loss (Bowlby, 1969, p. xvii), he had grave reservations about aspects of the Kleinian approach to child psychoanalysis. Klein held that children's emotional problems are almost entirely due to fantasies generated from internal conflict between aggressive and libidinal drives, rather than to events in the external world. She hence forbade Bowlby to talk to the mother of a 3-year-old whom he analyzed under her supervision (Bowlby, 1987). This was anathema to Bowlby who, in the course of his postgraduate training with two psychoanalytically trained social workers at the London Child Guidance Clinic, had come to believe that actual family experiences were a much more important, if not the basic, cause of emotional disturbance.

Bowlby's plan to counter Klein's ideas through research is manifest in an early theoretical paper (1940) in which he proposed that, like nurserymen, psychoanalysts should study the nature of the organism, the properties of the soil, and their interaction (p. 23). He goes on to suggest that, for mothers with parenting difficulties,

> a weekly interview in which their problems are approached analytically and traced back to childhood has sometimes been remarkably effective. Having once been helped to recognize and recapture the feelings which she herself had as a child and to find that they are accepted tolerantly and understandingly, a mother will become increasingly sympathetic and tolerant toward the same things in her child. (Bowlby, 1940, p. 23)

These quotations reveal Bowlby's early theoretical and clinical interest in the intergenerational transmission of attachment relations and in the possibility of helping children by helping parents. Psychoanalytic object-relations theories later proposed by Fairbairn (1952) and Winnicott (1965) were congenial to Bowlby, but his thinking had developed independently of them.

Bowlby's first empirical study, based on case notes from the London Child Guidance Clinic, dates from this period. Like the boy at the school for maladjusted children, many of the clinic patients were affectionless and prone to stealing. Through detailed examination of 44 cases, Bowlby was able to link their symptoms to histories of maternal deprivation and separation.

Although World War II led to an interruption in Bowlby's budding career as a practicing child psychiatrist, it laid further groundwork for his career as a researcher. His assignment was to collaborate on officer selection procedures with a group of distinguished colleagues from the Tavistock Clinic in London, an experience that gave Bowlby a level of methodological and statistical expertise then unusual for a psychiatrist and psychoanalyst. This training is obvious in the revision of his paper, "Forty-Four Juvenile Thieves: Their Characters and Home Lives" (Bowlby, 1944), which includes statistical tests as well as detailed case histories.

At the end of World War II, Bowlby was invited to become head of the Children's Department at the Tavistock Clinic. In line with his earlier ideas on the importance of family relationships in child therapy, he promptly renamed it the Department for Children and Parents. Indeed, in what is credited as the first published paper in family therapy, Bowlby (1949) describes how he was often able to achieve clinical breakthroughs by interviewing parents about their childhood experiences in the presence of their troubled children.

To Bowlby's chagrin, however, much of the clinical work in the department was done by people with a Kleinian orientation, who, he says, regarded his emphasis on actual family interaction patterns as not particularly relevant. He therefore decided to found his own research unit whose efforts were focused on mother–child separation. Because separation is a clear-cut and undeniable event, its effects on the child and the parent–child relationship were easier to document than more subtle influences of parental and familial interaction.

Mary Ainsworth

Mary Ainsworth (nee Salter), 6 years younger than Bowlby, finished graduate study at the University of Toronto just before World War II. Courses with William Blatz had introduced her to security theory (Blatz, 1940), which both reformulated and challenged Freudian ideas, though Blatz chose not to recognize his debt to Freud because of the anti-Freudian climate that pervaded the University of Toronto at that time (Ainsworth, 1983; Blatz, 1966).

One of the major tenets of security theory is that infants and young children need to develop a secure dependence on parents before launching out into unfamiliar situations. In her dissertation, entitled "An Evaluation of Adjustment Based Upon the Concept of Security," Mary Salter (1940) states it this way:

> Familial security in the early stages is of a dependent type and forms a basis from which the individual can work out gradually, forming new skills and interests in other fields. Where familial security is lacking, the individual is handicapped by the lack of what might be called a *secure base* [italics added] from which to work. (p. 45)

Interestingly, Mary Salter's dissertation research included an analysis of students' autobiographical narratives in support of the validity of her paper-and-pencil self-report scales of familial and extrafamilial security, foreshadowing her later penchant for narrative methods of data collection. Indeed, few researchers realize the enormous experience in instrument development and diagnostics she brought to attachment research.

Like Bowlby's, Mary Salter's professional career was shaped by her duties as a military officer during World War II (in the Canadian Women's Army Corps). After the war, as a faculty member at the University of Toronto, she set out to deepen her clinical skills in response to the request to teach courses in personality assessment. To prepare herself for this task, she signed up for workshops by Bruno Klopfer, a noted expert in the interpretation of the Rorschach test. This experience led to a coauthored book on the Rorschach technique (Klopfer, Ainsworth, Klopfer, & Holt, 1954), which is still in print.

In 1950, Mary Salter married Leonard Ainsworth and accompanied him to London, where he completed his doctoral studies. Someone there drew her attention to a job advertisement in the *London Times* that happened to involve research, under the direction of John Bowlby, into the effect on personality development of separation from the mother in early childhood. As Mary Ainsworth acknowledges, joining Bowlby's research unit reset the whole direction of her professional career, though neither Bowlby nor Ainsworth realized this at the time.

THE EMERGENCE OF ATTACHMENT THEORY

In 1948, 2 years before Ainsworth's arrival, Bowlby had hired James Robertson to help him observe hospitalized and institutionalized children who were separated from their parents. Robertson had had impeccable training in naturalistic observation, obtained as a conscientious objector during World War II, when he was employed as a boilerman in Anna Freud's Hampstead residential nursery for homeless children. Anna Freud required that all members of the staff, no matter what their training or background, write notes on cards about the children's behavior (Senn, 1977a), which were then used as a basis for weekly group discussions. The thorough training in child observation that Robertson thus obtained at the Hampstead residential nursery is Anna Freud's lasting personal contribution to the development of attachment theory.

After 2 years of collecting data on hospitalized children for Bowlby's research projects, Robertson protested that he could not continue as an uninvolved research worker, but felt compelled to do something for the children he had been observing. On a shoestring budget, with minimal training, a hand-held cinecamera, and no artificial lighting, he made the deeply moving film, *A Two-Year-Old Goes to Hospital* (Robertson, 1953a,

1953b; Robertson & Bowlby, 1952). Foreseeing the potential impact of this film, Bowlby insisted that it be carefully planned to ensure that no one would later be able to accuse Robertson of biased recording. The target child was randomly selected, and the hospital clock on the wall served as proof that time sampling took place at regular periods of the day. Together with Spitz's (1947) film, *Grief: A Peril in Infancy,* Robertson's first film helped improve the fate of hospitalized children all over the Western world, even though it was initially highly controversial among the medical establishment.

When Mary Ainsworth arrived at Bowlby's research unit late in 1950, others working there (besides James Robertson) were Mary Boston and Dina Rosenbluth. Rudolph Schaffer, whose subsequent attachment research is well known (Schaffer & Emerson, 1964), joined the group somewhat later, as did Christoph Heinicke (1956; Heinicke & Westheimer, 1966), who undertook additional separation and reunion studies, and Tony Ambrose (1961), who was interested in early social behavior. Mary Ainsworth, who was charged with analyzing James Robertson's data, was tremendously impressed with his records of children's behavior and decided that she would emulate his methods of naturalistic observation were she ever to undertake a study of her own (Ainsworth, 1983).

At this time, Bowlby's earlier writings about the familial experiences of affectionless children had led Ronald Hargreaves of the World Health Organization (WHO) to commission him to write a report on the mental health of homeless children in postwar Europe. Preparation of the WHO report gave Bowlby an opportunity to pick the brains of many practitioners and researchers across Europe and the United States who were concerned with the effects of maternal separation and deprivation on young children, including Spitz (1946) and Goldfarb (1943, 1945). The report was written in 6 months and translated into 14 languages, with sales of 400,000 copies in the English paperback edition; it was published in 1951 as *Maternal Care and Mental Health* by the WHO. A second edition, entitled *Child Care and the Growth of Love,* with review chapters by Mary Ainsworth, was published by Penguin Books in 1965.

It is interesting to examine the 1951 report from today's perspective. At that time Bowlby still used the terminology of traditional psychoanalysis (love object, libidinal ties, ego, and superego), but his ideas were little short of heretical. Perhaps following Spitz, he used embryology as a metaphor to portray the maternal role in child development:

> If growth is to proceed smoothly, the tissues must be exposed to the influence of the appropriate organizer at certain critical periods. In the same way, if mental development is to proceed smoothly, it would appear to be necessary for the undifferentiated psyche to be exposed during certain critical periods to the influence of the psychic organizer—the mother. (Bowlby, 1951, p. 53)

Then, seemingly doing away with the idea that the superego has its origin in the resolution of the Oedipus complex, Bowlby claims that during the early years, while the child acquires the capacity for self-regulation, the mother is a child's ego and superego:

> It is not surprising that during infancy and early childhood these functions are either not operating at all or are doing so most imperfectly. During this phase of life, the child is therefore dependent on his mother performing them for him. She orients him in space and time, provides his environment, permits the satisfaction of some impulses, restricts others. She is his ego and his super-ego. Gradually he learns these arts himself, and as he does, the skilled parent transfers the roles to him. This is a slow, subtle and continuous process, beginning when he first learns to walk and feed himself, and not ending completely until maturity is reached. . . . Ego and super-ego development are thus inextricably bound up with the child's primary human relationships. (Bowlby, 1951, p. 53)

This sounds more Vygotskian than Freudian. Moreover, despite his disagreements with Kleinian therapy, I detect remnants of Kleinian ideas in Bowlby's discussions of children's violent fantasies on returning to parents after a prolonged separation and "the intense depression that humans experience as a result of hating the person they most dearly love and need" (Bowlby, 1951, p. 57).

Bowlby's major conclusion, grounded in the available empirical evidence, was that to grow up mentally healthy, "the infant and young child should experience a warm, intimate, and continuous relationship with his mother (or permanent mother substitute) in which both find satisfaction and enjoyment" (Bowlby, 1951, p. 13). Later summaries often overlook the reference to the substitute mother and to the partners' mutual enjoyment. They also neglect Bowlby's emphasis on the role of social networks and on economic as well as health factors in the development of well-functioning mother–child relationships. His call to society to provide support for parents is still not heeded today:

> Just as children are absolutely dependent on their parents for sustenance, so in all but the most primitive communities, are parents, especially their mothers, dependent on a greater society for economic provision. If a community values its children it must cherish their parents. (Bowlby, 1951, p. 84)

True to the era in which the WHO report was written, Bowlby emphasized the female parent. In infancy, he comments, fathers have their uses, but normally play second fiddle to mother. Their prime role is to provide emotional support to their wives' mothering.

The proposition that, to thrive emotionally, children need a close and continuous caregiving relationship called for a theoretical explanation. Bowlby was not satisfied with the then current psychoanalytic view that love of mother derives from sensuous oral gratification, nor did he agree with social learning theory's claim that dependency is based on secondary reinforcement (a concept that was itself derived from psychoanalytic ideas). Like Spitz (1946) and Erikson (1950), Bowlby had latched onto the concept of critical periods in embryological development and was casting about for similar phenomena at the behavioral level when, through a friend, he happened upon an English translation of Konrad Lorenz's (1935) paper on imprinting.

From then on, Bowlby began to mine ethology for useful new concepts. Lorenz's (1935) account of imprinting in geese and other precocial birds especially intrigued him, because it suggested that social bond formation need not be tied to feeding. In addition, he favored ethological methods of observing animals in their natural environment, because this approach was so compatible with the methods Robertson had already developed at the Tavistock research unit.

One notable talent that stood Bowlby in great stead throughout his professional life was his ability to draw to himself outstanding individuals who were willing and able to help him acquire expertise in new fields of inquiry that he needed to master in the service of theory building. To learn more about ethology, Bowlby contacted Robert Hinde, under whose "generous and stern guidance" (see Bowlby, 1980b, p. 650) he mastered ethological principles to help him find new ways of thinking about infant–mother attachment. Conversely, Hinde's fascinating studies of individual differences in separation and reunion behaviors of group-living rhesus mother–infant dyads (Hinde & Spencer-Booth, 1967) were inspired by the contact with Bowlby and his co-workers (Hinde, 1991).

Bowlby's first ethological paper appeared in 1953. Somewhat surprisingly, however, various empirical papers on the effects of separation, published with his own research team during the very same period, show little trace of Bowlby's new thinking, because his colleagues were unconvinced that ethology was relevant to the mother–child relationship (Bowlby, personal communication, October 1986). Even Mary Ainsworth, though much enamored of ethology, was somewhat wary of the direction Bowlby's theorizing had begun to take. It was obvious to her, she said, that a baby loves his mother because she satisfies his needs (Ainsworth, personal communication, January 1992). A collaborative paper dating from this period (Bowlby, Ainsworth, Boston, & Rosenbluth, 1956) is nevertheless important, because it prefigures later work on patterns of attachment by Ainsworth. Her contribution to the paper was a system for classifying three basic relationship patterns in school-age children who had been reunited with parents after prolonged sanatorium stays: those with strong positive feelings toward their mothers; those with markedly ambivalent relationships; and a third group with nonexpressive, indifferent, or hostile relationships with mother.

THE FORMULATION OF ATTACHMENT THEORY AND THE FIRST ATTACHMENT STUDY

Theoretical Formulations

Bowlby's first formal statement of attachment theory, building on concepts from ethology and developmental psychology, was presented to the British Psychoanalytic Society in London in three now classic papers: "The Nature of the Child's Tie to His Mother" (1958), "Separation Anxiety" (1959), and "Grief and Mourning in Infancy and Early Childhood" (1960). By 1962 Bowlby had completed two further papers (never published; 1962a and b) on defensive processes related to mourning. These five papers represent the first basic blueprint of attachment theory.

The Nature of the Child's Tie to His Mother

This paper reviews and then rejects those contemporary psychoanalytic explanations for the child's libidinal tie to the mother in which need satisfaction is seen as primary and attachment as secondary or derived. Borrowing from Freud's (1905/1953) notion that mature human sexuality is built up of component instincts, Bowlby proposed that 12-month-olds' unmistakable attachment behavior is made up of a number of component instinctual responses that have the function of binding the infant to the mother and the mother to the infant. These component responses (among them sucking, clinging, and following, as well as the signaling behaviors of smiling and crying) mature relatively independently during the first year of life and become increasingly integrated and focused on a mother figure during the second 6 months. Bowlby saw clinging and following as possibly more important for attachment than sucking and crying.

To buttress his arguments, Bowlby reviewed data from existing empirical studies of infants' cognitive and social development, including those of Piaget (1951, 1954), with whose ideas he had become acquainted during a series of meetings by the "Psychobiology of the Child" study group, organized by the same Ronald Hargreaves at the World Health Organization who had commissioned Bowlby's 1951 report. These informative meetings, also attended by Erik Erikson, Julian Huxley, Baerbel Inhelder, Konrad Lorenz, Margaret Mead, and Ludwig von Bertalanffy, took place between 1953 and 1956. (Proceedings were published by Tavistock Publications.) For additional evidence, Bowlby drew on many years of experience as weekly facilitator of a support group for young mothers in London.

After his careful discussion of infant development, Bowlby introduced ethological concepts, such as sign stimuli or social releasers that "cause" specific responses to be activated and shut off or terminated (see Tinbergen, 1951). These stimuli could be external or intrapsychic, an important point in view of the fact that some psychoanalysts accused Bowlby of behaviorism because he supposedly ignored mental phenomena. Bowlby also took great pains to draw a clear distinction between the old social learning theory concept of dependency and the new concept of attachment, noting that attachment is not indicative of regression, but rather performs a natural, healthy function even in adult life.

Bowlby's new instinct theory raised quite a storm at the British Psychoanalytic Society. Even Bowlby's own analyst, Joan Riviere, protested. Anna Freud, who missed the meeting but read the paper, politely wrote: "Dr. Bowlby is too valuable a person to get lost to psychoanalysis" (Grosskurth, 1987).

Separation Anxiety

The second seminal paper (Bowlby, 1959) builds on observations by Robertson (1953b) and Heinicke (1956; later elaborated as Heinicke & Westheimer, 1966), as well as on Harlow and Zimmermann's (1958) groundbreaking work on the effects of maternal deprivation in rhesus monkeys. Traditional theory, Bowlby claims, can explain neither the intense attachment of infants and young children to a mother figure nor their dramatic responses to separation.

Robertson (Robertson & Bowlby, 1952) had identified three phases of separation response: protest (related to separation anxiety), despair (related to grief and mourning), and denial or detachment (related to defence mechanisms, especially repression). Again drawing on ethological concepts regarding the control of behavior, Bowlby maintained that infants and children experience separation anxiety when a situation activates both escape and attachment behavior but an attachment figure is not available.

The following quote explains, in part, why some psychoanalytic colleagues called Bowlby a behaviorist: "for to have a deep attachment for a person (or a place or thing) is to have taken them as the terminating object of our instinctual responses" (Bowlby, 1959, p. 13). The oddity of this statement derives from mixing, in the same sentence, experiential language (to have a deep attachment) with explanatory language representing an external observer's point of view (the attachment figure as the terminating object).

In this paper, Bowlby also took issue with Freud's claim that maternal overgratification is a danger in infancy. Freud failed to realize, says Bowlby, that maternal pseudoaffection and overprotection may derive from a mother's overcompensation for unconscious hostility. In Bowlby's view, excessive separation anxiety is due to adverse family experiences—such as repeated threats of abandonment or rejection by parents—or to a parent's or sibling's illness or death for which the child feels responsible.

Bowlby also pointed out that, in some cases, separation anxiety can be excessively low or be altogether absent, giving an erroneous impression of maturity. He attributes pseudoindependence under these conditions to defensive processes. A well-loved child, he claims, is quite likely to protest separation from parents but will later develop more self-reliance. These ideas reemerged later in Ainsworth's classifications of ambivalent, avoidant, and secure patterns of infant–mother attachment (Ainsworth, Blehar, Waters, & Wall, 1978).

"Grief and Mourning in Infancy and Early Childhood"

In the third, most controversial paper, Bowlby (1960) questioned Anna Freud's contention that bereaved infants cannot mourn because of insufficient ego development and therefore experience nothing more than brief bouts of separation anxiety if an adequate substitute caregiver is available. In contrast, Bowlby (citing Marris, 1958) claimed that grief and mourning processes in children and adults appear whenever attachment behaviors are activated but the attachment figure continues to be unavailable. He also suggested that an inability to form deep relationships with others may result when the succession of substitutes is too frequent.

As with the first paper, this paper also drew strong objections from many members of the British Psychoanalytic Society. One analyst is said to have exclaimed: "Bowlby? Give me Barrabas" (Grosskurth, 1987). Controversy also accompanied the published version of this paper in *The Psychoanalytic Study of the Child*. Unbeknownst to Bowlby, rejoinders had been invited from Anna Freud (1960), Max Schur (1960), and René Spitz (1960), all of whom protested various aspects of Bowlby's revision of Freudian theory. Spitz ended his rejoinder by saying:

> When submitting new theories we should not violate the principle of parsimony in science by offering hypotheses which in contrast to existing theory becloud the observational facts, are oversimplified, and make no contribution to the better understanding of observed phenomena. (p. 93)

Despite this concerted attack, Bowlby remained a member of the British Psychoanalytic Society for the rest of his life, although he never again used it as a forum for discussing his ideas. At a meeting of the society in memory of John Bowlby, Eric Rayner (1991) expressed his regret at this turn of events:

> What seems wrong is when a theorist extols his own view by rubbishing others; Bowlby received this treatment. . . . Our therapeutic frame of mind is altered by theory. John Bowlby was a great alterer of frames of mind.

Bowlby's controversial paper on mourning attracted the attention of Colin Parkes, now well known for his research on adult bereavement. Parkes saw the relevance of Bowlby's and Robertson's work on mourning in infancy and childhood for gaining insight into the process of adult grief. On joining Bowlby's research unit at the Tavistock Institute in 1962, Parkes set out to study a nonclinical group of widows in their homes to chart the course of normal adult grief, about which little was known at the time. The findings led to a joint paper with Bowlby (Bowlby & Parkes, 1970) in which the phases of separation response delineated by Robertson for young children were elaborated into four phases of grief during adult life: (a) numbness, (b) yearning and protest, (c) disorganization and despair, and (d) reorganization (see also Parkes, 1972).

Before the publication of the 1970 paper, Parkes had visited Elizabeth Kubler-Ross in Chicago, who was then gathering data for her influential book *On Death and Dying* (1970). The phases of dying described in her book (denial, anger, bargaining, depression, and acceptance) owe much to Bowlby's and Robertson's thinking. Bowlby also introduced Parkes to the founder of the modern hospice movement, Cicely Saunders. Saunders and Parkes used attachment theory and research in developing programs for the emotional care of the dying and bereaved. What they found particularly helpful in countering negative attitudes to the dying and bereaved was the concept of grief as a process toward attaining a new identity, rather than as a state (Parkes, personal communication, November 1989).

The First Empirical Study of Attachment: Infancy in Uganda

Let us now return to Mary Ainsworth's work. In late 1953, she had left the Tavistock Clinic, obviously quite familiar with Bowlby's thinking about ethology but not convinced of its value for understanding infant–mother attachment. The Ainsworths were headed for Uganda, where Leonard Ainsworth had obtained a position at the East African Institute of Social Research at Kampala. With help from the same institute, Mary Ainsworth was able to scrape together funds for an observational study, but not before writing Bowlby a letter in which she called for empirical validation of his ethological notions (Ainsworth, January 1992, personal communication).

Inspired by her analyses of Robertson's data, Ainsworth had initially planned an investigation of toddlers' separation responses during weaning, but it soon became obvious that the old tradition of sending the child away "to forget the breast" had broken down. She therefore decided to switch gears and observe the development of infant–mother attachment.

As soon as she began her data collection, Ainsworth was struck by the pertinence of Bowlby's ideas. Hence, the first study of infant–mother attachment from an ethological perspective was undertaken several years before the publication of the three seminal papers in which Bowlby (1958, 1959, 1960) laid out attachment theory.

Ainsworth recruited 26 families with unweaned babies (ages 1–24 months) whom she observed every 2 weeks for 2 hours per visit over a period of up to 9 months. Visits (with an interpreter) took place in the family living room, where Ganda women generally entertain in the afternoon. Ainsworth was particularly interested in determining the onset of proximity-promoting signals and behaviors, noting carefully when these signals and behaviors became preferentially directed toward the mother.

On leaving Uganda in 1955, the Ainsworths moved to Baltimore, where Mary Ainsworth began work as a diagnostician and part-time clinician at the Sheppard and Enoch Pratt Hospital, further consolidating her already considerable assessment skills. At the same time, she taught clinical and developmental courses at the Johns Hopkins University, where she was initially hired as a lecturer. Because of her involvement in diagnostic work and teaching, the data from the Ganda project lay fallow for several years.

REFINING ATTACHMENT THEORY AND RESEARCH: BOWLBY AND AINSWORTH

Before the publication of "The Nature of the Child's Tie to His Mother" in 1958, Mary Ainsworth received a preprint of the paper from John Bowlby. This event led Bowlby and Ainsworth to renew their close intellectual collaboration. Ainsworth's subsequent analysis of data from her Ganda project (Ainsworth 1963, 1967) influenced and was influenced by Bowlby's reformulation of attachment theory (published in 1969). In this sharing of ideas, Ainsworth's theoretical contribution to Bowlby's presentation of the ontogeny of human attachment cannot be overestimated.

Findings From Ainsworth's Ganda Project

The Ganda data (Ainsworth, 1963, 1967) were a rich source for the study of individual differences in the quality of mother–infant interaction, the topic that Bowlby had earlier left aside as too difficult to study. Of special note, in light of Ainsworth's future work, was an evaluation of maternal sensitivity to infant signals, derived from interview data. Mothers who were excellent informants and who provided much spontaneous detail were rated as highly sensitive, in contrast to other mothers who seemed imperceptive of the nuances of infant behavior. Three infant attachment patterns were observed: Securely attached infants cried little and seemed content to explore in the presence of mother; insecurely attached infants cried frequently, even when held by their mothers, and explored little; and not-yet attached infants manifested no differential behavior to the mother.

It turned out that secure attachment was significantly correlated with maternal sensitivity. Babies of sensitive mothers tended to be securely attached, whereas babies of less sensitive mothers were more likely to be classified as insecure. Mothers' enjoyment of breast-feeding also correlated with infant security. These findings foreshadow some of Ainsworth's later work, although the measures are not yet as sophisticated as those developed for subsequent studies.

Ainsworth presented her initial findings from the Ganda project at meetings of the Tavistock Study Group organized by Bowlby during the 1960s (Ainsworth, 1963). Participants invited to these influential gatherings included many now-eminent infant researchers of diverse theoretical backgrounds (in addition to Mary Ainsworth, there were Genevieve Appell, Miriam David, Jacob Gewirtz, Hanus Papousek, Heinz Prechtl, Harriet Rheingold, Henry Ricciuti, Louis Sander, and Peter Wolff), as well as renowned animal researchers such as Harry Harlow, Robert Hinde, Charles Kaufmann, Jay Rosenblatt, and Thelma Rowell. Their lively discussions and ensuing studies contributed much to the developing field of infant social development in general. Importantly for Bowlby, they also enriched his ongoing elaboration of attachment theory. Bowlby had always believed that he had much to gain from bringing together researchers with different theoretical backgrounds (e.g., learning theory, psychoanalysis, and ethology), whether or not they agreed with his theoretical position. Proceedings of these fruitful meetings were published in four volumes entitled *Determinants of Infant Behaviour* (1961, 1963, 1965, and 1969, edited by Brian Foss).

The Baltimore Project

In 1963, while still pondering the data from the Ganda study, Mary Ainsworth embarked on a second observational project whose thoroughness no researcher has since equalled. Again, she opted for naturalistic observations, but with interviews playing a somewhat lesser role. The 26 participating Baltimore families were recruited before their babies were born, with 18 home visits beginning in the baby's first month and ending at 54 weeks of age. Each visit lasted 4 hours to make sure that mothers would feel comfortable enough to follow their normal routine, resulting in approximately 72 hours of data collection per family.

Raw data took the form of narrative reports, jotted down in personal shorthand, marked in 5-minute intervals, and later dictated into a tape recorder for transcription. Typed narratives from all visits for each quarter of the first year of life were grouped together for purposes of analysis.

A unique (at the time) aspect of Ainsworth's methodology was the emphasis on meaningful behavioral patterns in context, rather than on frequency counts of specific behaviors. This approach had roots in her dissertation work, in which she classified patterns of familial and extrafamilial dependent and independent security, in her expertise with the Rorschach test, and in her work at the Tavistock Institute with Bowlby and Robertson.

Close examination of the narratives revealed the emergence of characteristic mother–infant interaction patterns during the first 3 months (see Ainsworth et al., 1978; see also Ainsworth, 1982, 1983). Separate analyses were conducted on feeding situations (Ainsworth & Bell, 1969), mother–infant face-to-face interaction (Blehar, Lieberman, & Ainsworth, 1977), crying (Bell & Ainsworth, 1972), infant greeting and following (Stayton & Ainsworth, 1973), the attachment–exploration balance (Ainsworth, Bell, & Stayton, 1971), obedience (Stayton, Hogan, & Ainsworth, 1973), close bodily contact (Ainsworth, Bell, Blehar, & Main, 1971), approach behavior (Tracy, Lamb, & Ainsworth, 1976), and affectionate contact (Tracy & Ainsworth, 1981).

Striking individual differences were observed in how sensitively, appropriately, and promptly mothers responded to their infants' signals. For some mother–infant pairs, feeding was an occasion for smooth cooperation. Other mothers had difficulties in adjusting their pacing and behavior to the baby's cues. In response, their babies tended to struggle, choke, and spit up, hardly the sensuous oral experience Freud had had in mind. Similar distinctive patterns were observed in face-to-face interactions between mother and infant during the period from 6 to 15 weeks (Blehar et al., 1977). When mothers meshed their own playful behavior with that of their babies, infants responded with joyful bouncing, smiling, and vocalizing. However, when mothers initiated face-to-face interactions silently and with an unsmiling expression, ensuing interactions were muted and brief. Findings on close bodily contact resembled those on feeding and face-to-face interaction, as did those on crying. There were enormous variations in how many crying episodes a mother ignored and how long she let the baby cry. In countering those who argued that maternal responsiveness might lead to "spoiling," Bell and Ainsworth (1972) concluded that "an infant whose mother's responsiveness helps him to achieve his ends develops confidence in his own ability to control what happens to him" (p. 1188).

Maternal sensitivity in the first quarter was associated with more harmonious mother–infant relationships in the fourth quarter. Babies whose mothers had been highly responsive to crying during the early months now tended to cry less, relying for communication on facial expressions, gestures, and vocalizations (Bell & Ainsworth, 1972). Similarly, infants whose mothers had provided much tender holding during the first quarter sought contact less often during the fourth quarter, but when contact occurred, it was rated as more satisfying and affectionate (Ainsworth, Bell, Blehar, et al., 1971). Ainsworth (Ainsworth et al., 1978) explains these findings by recourse to infants' expectations, based on prior satisfying or rejecting experiences with mother.

All first-quarter interactive patterns were also related to infant behavior in a laboratory procedure known as the Strange Situation (Ainsworth & Wittig, 1969). This initially very controversial laboratory procedure for 1-year-olds was originally designed to examine the balance of attachment and exploratory behaviors under conditions of low and high stress, a topic in which Harlow (1961) had aroused Ainsworth's interest during meetings of the Tavistock group, but which also reminded her of an earlier study by Arsenian (1943) on young children in an insecure situation and of her dissertation work on security theory.

The Strange Situation is a 20-minute miniature drama with eight episodes. Mother and infant are introduced to a laboratory playroom, where they are later joined by an unfamiliar woman. While the stranger plays with the baby, the mother leaves briefly and then returns. A second separation ensues during which the baby is completely alone. Finally, the stranger and then the mother return.

As expected, Ainsworth found that infants explored the playroom and toys more vigorously in the presence of their mothers than after a stranger entered or while the mother was absent (Ainsworth & Bell, 1970). Although these results were theoretically interesting, Ainsworth became much more intrigued with unexpected patterns of infant reunion behaviors, which reminded her of responses Robertson had documented in children exposed to prolonged separations, and about which Bowlby (1959) had theorized in his paper on separation.

A few of the 1-year-olds from the Baltimore study were surprisingly angry when the mother returned after a 3-minute (or shorter) separation. They cried and wanted contact but would not simply cuddle or "sink in" when picked up by the returning mother. Instead, they showed their ambivalence by kicking or swiping at her. Another group of children seemed to snub or avoid the mother on reunion, even though they had often searched for her while she was gone. Analyses of home data revealed that those infants who had been ambivalent toward or avoidant of the mother on reunion in the Strange Situation had a less harmonious relationship with her at home than those (a majority) who sought proximity, interaction, or contact on reunion (Ainsworth, Bell, & Stayton, 1974). Thus originated the well-known Strange Situation classification system (Ainsworth et al., 1978), which, to Ainsworth's chagrin, has stolen the limelight from her observational findings of naturalistic mother–infant interaction patterns at home.

The First Volume in the Attachment Trilogy: Attachment and Ethology

While Ainsworth wrote up the findings from her Ganda study for *Infancy in Uganda* (1967) and was engaged in collecting data for the Baltimore project, Bowlby worked on the first volume of the attachment trilogy,

Attachment (1969). When he began this enterprise in 1962, the plan had been for a single book. However, as he explains in the preface: "As my study of theory progressed it was gradually borne in upon me that the field I had set out to plough so light-heartedly was no less than the one Freud had started tilling sixty years earlier." In short, Bowlby realized that he had to develop a new theory of motivation and behavior control, built on up-to-date science rather than the outdated psychic energy model espoused by Freud.

In the first half of *Attachment*, Bowlby lays the groundwork for such a theory, taking pains to document each important statement with available research findings. He begins by noting that organisms at different levels of the phylogenetic scale regulate instinctive behavior in distinct ways, ranging from primitive reflexlike "fixed action patterns" to complex plan hierarchies with subgoals. In the most complex organisms, instinctive behaviors may be "goal-corrected" with continual on-course adjustments (such as a bird of prey adjusting its flight to the movements of the prey). The concept of cybernetically controlled behavioral systems organized as plan hierarchies (Miller, Galanter, & Pribram, 1960) thus came to replace Freud's concept of drive and instinct. Behaviors regulated by such systems need not be rigidly innate, but—depending on the organism—can adapt in greater or lesser degrees to changes in environmental circumstances, provided that these do not deviate too much from the organism's environment of evolutionary adaptedness. Such flexible organisms pay a price, however, because adaptable behavioral systems can more easily be subverted from their optimal path of development. For humans, Bowlby speculates, the environment of evolutionary adaptedness probably resembles that of present-day hunter–gatherer societies.

The ultimate functions of behavioral systems controlling attachment, parenting, mating, feeding, and exploration are survival and procreation. In some cases, the predictable outcome of system activation is a time-limited behavior (such as food intake); in others it is the time-extended maintenance of an organism in a particular relation to its environment (e.g., within its own territory or in proximity to particular companions).

Complex behavioral systems of the kind proposed by Bowlby can work with foresight in organisms that have evolved an ability to construct internal working models of the environment and of their own actions in it (a concept taken over from Craik, 1943, through the writings of the biologist J. Z. Young, 1964). The more adequate an organism's internal working model, the more accurately the organism can predict the future. However, adds Bowlby, if working models of the environment and self are out of date or are only half revised after drastic environmental change, pathological functioning may ensue. He speculates that useful model revision, extension, and consistency checking may require conscious processing of model content. In humans, communicative processes—initially limited to emotional or gestural signaling and later including language—also permit the intersubjective sharing of model content. On an intrapsychic level, the same processes are useful for self-regulation and behavioral priority setting.

In mammals and birds, behavioral systems tend to become organized during specific sensitive developmental periods. As initial reflexlike behavior chains come under more complex, cybernetically controlled organization, the range of stimuli that can activate them also becomes more restricted. This is the case in imprinting, broadly defined as the restriction of specific instinctive behaviors to particular individuals or groups of individuals during sensitive phases of development, as in filial, parental, and sexual imprinting.

Having laid out this general theory of motivation and behavior regulation in the first half of the volume, Bowlby goes on, in the second half, to apply these ideas to the specific domain of infant–mother attachment. He defines attachment behavior as behavior that has proximity to an attachment figure as a predictable outcome and whose evolutionary function is protection of the infant from danger, insisting that attachment has its own motivation and is in no way derived from systems subserving mating and feeding.

Although human infants initially direct proximity-promoting signals fairly indiscriminately to all caregivers, these behaviors become increasingly focused on those primary figures who are responsive to the infant's crying and who engage the infant in social interaction (Schaffer & Emerson, 1964). Once attached, locomotor infants are able to use the attachment figure as a secure base for exploration of the environment and as a safe haven to which to return for reassurance (Ainsworth, 1967; Schaffer & Emerson, 1964). How effectively the attachment figure can serve in these roles depends on the quality of social interaction—especially the attachment figure's sensitivity to the infant's signals—although child factors also play a role. Building on Ainsworth's Ganda study (1967) and preliminary findings from her Baltimore project, Bowlby (1969) comments that

> when interaction between a couple runs smoothly, each party manifests intense pleasure in the other's company and especially in the other's expression of affection. Conversely, whenever interaction results in persistent conflict each party is likely on occasion to exhibit intense anxiety or unhappiness, especially when the other is rejecting. . . . Proximity and affectionate interchange are appraised and felt as pleasurable by both, whereas distance and expressions of rejection are appraised as disagreeable or painful by both. (p. 242)

During the preschool years, the attachment behavioral system, always complementary to the parental caregiving system, undergoes further reorganization as the child attains growing insight into the attachment figure's motives and plans. Bowlby refers to this stage as *goal-corrected partnership*.

However, in emphasizing infant initiative and sensitive maternal responding, Bowlby's (1951) earlier theorizing on the mother as the child's ego and superego was regrettably lost.

Consolidation

The publication of the first volume of the attachment trilogy in 1969 coincided with the appearance in print of initial findings from Ainsworth's Baltimore project (reviewed earlier). However, many investigators strongly contested Ainsworth's claims regarding the meaning of Strange Situation behavior, often because they failed to note that Strange Situation classifications had been validated against extensive home observations. Some interpreted avoidant infants' behavior as independence. The controversy lessened somewhat after the publication of *Patterns of Attachment* (Ainsworth et al., 1978), which drew together the results from the Baltimore project and presented findings from other laboratories on the sequelae of attachment classifications in toddlerhood and early childhood (e.g., Main, 1973; Matas, Arend, & Sroufe, 1978).

During this period, many of Ainsworth's graduate students began to publish their own work. Silvia Bell (1970) examined the relationship between object permanence and attachment. Mary Main (1973) studied secure and insecure toddlers' capacity to become invested in play activities and problem solving. Mary Blehar (1974) undertook the first study of attachment and nonmaternal care, and Alicia Lieberman (1977) investigated attachment and peer relationships in preschoolers. Mary Ainsworth's influence is also evident in the fact that many Johns Hopkins undergraduate students who had helped with the analysis of data from the Baltimore project later produced innovative dissertations on attachment-related topics at their respective graduate institutions. Among these students were Robert Marvin (1972, 1977), who wrote on the goal-corrected partnership; Milton Kotelchuck (1972), who studied father attachment; Mark Cummings (1980), who investigated attachment and day care; Mark Greenberg (Greenberg & Marvin, 1979), who examined attachment in deaf children; and Everett Waters (1978), who documented the longitudinal stability of attachment patterns from 12 to 18 months.

Everett Waters's entry into graduate study at the University of Minnesota in 1973 had a profound effect on Alan Sroufe, who had read Mary Ainsworth's (1968) theoretical article about object relations and dependency but had not heard of the Strange Situation or the Baltimore project (Sroufe, personal communication, 1988). Sroufe's contact with Waters led to significant empirical and theoretical collaborations. In 1977, Sroufe and Waters wrote an influential paper that made attachment as an organizational construct accessible to a large audience. At the same time, Sroufe and Egeland, together with many of their students, undertook a large-scale longitudinal study of attachment with an at-risk population (disadvantaged mothers). The Minnesota study, summarized in Sroufe (1983) but still ongoing, stands as the second major longitudinal study of the relationship between quality of caregiving and security of attachment.

Elsewhere across the United States, much time was spent testing the predictive validity of Strange Situation reunion classifications. Many researchers sought to train with Mary Ainsworth or her former students to learn the procedure and classification system. Hundreds of studies using the Strange Situation appeared in print. It often seemed as if attachment and the Strange Situation had become synonymous.

ATTACHMENT THEORY AND MENTAL REPRESENTATION

Separation (Bowlby, 1973) and *Loss* (Bowlby, 1980a), the second and third volumes in Bowlby's attachment trilogy, were slower to make an impact on the field of developmental psychology than the first volume, in part because relevant empirical studies lagged behind. Like *Attachment*, these two volumes cover much more theoretical ground that their titles imply.

Separation

In this book, Bowlby (1973) revises Freud's (1926/1959) theory of signal anxiety, lays out a new approach to Freud's (1923/1961, 1940/1964) motivational theories, and presents an epigenetic model of personality development inspired by Waddington's (1957) theory of developmental pathways.

Elaborating on his seminal 1959 paper, Bowlby notes that two distinct sets of stimuli elicit fear in children: the *presence* of unlearned and later of culturally acquired clues to danger and/or the *absence* of an attachment figure. Although escape from danger and escape to an attachment figure commonly occur together, the two classes of behavior are governed by separate control systems (observable when a ferocious dog comes between a mother and her young child).

Although Bowlby regarded the systems controlling escape and attachment as conceptually distinct, he considers both as members of a larger family of stress-reducing and safety-promoting behavioral systems, whose more general function is that of maintaining an organism within a defined relationship to his or her environment. Rather than striving for stimulus absence, as Freud had suggested, Bowlby posits that humans are motivated to maintain a dynamic balance between familiarity-preserving, stress-reducing behaviors (attachment to protective individuals and to familiar home sites, retreat from the strange and novel) and antithetical exploratory and information-seeking behaviors.

After revising Freud's theories of fear and motivation, Bowlby reexamined Freud's concept of the "inner world" in light of modern cognitive theory. In *Separation*, he expands ideas proposed in *Attachment* by suggesting that, within an individual's internal working model of the world, working models of self and attachment figure are especially salient. These working models, acquired through interpersonal interaction patterns, are complementary. If the attachment figure has acknowledged the infant's needs for comfort and protection while simultaneously respecting the infant's need for independent exploration of the environment, the child is likely to develop an internal working model of self as valued and reliable. Conversely, if the parent has frequently rejected the infant's bids for comfort or for exploration, the child is likely to construct an internal working model of self as unworthy or incompetent. With the aid of working models, children predict the attachment figure's likely behavior and plan their own responses. What type of model they construct is therefore of great consequence.

In *Separation*, Bowlby also elucidates the role of internal working models in the intergenerational transmission of attachment patterns. Individuals who grow up to become relatively stable and self-reliant, he postulates, normally have parents who are supportive when called upon, but who also permit and encourage autonomy. Such parents tend not only to engage in fairly frank communication of their own working models of self, of their child, and of others, but also indicate to the child that these working models are open to questioning and revision. For this reason, says Bowlby, the inheritance of mental health and of ill health through family microculture is no less important, and may well be far more important, than is genetic inheritance (Bowlby, 1973, p. 323).

Loss

In the third volume of the attachment trilogy, Bowlby (1980a) uses information-processing theories to explain the increasing stability of internal working models as well as their defensive distortion. The stability of internal working models derives from two sources: (a) patterns of interacting grow less accessible to awareness as they become habitual and automatic, and (b) dyadic patterns of relating are more resistant to change than individual patterns because of reciprocal expectancies.

Given that old patterns of action and thought guide selective attention and information processing in new situations, some distortion of incoming information is normal and unavoidable. The adequacy of internal working models can be seriously undermined, however, when defensive exclusion of information from awareness interferes with their updating in response to developmental and environmental change.

To explain the workings of defensive processes, Bowlby cites evidence showing that incoming information normally undergoes many stages of processing before reaching awareness (see Dixon, 1971; Erdelyi, 1974). At every stage, some information is retained for further processing and the remainder discarded. That this may happen even after information has already undergone very advanced levels of encoding is shown by dichotic listening studies. In these studies, individuals who are presented with different messages to each ear through headphones are able to selectively attend to one of them. That the unattended message is nevertheless receiving high-level processing becomes obvious when the person becomes alerted to a word of personal significance (e.g., the person's name) that has been inserted into the unattended message.

Bowlby proposes that *defensive* exclusion of information from awareness derives from the same processes as *selective* exclusion, although the motivation for the two types of exclusion differs. Three situations are believed to render children particularly prone to engaging in defensive exclusion: situations that parents do not wish their children to know about even though the children have witnessed them, situations in which the children find the parents' behavior too unbearable to think about, and situations in which children have done or thought about doing something of which they are deeply ashamed.

Although defensive exclusion protects the individual from experiencing unbearable mental pain, confusion, or conflict, it is bound to interfere with the accommodation of internal working models to external reality. Indeed, a number of clinical studies reviewed in *Separation* (e.g., Cain & Fast, 1972) suggest that defensive exclusion leads to a split in internal working models. One set of working models—accessible to awareness and discussion and based on what a child has been told—represents the parent as good and the parent's rejecting behavior as caused by the "badness" of the child. The other model, based on what the child has experienced but defensively excluded from awareness, represents the hated or disappointing side of the parent.

In *Loss*, Bowlby attempts to shed further light on these repressive and dissociative phenomena with the aid of Tulving's (1972) distinction between episodic and semantic memory. According to Tulving, autobiographical experience is encoded in episodic memory, whereas generic propositions are stored in semantic memory, with each memory system possibly using distinct storage mechanisms. Generic knowledge may derive from information supplied by others and from actual experience. Bowlby surmises that severe psychic conflict is likely to arise when the two sources of stored information (generalizations built on actual experience and on communications from others) are highly contradictory. In such cases, defensive exclusion may be brought to bear on episodic memories of actual experience.

According to Bowlby, such processes are especially likely in bereaved children under 3 years of age.

Finally, in *Loss*, Bowlby also considers a more complex related problem, namely, the control of simultaneously active behavioral systems. In *Attachment* and *Separation*, the interplay among behavioral systems was implicitly treated as one of competition, not higher level regulation (see also Bretherton & Ainsworth, 1974). In *Loss*, Bowlby posits an executive structure that takes the place of Freud's (1923/1961) concept of ego. The central nervous system, Bowlby suggests, is organized in a loosely hierarchical way, with an enormous network of two-way communications among subsystems. At the top of the hierarchy, he posits one or perhaps several principal evaluators or controllers, closely linked to long-term memory. Their task is to scan incoming information for relevance. If evaluated as relevant, it may be stored in short-term memory to select aspects thereof for further processing.

Conscious processing is likely to facilitate high-level activities such as categorizing, retrieving, comparing, framing plans, and inspection of overlearned, automated action systems. In a unified personality, Bowlby claims, the principal system or systems can access all memories in whatever type of storage they are held. However, in some cases, the principal system or systems may not be unified or capable of unimpeded intercommunication with all subsystems. In this case, particular behavioral systems may not be activated when appropriate, or signals from these behavioral systems may not become conscious, although fragments of defensively excluded information may at times seep through.

Some of the dissociative or repressive phenomena involved in the deactivation of the attachment system occur during pathological mourning. For example, complete or partial disconnection of an emotional response from its cause is frequent. When the disconnection is only partial, emotional responses may be directed away from the person who caused them to third persons or to the self. Hence, a bereaved person may become morbidly preoccupied with personal reactions and sufferings, rather than attributing his or her feelings to the loss of a close relationship. Similarly, in disordered mourning, a bereaved person's disposition toward compulsive caregiving may derive from the redirection of attachment behavior. The individual may be taking the role of attachment figure instead of seeking care.

Attachment and Therapy

This discussion of defensive processes leads into the topic that preoccupied Bowlby during the last 10 years of his life: the uses of attachment theory in psychotherapy (Bowlby, 1988). Under attachment theory, a major goal in psychotherapy is the reappraisal of inadequate, outdated working models of self in relation to attachment figures, a particularly difficult task if important others, especially parents, have forbidden their review. As psychoanalysts have repeatedly noted, a person with inadequate, rigid working models of attachment relations is likely to inappropriately impose these models on interactions with the therapist (a phenomenon known as *transference*). The joint task of therapist and client is to understand the origins of the client's dysfunctional internal working models of self and attachment figures. Toward this end, the therapist can be most helpful by serving as a reliable, secure base from which an individual can begin the arduous task of exploring and reworking his or her internal working models.

NEW DIRECTIONS

Currently, attachment theory and research are moving forward along several major fronts, inspired by the second and third volumes of Bowlby's attachment trilogy, by methodological advances, and by the infusion into attachment theory of complementary theoretical perspectives.

Attachment and Representation

As a result of Mary Main's Berkeley study (Main, Kaplan, & Cassidy, 1985) and, I think, the publication of the Society for Research in Child Development Monograph, *Growing Points of Attachment Theory and Research* (Bretherton & Waters, 1985), we are now beginning to empirically explore the psychological, internal, or representational aspects of attachment, including the intergenerational transmission of attachment patterns that had been at the center of Bowlby's interests since his beginnings in psychiatry but that are most clearly elaborated in volumes 2 and 3 of the attachment trilogy (see Bretherton, 1987, 1990, 1991).

Interestingly, an additional source of inspiration for the study of internal working models came from attempts to translate Ainsworth's infant–mother attachment patterns into corresponding adult patterns. In the Adult Attachment Interview (George, Kaplan, & Main, 1984; Main & Goldwyn, in press), parents were asked open-ended questions about their attachment relations in childhood and about the influence of these early relations on their own development. Three distinct patterns of responding were identified: *Autonomous-secure* parents gave a clear and coherent account of early attachments (whether these had been satisfying or not); *preoccupied* parents spoke of many conflicted childhood memories about attachment but did not draw them together into an organized, consistent picture; and, finally, *dismissing* parents were characterized by an inability to remember much about attachment relations in childhood. In some of the dismissing interviews, parents' parents were idealized on a general level, but influences of early attachment experiences on later development were denied. Specific memories, when they did occur, suggested episodes of rejection.

Not only did the Adult Attachment Interview classifications correspond to Ainsworth's secure, ambivalent, and avoidant infant patterns at a conceptual level, but adult patterns were also empirically correlated with infant patterns (e.g., a dismissing parent tended to have an avoidant infant; Main & Goldwyn, in press). These findings have since been validated for prenatally administered interviews by Fonagy, Steele, and Steele (1991) and by Ward et al. (1990). Consonant findings were also obtained in a study of young adults in which Adult Attachment Interview classifications were correlated with peer reports (Kobak & Sceery, 1988).

In addition, representational measures of attachment have been devised for use with children. A pictorial separation anxiety test for adolescents, developed by Hansburg (1972), was adapted for younger children by Klagsbrun and Bowlby (1976) and more recently revised and validated against observed attachment patterns by Kaplan (1984) and Slough and Greenberg (1991). Likewise, attachment-based doll-story completion tasks for preschoolers were validated against behavioral measures by Bretherton, Ridgeway, and Cassidy (1990) and Cassidy (1988). In these tests, emotionally open responding tended to be associated with secure attachment classifications or related behaviors.

Finally, several authors have created interviews that examine attachment from the parental as opposed to the filial perspective (e.g., Bretherton, Biringen, Ridgeway, Maslin, & Sherman, 1989; George & Solomon, 1989). In addition, Waters and Deane (1985) developed a Q sort that can be used to assess a mother's internal working models of her child's attachment to her.

Attachment Across the Life Span

A related topic, attachment relationships between adults, began in the early 1970s, with studies of adult bereavement (Bowlby & Parkes, 1970; Parkes, 1972) and marital separation (Weiss, 1973, 1977). More recently, interest in adult attachments has broadened to encompass marital relationships (Weiss, 1982, 1991) and has taken a further upsurge with work by Shaver and Hazan (1988), who translated Ainsworth's infant attachment patterns into adult patterns, pointing out that adults who describe themselves as secure, avoidant, or ambivalent with respect to romantic relationships report differing patterns of parent–child relationships in their families of origin. Finally, Cicirelli (1989, 1991) has applied attachment theory to the study of middle-aged siblings and their elderly parents. Much future work will be needed to delineate more fully the distinct qualities of child–adult, child–child, and adult–adult attachment relationships (see

Ainsworth, 1989), as well as their interplay within the family system, a task begun by Byng-Hall (1985) and Marvin and Stewart (1990).

Attachment and Developmental Psychopathology

Attachment theory and research are also making a notable impact on the emerging field of developmental psychopathology (Sroufe, 1988), with longitudinal attachment-based studies of families with depression (Radke-Yarrow, Cummings, Kuczinsky, & Chapman, 1985), of families with maltreatment (e.g., Cicchetti & Barnett, 1991; Crittenden, 1983; Schneider-Rosen, Braunwald, Carlson, & Cicchetti, 1985), and of clinical interventions in families with low social support (Lieberman & Pawl, 1988; Spieker & Booth, 1988) and with behavior-problem children (Greenberg & Speltz, 1988). Much of this work is represented in a volume on clinical implications of attachment (Belsky & Nezworski, 1988). These topics hark back to Bowlby's seminal ideas from the 1930s, but they have been greatly enriched by Mary Ainsworth's notions on the origins of individual differences of attachment patterns.

The Ecology of Attachment

Although we have made progress in examining mother–child attachment, much work needs to be done with respect to studying attachment in the microsystem of family relationships (Bronfenbrenner, 1979). Despite studies by Belsky, Gilstrap, and Rovine (1984), Lamb (1978), and Parke and Tinsley (1987) that show fathers to be competent, if sometimes less than fully participant attachment figures, we still have much to learn regarding father attachment. Another important topic, sibling attachment, has been tackled by a few researchers (e.g., Stewart & Marvin, 1984; Teti & Ablard, 1989), but triadic studies of attachment relationships (modeled on Dunn, 1988) are sorely lacking. Especially crucial are attachment-theoretic studies of loyalty conflicts, alliances by a dyad vis-à-vis a third family member, and enmeshment of a child in the spousal dyad, as exemplified in a report by Fish, Belsky, and Youngblade (1991) in which insecure attachment in infancy was associated with inappropriate involvement in spousal decision making at 4 years of age. Finally, the interrelations of child temperament and developing attachment relationships with other family members remain conceptually unclear despite intensive research efforts (Belsky & Rovine, 1987; Sroufe, 1985).

The documentation of family and social network factors as they affect attachment relations (e.g., Belsky & Isabella, 1988; Belsky, Rovine, & Taylor, 1984) has been more successful. In the Pennsylvania project, attachment quality at the end of the first year was predictable from relative changes in levels of marital satisfaction after the child's birth, as well as from parental satisfaction with social support, but not its frequency.

An ecological perspective also calls for an examination of issues related to dual-worker families, especially in view of the continued sex/gender differentiation of parenting. Some feminist theorists have interpreted attachment theory as supporting the traditional view of women as primary caregivers (Chodorow, 1978; Johnson, 1988). This is not strictly justified, because attachment theory does not specify that caregiving must be done by mothers or be restricted to females (Marris, 1982). Most central to healthy development, according to attachment theory, is infants' need for a committed caregiving relationship with one or a few adult figures. Although the majority of attachment studies have focused on mothers because mothers tend to fill this role most often, we do have evidence that infants can be attached to a hierarchy of figures, including fathers, grandparents, and siblings (Schaffer & Emerson, 1964), as well as to day-care providers (Howes, Rodning, Galuzzo, & Myers, 1988). However, our knowledge about the range of societal options for successfully sharing the task of bringing up children is still woefully inadequate. The recent spate of studies documenting an increased risk of insecure attachment if day care begins in the first year and is extensive in duration (Belsky & Rovine, 1988; Belsky & Braungart, 1991) is worrisome and needs resolution. Cross-cultural studies of attachment and nonparental care in countries such as Sweden and Israel may ultimately provide more reliable answers.

Cross-Cultural Studies

Moving from family and other social networks to the larger societal matrix, we find that studies of Strange Situation classifications in other cultures have sparked a lively debate on their universal versus culture-specific meaning. In a north German study, avoidant classifications were overrepresented (Grossmann, Grossmann, Spangler, Suess, & Unzner, 1985), whereas ambivalent classifications were more frequent than expected in Israeli kibbutzim (Sagi et al., 1985) and in Japan (Miyake, Chen, & Campos, 1985).

Initially, these findings were interpreted in purely cultural terms. Thus, Grossmann et al. (1985) proposed that the high incidence of avoidant infants in Germany should be attributed not to parental rejection, but rather to a greater parental push toward infants' independence. Similarly, the high frequency of ambivalent classifications observed in Israeli kibbutzim and Japan was attributed to underexposure to strangers (Miyake et al., 1985; Sagi et al., 1985). Though persuasive on the surface, these explanations were not based on systematic assessments of parental beliefs and culturally guided practices.

More recently, van Ijzendoorn and Kroonenberg (1988) examined the frequency distributions of Strange Situation classifications from over a thousand U.S. and cross-national studies, pointing out that valid conclusions about cross-national differences should not be drawn from single samples. In addition, intercorrelational patterns of home and Strange Situation behavior in north Germany (Grossmann et al., 1985) closely resembled those in the Ainsworth's Baltimore study, at least in part undermining a purely cultural interpretation. Likewise, Sagi, Aviezer, Mayseless, Donnell, and Joels (1991) attribute the abundance of ambivalent classifications to specific nighttime caregiving arrangements in the kibbutzim they studied, rather than fewer experiences with strangers. Taken in combination, these findings suggest that Strange Situation classifications, and hence the concept of parental sensitivity, may have more cross-cultural validity in industrialized nations than was initially believed, but the issue is by no means resolved.

Systematic work on the more fascinating topic of how different cultures—especially non-Western cultures—fit attachment behaviors and relationships into their overall social organization has barely begun. There are, however, some tantalizing hints in the ethnographic literature (see Bretherton, 1985, for a review). For example, the Micronesian society of Tikopia (Firth, 1936) deliberately fosters attachment between an infant and its maternal uncle by prescribing face-to-face talk with the infant on a regular basis. This maternal uncle is destined to play an important quasi-parental role in the life of the child. Along somewhat different lines, Balinese mothers control their infants' exploratory behavior by using fake fear expressions to bring the infants back into close proximity to them (Bateson & Mead, 1942). In both cultures, a biological system is molded to a particular society's purposes (by fostering specific relationships or controlling exploration).

A recent study of parent–infant attachment among the Efe begins to provide systematic information in this area. The Efe, a seminomadic people, live in the African rain forest, subsisting on foraging, horticulture, and hunting (Tronick, Winn, & Morelli, 1985). Young Efe infants receive more care (including nursing) from other adult women than from their own mother, except at night. Despite this multiple mothering system, by 6 months, infants begin to insist on a more focalized relationship with their own mothers, although other female caregivers continue to play a significant role. Tronick et al. attributed Efe practices to their living arrangements, with closely spaced dwellings that offer little privacy and that make cooperation and sharing highly valued behaviors. In sum, attachment behavior is heavily overlain with cultural prescriptions, even in a society that much more closely resembles the conditions of human evolution than our own. To better explore such cultural variations in attachment organization, attachment researchers need to develop ecologically valid, theory-driven measures, tailored to specific cultures and based on a deeper knowledge of parents' and children's culture-specific folk theories about family relationships and attachment.

Attachment and Public Policy

Cultural differences in the regulation of attachment behaviors raise important questions about the value diverse societies place on attachment relations. In a thought-provoking chapter, Marris (1991) points to the fundamental tension between the desire to create a secure and predictable social order and the desire to maximize one's own opportunities at the expense of others. A good society, according to Marris, would be one which, as far as is humanly possible, minimizes disruptive events, protects each child's experience of attachment from harm, and supports family coping. Yet, in order to control uncertainty, individuals and families are tempted to achieve certainty at the expense of others (i.e., by imposing a greater burden of uncertainty on them or by providing fewer material and social resources). When powerful groups in society promote their own control over life circumstances by subordinating and marginalizing others, they make it less possible for these groups to offer and experience security in their own families. Valuing of attachment relations thus has public policy and moral implications for society, not just psychological implications for attachment dyads. This brings me back to one of Bowlby's early statements: "If a community values its children it must cherish their parents" (Bowlby, 1951, p. 84).

CHALLENGING TASKS FOR ATTACHMENT THEORY

In the preceding section, I have outlined the many new directions into which attachment research is branching out. It is difficult to predict which of these efforts will be most fruitful. No doubt, additions, revisions, and challenges to the theory will continue to arise out of future empirical studies. In this final section, however, I would like to focus briefly on some of the theoretical tasks that lie ahead. The idea that human motivation derives from an interplay of familiarity- and novelty-seeking systems needs further exploration, as does the notion that the human personality can be conceptualized as a hierarchy of interlinked systems. New theoretical treatments of defensive processes in the construction of internal working models of attachment need to be worked out in relation to insights from representational theories and research, and clinical attachment theory requires the development of an experiential language akin to that used by other psychoanalytic theories of interpersonal relatedness, such as Winnicott (1965) and Sullivan (1953). Most important, in my view, is that the development of internal working models of self and other within-attachment relations should be studied in conjunction with new approaches to the "dialogic" or "narrative" self, integrating the mental health perspective of attachment theory with the perspective of theorists interested in the social construction of reality (Hermans, Kempen, & van Loon, 1992).

These theoretical developments must go hand in hand or be followed by new methodological developments. Without Mary Ainsworth's work on patterns of attachment in the Strange Situation and Mary Main's Adult Attachment Interview that built on them, Bowlby's theoretical contributions to developmental and clinical psychology would not have had their current influence. I predict that, in the future, attachment theory may provide the underpinnings of a more general theory of personality organization and relationship development. Such a theory would build on, but also go beyond, Bowlby's reworking of Freud's ideas on motivation, emotion, and development.

In formulating the basic tenets of attachment theory, Bowlby's strategy was, wherever possible, to meticulously test intuitive hunches against available empirical findings and concepts from related domains, thus keeping the theory open to change. In his last work—a biography of Charles Darwin—Bowlby may have been talking about himself when he said of Darwin:

> Since causes are never manifest, the only way of proceeding is to propose a plausible theory and then test its explanatory powers against further evidence, and in comparison with the power of rival theories. . . . Since most theories prove to be untenable, advancing them is a hazardous business and requires courage, a courage Darwin never lacked. (Bowlby, 1991, p. 412)

Bowlby and Ainsworth, too, did not lack that courage. To explore the full future potential of attachment theory, others will need to exercise similar courage in refining, extending, and challenging it.

REFERENCES

Ainsworth, M. D. S. (1963). The development of infant–mother interaction among the Ganda. In B. M. Foss (Ed.), *Determinants of infant behavior* (pp. 67–104). New York: Wiley.

Ainsworth, M. D. S. (1967). *Infancy in Uganda: Infant care and the growth of love.* Baltimore: Johns Hopkins University Press.

Ainsworth, M. D. S. (1968). Object relations, dependency, and attachment: A theoretical review of the infant–mother relationship. *Child Development, 40,* 969–1025.

Ainsworth, M. D. S. (1974). *Citation for the G. Stanley Hall Award to John Bowlby.* Unpublished manuscript.

Ainsworth, M. D. S. (1982). Attachment: Retrospect and prospect. In C. M. Parkes & J. Stevenson-Hinde (Eds.), *The place of attachment in human behavior* (pp. 3–30). New York: Basic Books.

Ainsworth, M. D. S. (1983). A sketch of a career. In A. N. O'Connoll & N. F. Russo (Eds.), *Models of achievement: Reflections of eminent women in psychology* (pp. 200–219). New York: Columbia University Press.

Ainsworth, M. D. S. (1989). Attachments beyond infancy. *American Psychologist, 44*, 709–716.

Ainsworth, M. D. S., & Bell, S. M. (1969). Some contemporary patterns in the feeding situation. In A. Ambrose (Ed.), *Stimulation in early infancy* (pp. 133–170). London: Academic Press.

Ainsworth, M. D. S., & Bell, S. M. (1970). Attachment, exploration, and separation: Illustrated by the behavior of one-year-olds in a strange situation. *Child Development, 41*, 49–67.

Ainsworth, M. D. S., Bell, S. M., Blehar, M. C., & Main, M. (1971, April). *Physical contact: A study of infant responsiveness and its relation to maternal handling.* Paper presented at the biennial meeting of the Society for Research in Child Development, Minneapolis, MN.

Ainsworth, M. D. S., Bell, S. M., & Stayton, D. J. (1971). Individual differences in Strange Situation behavior of one-year-olds. In H. R. Schaffer (Ed.), *The origins of human social relations* (pp. 17–57). London: Academic Press.

Ainsworth, M. D. S., Bell, S. M., & Stayton, D. (1974). Infant–mother attachment and social development. In M. P. Richards (Ed.), *The introduction of the child into a social world* (pp. 99–135). London: Cambridge University Press.

Ainsworth, M. D. S., Blehar, M. C., Waters, E., & Wall, S. (1978). *Patterns of attachment: A psychological study of the strange situation.* Hillsdale, NJ: Erlbaum.

Ainsworth, M. D. S., & Bowlby, J. (1991). An ethological approach to personality development. *American Psychologist, 46*, 331–341.

Ainsworth, M. D. S., & Wittig, B. A. (1969). Attachment and the exploratory behaviour of one-year-olds in a strange situation. In B. M. Foss (Ed.), *Determinants of infant behaviour* (Vol. 4, pp. 113–136). London: Methuen.

Ambrose, J. A. (1961). *The development of the smiling response in early human infancy: An experimental and theoretical study of their course and significance.* Unpublished doctoral dissertation, University of London.

Arsenian, J. M. (1943). Young children in an insecure situation. *Journal of Abnormal and Social Psychology, 38*, 225–229.

Bateson, G., & Mead, M. (1942). *Balinese character: A photographic analysis.* New York: New York Academy of Sciences.

Bell, S. M. (1970). The development of the concept of the object as related to infant–mother attachment. *Child Development, 41*, 291–311.

Bell, S. M., & Ainsworth, M. D. S. (1972). Infant crying and maternal responsiveness. *Child Development, 43,* 1171–1190.

Belsky, J., & Braungart, J. M. (1991). Are insecure–avoidant infants with extensive day-care experience less stressed by and more independent in the
Strange Situation? *Child Development, 62,* 567–571.

Belsky, J., Gilstrap, B., & Rovine, M. (1984). The Pennsylvania Infant and Family
Development Project, I: Stability and change in mother–infant and father–
infant interaction in a family setting at one, three, and nine months. *Child
Development, 55,* 692–705.

Belsky, J., & Isabella, R. (1988). Maternal, infant, and social-contextual determinants of attachment security. In J. Belsky & T. Nezworski (Eds.), *Clinical
implications of attachment* (pp. 41–94). Hillsdale, NJ: Erlbaum.

Belsky, J., & Nezworski (1988). *Clinical implications of attachment.* Hillsdale, NJ:
Erlbaum.

Belsky, J., & Rovine, M. J. (1987). Temperament and attachment security in the
Strange Situation: An empirical rapprochement. *Child Development, 58,* 787–
795.

Belsky, J., & Rovine, M. J. (1988). Nonmaternal care in the first year of life and
the security of infant–mother attachment. *Child Development, 59,* 157–167.

Belsky, J., Rovine, M., & Fish, M. (in press). The developing family system. In
M. Gunnar (Ed.), *Systems and development: Minnesota symposia on child development* (Vol. 22). Hillsdale, NJ: Erlbaum.

Belsky, J., Rovine, M., & Taylor, D. (1984). The Pennsylvania Infant and Family
Development Project, II: Origins of individual differences in infant–mother
attachment: Maternal and infant contributions. *Child Development, 55,* 706–
717.

Blatz, W. (1940). *Hostages to peace: Parents and the children of democracy.* New
York: Morrow.

Blehar, M. C. (1974). Anxious attachment and defensive reactions associated with
day care. *Child Development, 45,* 683–692.

Blehar, M. C., Lieberman, A. F., & Ainsworth, M. D. S. (1977). Early face-to-
face interaction and its relation to later infant–mother attachment. *Child
Development, 48,* 182–194.

Bowlby, J. (1940). The influence of early environment in the development of
neurosis and neurotic character. *International Journal of Psycho-Analysis, XXI,*
1–25.

Bowlby, J. (1944). Forty-four juvenile thieves: Their characters and home lives.
International Journal of Psycho-Analysis, XXV, 19–52.

Bowlby, J. (1949). The study and reduction of group tensions in the family. *Human
Relations, 2,* 123–128.

Bowlby, J. (1951). Maternal care and mental health. *World Health Organization Monograph* (Serial No. 2).

Bowlby, J. (1958). The nature of the child's tie to his mother. *International Journal of Psycho-Analysis, XXXIX*, 1–23.

Bowlby, J. (1959). Separation anxiety. *International Journal of Psycho-Analysis, XLI*, 1–25.

Bowlby, J. (1960). Grief and mourning in infancy and early childhood. *The Psychoanalytic Study of the Child, VX*, 3–39.

Bowlby, J. (1962a). *Defences that follow loss: Causation and function*. Unpublished manuscript, Tavistock Child Development Research Unit, London.

Bowlby, J. (1962b). *Loss, detachment and defence*. Unpublished manuscript, Tavistock Child Development Research Unit, London.

Bowlby, J. (1969). *Attachment and loss, Vol. 1: Attachment*. New York: Basic Books.

Bowlby, J. (1973). *Attachment and loss, Vol. 2: Separation*. New York: Basic Books.

Bowlby, J. (1980a). *Attachment and loss, Vol. 3: Loss, sadness and depression*. New York: Basic Books.

Bowlby, J. (1980b). By ethology out of psycho-analysis: An experiment in interbreeding. *Animal Behavior, 28*, 649–656.

Bowlby, J. (1987). [Colloquium presented at the University of Virginia].

Bowlby, J. (1988). *A secure base: Parent–child attachment and healthy human development*. New York: Basic Books.

Bowlby, J. (1991). *Charles Darwin: A new biography*. London: Hutchinson.

Bowlby, J., Ainsworth, M., Boston, M., & Rosenbluth, D. (1956). The effects of mother–child separation: A follow-up study. *British Journal of Medical Psychology, 29*, 211–247.

Bowlby, J., & Parkes, C. M. (1970). Separation and loss within the family. In E. J. Anthony & C. Koupernik (Eds.), *The child in his family: International Yearbook of Child Psychiatry and Allied Professions* (pp. 197–216). New York: Wiley.

Bretherton, I. (1985). Attachment theory: Retrospect and prospect. In I. Bretherton & E. Waters (Eds.), *Growing points of attachment theory and research: Monographs of the Society for Research in Child Development, 50*(1–2, Serial No. 209), 3–35.

Bretherton, I. (1987). New perspectives on attachment relations: Security, communication, and internal working models. In J. Osofsky (Ed.), *Handbook of infant development* (pp. 1061–1100). New York: Wiley.

Bretherton, I. (1990). Open communication and internal working models: Their role in attachment relationships. In R. Thompson (Ed.), *Socioemotional de-*

velopment (*Nebraska Symposium, 1987*). Lincoln, NE: University of Nebraska Press.

Bretherton, I. (1991). Pouring new wine into old bottles: The social self as internal working model. In M. R. Gunnar & L. A. Sroufe (Eds.), *Self processes and development: The Minnesota symposia on child development* (Vol. 23, pp. 1–41). Hillsdale, NJ: Erlbaum.

Bretherton, I., & Ainsworth, M. D. S. (1974). One-year-olds in the Strange Situation. In M. Lewis & L. Rosenblum (Eds.), *The origins of fear* (pp. 134–164). New York: Wiley.

Bretherton, I., Biringen, Z., Ridgeway, D., Maslin, M., & Sherman, M. (1989). Attachment: The parental perspective. *Infant Mental Health Journal* (Special Issue), *10*, 203–220.

Bretherton, I., Ridgeway, D., & Cassidy, J. (1990). Assessing internal working models in the attachment relationship: An attachment story completion task for 3-year-olds. In M. T. Greenberg, D. Cicchetti, & E. M. Cummings (Eds.), *Attachment during the preschool years* (pp. 272–308). Chicago: University of Chicago Press.

Bretherton, I., & Waters, E. (1985). Growing points of attachment theory and research. *Monographs of the Society for Research in Child Development, 50*(1–2, Serial No. 209).

Bronfenbrenner (1979). *The ecology of human development.* Cambridge, MA: Harvard University Press.

Byng-Hall, J. (1985). The family script: A useful bridge between theory and practice. *Journal of Family Therapy, 7,* 301–305.

Cain, A. C., & Fast, I. (1972). Children's disturbed reactions to parent suicide. In A. C. Cain (Ed.), *Survivors of suicide* (pp. 93–111). Springfield, IL: Charles C Thomas.

Cassidy, J. (1988). The self as related to child–mother attachment at six. *Child Development, 59,* 121–134.

Chodorow, N. (1978). *The reproduction of mothering: Psychoanalysis and the sociology of gender.* Berkeley, CA: University of California Press.

Cicchetti, D., & Barnett, D. (1991). Attachment organization in maltreated preschoolers. *Development and Psychopathology, 3,* 397–411.

Cicirelli, V. G. (1989). Feelings of attachment to siblings and well-being in later life. *Psychology and Aging, 4,* 211–216.

Cicirelli, V. G. (1991). Attachment theory in old age: Protection of the attached figure. In K. Pillemer & K. McCartney (Eds.), *Parent–child relations across the life course* (pp. 25–42). Hillsdale, NJ: Erlbaum.

Craik, K. (1943). *The nature of explanation.* Cambridge, England: Cambridge University Press.

Crittenden, P. M. (1983). The effect of mandatory protective daycare on mutual attachment in maltreating mother–infant dyads. *Child Abuse and Neglect, 7,* 297–300.

Dixon, N. F. (1971). *Subliminal perception: The nature of a controversy.* London: McGraw-Hill.

Dunn, J. (1988). *The beginnings of social understanding.* Cambridge, MA: Harvard University Press.

Erdelyi, H. M. (1974). A new look at the new look: Perceptual defense and vigilance. *Psychological Review, 81,* 1–25.

Erikson, E. (1950). *Childhood and society.* New York: Norton.

Fairbairn, W. R. D. (1952). *An object-relations theory of the personality.* New York: Basic Books.

Firth, R. (1936). *We, the Tikopia.* London: Allen & Unwin.

Fish, M., Belsky, J., & Youngblade, L. (1991). Developmental antecedents and measurement of intergenerational boundary violation in a nonclinic sample. *Family Psychology, 4,* 278–297.

Fonagy, P., Steele, M., & Steele, H. (1991). Intergenerational patterns of attachment: Maternal representations during pregnancy and subsequent infant–mother attachments. *Child Development, 62,* 891–905.

Foss, B. M. (1961). *Determinants of infant behaviour* (Vol. 1). London: Methuen.

Foss, B. M. (1963). *Determinants of infant behavior* (Vol. 2). London: Methuen.

Foss, B. M. (1965). *Determinants of infant behaviour* (Vol. 3). London: Methuen.

Foss, B. M. (1969). *Determinants of infant behaviour* (Vol. 4). London: Methuen.

Freud, A. (1960). Discussion of Dr. John Bowlby's paper. *Psychoanalytic Study of the Child, 15,* 53–62.

Freud, S. (1953). Three essays on the theory of sexuality. In J. Strachey (Ed. and Trans.), *The standard edition of the complete psychological works of Sigmund Freud* (Vol. 7, pp. 125–245). London: Hogarth Press. (Original work published 1905)

Freud, S. (1955). The psychogenesis of a case of homosexuality in a woman. In J. Strachey (Ed. and Trans.), *The standard edition of the complete psychological works of Sigmund Freud* (Vol. 18, pp. 145–172). London: Hogarth Press. (Original work published 1920)

Freud, S. (1959). Inhibitions, symptoms and anxiety. In J. Strachey (Ed. and Trans.), *The standard edition of the complete psychological works of Sigmund Freud* (Vol. 20, pp. 77–175). London: Hogarth Press. (Original work published 1926)

Freud, S. (1961). The ego and the id. In J. Strachey (Ed. and Trans.), *The standard* edition of the complete psychological works of Sigmund Freud (Vol. 19, pp. 3–66). London: Hogarth Press. (Original work published 1923)

Freud, S. (1964). An outline of psycho-analysis. In J. Strachey (Ed. and Trans.), *The standard edition of the complete psychological works of Sigmund Freud* (Vol. 23, pp. 141–207). London: Hogarth Press. (Original work published 1940)

George, C., Kaplan, N., & Main, M. (1984). *Adult attachment interview.* Unpublished manuscript, University of California, Berkeley.

George, C., & Solomon, J. (1989). Internal working models of parenting and security of attachment at age six. *Infant Mental Health Journal, 10,* 222–237.

Goldfarb, W. (1943). The effects of early institutional care on adolescent personality. *Journal of Experimental Education, 14,* 441–447.

Goldfarb, W. (1945). Psychological privation in infancy and subsequent adjustment. *American Journal of Orthopsychiatry, 15,* 247–255.

Greenberg, M. T., & Marvin, R. S. (1979). Attachment patterns in profoundly deaf preschool children. *Merrill-Palmer Quarterly, 25,* 265–279.

Greenberg, M. T., & Speltz, M. L. (1988). Attachment and the ontogeny of conduct problems. In J. Belsky & T. Nezworski (Eds.), *Clinical implications of attachment* (pp. 177–218). Hillsdale, NJ: Erlbaum.

Grosskurth, P. (1987). *Melanie Klein: Her world and her work.* Cambridge, MA: Harvard University Press.

Grossmann, K., Grossmann, K. E., Spangler, G., Suess, G., & Unzner, L. (1985). Maternal sensitivity and newborns' orientation responses as related to quality of attachment in Northern Germany. In I. Bretherton & E. Waters (Eds.), *Growing points of attachment theory and research, Monographs of the Society for Research in Child Development, 50*(1–2, Serial No. 209).

Grossmann, K. E., & Grossmann, K. (1990). The wider concept of attachment in cross-cultural research. *Human Development, 13,* 31–47.

Hansburg, H. G. (1972). *Adolescent separation anxiety: A method for the study of adolescent separation problems.* Springfield, IL: Charles C Thomas.

Harlow, H. F. (1961). The development of affectional patterns in infant monkeys. In B. M. Foss (Ed.), *Determinants of infant behaviour* (pp. 75–97). London: Methuen.

Harlow, H. F., & Zimmermann, R. R. (1958). The development of affective responsiveness in infant monkeys. *Proceedings of the American Philosophical Society, 102,* 501–509.

Heinicke, C. M. (1956). Some effects of separating two-year-olds from their parents: A comparative study. *Human Relations, 9,* 105–176.

Heinicke, C. M., & Westheimer, I. (1966). *Brief separations.* New York: International Universities Press.

Hermans, H. J. M., Kempen, H. J. G., & van Loon, R. J. P. (1992). The dialogic self. *American Psychologist, 47,* 23–33.

Hinde, R. A. (1991). Relationships, attachment, and culture: A tribute to John Bowlby. *Infant Mental Health Journal, 12,* 154–163.

Hinde, R. A., & Spencer-Booth, Y. (1967). The effect of social companions on mother–infant relations in rhesus monkeys. In D. Morris (Ed.), *Primate ethology* (pp. 267–286). London: Weidenfeld and Nicolson.

Howes, C., Rodning, C., Galuzzo, D. C., & Myers, I. (1988). Attachment and child care: Relationships with mother and caregiver. *Early Childhood Research Quarterly, 3,* 403–416.

Johnson, M. M. (1988). *Strong mothers, weak wives.* Berkeley, CA: University of California Press.

Kaplan, N. (1984). *Internal representations of separation experiences in six-year-olds: Related to actual experiences of separation.* Unpublished master's thesis, University of California, Berkeley.

Klagsbrun, M., & Bowlby, J. (1976). Responses to separation from parents: A clinical test for young children. *British Journal of Projective Psychology, 21,* 7–21.

Klein, M. (1932). *The psycho-analysis of children.* London: Hogarth Press.

Klopfer, B., Ainsworth, M. D., Klopfer, W. F., & Holt, R. R. (1954). *Developments in the Rorschach technique (Vol. 1).* Yonkers-on-Hudson, NY: World Book.

Kobak, R. R., & Sceery, A. (1988). Attachment in late adolescence: Working models, affect regulation, and perceptions of self and others. *Child Development, 59,* 135–146.

Kotelchuck, M. (1972). *The nature of the child's tie to his father.* Unpublished doctoral dissertation, Harvard University.

Kubler-Ross, E. (1970). *On death and dying.* London: Tavistock.

Lamb, M. E. (1978). Qualitative aspects of mother–infant and father–infant attachments in the second year of life. *Infant Behavior and Development, 1,* 265–275.

Lieberman, A. (1977). Preschoolers' competence with a peer: Relations with attachment and peer experience. *Child Development, 48,* 1277–1287.

Lieberman, A. F., & Pawl, J. H. (1988). Clinical applications of attachment theory. In J. Belsky & T. Nezworski (Eds.), *Clinical applications of attachment* (pp. 327–351). Hilldale, NJ: Erlbaum.

Lorenz, K. Z. (1935). Der Kumpan in der Umwelt des Vogels [The companion in the bird's world]. *Journal fuer Ornithologie, 83,* 137–213. (Abbreviated English translation published 1937 in *Auk, 54,* 245–273.)

Main, M. (1973). *Exploration, play, and cognitive functioning as related to child–*

mother attachment. Unpublished doctoral dissertation, Johns Hopkins University, Baltimore.

Main, M., & Goldwyn, R. (in press). Interview-based adult attachment classifications: Related to infant–mother and infant–father attachment. *Developmental Psychology.*

Main, M., Kaplan, K., & Cassidy, J. (1985). Security in infancy, childhood and adulthood: A move to the level of representation. In I. Bretherton & E. Waters (Eds.), *Growing points of attachment theory and research, Monographs of the Society for Research in Child Development,* 50(1–2, Serial No. 209), 66–104.

Marris, P. (1958). *Widows and their families.* London: Routledge.

Marris, P. (1982). Attachment and society. In C. M. Parkes & J. Stevenson-Hinde (Eds.), *The place of attachment in human behavior* (pp. 185–201). New York: Basic Books.

Marris, P. (1991). The social construction of uncertainty. In C. M. Parkes, J. Stevenson-Hinde, & P. Marris (Eds.), *Attachment across the life cycle* (pp. 77–90). London: Routledge.

Marvin, R. S. (1972). *Attachment and cooperative behavior in 2-, 3-, and 4-year-olds.* Unpublished doctoral dissertation, University of Chicago.

Marvin, R. S. (1977). An ethological–cognitive model for the attenuation of mother–child attachment behavior. In T. M. Alloway, L. Krames, & P. Pliner (Eds.), *Advances in the study of communication and affect, Vol. 3: The development of social attachments* (pp. 25–60). New York: Plenum Press.

Marvin, R. S., & Stewart, R. B. (1990). A family system framework for the study of attachment. In M. Greenberg, D. Cicchetti, & M. Cummings (Eds.), *Attachment beyond the preschool years* (pp. 51–86). Chicago: University of Chicago Press.

Matas, L., Arend, R. A., & Sroufe, L. A. (1978). Continuity and adaptation in the second year: The relationship between quality of attachment and later competence. *Child Development,* 49, 547–556.

Miller, G. A., Galanter, E., & Pribram, K. H. (1960). *Plans and the structure of behavior.* New York: Holt, Rinehart & Winston.

Miyake, K., Chen, S., & Campos, J. (1985). Infants' temperament, mothers' mode of interaction and attachment in Japan: An interim report. In I. Bretherton & E. Waters (Eds.), Growing points of attachment theory and research, *Monographs of the Society for Research in Child Development,* 50(1–2, Serial No. 109), 276–297.

Parke, R. D., & Tinsley, B. J. (1987). Family interaction in infancy. In J. D. Osofsky (Ed.), *Handbook of infant development* (pp. 579–641). New York: Wiley.

Parkes, C. M. (1972). *Bereavement: Studies of grief in adult life*. New York: International Universities Press.

Piaget, J. (1951). *The origin of intelligence in children*. New York: International Universities Press.

Piaget, J. (1954). *The construction of reality in the child*. New York: Basic Books.

Radke-Yarrow, M., Cummings, E. M., Kuczinsky, L., & Chapman, M. (1985). Patterns of attachment in two- and three-year-olds in normal families and families with parental depression. *Child Development, 56*, 884–893.

Rayner, E. (1991, November). *John Bowlby's contribution, a brief summary*. Paper presented at the meeting of the British Psychoanalytic Society held in honor of John Bowlby, London, England.

Robertson, J. (1953a). *A two-year-old goes to hospital* [Film]. Tavistock Child Development Research Unit, London (available through the Penn State Audiovisual Services, University Park, PA).

Robertson, J. (1953b). Some responses of young children to loss of maternal care. *Nursing Care, 49*, 382–386.

Robertson, J., & Bowlby, J. (1952). Responses of young children to separation from their mothers. *Courrier of the International Children's Centre, Paris, II*, 131–140.

Sagi, A., Aviezer, O., Mayseless, O., Donnell, F., & Joels, T. (1991, April). *Infant–mother attachment in traditional and nontraditional kibbutzim*. Paper presented at the biennial meetings of the Society for Research in Child Development, Seattle, WA.

Sagi, A., Lamb, M. E., Lewkowicz, K. S., Shoham, R., Dvir, R., & Estes, D. (1985). Security of infant–mother, –father, and –metapelet among kibbutz reared Israeli children. In I. Bretherton & E. Waters (Eds.), *Growing points of attachment theory and research, Monographs of the Society for Research in Child Development, 50*(1–2, Serial No. 209), 257–275.

Salter, M. D. (1940). *An evaluation of adjustment based upon the concept of security: Child Development Series*. Toronto, Ontario, Canada: University of Toronto Press.

Schaffer, H. R., & Emerson, P. E. (1964). The development of social attachments in infancy. *Monographs of the Society for Research in Child Development, 29* (Serial No. 94).

Schneider-Rosen, K., Braunwald, K. G., Carlson, V., & Cicchetti, D. (1985). Current perspectives in attachment theory: Illustration from the study of maltreated infants. In I. Bretherton & E. Waters (Eds.), *Growing points of attachment theory and research, Monographs of the Society for Research in Child Development, 50*(1–2, Serial No. 209), 194–210.

Schur, M. (1960). Discussion of Dr. John Bowlby's paper. *Psychoanalytic Study of the Child, 15*, 63–84.

Senn, M. J. E. (1977a). *Interview with James Robertson*. Unpublished manuscript, National Library of Medicine, Washington DC.

Senn, M. J. E. (1977b). *Interview with John Bowlby*. Unpublished manuscript, National Library of Medicine, Washington, DC.

Shaver, P. R., & Hazan, C. (1988). A biased overview of the study of love. *Journal of Social and Personality Relationships*, 5, 473–501.

Slough, N., & Greenberg, M. (1991). Five-year-olds' representations of separation from parents: Responses for self and a hypothetical child. In W. Damon (Series Ed.) & I. Bretherton & M. Watson (Vol. Eds.), *Children's perspectives on the family* (pp. 67–84). San Francisco: Jossey-Bass.

Spieker, S., & Booth, C. (1988). Maternal antecedents of attachment quality. In J. Belsky & T. Nezworski (Eds.), *Clinical implications of attachment* (pp. 95–135). Hillsdale, NJ: Erlbaum.

Spitz, R. A. (1946). Anaclitic depression. *Psychoanalytic Study of the Child*, 2, 313–342.

Spitz, R. A. (1947). *Grief: A peril in infancy* [Film]. University of Akron Psychology Archives, Akron, OH (available through the Penn State Audiovisual Services, University Park, PA).

Spitz, R. A. (1960). Discussion of Dr. John Bowlby's paper. *Psychoanalytic Study of the Child*, 15, 85–208.

Sroufe, L. A. (1983). Infant–caregiver attachment and patterns of adaptation in preschool: The roots of maladaptation and competence. In M. Perlmutter (Ed.), *Minnesota symposium in child psychology* (Vol. 16, pp. 41–81). Hillsdale, NJ: Erlbaum.

Sroufe, L. A. (1985). Attachment classification from the perspective of infant–caregiver relationships and infant temperament. *Child Development*, 56, 1–14.

Sroufe, L. A. (1988). The role of infant–caregiver attachment in adult development. In J. Belsky & T. Nezworski (1988), *Clinical implications of attachment* (pp. 18–38). Hillsdale, NJ: Erlbaum.

Sroufe, L. A., & Waters, E. (1977). Attachment as an organizational construct. *Child Development*, 49, 1184–1199.

Stayton, D., & Ainsworth, M. D. S. (1973). Development of separation behavior in the first year of life. *Developmental Psychology*, 9, 226–235.

Stayton, D., Hogan, R., & Ainsworth, M. D. S. (1973). Infant obedience and maternal behavior: The origins of socialization reconsidered. *Child Development*, 42, 1057–1070.

Stewart, R. B., & Marvin, R. S. (1984). Sibling relations: The role of conceptual perspective-taking in the ontogeny of sibling caregiving. *Child Development*, 55, 1322–1332.

Sullivan, H. S. (1953). *The interpersonal theory of psychiatry.* New York: Norton.

Teti, D. M., & Ablard, K. E. (1989). Security of attachment and infant–sibling relationships: A laboratory study. *Child Development, 60,* 1519–1528.

Tinbergen, N. (1951). *The study of instinct.* London: Clarendon Press.

Tracy, R. L., & Ainsworth, M. D. S. (1981). Maternal affectionate behavior and infant–mother attachment patterns. *Child Development, 52,* 1341–1343.

Tracy, R. L., Lamb, M. E., & Ainsworth, M. D. S. (1976). Infant approach behavior as related to attachment. *Child Development, 47,* 571–578.

Tronick, E. Z., Winn, S., & Morelli, G. A. (1985). Multiple caretaking in the context of human evolution: Why don't the Efe know the Western prescription to child care? In M. Reite & T. Field (Eds.), *The psychobiology of attachment and separation* (pp. 293–321). San Diego: Academic Press.

Tulving, E. (1972). Episodic and semantic memory. In E. Tulving & W. Donaldson (Eds.), *Organization of memory* (pp. 382–403). San Diego: Academic Press.

Van Ijzendoorn, M. H., & Kroonenberg, P. M. (1988). Cross-cultural patterns of attachment: A meta-analysis of the Strange Situation. *Child Development, 59,* 147–156.

Waddington, C. H. (1957). *The strategy of the genes.* London: Allen & Unwin.

Ward, M. J., Carlson, E. A., Altman, S., Levine, L., Greenberg, R. H., & Kessler, D. B. (1990, April). *Predicting infant–mother attachment from adolescents' prenatal working models of relationships.* Paper presented at the Seventh International Conference on Infant Studies, Montreal, Quebec, Canada.

Waters, E. (1978). The reliability and stability of individual differences in infant–mother attachment. *Child Development, 49,* 520–616.

Waters, E., & Deane, K. E. (1985). Defining and assessing individual differences in attachment relationships: Q-methodology and the organization of behavior in infancy and early childhood. In I. Bretherton & E. Waters (Eds.), *Growing points of attachment theory and research, Monographs of the Society for Research in Child Development, 50*(1–2, Serial No. 209), 41–65.

Weiss, R. S. (1973). *Loneliness: The experience of emotional and social isolation.* Cambridge, MA: MIT Press.

Weiss, R. S. (1977). *Marital separation.* New York: Basic Books.

Weiss, R. S. (1982). Attachment in adult life. In C. M. Parkes & J. Stevenson-Hinde (Eds.), *The place of attachment in human behavior* (pp. 171–184). New York: Wiley.

Weiss, R. (1991). The attachment bond in childhood and adulthood. In C. M. Parkes, J. Stevenson-Hinde, & P. Marris (Eds.), *Attachment across the life cycle* (pp. 66–76). London: Routledge.

Winnicott, D. W. (1965). *The maturational process and the facilitating environment.* New York: International Universities Press.

Young, J. Z. (1964). *A model for the brain.* London: Oxford University Press.

16

SOCIAL LEARNING THEORY AND DEVELOPMENTAL PSYCHOLOGY: THE LEGACIES OF ROBERT R. SEARS AND ALBERT BANDURA

JOAN E. GRUSEC

This chapter offers an evaluation of social learning theory from a historical perspective. It focuses on the work of two major exponents of the position: Robert Sears and Albert Bandura. The undertaking is somewhat difficult in the case of Bandura, because he continues to be an active contributor to psychology. On the other hand, it is probably fair to say that Bandura's major substantive contributions to developmental psychology were in the work he and his students did during the 1960s and 1970s and that his energies now are directed more toward other fields, such as health psychology. Thus the main focus here is on his research and theory in the 1960s and 1970s, which, of course, is also more easily seen in its historical context.

I am grateful for very helpful comments made by Kay Bussey and an anonymous reviewer in response to an earlier version of this article.

Reprinted from *Developmental Psychology*, 28, 776–786. Copyright by the American Psychological Association.

This analysis of social learning theory involves consideration of the work of two individuals who were very different in their approaches, even though united by a common theoretical label. Sears and Bandura were not collaborators at any point in their respective careers, although they were colleagues at the same university and had a strong influence on each other. Bandura is clearly the intellectual heir of Sears, influenced by but also reacting against the tradition that Sears represented. The two overlapped in their published contributions to social developmental psychology by approximately 6 years (from *Adolescent Aggression* in 1959, the first book by Bandura and Richard Walters, to Sears, Rau, and Alpert's 1965 publication of *Identification and Child Rearing*). However, except for a very brief theoretical overlap in Bandura and Walters (1959), they charted quite distinct courses for developmental psychology. What they did have in common was their use of a set of learning principles to understand issues in human social development—hence the label of social learning theorist for each of them, although the form of learning theory was different for the two. For Sears, it was stimulus–response theory. For Bandura, it began with some influence from Skinner's radical behaviorism, although with added concepts such as modeling. It quickly evolved, however, into a form of learning theory heavily informed by concepts from information-processing theory.

The social learning theory of Sears has little direct influence on modern conceptualizations of development. Even Bandura's approach is less central as a formalized theory in developmental psychology than it once was. This is probably because it is not a theory that focuses primarily on age-related changes in behavior and thinking, although both Sears and Bandura were obviously developmentalists in the sense of being interested in processes of behavior acquisition and change. Nor do biology or notions of evolutionary adaptiveness figure strongly in Bandura's approach to development. It nevertheless continues to be a strong force in current thinking and provides, among other things, a critical skepticism that guards against too-ready acceptance of stage-theoretical, constructivist, or evolutionary theses. It should also be noted that social learning theory no longer holds center stage simply because its basic concepts, those of observational learning and learning through direct consequences, have become an accepted part of our knowledge base.

A brief comment about terminology is in order. As noted earlier, although Sears and Bandura are both social learning theorists, their brands of social learning theory are markedly different. Not only was the learning theory of Sears adapted from Hullian learning theory, but it also had a strong overlay of psychoanalytic theory. Bandura's social learning theory, somewhat more influenced by the operant tradition, completely disavowed the influence of psychoanalytic theory in anything other than its content areas. But, in Bandura's hands, the operant theory of Skinner quickly acquired a most non-Skinnerian cognitive flavor. As he struggled to make theoretical sense of the phenomenon of modeling, Bandura quickly abandoned mechanistic conditioning explanations and turned instead to the concepts of information processing. As his interest in self-regulative capacities and self-efficacy grew, he became even more distant from the anticognitive stance of the behaviorist tradition. In 1986, in fact, Bandura relabeled his approach "social cognitive theory" as a more suitable and adequate description of what he had been advocating since the late 1960s. The relabeling was useful because it made the features of his position clearer. On the other hand, there is nothing in the concept of learning that denies the importance of cognitive mechanisms in behavior change. It is only the historical association of the study of learning with strong anticognitivist views that may have led to misunderstanding or misinterpretation on the part of some of what Bandura was attempting.

In this chapter, the major theses of Sears and Bandura are outlined, along with a chronology of their theoretical developments. Then their contributions are evaluated in the context of current approaches to the study of social development.

SOCIAL LEARNING THEORY: SEARS AND HIS COLLEAGUES

Freud provided us with a first theory of personality development, one with impressive staying power. Through the work of his disciples, as well as his numerous critics, who nevertheless remained within the general structure he proposed, a rich and creative insight into human nature evolved over the years. It has always been the contention of psychoanalysts, however, that the hypotheses of psychoanalytic theory are not amenable to scientific testing but can be assessed only through use of the psychoanalytic method, that is, the free associations of patients undergoing analysis or the behavior of children during structured play. Academic psychologists, seriously interested in the development of a theory of personality and impressed by the insightfulness of Freud's, found these limitations on their scientific activities troublesome. A movement thus arose to make psychoanalytic principles amenable to scientific investigation in spite of objections that it could not be done. It was possible to operationalize psychoanalytic constructs and to make predictions, even if the operationalization was considered inadequate by exponents of the theory. But even further rigor could be achieved by joining psychoanalytic theory to theories more amenable to scientific investigation; during the 1930s and 1940s, behaviorism and learning theory provided the ultimate in scientific rigor.

The major formal effort to combine learning and psychoanalytic theories in order to understand personality and social development throughout the life span began at the Yale Institute of Human Relations. The institute's mission was to construct a unified science of behavior, which it started to do in 1935. The enterprise commenced under the direction of Mark May and with the intellectual leadership of Clark Hull (who had arrived at Yale in 1929 with an active program of research on hypnosis and a dedication to the principles of behaviorist psychology), as well as with input from representatives of a variety of related disciplines. From psychoanalytic theory and from "the closely charted regions of rigorous stimulus response theory" (Sears, 1975, p. 61), Hull, Sears, and others, including John Dollard and Neal Miller, welded together a new approach to the science of human development and behavior. Their first undertaking was an account of frustration and aggression (Dollard, Doob, Miller, Mowrer, & Sears, 1939) that included an analysis of the socialization of aggression throughout childhood, a problem on which Sears continued to work (e.g., Sears, 1941). In 1941, Miller and Dollard published *Social Learning and Imitation*, in which they presented the first major account of social learning theory supported in part by experiments on imitation in young children.

The attempt to marry psychoanalytic and stimulus–response (S-R) theories appeared promising. It was, of course, little more than a reinterpretation of Freudian hypotheses within the framework of S-R formulations, a translation made relatively straightforward by certain similarities between the two theories. Both, for example, viewed the goal of behavior as drive reduction, and reinforcement and the pleasure principle were concepts that could be equated easily. Certainly the individual integrity of each theory was to an extent violated by the marriage, but the exercise did serve to suggest that ideas based on the richness of clinical observation and interpretation could be subjected to rigorous scientific evaluation and therefore made acceptable to the scientific community. Yarrow and Yarrow (1955) summarized the contributions of social learning theory when they noted that

> Rather slowly, but very perceptibly, a new point of view is emerging in child psychology. It is not a point of view which is an irresponsible, radical departure from the conservative empiricism which has epitomized this discipline, but it is a reformulation of the problems in terms of a more dynamic conception of behavior and development. (p. 1)

In fact, the approach was particularly exciting because it was an attempt to account for developmental phenomena through concepts that formed part of a general theory of human behavior. Moreover, it offered a stimulating change from the more descriptive approaches characterizing the field in the 1940s and early 1950s, enabling the generation of theoretical propositions about social development that could be empirically tested.

Some Features of the Approach

It was the focus of Sears on socialization processes that had a particularly strong impact on research and theory in social developmental psychology. Much of his theoretical effort was expended on developing an understanding of the way that children come to internalize, or to take on as their own, the values, attitudes, and behavior of the culture in which they are raised. His interest centered on issues having to do with the control of aggression, the growth of resistance to temptation and guilt, and the acquisition of culturally approved sex-role behaviors. Sears stressed the place of parents in the fostering of internalization, concentrating on features of parental behavior that either facilitated or hampered the process, features that included both general relationship variables such as parental warmth and permissiveness and specific behaviors such as punishment in the form of love withdrawal and power assertion, as well as reasoning.

Aggression, Dependency, and Identification

Three content areas, largely dictated by the focus of psychoanalytic theory, attracted the attention of Sears: aggression, dependency, and identification (subsuming moral and sex-role development). With the exception of altruism, achievement, and peer social competence, they remain the major areas of interest to social developmentalists to this day, although the focus on dependency has been transformed into one on attachment.

The initial efforts of the Yale group had been directed toward an analysis of aggression. The work was influenced by Freud's early notions of aggression, in which he maintained that the cause of aggression is exposure to frustration. Thus frustration of an activity induces a behavior whose goal is injury to a person or object. Aggression is attributed to a drive—not the instinctual drive (Thanatos) of later Freudian theory but one whose strength is linked to experience with frustrating events. Although the early social learning view of aggression (Dollard et al., 1939) stated that frustration led inevitably to aggression, Sears (1941) argued that reactions to frustration could be altered through learning. Nevertheless, although dependency, regression, or increased problem solving could become the predominant response to frustration through learning, aggression was viewed as the dominant one in the hierarchy of responses elicited by frustration. Aggression's dominance was accounted for either on the basis of an innate connection between frustration and aggression or because aggression in response to frustration has a high probability of being acquired during socialization.

Several specific hypotheses amenable to empirical testing were derived from the general frustration—aggression hypothesis. One example of these hypotheses is that the strength of instigation to aggression would be a function of the strength of instigation to and the degree of interference with the frustrated response. Another is that the extent to which aggressive behavior was inhibited would be a function of the amount of punishment it elicited, although Dollard et al. (1939) also realized that punishment is frustrating and might therefore also increase the instigation to aggression.

In the latter case, one would expect displacement of aggression to another object or person, with increased amounts of punishment, meaning that increasingly dissimilar events would be sought out for the displacement. The Dollard et al. formulation also suggested that acts of aggression were functionally equivalent, so that all aggressive behaviors would work to reduce the aggressive impulse, a position corresponding to the psychoanalytic notion of catharsis. The problem with this conclusion, however, was that it failed to take into account another obvious prediction from learning theory, that aggressive responses that successfully remove sources of frustration will be reinforced and, hence, aggression is likely to be increased rather than decreased. In 1958, Sears addressed the as yet unclear issue of how an aggressive drive is acquired, suggesting that the motive to injure is learned through secondary reinforcement. The successful elimination of frustrating conditions by an aggressive response, as well as the possible evocation of pain in the frustrator by that act, is primarily reinforcing. Pairing of this primary reinforcement with the aggressive response thereby causes aggression to acquire secondary reinforcement properties.

The importance of secondary drives and their development is seen again in the manner in which Sears wrote about dependency. How does the young child learn to want to be near his or her primary caretaker? According to Sears, Whiting, Nowlis, and Sears (1953), dependency results from the fact that from birth the child has so many drive states reduced by others, particularly the mother. Through the pairing of the mother—her appearance, voice, and so on—with reduction of hunger and thirst and with the provision of warmth and comfort, her attributes take on secondary reward value. (In fact, Sears and his colleagues emphasized feeding experiences in their research on dependency apparently for no other reason than the major importance assigned to feeding by Freud.) Thus being near the mother and being held and touched by her become secondarily reinforcing events. And this desire to be near her produces "dependent" behaviors— clinging, following, and reaching out—that are reinforced by maternal attention.

Some would have been content to leave the story at this point, with the mother established simply as a secondary reinforcer. But both the Hullian and Freudian tradition necessitated further development of the concept of dependency. Some kind of motivational system had to be invoked, given that dependency seemed to be displayed even when all primary drives had been reduced and when, therefore, conditioned reinforcers ought to have lost their effectiveness. Thus, Sears et al. (1953) proposed that dependency acquires drive properties. The source of these drive properties, they proposed, lay in the fact that dependent behaviors are sometimes reinforced and sometimes punished. The incompatible expectancies of reward and frustration produce conflict that provides the drive strength for energization of the dependent action. From this viewpoint, it is easy to see that pun-

478   JOAN E. GRUSEC

ishment for dependency should heighten dependent behaviors by increasing the level of drive. Punishment also makes it likely that displacement will occur, with the new object of dependency being increasingly different from the mother as a function of the extent to which dependent behavior directed toward her has been punished. In later years, Sears (1963) acknowledged the lack of evidence to support these speculations but was not yet ready to give up the notion of drive completely.

Building on the notion of a dependency drive, Sears also proposed a theory of identification. Once a dependency drive has been established, young children, because they cannot discriminate between themselves and their mothers, perceive her actions as an integral part of their own action sequences. The reproduction of her actions is reinforcing, and thus a stable habit of responding imitatively is built up along with a secondary motivational system for which "acting like the mother" is the goal response (Sears, 1957). In this account, "what Sears has ingeniously accomplished is to restate in the language of learning theory Freud's theory of anaclitic identification" (Bronfenbrenner, 1960, p. 28). On the other hand, the formulation was far from totally satisfying. In the mid-1960s, Sears (Sears et al., 1965) noted the lack of a mechanism for explaining why the child begins to imitate the mother and suggested simple acceptance of the fact that observational learning (as the term was used by Bandura & Walters, 1963) occurs early in life and that this tendency to reproduce maternal acts provides a way in which children can reward themselves.

Testing Hypotheses: The Research

At the same time as these theoretical proposals were being made, Sears and his colleagues were engaged in a series of studies to test them. The results of the first large-scale assessment of parenting practices and children's social development guided by the social learning tradition were published in *Patterns of Child Rearing* (Sears, Maccoby, & Levin, 1957). The study was based on interviews of 379 mothers. In the research, Sears et al. determined how these mothers reared their children, what the effects of this rearing were, and what determined the choice of one rearing method over another, for example, the effects of marital satisfaction, self-esteem, and personal attitudes on parenting technique. Techniques of discipline, permissiveness, and severity of training were targeted as some variables important for socialization, and a variety of deductions from social learning theory were assessed. Sears et al. found a relationship between the use of withdrawal of love by warm mothers and conscience (compliance with parental dictate in the absence of surveillance); here the explanation was that the absence of valued parental attention motivates the child to imitate and, therefore, to incorporate parent behaviors, including standards for morality. Other predictions that also were supported in this work were that the strength of identification (or conscience development) would vary positively with the amount of affectionate nurturance given to the child, as well as with the severity of the demands placed on the child by the mother. (The more the demands, the more the mother would not provide immediate help, and the more the child would have to reproduce her behavior.) Punishment for aggression was correlated with immediate suppression of aggression but later high levels of aggression, presumably because punishment elicited hostility in the child and because physical punishment provided a model for aggressiveness.

Patterns of Child Rearing had serious methodological problems. Sears, trained as an experimentalist, was far from successful in his use of the interview method. Data about both child-rearing practices and child outcomes came from one source, the mother, and so were subject to maternal perceptual biases. Mothers were assumed to be giving accurate accounts of when and how such events as weaning and toilet training were carried out, even though we now know that they are highly likely to be inaccurate in their memories of such events. It is to his credit that Sears improved his assessment methods in a second major research program (Sears et al., 1965). Thus the methodology was extended from parent interviews to include also observations of mother–child interactions in a playroom, the administration of attitude scales, observations of child behavior, and doll play. The focus of the study now was exclusively on identification, with a search for the child-rearing correlates of behaviors such as self-control, prosocial aggression, guilt, and sex-role behaviors. The work nevertheless had little impact on the field, probably because social learning theory, as it had been developed by the Yale group, was being supplanted by newer approaches to the understanding of human behavior and development.

Mechanisms of Development

Social learning theory is not a stage theory. The developmental aspects of psychoanalytic theory—critical periods and stages—had been omitted in the translation from psychoanalytic to social learning theory. Instead, Sears (1957) offered a set of developmental mechanisms that are simple and straightforward, to say the least. First, there is learning, by which the child acquires appropriate actions or responses. Second, there is physical maturation of the child, a mechanism "so obvious as to require no discussion" (Sears, 1957, p. 151). In fact, the main impact of physical change is through its social implication; that is, influences on behavior do not come about directly because of physical change but rather through the differential reaction of agents of socialization as they expect new actions in accordance with increasing maturity. Changes in kind and amount of dependency, for example, are a reflection of what adults consider acceptable; clinging is rewarded in the very young but punished or extinguished as the child grows older and different forms of dependency are tolerated. The final change mechanism rests on the expectancies for action held by agents of socialization, expectancies determined not only by physical changes but also by realization that the child is learning new things.

Commentary and Evaluation

The contributions of Sears and his Yale colleagues to developmental psychology were substantial. They set the study of personality and social development on its scientific course, proposing a theory of human development in such a way that it was amenable to empirical study. They relied on a variety of methods in the course of this study, including parental interview, projective techniques, measures of parent attitudes, behavioral observations, and behavioral ratings. *Patterns of Child Rearing* provided a model for a multitude of subsequent studies addressing the central problem of socialization, that is, how parents transmit the values and standards of society in a variety of domains to their children. Socialization processes remain a central focus of study for developmental researchers, and Sears and his colleagues clearly demonstrated how one could begin to tackle these important issues. Probably the only recent breakthrough that is at all comparable in its importance for research in social development is the formulation of attachment theory and of a methodology for assessing the quality of caretaker–infant relationships.

The Limitations

Many of the details of the theory have not stood up to the test of time. Psychoanalytic and learning theory make such different basic assumptions about human behavior that they seem strange bedfellows indeed. For example, biological emphases and critical periods are central to the former and foreign to the latter, so Sears chose simply to ignore them. Clearly, Sears found himself in some difficulty in his attempts to explain the growth of drives, attempts necessitated by the importance of motivation for both psychoanalytic and stimulus–response theory; eventually he was forced to abandon the concept of drive and rely on notions of reinforcement and incentive alone. As a result, some of the theory's distinctiveness was lost.

The Successes

Data Generated

One criterion for a good theory lies not so much in whether its predictions are ultimately confirmed but in whether or not it generates data that are useful and important. By this criterion, social learning theory as formulated by Sears has been a success. He identified variables that are still of central interest to socialization researchers and established empirical relationships that have continued to be replicated. Distinctions between short- and long-term compliance with parental dictate; a concern with differential treatment of boys and girls; and a focus on the effects of maternal self-esteem, marital adjustment, perceptions of child-rearing self-efficacy, and social class on discipline practices are but a few examples of topics that have a very contemporary ring. In identifying specific relationships between parental discipline and internalization of societal standards, Sears et al. (1957) set the stage for a view of discipline effectiveness that has remained relatively unchanged to this day. Any modern textbook in developmental psychology still points to parental warmth and psychological techniques of discipline as facilitative of internalization. It is true that a variety of other theoretical explanations have been provided for the relationships, but the basic ideas remain unchanged even after more than 30 years of relatively intense investigation in the area.

The Importance of the Dyad

Sears (1951) was among the first to argue that the study of personality and social development must acknowledge not only that the external world acts on an individual, but also that the individual has an effect on the external world. He maintained that a dyadic rather than a monadic analysis of behavior was necessary for the understanding of social relationships. Personality is the result of learning experiences, but experiences are also determined by an individual's personality. This is a position developmentalists have all come to accept, and technological developments and modern methods of research design and analysis have made it easier to deal with the complexities of dyadic analyses. It was the social learning theorists, however, who first alerted researchers to the fact that both agents of socialization and the objects of their attention are subject to the laws of learning.

The Interview as a Research Tool

In addition to asking important questions, Sears also was responsible for methodological innovations that have left their imprint on current research practices. For example, he demonstrated that a wealth of information could be acquired from intensive but structured interviews of parents. Some of the features of the approach have been modified so that now we tend to focus on self-report concerning concrete and specific situations and actions that are reasonably fresh in the mind of the interviewee, rather than on self-report based on more generalized questions (e.g., "How do you handle it if X is saucy or deliberately disobedient?"). Nevertheless, it was

Sears et al. (1957) who demonstrated the usefulness of this major methodological tool for students of socialization.

Setting the Stage for Future Developments

A final contribution of Sears and his collaborators was their refinement of a way of thinking about development that was a precursor of Bandura's sociobehavioristic and, ultimately, social cognitive approach to social development. Sears sensitized Bandura to (a) the importance of identification as a process in personality development, (b) the crucial nature of a dyadic analysis of social behavior, and (c) the problems of pursuing a drive model.

SOCIAL LEARNING THEORY: BANDURA AND HIS COLLEAGUES

Albert Bandura did his graduate work at the University of Iowa, a choice dictated in part by the presence there of Kenneth Spence. Spence's association with Hullian theory made the activities of the Yale social learning group salient to Iowa psychologists. In addition, Bandura's first academic appointment was at Stanford University, where he arrived at the same time that Sears also joined the faculty there. It is hardly surprising, then, that his work should bear the strong impact of social learning theory. Bandura's first graduate student was Richard Walters, and the two began an immensely fruitful collaboration that resulted in two books. It was the second of these books that turned the study of social and personality development in yet another direction, inspired a large number of researchers for a great many years, and still remains a strong force in current thinking in developmental psychology.

The first book by Bandura and Walters was *Adolescent Aggression*, published in 1959; it was still very much in keeping with social learning theory as it then existed, a juxtaposition of psychoanalytic and learning principles. The data reported in the book came from interviews of adolescent boys—half of them engaged in delinquent activity—and their parents, as well as from the boys' responses to a projective test consisting of pictures and stories involving the possibility of deviant action. The theoretical structure drew on the old notions of drive and reinforcement. Specifically, Bandura and Walters elaborated a theory of dependency which suggested that aggressive boys were suffering from dependency anxiety arising from rejection and punishment of dependent responses and that the frustration created by neglect and rejection was in large part responsible for their antisocial behavior. Bandura and Walters also turned their attention to the role of identification in the internalization of controls over behavior. The theory of identification they put forward was that of Sears, and the predictions they made about the relationship between parental warmth, use of withdrawal of love, and conscience development were similar to those of Sears et al. (1957).

Even while the finishing touches were being put on *Adolescent Aggression*, however, its authors were being attracted to a different approach to social development. In their second book, *Social Learning and Personality Development* (Bandura & Walters, 1963), they rejected psychoanalytic ideas and adopted a "purer" learning approach. In fact, Bandura and Walters labeled the new theory a "sociobehavioristic approach," presumably to distinguish it both from the Yale form of social learning theory and also from the current operant or learning theory approach to personality development, deviant behavior, and psychotherapy that seemed to them deficient in its failure to consider social issues.

On the very first page of *Social Learning and Personality Development*, Bandura and Walters (1963) argued that most prior applications of learning theory (including Miller & Dollard's [1941] analysis of imitation) had relied too heavily on a limited range of principles established from studies of animal and human learning in situations involving only one organism. They noted as well the 1951 call of Sears for the study of principles developed in dyadic or group situations. Bandura and Walters used analyses of displacement as an example of failure to appreciate the operation of social forces in human life. On the basis of animal learning data, learning theorists (e.g., Miller, 1948) had hypothesized that when an organism was both reinforced and punished for a given response, this would give rise to an approach–avoidance conflict, with the behavioral outcome of that conflict dependent on the relative strengths of the approach and avoidance responses. Assuming that avoidance gradients are steeper than approach gradients, and using the notion that responses can generalize to stimulus situations similar to those in which they were originally learned, Miller was able to predict at what point along a continuum of stimulus similarity a punished response would reappear. The model, then, predicted behavior from knowledge of three variables only: the strength of instigation of a behavior, the severity of punishment of the response, and the dimension of stimulus similarity. What it failed to take into account, however, was the fact that original agents of punishment continue to act in ways that may influence the trajectory of the response in question. Through teaching, example, and control of reinforcement contingencies, they determine the exact nature of the displaced response. For example, the parents of highly aggressive boys punish aggression in the home but reward it outside the home (Bandura & Walters, 1959). Thus apparent displacement is, in reality, simply an account of discrimination training.

The most important omission of learning theories, however, lay in their account of observational learning:

The weaknesses of learning approaches that discount the influence of social variables are nowhere more clearly revealed than in their treatment of the acquisition of novel responses, a crucial issue for any adequate theory of learning. (Bandura & Walters, 1963, pp. 1–2)

Skinner suggested that novel responses could be acquired through the process of successive approximation, but the experimental work of both Bandura and Walters had drawn attention to a much more effective process: imitation. This process formed the central core of the new approach. Miller and Dollard (1941) had written a book about the role of imitation in social learning, but they saw it as a special case of instrumental conditioning, with social cues serving as discriminative stimuli and behavioral matches to those cues being reinforced. Indeed, in their book on personality and psychotherapy (Dollard & Miller, 1950), there were only three passing references to imitation, certainly an indication that it was not considered very important. But, for Bandura and Walters, imitation was elevated to a position of central importance. Contrary to the learning theory treatments of imitation, they documented that observational learning occurs even when a model's responses are not reproduced during acquisition and, therefore, could receive no reinforcement. In addition, they pointed to a fact previously unnoted, that the response consequence experienced by a model can influence the subsequent behavior of the observer by inhibiting or disinhibiting behavior. Thus behaviors that might previously have been displayed are suppressed even though the child has never actually had to engage in the behavior and be punished for it. Similarly, the stage can be set for acts that might have been suppressed in the past but that are engaged in again through the acquisition of information gained by observing an unpunished model.

In their conception of imitation, Bandura and Walters (1963) differed in several respects from Sears. First of all, they gave up the Freudian term of identification. Second, they had no need for the concept of drive or for imitative responses to be reinforced in order for observational learning to occur. Third, they moved observational learning into a primary position among learning mechanisms, arguing that it was a much more efficient technique of behavior change than either direct learning or successive approximation:

> One would not . . . permit an adolescent to learn to drive a car by means of trial-and-error procedures, nor would one entrust a firearm to an armed services recruit without a demonstration of how it should be handled. (Bandura & Walters, 1963, p. 52)

Some Features of the Approach

Throughout the 1960s and 1970s, Bandura presented a theory of social development that in fact has changed very little in its basic premises in the intervening years. It was markedly different from extant conditioning approaches, including that of Sears, as well as those put forward by individuals with a more Skinnerian bent. Bandura's theory is mainly concerned with how children and adults operate cognitively on their social experiences and with how these cognitive operations then come to influence their behavior and development. Individuals are believed to abstract and integrate information that is encountered in a variety of social experiences, such as exposure to models, verbal discussions, and discipline encounters. Through this abstraction and integration, they mentally represent their environments and themselves in terms of certain crucial classes of cognitions that include response-outcome expectancies, perceptions of self-efficacy, and standards for evaluative self-reactions. These cognitions are believed to affect not only how they respond to environmental stimuli but also the sorts of environments they seek out for themselves. The discussion that follows demonstrates how Bandura emphasized the role of cognition, abstraction, and integration in several areas that were of particular interest to him as he developed his own form of social learning theory. From now on, that form of social learning theory is referred to as social cognitive theory, in keeping with contemporary terminology.

Observational Learning, Self-Regulation, Self-Efficacy, and Reciprocal Determinism

Observational Learning

According to Bandura's theory of observational learning (see Bandura, 1969, 1977b, 1986), there are four components involved in the process of modeling. Each of these components has a role to play either in the acquisition of information about events and of rules or in the decision to put this information to use in guiding behavior. First, the observer must pay attention to events—live or symbolic—that are modeled. Attention is determined by a variety of variables, including the power and attractiveness of the model, as well as the conditions under which behavior is viewed: Television, for example, is a compelling medium for capturing and holding attention. Second, when material has been attended to, it must then be retained, with the observed behavior represented in memory through either an imaginal or a verbal representational system. In the third step, symbolic representation now must be converted into appropriate actions similar to the originally modeled behavior. For instance, motor reproduction of complex actions is much less likely to be successful than that of simple actions. The final process governing observational learning involves motivational variables. There must, for example, be sufficient incentive to motivate the actual performance of modeled actions.

Self-Regulation and Self-Efficacy

A significant challenge for any theory of socialization is to explain how control over behavior shifts from external sources to the individual. How does one move from prosocial behavior that is maintained by the expectation of externally administered consequences to behavior that is maintained by the self? Sears found the mechanism for internalization in identification. Bandura found it in self-regulation. People do not behave like weather vanes, constantly shifting their behavior in accordance with momentary influences; rather they hold to ideological positions in spite of a changing situation. They can do this because they bring judgmental self-reactions into play whenever they perform an action. Actions that measure up to internal standards are judged positively, and those that fall short of these standards are judged negatively (Bandura, 1977b).

The source of self-regulative functions lies in modeling and in direct tuition. Adults respond differentially to children's behaviors, and this differential responsivity is one kind of information children take into account when formulating personal standards or ideas about which behaviors are worthy of self-blame or self-praise. Children observe that people prescribe self-evaluative standards for themselves as well, and this behavior is also considered when formulating personal standards. In addition to imitating the evaluative behavior of others, children are also reinforced by agents of socialization for engaging in self-regulation. In the end, self-regulation depends, then, on external forces. It may, however, also produce personal benefits that maintain it, as, for example, when self-denial pays off in weight reduction for the fat person.

It is important to note that people do not passively absorb standards of behavior from whatever influences they experience. Indeed, they must select from numerous evaluations that are prescribed and modeled by different individuals, as well as by the same individual in differing circumstances. This conflicting information must be integrated so that rules can be generated, or general standards formed, against which individuals judge their own behavior. The selection of standards depends on the weighting of such factors as disparities in perceived competence between the model and the self, how much a specific activity is valued, and the extent to which individuals see their behavior as a function of their own effort and ability rather than external factors over which they have little control.

Self-efficacy is a major determinant of self-regulation and has been a central focus of Bandura's research since the late 1970s. Bandura's interest in self-efficacy arose from his studies of the role of participant modeling in the treatment of phobic disorders. A striking feature of the outcomes of these studies was the extent to which individuals' perceptions of their own feelings of effectiveness determined how easily changes in behavior and fear arousal were achieved and maintained. According to self-efficacy theory (first formalized in Bandura, 1977a), people develop domain-specific beliefs about their own abilities and characteristics that guide their behavior by determining what they try to achieve and how much effort they put into their performance in that particular situation or domain. Thus self-percepts provide a framework or structure against which information is judged: They determine how or whether individuals put into action the knowledge they have. (Self-efficacy should be distinguished from locus of control, which refers to individuals' beliefs that outcomes are a result either of their own actions or of chance.) When people have negative self-percepts about a situation, believing they are ineffective and do not have the ability to perform well, they become preoccupied with themselves as well as being emotionally aroused, two conditions that distract them from performing effectively. Beliefs about self-efficacy arise from the individual's history of achievement in a domain, from observation of what others are able to accomplish, from attempts of others to mold feelings of self-efficacy through persuasion, and from consideration of one's own physiological state during a task as a reflection of personal capabilities and limitations.

Self-efficacy theory has guided research in a variety of domains, including academic achievement, health-related behavior, parenting styles, children's self-concept, athletic performance, and clinical disorders. Recently, researchers interested in age-related changes in memory functioning have used it in an attempt to understand performance deficits in the elderly, suggesting that concerns over a believed decline in memory ability will be reflected in choice of activities, effort expended, and persistence of actions in tasks requiring memory. Thus training designed to show the elderly how efficacious they can actually be in the domain of memory should lead to an increase in self-efficacy and in subsequent memory performance (e.g., Rebok & Balcerak, 1989). The results of current research on maternal responsiveness and infant security, although guided by attachment theory, can also be fitted into a self-efficacy framework. Thus Bandura (1986, 1989) suggests that the social and cognitive competence observed in infants who are classified as securely attached in the Infant Strange Situation is a result of their highly developed sense of self-efficacy. This sense of self-efficacy is fostered by responsive parents, who react to the communicative behavior of their babies and who provide enriched environments that allow the babies to see that their actions on that environment can be efficacious. In this way, accelerated social and cognitive development is promoted.

Reciprocal Determinism

Social cognitive theory acknowledges the interrelationship between the individual, the environment, and behavior. In his formalization of triadic reciprocal determinism, Bandura (1977b, 1986) argues that behavior, the environment, and cognition, as well as other personal factors, operate as interacting determinants that have a bidirectional influence on each other. Thus expectations, self-perceptions, goals, and physical structures direct behavior, with the results of that behavior having an impact on those cognitions and biological properties. Environmental events in the form of modeling, instruction, and social persuasion affect the person, and the person in turn evokes different reactions from the environment, depending on his or her personality and physical features. Finally, behavior determines aspects of the environment to which the individual is exposed, and behavior is, in turn, modified by that environment.

The concept of reciprocal determinism handles well one of the central and intriguing phenomena of human behavior to which attachment theorists, among others, have currently addressed themselves: the relative lack of plasticity of human behavior and the fact that some people seem continually to seek out relationships that have similar negative outcomes for them. Bandura argues that people contribute to their own life course by selecting, influencing, and constructing their own circumstances:

> We are all acquainted with problem-prone individuals who, through their obnoxious conduct, predictably breed negative social climates wherever they go. Others are equally skilled at bringing out the best in those with whom they interact. (Bandura, 1977b, p. 197)

Competencies, self-efficacy beliefs, and self-regulatory capacities are acquired through experience, but they in turn determine the individual's experience in such a way that they are maintained.

Testing Hypotheses: The Research

Bandura's theoretical writings have continued to be supported by his reports of empirical research. The research has been of two sorts: experimental analogues of socialization situations (particularly modeling) and demonstrations of procedures for achieving therapeutic change, such as vicarious desensitization and training in self-efficacy. The experimental analogues of socialization were hailed at the time of their appearance as clever simulations of complex social situations and relationships that enabled developmental psychologists to make major progress in their studies of processes involved in socialization. Thus they opened up new modes of investigation that freed researchers from reliance on interviews, with their attendant limitations, and enabled them to make causal inferences from data, rather than having to guess at the direction of an effect. The following are but a few examples of this work. Bandura, Ross, and Ross (1963) were able to take the complex and often nebulous concepts of three theories of identification—social power, status envy, and secondary reinforcement—and test them in a manageable way through manipulations of the characteristics and behavior of models to whom young children were exposed. A series of studies in which children viewed aggressive models showed with startling clarity how such exposure could lead to increases in the children's own aggression, rather than serving some cathartic function. It also demonstrated how knowledge could exist in the absence of performance, and that children could be fully cognizant of the nature and consequences of a given behavior without ever having engaged in it (see Bandura, 1973). Bandura and McDonald (1963) questioned the basic tenets of cognitive developmental theorizing concerning moral development by showing that, through a training procedure involving social reinforcement and modeling, the moral judgments of young children could be modified. Bandura and Schunk (1981) demonstrated how the enhancement of perceived self-efficacy could improve children's cognitive skill development and their intrinsic interest in academic subjects.

Mechanisms of Development

Bandura's analysis of development (e.g., Bandura, 1977a, 1986, 1989) is much more elaborated than was that of Sears and is a reflection of the refocusing on developmental issues that took place among North American psychologists in the 1960s. His position, however, stands in marked contrast to a traditional Piagetian one, being informed as well by a large body of recent research on children's changing information-processing capacities.

Bandura maintains that cognition involves knowledge and the skills for acting on that knowledge: Rather than conceptualizing the development of thinking in terms of discrete and uniform stages, he argues that it is best regarded as guided by specialized cognitive capacities that change over time as a function of maturation and experience. These capacities or skills involve a number of domains. One is attention. The ability to attend to relevant parts of the environment is essential for children to begin to see connections between or to acquire information about relations between actions and outcomes. But when they are young, children have attentional deficiencies—including difficulty in attending simultaneously to multiple cues and in maintaining attention for sufficiently long periods of time—that limit their proficiency. Children must also transform observed material to symbolic form, first by using imaginal symbols and then, as language develops, verbal ones. Memory is another important cognitive skill, enabling information about observed and personally experienced events to be retained so that it can guide the formulation of rules for behavior. Memory improves over time with the acquisition of language and a knowledge base that allows new information to be related to what is already known and hence remembered better. The ability to monitor the match between ideas about relations of actions and outcomes and the actual effects of actions, as well as to correct mismatches, is yet another cognitive ability necessary for successful behavioral functioning. And, finally, children's reasoning skills must be refined so that they can make and apply decision rules governing behavior.

Piaget argues that cognitive conflict produced by discrepancies between existing mental schemata and perceived events motivates changes in thinking. The social cognitive approach finds the source of change in maturation, exploratory experiences, and, most important, the imparting of information by social agents in the form of guided instruction and modeling. Parents and other teachers, for example, help young infants to learn contingencies between their actions and outcomes by making connections salient. They teach them ways to improve their attention and memory skills. They increase their knowledge base so as to aid comprehension and retention. When imparting moral standards, they use physical sanctions initially because of their children's poor command of language, but switch to more cognitively sophisticated techniques as language improves. As the child's social reality expands, and as the nature and potential seriousness of possible transgressions change with age, moral standards of a more complex and generalized nature are introduced. Parents both foster and respond, then, to their children's improved attentional skills, ability to process greater amounts of information, and increasing knowledge so as to promote greater sophistication in cognitive functioning over age. They also take changing social needs into consideration in their interactions.

Commentary and Evaluation

Bandura's contributions to a theoretical understanding of human development have been of major significance for the field. To begin with, he rescued the process of identification from the confusion of hypothesized roots in dependency and acquired reinforcement and motivation, directing the theoretical focus to a more fruitful basis in cognitive processes, including attentional and memorial factors. Bandura's empirical contributions during the 1960s and 1970s provided ample evidence of the central role of observational learning in a diversity of areas, particularly aggression and self-regulation. The research also highlighted the variety of mechanisms mediating the acquisition of behavior through observational learning. It is doubtful that anyone today would argue that modeling does not play a dominant role in socialization. The concept of self-efficacy, although developed largely in the context of understanding therapeutic change, has major potential for explaining how children's changing self-concepts can affect their social and cognitive behavior.

Bandura must also be credited with quickly moving the social learning orientation from its roots in stimulus–response theory to one within information-processing theories of memory, imagery, and problem solving. The antipathy to mentalistic constructs evident in many learning theory formulations is in no way evident in even early presentations of his position:

Mental processes are not discussed at length by Bandura and Walters in 1963, but they begin to appear in published work soon thereafter (e.g., Bandura, 1965). Bandura's analysis of modeling draws strongly on concepts of information coding, information storage, and the development of rule-governed behavior. His descriptions of how human beings select and transform information and how they generate rules to guide their own behavior was a major achievement in understanding social developmental processes. Bandura did not break new ground in his specific cognitive formulations that relate directly to current information-processing approaches, but he was a pioneer in his fundamental interest in relating thought to behavior.

Some Issues and Reactions

One question is why, in spite of being in the mainstream of North American cognitive psychology, social cognitive theory lost its position of preeminence in North American developmental psychology. This is not to say that Bandura's contributions went unheeded. Indeed, many of social cognitive theory's basic premises and mechanisms have simply become an accepted and thoroughly entrenched part of our beliefs about human social behavior. Yet, it is also true that the methodology favored by Bandura, as well as his less than central focus on development, was not in keeping with the changing zeitgeist of developmental psychology during the 1970s and 1980s.

Turning first to the (less important) matter of methodology, it was noted earlier that one of the exciting features of Bandura's work was his very clever use of laboratory analogues of real-life situations to test hypotheses, an approach influenced not only by that of learning researchers but also by the experimental work of Kurt Lewin. The ability to manipulate independent variables in controlled settings and to draw causal conclusions provided a solution to one of the great problems of the correlational approach of Sears, and it appeared to be another giant step forward in making the study of social development a truly scientific undertaking. The methodological soul-searching of the 1970s, however, detracted somewhat from Bandura's achievement in this regard, as a myriad of arguments were presented concerning the difficulties of the experimental approach: Experimental analogues of reality lacked ecological validity (Bronfenbrenner, 1977), psychology had missed out on the important first stage of science that involves observation and identification of phenomena later to be explained (McCall, 1977), and so on. Along with these warnings came technological advances that facilitated the use of observational methodology, as well as statistical developments that enabled at least the inference of causal relationships from correlational data. In all this flurry of discussion and changing focus, experimentation lost its place of favor, and social cognitive theory, through association, may have lost some of its luster as well.

Nonetheless, the use of experimental analogues of social situations is not integral in any way to assessment of the tenets of social cognitive theory. The theory can be tested using either experimental or correlational methodologies and does, in fact, guide many current correlational investigations. Bandura's preference for the experimental method, moreover, is a useful reminder that no amount of statistical sophistication can allow us to draw causal conclusions in the absence of experimental manipulation, and that greater use of this methodology in the many areas that lend themselves to such an approach could prove beneficial in augmenting our understanding of social developmental processes.

More important to an understanding of the changed role of social cognitive theory in developmental psychology was the fact that Bandura was less concerned with developmental issues than he was with other parts of his theory. As Piagetian approaches became more familiar to developmental psychologists during the late 1960s and early 1970s, social cognitive theory began to be criticized for its lack of attention to the importance of changes with age that might have an impact on behavior (e.g., Coates & Hartup, 1969). Although Bandura responded to the increasing emphasis on changing cognitive capacities in his theoretical writings, there was little accompanying research that specifically addressed developmental issues and that seemed specifically generated by social cognitive theory. For that reason, other approaches that concentrated more clearly on matters of age-related changes in development moved to the forefront of interest for many developmental psychologists. This is probably the main reason social learning theory lost its central position.

Current Status of the Theory and Issues for Further Exploration

Social cognitive theory has evolved over the years in a way that is responsive to new data. The fact that modifications have been accomplished with relative ease speaks to the strength of the initial formulations: There is as yet no evidence of distortion or convolution that might ultimately lead one to a recommendation of abandonment. Its position in the mainstream of current cognitive psychology suggests that it can continue to guide the acquisition of new data as well as to accommodate research findings that have been generated by other theoretical approaches.

There are, of course, areas of social learning and social cognitive theory whose full potential has yet to be realized. Two are briefly mentioned. The first is obvious from the immediately preceding discussion: More attention needs to be paid to development. The second concerns the basic building blocks of social learning and social cognitive theory: reinforcement, punishment, reasoning, and modeling. Bandura concentrated his theoretical and empirical efforts on the latter; however, we still have much to learn about the first three techniques of behavior change.

A Theory of Development

Both Sears and Bandura set out to formulate a general theory of human behavior. In the course of this activity, their interests spanned the entire range of human psychological functioning. Thus their concern was not exclusively with developmental issues. This is particularly the case for Bandura, whose interest in clinical matters has always been at least as strong as his interest in child development. Although Sears was more clearly focused than Bandura on issues of personality and social development, his adherence to a theory which suggested that development could be viewed most easily as the acquisition of new behaviors caused him to pay relatively little attention to specific developmental issues. For Bandura, this has not been the case. What has been less emphasized in the empirical work, however, is the interaction between age and experience. The theoretical underpinning of such work has been provided by Bandura. But what we need now is a more elaborated demonstration of how cognitive skills in the domains of memory, attention, self-monitoring, and reasoning are modified through maturation and experience and how they then influence social behavior. We need to know how children at different ages go about the process of weighing and synthesizing information that leads to the kinds of cognitions emphasized by social cognitive theory. With such an elaboration, social cognitive theory may well hold greater promise than any other contemporary developmental theory for providing an integrated view of processes of social development.

Further Analyses of Socialization Techniques and Processes

The great contribution of social learning/social cognitive theory has been in aiding our understanding of how children are socialized to accept the standards and values of their society. Sears and his colleagues oriented psychologists to the importance of internalization, reinforcement, punishment, modeling, reasoning, and affectional relationships in their understanding of socialization. Bandura developed conceptions of modeling, dealt with the issue of affectional relationships particularly as they relate to modeling, and focused on mechanisms of internalization. However, in his belief in the primacy of modeling, he has been less concerned with reinforcement and punishment, which are, after all, central concepts of learning theory. Nor does reasoning receive the detailed attention it has been given by others.

It is notable that views about the relative effectiveness of punishment and reasoning in socialization have changed remarkably little since *Patterns of Child Rearing*. And yet there are a number of anomalies in the research and a number of unanswered questions which indicate that the topic needs to be revisited. Is punishment always detrimental to the socialization process? Why are mothers who are flexible in their responses to children's misdeeds more effective as agents of socialization (Hoffman, 1970)? Why do children rate certain forms of reasoning as more acceptable than others, depending on the domain of misdeed (Nucci, 1984)? Why are relationships between reasoning and internalization dependent on age of child, gender of parent, and socioeconomic class (Brody & Shaffer, 1982)? Does reasoning serve any other function than clarifying the contingency between behavior and outcome? Do different forms of punishment (e.g., withdrawal of love, physical punishment, withdrawal of privileges, and criticism) have different affective and cognitive impacts on children? Similarly, we still have much to learn about reinforcement. Reinforcement can be material in nature and presumably has a detrimental effect on the internalization of values. But it can also be psychological in its form, running the gamut from praise of a specific act, positive attributions about the physical or psychological characteristics of the actor, reflection of the pleasurable feelings of the object of an action, a positive social comparison, or a simple acknowledgement that an act has occurred. Are some of these more detrimental to internalization than others? How do they vary in their effects on behavior, and why? It is the answers to these sorts of questions that will be needed before we have a really complete understanding of how these basic and fundamental processes—ones that form the cornerstones of learning theory approaches—make their contribution to children's internalization of societal standards and values and, hence, to their social development.

CONCLUSION

In the hands of Robert Sears and Albert Bandura, social learning theory has progressed from the initial achievement of bringing the language and data of learning theory to bear on an understanding of complex human functioning to a sophisticated application of modern information-processing concepts. Clearly, the theory in its present form offers an extremely useful way of organizing existing data, as well as providing a framework for future research. The theory's potential for developmental psychology has yet to be fully realized. However, both Sears and Bandura, in company with their colleagues, have given us a substantial lead along the way. Our debt to them is great.

REFERENCES

Bandura, A. (1965). Vicarious processes: A case of no-trial learning. In L. Berkowitz (Ed.), *Advances in experimental social psychology* (Vol. 2, pp. 1–55), San Diego: Academic Press.

Bandura, A. (1969). Social-learning theory of identificatory processes. In D. A.

Goslin (Ed.), *Handbook of socialization theory and research* (pp. 213–262). Chicago: Rand McNally.

Bandura, A. (1973). *Aggression: A social learning analysis.* Englewood Cliffs, NJ: Prentice-Hall.

Bandura, A. (1977a). Self-efficacy: Toward a unifying theory of behavioral change. *Psychological Review, 84,* 191–215.

Bandura, A. (1977b). *Social learning theory.* Englewood Cliffs, NJ: Prentice-Hall.

Bandura, A. (1986). *Social foundations of thought and action: A social cognitive theory.* Englewood Cliffs, NJ: Prentice Hall.

Bandura, A. (1989). Social cognitive theory. *Annals of Child Development, 6,* 1–60.

Bandura, A., & McDonald, F. J. (1963). The influence of social reinforcement and the behavior of models in shaping children's moral judgments. *Journal of Abnormal and Social Psychology, 67,* 274–281.

Bandura, A., Ross, D., & Ross, S. A. (1963). A comparative test of the status envy, social power, and secondary reinforcement theories of identificatory learning. *Journal of Abnormal and Social Psychology, 67,* 527–534.

Bandura, A., & Schunk, D. H. (1981). Cultivating competence, self-efficacy, and intrinsic interest through proximal self-motivation. *Journal of Personality and Social Psychology, 41,* 586–598.

Bandura, A., & Walters, R. H. (1959). *Adolescent aggression.* New York: Ronald Press.

Bandura, A., & Walters, R. H. (1963). *Social learning and personality development.* New York: Holt, Rinehart & Winston.

Brody, G. H., & Shaffer, D. R. (1982). Contributions of parents and peers to children's moral socialization. *Developmental Review, 2,* 31–75.

Bronfenbrenner, U. (1960). Freudian theories of identification and their derivatives. *Child Development, 31,* 15–40.

Bronfenbrenner, U. (1977). Toward an experimental ecology of human development. *American Psychologist, 32,* 513–531.

Coates, B., & Hartup, W. W. (1969). Age and verbalization in observational learning. *Developmental Psychology, 1,* 556–562.

Dollard, J., Doob, L. W., Miller, N. E., Mowrer, O. H., & Sears, R. R. (1939). *Frustration and aggression.* New Haven, CT: Yale University Press.

Dollard, J., & Miller, N. E. (1950). *Personality and psychotherapy: An analysis of thinking, learning, and culture.* New York: McGraw-Hill.

Hoffman, M. L. (1970). Conscience, personality, and socialization techniques. *Human Development, 13,* 90–126.

McCall, R. B. (1977). Challenges to a science of developmental psychology. *Child Development, 48,* 333–344.

Miller, N. E. (1948). Theory and experiment relating psychoanalytic displacement to stimulus–response generalization. *Journal of Abnormal and Social Psychology, 43,* 155–178.

Miller, N. E., & Dollard, J. (1941). *Social learning and imitation*. New Haven, CT: Yale University Press.

Nucci, L. (1984). Evaluating teachers as social agents: Students' ratings of domain appropriate and domain inappropriate teacher responses to transgression. *American Educational Research Journal, 21*, 367–378.

Rebok, G. W., & Balcerak, L. J. (1989). Memory self-efficacy and performance differences in young and old adults: The effect of mnemonic training. *Developmental Psychology, 25*, 714–721.

Sears, R. R. (1941). Non-aggressive reactions to frustration. *Psychological Review, 48*, 343–346.

Sears, R. R. (1951). A theoretical framework for personality and social behavior. *American Psychologist, 6*, 476–483.

Sears, R. R. (1957). Identification as a form of behavioral development. In D. B. Harris (Ed.), *The concept of development* (pp. 149–161). Minneapolis: University of Minnesota Press.

Sears, R. R. (1958). Personality development in the family. In J. M. Seidman (Ed.), *The child* (pp. 117–137). New York: Rinehart.

Sears, R. R. (1963). Dependency motivation. In M. R. Jones (Ed.), *Nebraska Symposium on Motivation* (Vol. 11, pp. 25–64). Lincoln, NE: University of Nebraska Press.

Sears, R. R. (1975). Your ancients revisited: A history of child development. In E. M. Hetherington (Ed.), *Review of child development research* (Vol. 5, pp. 1–80). Chicago: University of Chicago Press.

Sears, R. R., Maccoby, E. E., & Levin, H. (1957). *Patterns of child rearing*. Evanston, IL: Row, Peterson.

Sears, R. R., Rau, L., & Alpert, R. (1965). *Identification and child rearing*. Stanford, CA: Stanford University Press.

Sears, R. R., Whiting, J. W. M., Nowlis, V., & Sears, P. S. (1953). Some child-rearing antecedents of dependency and aggression in young children. *Genetic Psychology Monographs, 47*, 135–234.

Yarrow, M. R., & Yarrow, L. J. (1955). Child psychology. *Annual Review of Psychology, 6*, 1–28.

17

A SINGULAR CAREER: NANCY BAYLEY

JUDY F. ROSENBLITH

One might call Nancy Bayley the "very model of a model developmentalist." She was interested in the course of physical development and growth of many different systems, including head circumference (Bayley, 1936a; Eichorn & Bayley, 1962), rectal temperature (Bayley & Stolz, 1937), height, weight, skeletal maturation, body build, and motor and intellectual development.[1] Her first publication in 1926 (based on her master's thesis) was "Performance Tests for 3-, 4-, and 5-Year-Olds," and the last I found (Werner & Bayley, 1966) was "The Reliability of Bayley's Revised Scale of Mental and Motor Development During the First Year of Life." There are several unusual aspects to her life's work: (a) She pursued the same set of topics for her entire career; (b) her work covered a broad span of developmental characteristics; and, as everyone knows, (c) her infant tests

I am indebted to the reference librarians at Wheaton College for assembling Bayley's publications, to Marylyn Rands for editorial help, and to Robert McCall for helpful suggestions for improving the manuscript.

Reprinted from *Developmental Psychology*, 28, 747–758. Copyright by the American Psychological Association.

[1] Bayley also studied fear by using the psychogalvanic technique (1928) for her doctoral dissertation, and crying and the situations during testing that evoked it (1932).

are the standard used in research in this country and throughout much of the world. She was also unusual in that many of her articles were authored solely by her.

CAREER HIGHLIGHTS

Nancy Bayley, after 2 years as an instructor at the University of Nebraska, went in 1928 to Berkeley's Institute of Child Welfare (now the Institute of Human Development) at the invitation of Harold Jones. There she initiated the study that became known as the Berkeley Growth Study (BGS). She remained at Berkeley until 1954, when she became chief of the section on child development at the National Institute of Mental Health, returning to Berkeley in 1964 as first head of the Harold E. Jones Child Study Center.[2]

In addition to Bayley's many professional publications and papers for professional meetings, she took the time to write or collaborate on articles for popular consumption. These efforts span the period from 1930 to 1961. In the 1930s, she and Harold E. Jones produced movies on the development of locomotion and on a case history (Case 75). She also lectured widely to medical persons and other professional groups concerned with children.

With this overview, we can turn to some of her substantive contributions. Her major contributions were in the areas of growth and skeletal maturation, body build and androgyny, issues of measurement and methodology, and motor and mental development. First, her general contributions to issues of measurement are addressed. Then I will proceed to selected topics she dealt with, starting with those less known to current-day psychologists. Because different threads of her research crop up at different times, I will be chronological within topics.

MEASUREMENT

A hallmark of all of Nancy Bayley's work has been a concern with good measurement, be it of motor or intellectual behaviors, of height in young children, or of the radiographs used in judging skeletal maturity to predict adult height (Bayer & Bayley, 1947). She was always alert to pointing out problems in her own data, as, for example, in calling attention to the fact that in longitudinal studies, consistency over time can be caused by sampling errors that persist in the constant sample; hence, replication in other samples is always needed. She often achieved replication by using

---

[2]More detailed information on Nancy Bayley and her career can be found in a recent chapter by Lipsitt and Eichorn (1990).

data from the Berkeley Guidance sample in addition to that of the BGS, and, in some work,. the Terman sample of the gifted. Her consultancies often involved helping other people achieve good measurement.

In achieving satisfactory measurement of some feature, be it physical or psychological, Bayley was always careful to call attention to individual differences, not just to group characteristics. The publication practices at the time of most of her work allowed for large amounts of descriptive data, as well as for brief case studies illustrating individual differences and many charts showing growth curves for individual cases. For those of us accustomed to current publication practices, the detail of her descriptive data makes it difficult to read some of her studies. However, the point conveyed by them is always given in verbal description, and many tables can be lightly skimmed unless one has a particular interest in the topic.

BODY BUILD AND ANDROGYNY

In 1946, long before psychologists were much concerned with androgyny but when somatotyping was somewhat popular, Bayley and Bayer developed a scheme for classifying the photos of the backs of boys and girls as they approximated physical maturity (about 17.5 years of age). This work built on Jones and Bayley (1941). Bayley and Bayer determined which characteristics were related to sex differences and which varied without regard to sex, a procedure which they describe as "taking practical cognizance of the accepted biological fact that every individual is a composite of both masculine and feminine endowments, and that the only mutually exclusive sex element is the gamete" (Bayley & Bayer, 1946, p. 435). Eight items that were reliably rated and that had bimodal distributions with varying amounts of overlap were used to determine maleness, femaleness, and androgynous characteristics. The last included both bisexual and asexual forms. They believed that with this measuring tool it should be possible to determine the relation of body type to personality, as well as to other physical and hormonal factors. Other researchers had looked at feminine bodily characteristics in men, but women had been largely ignored.

Bayley (1951b) compared girls who were hyperfeminine, feminine, hypofeminine, hypo-bisexual, and bisexual with boys in the five parallel masculine categories on height, weight, strength, and masculinity (M) and feminity (F) of interests (on the Kuder Interest Record). Among the physical variables, strength was related to androgyny within each sex. Hyperfeminine females were heavier than hypofeminine females, and bisexual males, the heaviest of all groups, were weaker than hypermasculine or masculine males. The Kuder M-F scores were unrelated to height, strength, or skeletal age but were slightly related to IQ for males. For both sexes, mean M-F scores were more feminine for the typical androgyny group. That is, there was some tendency for those of either sex whose body builds were not completely sex appropriate (but especially the hypomasculine and bisexual males) to have interest scores that deviated in the masculine direction from the average of their own sex. Unfortunately, neither Bayley nor anyone else, to my knowledge, has pursued the many research ideas contained in these articles, ideas that are well worth study today.

The relation of physical characteristics to psychological functioning was also addressed in Jones and Bayley (1950). Early-maturing boys were seen by adults as more attractive, showed earlier signs of appropriate grooming, were more masculine on the androgynic scale, and were more matter of fact, unaffected, and relaxed. Late-maturing boys were more eager (more childish?). Peer ratings were less affected than those of adults. In this, as in virtually all of her work, Bayley stressed not only the individual differences, but also the multiplicity of factors that contribute to basic personality patterns. This early work foreshadows our current concerns with the timing of puberty in studies of adolescence (Magnusson, 1988).

GROWTH IN BODY SIZE AND PROPORTIONS

In 1935, Bayley and Davis published their detailed account of growth changes in the first 3 years. Nine measures of size had been made at 17 times during the child's first 36 months. The measures that showed the greatest correlations from one time to another were head circumference, length, and stem length. Weight and width did not become consistent until after 12 months. Although it is inappropriate to go into the findings on physical growth, I note the evaluation of Bayley's work provided by Tanner, one of the world's leading authorities on human growth. He described the contributions of Nancy Bayley to human growth (in his book, A *History of the Study of Human Growth*, 1981) as classic in their penetration and simplicity. Tanner also noted that Bayley (1940c) published the first correlations that related infants' size to their adult size and made the first effort (Bayley, 1956a) to produce standards for heights that took account of an individual's tempo of growth. This radical departure in the approach to standards of growth built on Shuttleworth's (1939). Bayley's (1956a) was seen as a tool for use rather than as an analytical dissection. It was published appropriately in the *Journal of Pediatrics*, but to an audience that Tanner describes as lacking an understanding of tempo and accustomed only to cross-sectional data. He credits Bayley's 1956a article with being at the base of his own much-quoted article on longitudinal-type standards (Tanner, Whitehouse, & Takaishi, 1966).

SKELETAL MATURING

In two major articles, Bayley (1943a, 1943b) related early and late skeletal maturing to individual differences in body build. Most early-maturing boys were consistently tall and broad hipped, whereas late maturers were characteristically slender hipped and long legged. Early-maturing girls tended to be relatively large at an early age (at 10 to 12 or 13 years) and small as adults, whereas late-maturing girls were more often the reverse. There were sex differences in age of reaching bone maturity (girls about 2 years earlier). The *rate* of growth change differed for boys and girls with curves that are separated, not just bimodal. But, if the groups were equated for skeletal maturity, and if percentage of mature height and stem length were plotted against age, sex differences were eliminated. There thus "appears to be a relation between the maturity of the skeleton and the proportion of completed growth, which is independent of sex" (Bayley, 1943a, p. 86). Among boys, deviations in maturing showed some evidence of being accompanied by differences in strength, motor abilities, and personality characteristics.

In 1946, Bayley published the first of her famous tables for predicting adult height from a knowledge of the child's present height and skeletal age, as determined from X-rays (usually of the hand), to determine whether bone growth was still active. The tables (applicable to children over 7 years of age) took account of children's velocity of growth and sex, and they were based both on data from the Harvard Growth Study and on the California children.

Because the standards for judging skeletal age from X-rays changed over time, Bayley and Pinneau (1952) revised the tables. This later article contains a clearer presentation of method than the earlier one. Predictions made from a single X-ray and height measurement (prior to 12 years for girls or 14 years for boys) were accurate to within 1 inch (see also Bayley, 1962). As psychologists, you may wonder why it is important to be able to do this. For children with growth problems, some of which may be treatable with growth hormones, such prediction can be extremely important (see, e.g., Bayer & Bayley, 1949). Tanner (1981) has noted that these tables are still extensively used by pediatricans and endocrinologists.

MOTOR DEVELOPMENT

In 1935, Bayley published a monograph titled "The Development of Motor Abilities During the First Three Years: A Study of Sixty-One Infants Tested Repeatedly." In it, she called attention to the fact that McGraw (1932) had noted that "sitting," "standing with help," "walking," and so on are of little significance until the processes through which they have been achieved are understood. Certainly Bayley's detailed studies helped in this direction.

The California Infant Scale of Motor Development (Bayley, 1936b) was made up of items from several sources and included 12 items from the mental development scale (mostly tests of eye–hand coordination and prehension), which are discussed later. After establishing appropriate measurement qualities, the growth trends of motor abilities were plotted. Motor development showed a very rapid rise in the first 21 months, then an abrupt decrease, for both boys and girls. Gross motor coordinations related to gaining control of the body appeared to grow more rapidly during the first 2 years than did more intellectual abilities. During the third year, the situation was reversed (Bayley, 1935).

The motor scale had a fair degree of reliability, but less than that of the mental scale. Hence Bayley (1935) addressed the question of how well motor performance in the first year of life would predict later motor performance, a question previously addressed only by Shirley (1931), who believed there was high predictability but who had an inadequate data base. Bayley found the correlations between early and later tests to be low, except for adjacent age groups. She also asked how the predictive power of motor scores would compare with that for mental scores. It is intriguing to note that the antigravity items on the motor scale correlated highly with mental scores at 6 months. This fits well with current work on the importance of control of the upper body in achieving sophisticated reaching behaviors (see, e.g., Rochat & Senders, 1990; Rochat & Stacy, 1989). Until now this area has been little examined since Bayley (1935) had noted that the relation between sitting erect and mental achievements could be due to the new position stimulating the perceptual and manipulatory functions that were scored in the mental tests. The new work indicates that artificially providing positions and stability not yet achieved developmentally may also stimulate these functions.

The correlations between motor and mental scales were very low after 15 months. Extremely thin or chubby children had a slight tendency to make poorer than average motor scores. The age of walking correlated higher than that of prewalking behaviors with both motor and mental scores; even in the third year the correlations are substantial (.40 and .63) but are inadequate for individual prediction. The age of first walking was as closely related to 3-year-olds' motor and mental ability as was the whole battery of tests given at 1 year.

Bayley (1935) concluded that the developmental sequence depended on rapid increments in the entire level of ability, rather than on a regular order of appearance of specific abilities. Her data did not confirm Shirley's postulated invariable sequence of motor growth but were compatible with that espoused earlier by Gesell. Bayley saw the correlation of .39 between age of walking and talking as an instance of the tendency for all behavior to conform to a general maturational trend in early life, when both behaviors are a function of a general stage of maturity. The general level of maturity becomes less important as age increases and as the rate of development becomes slower. She called attention to factors that might operate to make motor abilities in infants seem more related to mental abilities than they are in older persons.

In her 1935 paper, Bayley found that motor scores, unlike mental scores, were not correlated with the level of parental education. In 1937, together with Harold E. Jones, she published a paper examining environmental correlates of mental and motor development from infancy to 6 years. At the time of this publication, some studies had found parental education and occupation to be related to development and others had not. One of the early points made in the article was that, for the first 15 months, the reliability of any single test was unsatisfactory, so that three successive tests were combined to yield a more reliable score. This practice of combining scores from repeated tests is currently used by some researchers who work with the Brazelton test for newborns and is built into Korner and Thom's (1991) test for use with premature babies.

Social factors such as income, education, and ratings of social class tended to be slightly negatively correlated with motor scores during the first year.[3] Bayley and Jones (1937) noted that this could be explained by a biological hypothesis (precocity associated with a lower limit on final development) or by an environmental hypothesis. This hypothesis was that children from superior homes are less motorically advanced because they have less incentive for independent action, owing to being more sheltered and cared for in infancy, a hypothesis that may not make sense in today's child-rearing environments.

In a review of mental and motor development from 2 to 12 years, Bayley (1939b) summarized the findings thus:

> These recent studies of motor abilities tend to agree in reporting age changes in the abilities measured, although most of the data are for young children; in positive correlations between scores on different tests, . . . in absence of correlation with socio-economic factors; and in improvement with practice on certain skills. Sex differences vary widely according to the specific ability under consideration. (p. 37)

In 1940, Bayley's monograph, *Studies in the Development of Young Children* (Bayley, 1940c), appeared. In one chapter titled "Gaining Control Over the Body," she noted that motor abilities were not affected by past routine illnesses, the maturity of the skeleton, or vegetative functions. As in all of her work, Bayley stressed the individual differences in development.

---

[3] In looking at socioeconomic factors, it is worth noting that at the time of her study, approximately half of the sample had annual incomes under $1,560.

The growth curve for the first 6 or 8 months was of sensorimotor development rather than of intelligence and was unrelated to later mental development, except for preceding it. Bayley's conclusion was

> we have measured, at successive ages, varying composites of more or less independent functions; not until after the age of two years do these composites exhibit a significant degree of overlapping with the aggregations of traits constituting 'intelligence.' (1933a, p. 82)

This view is compatible with Gardner's (1985) view of multiple intelligences, except that he sees them as operating throughout the life span.

In one of Bayley's 1940 chapters for the *Yearbook of the National Society for the Study of Education*, she (1940b) surveyed her data on mental growth to that time when 48 of the children in the BGS had been tested through 9 years of age. The sample, from somewhat above-average backgrounds, "test wise," and tested by an examiner who had much experience in dealing with them, scored above average at ages 5 through 8 (on the California Preschool Scale at 5 and the Stanford-Binet later). Children's rates of mental growth became fairly stable at about 4 years. It appeared that tests given at 4 years might be predictive to grade school (rs about .75). Tests at 2 to 4 years correlated only at $r = .55$ with 8- and 9-year performance, and those before 18 months were useless in prediction of school-age abilities, a result in agreement with findings of Honzik (1962). Bayley noted that one fourth of the group changed 10 or more IQ points over a single year and 17 or more points over a 3-year interval. The growth curves of individual children exemplified differing patterns of growth, and some had no pattern. Rates of intellectual growth became more stable between 2 and 4 years of age, with some children becoming consistent earlier than others. The more stable cases were those near the average; those with extreme scores in the first 2 years were more apt to regress toward the mean. After a number of analyses attempting to find greater stability in different components, Bayley (1940b) concluded:

> It is possible, of course, that tests might be devised for use in infancy that would predict later intelligence. But the present efforts have been fruitless. Neither a more widely inclusive measure of the development of behavior nor various selections restricting the nature of the abilities measured has yielded greater prediction from the first two years. . . . It seems more reasonable to conclude . . . that there is a pervasive change in mental organization during the early preschool period . . . most rapid between one and two years of age. (p. 43)

She went on to point out that although the break (i.e., change point) occurs at about the time language is acquired, her data on nonlanguage and language aspects of the tests make this (i.e., acquisition of language as an explanation) unlikely, especially since language itself was unpredictable.

By 1949, data collection and analysis had proceeded to the point that Bayley was able to write "Consistency and Variability of Growth of Intelligence From Birth to Eighteen Years." It included an excellent survey of the problems of comparing MAs and IQs from different tests that should receive more attention currently.

An interesting discussion included data from other tests and samples that corroborated her earlier findings of age changes in variability. She noted that

> During growth of a structure or function variability increases, in part because of increasing individual differences in capacity, and in part because of individual differences in the speed with which the maturing process takes place. These two factors are known to be operative in physical growth, and it seems reasonable to expect that they may be characteristic of many growth processes. During the stage of development when both factors operate freely, the variability of measures or scores will become greater with the general increments in the structure or function concerned. But as an increasing number of individuals stop growing, and the means level off to a constant value, the individual differences which remain become restricted to those of the achieved mature state. (Bayley, 1949, p. 179)

Inasmuch as restricted variability necessarily brings the MA/CA (mental age/chronological age) ratio closer to average, Bayley computed standard scores at each age to analyze the correlations between tests at different ages (Bayley, 1956c). She plotted both these scores and IQs for a number of cases to show their lack of strict comparability. Children in the BGS were assigned an "intelligence lability score" based on the mean and standard deviation of their standard scores. Such lability was not different for boys and girls, nor was it correlated with intelligence level. Lability, too, showed wide individual differences and differed from one stage to another. She advocated further study of the meaning of lability, which to the best of my knowledge has not occurred. Indeed, too little attention has been paid in developmental psychology to variability per se.

Because of the low predictability from the mental scale (Bayley, 1940b), she attempted in 1949 to determine whether specific items would differentiate the brightest from the dullest. Thirty-one items on the First-Year Scale had been passed by the brightest 16- to 17-year-olds at least 2 months earlier than by the 6 dullest. But scores on these items still did not differentiate the two groups during the first year.

Later cluster analyses of Bayley's First Year Mental Scale (Cameron, Livson, & Bayley, 1967) found that one of the six clusters (composed chiefly of vocalizations) correlated with later intelligence for girls (higher to verbal than to performance scores). These correlations actually increased with age (up to 26 years, declining after 36 years). Correlations were negative for boys after 4 years.

Relation of Mental Performance to Environmental Factors

As noted earlier, one of the questions Bayley had posed was the extent to which mental growth is affected by environmental factors. Hence, as she had done in relation to motor development, she examined the relation of the infant test scores to various socioeconomic factors (1933a). At that time, some studies had found parental education and occupation to be related to development and others had not. Bayley found that midlevel parent education was negatively related to mental test scores from months 3 through 7, when it returned to zero, which it had been at birth. After 15 months, the correlations became positive (around .40 from 24 to 36 months). Play school had a small positive effect on scores in the third year.

Bayley and Jones (1937) reported on environmental correlates of mental development up to age 6.[5] Mental development was most highly correlated with mother's education ($r = .50$ at 2 years). Similar correlations with father's education were not found until 5 years. Midlevel parent education was most, and income was least, related to mental scores. For all social measures, correlations with mental scores tended to increase with age. While noting that their data could not determine the roles of educational and genetic factors in mental scores, Bayley and Jones called attention to the fact that the higher correlations with maternal than with paternal education could not be explained on a genetic basis. Mental growth curves of children of the most educated parents were nearly identical with those of the least educated until 42 months, after which the latter leveled off and the former continued to rise. The importance of parental education for infant performance was further shown by the fact that both siblings and unrelated pairs matched for midlevel parent education showed remarkably similar growth curves. They noted that

> the increasing correspondence between mental score and environmental variables is not necessarily attributable to the influence of the environment; it may equally well be a phenomenon of infant development, that inherited parent–child resemblances become evident only after a certain stage in the process of maturation has been reached. . . . the probability is that each has some validity, and that the growth of children involves both an increasing assimilation of environmental pressures and an increasing manifestation of complex hereditary potentialities. (Bayley & Jones, 1937, p. 339)

Bayley's conclusions are compatible with the views more recently espoused by Scarr and her colleagues (Scarr, 1987; Scarr & McCartney, 1983) and by Plomin and his (see, e.g., Bergeman, Plomin, McClearn, Pedersen, & Friberg, 1988; Plomin, 1986).

---

[5] An interesting sidelight is the fact that this article and several others acknowledge the assistance of the Works Progress Administration in preparing materials.

Bayley (1939a) also reviewed the studies of others on mental development, an account that is interesting to anyone concerned with the history of studies in this area. In her comments on nature and nurture, she said:

> It is apparent, from the various studies here reviewed, that inheritance is not the sole determiner of a child's intellectual status, and that many factors in his environment serve either to stimulate or to retard his mental development. It is extremely difficult, however, to control or to take account of all of the determiners of mental test performance so as to study the influence of any one of them; and most experimenters resort in part, at least, to hunches or preferences when interpreting their material. (Bayley, 1939a, pp. 26–27)

This comment seems as valid now as it was then.

Bayley (1940a) found that health and histories of illness were not related to mental development in general, but may have been in individual cases. Body build and skeletal maturity were unrelated to intelligence, but larger, more physically mature children were slightly more likely to be advanced mentally. Nursery school attendance and being first or last born, only children, or children of divorced parents were not differentiating factors, nor was having been very shy in the testing situation during infancy. The relation to attitudes and test-relevant behaviors do tend to be positive and are marked for some children, but for others are nonexistent. One of Bayley's conclusions was

> Attempts to isolate the factors influencing rates of mental growth . . . point repeatedly to the great complexity of these factors, and at the same time to minimize the influences of environmental factors on intelligence under relatively normal conditions. (Bayley, 1940a, pp. 77–78)

Focus on Variability in Relation to Age of Testing

One of Bayley's important contributions was to point to the patterns of change in standard deviations on tests with age: They increased rapidly from 1 to 6 months, dropped sharply to 12 months, then increased steadily to 36 months. She linked this pattern to the possibility that there was a shift in the type of abilities measured, so that as infants reached the limit of the development in one type of ability, there would be little variability (low standard deviations), and then, as a new function was being measured, variability would increase (high standard deviations).

In 1949, she corroborated her earlier findings on age changes in variability by using data from other tests and samples. There was less variability at 1 year than earlier or later, and the increase in variability after 1 year was followed by a decrease until 6 years, then another increase lasting till 11 or 12 years, after which it dropped again. To my knowledge this interesting hypothesis has not been tested subsequently.

Intelligence in Adulthood

Bayley was rather alone in the 1950s in looking at changes in intelligence in adulthood and the types of intellectual performance that change, especially in longitudinal samples that use tests with high enough ceilings to differentiate changing abilities at the upper levels of intelligence. She collaborated with Oden on a study of Terman's gifted sample (Bayley & Oden, 1955). There was marked stability of performance from about 29 to about 41 years of age on the Concept Mastery Test (.88 for both males and females and .92 for their respective spouses). Most increased their scores, 9% by more than 1 standard deviation (35 points), although about 9% lost more than 5 points. Regression toward the mean did not account for these changes: Increases occurred in all occupational and educational levels represented, in both sexes, in spouses as well as in the gifted, and at all levels of ability, except where the test ceiling prevented higher scoring.

Much of Bayley's work on intellectual growth was drawn together in her much reprinted and cited (1955) paper, "On the Growth of Intelligence," based on her presidential address to the Western Psychological Association. In it, she also developed an age curve for the growth of intelligence based on the BGS, a study by Owens (1953), and the Bayley and Oden (1955) data. The curve is based on scores that take as their reference point performance at 16 years of age. She concluded that

> The question . . . is whether more adequate studies, of the same individuals through time, will not show that the age of highest intellectual capacity is later than we thought, and that the decrements in abilities are, correspondingly, deferred. (Bayley, 1955, p. 817)

Bayley (1957) found that intelligence increased from 16 to 18 and 21 years for 33 cases tested on the Wechsler-Bellevue Intelligence Scale. Increases were about equal for both sexes and occurred at all levels of intelligence in the sample. Some seemed to have reached their top capacities by 16 to 18 years, but others appeared still to be growing at 21. Different components of the test changed differentially with age.

Bayley (1955) made a plea for testing her curve with more research and broader samples covering the entire life span. It is only relatively recently that substantial efforts have been made to understand changes in intellectual performance with increased age (see Salthouse, 1985; Schaie, 1983).

THE REVISED BAYLEY SCALES OF MOTOR AND MENTAL DEVELOPMENT

Perhaps the greatest tribute to the care with which Bayley had done her early work on motor and mental development and to the generality of her conclusions is to be found in the results obtained with her revision of both scales (Bayley, 1965a). The revision was undertaken when these scales were selected for the assessment at 8 months of the 50,000 children ultimately enrolled in the National Collaborative Perinatal Project. Bayley supervised the new standardization, in which the scales were administered to over 1,400 infants (from 1 to 15 months of age) from 12 metropolitan areas. This sample (quite representative of the population of the United States) replicated her earlier findings of no sex, birth order, or educational level differences on either scale. There were also no geographical differences or ethnic differences on the mental scale, although Blacks were superior on the motor scale. The growth curves for both mental and motor development were highly similar to those she had found almost 30 years earlier, although the point at which the rate of growth declined was 2 months earlier in the 1958–1961 sample. These babies were more precocious in the first 6 months, but not after 10 months. Motor scores showed an opposite trend, being higher after 8 months of age for the later tested infants. The 1965 data agreed with her earlier conclusion that if there is a minimally adequate environment, the human infant will develop rapidly in the first year.

At the time of her 1965a article, Bayley speculated about a possible genetic component to the Black superiority on the Motor Scale and ruled out environmental factors, partly in the light of Geber's (1958) report, later found to be faulty. Today we would not be able to rule out environmental sources for the motor superiority, unless we knew how many of the Blacks were from subcultures in which massage, practice, teaching, and other forms of stimulation were common (Rosenblith, 1992, chap. 8).

Werner and Bayley (1966) published data on two types of reliability: that between the scoring by the tester and an observer and that between the infant's performance on the same test given by the same examiner 1 week later. The only tester–observer reliability reported earlier than this was by Knobloch and Pasamanick (1960), who did not examine consistency over time. The Werner and Bayley study was also the first to report on the test–retest reliability of individual items of the scales, an effort that was particularly focused on the possibility that some items might be of particular use in trying to identify diagnostic signs of mental retardation.

Tester–observer reliability was determined for 90 eight-month-old infants and averaged over 89%. Test–retest agreement for 28 infants averaged over 75%. Items from the mental scale involving eye–hand coordination, sustained attention, awareness of object constancy, and vocabulary were highest on both types of reliability. Those that were lowest involved interaction with the examiner or spontaneous behaviors (vocalizations or exploration). Items from the motor scale with high test–retest reliabilities were those that represented finished products of maturation involving independent control of head, trunk, and lower extremities. Items with low reliability either involved assistance from an adult or were items that were rapidly emerging at 8 months. It is important to note that the items that Honzik (1962) found to differentiate between "suspect" and normal babies at 8 months were usually items that had high tester–observer and test–retest reliabilities.

A subtheme in Bayley's work was to examine the ages at which children became more similar to their parents. If we are to understand the contributions of heredity and environment to development, we must be able to make sense out of the pattern of ages at which similarities become maximal, an issue as yet not addressed by those who worry about this problem. Her 1954 article presented data on similarities in physical as well as mental characteristics. (There were also interesting age and sex differences in the correlations of children's and parents' physical characteristics, which I will not go into.) Overall, the children were favored both physically and mentally compared with their parents. The correlations for mental level became positive and significant at 21 months, were above .50 from 48 months on, and reached .65 at 17 years. One has to posit either that mental development at different ages is different, and hence differently inherited, or that environment plays an increasing role in the similarities between parents and offspring. However, the patterns of correlation were different for boys than for girls, which makes interpretation even more complex. Boys' mental test scores were more highly correlated with their mother's education than with their father's at 3, 6, and 8 years. Girls' scores were more highly correlated with both parents' education than boys' at most ages, but with no pattern of being higher for mother or father. These data need, at some point, to be understood in terms of the roles of environment, genetics, and biology. As part of this effort, some of the adoption studies need to have their data examined separately for the sexes.

PARENTAL ATTITUDE AND CIRCUMPLEX MODEL RESEARCH

Bayley's move from Berkeley to the National Institutes of Health led to a new phase in her work and to her collaboration with Schaefer, who had developed his circumplex model of maternal behavior (1959), and with Bell (Schaefer, Bell, & Bayley, 1959). Their work built on the Schaefer and Bell (1958) development of a parental attitude research instrument (PARI, based on BGS materials). This work was pioneering in considering the effects of child-rearing attitudes and behaviors, work which was fairly rapidly replaced by that looking at interactions. Although Sears (1951) had earlier called for considering the dyadic mother–infant relationship, little work on mother–infant interaction had appeared when Bayley and her colleagues did their work. A number of studies contemporary with Bayley and Schaefer's work looked at mother–infant relationships but did not focus on mental development. Examples are Harlow's (1958) on the artificial monkey mothers, Bowlby's (1958) on the nature of the child's tie to his mother, and Rheingold's (1956) on the modification of social responsiveness in institutional babies. Subsequent work has paid no more than sporadic attention to mental development in this context.

Consistency Over Time

Bayley and Schaefer used the maternal behavior model to examine a long-time Bayley theme—consistency over time—but now in maternal and child behaviors (Bayley, 1964; Schaefer & Bayley, 1960, 1963). Notes on maternal behavior in home interviews between birth and 3 years were converted into ratings or numerical scores and then compared with those at 9 to 14 years separately for boys and girls (Bayley, 1964). Consistency tended to be moderate. Mothers of girls were consistent on more and different variables than those of boys ($r > .20$ on 14 vs. 10 variables). For girls, mothers were more consistent on autonomy, emotional involvement, fostering dependency, and achievement demands; for boys, they were more consistent on positive evaluation, equalitarian treatment, and using fear to control. However, the greatest consistency for both sexes occurred for expressing affection, emotional involvement, irritability, and ignoring ($rs \geq .50$). Over time, mothers' relationships to daughters' behaviors diminished, whereas those to sons' behaviors increased. Although the precise variables examined differ from those studied in attachment research, these consistency data ought to be looked at in connection with the issue of whether early or current interactions lead to current attachment in infants (see, e.g., Solomon, George, & Ivins, 1987).

Interrelations Between Maternal and Child Behaviors

Schaefer and Bayley (1963) used the circumplex models of maternal and child behavior to establish patterns of correlations. Ratings of activity and rapidity (interpreted as extraversion) had the highest correlations with later behaviors. Both were significantly negatively correlated with ratings of positive task-oriented behavior (in boys through 12 years and in girls throughout childhood). They were positively correlated with extraverted aggressive behaviors in adolescent girls. As was suggested by Schaefer and Bayley, activity is currently studied as a possible enduring temperamental trait (Eaton, Chipperfield, & Singbiel, 1989; Eaton & Saudino, in press; Gandour, 1989), as is shyness (Kagan, 1989; Kagan, Reznick, & Snidman, 1989), and both are studied, sometimes under different names, by Plomin and colleagues (see, e.g., Plomin, 1987; Plomin & Dunn, 1986) and by Riese (see, e.g., Riese, 1986, 1987).

Schaefer and Bayley (1963) called attention to the fact that efforts to facilitate positive relationships were more likely to be successful than those to change negative relationships. Relatively recent studies have found this to be true, both in intervention programs dealing with mothers (see, e.g., Andrews et al., 1982) and in one dealing with interventions directed toward day-care providers (Beller, Laewen, & Stahnke, 1981).

The BGS data showed that social adjustment in the first 2 years correlated very little with later behavior for either sex, but both social and task-oriented behaviors became relatively consistent for both sexes after about 4 years. The evidence did not support a hypothesis that social patterns were fixed in infancy; rather, the more enduring behavioral traits were developed during latency. Much current temperament research finds the same lack of consistency prior to 3 or 4 years of age. Social and emotional behaviors showed marked and relatively rapid changes still later, in adolescence.

Maternal behaviors were more related to sons' than to daughters' behaviors. Because their findings differed markedly for boys and girls, Schaefer and Bayley (1963) suggested that all future studies of maternal or paternal behavior in relation to that of offspring be examined separately in the two sexes, a suggestion that has only sometimes been heeded. They concluded:

> the child's social, emotional, and task-oriented behaviors are, to some extent, a reaction to the parental behaviors he has received throughout the period of childhood. . . . the consistency of a dimension of activity–passivity, and its relative independence of parent–child relationships, also supports hypotheses that the human infant is not completely plastic but responds to his environment in accordance with his innate tendencies. (Schaefer & Bayley, 1963, p. 96)

This is a view that has only come to be commonly espoused in the 1980s, as seen in the earlier cited work of Scarr and Plomin.

Maternal and Child Behavior in Relation to Later Development

Bayley and Schaefer (1964) and Bayley (1964) also found marked sex differences in the relations between maternal and child behaviors and the child's intelligence:

> Mothers who evaluate their boy babies positively, behave toward them in an equalitarian way, and to some degree both grant them autonomy and express affection for them—such mothers more often have sons who as infants are happy, positive in their responses, and calm. These boys tend to make below-average mental scores in the first year but to make rapid gains in the next two or three years, so that by five and thereafter they are more likely to have high IQs. (Bayley & Schaefer, 1964, p. 67)

Daughters whose mothers are both loving and controlling tend to have above-average mental scores over the first 3 years, but early maternal or child behaviors have little or no relation to their intelligence after 5 years. Generalizing from the BGS sample, Bayley and Schaefer saw male infants' responses to their emotional climate as more readily fixed than females' and, hence, as coloring all later development. Bayley and Schaefer (1964) noted:

> one should at least be warned against making across-the-board general statements about the effects of "mothering" in infancy on later development. . . . The nature of the maternal behaviors, the nature of the child's own behaviors, the sex of the child, as well as a multitude of other genetic and environmental conditions all play some part. (pp. 69–70)

The caution against generalizations about the effects of mothering in infancy needs to be heeded more in our current work.

Bayley and Schaefer's data showed that the love–hostility dimension of maternal behavior was correlated with happy, calm, and positive behaviors for both boys and girls in the first 3 years, but with positive task-oriented behaviors of sons through 12 years. An integration of these results with some of the sex differences reported in the attachment data is much needed.

Origins of Maternal Behaviors

This topic was explored in Bayley and Schaefer (1960) and in Schaefer and Bayley (1963). The data in the latter suggested that mothers' hostility toward their children was highly related to poor relationships (with husband and others), to environmental stresses, and to emotional maladjustment. In the 1960 article, they proposed that social class differences in maternal behavior are more relevant to practices with boys than with girls. Their data shed light on the controversy (see Havighurst & Davis, 1955; Maccoby et al., 1954) over the role of historical timing in the differences between the findings of Sears, Maccoby, and Levin (1957) and of Baldwin, Kalhorn, and Breese (1945). The better educated and more intelligent BGS mothers might have been expected to follow the rigid schedules and training procedures advocated at that time, but the patterns of socioeconomic and sex differences found in Schaefer and Bayley (1960) based on the BGS were similar to those in the Sears et al. studies despite the temporal interval. They were also similar despite the fact that the Sears et al. data were based on maternal interviews about their practices, and the Schaefer and Bayley data on behaviors shown by mothers.

A slight tendency for mothers of higher socioeconomic status to be warmer and more understanding and accepting and for those of lower status to be more controlling, irritable, and punitive that existed in the first 3 years and at 9 to 14 years was stronger for mothers of boys than for those of girls. For Autonomy versus Control, higher status boy babies and lower status girl babies seem to have had more freedom from maternal supervision.

OUTLOOK ARTICLES FROM BAYLEY'S MATURE YEARS

Bayley's Research Philosophy

In 1956, Bayley published an article on "Implicit and Explicit Values in Science as Related to Human Growth and Development." In it, she made her philosophy of research clear. She stated that

> Although many of us experience deep satisfaction in the activities of inquiry and discovery for their own sake, their ultimate values lie in the application of scientific knowledge in the interests of human welfare and happiness. (Bayley, 1956b, p. 121)

In order to understand any psychological process (emotions, perceptions, learning, etc.), Bayley felt that it was of fundamental importance to know about its earliest appearance—the time at which it becomes differentiated—and progressive differentiation, as well as the interdependencies of the various processes. Her concern with the welfare of those she (or anyone) studied was spelled out in that article, and her focus on studying the child in a normal environment voiced there is being returned to today by those concerned with ecological psychology (see, e.g., Bronfenbrenner, 1986, 1990). She also made the tie between the ethics of a study and its likelihood of obtaining the desired information. Altogether, her 1956 article might serve as a required topic for discussion in seminars of psychologists about to enter the profession.

Pitfalls and Advantages of Life-span and Longitudinal Studies

In 1963, an adaptation of her 1958 presidential address to Division 20 (Adult Development and Aging) of the American Psychological Association appeared. It focused on a life-span frame of reference for psychological research and called attention to the lack of any precise definition for maturity with which infancy and decline are often compared. Bayley stressed the fact that change is continuous throughout life. While acknowledging that psychological processes are so complex that they must be broken into small, meaningful segments for study, she charged that investigators often forget to take account of the context from which they were abstracted. Her discussion of longitudinal studies presaged her 1965b article. The relations between growth and decline were discussed, and more study was asked for, as was her work and that of others on constancies in personality over time, especially as seen in longitudinal studies.

In her 1965 article on the longitudinal perspective in child development research, Bayley (1965b) discussed the criticisms that had been leveled at longitudinal studies in a way that acknowledged the problems but that also pointed to the questions that could only be answered by longitudinal research. This article is highly recommended to anyone contemplating a longitudinal study.

Her 1958 article, "Value and Limitations of Infant Testing," should, in my opinion, be required reading for all parents and professionals who are looking for the grail of an early indicator of adult intelligence.

SUMMARY

Nancy Bayley's work provided psychology with a number of useful tools.[6] Many who have used them have not had the understanding that Bayley had of the importance of individual differences, and few have used them in the ways she did to study patterns of change over time.

Bayley provides us with a role model both for being concerned with many aspects of development and for pursuing a set of problems (and a population) over a long time span. Her ability to follow her participants is itself a tribute to the sensitive concern she evidenced for them. We also must remember that most of her work was done when the support did not allow for assembling teams of workers, with the result that she herself did a phenomenal amount of the testing on which she has reported, a factor that contributed to the rapport and mutual respect.

In addition, Bayley anticipated many topics currently considered important, such as behavior genetics, the importance of timing of maturation in adolescence, the relation of size and structure to motor development, the importance of life-span approaches to cognitive development, and parental attitudes and behaviors as they affect both personality and intellectual development. Finally, Bayley has left us with a legacy of interesting facts and questions that still need to be addressed.

REFERENCES

Andrews, S. R., Blumenthal, J. B., Johnson, D. L., Kahn, A. J., Ferguson, C. J., Laseter, T. M., Malone, P. E., & Wallage, D. B. (1982). The skills of mothering: A study of parent–child development centers. *Monographs of the Society for Research in Child Development, 47*(6, Serial No. 198).

---

[6]The reference librarians at Wheaton College were startled when they looked in the Citation Index by the number of references to Bayley—316 between 1983 and 1991—mostly to the use of the Bayley Scales in the studies being reported.

Baldwin, A. L., Kalhorn, J. C., & Breese, F. H. (1945). Patterns of parent behavior. *Psychological Monographs, 58* (Whole No. 268).

Bayer, L. M., & Bayley, N. (1947). Directions for measures and radiographs used in predicting height. *Child Development, 18,* 85–87.

Bayer, L. M., & Bayley, N. (1949). Stature prediction in stature control. *Stanford Medical Bulletin, 7,* 130–136.

Bayley, N. (1926). Performance tests for three, four and five year old children. *Journal of Genetic Psychology, 33,* 435–454.

Bayley, N. (1928). A study of fear by means of the psychogalvanic technique. *Psychological Monographs, 38,* 1–38.

Bayley, N. (1932). A study of the crying of infants during mental and physical tests. *Journal of Genetic Psychology, 40,* 306–329.

Bayley, N. (1933a). Mental growth during the first three years: A developmental study of sixty-one children by repeated tests. *Genetic Psychology Monographs, 14,* 1–92.

Bayley, N. (1933b). *The California First-Year Mental Scale.* Berkeley, CA: University of California Press.

Bayley, N. (1935). The development of motor abilities during the first three years: A study of sixty-one infants tested repeatedly. *Monographs of the Society for Research in Child Development, 1,* 26–61.

Bayley, N. (1936a). Growth changes in the cephalic index during the first five years of life. *Human Biology, 8,* 1–18.

Bayley, N. (1936b). *The California Infant Scale of Motor Development.* Berkeley, CA: University of California Press.

Bayley, N. (1939a). Mental and emotional growth in personality adjustment. In C. E. Skinner & P. A. Witty (Eds.), *Mental hygiene in modern education* (pp. 25–65). New York: Farrar & Rinehart.

Bayley, N. (1939b). Mental and motor development from two to twelve years. *Review of Educational Research, 9,* 18–37.

Bayley, N. (1940a). Factors influencing the growth of intelligence in young children. In G. M. Whipple (Ed.), *Intelligence: Its nature and nurture: Yearbook of the National Society for the Study of Education, Vol. 39* (Part II, pp. 49–79). Bloomington, IL: Public School Publishing.

Bayley, N. (1940b). Mental growth in young children. In G. M. Whipple (Ed.), *Intelligence: Its nature and nurture: Yearbook of the National Society for the Study of Education, Vol. 39* (Part II, pp. 11–47). Bloomington, IL: Public School Publishing.

Bayley, N. (1940c). *Studies in the development of young children.* Berkeley, CA: University of California Press.

Bayley, N. (1943a). Size and body build of adolescents in relation to rate of skeletal maturing. *Child Development, 14,* 51–89.

Bayley, N. (1943b). Skeletal maturing in adolescence as a basis for determining percentage of completed growth. *Child Development, 14,* 1–46.

Bayley, N. (1949). Consistency and variability in the growth of intelligence from birth to eighteen years. *Journal of Genetic Psychology, 75*, 165–196.

Bayley, N. (1951a). Development and maturation. In H. Helson (Ed.), *Theoretical foundations of psychology* (pp. 145–199). New York: Van Nostrand.

Bayley, N. (1951b). Some psychological correlates of somatic androgyny. *Child Development, 22*, 47–60.

Bayley, N. (1954). Some increasing parent–child similarities during the growth of children. *Journal of Educational Psychology, 45*, 1–21.

Bayley, N. (1955). On the growth of intelligence. *American Psychologist, 10*, 805–818.

Bayley, N. (1956a). Growth curves of height and weight by age for boys and girls, scaled according to physical maturity. *Journal of Pediatrics, 48*, 187–194.

Bayley, N. (1956b). Implicit and explicit values in science as related to human growth and development. *Merrill-Palmer Quarterly, 2*, 121–126.

Bayley, N. (1956c). Individual patterns of development. *Child Development, 27*, 45–74.

Bayley, N. (1957). Data on the growth of intelligence between 16 and 21 years as measured by the Wechsler–Bellevue scale. *Journal of Genetic Psychology, 90*, 3–15.

Bayley, N. (1958). Value and limitations of infant testing. *Children, 5*, 129–133.

Bayley, N. (1962). The accurate prediction of growth and adult height. *Modern Problems in Paediatrics, 7*, 234–255.

Bayley, N. (1963). The life span as a frame of reference in psychological research. *Vita Humana, 6*, 125–139.

Bayley, N. (1964). Consistency of maternal and child behaviors in the Berkeley Growth Study. *Vita Humana, 7*, 73–95.

Bayley, N. (1965a). Comparisons of mental and motor test scores for ages 1–15 months by sex, birth order, race, geographical location, and education of parents. *Child Development, 36*, 379–411.

Bayley, N. (1965b). Research in child development: A longitudinal perspective. *Merrill-Palmer Quarterly, 11*, 183–208.

Bayley, N., & Bayer, L. M. (1946). The assessment of somatic androgyny. *American Journal of Physical Anthropology, 4*, 433–461.

Bayley, N., & Davis, F. C. (1935). Growth changes in bodily size and proportions during the first three years: A developmental study of sixty-one children by repeated measurements. *Biometrica, 27*, 26–87.

Bayley, N., & Espenchade, A. (1944). Motor development from birth to maturity. *Review of Educational Research, 14*, 381–389.

Bayley, N., & Espenchade, A. (1950). Motor development and decline. *Review of Educational Research, 20*, 367–374.

Bayley, N., & Jones, H. E. (1937). Environmental correlates of mental and motor development: A cumulative study from infancy to six years. *Child Development, 8*, 329–341.

Bayley, N., & Oden, M. H. (1955). The maintenance of intellectual ability in gifted adults. *Journal of Gerontology, 10,* 91–107.

Bayley, N., & Pinneau, S. R. (1952). Tables for predicting adult height from skeletal age: Revised for use with the Greulich–Pyle hand standards. *Journal of Pediatrics, 40,* 423–444.

Bayley, N., & Schaefer, E. S. (1960). Maternal behavior and personality development: Data from the Berkeley Growth Study. In C. Shagass & B. Pasamanick (Eds.), *Child Development Research Reports of the American Psychiatric Association* (Vol. 13, pp. 155–173).

Bayley, N., & Schaefer, E. S. (1964). Correlations of maternal and child behaviors with the development of mental abilities: Data from the Berkeley Growth Study. *Monographs of the Society for Research in Child Development, 29*(6, Serial No. 97).

Bayley, N., & Stolz, H. R. (1937). Maturational changes in rectal temperatures of 61 infants from 1 to 36 months. *Child Development, 8,* 195–260.

Beller, E. K., Laewen, H., & Stahnke, M. (1981). A model of infant education in day care. In M. J. Begab, H. Gardner, & H. C. Haywood (Eds.), *Psychosocial influences in retarded performance: Strategies for improving competence* (Vol. 2, pp. 127–146). Baltimore: University Park Press.

Bergeman, C. S., Plomin, R., McClearn, G. E., Pedersen, N. L., & Friberg, L. T. (1988). Genotype–environment interaction in personality development: Identical twins reared apart. *Psychology and Aging, 3,* 399–406.

Bowlby, J. (1958). The nature of the child's tie to his mother. *International Journal of Psychoanalysis, 39,* 350–373.

Bronfenbrenner, U. (1986). Ecology of the family as a context for human development: Research perspectives. *Developmental Psychology, 22,* 723–742.

Bronfenbrenner, U. (1990). Who cares for children? *Research and Clinical Center for Child Development, 12,* 27–40.

Cameron, J., Livson, N., & Bayley, N. (1967). Infant vocalizations and their relationship to mature intelligence. *Science, 157*(3786), 331–333.

Eaton, W. O., Chipperfield, J. G., & Singbiel, C. E. (1989). Birth order and activity level in children. *Developmental Psychology, 25,* 668–672.

Eaton, W. O., & Saudino, K. J. (in press). Prenatal activity level as a temperament dimension? Individual differences and developmental functions in fetal movement. *Infant Behavior and Development.*

Eichorn, D., & Bayley, N. (1962). Growth in head circumference from birth through young adulthood. *Child Development, 33,* 257–271.

Gandour, M. J. (1989). Activity levels as a dimension of temperament in toddlers: Its relevance for the organismic specificity hypothesis. *Child Development, 60,* 1092–1098.

Gardner, H. (1985). *The theory of multiple intelligence.* New York: Basic Books.

Geber, M. (1958). The psycho-motor development of African children in the first year, and the influence of maternal behavior. *Journal of Social Psychology, 47,* 185–195.

Harlow, H. F. (1958). The nature of love. *American Psychologist, 13,* 673–685.

Havighurst, R. J., & Davis, W. A. (1955). A comparison of the Chicago and Harvard studies of social class differences in childrearing. *American Sociological Review, 20,* 438–442.

Honzik, M. (1962, May). *The mental and motor test performances of infants diagnosed or suspected of brain-injury.* (Contract No. SA 43 PH 2426). Washington, DC: National Institutes of Health, National Institute of Neurological Diseases and Blindness, Collaborative Research.

Jones, H. E., & Bayley, N. (1941). The Berkeley growth study. *Child Development, 12,* 167–173.

Jones, H. E., & Bayley, N. (1950). Physical maturing among boys as related to behavior. *Journal of Educational Psychology, 41,* 129–148.

Kagan, J. (1989). Temperamental contribution to social behavior. *American Psychologist, 44,* 668–674.

Kagan, J., Reznick, J. S., & Snidman, N. (1989). Issues in the study of temperament. In G. A. Kohnstamm, J. E. Bates, & M. K. Rothbart (Eds.), *Temperament in childhood.* New York: Wiley.

Knobloch, H., & Pasamanick, B. (1960). An evaluation of the consistency and predictive value of the 40-week Gesell Development Schedule. *Psychiatric Research Reports, 13,* 10–31.

Korner, A. F., & Thom, V. A. (1991). *Neurobehavioral assessment of the preterm infant.* Orlando, FL: Harcourt-Brace-Jovanovich.

Lipsitt, L. P., & Eichorn, D. H. (1990). Nancy Bayley. In A. N. O'Connell & N. F. Russo (Eds.), *Women in psychology: A biobibliographic sourcebook.* New York: Greenwood Press.

Maccoby, E. E., Gibbs, P. K., & the staff of the Laboratory of Human Development, Harvard University. (1954). Methods of childrearing in two social classes. In W. E. Martin & C. B. Stendler (Eds.), *Readings in child development* (pp. 380–396). New York: Harcourt Brace.

Magnusson, D. (1988). *Individual development from an interactional perspective: A longitudinal study. Vol. 1.* Hillsdale NJ: Erlbaum.

McGraw, M. B. (1932). From reflex to muscular control in the assumption of an erect posture and ambulation of the human foot. *Child Development, 3,* 291–297.

Owens, W. A. (1953). Age and mental abilities: A longitudinal study. *Genetic Psychology Monographs, 48,* 3–54.

Plomin, R. (1986). *Development, genetics and psychology.* Hillsdale, NJ: Erlbaum.

Plomin, R. (1987). Developmental behavioral genetics and infancy. In J. D. Osofsky (Ed.), *Handbook of infant development* (2nd ed., pp. 363–414). New York: Wiley.

Plomin, R., & Dunn, J. (1986). *The study of temperament: Changes, continuities and challenges.* Hillsdale, NJ: Erlbaum.

Rheingold, H. L. (1956). The modification of social responsiveness in institutional babies. *Monographs of the Society for Research in Child Development, 21* (2, Serial No. 63).

Riese, M. L. (1986). Implications of sex differences in neonatal temperament for early risk and developmental/environmental interactions. *Journal of Genetic Psychology, 147,* 507–513.

Riese, M. L. (1987). Temperament stability between the neonatal period and 24 months. *Developmental Psychology, 23,* 216–222.

Rochat, P., & Senders, S. J. (1990, April). *Sitting and reaching in infancy.* Introduction to the Symposium on Posture and Action in infancy, presented at the International Conference on Infant Studies, Montreal, Canada.

Rochat, P., & Stacy, M. (1989, April). *Reaching in various postures by 6- and 8-month-old infants: The development on monomanual grasp.* Paper presented at the meeting of the Society for Research in Child Development, Kansas City, MO.

Rosenblith, J. F. (1992). *In the beginning: Development from conception to age two.* Newbury Park, CA: Sage.

Salthouse, T. A. (1985). *A theory of cognitive aging.* Amsterdam, Netherlands: North-Holland.

Scarr, S. (1987). Three cheers for behavior genetics: Winning the war and losing our identity: A presidential address to the Behavior Genetics Association. *Behavior Genetics, 17,* 219–228.

Scarr, S., & McCartney, K. (1983). How people make their own environments: A theory of genotype–environment effects. *Child Development, 54,* 424–435.

Schaefer, E. S. (1959). A circumplex model for maternal behavior. *Journal of Abnormal and Social Psychology, 59,* 226–235.

Schaefer, E. S., & Bayley, N. (1960). Consistency of maternal behavior from infancy to preadolescence. *Journal of Abnormal and Social Psychology, 1,* 1–6.

Schaefer, E. S., & Bayley, N. (1963). Maternal behavior, child behavior and their intercorrelations from infancy through adolescence. *Monographs of the Society for Research in Child Development, 28*(3, Serial No. 87).

Schaefer, E. S., & Bell, R. Q. (1958). Development of a parental attitude research instrument. *Child Development, 29,* 339–361.

Schaefer, E. S., Bell, R. Q., & Bayley, N. (1959). Development of a maternal behavior research instrument. *Journal of Genetic Psychology, 95,* 83–104.

Schaie, K. W. (Ed.). (1983). *Longitudinal studies of adult psychological development.* New York: Guilford Press.

Sears, R. R. (1951). A theoretical framework for personality and social behavior. *American Psychologist, 6,* 476–483.

Sears, R. R., Maccoby, E. E., & Levin, H. (1957). *Patterns of child rearing.* New York: Harper & Row.

Shirley, M. M. (1931). *The first two years.* Minneapolis: University of Minnesota Press.

Shuttleworth, F. K. (1939). Physical and mental growth of girls and boys age six

·to nineteen in relation to maximum growth. *Monographs of the Society for Research in Child Development, 4* (3, Serial No. 22).

Solomon, J., George, C., & Ivins, B. (1987, April). *Mother–child interaction in the home and security of attachment at age 6.* Paper presented at the Society for Research in Child Development, Baltimore, MD.

Tanner, J. M. (1981). *A history of the study of human growth.* Cambridge, England: Cambridge University Press.

Tanner, J. M., Whitehouse, R. N., & Takaishi, M. (1966). Standards from birth to maturity for height, weight, height velocity, and weight velocity: British children, 1965. *Archives of Disease in Childhood, 41,* 454–471, 613–635.

Thelen, E. (1984). Learning to walk: Ecological demands and phylogenetic constraints. In L. P. Lipsitt (Ed.), *Advances in infancy research* (Vol. 3, pp. 213–250). Norwood, NJ: Ablex.

Thelen, E. (1985). Developmental origins of motor coordination: Leg movements in human infants. *Developmental Psychology, 18,* 1–22.

Thelen, E., & Cooke, D. W. (1987). Relationship between newborn stepping and later walking: A new interpretation. *Developmental Medicine and Child Neurology, 29,* 380–393.

Thelen, E., & Fisher, D. M. (1982). Newborn stepping: An explanation for a "disappearing reflex." *Developmental Psychology, 18,* 760–775.

Thelen, E., Fisher, D. M., & Ridley-Johnson, R. (1984). The relationship between physical growth and a newborn reflex. *Infant Behavior and Development, 7,* 479–493.

Thelen, E., Fisher, D. M., Ridley-Johnson, R., & Griffin, N. (1982). The effects of body build and arousal on newborn stepping. *Developmental Psychobiology, 15,* 447–453.

Thelen, E., Skala, K. D., & Kelso, J. S. (1987). The dynamic nature of early coordination: Evidence from bilateral leg movements in young infants. *Developmental Psychology, 23,* 179–186.

Werner, E. E., & Bayley, N. (1966). The reliability of Bayley's revised scale of mental and motor development during the first year of life. *Child Development, 36,* 39–50.

18

ELEANOR J. GIBSON:
LEARNING TO PERCEIVE AND
PERCEIVING TO LEARN

HERBERT L. PICK, JR.

Imagine yourself a participant in an experiment. You are shown a complex graphic "scribble" consisting of a four-coil spiral. You are then shown successively a series of similar and identical drawings. Your task is to pick out the identical ones in the series. The first few scribbles seem about the same as each other and the same as what you remember of the original standard. However, you gradually notice that there is variation in number of coils in the spiral, perhaps degree of tightness of the spiral, and even direction of rotation of the spiral (clockwise vs. counterclockwise). You do not know if you have noticed all the ways the scribbles differed or all the particular differences among them, because the experimenter never tells you specifically whether you are right or wrong. However, at the end of the series the experimenter asks you to repeat the procedure, giving you another opportunity to look at the standard, and then to go through the series again. This time you are more certain that you have noticed the types

Reprinted from *Developmental Psychology*, 28, 787–794. Copyright by the American Psychological Association.

of difference among the scribbles, and you are fairly sure you have detected most of the scribbles that were not identical to the standard. Once more you are asked to examine the standard and to select those identical to it in the series. At the end of this trial the experimenter tells you, finally, that you have now gotten them all correct and thanks you for your participation.

You have been participating vicariously in a now classical experiment, conducted by Eleanor Gibson in the early fifties and published in one of the few papers jointly authored by her and her husband, James Gibson (J. J. Gibson & E. J. Gibson, 1955). The experiment was carried out with two groups of children (7- and 9-year-olds) and a group of adults. Not surprisingly, the initial level of performance of the adults was better than that of the children. That is, the number of similar scribbles incorrectly judged as identical to the standard the first time through was a decreasing function of age. In addition, the number of such confusion errors decreased with trials for participants of all ages.

Why is this experiment considered a classic? Consider the time when it was carried out. It was the early mid-fifties, in the heyday of behaviorism, with its emphasis on the association of stimuli and responses (e.g., Hull and Spence) or in some cases the association of stimuli and stimuli (e.g., Guthrie). Psychologists interested in learning generally agreed that learning was the forming of associations or, at the very least, emphasized the response side of learning. The scribble experiment was a simple and vivid demonstration that a change in performance as a function of experience did not have to involve the formation of associations between stimuli and responses but could consist of improvement in perception. Moreover, this improvement in perception occurred without reinforcement in the sense of drive reduction or even reinforcement in the sense of extrinsic information about correctness (i.e., knowledge of results). What was required was merely the opportunity to examine and to study the stimuli. What was learned was not a new association, but rather how the stimuli differed from one another. Besides the quantitative data about errors from the experiment, the spontaneous comments of the subjects—especially the children—during the learning task supported the claim that they were in fact noticing more and more of the types of variation as they progressed through the trials.

The article that described this scribble experiment was part of an exchange between the Gibsons and Postman (1955) on the nature of perceptual learning. In their article, the Gibsons drew a distinction between two senses of perceptual learning. One was the improvement in perception as a function of experience (*learning to perceive*); the other was a change in performance as a function of perceiving in a new or different way (*perceiving to learn*). Eleanor Gibson's elaboration of this initial analysis over the next decade or so essentially defined the domain of this important but relatively ignored form of learning. It culminated in her book, *Principles of Perceptual*

Learning and Development (E. J. Gibson, 1969). The book integrated a rapidly increasing research literature on the topic of perceptual learning (a considerable amount was her own contribution) and applied it to understanding the perceptual development of children. The central concept in Gibson's analysis of the process of perceptual learning has been that of *differentiation*. What is differentiation, and how has it figured in the development of her ideas?

DIFFERENTIATION

All previous perceptual theorists had agreed that the stimulation impinging on our sensory systems was too impoverished to account for the richness and veridicality of our perception. Associationism, in the form of classical structuralism as well as behaviorism, was one solution to this problem. The impoverished sensory stimulation, meaningless in itself, was enriched by association to provide a final meaningful perception. (Innate organization of the brain, as represented, for example, by Gestalt psychology, was an alternative solution.) The position of the Gibsons, in contrast, was that the stimulation impinging on us is rich, perhaps infinitely rich, and provided all the information necessary to account for our perception. This was a radical idea. It turns upside down the problem of how perception improves. The Gibsons' thesis in the exchange with Postman was that differentiation rather than enrichment is the basis of perceptual learning. Our perception improves because we come to detect or differentiate more of the aspects, features, and nuances of the tremendously complex stimulation that impinges on us. The Gibsons were arguing against the alternative that our perception improves because we form associations between simple aspects of the impoverished stimulation impinging on us and our own responses or other concurrent stimuli.

Eleanor Gibson had first emphasized the issue of differentiation in her doctoral dissertation on verbal learning, undertaken at Yale in the late thirties. She had come to Yale from Smith College, where she received her bachelor's degree in 1931. Smith was a good environment. Besides obtaining a thorough undergraduate grounding in psychology, she met and married James Gibson, one of her instructors. She stayed at Smith to teach and work on her master's degree. She went to Yale hoping to work on primate behavior with Robert Yerkes. However, Yerkes informed her that he accepted no women in his laboratory. She found Clark Hull a more sympathetic mentor and completed her dissertation with him in 1938.

Her thesis involved the study of the effects of paired associate learning of one set of items on subsequent sets (E. J. Gibson, 1939, 1940, 1941, 1942). In some of her thesis experiments, the task consisted of associating verbal responses with visual shapes. One innovative aspect of her design was varying the degree of similarity between the shape stimuli on an initial list and a subsequent list. She found that the lower the similarity (or the greater the differentiation) among the stimuli of the two lists, the less the interference from learning of one list on learning subsequent lists. Her careful theoretical development, as well as the systematic series of experiments to verify that analysis, served for many years as a research approach to be emulated.

The rigorous demonstration of differentiation in traditional learning tasks made it a plausible candidate for the basis of perceptual learning, as exemplified by the scribble experiment. Stemming from Gibson's thesis experiments, there had developed by the time of the scribble experiment a lively interest in the effects of predifferentiation of the stimuli used in learning studies. What were the effects on learning if subjects were given various kinds of prior experience in differentiating the stimuli that would be subsequently used in the learning task?

The role of such prior experience became the focus of considerable controversy in developmental research on discrimination learning. The controversy arose as part of the analysis of what came to be called *acquired distinctiveness* and *acquired equivalence* of cues. In the fifties and sixties, there was a lively interest in children's discrimination learning. The typical paradigm, adapted from research on animals, was to give the child a task of learning a distinctive response to each of a pair of stimuli. For example, the distinctive responses might be the vocalizing of a particular nonsense syllable to one of the stimuli and a different nonsense syllable to the other. Prior learning of different responses to the two stimuli facilitated subsequent discrimination learning. Conversely, prior learning of similar or identical responses to the two stimuli slowed subsequent discrimination learning. One explanation, following learning theories like those of Hull and Spence, involved associating distinctive or similar motor responses to the original stimuli. Suppose a child is faced with two fairly similar stimuli and learns to make a distinctive motor response to each of them. When these stimuli are presented for subsequent discrimination learning, the initial stimuli plus the distinctive proprioceptive feedback (implicit or explicit) from the motor response make the total stimulus configuration more distinctive than the initial similar stimulus pair. This would illustrate acquired distinctiveness of cues.

Gibson argued cogently that, to learn distinctive motor responses to the two similar stimuli in the first place, the stimuli would already have to be differentiated. (See E. J. Gibson [1963, 1969] for a review of the relevant data and issues.) In brief, predifferentiation, which yielded faster subsequent discrimination learning, did not necessarily involve distinctive response or motor learning. Experiments simply requiring children to make same–different judgments about the stimuli or to judge the similarity and differences would work equally well. She did not deny that learning one discrimination could facilitate or retard a subsequent discrimination learning task. Rather, she rejected the idea that these effects were based on the association of the responses.

The controversy continued for a number of years and became ever more particularistic. However, Gibson did not stay embroiled in this scholastic exercise. Instead, she proceeded to exploit her concept of differentiation as the underlying mechanism of improvement in perception in more positive ways. One example comes from her studies of the development of reading skills in children. In her analysis, an early stage of reading must involve differentiating among the various letter shapes. This should occur prior to, or at the most in parallel with, learning the letter names. To investigate this process, she and her colleagues (E. J. Gibson, J. J. Gibson, Pick, & Osser, 1962) assessed how well children could discriminate among variations of nonsense shapes that were similar to letters. To rule out variability caused by different children's experience with the actual letters of the alphabet, Gibson et al. generated a set of letterlike forms and, for each of these standard forms, a set of transformations. The transformations captured some ways in which one letter of the alphabet differs from another. Thus, for example, one type of transformation involved changing a straight line segment of the standard to a curve (or vice versa). Such a difference would distinguish a D from an O or a U from a V. Are children at the prereading and early reading ages sensitive to such variations? Children between the ages of 3 and 7 years were shown a standard form and were asked to pick out copies of it from a row of forms containing both copies of the standard and the variations. Even the young children were good at picking out transformations that would ordinarily distinguish one physical object from another, such as a transformation differing from the standard by having a segment added or removed. Children did not improve until the early school ages at differentiating those variations from the standard which distinguished among letters but not physical objects. These were the transformations involving straight-line-to-curve changes or rotations of the standard. Children showed the least improvement across the whole age range in differentiating transformations from the standard that do not distinguish among either the physical objects of the world or the letters of the alphabet. The study is a compelling example of how improvement in perception — in this case, of letters of the alphabet by children — can be understood in terms of differentiation based on detection of types of variation. At the same time, it illustrates the idea of how sensitivity to types of variation or dimensions of difference in one domain might generalize to another. In this case, the properties used to differentiate objects seem to be the ones used first to differentiate among graphic symbols.

This research on reading was undertaken at Cornell University. Gibson and her husband had moved to Ithaca with their two children after the Second World War when he accepted a position in the Cornell Psychology

Department. Cornell, unlike Smith, had nepotism rules, and she could not be hired on the faculty. She could become a research associate, and in that capacity, conducted research, first on conditioning and maternal–infant bonding in goats at the Cornell Behavior Farm and then in the Psychology Department proper on perceptual learning and development. Finally, after 16 years at Cornell, the nepotism rules were relaxed, and in 1966 in one step she became a full professor. In 1974, she was appointed as the Susan Linn Sage Endowed Professor of Psychology.

PERCEPTION AND COGNITION

Learning to Perceive Meaningful Properties

The traditional enrichment theories of perception were in a sense cognitive approaches. Consider, for example, the very idea of Helmholtz's unconscious inference to explain such phenomena as size constancy. At first blush, one might think a differentiation approach to perception would be *a*cognitive. However, this is far from the case. Gibson (1991) writes,

> perception *is* cognitive. . . . Many psychologists think of cognition exclusively as problem solving, reasoning, remembering, and so on, however. I like to point out that these processes begin with and depend upon knowledge that is obtained through perception, which extracts information from arrays of stimulation that specify the events, layout and objects of the world. (p. 493)

The roots of this strong assertion about perception being cognitive can itself be traced to Gibson's view of perceptual learning and the process of differentiation. Her interpretation of the improvement in discrimination of the letterlike forms in her reading research focused on the detection of distinctive features that distinguished among these graphic symbols and the actual letters of the alphabet. However, recall that the features initially discriminated were those that distinguished among the objects of the world. That is, the children were using discriminations that they were making among the meaningful objects of the world. They were applying their sensitivity to such differences to these strange graphic objects. More and more, Gibson has come to believe that progressive differentiation occurs with respect to information specifying the meaningful properties of the world.

An early example of this emphasis in Gibson's thinking on meaning in discrimination can also be taken from her research on reading. Although her initial studies focused on letter discrimination in children's learning to read, she quickly moved to larger units of letter clusters and whole words. One issue concerned how meaning was accessed through words. Pictures seem to convey meaning by virtue of being an iconic representation of the thing depicted. A reasonable prediction would be that children learning to read would be able to extract meaning from pictures more easily than from words. Gibson, Barron, and Garber (1972) confirmed this in an experiment in which second, fourth, and sixth graders and adults were asked to judge whether two pictures, two words, or a word and a picture were from the same category (i.e., had the same meaning). The matches could not be made on the basis of identical physical shape, because pairs of pictures from the same category were taken from different viewpoints and the pairs of words were in upper- and lowercase. For the younger children picture matching was faster than word matching, whereas for the adults word matching was faster than picture matching. Quick access to the abstract meaning of a word, as opposed to the more iconic meaning of a picture, seems to be a relatively slow development as reading skills develop.

Most recently, Gibson's empirical research has implicated meaning in perception, perceptual learning, and development through the concept of *affordance*. Affordance, a concept elaborated by James Gibson (1979), refers to the utility of aspects of the environment for organisms. It is an intriguing concept cutting across the subjective–objective dimension or bipolarity of Western philosophy and implying a very close reciprocity between organism and environment. As conceived by James Gibson, an object's affordance is objective in the sense that it is a real property of an object, but it is a property of an object taken with respect to an organism and, in that sense, subjective. It is that relationship between the object and organism that accounts for its utility. Thus an affordance of an airplane seat is the provision of sitting support for a normal-size child or adult. The airplane seat does not afford sitting support for an obese adult, much less for an elephant. In his formulation of this concept, J. J. Gibson argued that affordances were one of the primary perceivable aspects of the environment.

Eleanor Gibson has been exploiting the concept of affordance in her current research on infant perceptual development. She suggests that affordances may be among the first properties of the environment differentiated in perceptual development. However, affordances not only are determined by the relation between the physical characteristics of the environment and the physical characteristics of the organism, they also depend on the relation between the properties of the environment and the capacities of the organism. For example, whether a staircase affords stepping up depends on the riser height of the step in relation to leg length (Ulrich, Thelen, & Niles, 1990; Warren, 1984), but it also depends on the capabilities of the stepper. If one has a broken leg, a previously "steppable" staircase may no longer be so. Do young perceivers and infants perceive the affordances of their environment as determined by the physical characteristics of the environment, as well as themselves and their own capabilities? An example of one approach to this question is provided in an investigation by Gibson and her colleagues of infant and toddler locomotion across surfaces varying in rigidity.

Mothers at one end of a criblike enclosure called to their infants at the other end to come to them. The surface of the enclosure consisted of two possible walkways. One was a rigid surface covered with a textured fabric pattern. The other walkway was a nonrigid surface (a waterbed) covered with the same pattern. The nonrigid waterbed surface was set into gently undulating motion at the beginning of each trial. Two groups of infants participated: One group consisted of recently walking children about 14 months of age, whereas the other group included only crawlers about 11 months of age. The walking infants predominantly chose the rigid surface to cross to their mother. The few who did cross the nonrigid surface got down on their hands and knees and crawled across it. The crawlers did not show any particular preference for either surface. This pattern of results (supported by four additional experiments) was interpreted as suggesting that infants detect the affordances of surfaces relevant to their current mode of locomotion. In a similar manner, Gibson had been applying the concept of affordance to understand infants' and young children's perception of objects and possible paths of locomotion (Adolph, E. J. Gibson, & Eppler, 1990; E. J. Gibson, 1982). The results support the idea that perceptual development and learning in young children involve a progressive increase in discrimination and detection of the meaningful properties of the environment, the affordances.

Perceiving to Learn

The second connotation of perceptual learning raised by the Gibsons in their exchange with Postman was the idea that learning itself could be perceptual in nature. That is, our performance could change or improve, not because we had learned a new response but because we were perceiving in a different way. Our knowledge had increased, not in the sense that we had learned new responses, but because we were perceiving new things.

The scribble experiment, as mentioned, demonstrates improvement in performance without reinforcement in the sense of reduction of need or drive. That is not especially surprising today, but in the associative learning–theoretic atmosphere of the time it was a radical idea. What was the motivation for such learning? Gibson suggested it was something like a search for meaningfulness or information in the stimulation. This did not require external reinforcement or even extrinsic knowledge of results. As she put it, there was a "kind of intrinsic knowledge of results" (E. J. Gibson, 1963, p. 48) that the perceiver discovered. The idea that perception involves an effort toward meaning or making sense out of the world has been a persistent theme in Gibson's thinking over the years. She is fond of referring to an article by Woodworth (1947) on the reinforcement of perception that emphasizes an intrinsic motive to perceive clearly.

The search for meaning in perception, in fact, influenced Gibson's whole interpretation of the reading process. In spite of the fact that much of her own empirical research on reading was concentrated at the prereading and perceptual discrimination levels, she never lost sight of the fact that the goals of reading, in general, are comprehension and the extraction of meaning for a variety of purposes, such as the acquisition of information or entertainment. This is vividly reflected in a section of her book, *The Psychology of Reading* (E. J. Gibson & Levin, 1975), which contains delightful responses by skilled readers who were asked how they read various types of material. The examples, ranging from reading scientific material to reading newspapers to reading poetry, illustrate how skilled readers use a number of active strategies. Depending on the type of information desired, mature readers use flexible attentional strategies, which are adapted to the characteristics of the text, the newness of the information, and their appraisal of their own comprehension. The centrality of comprehension and extraction of meaning to Gibson's view of the reading process is also reflected in the final section of the book, with suggestions of what parents might do to help their children with reading. A variety of possibilities are mentioned. One is for the parents themselves to be good models, showing the child that reading is an interesting activity by engaging in it themselves. A second obvious recommendation is reading to the child, "which provides the best opportunity for [the child] discovering that books have something to say; it increases knowledge about other places and other people; and above all, it can increase a child's language skills" (E. J. Gibson & Levin, 1975, p. 553).

MECHANISM OF CHANGE IN PERCEPTUAL DEVELOPMENT AND LEARNING

Gibson has documented the fact of changes in perception with experience and the fact of learning as a function of changes in perception. She has argued compellingly that these changes reflect increased differentiation of the stimulation impinging on any developing organism. But what accounts for this differentiation? What is the mechanism underlying that change? The question of mechanism can be posed at several levels. Eschewing reductionism, Gibson has not been interested in specifying the physiological mechanism, but she has been very interested in understanding the mechanism at a behavioral level. Central to her view of the mechanism is conceptualizing perception as an active process. Implicit already in the scribble experiment was the idea that increased differentiation was a matter of attending to more or new dimensions of a stimulus. But how did that occur? One important way was through peripheral mechanisms of attention, the exploratory adjustments of sense organs.

Gibson followed in detail a body of Soviet research in the late fifties and early sixties, which searched for commonalities between hand movements and eye movements in children (Zaporozhets, 1965; Zinchenko, Van, & Tarakanov, 1963). This research itself was indebted to Pavlov's suggestion of an investigatory or orienting reflex. More generally, she found a distinction the Soviets made between executive and investigatory movements quite appealing. Indeed, in her book on perceptual learning and development, she writes, "Perception is action, but it is exploratory action, not executive action in the sense of manipulating the environment" (E. J. Gibson, 1969, p. 120).

Exploratory activity remains a primary mechanism in perceptual learning and development in Gibson's thinking. It figures importantly in her recent work on infant sensitivity to affordances. In the case of the research comparing crawling and walking infants in responding to rigid and water bed surfaces, she and her colleagues carefully observed both the visual and haptic exploratory activity of the infants when faced with these two types of surface. The older infants who walked only across the rigid surface spent much more time exploring the water bed surface haptically than they did the rigid surface. The younger infants, the crawlers, who showed no differential preference for either surface, did not differentially explore the two surfaces. The exploratory behavior of the infants appears to provide the information for differentiating their paths of movement in relation to their mode of locomotion.

A similar analysis of exploratory haptic activity was part of an investigation of a very different topic, the sensitivity of 1-year-old infants to visual–tactual correspondence (E. J. Gibson & Walker, 1984). During a habituation period, the infants were given an opportunity to explore tactually (in the dark) a rigid or a deformable spongy object. After this exposure, their visual preference was tested. Would the infants look more at a filmstrip depicting rigid motion of an object like the one they had been feeling in the dark or more at a filmstrip depicting an elastic deforming motion? The infants showed a significant visual preference for the same or familiar type of object as the one they had been exploring tactually. Of particular interest here was the haptic exploratory activity that was recorded in the dark with an infrared video camera. Five categories of haptic exploratory activity could be reliably coded from the videotape, and the frequency of two of these differed depending on whether the infants were exploring the rigid or deformable object. They pressed or squeezed the deformable object more than the rigid. They struck or hit the rigid object against the table surface more than the deformable object. These results indicate, first of all, by means of their exploratory activity, that even at this early age the infants are differentiating the material substance of these objects. Furthermore, the exploratory activity suggests a way the infants are acquiring the information about how the objects differ, in this case, information that affects their subsequent visual behavior.

CURRENT AND FUTURE IMPACT OF ELEANOR GIBSON'S RESEARCH AND IDEAS

Infants as young as 1 month of age are sensitive to the equivalence of a tactually pliable and visibly deforming moving object; likewise, they are sensitive to the equivalence of a tactually firm and visibly rigidly moving object (E. J. Gibson & Walker, 1984). As soon as infants are able to locomote and to crawl, they choose appropriate textured surfaces for locomotion in preference to transparent surfaces (Walk & E. J. Gibson, 1961). These previously mentioned examples of Gibson's research showing infant sensitivity to meaningful properties of the environment are both instigations of and contributions to the explosion of research on early infant cognitive development. This revolution began with the methodological breakthrough in the late fifties and early sixties in exploiting the orienting response and the habituation paradigm. However, for many years infant perceptual research was focused on psychophysical sensory dimensions such as brightness, amount of contour, and hue, only occasionally getting to the complexity of two-dimensional shapes and only rarely getting to the level of meaningful objects such as faces. Even then, the faces were often schematic outlines or, at the most, photographs. However, from the late seventies on, the emphasis has gradually shifted, and the research is showing precocious sensitivity to ever more complex and meaningful aspects of the world. There is substantial disagreement on how to interpret these results. Gibson prefers explanation in terms of perception: detection of affordances. Others (e.g., Spelke or Baillargeon) prefer explanation in terms of innate "higher" cognitive or conceptual processes. This disagreement is yet to be resolved (and may be unresolvable). However, the shift in emphasis to the meaningful features of the environment owes much to Gibson's influence.

A caricature of current views of infant cognitive development is that they leave the baby wrapped in thought; they regard the infant as a theoretician. It is the case that there is a contemplative emphasis in how the infant is regarded in current cognitive developmental research (e.g., Carey, 1991; Keil, 1991). More generally, action is largely ignored in current cognitive developmental theory. Conversely, cognition and cognitive development are largely ignored by researchers interested in the development of motor control. Gibson's view of perception and perceptual activity being important aspects of cognitive development provides a way to bridge the gap between cognition and action. For her, perception and action are integral; we perceive in order to act, and we act in order to perceive. The close coupling of perception and action in development may be reflected in the congruity between the maturation of action systems (Reed, 1982) such as manipulatory behavior and the development of sensitivity to relevant environmental features such as object properties (Eppler, 1990). A complete theory of cognitive development must explain how our knowledge is acquired and how our knowledge guides our behavior. Gibson's framework, emphasizing active perception of meaningful properties of the world, is and will continue to be a very fruitful way of approaching these issues.

In spite of the considerable current interest in perceptual development, especially in infants and young children, interest in perceptual learning has waned since the publication of Gibson's book, *Principles of Perceptual Learning and Development* (1969). Thus the emphasis in recent years in the study of perceptual development has been to document the perceptual achievements of infants and to note how these change as a function of age. There has been relatively little interest in the investigation of the role of experience in the improvements in perception. The trend appears to be reversing. One example is the research by Bertenthal and his colleagues on the role of locomotor experience in cognitive development (Bertenthal, Campos, & Barrett, 1984). Their research suggests that self-produced locomotor experience facilitates development of sensitivity to the kind of information provided by the visual cliff and also facilitates using geographic rather than egocentric frames of reference in spatial orientation. Another example is research by Bahrick (1988) on infant sensitivity to bimodal visual–auditory stimulation. Her results suggested that infants could detect the correspondence in bimodal stimulation if it arose from an actual event with bimodal information, but not if it were the result of an arbitrary association or coincidence of unrelated events in the two modalities. With the large knowledge base available now about what and when infants perceive, it is not unreasonable to expect a big increase in the near future in research on the next step: how experience affects these norms.

The role of experience in perceptual learning and development is an initial step in addressing the mechanism of change. Interest in the mechanism is bound to increase in the near future. As noted earlier, Gibson has focused on mechanism at the behavioral level, emphasizing overt exploratory behavior. From overt exploratory behavior, it is often possible to see how an organism is making available new information about the environment. However, not all exploratory behavior is overt, and good techniques need to be found for inferring implicit exploratory behavior. It is likely that such techniques will be developed in the near future and will include methods as mundane as direct questioning for older subjects, as well as inferences from reaction time measures and types of errors, and experimental manipulation of the availability of perceptual information.

Gibson (e.g., 1969) has also hypothesized processes of abstraction and filtering as mechanisms underlying perceptual learning, but these have received much less attention than exploratory behavior. One reason may be that they also have to be inferred indirectly. The use of the various new less intrusive techniques for observing brain functioning may be one way to investigate these implicit processes. More generally, the rapid advances in brain physiology are very likely to elucidate the mechanisms of perceptual learning at the neurological level. For example, the work of Greenough and his colleagues (e.g., Greenough & Black, 1992) illustrates how early experience affects both brain anatomy and neural functioning in relation to perceptual and cognitive development.

Gibson herself is not so sanguine about the possibility of a rapid payoff in seeking mechanisms at the neurological level. She feels that we must know more about the things we want the neuropsychologists to explain. She writes,

> On the whole, I have not found my sallies into the neurological literature very productive. As psychologists we are still needed as the scientists who know how to study behavior, who can define the intricate intertwining of perceiving and acting in the adaptive life of a human animal, and who can observe the development of this activity with insight into the constraints, opportunities, and environmental offerings that underlie the dynamics of change. (E. J. Gibson, 1992, p. 234)

ELEANOR GIBSON AS A DEVELOPMENTAL EXPERIMENTER

It is no accident that the aforementioned description of Gibson's approach and contributions includes so many detailed examples of the results of her research. Starting with her early dissertation research, she was regarded as a consummate experimenter. Her dissertation included a detailed and systematic theoretical analysis of how differentiation and generalization—concepts elaborated from the classical conditioning paradigm—might be applied in the voluntary verbal learning domain. This was followed by an equally systematic as well as rigorous series of experiments based on the theoretical analysis.

Throughout her career, she has continued to be a model experimenter who has been widely recognized—for example, by her election to the National Academy of Science and the awarding to her of the National Medal of Science (1992). In 1980 Eleanor Gibson became professor emeritus at Cornell University, but she has not retired. Since then, she has continued her very active research program, first as director of the Eleanor J. Gibson Laboratory of Perceptual Development at Cornell and then as visiting professor for various lengths of time at Emory University, the University of Connecticut, and the University of Minnesota.

It is instructive to try to characterize Gibson's experimental approach. First, her experiments are always theoretically motivated. As is obvious from the foregoing, she has a strong theoretical orientation. This has always been evident in the conceptualization of her empirical research, ranging from the testing with goats of Mowrer's two-factor theory of conditioning (E. J. Gibson, 1952), to the study of the nature of improvement in adults' judgments of distance over natural terrain (e.g., E. J. Gibson, Bergman, & Purdy, 1955), to the investigation of toddlers' sensitivity to the affordances for locomotion of surfaces with different degrees of slope (Adolph et al., 1990). The empirical results by themselves are of considerable interest, but the theoretical context in which she embeds the problems generates an added richness, depth, and provocativeness. For example, as an empirical investigation, Adolph et al. had parents call to their 14-month-old children to come to them across an inclined surface. On different occasions the slope varied from 10° to 40°. A basic empirical question was how their mode of locomotion depended on the degree of slope. Although all the children were walkers, would they revert to crawling at the steeper slopes? The theoretical context raised such questions as whether toddlers were sensitive to the affordances of this situation, and if so, did they detect these affordances by active exploration? Because affordances by definition implicate the relation between the organism and the environment, a subsidiary question was whether it would be possible to predict the modes of locomotion that would be used on the basis of physical characteristics and skill level of the individual child. The results indicated that body dimensions were unrelated to mode of locomotion in this situation, but locomotor skill as reflected in step length was related. Children with longer step lengths tended to walk up steeper inclines than children with shorter step lengths.

Second, in characterizing her experimental approach, perhaps because her research has theoretical implications, Gibson poses the questions of her experiments sharply and clearly. This permits the use of simple and rigorous designs in answering them. The series of studies on infants' ability to distinguish rigid and elastic motion—a characteristic that ordinarily specifies a difference in object substance and object affordances—is a good illustration of this characteristic (E. J. Gibson, Owsley, & Johnston, 1978; E. J. Gibson, Owsley, Walker, & Megaw-Nyce, 1979; Walker, E. J. Gibson, Owsley, Megaw-Nyce, & Bahrick, 1980). Those studies indicated that infants could distinguish between rigid and elastic movements of an object. Furthermore, the infants generalize this distinction across a change of sense modality from touch to vision as early as 1 month of age. This was demonstrated by means of a habituation–dishabituation design, in which infants who habituated to rigid or elastic movements dishabituated more to the opposite kind of movement than to a completely new exemplar of the same kind of motion. (These studies indicated that infants could also detect the difference from new to old exemplar and that they could detect changes of kind of motion across changes in the particular shapes used as carriers of the motion.)

Third, Gibson uses simple and elegant experimental situations to investigate these questions. Perhaps the most notable example of this is her research with Richard Walk in investigating infant and animal depth perception with the visual cliff (Walk & E. J. Gibson, 1961). As is well known, using this simple but powerful situation, they studied depth perception in a wide variety of species. Most of these species discriminated an optically deep drop-off from a shallow one by the time they were able to locomote. However, that research itself arose out of a series of experiments investigating the effects on rats of early exposure to visual forms on their later ability to discriminate similar shapes (E. J. Gibson & Walk, 1956). This set of studies also used a traditional, very simple, but powerful Grice discrimination box to investigate a fundamental question about whether perceptual learning would occur without differential reinforcement of particular responses. (The visual cliff was invented as a quick test to determine whether dark-reared rats in these shape studies were functionally blind [Walk, E. J. Gibson, & Tighe, 1957].) The visual cliff situation derives its elegance from the fact that it exploits a simple natural response of the organisms under investigation. The use of such natural responses, more generally, is a characteristic of most of Gibson's infant research. She uses naturally occurring locomotor and manual (and even oral) exploratory behavior to index perception and its developmental changes, as is evident from the studies of infants' discrimination of surfaces and object substance.

In the early part of her career (up till the mid-fifties), Gibson was primarily concerned with perceptual learning in adults. Not only had she demonstrated that an important aspect of traditional verbal learning had a perceptual learning component, but she also had suggested that there was a perceptual learning component reflected in traditional psychophysical data (E. J. Gibson, 1953). However, she had always been interested in phylogenetic development and in a comparative approach and, as noted earlier, originally went to Yale with the intention of doing research on nonhuman primates. Although that goal was frustrated, she was able to pursue comparative research later on at Cornell University. There she worked first on traditional conditioning problems with goats and then later on the perceptual learning experiments with rats reared with visual forms on the sides of their cages. In those experiments, the animals were a convenient experimental subject. However, her comparative developmental and phylogenetic perspective was reflected more in the visual cliff experiments, in which the adaptive value of avoiding drop-offs was evident. Functionally, findings suggesting that precocial species discriminated depth very early in life made a great deal of sense. The comparative developmental perspective is reflected in a functional orientation in much of Gibson's writing. It appears particularly strongly in her recent emphasis on affordances, although she has not recently engaged in comparative work with animals herself.

The scribble experiment represents one of Gibson's first investigations of the relation between perceptual learning and perceptual development. Her analysis suggested that improvement in perception was a matter of increased differentiation. That increase was more manifest in the younger children than in the adults, whose perception already reflected a much greater degree of differentiation. Gibson was recognized as an experimental psychologist first and then as a developmental psychologist. She has always been interested in perceptual learning as a basic psychological process in adults and children and in animals and humans, as well as in its relation to perceptual development in children. Understanding perceptual development is vital in its own right as the foundation for understanding cognitive development, but it is also important for the light it sheds on understanding perceptual learning and perception in general. A vivid illustration of her view is expressed by the title (and content) of an article in the *Journal of Experimental Psychology: Human Perception and Performance*: "What Does Infant Perception Tell Us About Theories of Perception?" (E. J. Gibson, 1987). Her contributions are a splendid example of Vygotsky's dictum that to understand a phenomenon requires understanding its development.

REFERENCES

Adolph, K. E., Gibson, E. J., & Eppler, M. A. (1990). *Perceiving affordances of slopes: The ups and downs of toddlers' locomotion* (Emory Cognitive Project, No. 16). Atlanta: Emory University, Department of Psychology.

Bahrick, L. E. (1988). Intermodal learning in infancy: Learning on the basis of invariant relations in audible and visible events. *Child Development, 59,* 197–209.

Bertenthal, B. I., Campos, J. J., & Barrett, K. C. (1984). Self-produced locomotion: An organizer of emotional, cognitive, and social development in infancy. In R. N. Emde & R. J. Harmon (Eds.), *Continuities and discontinuities in development* (pp. 175–210). New York: Plenum Press.

Carey, S. (1991). Knowledge acquistion: Enrichment or conceptual change? In S. Carey & R. Gelman (Eds.), *The epigenesis of mind: Essays on biology and cognition* (pp. 257–292). Hillsdale, NJ: Erlbaum.

Eppler, M. A. (1990). *Perception and action in infancy: Object manipulation skills and detection of auditory–visual correspondences.* Unpublished doctoral dissertation, Emory University, Atlanta.

Gibson, E. J. (1939). Sensory generalization with voluntary reactions. *Journal of Experimental Psychology, 24,* 237–253.

Gibson, E. J. (1940). A systematic application of the concepts of generalization and differentiation to verbal learning. *Psychological Review, 47,* 196–229.

Gibson, E. J. (1941). Retroactive inhibition as a function of degree of generalization between tasks. *Journal of Experimental Psychology, 28,* 93–115.

Gibson, E. J. (1942). Intra-list generalization as a factor in verbal learning. *Journal of Experimental Psychology, 30*, 185–200.

Gibson, E. J. (1952). The role of shock in reinforcement. *Journal of Comparative and Physiological Psychology, 45*, 18–30.

Gibson, E. J. (1953). Improvement in perceptual judgments as a function of controlled practice or training. *Psychological Bulletin, 50*, 401–431.

Gibson, E. J. (1963). Perceptual learning. *Annual Review of Psychology, 14*, 29–56.

Gibson, E. J. (1969). *Principles of perceptual learning and development.* New York: Appleton-Century-Crofts.

Gibson, E. J. (1982). The concept of affordances in perceptual development: The renascence of functionalism. In W. A. Collins (Ed.), *The Minnesota Symposia on Child Psychology, Vol. 15* (pp. 55–81). Hillsdale, NJ: Erlbaum.

Gibson, E. J. (1987). What does infant perception tell us about theories of perception? *Journal of Experimental Psychology: Human Perception and Performance, 13*, 515–523.

Gibson, E. J. (1991). *An odyssey in learning and perception.* Cambridge, MA: MIT Press.

Gibson, E. J. (1992). How to think about perceptual learning: Twenty-five years later. In H. L. Pick, P. van den Broek, & D. C. Knill (Eds.), *Cognitive psychology: Conceptual and methodological issues* (pp. 215–237). Washington, DC: American Psychological Association.

Gibson, E. J., Barron, R. W., & Garber, E. E. (1972). *The development of convergence of meaning for words and pictures* (Appendix to Final Report No. 90046, pp. 12–26). Ithaca, NY: Cornell University and Office of Education.

Gibson, E. J., Bergman, R., & Purdy, J. (1955). The effect of prior training with a scale of distance on absolute and relative judgments of distance over ground. *Journal of Experimental Psychology, 50*, 97–105.

Gibson, E. J., Gibson, J. J., Pick, A. D., & Osser, H. A. (1962). A developmental study of the discrimination of letter-like forms. *Journal of Physiology and Psychology, 55*, 897–906.

Gibson, E. J., & Levin, H. (1975). *The psychology of reading.* Cambridge, MA: MIT Press.

Gibson, E. J., Owsley, C. J., & Johnston, J. (1978). Perception of invariants by five-month-old infants: Differentiation of two types of motion. *Developmental Psychology, 14*, 407–415.

Gibson, E. J., Owsley, C. J., Walker, A. S., & Megaw-Nyce, J. S. (1979). Development of the perception of invariants: Substance and shape. *Perception, 8*, 609–619.

Gibson, E. J., & Walk, R. D. (1956). The effect of prolonged exposure to visually presented patterns on learning to discriminate them. *Journal of Comprehensive Physiology and Psychology, 49*, 239–242.

Gibson, E. J., & Walker, A. S. (1984). Development of knowledge of visual–tactual affordances of substances. *Child Development, 55*, 453–460.

Gibson, J. J. (1979). *The ecological approach to visual perception*. Boston: Houghton-Mifflin.

Gibson, J. J., & Gibson, E. J. (1955). Perceptual learning: Differentiation or enrichment? *Psychological Review, 62*, 32–41.

Greenough, W. T., & Black, J. E. (1992). Induction of brain structure by experience: Substrates for cognitive development. In M. R. Gunnar & C. A. Nelson (Eds.), *Developmental behavioral neuroscience: The Minnesota Symposium on Child Psychology, Vol. 24* (pp. 155–200). Hillsdale, NJ: Erlbaum.

Keil, F. C. (1991). The emergence of theoretical beliefs as constraints on concepts. In S. Carey & R. Gelman (Eds.), *The epigenesis of mind: Essays on biology and cognition* (pp. 257–292). Hillsdale, NJ: Erlbaum.

Postman, L. (1955). Association theory and perceptual learning. *Psychology Review, 62*, 438–446.

Reed, E. S. (1982). An outline of a theory of action systems. *Journal of Motor Behavior, 14*, 98–134.

Ulrich, B. D., Thelen, E., & Niles, D. (1990). Perceptual determinants of action: Stairclimbing choices of infants and toddlers. In J. Clark & J. Humphrey (Eds.), *Advances in motor development research, Vol. 3* (pp. 1–5). New York: AMS Publishers.

Walk, R. D., & Gibson, E. J. (1961). A comparative and analytical study of visual depth perception. *Psychological Monographs, 75* (No. 15).

Walk, R. D., Gibson, E. J., & Tighe, T. J. (1957). Behavior of light- and dark-reared rats on a visual cliff. *Science, 126*, 80–81.

Walker, A., Gibson, E. J., Owsley, C. J., Megaw-Nyce, J., & Bahrick, L. E. (1980). Detection of elasticity as an invariant property of objects by young infants. *Perception, 9*, 713–718.

Warren, W. H. (1984). Perceiving affordances: Visual guidance of stair climbing. *Journal of Experimental Psychology: Human Perception and Performance, 10*, 683–703.

Woodworth, R. S. (1947). Reenforcement of perception. *American Journal of Psychology, 60*, 119–124.

Zaporozhets, A. V. (1965). The development of perception in the pre-school child. In P. H. Mussen (Ed.), *European research in child development: Monographs for the Society for Research in Child Development, 30* (Serial No. 100), 82–101.

Zinchenko, V. P., Van, C.-T., & Tarakanov, V. V. (1963). The formation and development of perceptual activity. *Soviet Psychology and Psychiatry, 2*, 3–12.

V

REFLECTIONS ON A CENTURY OF DEVELOPMENTAL PSYCHOLOGY

INTRODUCTION

REFLECTIONS ON A CENTURY OF DEVELOPMENTAL PSYCHOLOGY

In this final section, major contemporary developmental psychologists offer their reflections on the past and their hopes for the future of our field. Several recurring themes are evident in these chapters. First, our field is becoming less compartmentalized into clearly defined subdisciplines, such as cognitive, biological, social, or perceptual development. Both theory and empirical research suggest that we are becoming more integrated, as evidenced by the recognition of the interrelationships among different domains of development. All contributors recognize the increased interplay between biology and other aspects of development, but links among affect, cognition, and social processes are being increasingly recognized as well. Indeed, social, cognitive, and linguistic issues are often likely to be examined in a single study rather than in separate investigations. Several exciting efforts have provided integrative theoretical frameworks that can serve to unify both empirical evidence of shifts in biological, social, cognitive, and perceptual development and related domain-based minitheories. For example, dynamic systems theory, evolutionary psychology, comparative developmental psychology, connectionism, and neuropsychology all hold promise of offering integrative viewpoints.

Second, the authors note the increasing trend toward a more inter-disciplinary developmental psychology. This is a continuing trend in many areas of psychology and a recognition that the interesting cutting-edge issues are often at the boundaries between disciplines. The sustained collaboration between psychology and pediatrics is one example of this interdisciplinary cooperation, with the emerging area of how developmental factors affect children's physical health reflecting this cross-disciplinary trend. Another example is recent work on children's eyewitness testimony that links law and psychology.

Third, the distinction between applied and nonapplied research is an increasingly blurry and, perhaps, dubious one as researchers continue to recognize the multifaceted value of social experiments, such as Head Start, for evaluating both basic theoretical issues and social policy concerns.

Fourth, the scope of research projects has continued to increase, with many investigators launching multimethod, multimeasure studies that often use longitudinal designs. This trend is a welcome one for the field because it permits the unraveling of the interdependencies that exist among developmental phenomena.

Fifth, we are becoming more appreciative of cultural diversity as a field than we have been in the past. Cross-cultural work has flourished (e.g., Tronick, 1992), and our appreciation of intracultural variation is increasing (McLoyd, 1990). However, the number of projects devoted to ethnically and racially diverse samples is still low. As a scientific community, we need to do a better job of investigating and of publishing reports that go beyond the traditional samples. This is one of our most important challenges for the future.

A sixth, closely related theme is that we are coming to recognize that historical cycles in values and concerns can seriously influence the choice of problems and the interpretation of data. As life course theorists have argued, attention to secular change and historical events is crucial for understanding development (e.g., Elder, Modell, & Parke, 1993).

Seventh, our views of children have changed with the recognition that children are active constructors of both their cognitive and social worlds. Eighth, we are beginning to appreciate the complexity of the levels of context in which children are embedded and the need to study units of analysis (individual, dyadic, family, community, etc.) that reflect these levels. At the same time, more attention needs to be paid to the links across levels of functioning. And ninth, our field is showing an increased awareness of the need to understand subjective as well as objective aspects of experience.

In sum, the contributors to this book agree that the century has been marked by considerable progress; but at the same time, they suggest that the past 100 years represent only the first steps in unraveling the complexities of development. Their concerns and cautions, as well as their wisdom and wishes, provide our field with a fine start on the agenda for the next century of progress.

REFERENCES

Elder, G. H., Modell, J., & Parke, R. D. (Eds.). (1993). *Children in time and place*. Cambridge, England: Cambridge University Press.

McLoyd, V. (1990). Minority children: Introduction to the special issue. *Child Development, 61,* 263–266.

Tronick, E. Z. (1992). Cross-cultural studies of development. *Developmental Psychology, 28,* 566–567.

19

YESTERDAY'S PREMISES, TOMORROW'S PROMISES

JEROME KAGAN

Nature presents the uniform and the variable in every phenomenon, allowing scientists to choose which face they wish to explore. Because living events are usually more variable than the inorganic at the macroscopic level—compare the growth of an embryo with that of a crystal—biologists and psychologists have been less successful than physicists and chemists in formulating abstract, nomothetic laws that ignore local context and apply across a broad swath of different phenomena.

Developmental psychologists, too, carve growth into universal and variable qualities. Some study the form and time of appearance of stranger anxiety, language, empathy, and conservation; others increase the magnification to explain why some 8-month-old infants cry with intensity to all strangers whereas others fret to only a few. Obviously, the reasons why most infants will cry to a stranger during the last months of the first year

This article was supported in part by the John D. and Catherine T. MacArthur Foundation and the Leon Lowenstein Foundation. I thank Nancy Snidman, Doreen Arcus, and J. Steven Reznick, who have been close friends and wise collaborators in the research on temperament.

Reprinted from *Developmental Psychology*, 28, 990–997. Copyright by the American Psychological Association.

are different from the bases for the variation in fear. Most of this essay is a historical analysis of the study of inquiry into variation in development; however, some general reflections on the last century of scholarship may be helpful.

NEW CONCEPTIONS

Although the five fundamental premises of gradual change, connectedness between phases of development, internalization of external events, the law of effect, and freedom as a telos remain almost as strong today as they were a century ago (Kagan, 1983), there have been at least four changes in the traditional conceptions of psychological growth. One of the most important is the willingness to award more influence to the child's reciprocal encounters with others—adults and children—and the changing symbolic constructions of these relationships (Emde & Buchsbaum, 1990; Lewis, 1987; Parke, 1992; Sameroff, 1975). As a result, psychologists have invented constructs that refer to a relationship: The concept of attachment is, perhaps, the best example (Ainsworth, 1967). The older view conceived of the child as the primary unit, acting on the world in Piaget's prose, or acted upon in Watson's. In the contemporary view, the child is a strand of ivy in a forest rather than a violet seedling in a greenhouse.

It is often the case that when a new philosophical premise appears in one discipline it emerges in others, because changes in the larger society have made theorists receptive to a fresh conception. Thus, it is not surprising that evolutionary biologists have begun to suggest that the behavioral relationships among members of a species are a factor in evolution. Because these relations are a strict derivative of neither genes nor ecology, they represent a new set of conditions to acknowledge (Plotkin, 1988).

A second, more novel change is recognition that historical cycles in values, motives, and uncertainties that permeate an entire society can affect children, independently of any child's particular familial circumstances. Elder (1974) has demonstrated that the American depression of the 1930s influenced the adult values of those children who were young adolescents during that sorrowful decade. Psychologists should perform comparable analyses on the effect of the Vietnam War protests on American adolescents living in metropolitan areas at the end of the 1960s. The values of a child born in 1950 in Boston to a middle-class professional family were shaped at a critical period by the civil rights movement, pacifism, celebration of sexual freedom, and egalitarianism. It would be more difficult for this person than for one born in 1940 or 1970 to the same family in the same place to oppose premarital sexuality, abortion, or affirmative action.

History also influences the phenomena selected for inquiry. During the first two decades of this century, a large number of developmental psychologists described the development of motor coordinations and language. Although these two domains remain popular targets of inquiry, the earlier investigators showed little interest in the attachments of infants, prosocial behavior, or peer relationships. The current attractiveness of these latter three universal phenomena is due, I believe, to the growing ethical conviction among Americans and Europeans that communitarian values should be placed in a more harmonious balance with individualistic ones. This emphasis is seen as necessary because personal achievement has become the only imperative standard for too many young adults. No particular single goal enjoys transcendence; it is important only to gain the prized goal the person selected as desirable.

Historical events have also tainted to some degree the idea of intelligence, because of the presumption that IQ tests do not accurately evaluate the mental abilities of poor children of color. As a result, the hypothesis of profiles of varied cognitive talents has become popular (Gardner, 1983).

These new emphases on the power of social relationships and historical eras award salience to specific contexts of growth, as Bronfenbrenner (1979) has urged. Analogous views are developing in biology; for example, the genetic material that surrounds the sequence of DNA that controls an animal's eye color—the chemical context—can influence the final phenotype. Indeed, one of the most significant changes in psychology, which is affecting all domains of the science, is the recognition that the current constructs for psychological processes should name the particular contexts to which they apply.

Developmental psychologists now appreciate that statements about learning, memory, and anxiety must specify not only the child's age but also the detailed experimental procedures that form the referent for the inferred process. A dramatic example of this principle of context specificity is found in prosopagnosics who are unable to recognize a static photograph of a face of a familiar person but who can recognize the same person walking. The cognitive impairment is limited to static, visual representations of the face. That statement is dramatically more constrained than the casual, broad conclusion that these brain-damaged patients suffer from a defect in recognition memory (Damasio, 1989).

The current interest in temperamental concepts, after almost 75 years of exile, is a third novelty, although it is the return of an old idea that can be traced to two ancient physicians, Hippocrates and Galen of Pergamon. The study of temperamental differences lost favor in the United States during the second decade of this century, because it became politically necessary to affirm that the first-generation children of European immigrants, many of whom were unsuccessful in school, were not biologically different from those of indigenous families. This hope became dogma following two independent events: the dissemination of Hitler's propaganda on racial purity and the laboratory research of the major behaviorists, especially Skinner, Hull, Miller, Spence, and their students, demonstrating the extraordinary power of experience to shape habit.

However, the observation that all infants do not react to a particular context or incentive in the same way remains a stubborn fact. For example, unpublished data on 4-month-old Chinese infants born in Beijing (Kagan et al., 1992) verify an earlier suggestion by Freedman and Freedman (1969) that Chinese infants are less aroused by visual and auditory stimuli than white infants (Kagan & Snidman, 1991). Even though delinquency is most common among children in economically disadvantaged neighborhoods, the fact that only a small proportion of adolescents living in these contexts becomes chronically delinquent implies that this profile requires a combination of temperament and experiential factors. Social scientists are beginning to appreciate that, most of the time, they should expect an interaction between children's temperaments and past history with respect to a profile of interest, whether it be aggression, avoidance, prosocial behavior, coping strategy, or illness (Boyce & Jemerin, 1990).

However, temperamental constructs have the philosophical disadvantage of appearing to rob children of their will. A child born with a physiology that biases him or her to become fearful of strangers cannot easily approach every group of unfamiliar peers. Acknowledging the power of temperamental factors dilutes to some degree the Western ideal of a sovereign agent with an autonomous will acting on his or her world in the most adaptive fashion.

Finally, the invention of new methodologies has contributed to altered conceptions. The VCR, which has permitted detailed analyses of facial expression not possible earlier, has led to new hypotheses about affect. The availability of techniques to measure brain electrical activity, heart rate, blood pressure, muscle tension, cortisol, and chemicals in plasma and cerebrospinal fluid have motivated scientists to probe the psychological correlates of these biological characteristics, even though most social scientists acknowledge that the biology is not the primary or direct cause of the psychological phenomena. This work has produced some interesting information. For example, enhancement of vagal tone on the heart occurs in all infants between 6 and 12 weeks (Schechtman, Harper, & Kluge, 1989), the same time that recognition memory improves (Kagan, 1984). Enhanced coherence of the EEG occurs at 4 to 6 years of age, just prior to the display of concrete operations (Thatcher, Walker, & Giudice, 1987). Finally, some conduct-disorder children show very low plasma levels of dopamine beta-hydroxalase (Rogeness, Hernandez, Macedo, Amyrony, & Hoppe, 1986). Because this enzyme is involved in the synthesis of norepinephrine, and norepinephrine can influence the threshold for anxiety, it is possible that low levels of the enzyme contribute to the probability of delinquency. These are tiny facts at the moment, but one day creative scientists may use them in bold developmental propositions that describe coherent profiles of behavioral, affective, and biological qualities.

The remainder of this chapter, which focuses on variation in development, deals with five themes: (a) the factors that guide the selection of phenomena, (b) the choice of continua versus categories in description, (c) continuity versus discontinuity in development, (d) the influence of temperament, and (e) the relation between the meaning of a construct and its source of evidence.

WHAT SHALL WE STUDY?

No scientific discipline is immune to the influence of local factors in the selection of phenomena. The naturalists who studied heat were aware of its relevance to the work that machines might do to make human labor easier; Pasteur's discoveries were in the service of helping a winemaker. The choices of developmental psychologists are influenced by both pragmatic considerations and deeply held philosophical beliefs regarding the ideal traits children should develop—the American version of the Greek paideia.

As the century began, wise commentators in America were certain that children should become independent, intelligent, honest, and sociable. Thus, it is not surprising that early studies of development emphasized these qualities. Because standard instruments for assessing cognitive ability were available (this was less true for behavioral traits), a significant number of longitudinal studies asked about the predictability and consequences of early variation in intellectual function (see Bayley, 1949; Terman, 1925). The consensus that emerged from these studies was that motor and social skills assessed by infant tests before the second birthday were not predictive of future performance on IQ tests. Because that conclusion bothers some contemporary psychologists who believe that cognitive ability is an inherited unity that must be preserved, scholars like Fagan (1984) and Bornstein and Sigman (1986) have searched for different indexes of infant competence. They report that rate of habituation to visual stimuli and reactivity to novelty appear to be sensitive, prophetic signs of later intelligence. Although it is likely that children differ inherently in their profile of cognitive talents, I agree with Garcia (1981) that it does not make biological sense to postulate a single problem-solving capacity (g factor) to account for the differences in behavior among members of a species. The key to species survival is heritable variation in a broad profile of characteristics so that some members will be best adapted during one era, whereas others will be better adapted when conditions change and new talents are required. I doubt that the endurance and control of fear required by Spartan society is highly correlated with the ability to program a computer.

The classic longitudinal studies, originating in the 1920s and 1930s in Berkeley, Denver, and Yellow Springs, focused on social and mastery behaviors. I leave for later discussion of the referential meanings of these constructs. The prejudices of this period can be seen in the principle variables Kagan and Moss (1962) chose when they analyzed the corpus of data at the Fels Institute: dependence, independence, aggression to peers and parents, achievement, anxiety, and sociability. The definitions of these variables reflected the assumption, popular at the time, that family experiences shaped these habits, and if the child's environment did not change, the habits would be preserved. Each of these variables was conceived as a characteristic of the child, not of the child in a particular context—admittedly an error.

The failure of these investigators to quantify attachment to a parent, empathy with peers, or prosocial behavior is not unlike Osgood's (1962) failure to include adjective pairs such as natural–unnatural in constructing the semantic differential. Had Osgood done so, he might have found the construct that Levy–Strauss used so profitably in his anthropological treatises. Remember, the idea of alienation from society never occurred to Freud. Every investigator's vision is foreshortened by his or her historical moment.

Many changes in the favored status of developmental ideas have been the product of history, rather than of new knowledge. The current popularity of the concept of attachment provides a clear example. When most middle-class mothers remained at home caring for their young children in the period before the Second World War, the presumed threat to the child was overprotection. Kanner (1944) wrote with passion on the danger of an overly sensitive, affectionate mother who might produce an extremely dependent child, afraid to sever his or her emotional tie to the parent. Today, when over half of the mothers of young children work outside of the home and place their children in surrogate care, the node of community worry has shifted to the real possibility of insufficient affection for and sensitivity to the child. Because society wishes to guarantee that every young child has a minimal emotional bond to his or her parents—this was not a hypothesis 60 years ago—the idea of attachment has become ascendant.

CONTINUOUS DIMENSIONS AND CATEGORIES OF CHILDREN

History has had a more modest influence on the choice of continua or qualitative categories to describe children, although continua remain the preferred alternative. Consider the following two descriptions: (a) "Mary is more sociable than Joan" and (b) "Mary is extraverted and Joan is introverted." The use of the category terms *introverted* and *extraverted* in the second sentence implies that the two women differ on a set of correlated characteristics, not just one, and, therefore, the women may be qualitatively different.

Most theoretical constructs in the life sciences—species, enzyme, cell, neurotransmitter, and developmental stage—are defined by a profile of values rather than a single dimension. An animal species is not defined by the linear addition of separate continuous dimensions (e.g., weight, length, and life span) but by a distinct profile of features. A factor analysis of a dozen continuous vertebrate traits—weight, crown-to-rump length, ratio of head to trunk, number of offspring, gestational period, speed of loco- motion, basal metabolic rate, life span, etc.—would not produce, as major factors, the families, genera, and species that are now accepted as the best taxonomic categories. This is because each taxon is defined by a profile of characteristics, many of which are uncorrelated. Turtles and birds are similar in size but are very different in speed of locomotion; lizards and seals are different in size but similar in speed of locomotion. A comparison of the behavior and physiology of three closely related macaque species—rhesus, bonnets, and crabeaters—reveals that it is not possible to arrange the three species on a continuum of either fearfulness or arousal to unfamiliarity. The three groups must be viewed as qualitatively different categories of animals (Clarke, Mason, & Moberg, 1988).

However, many psychologists continue to compare children with re- spect to their position on single continuous dimensions. The constructs of motivation for achievement, anxiety, and aggression are a few examples. Consider the characteristic called *sociability with peers*. Parents and teachers are asked to compare school-age children on this characteristic, with the tacit assumption that it is continuous and that all highly sociable children belong to a homogeneous group. However, this behavioral quality is part of a correlated cluster for about one third of highly sociable children who also display low sympathetic tone, low levels of cortisol, a mesomorphic body build, dark eyes, and frequent positive affect. This diverse, correlated set of features defines a temperamental category that has been called *un- inhibited to the unfamiliar* (Kagan & Snidman, 1991). Uninhibited children are qualitatively different from those who are equally sociable with peers but do not possess these other features. Thus, the two sentences, (a) "Mary is more sociable than most of her friends" and (b) "Mary is an uninhibited child," have different meanings.

The usefulness of continua or categories will depend on the scientist's purpose. If investigators wish to explain a single particular event (for ex- ample, why Mary was elected class president), they will probably choose the continuous dimension of sociability. However, if they wish to explain a large, diverse set of behaviors that persists over an extended period of time, they should consider selecting a categorical description.

One reason why psychologists prefer continua derives from a greater interest in the consequences of an agent's actions than in the nature of the agent. Acts of aggression have undesirable consequences. Scientists count them and examine their distribution, usually ignoring whether the aggression was performed by an adolescent with a birth defect, a record of school failure, or a chromosomal anomaly. In addition, qualitative categories imply individual characteristics that are presumed to be resistant to change, an idea that has been unacceptable to most social scientists during this century.

Psychology has cycled from a preference for categories of people, characteristic of 19th- and early 20th-century theorists (*hysteria* was a category for Freud and Breuer, as was *introvert* for Jung), to the more malleable, single dimensions invented after the Second World War, because of a politically motivated desire to believe that all human qualities were amenable to change through education and altered social conditions.

A third factor favoring continuous dimensions was dissemination of the statistical methods of analysis of variance and regression coefficients, both of which assume that the data represent continuous dimensions, compared, for example, with latent class analyses. A fourth reason for choosing continua is that most psychologists are interested in processes rather than organisms. Variation in memory ability, anxiety, and perceptual accuracy appears to be continuous; mice and monkeys are qualitatively different. Hence, psychologists push against limitations on the generality of a process, hoping that it will be applicable to a broad group of phenotypically different species: The construct of learning is a prime example. But, even though EEG spectra are defined by continuous distributions of frequency and amplitude, no physiologist claims that the state of sleep, with its characteristic signature of frequency and amplitude, differs only quantitatively from the state of alertness in a performing violinist.

Finally, adults in the child's social environment typically react to the whole child, not to a single characteristic of that child. Teachers will chastise an academically retarded child whose history contains no stigmata, but they are likely to be more supportive of one who has known organic deficit. After studying a large group of Swedish youth and young adults from 10 to 26 years of age, David Magnusson (1988) came to a similar conclusion. Single continuous dimensions, like aggressive behavior, were not related in a simple way to adult outcomes. However, a small group of boys who were restless and aggressive and who had lower levels of epinephrine in their urine were at significantly greater risk for adolescent delinquency. Magnusson concluded that there was continuity and stability in the patterns of individual functioning, but it was individuals who were stable across time, not variables.

CONTINUITY VERSUS DISCONTINUITY OF DISPOSITIONS

Indefinite preservation of a young child's salient qualities, whether intellectual ability or a secure attachment, remains an ascendant assumption in developmental work. This entrenched premise is difficult to disprove in a single study. There is no era in the history of Western society without a large group of scholars, clergy, or statesmen who declared that adult characteristics were formed during the opening years of life. Plato was certain that the infant who was rocked frequently became a better athlete. Nineteenth-century New England ministers told parents in Sunday sermons that the way they handled their infants would determine the child's future character. As I have written elsewhere (Kagan, 1984), the concern with the first years of development rests on the premise that each life is an unbroken trail on which one can trace a psychological quality from any point back to its beginning. This view is to be contrasted with the classic Chinese belief in change rather than permanence, a flowing river rather than a statue (Chan, 1963). It may not be a coincidence that a majority of Western physicists believe, despite some logical difficulties, that the universe began with a big bang and has been cooling continuously, without any discontinuity, since that time. A small number of scientists—for example, Burbidge (1992)—recognize that the big bang premise rests on faith in a single original act of creation. Burbidge adds that this faith "properly lies in the realm of metaphysics, not science" (p. 120).

One reason for the commitment to preservation of early habits and moods is the nature of the English language. The English adjectives used to describe children rarely refer to the child's age or the context of action. Like the names of colors, they imply a stability over time and location. Americans use words like *intelligent*, *fearful*, *secure*, or *aggressive* to describe 2-year-olds, 10-year-olds, and adolescents as if the meanings of those words were not altered by growth. The use of the same word invites the belief that one is talking about the same characteristic. This feature is not present in all languages; for example, the Japanese use different adjectives to describe intellectual ability in very young or older persons: *kashikoi* for infants, *yùno* for adults.

There is an inconsistency between the contemporary commitment to the importance of the local context, which changes, and a belief in the capacity of early encounters to create immutable structures that will be preserved. Both hypotheses cannot be true. The belief in the indefinite preservation of habits, beliefs, and moods rests on a static conception of psychological structures. Even children who display the qualities of an inhibited temperament, which is heritable, have the capacity to change their behavioral phenotype. Almost one third of a group of children who were highly aroused by unfamiliar visual and auditory stimuli at 4 months and showed the behavior and physiology of an inhibited child in the 2nd year were not unusually shy or fearful when assessed in the 4th year (Kagan & Snidman, 1991). Additionally, 20% of the children with the opposite profile—minimally aroused at 4 months and sociable and fearless in the 2nd year—were shy with adults and children at 4 years of age. Phenotypes can change.

TEMPERAMENT

The current revival of interest in categories of temperament is due, in part, to the loss of faith in the strong form of both behaviorism and the American transformation of Freud's theory. The failing faith permitted Alexander Thomas and Stella Chess (1977) to reintroduce the idea of temperament to the psychiatric community in the 1960s. A second relevant factor is the recent interest in inter- and intraspecific differences in the behavior of varied animal species. Dogs, mice, rats, wolves, cats, cows, monkeys, and even paradise fish differ within species in their tendency to approach or to avoid novelty. One of the most extensive studies of the genetic origins of behavior in animals showed dramatic variation in the degree of timidity displayed in unfamiliar situations by five different breeds of dog (Scott & Fuller, 1974). Even rats from within a single Wistar strain bred over many generations vary in both brain biochemistry and behavior. Some animals display large potentials in the dentate gyrus of the hippocampus after stimulation of the lateral amygdala, whereas others do not. The former are protected from ulceration of the stomach following immobilization, whereas the latter, which did not display any such potentials, were more likely to develop ulcers following stress (Hencke, 1990).

Perhaps the most important reason for the current interest in temperament lies with extraordinary advances in neuroscience. The brain contains over 150 different chemicals, each of which influences the excitability of specific sites (Siegel, Albers, Agranoff, & Katzman, 1981). Individuals inherit different concentrations of many of these chemicals, as well as the density of associated receptors. Therefore, it is now easier to imagine how a particular child might be vulnerable to sadness or to anxiety. Scientists are appropriately conservative and resist explanations that do not rest on a rationale built of robust facts arranged in a logical argument. The familiar environmental explanation of why a child was excessively fearful was reasonable; hence, psychologists were reluctant to relinquish it until another equally commanding account was provided. Neuroscientists are supplying these new arguments with robust facts that suggest that inherited variation in neurochemistry and neurophysiology can contribute to differences in behavior through activity of the sympathetic nervous system and the hypothalamic-pituitary-adrenal axis, as well as the distribution and concentration of catecholamines, glucocorticoids, and endogenous opioids.

However, behaviors that are influenced by temperament are not immutable, as was noted earlier. Membership in a temperamental category implies only a slight, initial bias for certain emotions and actions. Most children can learn to control the urge to withdraw from a stranger or a large dog. The environment is probably more important in helping a very fearful 1-year-old overcome his or her fear than it is in making that child timid in the first place.

Ideally, a category of temperament should be defined by both a behavioral and a related physiological profile that is under some genetic control. At present, psychologists must rely on the behavioral profile, because scientists have not yet discovered the physiology that is reliably and selectively linked to the behavior. The category of temperament called *uninhibited to the unfamiliar* is defined by very low motor activity and low crying to stimuli at 4 months and sociable, fearless behavior in the 2nd year. Although a proportion of these children have very low and variable heart rates at 4 months (heart period greater than 450 ms and variability greater than 30 ms) and low levels of cortisol as older children (less than 2,000 pmol/l), the correlations between these physiological profiles and behavior are modest. Hence, it is not clear whether these biological markers should be added to the definition and scientists should require that all children classified as uninhibited must possess these characteristics, too.

One reason for the caution is a recent discovery from our laboratory suggesting that high levels of salivary cortisol in 5- to 7-month-old infants is more closely related to a propensity to display high levels of affective arousal in the 2nd year than to a vulnerability to fear. Because the current popular belief is that high levels of cortisol should be always associated with fear, this unexpected result serves as a useful caution to premature judgments about the meaning of particular physiological variables. One day scientists will discover the physiology that biases some children to become uninhibited. For the present, the behavioral evidence must remain primary. This is a common historical sequence in medicine. All of the infectious diseases had to be defined by their public symptoms before their pathophysiology became known.

The definition of a category of temperament as a changing but coherent profile of behavior and emotion linked probabilistically to a distinct physiology can apply to a very large number of categories. It is likely that during the next century psychologists will discover these categories and learn that the hyperactive child and the listless child belong to different temperamental groups. The potentially large variety is one reason why the extensive variety in breeds of puppies provides a useful metaphor for the temperamental categories of children. Let us hope that the final number will be smaller than the 810 different character types Fourier posited in a deductive scheme that began with 12 basic feelings and emotions (Roback, 1931).

SOURCES OF EVIDENCE

The theoretical meaning of every scientific construct combines sense and referential meanings (Kagan, 1989). Thus, the term *intelligence* has one meaning in Piaget's writings but a different meaning when IQ scores are the source of evidence. Biologists are more sensitive to this issue than are social scientists. For example, biologists are now questioning the extrapolation of the carcinogenic potential of environmental or dietary factors when inbred strains of rats are the source of risk estimates for humans (Abelson, 1992). Psychologists are generally less critical of extrapolation from animals to humans, especially when conclusions concern the effect of social interaction on behavioral development.

Developmental psychologists usually rely on three very different sources of evidence: (a) behavioral observations, including performances on laboratory tests (fortunately, films are now being used to supplement the notes of human observers); (b) questionnaires and interviews that rely on verbal statements; and, less often, (c) physiological information. Most of the time, each class of evidence is used, appropriately, as the referent for a specific concept whose meaning derives from one of the classes of data. When psychologists describe a child as intelligent, they rely on test performance, not on autonomic function or parental report; when they say that an infant has sympathetic reactivity to stress, they rely on heart rate or blood pressure changes, not on cognitive test performance.

But investigators occasionally use the same construct when the referent is any one of the three different sources of evidence. For example, some psychologists will describe a group of children as fearful whether the evidence is behavioral observation, parental report, or, less frequently, a physiological reaction like skin conductance or heart rate. This practice is creating mischief, because the correlations among the different sources of evidence will be low when each source is measuring a different process. Hence, psychologists should not use the same term for the three different sources of data without a strong empirical or theoretical basis for doing so.

An illustration of this error is the tendency to use the same terms for categories of temperament that originate in parental report, which relies on familiar words, compared with direct observations of the child's behavior. The correlations between parental descriptions of children's emotions and reactivity to stimuli, on the one hand, and behavioral data gathered by observers, on the other, is modest at best and, in some studies, minimal. In one study (Seifer, Sameroff, Barrett, & Krafchuk, 1992), infants were observed at home weekly from 4 to 6 months of age. Even though both parents and observers were consistent over time, the correlations between parents' ratings of temperamental qualities in their infants and the observers' evaluations of the same children hovered around .2 (see Bornstein, Gaughran, & Segui, 1991). (The relation between the statements of parents and those of their older children regarding the degree of anxiety and pathology in the child is equally poor [Klein, 1991].) However, agreement between parental report and direct observation can be high for some qualities. For example, parental assessment of a child's vocabulary in the 2nd year is highly correlated with observational data (Dale, Bates, Reznick, & Morisett, 1989). The issue is not whether parental report is valid or not, but rather the characteristics for which it is or is not an accurate index of a construct of interest.

There are four reasons why there may be a poor relation between direct behavioral observations of emotionally based, complex behaviors in specific contexts and parental report of presumably similar characteristics. First, parents are not equally discerning in their observations and subsequent interpretations of all of their children's behaviors. The fact that two mothers say that their child is highly fearful does not mean that impartial observations would reveal the same conclusion. A young mother who has not had extensive experience with infants has a less accurate base for judging her first child than a mother who is evaluating her third child. Furthermore, parents of more than one child are vulnerable to contrast effects. If the first child was extremely fearful and the second only a little less so, but still more fearful than most children, the mother will rate the second child as far less fearful than observations reveal, because she is contrasting the second with the first child.

Second, a scientist can only ask a parent to describe psychological qualities that he or she can detect easily. The average parent is not good at discriminating among infant cries that are occasioned by fear, frustration, hunger, or overarousal and may have a difficult time detecting the difference between smiles of assimilation and smiles of excitement. Thus, investigations that rely on questionnaires must limit their inquiry to behaviors that are easily understood and not limited to extremely specific contexts. Hence, questionnaires usually ask, "Does your child smile (or cry) a great deal?" For these reasons, the parental statement that a child cries frequently is not equivalent to an observer's evaluation of the degree to which an infant cries when aroused by the sound of a truck or when frightened by a stranger.

In addition, psychologists can only ask parents to describe qualities with words that all parents understand in a similar way. However, investigators often synthesize a construct from disparate sources of information— some of which is not available to parents—and give it a special name. For instance, there is a small group of infants who, in addition to low irritability, have very low and variable heart rates, high vagal tone, and low muscle tension. Psychologists invent a new name for this combination of qualities. However, they cannot ask a mother to rate her child on this characteristic, because she does not have access to the child's heart rate and muscle tension and, furthermore, will not understand the term invented to name the synthetic construct. Anthropologists do not ask informants, "Is your society matrilocal?" ecologists do not ask residents of a forested area if their land is acidic, and Ainsworth's students do not ask a mother if her child is insecurely attached to her.

Third, parents often impose different meanings on the same behavior. Some parents will regard shy behavior as an index of sensitivity, others interpret it as caution, and still others will regard it as a sign of fear. If a questionnaire asks, "Is your child fearful with strangers," the first two groups of parents will answer negatively, whereas the third may answer in the affirmative, even though the children behave similarly with strangers. Moreover, some mothers distort their child's behavior to fit their ego ideal. The parent who wants an outgoing child and is threatened by a quiet one may deny the child's introverted style and exaggerate his or her sociability.

Finally, there is a philosophical reason to question parental report of complex qualities. The primary properties of words are different from those of behavior. Many words are intended to name abstract classes and to generalize across a large number of situations (e.g., "Mary is fearful with strangers"). Behaviors are concrete events that change over time and have latency, frequency, and intensity as some of their defining characteristics. No two film records of a particular child encountering different strangers on two occasions would be identical.

Therefore, there are many special influences on parental descriptions of infants and children that are absent when behaviors are coded by disinterested but trained observers in specific contexts. That is why agreement between parents and observers can be low, and much of the time the parental descriptions are not close enough to the phenomena the scientist wishes to understand. I borrow from Paul Meehl an analogy that captures the nature of the problem:

Imagine a botanist who wished to know the relation between the amount of rainfall and the growth of grass in a specific region of the country over a 2-year period. However, the scientist was unable to obtain direct measurements of either the amount of rainfall or the amount of grass growth. The only available data were the number of telephone calls to plumbers—to index heavy rainfall—and the number of telephone calls to stores that sold lawn mowers—to index grass growth. It is likely that the relation between the two measured variables would be very different from the relation between the unmeasured variables of primary interest. For many questions in psychology, the indexes used are as indirect as those in this hypothetical example.

Progress in the study of personality and temperament is likely to remain slow if scientists continue to rely only on verbal statements from parents and teachers with no additional evidence. That is why the development of the Laboratory Temperament Assessment Battery by Goldsmith and Rothbart (1992) is to be celebrated. Developmental scientists who study the uniformities in cognitive growth regularly use behavioral observations and rarely rely on parental report. These investigators appreciate that parental descriptions of infants could not capture the subtle development of recognition or recall memory, cross-modal perception, or the object concept, each of which is an established milestone. Yet, scientists interested in individual differences in temperament, an equally complex set of phenomena, are more trusting of parental report. If talking to parents about their children were such an accurate source of information, the field of emotional and personality development would be one of the most advanced domains in the social sciences, rather than one trying to find its way. Wise people have been observing children and constructing theories of their development for a very long time. I interpret the current level of progress to mean that verbal statements describing the behaviors and emotions of children by parents, friends, or teachers has some, but limited, value.

THE FUTURE

Although estimates of the future are rarely accurate—witness the failure of the wisest scholars to predict the dissolution of the Soviet Union— three tentative guesses are offered.

First, the next cohort of scientists studying personality development will routinely add biological measurements to their behavioral observations. Most of the time, a behavioral phenotype hides several qualitatively different groups; for example, not every shy 5-year-old is a temperamentally inhibited child. One way to separate the phenotype into its different etiological categories is to gather physiological information. A shy child who has an inhibited temperament will show both signs of fear and sympathetic reactivity, whereas one who acquired that demeanor as a result of stress will not.

Second, concepts representing categories of children, defined by a profile of temperament, home experience, and social context, will supplement those that assume continuous variation in single traits. Finally, there will be greater acceptance of the fact that, for some qualities, self-report data are of limited validity. As a result, behavioral observations in both natural and laboratory contexts will become a primary referent in the study of individual differences, as it was in the opening decades of this century.

Psychologists know considerably more about development than Preyer, Baldwin, or Freud, which is a just cause for celebration. These victories were the product of careful observations by investigators open to unexpected discoveries. The major longitudinal studies of the 1930s, Harlow's discovery of the isolation syndrome in rhesus monkeys, and Ainsworth's early research in Uganda were in this receptive frame characteristic of biology. Biologists, unlike social scientists, are typically inductive rather than deductive, analytic rather than synthetic in description, and always exploitative of new technology. The discovery of the cell, the gene, mutation, nerve growth factor, and retroviruses, to name only a few, were Baconian victories that required the use of complex laboratory techniques by minds open to any possibility. In a review of a biography of Niels Bohr, Wilczek (1992) described three features that marked Bohr's personality: remaining close to experimental reality; a willingness to entertain ideas that were provisional; and, lurking in the background, the suspicion that virtually all knowledge is incomplete. Surely, Bohr would have urged psychology toward direct observations that never failed to acknowledge context, a motivation to invent and a willingness to exploit new methods, and always a preparedness for surprises.

REFERENCES

Abelson, P. H. (1992). Diet and cancer in humans and rodents. *Science, 255,* 141.

Ainsworth, M. D. S. (1967). *Infancy in Uganda.* Baltimore: Johns Hopkins University Press.

Bayley, N. (1949). Consistency and variability in the growth of intelligence from birth to eighteen years. *Journal of Genetic Psychology, 75,* 165–196.

Bornstein, M. H., Gaughran, J. M., & Segui, D. (1991). Multimethod assessment of infant temperament. *International Journal of Behavioral Development, 14,* 131–151.

Bornstein, M. H., & Sigman, M. D. (1986). Continuity in mental development from infancy. *Child Development, 57,* 251–274.

Boyce, W. T., & Jemerin, J. M. (1990). Psychobiological differences in childhood stress response. *Developmental and Behavioral Pediatrics, 11,* 86–94.

Bronfenbrenner, U. (1979). *The ecology of human development.* Cambridge, MA: Harvard University Press.

Burbidge, G. (1992). Why only one big bang? *Scientific American, 266,* 120.

Chan, W.-S. (1963). *A source book in Chinese philosophy.* Princeton, NJ: Princeton University Press.

Clarke, A. S., Mason, W. A., & Moberg, G. P. (1988). Differential behavioral and adrenocortical responses to stress among three macaque species. *American Journal of Primatology, 14,* 37–52.

Dale, P., Bates, E., Reznick, J. S., & Morisett, C. (1989). The validity of a parent report instrument of child language at 20 months. *Child Language, 16,* 239–250.

Damasio, A. R. (1989). Reflections on visual recognition. In A. M. Galaburda (Ed.), *From reading to neurons* (pp. 361–376). Cambridge, MA: MIT Press.

Elder, G. H. (1974). *Children of the Great Depression.* Chicago: University of Chicago Press.

Emde, R. N., & Buchsbaum, H. K. (1990). "Didn't you hear my mommy?" Autonomy with connectedness in moral self emergence. In D. Cicchetti & M. Beaghly (Eds.), *The self in transition* (pp. 35–60). Chicago: University of Chicago Press.

Fagan, J. F. (1984). The relationship of novelty preferences during infancy to later intelligence and later recognition memory. *Intelligence, 8,* 339–346.

Freedman, D. G., & Freedman, N. (1969). Behavioral differences between Chinese-American and European-American newborns. *Nature, 224,* 1227.

Garcia, J. (1981). The logic and limits of mental aptitude testing. *American Psychologist, 36,* 1172–1180.

Gardner, H. (1983). *Frames of mind.* New York: Basic Books.

Goldsmith, H. H., & Rothbart, M. K. (1992). *The Laboratory Temperament Assessment Battery.* Eugene, OR: Personality Development Laboratory.

Hencke, P. (1990). Potentiation of inputs from the posterolateral amygdala to the dentate gyrus and resistance to stress ulcer formation in rats. *Physiology and Behavior, 48,* 659–664.

Kagan, J. (1983). Classifications of the child. In P. H. Mussen (Series Ed.) & W. Kessen (Vol. Ed.), *History, theory, and methods: Vol. 1. Handbook of child psychology* (pp. 477–526). New York: Wiley.

Kagan, J. (1984). *The nature of the child.* New York: Basic Books.

Kagan, J. (1989). *Unstable ideas.* Cambridge, MA: Harvard University Press.

Kagan, J., Arcus, D., Snidman, N., Wang, Y. F., Hendler, J., & Greene, S. (1992). *Ease of arousal in infants.* Unpublished manuscript.

Kagan, J., & Moss, H. A. (1962). *Birth to maturity.* New York: Wiley.

Kagan, J., & Snidman, N. (1991). Temperamental factors in human development. *American Psychologist, 46,* 856–862.

Kanner, L. (1944). Behavior disorders of childhood. In J. McV. Hunt (Ed.), *Psychology and behavior disorders* (pp. 110–140). New York: Ronald.

Klein, R. G. (1991). Parent–child agreement in clinical assessment of anxiety and other psychopathology. *Journal of Anxiety Disorders, 5,* 187–198.

Lewis, M. L. (1987). Social development in infancy and early childhood. In J. D. Osofsky (Ed.), *Handbook of infant development* (2nd ed., pp. 419–493). New York: Wiley.

Magnusson, D. (1988). *Individual development from an interactional perspective.* Hillsdale, NJ: Erlbaum.

Osgood, C. E. (1962). Studies on the generality of affective meaning systems. *American Psychologist, 17,* 10–28.

Parke, R. D. (1992). Social development in infancy: Looking backward, looking forward. In G. A. Suci & S. S. Robertson (Eds.), *Future directions in infant development research* (pp. 1–24). New York: Springer-Verlag.

Plotkin, H. C. (1988). *The role of behavior in evolution.* Cambridge, MA: MIT Press.

Roback, A. A. (1931). *The psychology of character.* New York: Harcourt Brace.

Rogeness, G. A., Hernandez, J. M., Macedo, C. A., Amyrony, S. A., & Hoppe, S. K. (1986). Near zero plasma dopamine beta hydroxylase and conduct disorder in emotionally disturbed boys. *Journal of American Academy of Child Psychiatry, 25,* 521–527.

Sameroff, A. J. (1975). Transactional models in early social relations. *Human Development, 18,* 65–79.

Schechtman, V. L., Harper, R. M., & Kluge, K. A. (1989). Development of heart rate variation over the first six months of life in normal infants. *Pediatric Research, 26,* 343–346.

Scott, J. P., & Fuller, J. L. (1974). *Dog behavior: The genetic basis.* Chicago: University of Chicago Press.

Seifer, R., Sameroff, A. J., Barrett, L. C., & Krafchuk, K. E. (1992). *Infant temperament measured by multiple observations and mother report.* Unpublished manuscript.

Siegel, G. J., Albers, R. W., Agranoff, B. W., & Katzman, R. (1981). *Basic neurochemistry* (3rd ed.). Boston: Little Brown.

Terman, L. M. (1925). *Genetic studies of genius.* Stanford, CA: Stanford University Press.

Thatcher, R. W., Walker, R. A., & Giudice, S. (1987). Human cerebral hemispheres develop at different rates and ages. *Science, 236,* 1110–1112.

Thomas, A., & Chess, S. (1977). *Temperament and development.* New York: Brunner/Mazel.

Wilczek, F. (1992). What did Bohr do? *Science, 255,* 345–347.

20

COGNITIVE DEVELOPMENT: PAST, PRESENT, AND FUTURE

JOHN H. FLAVELL

This chapter has two objectives. The first and most important one is to summarize where we developmental psychologists currently are in our understanding and conceptualization of human cognitive development. That is, what do we know about it, and how do we think about it? What are and have been the field's different images of what cognitive development is like? The focus is thus on our past and, especially, our present ideas about it. The second objective is to speculate briefly about the future of the field — some possible directions in which it could or should go. Space limitations preclude consideration of two important topics one might expect to see included in an overview of cognitive development, namely, language acquisition and cognitive changes during adulthood.

I am very grateful to Robbie Case, Eleanor Flavell, Rochel Gelman, Frances Green, Eleanor Maccoby, Ellen Markman, Robert Siegler, Robert Sternberg, and Henry Wellman for their helpful comments on an earlier draft of this article.

Reprinted from *Developmental Psychology*, 28, 998–1005. Copyright by the American Psychological Association.

THE PAST AND PRESENT

What have developmentalists come to believe about human cognitive development after over a century of study? First, some obvious things: Children do undergo extensive and varied cognitive growth between birth and adulthood. That is, there is most definitely a phenomenon called *cognitive development*, and it is an extremely rich, complex, and multifaceted process. Moreover, it has proved amenable to productive scientific inquiry. Cognitive development has become a large and thriving scientific field, a fact that would have surprised some of our forebears: "Titchener, like his mentor Wundt, thought an experimental psychology of children impossible" (Kessen, 1983, p. viii). Studies have yielded a large number and variety of interesting facts about cognitive development, many of them quite surprising. Some are surprising because they show that children of a certain age have not yet acquired something we would have expected them to have acquired by that age, if indeed it needed acquiring at all. The Piagetian conservations are everyone's favorite examples. Others surprise us for the opposite reason. The remarkable infant competencies revealed by recent research are cases in point—for example, the young infant's capacities for speech perception and intermodal matching. Actually most of what developmentalists have discovered about cognitive development is surprising at least in the sense of being unexpected, and perhaps virtually nonexpectable, without a scientific background in the field. For example, what newcomer to the field could anticipate the possible existence of such "developables" as Piagetian concrete-operational skills or a naive "desire psychology" (Wellman, 1990)?

The Child as Constructive Thinker

Another thing developmentalists have come to believe about children is that they are very active, constructive thinkers and learners. Children are clearly not blank slates that passively and unselectively copy whatever the environment presents to them. Rather, the cognitive structures and processing strategies available to them at that point in their development lead them to select from the input what is meaningful to them and to represent and transform what is selected in accordance with their cognitive structures. As Piaget correctly taught us, children's cognitive structures dictate both what they accommodate to (notice) in the environment and how what is accommodated to is assimilated (interpreted). The active nature of their intellectual commerce with the environment makes them to a large degree the manufacturers of their own development:

> One major impetus to cognitive development is the child himself. Much of cognitive development is *self-motivated*. Children are knowledge seekers, they develop their own theories about the world around them, and

continually subject their theories to tests, even in the absence of external feedback. They perform thought and action experiments on their own, continually, and without external pressure. Children as well as adults "play" with their developing knowledge. . . . They engage in knowledge-extending and knowledge-refining activities spontaneously, arguing with themselves via an internal dialogue. They question the veracity or range of applicability of their theories, they perform *thought experiments*, question their own basic assumptions, provide counterexamples to their own rules, and reason on the basis of what ever knowledge they have, even though it may be incomplete, or their logic may be faulty. . . . This metaphor of the child as *little scientist* is compelling and central to many theories of development. (Brown, 1983, pp. 31–32)

New Methods

Acquiring all these facts and beliefs about the cognition of infants, children, adolescents, and adults required the invention of new research methods. Historically, there seems to have been at least a rough and irregular trend from an almost exclusive reliance on observational methods and highly verbal, talky testing procedures to the addition of mixed verbal–nonverbal and wholly nonverbal experimental methods. To illustrate the early emphasis on verbal methods, in the 1880s G. Stanley Hall used the newly invented questionnaire in his pioneering study of the "contents of children's minds" (Cairns, 1983). Likewise, most of Piaget's early research made use of the interview method, in which both the questions and problems posed by the experimenter and the responses given by the child subject were entirely verbal (J. H. Flavell, 1963).

There is now a variety of different methods at the developmentalist's disposal, most of them not wholly verbal in nature. Recent innovations intended mainly for use with older, postinfancy subjects include procedures involving modeling and imitation (Watson & Fischer, 1980), double imitation (Smith, 1984), information integration (Anderson & Cuneo, 1978), rule assessment (Siegler, 1981), double assessment (Wilkinson, 1982), surprise (Gelman, 1972), and deception (Chandler, Fritz, & Hala, 1989). For example, what children can and cannot successfully imitate gives us some indication of what they do and do not understand.

However, it is in cognitive research with infants that the historical movement toward nonverbal measures is most clearly seen. The nonverbal methods devised for use with infants have been ingenious and their scientific payoff enormous. Before their invention, developmentalists knew very little about the young infant's cognitive capabilities, Piaget's astute observations notwithstanding—"infancy was like the dark side of the moon," as Bower put it (1977, p. 5). The key to studying infant cognition proved to be the exploitation by experimenters of nonverbal response patterns, patterns that provide information about the infant's perceptual—cognitive states and activities. The main patterns exploited in this way have been sucking, heart-rate changes, head turning, reaching, and—most useful of all—looking. It seems that infants will look longer at one object or event than another for much the same reasons that adults would: because they like it better, because it takes longer to process completely, and because it violates their expectations. If we find that infants seem surprised—as indexed by prolonged looking time—at a display that violates some physical law (e.g., a display suggesting that two solid objects are occupying the same space at the same time), it seems reasonable to credit them with some sort of tacit knowledge of that law. Recent studies of infants' knowledge about objects by Baillargeon (in press) and Spelke (1988) illustrate this research strategy. Technological advances—for example, eye-movement cameras, video recorders, and computers—have also played an important role in research with both infants and older subjects.

The Diagnosis Problem

Despite the impressive array of different methods now at their disposal, present-day developmentalists are still often unable to characterize a given child's knowledge or abilities with precision and confidence. The diagnosis problem in cognitive development has proved to be a formidable one (e.g., Brown, 1983; J. H. Flavell, 1985; Greeno, Riley, & Gelman, 1984). It turns out that a child is likely to "have" a target competency in different degrees, ways, and forms at different ages, and precisely how best to characterize each child's "has," both in itself and in relation to its preceding and succeeding "haves," is a difficult problem. Some common ways that competencies change with age are the following:

> A competency may be improved in the course of development by becoming more reliably invoked and used on any one task, more generalized and differentiated in its use across tasks, more dominant over competing, inappropriate approaches, more integrated with other competencies, more accessible to conscious reflection and verbal expression, and more consolidated and solidified. (J. H. Flavell, 1985, pp. 116–117)

A good example of a current developmental diagnosis problem is to be found in the area of theory-of-mind development: Despite a great deal of recent research using a variety of methods, researchers in this area are still not sure exactly what the average 3-year-old does and does not understand about the mental state of belief (Perner, 1991; Wellman, 1990).

Revised Estimates of Competence

Recent research with these new methods has led to a somewhat different estimate of subjects' cognitive abilities than that suggested by Piagetian and other earlier work. Infants and young children now seem more competent, and adults less competent, than developmentalists used to think (Brown, 1983; J. H. Flavell, 1985; Gelman & Brown, 1986; Siegler, 1991). For example, recent research suggests that infants can perceptually discriminate most of the speech sounds used in human language, discriminate between small numerosities (e.g., sets of two vs. three objects), distinguish causal from noncausal event sequences, understand a number of basic properties of objects including object permanence, distinguish between animate agents and inanimate objects, detect intermodal correspondences, imitate facial gestures, form concepts and categories, and recall past events. As precocious infant abilities continue to be discovered, the difference between infant and postinfant competencies, although still substantial, seems less and less discontinuous and qualitative. Similarly, young children also turn out to be not as incompetent—not as "pre" this and "pre" that (precausal, preoperational, and so on)—as we once thought. To mention but two of many examples, their understanding of numbers and mental states, although still elementary, is more advanced than previously believed. For instance, even 2-year-olds are nonegocentric in the sense that they realize that another person will not see an object they see if the person is blindfolded or is looking in a different direction (Lempers, E. R. Flavell, & J. H. Flavell, 1977). Finally, adult cognition is less developmentally advanced than we had assumed:

> At the other end of the age spectrum, adults' reasoning has turned out to be not as rational as was once thought. Without training, even high school and college students rarely solve Piagetian formal operations tasks. . . . These difficulties are not limited to Piaget's tasks or scientific reasoning. Shaklee (1979) reviewed a host of irrational aspects of adults' thinking. (Siegler, 1991, p. 350)

In summary,

> The recent trend in the field has been to highlight the cognitive competencies of young children . . . , the cognitive shortcomings of adults, and the cognitive inconsistencies of both, effectively pushing from both ends of childhood towards the middle and blurring the difference between the two groups. (J. H. Flavell, 1985, p. 84)

The Question of General Stages

A long-standing controversial issue in the field has been whether the mind develops in a more general, unified fashion or in a more specific, fractionated manner (e.g., Case, 1992; Demetriou & Efklides, in press; Fischer & Silvern, 1985; J. H. Flavell, 1982, 1985). Development would be very general and unified if it proceeded through a fixed sequence of broad, across-tasks-and-domains structures of the whole, such as the sensory-motor, concrete-operational, and formal-operational stages described by Piaget. If development were very general in this sense, the child's mind would be uniformly and homogeneously stage-x-like (e.g., concrete operational-like) in its approaches to all cognitive tasks while the child was in that stage. That is, the child would have a characteristic mental structure at that stage and would apply it to all content areas. In contrast, development would be very specific and fractionated if each developmental acquisition proceeded at its own rate and in its own manner, independent of all the others. If this were true, there would be nothing homogeneous or unified about the child's mind at any age. Rather, it would be as if the child's mind were a collection of different and unrelated "mindlets," each developing independently of the others according to its own timetable.

Virtually all contemporary developmentalists agree that cognitive development is not as general stagelike or grand stagelike as Piaget and most of the rest of the field once thought. They disagree, however, as to just how general or specific it is. Neo-Piagetian theorists recognize that development is specific in many respects but also believe that it contains important general properties (Case, 1987, 1992; Demetriou & Efklides, in press; Fischer & Farrar, 1987; Halford, in press; Pascual-Leone, 1987; see also Sternberg, 1987). They assume that there is a regular, probably maturation-based increase with age in some aspect of the child's information-processing capacity, such as the child's processing speed or processing efficiency. As the child's information-processing capacity increases with increasing age, it makes possible new and more complex forms of cognition in all content domains, because the child can now hold in mind and think about more things at once. Conversely, capacity limitations at any given age constrain and limit the possible forms of cognition the child can enact. Thus, capacity limitations and their progressive reduction with age act as governors and enablers of cognitive growth, making for important across-domain similarities in the child's cognitive functioning at each point in development. In support of this view, neo-Piagetians have obtained empirical evidence suggesting that cognitive development does have some general stagelike as well as specific properties. Indeed, for it not to have any general-stage properties at all would seem counterintuitive: An extreme "unrelated mindlets" view does not seem to me any more likely to be right than Piaget's "grand stage" view.

Effects of Expertise

Most contemporary developmentalists seem either to ignore or to doubt the existence of such general, transdomain developmental similarities and synchronisms, focusing instead on more specific developments within a single content area or knowledge domain. Some emphasize the surprisingly powerful effects of well-organized content knowledge or expertise on the child's cognitive level within that specific content area (e.g., Chi & Glaser, 1980). They argue that a child may function at a higher developmental level or stage in one content area than in another if he or she has acquired expertise in that area through extensive practice and experience. The result is that the child may operate less consistently and uniformly across domains at a single general stage of development than general-stage theorists would predict. One way that domain-specific knowledge and experience benefits children's thinking is that it permits them "to solve many problems more by memory processes than by complex reasoning processes—that is, by recognizing familiar problem patterns and responding to them with over-learned solution procedures" (J. H. Flavell, 1985, p. 115).

Natural Domains and Constraints

Other developmentalists stress the importance of cognitive acquisitions in special, biologically natural rather than arbitrary knowledge domains (Carey & Gelman, 1991; Wellman & Gelman, 1992; see also Gardner, 1983). Unlike Piagetians, neo-Piagetians, or advocates of the expertise approach, these developmentalists emphasize the fact that, as members of a biological species, humans have evolved to find some things much easier and more natural to acquire than others. Humans are born with, or develop early on through maturation, specific predispositions and potentials for achieving these "privileged acquisitions" (Gallistel, Brown, Carey, Gelman, & Keil, 1991, p. 5). We are equipped with specific, possibly modular or encapsulated processing biases or constraints that give us a crucial leg up in developing these biologically natural competencies (Leslie, 1991). The most obvious and long-recognized of these natural domains is language. Chomsky and his followers have convinced virtually everyone that human beings have evolved very powerful mechanisms dedicated to extracting grammatical knowledge about a language from fairly impoverished linguistic input (Cook, 1988). The young infant's innately given ability to discriminate subtle differences in speech sounds mentioned previously suggests that phonological learning is also a natural domain for humans. Children may also be endowed with additional constraints (e.g., mutual exclusivity) that facilitate lexical and perhaps other nonlinguistic acquisitions (Markman, 1992).

Cognitive Development as Theory Development

For some domains, the knowledge that children acquire may be such as to warrant being called an informal, naive, nonscientific "theory" (e.g., Carey, 1985; Keil, 1989; Wellman, 1990). Wellman and Gelman (1992) argued that children can be said to possess a "framework" or "foundational" theory in a domain if (a) they honor the core ontological distinctions made in that domain, (b) they use domain-specific causal principles in reasoning about phenomena in the domain, and (c) their causal beliefs cohere to form an interconnected theoretical framework. Wellman and Gelman reviewed evidence suggesting that children acquire naive foundational theories in at least three areas: physics, psychology, and biology. Children's naive physics includes their understanding of the physical properties and behavior of inanimate objects and their physical–causal interactions. Children's naive psychology consists of their knowledge of mental states and how these states interact in a psychological–causal way with one another, with environmental input, and with behavioral output. Their naive biology comprises an ontology of biological kinds and beliefs about specifically biological–causal mechanisms that affect these kinds. This view of cognitive development as domain-specific theory development is new and exciting and poses numerous important questions for the field. One that Wellman and Gelman rightly cited as being particularly critical is that of how one would "test and therefore potentially disconfirm the hypothesis that early understandings develop within distinct domains of thought" (1992, p. 365; see also Gallistel et al., 1991).

Synchronisms, Sequences, and Qualitative Changes

A large number of cognitive–developmental entities (concepts, skills, etc.) enter a person's cognitive repertoire during childhood. Developmentalists have long been interested in determining whether or how these entities might be related to one another psychologically (J. H. Flavell, 1985). Research suggests that many of them are indeed interrelated. Some may enter the child's repertoire at the same time, be substantially positively intercorrelated within children of the same age, and appear to be psychologically related within some theory. This suggests that they are different manifestations of the same underlying ability or conceptual structure and thus comprise an emerging psychological unit. Whether there are some units of this sort that are very general and transdomainal, such as Piaget's concrete-operational structures, is of course the general-stage issue that was previously noted as being controversial. However, developmentalists of both domain-general and domain-specific persuasion sometimes find more modest-sized units within individual domains as well. Here is an example from the domain of naive psychology: Children's understanding of so-called Level 2 visual-perspective differences (e.g., recognizing that something may look upside down from one person's side but right side up from another's), of the appearance–reality distinction, and of false beliefs all emerge at about the same time in early childhood, are substantially correlated within 3-year-olds, and can be plausibly interpreted as being different expressions of an emerging representational theory of mind (J. H. Flavell, Green, & E. R. Flavell, 1990).

Other cognitive entities within a domain may develop in a fixed sequence rather than synchronously—another kind of orderliness and connectedness in development. The entities comprising such sequences may be linked by one or more of at least five major types of sequential relationships: addition, substitution, modification, inclusion, and mediation (J. H. Flavell, 1985). As an example of an addition sequence, Wellman (1990) cites evidence suggesting that earlier in their development of knowledge about the mind children acquire some understanding of people's desires (a *desire psychology*); later, they add to it some understanding of beliefs (a *belief–desire psychology*). As is well known, the Piagetians have also described a prodigious number of varied and interesting cognitive–developmental sequences over the years.

A perennial question about developmental sequences has been whether at least some of them represent big, qualitative-looking changes in the child's thinking about whatever the sequences concern. The answer is that many changes do look quite qualitative at face value, even though they are probably produced by a succession of underlying changes of a more quantitative and continuous nature. Again, Piagetian psychology has shown us many qualitative-looking changes. For a striking example, Carey (1991) proposed that the child's intuitive theory of physical objects is not just qualitatively different from the adult's intuitive theory of material entities but is actually incommensurable with it, that is, so different that the concepts contained in one theory cannot be defined or expressed by the concepts contained in the other.

Mechanisms of Development

It is not easy to describe cognitive development, but it is even harder to explain it:

> Serious theorizing about basic mechanisms of cognitive growth has actually never been a popular pastime, now or in the past. It is rare indeed to encounter a substantive treatment of the problem in the annual flood of articles, chapters and books on cognitive development. The reason is not hard to find: good theorizing about mechanisms is very, very hard to do. (J. H. Flavell, 1984, p. 189)

Understanding mechanisms is important because they can help explain the various developments that are described. The question of mechanisms is similar to that of stages in that one can distinguish domain-specific and domain-general approaches. The main developmental mechanisms of any putatively natural, privileged acquisition such as language development would presumably be some specialized, perhaps modular neural system dedicated to engendering that development and controlling its timing and form (Gallistel et al., 1991). Psychologists who study development in specific, natural domains may also consider the possibility of general, domain-neutral mechanisms (true for many developmental psycholinguists, for example), but domain-specific ones will understandably be of particular interest to them (Gallistel et al., 1991, pp. 32–33).

Other developmentalists have been more concerned with describing general mechanisms, ones potentially capable of engendering cognitive growth in any domain. The best known general mechanism is the process of equilibration that Piaget (1985) spent much of his professional life elaborating; the clearest and most readable exegesis of this abstractly described and difficult-to-understand change process is probably that of Chapman (1988). For a current and very interesting attempt to work with the concept experimentally, see Acredelo and O'Connor (1991).

Another undoubtedly important general mechanism already mentioned is the increase with age in some aspect of information-processing capacity that neo-Piagetians regard as the main engine of development. Recent work by Kail (1991) makes it seem increasingly likely that this capacity increase is the result of some hard-wired maturational change in the brain, rather than just the result of age-associated accumulations of specific or nonspecific cognitive experience (although experience can also lead to capacitylike increases). Developmentalists have long searched for a maturational process that could serve as a kind of universal regulator and pacesetter for cognitive growth, thereby making for similarities among all of the cognitive–development courses. This might be one such process. Another might be maturational changes in the brain that make it possible for the child to delay or inhibit responding (e.g., Llamas & Diamond, 1991).

Finally, the quest for general mechanisms has been reinvigorated by some of Siegler's (1989; Siegler & Crowley, 1991) work. Siegler defined a mechanism of cognitive development broadly as "any mental process that improves children's ability to process information" (1989, p. 354) and described recent research on five classes of such mechanisms: (a) *neural mechanisms*, including synaptogenesis, segregation of neuronal input, and experience-expectant and experience-dependent processes; (b) *associative competition*, especially connectionist models; (c) *encoding*, including his scale-balance research and others' work on transitive inference; (d) *analogy*, particularly the work of Brown and Gentner; and (d) *strategy choice*, featuring Siegler's own theory and research. He concluded by arguing that most mechanisms involve the creation and subsequent resolution of *competition* between neurological or psychological entities, a position that he notes to be similar to Piaget's. In a subsequent article, Siegler and Crowley (1991) described a microgenetic method for obtaining information about mechanisms and presented two interesting conclusions about the typical course of cognitive growth that the use of such methods has suggested: (a) Even after children discover a new competency, they may continue for some time to use previous, less adequate approaches; and (b) contrary to what might be predicted from Piaget's equilibration model, cognitive change often follows successes rather than failures in the use of current approaches (see also Karmiloff-Smith, 1984).

Sociocultural Influences

Not all mechanisms of cognitive development are situated wholly within the child. Although not usually classified as "mechanisms of development," activities and environmental settings involving other people clearly play a critical role in children's cognitive development. The crucial importance of the sociocultural environment in this development has been particularly emphasized by Vygotsky (1978) and other theorists (e.g., Bronfenbrenner, 1979; Bruner, 1990; Cole, 1985; Laboratory of Comparative Human Cognition, 1983; Rogoff, 1990; Wertsch, 1985). Rogoff's (1990) ideas will serve to illustrate this sociocultural or contextualistic approach. She views cognitive development as an apprenticeship in which children acquire knowledge and skills by participating in societally structured activities together with their parents, other adults, and children. Children learn in specific contexts through a process of guided participation in which others provide various kinds of help tailored to the children's current level of knowledge and skill (within their "zone of proximal development," in Vygotsky's words). Rogoff (1990) differs from many theorists of both domain-general and domain-specific orientation on at least two points. First, she expects to see multiple, highly specific, and variable developments as a function of individual children's specific and variable cultural experiences, rather than universal, specieswide developmental outcomes (1990, p. 30). Second, unlike most developmentalists, she does not view the child as a separate entity interacting with another separate entity, namely, an environment that can be differentiated from the child. Rather, "the child and the social world are mutually involved to an extent that precludes regarding them as independently definable" (Rogoff, 1990, p. 28). It is clear that her image of the developing child is most decidedly not that of the solitary little scientist constructing naive theories about the world through his or her own unaided effects.

Individual Differences

One can distinguish between developmentalists who focus more on similarities among children and specieswide, universal developmental outcomes (either transdomainal or domain-specific) and those who focus more on individual differences among children and their developmental outcomes. As Maccoby (1984) has pointed out, the former focus has been dominant in cognitive development since the ascendance of Piagetian psychology, whereas the latter has been dominant in social–emotional and personality development. Nevertheless, there have always been developmentalists with strong interests in individual variation in children's cognitive behavior and development (Wohlwill, 1973).

For example, since Binet, a number of developmentalists have been interested in individual differences in tested intelligence. Others have examined individual variation in cognitive traits such as cognitive style and creativity (Kogan, 1983). Some have studied genetic and environmental contributions to individual differences using the powerful tools of behavior genetics (e.g., Loehlin, Willerman, & Horn, 1988; Plomin & Rende, 1991)—another example of how new methods lead to new knowledge. Developmental behavior geneticists have not only documented the power of genetic differences to produce cognitive differences between children, but more surprisingly, they have also shown how the different nonshared environments that individual children experience even within the same family can increase these individual differences (Plomin & Rende, 1991). Other developmentalists have recently succeeded in doing something that the field had long given up on as being impossible: Predict individual differences in cognition in later childhood from individual differences in cognition during infancy (Bornstein & Sigman, 1986; Thompson, Fagan, & Fulker, 1991). For example, it turns out that infants who show greater preference for visual novelty tend in later childhood to perform better on intelligence measures.

Practical Applications

Finally, another very important thing developmentalists have learned about cognitive development is that what has been learned can be applied to the solution of real-world problems involving children. That is, scientific information about children's cognitive growth has been very useful to parents, educators, child-care givers, mental health professionals, jurists, and others concerned with promoting the welfare and optimal development of children. Palincsar and Brown's (1984) reciprocal teaching method for fostering comprehension-monitoring activity during reading is but one of many examples that could be cited here. Of this accomplishment the field can be justly proud.

The Development of the Child

A quick way to suggest what developmentalists think cognitive development is like is simply to list the main things that seem to develop. Here are two such lists (see also Sternberg & Powell, 1983). Siegler (1991) follows Brown and DeLoache (1978) in proposing that the main things that develop are (a) basic processes, (b) strategies, (c) metacognition, and (d) content knowledge. I (J. H. Flavell, 1985) have suggested that there are seven cognitive–developmental trends during middle childhood and adolescence: (a) increases in information-processing capacity, (b) increases in domain-specific knowledge, (c) concrete and formal operations, (d) the ability to engage in quantitative thinking, (e) the acquisition of "a sense of the game" of thinking, (f) the acquisition of metacognitive knowledge and experiences, and (g) improvement of the cognitive competencies the child already possesses.

The Development of the Field[1]

Another way to convey what developmentalists think cognitive development is like is to summarize the history of that thinking. Although the following is obviously a much oversimplified account of that history, it may provide a useful additional perspective. A century ago, we knew virtually nothing about children's cognitive growth and were not even sure it could be studied scientifically. In subsequent years, a large number of facts were accumulated about what children know and can do at different ages, but there was no general theory that could integrate them. Piaget provided such a theory and also added vastly to the store of facts. Since Piaget, the field has made progress in at least three ways. First, the invention of new methods (e.g., infant looking measures) allowed developmentalists to challenge both Piagetian and common-sense assumptions about the competencies of infants and young children. New data were also gathered to support or refute key aspects of Piagetian theory (e.g., concerning general stages). Second, new "developables" (e.g., memory strategies) were identified, making it possible to learn about acquisitions not previously envisioned by Piaget or others. Finally, new ways of thinking about cognitive development (e.g., as theory change or as the growth of information-processing capacity) have emerged to supplement or compete with Piagetian approaches.

THE FUTURE

Attempts to predict the future of the field have been few in number (e.g., Siegler, 1983). One has only to try to make such predictions to understand why. On the one hand, the most accurate-seeming ones are also the most obvious-seeming and, therefore, less revealing to reader and forecaster alike. Thus, although likely to be right, these predictions are also likely to be unsurprising and uninteresting. On the other hand, lines of research that may seem novel and nonobvious to the forecaster may have

---

[1] I am indebted to Robbie Case for most of the content of this paragraph.

already been tried and quietly abandoned as unpromising by others. After all, many child researchers have tried to study many things in many ways during the past century. Still, the temptation to do a little crystal ball gazing is hard to resist.

Probably the most obvious prediction one could make is that currently productive lines of work will continue to be active, at least for a while. A number of such lines were described in the previous section. Among these, the biological-constraints and cognitive-development-as-theory-development approaches strike me as being particularly promising. I am somewhat less optimistic about the future of general-stage theories and contextualistic approaches. Almost as obvious is the prediction that some newly emerging approaches in related fields will invigorate future research in this one. Possible candidates here are connectionism and neuropsychology (Llamas & Diamond, 1991; McClelland, 1991), dynamic systems theory (Thelen & Ulrich, 1991), comparative developmental psychology (Parker, 1990; Povinelli & deBlois, 1991; Whiten, 1991), evolutionary psychology (Cosmides, 1989), and perhaps "gains-losses" and other conceptualizations of adult cognitive changes (Baltes, 1987).

A less obvious prediction emerges from consideration of what developmentalists have and have not learned about children's mental lives. Quite a lot has been learned about their knowledge and abilities at different ages: the tasks they can and cannot solve, the concepts they have and have not acquired, and so forth. Developmentalists have even learned something about how what children have acquired cognitively affects their everyday social and nonsocial behavior—for example, the character of their play and peer relationships, as well as their response to curricula in school. These are the things developmentalists have been studying all these years. However, we have seldom examined the implications of the knowledge and skills children have and have not developed for the nature of their inner lives. That is, we have seldom tried to infer what it is like to be them and what the world seems like to them, given what they have and have not achieved cognitively. When knowledge and abilities are subtracted from the totality of what could legitimately be called "cognitive," an important remainder is surely the person's subjective experience: how self and world seem and feel to that person, given that knowledge and those abilities. This gap between what developmentalists have and have not learned is clearest in the case of infants. We have learned at least a fair amount about what infants know and can do. However, one rarely sees detailed accounts of what it might be *like* to be an infant of this or that age, based on what infants know and can do. The only good account of this kind that I have found is presented in a book by Stern (1990).

Some might object that such an effort could not be scientific, because there is no way to obtain objective, scientific data about the phenomenological experience of a nonverbal subject. Although this objection certainly has some force, it still seems possible that developmental psychologists, working together with highly skilled writers, filmmakers, and the like, could effectively convey a rich, evidence-based, and convincing picture of an infant's or child's inner world. This picture might be regarded more as an applied science or engineering feat than a basic science one, but this would not make it any the less valuable a contribution to our understanding of children. To be convinced of this, just ask yourself if you would like to see an age-graded series of such portraits and if you would want students, teachers, and parents to see them. Moreover, well-done portraits of this kind, based on basic scientific thinking and research, might in turn lead to new thinking and new research. For example, it is possible that cognitive development would appear more compellingly saltatory or stagelike (that is, showing large, qualitative-looking differences between children of different ages) if portraits rather than task performance were considered.

Whether cognitive developmentalists will actually pursue this line of inquiry in the future is of course hard to predict. They might not try it, or they might try it but find it unprofitable. The argument for at least trying it seems strong, however: If we are going to study the development of the mind, we should study the development of all of it.

REFERENCES

Acredelo, C., & O'Connor, J. (1991). On the difficulty of detecting cognitive uncertainty. *Human Development, 34*, 204–223.

Anderson, N. H., & Cuneo, D. O. (1978). The height + width rule in children's judgments of quantity. *Journal of Experimental Psychology: General, 107*, 335–378.

Baillargeon, R. (in press). The object concept revisited: New directions. In C. E. Granrud (Ed.), *Visual perception and cognition in infancy* (Carnegie-Mellon Symposia on Cognition, Vol. 23). Hillsdale, NJ: Erlbaum.

Baltes, P. B. (1987). Theoretical propositions of life-span developmental psychology: On the dynamics between growth and decline. *Developmental Psychology, 23*, 611–626.

Bornstein, M. H., & Sigman, M. D. (1986). Continuity in mental development from infancy. *Child Development, 57*, 251–274.

Bower, T. G. R. (1977). *A primer of infant development.* New York: Freeman.

Bronfenbrenner, U. (1979). *The ecology of human development.* Cambridge, MA: Harvard University Press.

Brown, A. L. (1983). *Cognitive development.* Unpublished manuscript, National Institute of Child Health and Human Development, Bethesda, MD.

Brown, A. L., & DeLoache, J. S. (1978). Skills, plans, and self-regulation. In R. S. Siegler (Ed.), *Children's thinking: What develops?* (pp. 3–33). Hillsdale, NJ: Erlbaum.

Bruner, J. S. (1990). *Acts of meaning*. Cambridge, MA: Harvard University Press.

Cairns, R. B. (1983). The emergence of developmental psychology. In P. H. Mussen (Series Ed.) & W. Kessen (Vol. Ed.), *Handbook of child psychology: Vol. 1. History, theory, and methods* (4th ed., pp. 41–102). New York: Wiley.

Carey, S. (1985). *Conceptual change in childhood*. Cambridge, MA: MIT Press.

Carey, S. (1991). Knowledge acquisition: Enrichment or conceptual change? In S. Carey & R. Gelman (Eds.), *The epigenesis of mind: Essays on biology and cognition* (pp. 257–291). Hillsdale, NJ: Erlbaum.

Carey, S., & Gelman, R. (Eds.). (1991). *The epigenesis of mind: Essays on biology and cognition*. Hillsdale, NJ: Erlbaum.

Case, R. (1987). Neo-Piagetian theory: Retrospect and prospect. *International Journal of Psychology, 22*, 773–791.

Case, R. (Ed.). (1992). *The mind's staircase: Exploring the conceptual underpinnings of children's thought and knowledge*. Hillsdale, NJ: Erlbaum.

Chandler, M., Fritz, A. S., & Hala, S. (1989). Small scale deceit: Deception as a marker of 2-, 3-, and 4-year-olds' early theories of mind. *Child Development, 60*, 1263–1277.

Chapman, M. (1988). *Constructive evolution: Origins and development of Piaget's thought*. Cambridge, England: Cambridge University Press.

Chi, M. T. H., & Glaser, R. (1980). The measurement of expertise: Analysis of the development of knowledge and skill as a basis for assessing achievement. In E. L. Baker & E. S. Quellmalz (Eds.), *Educational testing and evaluation: Design, analysis and policy* (pp. 37–47). Beverly Hills, CA: Sage.

Cole, M. (1985). The zone of proximal development: Where culture and cognition create each other. In J. V. Wertsch (Ed.), *Culture, communication, and cognition: Vygotskian perspectives*. Cambridge, England: Cambridge University Press.

Cook, V. J. (1988). *Chomsky's universal grammar: An introduction*. Oxford, England: Basil Blackwell.

Cosmides, L. (1989). The logic of social exchange: Has natural selection shaped how humans reason? Studies with the Watson selection task. *Cognition, 31*, 187–276.

Demetriou, A., & Efklides, A. (in press). Experiential structuralism: A frame for unifying cognitive developmental theories. *Monographs of the Society for Research in Child Development*.

Fischer, K. W., & Farrar, M. J. (1987). Generalizations about generalization: How a theory of skill development explains both generality and specificity. *International Journal of Psychology, 22*, 643–677.

Fischer, K. W., & Silvern, L. (1985). Stages and individual differences in cognitive development. *Annual Review of Psychology, 36*, 613–648.

Flavell, J. H. (1963). *The developmental psychology of Jean Piaget*. Princeton, NJ: Van Nostrand.

Flavell, J. H. (1982). On cognitive development. *Child Development, 53*, 1–10.

Flavell, J. H. (1984). Discussion. In R. J. Sternberg (Ed.), *Mechanisms of cognitive development* (pp. 187–209). New York: Freeman.

Flavell, J. H. (1985). *Cognitive development* (2nd ed.). Englewood Cliffs, NJ: Prentice-Hall.

Flavell, J. H., Green, F. L., & Flavell, E. R. (1990). Developmental changes in young children's knowledge about the mind. *Cognitive Development, 5,* 1–27.

Gallistel, C. R., Brown, A. L., Carey, S., Gelman, R., & Keil, F. C. (1991). Lessons from animal learning for the study of cognitive development. In S. Carey & R. Gelman (Eds.), *The epigenesis of mind: Essays on biology and cognition* (pp. 3–36). Hillsdale, NJ: Erlbaum.

Gardner, H. (1983). *Frames of mind: The theory of multiple intelligences.* New York: Basic Books.

Gelman, R. (1972). Logical capacity of very young children: Number invariance rules. *Child Development, 43,* 75–90.

Gelman, R., & Brown, A. L. (1986). Changing views of cognitive competence in the young. In N. J. Smelser & D. R. Gerstein (Eds.), *Behavioral and social sciences: Fifty years of discovery* (pp. 175–207). Washington, DC: National Academy Press.

Greeno, J. G., Riley, M. S., & Gelman, R. (1984). Conceptual competence and children's counting. *Cognitive Psychology, 16,* 94–143.

Halford, G. S. (in press). *Children's understanding: The development of mental models.* Hillsdale, NJ: Erlbaum.

Kail, R. (1991). Development of processing speed in childhood and adolescence. *Advances in Child Development and Behavior, 23,* 151–185.

Karmiloff-Smith, A. (1984). Children's problem solving. In M. Lamb, A. L. Brown, & B. Rogoff (Eds.), *Advances in developmental psychology* (Vol. 3, pp. 39–90). Hillsdale, NJ: Erlbaum.

Keil, F. C. (1989). *Concepts, kinds, and cognitive development.* Cambridge, MA: Bradford Books/MIT Press.

Kessen, W. (Ed.). (1983). *Handbook of child psychology: Vol. 1. History, theory and methods* (4th ed., P. H. Mussen, Series Ed.). New York: Wiley.

Kogan, N. (1983). Stylistic variation in childhood and adolescence: Creativity, metaphor, and cognitive styles. In P. H. Mussen (Series Ed.) & J. H. Flavell & E. M. Markman (Vol. Eds.), *Handbook of child psychology: Vol. 3. Cognitive development* (4th ed., pp. 630–706). New York: Wiley.

Laboratory of Comparative Human Cognition. (1983). Culture and cognitive development. In P. H. Mussen (Series Ed.) & W. Kessen (Vol. Ed.), *Handbook of child psychology: Vol. 1. History, theory, and methods* (4th ed., pp. 295–356). New York: Wiley.

Lempers, J. D., Flavell, E. R., & Flavell, J. H. (1977). The development in very young children of tacit knowledge concerning visual perception. *Genetic Psychology Monographs, 95,* 3–53.

Leslie, A. (1991, April). *Information processing and conceptual development: The theory of ToMM.* Paper presented at the Biennial Meeting of the Society for Research in Child Development, Seattle, WA.

Llamas, C., & Diamond, A. (1991, April). *Development of frontal cortex abilities in children between 3–8 years of age.* Paper presented at the Biennial Meeting of the Society for Research in Child Development, Seattle, WA.

Loehlin, J. C., Willerman, L., & Horn, J. M. (1988). Human behavioral genetics. *Annual Review of Psychology, 39*, 101–133.

Maccoby, E. E. (1984). Socialization and developmental change. *Child Development, 55*, 317–328.

Markman, E. M. (1992). Constraints on word learning: Speculations about their nature, origins, and domain specificity. In M. R. Gunnar & M. P. Maratsos (Eds.), *Minnesota Symposia on Child Psychology* (Vol. 25). Hillsdale, NJ: Erlbaum.

McClelland, J. L. (1991, April). *Connectionist models of developmental change.* Paper presented at the Biennial Meeting of the Society for Research in Child Development, Seattle, WA.

Palincsar, A. S., & Brown, A. L. (1984). Reciprocal teaching of comprehension-monitoring activities. *Cognition and Instruction, 1*, 117–175.

Parker, S. T. (1990). The origins of comparative developmental evolutionary studies of primate mental abilities. In S. T. Parker & K. R. Gibson (Eds.), *"Language" and intelligence in monkeys and apes* (pp. 3–63). New York: Cambridge University Press.

Pascual-Leone, J. (1987). Organismic processes for Neo-Piagetian theories: A dialectical causal account of cognitive development. *International Journal of Psychology, 22*, 531–570.

Perner, J. (1991). *Understanding the representational mind.* Cambridge, MA: Bradford Books/MIT Press.

Piaget, J. (1985). *The equilibration of cognitive structures: The central problem of intellectual development.* Chicago: University of Chicago Press.

Plomin, R., & Rende, R. (1991). Human behavioral genetics. *Annual Review of Psychology, 42*, 161–190.

Povinelli, D. J., & deBlois, S. (1991). *Young children's (Homo sapiens) understanding of knowledge formation in themselves and others.* Unpublished manuscript, Yale University, New Haven, CT.

Rogoff, B. (1990). *Apprenticeship in thinking: Cognitive development in social context.* New York: Oxford University Press.

Shaklee, H. (1979). Bounded rationality and cognitive development: Upper limits on growth? *Cognitive Psychology, 11*, 327–345.

Siegler, R. S. (1981). Developmental sequences within and between concepts. *Monographs of the Society for Research in Child Development, 46*(2, Serial No. 189).

Siegler, R. S. (1983). Information processing approaches to development. In P. H. Mussen (Series Ed.) & W. Kessen (Vol. Ed.), *Handbook of child psychology: Vol. 1. History, theory, and methods* (4th ed., pp. 129–211). New York: Wiley.

Siegler, R. S. (1989). Mechanisms of cognitive development. *Annual Review of Psychology, 40*, 353–379.

Siegler, R. S. (1991). *Children's thinking* (2nd ed.). Englewood Cliffs, NJ: Prentice-Hall.

Siegler, R. S., & Crowley, K. (1991). The microgenetic method: A direct means for studying cognitive development. *American Psychologist, 46,* 606–620.

Smith, L. B. (1984). Young children's understanding of attributes and dimensions: A comparison of conceptual and linguistic measures. *Child Development, 55,* 363–380.

Spelke, E. S. (1988). Where perceiving ends and thinking begins: The apprehension of objects in infancy. In A. Yonas (Ed.), *Perceptual development in infancy. Minnesota Symposia on Child Psychology* (Vol. 20, pp. 197–234). Hillsdale, NJ: Erlbaum.

Stern, D. N. (1990). *Diary of a baby.* New York: Basic Books.

Sternberg, R. J. (1987). A day at Developmental Downs: Sportscast for Race #2 — neo-Piagetian theories of cognitive development. *International Journal of Psychology, 22,* 507–529.

Sternberg, R. J., & Powell, J. S. (1983). The development of intelligence. In P. H. Mussen (Series Ed.) & J. H. Flavell & E. M. Markman (Vol. Eds.), *Handbook of child psychology: Vol. 3. Cognitive development* (4th ed., pp. 341–419). New York: Wiley.

Thelen, E., & Ulrich, B. D. (1991). Hidden skills. *Monographs of the Society for Research in Child Development, 56*(1, Serial No. 223).

Thompson, L. A., Fagan, J. F., & Fulker, D. W. (1991). Longitudinal prediction of specific cognitive abilities from infant novelty preferences. *Child Development, 62,* 530–538.

Vygotsky, L. S. (1978). *Mind in society: The development of higher psychological processes.* Cambridge, MA: Harvard University Press.

Watson, M. W., & Fischer, K. W. (1980). Development of social roles in elicited and spontaneous behavior during the preschool years. *Developmental Psychology, 16,* 483–494.

Wellman, H. M. (1990). *The child's theory of mind.* Cambridge, MA: Bradford Books/MIT Press.

Wellman, H. M., & Gelman, S. A. (1992). Cognitive development: Foundational theories of core domains. *Annual Review of Psychology, 43,* 337–375.

Wertsch, J. V. (1985). *Vygotsky and the social formation of mind.* Cambridge, MA: Harvard University Press.

Whiten, A. (Ed.). (1991). *Natural theories of mind: Evolution, development and simulation.* Oxford, England: Basil Blackwell.

Wilkinson, A. C. (1982). Partial knowledge and self-correction: Developmental studies of a quantitative concept. *Developmental Psychology, 18,* 876–893.

Wohlwill, J. F. (1973). *The study of behavioral development.* San Diego: Academic Press.

21

THE ROLE OF PARENTS IN THE SOCIALIZATION OF CHILDREN: AN HISTORICAL OVERVIEW

ELEANOR E. MACCOBY

The approach of the next century is an appropriate time to take stock of psychology's progress in the study of human development and to consider where developmental psychology has been, where it stands, and where it is going. Attempting to understand the socialization process has been a long-standing enterprise in both social and developmental psychology. When broadly conceived, the outcomes of interest have not changed greatly over time. That is, students of socialization continue to be concerned with the cluster of processes that lead to adults being able to function adequately within the requirements of the social group or groups among which they live. Therefore the target or outcome behaviors of interest have continued to be some aspect of adequate functioning.

What is meant by "adequate"? The meaning has varied, of course, but there is a common core of meaning stemming from the understanding that if children are to be adequate adults, they must acquire habits, skills,

Reprinted from *Developmental Psychology*, 28, 1006–1017. Copyright by the American Psychological Association.

values, and motives that will enable them to (a) avoid deviant behavior, that is, avoid behaviors that disrupt or place undue burdens on the functioning of other persons in the nested hierarchy of social groups within which individuals live their lives; (b) contribute, through work, to the economic support of self and family; (c) form and sustain close relationships with others; and (d) be able to rear children in their turn.

Although parents are not the only agents contributing to the socialization of children, the family has continued to be seen as a major—perhaps the major—arena for socialization. This reflects the pervasive assumption that even though socialization and resocialization can occur at any point in the life cycle, childhood is a particularly malleable period, and it is the period of life when enduring social skills, personality attributes, and social orientations and values are laid down. The idea that "the child is father to the man" goes back to biblical times and probably before. So does the idea that an adult's rectitude depends on having received proper training earlier in life from parents and other educators. Over many centuries, the writings of religious leaders and philosophers—as well as popular wisdom—have been replete with theories and speculations concerning what kinds of child training will produce well-socialized adults. It is only in this century, however, that childhood socialization processes have become the focus of scientific study.

Most students of socialization have understood that societies, particularly modern ones, cannot rely on the ubiquitous presence of policemen or monitors to keep individual members of society in line. (Among other problems, relying on monitors raises the recursive question of who would monitor the monitors.) Developmentalists have continued to recognize that socialization practices must be such as to bring children to some degree of self-regulation with respect to social norms. This aspect of socialization has been studied in various guises with various labels, among them conscience, resistance to temptation, internalization of values, postponement of gratification, moral development, and out-of-sight compliance with parental requirements. Changes in theoretical points of view have dictated changes in the way these outcomes have been defined, but some aspect of internalization has remained a common theme.

The affective aspects of relationships between parents and children—love, hate, fear, and empathy—have also continued to occupy a central place in most conceptions of the socialization process. As readers will see, there have been changes in the role attributed to emotions, and some theories have given them minimal attention, but recognition of their importance has recurred repeatedly.

While these and other continuities can be seen in the field of socialization research, there have also been sweeping changes. The first major change has to do with how inclusive the theories have been. There was an early period of grand, all-encompassing theories, which gave way to more modest theories that were more limited to specific behavioral domains or specific age periods. A second major change concerns the direction of effects. What began as top-down conceptions in which parents were seen primarily as trainers or transmitters of culture and children as empty vessels who were gradually filled up with the necessary social repertoires has shifted to a conception of socialization as involving mainly bidirectional and interactive processes. A third change has involved the development of more complex process models. Whereas early work consisted largely of a search for direct connections between given parental practices (or clusters of practices) and a given child outcome, current work adds a focus on processes that may mediate the way in which a parental practice affects a child.

TWO GRAND THEORIES

In the early part of this century, there was relatively little empirical research on family processes and their relation to children's development. Nevertheless this period did see the introduction of theoretical points of view that strongly influenced the empirical work that was to come. The period has been thoughtfully reviewed by Cairns (1983), and here I mention only some highlights.

Behaviorism

The dawn of behaviorism ushered in a long period in which the socialization of children was seen by psychologists as analogous to the processes of *learning* being studied in the laboratory. Parents were teachers, and children were learners. The principles of classical and instrumental conditioning were seen as specifying the processes whereby children learned the required forms of behavior. Parents were the primary persons who set the agendas for what children were to learn and who administered the rewards and punishments that would strengthen desired behaviors and eliminate undesired ones from children's repertoires. Parents also set up the contingencies that enabled children to discriminate between situations in which a given behavior was permissible and situations in which it was not. (See the review by Gewirtz, 1969, for a detailed account of stimulus–response learning theories as applied to socialization.)

Habits once learned could be unlearned if they no longer received external reinforcement, and early learned behaviors were not considered any more difficult to unlearn or replace than behaviors acquired later in life (Gewirtz, 1969, p. 61). In behaviorists' writings, the question of how to define behavioral units was seldom clearly posed (or answered!), but it was recognized that emotions, as well as actions, could be conditioned, and both were subsumed under the more general concept of "responses." Responses could be quite small, isolated units (e.g., an eye blink or a smile), but smaller units of behavior could also be organized into smoothly articulated chains or clusters of acts that would make up a larger whole. Socialization, in sum, was seen as a process of accretion of a repertoire of habitual social responses that had acquired a specifiable probability of occurring under specific conditions. The theory was not developmental except in its assumption that the younger the child, the more limited was the repertoire and the more there was still to be learned. But new behaviors were thought to be acquired in the same way in childhood as at any other time of life.

Psychoanalytic Theory

The second major theme, introduced early in the 1900s and strongly elaborated thereinafter, was psychoanalytic theory. Many elements of this theory had to do with the socialization process and the role of parents therein. Some of the major propositions were as follows:

1. Early childhood is a time of high plasticity. Characteristics acquired at that time are nearly irreversible, although they may change the way in which they are manifested as children grow into adulthood.

2. There are two major intrapsychic forces—sexuality (libido) and aggression—and these progress through a series of predetermined psychosexual stages during the first 4 or 5 years of life. The theory was dynamic in that it was greatly concerned with children's emotional states (anger or love), rather than merely with the details of behavior.

3. Parental practices determine the quality of a child's experiences at each stage and are crucial in determining what the long-range consequences of these experiences will be. Parents must impose unwanted restrictions on the free expression of children's wishes and impulses. Children will become angry at parents when restrictions are imposed, and parents must then deal with this anger, suppressing it in some way. Parents are the ones who channel their children's aggression into acceptable channels during the early plastic years, and they must turn the child's sexual impulses away from the parents themselves.

4. Children experience intense conflict: They love their parents and need their devoted, nurturing presence; they intensely fear the loss of this nurturance and come to understand that their feelings of anger and sexuality directed toward parents entail the danger of parental rejection and the loss of parental nurturance.

5. The conflict is resolved through identification. Children "internalize" their parents and "introject" their values, forming a superego or conscience that is an internal representation of the parents (primarily in their regulatory capacity). Because the child's incestuous wishes are directed primarily toward the opposite-sex parent, there is greater risk of retaliation

or rejection by the same-sex parent, and conflict resolution therefore takes the form of identification primarily with the same-sex parent. This identification carries with it an adoption of appropriately sex-typed behavior and attitudes, along with an adoption of a more general set of prosocial values. A crucial outcome of the identification process is presumed to be the capacity to self-regulate primitive impulses.

Psychoanalytic theory underwent considerable criticism and modification during the years following the initial formulations by Sigmund Freud. In particular, many argued that the energy or drive manifested in young children's behavior was not specifically sexual. Still, the propositions listed here remained major ones that influenced the socialization research that followed.

Each of the two theories just outlined was a grand, overarching theory that presumed to encompass most of what was significant about the socialization of children. The theories differed in that, for learning theorists, the child was close to being a tabula rasa (except for some inborn reflexes and need states such as hunger and thirst), whereas for psychoanalytic theory, children entered the early childhood years equipped with a set of primitive impulses that needed to be brought under social control. Nevertheless, for both theories, it was primarily through parental control and teaching that the adult culture was seen as being passed on to each new generation of children.

EARLY EFFORTS AT EMPIRICAL TESTS

The late 1930s saw the initiation of an active period of research, which continued and expanded through the 1940s, 1950s, and into the 1960s. Some studies were straightforward applications of behavior theory and demonstrated that specific infant behaviors (such as smiles or vocalizations) could be instrumentally conditioned or extinguished. However, the most important development of this period was the effort to reconcile the two grand theories. Or more precisely, the effort was to derive hypotheses from psychoanalytic theory and to reformulate them into testable propositions stated in behavior-theoretical terms.

This work had its origin in the Yale Institute of Human Development in the 1930s (see Dollard, Doob, Miller, Mowrer, & R. R. Sears, 1939; Miller & Dollard, 1941), and for convenience, I refer to it as "the Yale school." A segment of this work that dealt with child rearing and its effects was undertaken in the 1940s and 1950s by psychologists Robert and Pauline Sears and anthropologists John and Beatrice Whiting (see R. R. Sears, Whiting, Nowlis, & P. S. Sears, 1953).

In this work, reinforcement and punishment, as well as their schedules and combinations, were the primary antecedent constructs. Secondary drives were seen as being created out of primary biological needs, by means of associationist principles. If the research had been based on behavior theory alone, it might have dealt with a range of socialization outcomes, such as children's learning to share toys, to comply with adult requests, to become polite and well mannered, to acquire language efficiently, and to read. Instead, the choice of outcome variables was dictated primarily by psychoanalytic theory. Children's aggression and their seeking of parental nurturance (translated as *dependency*) were a central focus of study, as were sex typing and manifestations of identification with parents (e.g., *conscience*). Weaning and toilet training received research attention, on the grounds that manifestations of fixations at one of the early psychosexual stages might be detectable. Conditioned anxiety was emphasized as a mediating process underlying fixations and as having long-term inhibitory effects within each of the behavioral domains. The studies dealt almost exclusively with socialization events occurring in the first 5 years of life, the years that were crucial for personality formation, according to psychoanalytic theory.

The results of this body of work were in many respects disappointing. In a study of nearly 400 families (R. R. Sears, Maccoby, & Levin, 1957), few connections were found between parental child-rearing practices (as reported by parents in detailed interviews) and independent assessments of children's personality characteristics—so few, indeed, that virtually nothing was published relating the two sets of data. The major yield of the study was a book on child-rearing practices as seen from the perspective of mothers (R. R. Sears et al., 1957). This book was mainly descriptive and included only very limited tests of the theories that had led to the study. Sears and colleagues later conducted a study with preschoolers focused specifically on the role of identification with the same-sex parent in producing progress toward social maturity. They used a much expanded range of assessment techniques, including observations of parent–child interaction. The hypothesis that identification with parents was a primary mechanism mediating children's acquisition of a cluster of well-socialized attributes was, once again, not supported (see especially R. R. Sears, Rau, & Alpert, 1965, Table 40, p. 246).

One can see, then, that these large-scale efforts to merge psychoanalytic and behavior theory, and then to predict children's personality attributes from parental socialization methods, were largely unsuccessful. For one thing, the two theories were probably more intrinsically incompatible than was acknowledged at the time. But it is important to note that the weakness of the research results did not disprove either of the grand theories. Rather, the theories began to fall of their own weight. New developments within the field of developmental psychology were making it more and more evident that neither theory, as originally formulated, could succeed. More limited theories began to appear, each growing up in a more limited domain and attempting to encompass a more limited body of data than the two theories of grand design. Before turning to these new developments, however, I need to mention a different line of thought and research that was occurring concurrently with the events just described.

A MORE MODEST EARLY THEORY

In the 1930s and into the 1940s, a research group headed by Alfred Baldwin at the Fels Institute in Ohio undertook a longitudinal study of children and their families, making repeated home visits to observe parent–child interaction and assessing the development of the children at several successive ages. The group's thinking about what was important to observe and measure was influenced by the writings of Piaget and by the work of Kurt Lewin and his colleagues. Their theory, like the two theories of grand design, was a top-down theory, but it was also strongly developmental. They were the first to emphasize and to demonstrate that parenting must undergo systematic change with the increasing cognitive capacities of children. In conceptualizing what was important about parenting, they took their lead from the work on group atmospheres done by Lewin and colleagues in the late 1930s (Lewin, Lippitt, & White, 1939; see also Maccoby, 1992). In that work, it had been shown that under democratic leadership, groups of school-age children became more fully involved in group projects, displayed less hostility, and were able to work in the absence of supervision more effectively than children under autocratic leadership. Baldwin and colleagues contrasted democratic with autocratic home atmospheres and were able to identify meaningful connections between these atmospheres and the quality of children's functioning in out-of-home settings (Baldwin, 1949, 1955).

THEMES IN THE WORK THAT FOLLOWED

Although elements of the two grand theories can be traced into the socialization research of the 1960s, 1970s, and 1980s, several profound changes occurred in theories about the nature of the socialization processes. These theoretical developments began to occur fairly independently of one another, being largely domain specific and not always compatible. I turn to them now.

The Decline of Simple Reinforcement Theory

The cognitive revolution that swept through much of psychology in the 1950s and 1960s did much to weaken the grip of simple S–R theorizing in general and reinforcement theory in particular. The impact on conceptions of socialization processes came first of all through the mushrooming work on developmental psycholinguistics.

Developmental Psycholinguistics

It had long been understood that a child's early learning of the language of his or her culture was a prerequisite for the smooth accomplishment of subsequent socialization steps. B. F. Skinner (1957) made a valiant attempt to bring language acquisition within the embrace of behavior theory, but the attempt was notably unsuccessful. The devastating review by Chomsky (1959), as well as reports by early students of children's language acquisition in the first few years of life, made it clear that the acquisition process had little to do with parental reinforcement. Parents were important in that they were the primary source of children's exposure to their culture's language. But children's early language was clearly not a simple imitation of phrases spoken by adults in their presence. Nor was it a process of selection, through parental reinforcement, from an initial large random repertoire of sounds, words, or phrases.

From the time of Chomsky's postulation of an innate *language acquisition device* to the current research on constraints in the acquisition of concepts (Markman, 1992), it has been clear that children do not come to language learning *de novo*. They are equipped with capacities or readinesses that are language specific, and they do much of the work of language acquisition themselves. While parents of course help to teach the meanings of words, children acquire the prosody and syntax of their language fairly independently of parental guidance, and their own inductive processes guide semantic development as well. These processes are clearly not top down: The role of the learner is fully as important as that of the teacher. The revelations from developmental psycholinguistics served to demote considerably the power of parents as socialization agents. Parental inputs began to be seen as being used by children, rather than as determining what children do or learn. Readers will recognize that this was the same message that was conveyed by Piaget and his followers for a whole range of children's cognitive acquisitions.

Did researchers' increasing focus on cognition mean that the interest in socialization died out? By no means—only that the field of developmental psychology became bifurcated. Whereas earlier, when behavior theory had sought to encompass all aspects of development through its emphasis on learning as the central process, now one group studied language and thought, and another studied personality and socioemotional development. It was in the latter portion of the field that socialization processes remained important and where the language and concepts of behaviorism were retained for a longer period.

Attachment Theory

A second body of work that served to weaken reinforcement theory was the research on attachment. As in the case of language acquisition, innate mechanisms were postulated. John Bowlby (1969) brought ethological theory squarely into the socialization arena. Drawing on work with nonhuman primates, he emphasized the evolutionary heritage that human beings brought to the early infant–mother relationship. Parent and infant were seen to be in a state of prepared readiness to develop reciprocal behaviors that would sustain the infant's development during the long period of dependency of human young. In this sense, parental behavior—in particular, *maternal* behavior—could be seen as instinctive, although it was by no means stereotyped or rigidly determined. There was a normal course of development of attachment behavior in human infants that depended on the responsiveness of the caregiver (Ainsworth & Bell, 1969). The process could be disrupted or deflected into maladaptive forms if the mother failed to perform her side of the interactive duet, but within a fairly wide range of maternal behaviors, the adaptive function of the interaction would be achieved, making it possible for the infant to proceed smoothly to succeeding developmental steps.

Many of the behaviors identified by attachment theorists as part of the attachment syndrome were the same as what had previously been called *dependency* (e.g., clinging, staying close to the mother, and resisting separation), but their meaning and consequences were seen quite differently. In the Yale school formulation, dependency was a kind of necessary side effect of the early nurturance of the infant—a set of habits that reflected the reinforcing properties of the mother but that needed to be dropped out if the child was to become able to function independently. The strongly contrasting view of the attachment theorists was that the attachment relationship was itself the necessary mediator of the child's ability to take on independent functioning. Parental responsiveness was not seen as reinforcing dependent behavior. In fact, parental responsiveness to children's dependency bids (crying or approaching) led children to behavior that was the opposite of what had been "reinforced": to a decrease in crying and to moving away from the parent to explore the environment (see Sroufe & Waters, 1977, for a detailed comparison of the two theories).

Nonreinforced Learning Through Modeling

In the 1960s, Albert Bandura published some ground-breaking studies of imitative learning (e.g., Bandura, 1962, 1965). Early work by the Yale school had included studies of imitation (Miller & Dollard, 1941), but they conceived of imitation in reinforcement terms. That is, children were so frequently reinforced for behaving like adults that adult behavior—or at least, the behavior of certain adults—acquired secondary reinforcer power.

The Bandura formulation was quite different: Performance was controlled by external contingencies, whereas learning was not. He spoke of "no trial learning" and was able to demonstrate that children could acquire new behaviors without ever performing them overtly and without their ever being reinforced, merely by observing them being performed by others.

Even after learning theory was expanded to incorporate observational learning, the viewpoint concerning socialization remained a top-down one. By seeing siblings punished for certain behavior, children could learn that this behavior was not acceptable to their parents and avoid it without ever having been punished directly. But the contingencies applied by adults were still what children had to learn about and what mainly affected the probabilities that they would act in given ways.

Social learning theory was revised and expanded over the subsequent years, becoming progressively more cognitive. (See Cairns's [1979] account of three generations of social learning theories.) In Bandura's writing, the label *imitation* was replaced by *modeling*, which in turn was replaced by *psychological matching*, to indicate that the process was not one of simple mimicry of acts. Social learning theory remained essentially nondevelopmental, but developmentalists know that the body of knowledge concerning cognitive development is highly relevant to the processes of psychological matching. What information children will take in from the behavior of others, what kind of symbolic representation they will store, and how they will process the stored information in relation to specific situations they encounter—all these things must surely depend on their level of cognitive development. I return later to the implications of this fact for the processes known as identification.

Microanalytic Analyses

In the 1970s, sophisticated computer technologies became available that made possible the analysis of moment-to-moment sequences of parent–child interaction. These sequences were first examined from the perspective of operant conditioning, in terms of the immediate contingencies members of a dyad were providing for each other's behavior. An important example of this approach is found in the work of G. R. Patterson and his colleagues (1980, 1982), who initiated a research program aimed at understanding the development of aggressive behavior in children (primarily boys). They began with the top-down assumption that "most deviant behaviors, and particularly those relating to child aggression, are caused by inept performance of child management skills" on the part of the parents (Patterson, 1980, p. 1.) The group carried out detailed observations of the children's interactions with their parents, recorded in small units of real time. From the sequential data, they studied the moment-to-moment consequences that parents provided for aggressive children's behavior and compared them with the sequences found in the homes of nonaggressive (or at least normally aggressive) children.

The microanalyses had disappointing results from the standpoint of the initial theorizing. The studies did not show that parents of aggressive boys provided higher rates of either positive or negative reinforcement for aggressive behavior. (See Maccoby & Martin, 1983, pp. 42–43, for detailed analysis of the findings.) However, the yield of the studies was very rich in other respects. It was clearly shown that the interactions occurring between parents and children were indeed quite different in the households of aggressive children. There were long chains of mutually coercive behaviors; parents used somewhat more punishment with aggressive boys, but more important, punishment was less effective with these boys than with controls. Therapeutic interventions with the families demonstrated that it was possible in some families to improve the behavior of the children by establishing firm and rule-oriented (rather than capricious) parental control. By this means, the mutual avoidance among family members was lessened, so that joint problem solving became possible, and there was even a rebirth of mutual affection. The theorizing of the Patterson group evolved from a social learning approach to a social interactionist perspective (Patterson, Reid, & Dishion, 1992, pp. 2–4).

The moment-to-moment interactions of mothers with their infants and toddlers have also been observed and microanalyzed. With the availability of videotaping technology, it became possible to make detailed video records of interaction sessions, which could then be segmented into tiny time units for coding. It was quickly evident that mothers were getting into communication with their infants by, among other things, imitating them and coordinating their own activities to the infant's attentional states. In interaction with a skillful and responsive mother, the infant's social capabilities expanded, and the pair could build a more and more reciprocal system. While maternal responsivity could have been described as reinforcement—and there were attempts to do so—this conceptual framework turned out to be inappropriate on the whole. For example, infants did not simply increase the frequency of the responses for which they were being "reinforced" (e.g., smiling or crying). Instead, they learned a turn-taking schema and became able to wait for the mother to perform her response before initiating their own next action.

It is not possible in this space to do justice to the richness of the detailed work on mother–infant interaction, but a few contributions can be mentioned. The work has shifted attention from individuals to dyads, and this forms an important part of the growing "science of relationships" (Berscheid & Peplau, 1983; Hartup & Rubin, 1986; and see summary in

Maccoby & Martin, 1983, pp. 26–36). The work has emphasized the importance of shared understandings, joint focus of attention, awareness by each of the other's intentions, and shared emotional states in the achievement of communication between parent and child (see Trevarthan & Hubley, 1978, on intersubjectivity). And the work has been highly influential in the redefinition of the socialization process, from one in which influence flows from adults to children to an interactive perspective.

Work on Intrinsic Motivation

In social psychology, there was a body of work on *overjustification* that dealt with whether individuals believed that their actions were self-motivated or were produced by external pressure. Studies with children were done in which their initial level of interest in a given activity was assessed, and then they were offered rewards for doing what they already wanted to do. It was shown that the children's interest in doing the activity declined (compared with pretreatment levels) when rewards were no longer offered. (Deci, 1975; Lepper & Greene, 1975) This work, of course, contributed to the decline of simple reinforcement theory and underlined the importance of children's interpretations of their own behavior and its causes.

Changing Conceptions of Children's Identification With Their Parents

As mentioned earlier, Freud's theory conceived of identification as a unitary process that brought about advances in several aspects of personality, including the adoption of sex-typed behaviors, taking adult roles in enforcing rules on self and others, resisting temptation, and feeling guilt over transgressions. As was noted, this theory was not sustained by research evidence. A major problem was that the different presumed outcomes of identification did not cluster together, nor did they have similiar socialization antecedents. Subsequent developments involved reformulations of the concept of internalization, and studies looked for relevant parental antecedents for different personality domains separately.

The Work on Modeling

Bandura explicitly discarded the terms *identification* and *internalization* on the grounds that they had too many surplus meanings. In early experiments, he did draw on psychoanalytic conceptions of identification to examine whether preestablished relationships between model and child would affect the likelihood that the child would imitate the model. The experiments showed that children were more likely to imitate a model who had previously been nurturant toward them or who had power over resources that children wanted (Bandura, 1965). The implications for the role of parents were clear: Because parents are both nurturant and powerful, children should be more likely to learn by observing them than by observing strangers.

Still, subsequent studies on the acquisition of aggressive behavior from filmed models showed that children would copy the behavior of unfamiliar models. It was clear, then, that the process of observational learning did not depend on a child's preestablished relation of dependency or fear in relation to a given model. Observational learning, then, was a much broader process than what had been previously called identification, and the interpersonal dynamics that had been presumed to underlie children's spontaneous taking on of parental characteristics were deemphasized.

Work on the acquisition of sex-typed behavior raised further questions about the role of identification. The psychoanalytic viewpoint was that boys became masculine and girls feminine by identifying with the same-sex parent. However, studies on parent–child similarities did not find that a child's sex-typed characteristics were related to those of the same-sex parent. And work by Perry and Bussey (1979) indicated that, with respect to the behavior displayed, children would preferentially imitate same-sex models only when there was consensus within a same-sex group of models and clear differentiation from a group of the other sex. This work helped to explain why children's sex typing was so poorly related to that of the same-sex parent. It indicated that the child's acquisition of sex-typed behavior could not be seen as a process of incorporation of the characteristics of a single model. It reflected the more general point that children were choosing whom and what to imitate on the basis of their growing conceptions of what was relevant to their own self-definitions and aspirations. Identification then became more a consequence than a cause of children's sex typing.

The View From Attachment Theory

Following the period of frequent, overt manifestation of attachment behaviors in the first 2 years of life, attachment theory postulates the formation of an *internal representation* of the attachment relationship, an internal schema that then affects the nature of new relationships formed later in life (see Main, Kaplan, & Cassidy, 1985). How similar is this schema to the internalized parent that Freudians postulated? Not very similar. It is quite unlike the conscience or superego presumably derived from identification with a powerful, punitive, often critical parent. Nor is it equivalent to anaclitic identification, which is a child's internalization of a parent's nurturant qualities. Rather, the child's internal representation of the early attachment relationship reflects how secure and trusting that relationship was (and probably continues to be) and determines whether the child will be open and trusting, or apprehensive and wary, in approaching a new person with whom an intimate relationship might be formed. What is being "internalized" from a child's attachment experience is the quality of a relationship with a parent—importantly, the roles of both partners—not the personality characteristics of a parent (Sroufe & Fleener, 1986).

Work on Morality and Altruism

Hoffman (1975) assessed several dimensions of morality in school-age children, including whether their moral reasoning was based on fear of punishment or hope of reward, as distinct from principled reasoning or concern for the well-being of others. The child's level of social responsibility was assessed from the reports of teachers and classmates. The researchers looked for relationships between children's moral status and their parents' child-rearing methods. Psychoanalytic theory would suggest that parental use of withdrawal of love would be a predictor of these various aspects of internalization, but it did not prove to be. Rather, parents who used *other-oriented induction*—that is, those who frequently reminded their children of the effect of their actions on others—were the ones whose children were most likely to manifest internalized morality.

The importance of other-oriented induction emerged again, with much younger children, in the work of Radke-Yarrow and colleagues (Zahn-Waxler, Radke-Yarrow, & King, 1979). They found that children as young as 2 years old would respond to the distress of others by efforts to help or comfort. The children most likely to do so were those whose mothers, when the children were guilty of wrongdoing, most often stressed the effects of their actions on others, rather than simply threatening or punishing.

One theme that emerged clearly from the large body of work on conscience was that parental use of power-assertive socialization techniques was counterproductive for children's development of internalized standards and controls.

Out-of-Sight Compliance

In several studies, it has been found that the parental behaviors that are associated with children complying with adult demands in the parent's presence are different from those associated with compliance when no parent is present (see review by Maccoby & Martin, 1983). If out-of-sight compliance can be encompassed within the range of meanings of internalization, this research bears on my topic and shows some consistency with other findings. The findings are that even though power-assertive methods are often effective in obtaining immediate compliance, delayed, out-of-sight compliance is more likely if parents have used other-oriented induction and attribution of prosocial motives to their children. Parents behave as though they were aware of these connections. As Grusec and Kuczynski (1980) have shown, most parents use a variety of socialization techniques, including both power assertion and induction or reasoning. Their choice depends largely on the nature of the child's infraction; power assertion is more often used for immediate control, induction and reasoning for moral training.

Scaffolding

There has been a strong recurrence of Vygotskian thinking concerning the role of parents in children's cognitive development. According to this point of view, cognitive as well as social development occurs mainly in a social context, through interaction with trusted, more competent partners (see Rogoff, 1990, for a review). Of course, it is stretching the concept of internalization to include the scaffolding work here. It is similar to internalization work in that it attempts to understand the processes whereby children come to be self-regulating. However, students of scaffolding describe a different route to this outcome, one that does not involve the dynamic aspects of identification. And although the parent is seen as teacher in one sense, the scaffolding work does not see the parental teaching role as one of applying "contingencies"—rewards, punishments, or corrections—following children's correct or incorrect responses. Rather, their role is to provide a structure for learning that will increase the likelihood of children's succeeding in their attempts to learn.

The kind of scaffolding that parents need to provide changes greatly with the child's age. At any age, however, the parent can function to simplify problems by breaking them up into component parts so that the child only has to do one simplified part at a time. The parent also functions to focus the child's attention on each successive **element** of a task as it becomes most relevant. Rogoff says,

> In addition to the executive role of adult–child interaction, structuring the goals and subgoals of an activity, adult–child interaction may provide children with routines that they can use as their contribution to more complex activities. That is, routines of adult–child interaction may provide ready-made pieces of meaningful actions on which children can build their further efforts. (1990, p. 95)

Clearly, this kind of analysis could be applied much more broadly—in particular, to children's understanding of social routines and scripts. The work of Trabasso, Stein, Rodkin, Munger, and Raughn (1992) on children's progress between the ages of 3 and 5 in understanding the intentions, goals, and plans of storied characters indicates that when mothers tell pictured stories to their children, they incorporate information about characters' goals and plans that is slightly in advance of their child's current level of understanding, thus providing a structure for the child's next steps in achieving social meanings. At a more molar level, the role of parents both in structuring the household environment so that children will be able to explore without getting into trouble and in managing daily routines so as to be predictable and satisfying to children has surely not been given the attention in traditional socialization research that it deserves. However, instances of attention to these processes are beginning to surface in the socialization literature. For example, in a study of the children of divorced families, the structure provided by predictable household routines has proved to be a strong predictor of adolescents' adjustment (Buchanan, Maccoby, & Dornbusch, in press).

I should note here that students of interaction between parents and adolescents stress that this interaction strongly affects adolescent ego development, but not through a process of identification or internalization (Powers, Hauser, Schwartz, Noam, & Jacobson, 1983). They point out that parental influence need not take the form of making the child similar to the parent; indeed, the ego developments of the two generations are not directly related to each other (see Powers et al., 1983, p. 20). Here one can see that Vygotskian approaches to self-regulation have moved very far from the earlier conceptions of the origins of self-regulation in internalization.

Changing Definitions of Optimal Parenting

Popular interpretations of psychoanalytic theory and some early research findings on the undesirable effects of punishment or rigid restriction of children led to the view that the ideal parent was the permissive parent. As noted earlier, Baldwin and colleagues advocated *democratic parenting*, by which was meant minimal restrictions and the involvement of children in family decision making to the maximum possible extent. Diana Baumrind began her career studying adult leadership styles (see Maccoby, 1992, for more detail on this history), and she became convinced that an optimal leadership style was not best described as a collegial arrangement in which leaders essentially became resource persons and co-workers, but rather that elements of democracy needed to be combined with elements of authority. She applied this viewpoint to studies of the socialization of children, being motivated in part by a conviction that a simple permissive philosophy of child rearing did not lead to optimal outcomes for children's adjustment.

Baumrind's initial typology of parenting styles is well known (Baumrind, 1973). Compared with either an authoritarian or permissive style, she regarded the *authoritative* style as optimal, and this style involved a combination of affection and attentive responsiveness to children's needs, along with parental imposition of clear requirements for prosocial, responsible behavior (to the degree consistent with the child's developmental level). Achievement of this pattern was seen to require considerable negotiation— even confrontation—with children, and parents needed to be firm, as well as kind and understanding.

Baumrind's concept of authoritative parenting has been widely adopted by other students of socialization and has been notably successful in distinguishing effective from ineffective parenting. Current examples may be found in the work of Dornbusch, Ritter, Leiderman, Roberts, and Fraleigh (1987) and in the large-scale study of family structures by Hetherington and colleagues (Hetherington & Clingempeel, 1992).

A number of definitions and redefinitions of parenting types have emerged as new groups of families have been studied and the age range of the children has been expanded. It is difficult indeed to identify the "same" parental attributes across time, because a parent deals with a child who is first an infant or toddler, then a preschooler, then in middle childhood, and then an adolescent. Especially for families in which the children are preadolescent or adolescent, a disengaged parenting pattern can now be seen to be frequent, and its outcomes contrast with those of the authoritative or authoritarian patterns (Baumrind, 1991; Hetherington & Clingempeel, 1992; Lamborn, Mounts, Steinberg, & Dornbusch, 1991; Maccoby & Martin, 1983). Increasingly, researchers are finding that some parents are more fully committed to their parenting role than others (see Greenberger & Goldberg, 1989; Pulkkinen, 1982)—or at least maintain a fully engaged commitment over a longer period of the child's development—and that the degree of commitment may be even more important than the style with which that commitment is expressed.

For Steinberg, Elmer, and Mounts (1989), the optimal parenting cluster includes not only high acceptance—warmth and firm control (the two major Baumrind elements)—but also a quality which Steinberg et al. call *psychological autonomy* or *democracy*. Democracy may be particularly important as children grow older and progressively more skillful in negotiating with their parents. Steinberg and Dornbusch (in press) have shown that when parents and adolescents are jointly involved in making decisions that affect the children's lives, the children have better self-regulation and impulse control than when parents either impose decisions unilaterally or leave the decisions to their children.

However authoritative parenting is defined, and whatever the age of the child, there appears to be a common core of meaning that defines the optimal cluster, and it has to do with inducting the child into a system of reciprocity. An authoritative parent assumes a deep and lasting obligation to behave so as to promote the best interests of the child, even when this means setting aside certain self-interests. At the same time, the parent insists that the child shall progressively assume more responsibility for responding to the needs of other family members and promoting their interests as well as his or her own within the limits of a child's capabilities.

The Role of Affect

Freud and subsequent psychoanalytic theorists have stressed the power of children's emotions—love, anger, and fear—in the formation of their internal personality structures. In a different way, so have the attachment theorists, who have stressed the function of the child's attachment to the parent in lessening children's anxieties. Recent work has greatly enriched the picture of the way in which affect is involved in parent–child interaction.

Emotions constitute the first language whereby parents and children communicate with one another before the child acquires speech. Infants respond to their parents' facial expressions and tones of voice. Parents in their turn "read" the affective quality of their infants' arousal states, responding appropriately when their infants are either distressed or in a happy, playful mood. It is important to note that in responding appropriately to a child's mood state, parents are not simply matching it empathically. They respond to a child's distress with soothing, rather than by manifesting distress themselves, a reaction that sometimes calls for considerable emotional control on the parent's part.

Fernald (1992) has identified some cross-cultural similarities in the affective meaning of the tones of voice mothers use to infants, and facial expressions, too, have been found to have similar meanings for people from different cultures (Ekman, 1972). The initial phases of parent–child bonding, then, are based on affectively charged parent–child exchanges. Furthermore, the work on social referencing suggests that by the end of the first year, a mother's facial expression—either a smile or a fear face— influences whether an infant will explore an unfamiliar environment. And Cummings's (1987) work on overheard quarrels between adults shows that young children react to adult anger with distressed facial expressions and inhibited play.

It is becoming evident that ambient mood states have a good deal to do with the quality of parent–child interaction. Lay, Waters, and Park (1989) have shown that when a positive mood has been induced in a child, the child is more likely to comply with a mother's directions. Dix (1991) has shown that when a mother is in an angry mood—one that has not arisen as a result of anything the child has done—she is more likely to believe that subsequent interaction with her child will be unpleasant and that more sternness will be required. Patterson, in studying a group of exceptionally well-functioning families, observed that an important ingredient of their interactions was humor: They made one another laugh, and light, pleasant mood states served to defuse conflicts. Several theorists have pointed to parent–child interaction as a context in which strong emotions, both positive and negative, are especially likely to be aroused (Berscheid, 1986; Dix, 1991), because the achievement of each individual's goals depends on the coordinated actions of the partner. Dix (1991) has assembled evidence to show that strong emotions, once aroused, serve to organize, motivate, and direct parental behavior. He has also noted that the frequency of episodes of mutual anger is greatly reduced if parents are able to adopt children's goals as their own.

Affective exchanges between parents and very young children appear to play an important role in whether toddlers will react empathically to others' distress (Zahn-Waxler & Radke-Yarrow, 1990; Zahn-Waxler et al., 1979). Follow-up work at ages 8–10 years with children who had been studied as toddlers (Kochanska, 1991) points to a connection between the parent–child affective exchanges in early childhood and the children's subsequent empathy with victims of others' wrongdoing. Kochanska, building on Hoffman's earlier work, argues that children's ability to experience discomfort, guilt, and anxiety associated with actual or anticipated wrongdoing is a necessary but insufficient condition for the emergence of conscience (a self-regulatory component is needed, too), and she sees parental affective responses as central for the development of the relevant emotions.

From Individuals to Interactions to Relationships

As was mentioned earlier, in early socialization research, parent behaviors were called *antecedents*, and child behaviors were called *outcomes*, and when a correlation between the two was found it was usually interpreted as an effect of one person's behavior (the parent) on another individual (the child). In the 1970s, insistent voices began to be raised pointing out that the causal arrow might point the other way (Bell & Harper, 1977; Parke, 1977). Clearly, a simple concurrent correlation between attributes of two interacting persons tells one nothing about the direction of effects. Researchers began to use time sequences and change scores to try to identify the direction of influence within a dyad. Several microanalyses of parent–infant interaction sequences provided strong evidence for the view that the infant's behavior, more than the parent's, was driving moment-to-moment sequences as they unfolded (see summary, Maccoby & Martin, 1983, p. 30). Evidence for the power of children to affect the course of bouts of parent–child interaction has continued to appear up to the present time (e.g., Kuczynski & Kochanska, 1990; Lytton, 1990; Patterson, 1986; Patterson, Bank, & Stoolmiller, 1990). Even more commonly, it has been evident that cycles of successive and mutual influence prevailed (Patterson, 1982).

The idea of bidirectional influence was originally one in which each participant in the interaction of the parent–child dyad was seen as shaping the other, by providing reinforcements or aversive consequences for one another's behavior (e.g., Sears, 1951). In recent years, however, this conception has given way to one that stresses the development of reciprocity and linked streams of behavior between the members of a familiar pair. In short, the interest has shifted to relationships (Hartup & Rubin, 1986; Hinde, 1987; Youniss, 1983). From this point of view, children are socialized mainly through participating in the interaction within close relationships. Interactions between intimate pairs (friends or family members) are quite different from those between strangers. Relationships are constructed over time. Patterson and colleagues have shown how the frequent occurrence of coercive cycles between parent and child can undermine the child's acquisition of prosocial behavior and positive social interactional skills. In part, this failure of socialization occurs because mutually coercive cycles do not allow children to gain experience in sustained joint activity with others. When a parent–child pair is able to engage in noncoercive joint activity, the two streams of behavior become interwoven, so that the smooth continuation of one person's behavior depends on the partner's performing the reciprocal portion of the action. Partners develop coherent expectations concerning each other's behavior, joint goals, shared scripts from which each acts, and shared meanings that make fuller coordination of their activities possible.

Youniss (1983) argues that socialization should not be described as a process whereby control of children is shifted from adults to the children themselves, who become progressively more autonomous and self-regulating. Rather, he says, at every stage of life, relationships involve coregulation, and individuals never graduate to being free of the regulatory requirements of intimate others unless they become social isolates. (See also Maccoby, 1984, on coregulation between parents and children in middle childhood.) This view implies that any enduring parental influence stems mainly from the nature of the relationships parents have coconstructed and continually reconstructed with their children. These relationships can vary in many ways from one parent–child pair to another. Some are such as to foster children's development, others inhibit it (see Hauser et al., 1987, on parents' enabling and restrictive interactive styles).

PRESENT AND FUTURE

This chapter has shown that the study of socialization has been a highly active research field and has been undergoing major change. What questions remain open, and what directions are promising? One broad question concerns the sequencing of steps or phases in socialization. To what extent do early socialization events constrain what the parent–child relationship can become at later times? That is, to what extent does the ability of a parent to cope effectively with socialization issues at one period of a child's life depend on the socialization that occurred previously? Although there are several domain-specific accounts concerning how early parent–child relationships feed into the child's subsequent social behavior (e.g., early secure attachment is associated with later positive reactions to the social initiations of new partners), we do not yet have a coherent theory of the ways in which parent–child relationships themselves evolve. What does a parent's ability to use an authoritative parenting style with a child 6–8 years old depend on? A secure attachment in infancy? Sufficiently skillful earlier scaffolding so that the child acquired the competencies needed for him or her to be treated democratically? Can one trace trajectories in which early parenting styles set a given parent–child relationship in a given direction so that its subsequent characteristics are predictable? Can such trajectories be redirected?

Mutual cognitions no doubt play a role in the carry-over of one phase of socialization to the next. As parents and children accumulate a long history of interacting with one another, each acquires a set of expectations concerning the other's behavior and stereotyped ways of interpreting the other's reactions. Probably, each progressively reacts to the other more in terms of these stereotypes than in terms of the other's actual moment-to-moment behavior. (Note that Patterson, 1980, has found that aggressive children often react coercively to other family members' approaches even when those approaches are benign, as though they interpreted them as having hostile intent.) If this is so, the rate of new learning that is derived from the interaction of a given parent–child pair should decline as time goes on, and relationships could become more rigid, because each person's stereotypes function to keep the partner from changing. However, stereotypes can and do change, and we do not know the extent to which early-formed stereotypes can set the trajectories that relationships will take over extended periods of time.

On a related issue, is each period of childhood a kind of window of developmental time during which certain socialization lessons are best learned? Perhaps it is time to reconsider the old question of critical periods. Are children more open in early childhood to the emotional conditioning processes that underlie empathy and interpersonal trust than they will be later? Learning to self-regulate affect is one of the major achievements of childhood, but it seems likely that as children achieve it, they are rendered less susceptible to any aspect of socialization that involves the arousal of intense affect. Or to put the matter differently, it is possible that the effects of socialization experiences involving strong affect are more enduring and more resistant to change than less intense encounters and that the encounters of early childhood are more affectively intense. There are echoes of earlier psychodynamic thinking here. Although I do not believe developmental psychology will go back to psychoanalytic socialization theory in any serious way, the question of whether and in what ways early childhood is a period of special importance still exists and needs to be dealt with.

The most central assumption of all the socialization viewpoints I have examined is that events that occur in the context of parent–child interaction affect children's social behavior in other settings and at later times. Nowadays, considering the intellectual history I have reviewed, one can hardly see this as a matter of simple generalization of habits learned in one setting (with parents) to interaction with new partners. Every partner is different; each new relationship is coconstructed with a partner who brings something different to the relationship than any previous partner has done. How, then, do children build on their previous interactive experience with parents in the context of new relationships? Attachment theorists argue that even though specific behaviors are not carried over, the quality of relationships is likely to be: Children seek to reconstruct, with peers and later with intimate romantic partners, the relationship they had with a parent (Sroufe & Fleener, 1986). Others appear to believe that new developmental periods, new settings, and new partners open up possibilities for qualitatively quite new relationships. I suspect that the experiences children have in their same-sex peer groups in middle childhood (Maccoby, 1990) must be integrated in some way with in-family experiences to influence the quality of the relationships young adults form with romantic partners, but these questions remain to be explored.

As mentioned, research on adult relationships has some connections with the recent advances in the understanding of parent–child relationships. Nevertheless the fact remains that the parent–child relationship is unique in a number of respects, most especially in its asymmetry. Although this article has shown that influence is a bidirectional matter from infancy onward, there can be no doubt that the differential between parents and young children in power and competency is enormous. Parents select and design the settings in which children will spend their time and, to some extent, the identity of the cast of characters with whom the children will have an opportunity to interact. Parents control access to things children want. Parents are larger and stronger and can control children's movements physically (witness Japanese parents applying gentle pressure to the top of a small child's head to cause the child to bow—an early bit of training in deference). Parents have vastly greater knowledge, and children need to rely on this knowledge, especially in unfamiliar situations.

What are the implications of this asymmetry? A number of themes have emerged. One is that parents derive authority from their greater power and competence, and they cannot abdicate this authority without endangering their children. The work on authoritative parenting points to the importance of parents' carrying out the managerial and control functions in family life, and the writings of family systems theorists stress that the boundaries between the parent and child generations should be kept clear: Families become dysfunctional if roles are reversed so that children become the ones who nurture or control parents; furthermore, there is evidence that children are less competent when their parents "disengage."

The research reviewed earlier indicates that it matters how parents exercise their authority. Simple unqualified power assertion seems effective for immediate behavioral control but appears to undermine children's progress toward becoming independently prosocial and self-regulating. In other words, although parents have great power (especially when children are quite young), they had best use it sparingly or selectively in disciplinary encounters. But the implications of the parent–child asymmetries in power and competence go much beyond the question of whether and how parents should punish or issue orders. Parents must use their greater interactive skills to adapt themselves to the child's capacities and current states. Thus in the first year, they need to speak the emotional language that infants understand, even though this language is quite different from speech to adults. The work on scaffolding points to the importance of the way parents arrange situations and event sequences so that the demands of a situation will be within the child's "zone of proximal development"; the time is ripe for extending the scaffolding work beyond cognitive development and exploring its relevance to the growth of social competence.

The parent role calls for a very demanding admixture of childlike and adult perceptions. Clearly, parent–child interaction goes more smoothly when parents adopt the child's momentary goals as their own. To do so calls for considerable empathy with children's emotional states and ways of thinking. Yet a parent cannot fully adopt a child's point of view. There are longer term goals, in the child's best interests, that the child cannot appreciate and may indeed resist. And some of the parent's own goals may be independent of what is needed to serve the child's momentary goals or long-term interests. There is plentiful evidence that skill in role taking is important for smooth and mutually beneficial interaction among equals in status, but socialization researchers have devoted little attention to what is required for successful role taking with much less mature partners. More important, little is known about the process whereby parents maintain multiple perspectives at the same time: taking the child's perspective affectively and cognitively, while at the same time maintaining their own adult orientations. One thing seems obvious: To maintain these multiple perspectives calls for considerable effort and skill, and these in their turn must rest on parents having accepted almost unlimited, long-term commitment to promoting the child's welfare. It is in this respect that the parent–child relationship continues to be unique, and it may be expected to remain a distinct branch of the growing science of relationships.

REFERENCES

Ainsworth, M. D. S., & Bell, S. M. (1969). Some contemporary patterns of mother–infant interaction in the feeding situation. In A. Ambrose (Ed.), *Stimulation in early infancy* (pp. 133–170). San Diego: Academic Press.

Baldwin, A. L. (1949). The effect of home environment on nursery school behavior. *Child Development, 20,* 49–62.

Baldwin, A. L. (1955). *Behavior and development in childhood* (pp. 493–494). New York: Dryden Press.

Bandura, A. (1962). Social learning through imitation. In M. R. Jones (Ed.), *Nebraska Symposium on Motivation* (Vol. 10, pp. 211–274). Lincoln, NE: University of Nebraska Press.

Bandura, A. (1965). Vicarious processes: A case of no-trial learning. In L. Berkowitz (Ed.), *Advances in experimental social psychology* (Vol. 2, pp. 1–55). San Diego: Academic Press.

Baumrind, D. (1973). The development of instrumental competence through socialization. In A. D. Pick (Ed.), *Minnesota Symposium on Child Psychology* (Vol. 7, pp. 3–46). Minneapolis: University of Minnesota Press.

Baumrind, D. (1991). The influence of parenting style on adolescent competence and substance abuse. *Journal of Early Adolescence, 11,* 56–94.

Bell, R. Q., & Harper, L. V. (1977). *Child effects on adults.* Hillsdale, NJ: Erlbaum.

Berscheid, E. (1986). Emotional experience in close relationships: Some implications for child development. In W. W. Hartup & Z. Rubin (Eds.), *Relationships and development* (pp. 135–166). Hillsdale, NJ: Erlbaum.

Berscheid, E., & Peplau, L. A. (1983). The emerging science of relationships. In M. H. Kelley, E. Berscheid, A. Christensen, J. H. Harvey, T. L. Huston, G. Levinger, E. McClintock, L. A. Peplau, & D. R. Peterson (Eds.), *Close relationships* (pp. 1–19). New York: Freeman.

Bowlby, J. (1969). *Attachment.* New York: Basic Books.

Buchanan, C. M., Maccoby, E. E., & Dornbusch, S. M. (in press). Adolescents and their families after divorce: Three residential arrangements compared. *Journal of Research on Adolescence.*

Cairns, R. B. (1979). *Social development: The origins and plasticity of interchanges.* New York: Freeman.

Cairns, R. B. (1983). The emergence of developmental psychology. In P. H. Mussen (Series Ed.) & W. Kessen (Vol. Ed.), *Handbook of child psychology* (Vol. 1, pp. 41–102). New York: Wiley.

Chomsky, N. (1959). Review of *Verbal Behavior,* by B. F. Skinner. *Language, 35,* 26–58.

Cummings, E. M. (1987). Coping with background anger in early childhood. *Child Development, 58,* 976–984.

Deci, E. L. (1975). *Intrinsic motivation.* New York: Plenum Press.

Dix, T. (1991). The affective organization of parenting: Adaptive and maladaptive processes. *Psychological Bulletin, 110,* 3–25.

Dollard, J., Doob, L. W., Miller, N. E., Mowrer, O. H., & Sears, R. R. (1939). *Frustration and aggression.* New Haven, CT: Yale University Press.

Dornbusch, S. M., Ritter, P., Leiderman, P. H., Roberts, D. F., & Fraleigh, M. J. (1987). The relation of parenting style to adolescent school performance. *Child Development, 58,* 1244–1257.

Ekman, P. (1972). Universals and cultural differences in facial expressions of emotion. In J. Cole (Ed.), *Nebraska Symposium on Motivation* (pp. 207–283). Lincoln, NE: University of Nebraska Press.

Fernald, A. (1992). Human maternal vocalization to infants as biologically relevant signals: An evolutionary perspective. In J. H. Barkow, L. Cosmides, & J. Tooby (Eds.), *The adapted mind: Evolutionary psychology and the generation of culture* (pp. 345–382). Oxford, England: Oxford University Press.

Gewirtz, J. L. (1969). Mechanisms of social learning: Some roles of stimulation and behavior in early human development. In D. A. Goslin (Ed.), *Handbook of socialization theory and research* (pp. 57–212). Chicago: Rand McNally.

Greenberger, E., & Goldberg, W. (1989). Work, parenting, and the socialization of children. *Developmental Psychology, 25*, 22–35.

Grusec, J. E., & Kuczynski, L. (1980). Direction of effects in socialization: A comparison of the parent's versus the child's behavior as determinants of disciplinary techniques. *Developmental Psychology, 16*, 1–9.

Hartup, W. W., & Rubin, Z. (1986). *Relationships and development.* Hillsdale, NJ: Erlbaum.

Hauser, S. T., Book, B. K., Houlihan, J., Powers, S., Weiss-Perry, B., Follansbee, D. J., Jacobson, A. M., & Noam, G. G. (1987). Sex differences within the family: Studies of adolescent and parent family interactions. *Journal of Youth and Adolescence, 16*, 199–220.

Hetherington, E. M., & Clingempeel, W. G. (1992). Coping with marital transitions: A family systems perspective. *Monographs of the Society for Research in Child Development, 57*(Serial No. 23).

Hinde, R. A. (1987). *Individuals, relationships and culture. Links between ethology and the social sciences.* Cambridge, England: Cambridge University Press.

Hoffman, M. L. (1975). Moral internalization, parental power and the nature of parent–child interaction. *Developmental Psychology, 11*, 228–239.

Kochanska, G. (1991). Socialization and temperament in the development of guilt and conscience. *Child Development, 62*, 1379–1392.

Kuczynski, L., & Kochanska, G. (1990). Development of children's noncompliance strategies from toddlerhood to age 5. *Developmental Psychology, 26*, 398–408.

Lamborn, S. D., Mounts, N. S., Steinberg, L., & Dornbusch, S. M. (1991). Patterns of competence and adjustment among adolescents from authoritative, authoritarian, indulgent, and neglectful families. *Child Development, 62*, 1049–1065.

Lay, K., Waters, E., & Park, K. A. (1989). Maternal responsiveness and child compliance: The role of mood as a mediator. *Child Development, 60*, 1405–1411.

Lepper, M. R., & Greene, D. (1975). Turning play into work. Effects of adult surveillance and extrinsic reward on children's intrinsic motivation. *Journal of Personality and Social Psychology, 31*, 479–486.

Lewin, K., Lippitt, R., & White, R. K. (1939). Patterns of aggressive behavior in experimentally created "social climates." *Journal of Social Psychology, 10,* 271–299.

Lytton, H. (1990). Child and parent effects in boys' conduct disorders: A reinterpretation. *Developmental Psychology, 26,* 683–697.

Maccoby, E. E. (1984). Middle childhood in the context of the family. In W. A. Collins (Ed.), *Development during middle childhood: The years from six to twelve* (pp. 184–239). Washington, DC: National Academy Press.

Maccoby, E. E. (1990). Gender and relationships. *American Psychologist, 45,* 513–520.

Maccoby, E. E. (1992). Trends in the study of socialization: Is there a Lewinian heritage? *Journal of Social Issues, 48,* 171–186.

Maccoby, E. E., & Martin, J. A. (1983). Socialization in the context of the family: Parent–child interaction. In E. M. Hetherington (Ed.), *Mussen manual of child psychology* (Vol. 4, 4th ed., pp. 1–102). New York: Wiley.

Main, M., Kaplan, N., & Cassidy, J. (1985). Security in infancy, childhood and adulthood: A move to the level of representation. In I. Gretherton & E. Waters (Eds.), *Monographs of the Society for Research in Child Development,* 50(1–2, Serial No. 209).

Markman, E. M. (1992). Constraints on word learning: Speculations about their nature, origins, and domain specificity. In M. R. Gunnar & M. P. Maratsos (Eds.), *Minnesota Symposium on Child Psychology* (Vol. 25, pp. 59–101). Hillsdale, NJ: Erlbaum.

Miller, N. E., & Dollard, J. (1941). Social learning and imitation. New Haven, CT: Yale University Press.

Parke, R. D. (1977). Punishment in children: Effects, side effects, and alternative strategies. In H. L. Hom, Jr., & P. Robinson (Eds.), *Psychological processes in early education* (pp. 71–97). San Diego: Academic Press.

Patterson, G. R. (1980). Mothers: The unacknowledged victims. *Monographs of the Society for Research in Child Development, 45*(Serial No. 5).

Patterson, G. R. (1982). *Coercive family processes.* Eugene, OR: Castalia Press.

Patterson, G. R. (1986). Maternal rejection: Determinant or product for deviant child behavior? In W. W. Hartup & Z. Rubin (Eds.), *Relationships and development* (pp. 73–94). Hillsdale, NJ: Erlbaum.

Patterson, G. R., Bank, L., & Stoolmiller, M. (1990). The preadolescent's contributions to disrupted family process. In R. Montemayor, G. R. Adams, & T. P. Gulotta (Eds.), *From childhood to adolescence: A transitional period?* (pp. 107–133). Newbury Park, CA: Sage.

Patterson, G. R., Reid, J. B., & Dishion, T. J. (1992). *Antisocial boys.* Eugene, OR: Castalia Press.

Perry, D. G., & Bussey, K. (1979). The social learning theory of sex differences: Imitation is alive and well. *Journal of Personality and Social Psychology, 37,* 1699–1712.

Powers, S. I., Hauser, S. T., Schwartz, J. M., Noam, G. G., & Jacobson, A. M.

(1983). Adolescent ego development and family interaction: A structural-developmental perspective. In H. D. Grotevant & C. R. Cooper (Eds.), *Adolescent development in the family: New directions for child development* (No. 22, pp. 5–25). San Francisco: Jossey-Bass.

Pulkkinen, L. (1982). Self-control and continuity from childhood to adolescence. In P. B. Baltes & O. G. Brim (Eds.), *Life-span development and behavior* (Vol. 4, pp. 63–105). San Diego: Academic Press.

Rogoff, B. (1990). *Apprenticeship in thinking.* New York: Oxford University Press.

Sears, R. R. (1951). A theoretical framework for personality and social behavior. *American Psychologist, 6,* 476–483.

Sears, R. R., Maccoby, E. E., & Levin, H. (1957). *Patterns of child rearing.* Evanston, IL: Row-Peterson.

Sears, R. R., Rau, L., & Alpert, R. (1965). *Identification and child rearing.* Stanford, CA: Stanford University Press.

Sears, R. R., Whiting, J. W. M., Nowlis, V., & Sears, P. S. (1953). Some child-rearing antecedents of aggression and dependency in young children. *Genetic Psychology Monographs, 47,* 135–234.

Skinner, B. F. (1957). *Verbal behavior.* New York: Appleton Century.

Sroufe, L. A., & Fleener, J. (1986). Attachment and the construction of relationships. In W. W. Hartup & Z. Rubin (Eds.), *Relationships and development* (pp. 51–72). Hillsdale, NJ: Erlbaum.

Sroufe, L. A., & Waters, E. (1977). Attachment as an organizational construct. *Child Development, 48,* 1184–1199.

Steinberg, L., & Dornbusch, S. M. (in press). Authoritative parenting and adolescent adjustment across varied ecological niches. *Journal of Adolescent Research.*

Steinberg, L., Elmer, J. D., & Mounts, N. S. (1989). Authoritative parenting, psychosocial maturity, and academic success among adolescents. *Child Development, 60,* 1424–1436.

Trabasso, T., Stein, N. L., Rodkin, P. C., Munger, M. P., & Raughn, C. R. (1992). Knowledge of goals and plans in the on-line narration of events. *Cognitive Development, 7,* 133–170.

Trevarthan, C., & Hubley, P. (1978). Secondary intersubjectivity: Confidence, confiding, and acts of meaning in the first year. In A. Locke (Ed.), *Action, gesture and symbol: The emergence of language.* San Diego: Academic Press.

Youniss, J. (1983). Social construction of adolescence by adolescents and parents. In H. D. Grotevant & C. R. Cooper (Eds.), *Adolescent development in the family: New directions for child development* (No. 22, pp. 93–109). San Francisco: Jossey-Bass.

Zahn-Waxler, C., & Radke-Yarrow, M. (1990). The origins of empathic concern. *Motivation and Emotion, 14,* 107–130.

Zahn-Waxler, C., Radke-Yarrow, M., & King, R. A. (1979). Child-rearing and children's prosocial initiations toward victims of distress. *Child Development, 50,* 319–330.

22

DEVELOPMENTAL PSYCHOLOGY IN THE CONTEXT OF OTHER BEHAVIORAL SCIENCES

ROBERT A. HINDE

That developmental psychology has made enormous progress since its birth some 100 years ago hardly needs underlining. Indeed, self-congratulatory backslapping would be out of place in a volume such as this. Rather, the approach of the next millenium is a time to look forward, to assess the present constraints on further progress and ask how they can be overcome. Let us then start with some gross generalizations, not because I believe for a moment that they are without exceptions, but because they help focus attention on some current problems in developmental psychology.

In its early days, psychology needed to establish itself as a distinct discipline and to achieve recognition as a respectable branch of science. It achieved distinctiveness from biology/physiology by focusing on the psyche and from philosophy primarily by adopting an experimental approach. It

I am grateful to Patrick Bateson (1991) for editing a series of essays that brought together many of the issues discussed in this article, and to him, John Fentress, and Joan Stevenson-Hinde for comments on an earlier draft of the article.

Reprinted from *Developmental Psychology*, 28, 1018–1029. Copyright by the American Psychological Association.

achieved respectability by attempting to ape physics—again by the use of the experimental method—and also by attempting a hypothetico-deductive approach, by an emphasis on objectivity, and by the use of statistical tools.

Each of these, taken too far, has brought problems. A focus on the psyche came into conflict with pressures to study *behavior* objectively, which in turn led to a neglect of process. An overemphasis on an experimental approach led to an underemphasis on people in the real world and to single-variable studies. Attempts to ape physics led to an underestimation of the importance of description: Much of classical physics dealt with everyday events for whose analysis description was unnecessary, but the complexity of human behavior demands an initial descriptive phase.

The undervaluing of description led also to a belief that research should always be theory driven. This is fair enough if not overstated, but it can lead to an unwillingness to allow the data to suggest problems. During the forties and fifties, a hypothetico-deductive approach led to a particularly narrow, theory-driven approach, with a focus on limited experimental situations. Although theory-driven research is often a first priority, important advances can also follow if novel phenomena are seized and studied with the best tools available. Examples are provided by Bowlby's (e.g., 1969) following up of the finding that disturbed adolescents had had major and repeated separation experiences in childhood, Andrew's (1991) discovery of the effects of testosterone on the persistence of motor patterns and the duration for which events are held in the working memory, and Horn's (1985, 1991) discovery of asymmetries in brain function in chicks. Finally, an overemphasis on statistics can lead to a focus on group means, with a neglect of individual differences.

These caveats are not intended to play down in any way the extraordinary progress made by psychology in general or by developmental psychology in particular. But a retrospective view and a recognition of past constraints can warn us of future dangers. And there is one further issue that is a direct result of psychology's success: its fragmentation into subdisciplines. Developmental psychology has, properly, become a field in its own right but, as a result, has become partially cut off from clinical, personality, physiological, and social psychology and from biology. Developmental psychology has focused largely on changes with age and on group averages, but we need also to understand individuals, the primary concern of much clinical and personality psychology. Physiological analysis leads to functions of parts, and although individuals function as wholes, that functioning depends on, but cannot be entirely explained by, processes within parts. And physiological analysis can aid behavioral understanding. A recent example is the manner in which Rosenblatt's (1991) survey of the physiology of parturition poses new questions about the onset of maternal responsiveness. Social psychology is concerned largely with group phenomena, and developmentalists—knowing that children grow up in groups, that relationships are crucial to their development, and that values, expectations, and hopes held by the child and others shape development— need social psychological expertise. And ethology, as we shall see, can contribute principles and perspectives of importance to developmental psychologists.

We have here demands that could conflict: Science proceeds by analysis, but one needs synthesis and the study of wholes as well; one needs to specialize, but that means studying only parts of a whole; one needs to describe phenomena, but one also needs to understand process; one needs concepts to cope with intangibles, but one must not lose discipline. It would be folly to suggest that these problems can be readily solved, but the following sections address a series of relevant and interrelated issues.

There are three main themes. The first concerns the need to focus not only on individuals, but also on individuals in a network of relationships, and this in turn requires us both to distinguish levels of social complexity and to come to terms with the dialectical relations between them. The second is that description is a necessary first step, but can never be perfect. Our categories and concepts are essential heuristically but are never absolute, because we have at present no entirely satisfactory way of coping with entities that are both isolatable and interconnected and mutually influence each other. The third is the need to integrate developmental psychology with other disciplines. Here, because of my own biases, I refer especially to ethology, though I am aware that some of the ideas I ascribe to ethology also had other roots.

LEVELS OF COMPLEXITY

Children grow up in a network of relationships and usually within families, which form parts of larger groups. It is thus necessary to come to terms with a series of levels of social complexity: physiological and psychological systems, individuals, short-term interactions between individuals, and relationships involving a succession of interactions between two individuals known to each other, groups, and societies (Figure 1). Each of these levels has properties not relevant to lower levels, and at each level new descriptive and explanatory concepts are needed. For instance, we may describe the behavior of two individuals in an interaction as "meshing" well, but meshing is a concept irrelevant to the behavior of an individual in isolation. Furthermore, each level affects and is affected by other levels. Thus the course of an interaction depends both on the natures of the participating individuals and on the relationship of which it forms a part, and the nature of a relationship is influenced both by the component interactions and by the group in which it is embedded. Furthermore, each of these levels influences, and is influenced by, the physical environment

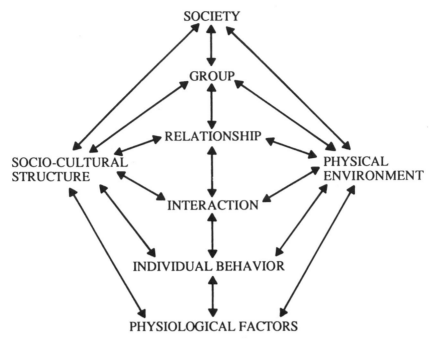

Figure 1. The dialectical relations between successive levels of social complexity.

and the sociocultural structure of ideas, values, myths, beliefs, institutions with their constituent roles, and so on, more or less shared by the individuals in the relationship, group, or society in question.

Recognition of these levels is in no way an argument for unidirectional reductionism, because the dialectical relations between levels are crucial (cf. Fentress, 1991). Each level, including that of the individual, must be thought of not as an entity but rather in terms of processes continually influenced by the dialectical relations between levels (Hinde, 1987, 1991a). It will be apparent that such an approach always demands liaison between a variety of disciplines.

Each level, as well as the sociocultural structure, has both objective and subjective aspects. For example, relationships have objective aspects that are apparent to an outside observer and subjective aspects that are specific to each participant, known in their entirety only to him or her, and shared only partially. Similarly, the objective aspects of the sociocultural structure may be partially codified in laws and customs, but the sub-jective aspects may be subtly different for each individual.

The position taken here is not so extreme as that of some who espouse dialectical determinism (review Hopkins & Butterworth, 1990). It is, of course, basic that development must be studied at several levels simulta-neously and that stability is, if not always momentary, at least dynamic. But though emphasizing process, I would argue that the view that organism and environment are inseparable is not helpful. Although the difficulties of boundary definition matter and must be borne in mind, the essential thing is to come to terms with the continuous interplay (e.g., Markova, 1990; Mead, 1934). And while rejecting linear causal chains, I would stop short of saying that development can never be adequately predicted on the basis of individual elements, although that perhaps reflects an aspiration rather than an achievable goal.

DESCRIPTION

How can one cope with multiple levels of analysis simultaneously? How can one nail down entities constituted by continuous dynamic processes? Description and categorization are clearly necessary as a preliminary to—or as a part of (Carey, 1990)—analysis, but in describing such phenomena, one inevitably simplifies the complexity of real life. A delicate balance must be struck between using categories and concepts that one can handle and distorting nature. And that one is compromising must not be forgotten.

This is a lesson that is being learned slowly by ethologists. For example, the early concept of the Fixed Action Pattern (FAP), used to refer to a species' characteristic movement pattern, seemed clear cut. Gradually, it became apparent that all FAPs were variable, and the concept was replaced with that of the Modal Action Pattern (Barlow, 1977). Similar issues arise in child development. In studies of preschoolers, "aggressive behavior" seemed a clear-cut category, but experience soon showed that the category boundaries are hard to define and that the category is itself heterogeneous. But subdivision met similar problems. The subcategories into which it is usually divided (e.g., instrumental aggression and teasing aggression [Feshbach, 1970]) themselves have shady boundaries. It is nearer the truth (though not necessarily facilitatory of research) to recognize that aggressive acts involve other behavioral systems—for instance, tendencies to acquire objects (*acquisitiveness*) or status (*assertiveness*)—and that the nature of the aggression shown depends on interactions between these systems (Figure 2). As another example, Stevenson-Hinde (1991) has argued that although *fear behavior* and *attachment behavior* are to be thought of as discrete behavioral systems, "the postulation of discrete behavioural systems should not obscure relations between them. Activation of a fear behaviour system may lead to activation of an attachment behaviour system" (pp. 325–326), and activation of the attachment behavior system may inhibit the fear.

This tendency for systems to change their state or even their properties according to the broader context within which they are operating has been repeatedly stressed by Fentress (e.g., 1991). For instance, at a lower level of analysis, Getting and Dekin (1985) have shown that the neural networks operative in the swimming of the mollusc Tritonia are reconfigured into

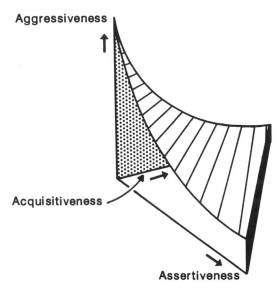

Aggressiveness

Acquisitiveness

Assertiveness

Figure 2. Model of the relations among three propensities and aggressive behavior. (Aggression would be shown if the current state were represented by a point above the striped surface.)

different functional circuits according to the behavioral state of the animal and that the neurones involved cannot be clearly categorized as motor neurones, central pattern generators, and so forth. And at higher levels of social complexity, relationships or families may change their characteristics with the context. Fentress sees the difficulties in understanding behavior and development as stemming in large part from the difficulty of comprehending that, at all levels of complexity, systems must be both self-organizing and interactive with other systems: "Varying forms of behavioural taxonomy clarify certain properties of expression while potentially obscuring others. Unitary 'boxes connected by arrows' taxonomies often do not work, in part because they too easily draw our attention away from the properties of the arrows that in turn may affect the properties of the boxes" (Fentress, 1991, p. 98).

From this perspective, it is not surprising that individuals behave differently in different social contexts. Stevenson-Hinde (1986) has pointed out that so-called child characteristics refer to characteristics that lie on a continuum from individual characteristics to relationship or situation characteristics, with height and weight but few, if any, psychological characteristics at the individual end, temperament dimensions close to but at varying distances from it, and attachment categories near the relationship end.

It is possible that we should view some age changes in the same way. We are accustomed to the concept of "age-appropriate behavior," ascribing underlying similarities across ages to "heterotypic continuity" (Kagan, 1971) and the changes to changes in the system concerned, but they could also be caused by changes in relations with other systems. For example, digit span increases between infancy and adulthood, but the evidence indicates that memory span remains constant after about age 4, the changes being caused by a domain-specific increase in knowledge about the materials (Carey, 1990).

Because of this lability in the elements and in the relations between elements, every generalization should be accompanied by a statement of its limitations—a requirement that makes description of both behavior and context even more necessary. As an example of the importance of this, Radke-Yarrow, Richters, and Wilson (1988) found that higher rates of initial child compliance were related to more positive mother–child relationships only in families categorized as "stable," and maternal use of harsh enforcement was associated with more negative mother–child relationships only in "chaotic" families. Again, Stevenson-Hinde and Shouldice (1990) found that mothers of securely attached children tended to overestimate their children's shyness, whereas mothers of insecurely attached children tended to underestimate.

Therefore, we must recognize that description and classification nearly always involve trying to push nature into pigeonholes when the fit is by no means perfect and that, for psychologists, description must embrace the several levels of social complexity.

Developmental psychology, concerned with what children do or can do at different ages, has not neglected description, but it is worth emphasizing two issues. First, at the behavioral level, there are two routes to description: (a) one that refers ultimately to patterns of muscular contraction and (b) one that refers to the consequences of action or the meanings behind action. Each has its uses and advantages (Hinde, 1966). Taking a lead from studies of lower species, such as fish, some researchers (e.g., Blurton-Jones, 1972) have attempted to describe children's behavior by focusing solely on the former route. However, children are not fish, and such attempts have proved on the whole sterile. Better ways for describing children's behavior, which do not assume that behavior is all we are interested in and take account of the meanings behind actions, are available (e.g., Caldwell, 1969; Lytton, 1973).

Second, description is necessary at each level of social complexity, and the more complex the phenomenon, the more selective description must be. A special problem arises in the description of relationships (and higher order phenomena). Developmental psychologists normally study interactions, for instance, studying mother–child play across a number of dyads and making generalizations across dyads. Relationships involve a number of types of interaction and cannot be described from generalizations across dyads about interactions, because the different interactions within each relationship affect each other. Rather, each relationship must be

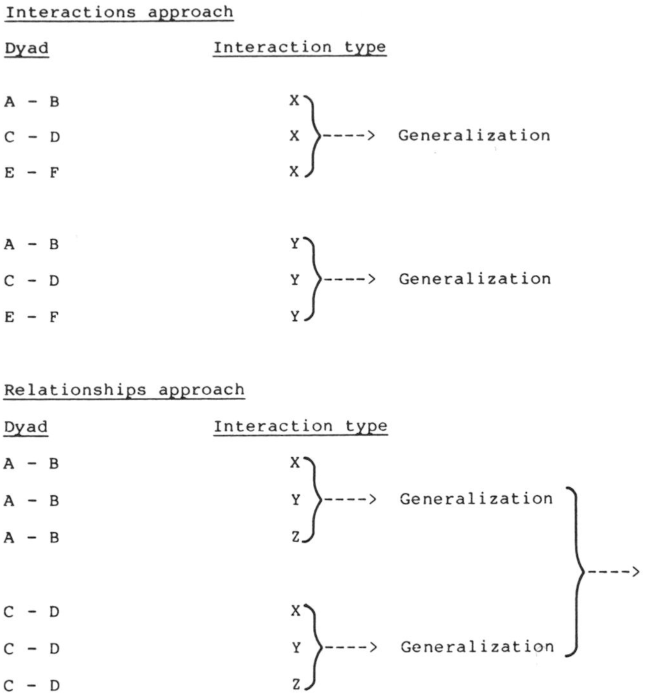

```
Interactions approach

Dyad                    Interaction type

A - B                        X ⌉
C - D                        X ⌡}----> Generalization
E - F                        X ⌡


A - B                        Y ⌉
C - D                        Y }----> Generalization
E - F                        Y ⌡


Relationships approach

Dyad                    Interaction type

A - B                        X ⌉
A - B                        Y }----> Generalization ⌉
A - B                        Z ⌡                      }
                                                       }---->
C - D                        X ⌉                      }
C - D                        Y }----> Generalization ⌡
C - D                        Z ⌡
```

Figure 3. The contrast between achieving generalizations about interactions and generalizations about relationships.

described, and only then can generalizations be made across dyads (Figure 3).

Attachment theory involves a procedure for categorizing some aspects of mother–child relationships (Ainsworth, Blehar, Waters, & Wall, 1978; Cassidy & Marvin, 1989). A means for classifying other characteristics of relationships is given by Hinde (1979, 1991a).

RELATIONS BETWEEN LEVELS

Even though analysis tends to move from more complex levels to less, the importance of crossing and recrossing in both directions cannot be overestimated. The relations between levels of social complexity are well established in studies of physiology and behavior (e.g., Andrew, 1991; Horn, 1991; Hutchison, 1991), but they are equally important in developmental studies. It is not only that similar principles of organization may be repeated at different levels; it is also necessary to trace causal relations between them.

Both the experiences a child has in interactions with others and the effects of those experiences on the child himself or herself depend on the child's nature. Those interactions will affect and be affected by the rela-

624   *ROBERT A. HINDE*

tionships of which they form a part, and those relationships are similarly related to the family or group. Each of these levels may also be affected by the sociocultural structure—by the myths and values current in the family, group, or society. Thus we need to come to terms with the dialectical relations between levels.

Consider, as an example, the genesis of a fear of snakes. Children brought up in an institution who have never seen a snake show little fear if they first encounter one at 30 months, but they avoid a snake crawling on the ground from about 3 years (Prechtl, 1950). Children also show spontaneous fears of other objects or situations that might have posed a real threat in humans' environment of evolutionary adaptedness, such as spiders, heights, darkness, and being alone. Humans are much less prone to develop spontaneous fears of other situations that are genuinely lethal in modern society but that were not present earlier in evolutionary history, such as cars or bombs (Marks, 1987). It is thus not unreasonable to suppose that a propensity to fear, or to learn to fear, snakes is part of the human biological heritage.

Anecdotal evidence suggests that the extent of the fear is much influenced by social referencing. The child looks at others, and especially at a trusted other, and imitates their response (Emde, 1980; Klinnert, Campos, Sorce, Emde, & Svedja, 1983). Comparative evidence provides strong support for this view, thus: (a) Wild-reared rhesus monkeys tested in the laboratory nearly always show fear of snakes; (b) laboratory-reared monkeys do not show fear of snakes; (c) laboratory-reared monkeys shown a videotape of a wild-reared monkey showing fear of a snake become afraid of snakes thereafter; and (d) laboratory-reared monkeys shown a "doctored" videotape of a wild-reared monkey apparently showing fear of a flower do not become afraid of either flowers or snakes (Mineka, 1987). There is thus clear evidence that rhesus monkeys have a propensity to fear snakes that depends for its full realization on the experience of seeing others respond fearfully to snakes. This in turn increases the plausibility of a similar explanation of snake fears in humans.

Some individuals develop snake phobias, showing a fear of snakes out of all proportion to the threat they present, a fear that is irrational and is beyond voluntary control. It is reasonable to suggest that the role of snakes as a symbol in our culture is related to these issues. Snakes play an important part, and have played an even more important part, in our mythology. In the myth of the garden of Eden, and in the Rubens paintings of snakes gnawing at the genitals of those cast down into Hell, snakes symbolize evil. Therefore, if we are really to understand fear of snakes and the symbolic role of snakes, we must come to terms with a series of dialectical relations among the propensity to fear snakes, social referencing within relationships, and snake myths within the sociocultural structure (see Figure 4 and further discussion in Hinde, 1991a).

Fear of Snakes

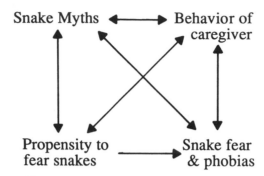

Figure 4. The genesis of fear of snakes.

Let us consider a very different example that also suggests complex links between the levels of social complexity. In a study of families in Bethesda, Maryland, Radke-Yarrow et al. (1988) found the following: (a) There was a high level of concordance in negative affect between the members of mother–child dyads, indicating strong interdependence within the dyad. (b) In families in which the mother–younger child were concordant in negativity, both mother–older child relationships and sibling relationships tended also to be concordant. (c) Mothers showed more negative affect in families of low socioeconomic status (SES). When the instability and unpredictability of life circumstances in the families were examined, it appeared that the link between low SES and maternal negative affect was primarily due to the corrosive hardship of unpredictability and disorganization. (d) As mentioned earlier, the relations between indices of maternal control interactions and the nature of the mother–child relationship varied with family stability. Thus higher rates of child compliance were related to more positive mother–child relationships only in stable families, and maternal use of harsh enforcement was related to more negative mother–child relationships only in more negative ones. (e) The relation between child characteristics and the mother–child relationship differed according to the sex of the child. Thus shy girls had more positive relationships with their mothers than nonshy girls, whereas shy boys had worse relationships than nonshy boys. Radke-Yarrow et al. ascribed this difference to other child characteristics associated with shyness. A very similar finding in Britain by Simpson and Stevenson-Hinde (1985) was ascribed to maternal values: Maccoby and Sants (personal communication) showed that Californian mothers like little girls to be shy and little boys not to be. Although these data were cross sectional, they strongly suggest influences among individual characteristics, relationships, family characteristics, and the sociocultural structure of beliefs and values. Dunn's (1991) important studies of sibling relationships within the family led to a similar conclusion.

Not clearly demonstrated by these data, but important in the long run, are influences up the levels of complexity. The nature of the family depends on the natures of the family members and on their relationships, and the values and beliefs of a society stem ultimately from processes in individuals.

NATURE–NURTURE: RELATIVELY STABLE CHARACTERS, CONSTRAINTS ON LEARNING

For logistical reasons, every study in developmental psychology has limits. One cannot trace all the dialectical relations shown in Figure 1 in every investigation. A starting point is therefore needed. Can one identify simple items or properties of behavior that can fill this role? The previous discussion of the difficulties of describing behavior indicates that one must be content with approximations, with categories heuristically useful but shady at the edges.

A false start involved the view that behavior or propensities could be divided into those that are innate and those that are learned or otherwise acquired. Although this error has long been recognized (Bateson, 1991a, 1991b; Oyama, 1985), it still persists. Development involves an interplay between the individual and the environment. The current state of the individual influences which genes are expressed, and individuals influence and change the world they encounter. At the present time, twin and adoption studies are providing new insights into the interactions between genetic and environmental factors in development (e.g., Plomin & de Fries, 1983; Scarr & Kidd, 1983).

Although the dichotomy of innate versus learned behavior is false, it is possible to arrange characters along a continuum from those that are relatively stable with respect to environmental influence to those that are relatively labile (Barlow, 1989; Hinde, 1966, 1991a). Thus there are some characters that appear in virtually the whole range of environments in which life is possible ("stable" characters): Either the processes involved in their development are so regulated that they appear over a wide range of experiential influences, or the factors relevant to their development are ubiquitous. By contrast, characters at the labile end of the continuum appear only over a narrow range of conditions. It will be noted that this formulation differs from the innate–learned dichotomy in that (a) it involves a continuum and (b) a characteristic may be influenced by experience but yet is stable because the relevant influences lack specificity or are ubiquitous.

However, the level of analysis at which the character is defined may be crucial. Thus the broad details of the motor pattern of smiling form a stable human characteristic, yet its fine details and the circumstances in which it is given are labile. Furthermore, development may be stable up to a certain point and labile thereafter, or labile first and stable later.

For some (but not all) problems, such relatively stable characters can provide us with starting points, provided, however, that we remember that they will be subject to variation. It is impracticable to make a list of such characters, partly because a list of mundane characters would be tedious and partly because the cross-cultural data are not adequate to prove cross-cultural stability for any characters. However, they might include aspects of perception, motor patterns, stimulus responsiveness, motivation, cognitive processes, predispositions to learn (including the capacity for language), and so on (see Hinde, 1991a).

Of course, each such "relatively stable" character itself poses a developmental problem. Because the degree to which genes are expressed may depend on the environment, and because susceptibility to the environment may depend on the genetic constitution, the constraints on their variability themselves involve an interplay between genetic and environmental influences. The same is true for subsequent development.

The importance of constraints on learning and predispositions to learn must be emphasized here (Hinde & Stevenson-Hinde, 1973; Seligman & Hager, 1972). The earlier work on this subject concerned animals, where cross-species comparisons threw genetic constraints on development into relief. For instance, the chaffinch (a small bird) has to learn its song, but it will learn only songs with a note structure similar to the species-characteristic song. The bullfinch learns preferentially the song its father (biological or adoptive) sang (Thorpe, 1961). Even the capacity to acquire individual distinctiveness in singing behavior, essentially creative in nature, is to be seen in this light (Marler, 1991).

Humans as a species presumably also have similar constraints, though we recognize them only in the observation that some tasks or experiences are difficult to learn. Indeed it can be agreed that efficient learning requires inbuilt constraints (Johnson-Laird, 1990). Within the human species, similar constraints probably operate in autism. Autism is known to have genetic "bases" and involves specific deficits in understanding of emotion caused by beliefs (Baron-Cohen, 1991). It has also been suggested that male and female humans differ in their predispositions to learn (Hinde, 1987).

Constraints or predispositions may equally well be environmental in origin in both animals (Bateson, 1987; Gottlieb, 1991) and humans (e.g., Butterworth & Bryant, 1990; Sameroff & Chandler, 1975). Insofar as an individual is what he or she is as a consequence of prior experience, and future development depends on current state, all development is channeled by experience.

RELATIONSHIPS AND INDIVIDUALS

The critical question for the developmental psychologist is how individual characteristics are affected by the relationships experienced. Strong associations between parenting practices and child characteristics, involving social behavior (e.g., Baumrind, 1971; Bretherton, 1985; Maccoby & Martin, 1983), affective behavior (e.g., Easterbrooks & Emde, 1988; Radke-Yarrow et al., 1988), and cognitive dimensions (e.g., Goswami & Bryant, 1990) have been demonstrated, and although it must be assumed that influences operate both ways, in at least some cases there is an effect of parenting practices on the child.

But the issues are not simple. First, some individual characteristics may be influenced by relationships more than others, and the extent to which any one characteristic is affected may change during development. Thus the propensity to show fear may be relatively independent of relationships from 0 to 6 months, subsequently modified by relationships and reinforcement, and later still become relatively fixed (Stevenson-Hinde, 1988).

Second, in the case of relatives, and especially parents, it is by no means easy to distinguish genetic from experiential influences. First, similarities in genetic constitution may predispose the child to respond to environmental events similarly to, for example, the parents. Second, similarities in genetic constitution may cause the child to select or create an environment similar to that to which the parents preferentially respond. Third, parents may be predisposed genetically to provide their children with an environment conducive to the development of particular characteristics. For example, shy parents may both pass on genes associated with a predisposition to develop a behavioral style that might be labeled as shy and create an environment in which their children saw few strangers. Finally, parents and others may react differently to children of different genotypes (e.g., Jaspers & Leeuw, 1980; Plomin, 1986; Plomin & de Fries, 1983; Scarr & McCartney, 1983).

With regard to the processes whereby interactions within relationships have long-term effects on child behavior, until recently most work focused on reinforcement and modeling. Current interest centers on possible cognitive intermediaries between attachment relationships and subsequent interactions. The quality of the child's attachment relationship with the mother predicts the character of later peer interactions (e.g., Sroufe, 1983; Sroufe & Fleeson, 1986; Turner, 1991), suggesting that it affects some aspects of the child. Bowlby (1969), taking a lead from Craik (1943), postulated that the child forms internal working models of self, of others, and of their relationships. During the last decade, this idea has achieved increasing prominence. Initially, although heuristically useful, it was too ill defined to serve as a scientific concept (cf. MacCorquodale & Meehl, 1954). For instance, Main, Kaplan, and Cassidy (1985, p. 68) described it as "a mental representation of an aspect of the world, others, self, or relationships to others that is of special relevance to the individual," and elsewhere as "a set of conscious and/or unconscious rules for the organization of information." In this and other articles, additional properties were ascribed to the concept, many of which were isomorphic with the phenomena they were seeking to explain (Hinde, 1989a). Furthermore, there were both methodological and conceptual differences in the way in which the concept was used by different workers (Crittenden, 1990). Now, however, the concept of internal working model is in an exciting stage of development, involving inputs from work on cognition by both cognitive psychologists (e.g., Johnson-Laird, 1983, 1990) and developmental psychologists/psychiatrists (e.g., Stern, 1985, 1991). Bretherton (1990) conceptualized internal working models as systems of hierarchically organized schemata, with the models of self, others, and the world interlinked and mutually influencing each other (cf. Fentress, 1991). Used in this way, the concept is becoming more than a useful metaphor and is able to integrate data on psychopathology, the transmission of patterns of parenting across generations, and the relations between communication within attachment relationships and communication about such relationships to third parties.

EFFECTS OF RELATIONSHIPS ON RELATIONSHIPS

A child grows up in a network of relationships, and the different relationships may affect each other (Hinde & Stevenson-Hinde, 1988a, 1988b). The influence of relationships on relationships has been of interest to three groups of workers. Primatologists have come to recognize that relationships affect relationships within primate groups and, with observational and experimental evidence, that the mother–infant relationship is crucially affected by others (Hinde, 1972, 1983). Child developmentalists have demonstrated that the quality of a particular relationship in the family may be related to that of another. For instance, the marital relationship may be related to the mother–child relationship (Christensen & Margolin, 1988; Easterbrooks & Emde, 1988; Engfer, 1988; Meyer, 1988), the mother–child relationship may be related to the sibling relationship (Dunn, 1988a, 1988b), divorce may have long-term sequelae for the children (Hetherington, 1988; see also Rutter, 1988), and effects of inadequate parenting may be transmitted across generations (Belsky & Pensky, 1988; Caspi & Elder, 1988; K. Grossman, Fremmer-Bombik, Rudolph, & K. E. Grossman, 1988;

Patterson & Dishion, 1988). Some of the mechanisms involved are summarized by Hinde and Stevenson-Hinde (1988b).

A third group that has been concerned with the effects of relationships on relationships is the family systems theorists. Although there are many points of contact between them and developmental psychologists working on similar problems (Minuchin, 1985), the family systems theorists (themselves diverse) have developed a rather distinctive orientation and vocabulary. They emphasize the family as an open system, with organized patterns of interaction that are circular in form. The family system has homeostatic features that maintain the stability of the patterns within it, but may periodically undergo perturbations requiring a reorganization of patterns. The individuals constituting the family are seen as interdependent and distributed across subsystems which have their own integrity and whose interactions are governed by implicit rules and boundaries (e.g., Minuchin, 1988).

It will be apparent that many of the properties emphasized by family systems theorists are compatible with the interdependent yet self-organizing systems whose importance is emphasized by Fentress (1991) at lower levels of analysis (see earlier discussion). It is important to recognize that the family as a whole can have properties with some degree of independence from the behavior of its component units—analogous (only) to Hoyle's (1964) finding at a quite different level that the regular stepping movements of insects are not accompanied by fixed patterns of electrical activity in the motor neurones. Furthermore, the concepts of family systems theorists are clearly potentially compatible with the dialectical relations between levels shown in Figure 1.

My own view is that the level of dyadic relationships merits special attention for developmental psychologists, in that it is by interactions within relationships that development is affected. From there, it is possible to assess how interactions and relationships are affected by third parties (e.g., Clarke-Stewart, 1978; Corter, Abramovitch, & Pepler, 1983; Barrett & Hinde, 1988), other relationships, and the sociocultural structure. To foster further links between family systems theorists and developmental psychologists, it would be desirable to clear up a few conceptual issues (Hinde, 1989b). For instance:

1. Family systems theorists emphasize the family as an "organized whole" and ascribe to it homeostatic properties. But the maintenance of the family as a functioning unit depends on the behavior of individuals within their relationships. Family organization may derive from personal goal seeking—in which individuals attempt to create a family that suits their own personal needs and the resulting pattern of relationships is a consequence but not a goal of the behavior of individuals—as well as from interpersonal goal seeking, involving efforts to make the constituent relationships conform to an ideal or desired pattern. In both cases, the goals

may be unconscious or loosely defined. In any case, the processes that contribute to stability are diverse and may reside in one or more individuals or relationships. And they may involve attempts to approach an equilibrium or goal state whatever the current state, to approach it only so long as the current state remains within certain limits, or to avoid an undesirable state.

2. The same individual may belong to more than one subsystem. Thus the mother is part of both the spouse and the mother–child subsystem. An advantage of this subsystem approach is that it permits description of separate patterns for different subsystems composed of the same people (e.g., spouses are also parents). An advantage of the relationships approach advocated here is that it calls attention to the effects of interactions on interactions within a relationship and between relationships, so that a mother's marriage may affect (or be affected by) the mother–child relationship. But there is a clear need for an unambiguous definition of the subsystem concept. For instance, does the concept have a subjective reality for the participants? If it does, how does it differ from relationships? If it does not, as would appear to be the case with the "three-generational subsystem" postulated by Minuchin (1985), is its reality confined to the mind of the therapist?

3. Some family therapists downplay the role of the individual so far as to hold that attempts "to quantify the relative input of members of a system" do not make sense in a systems framework (Minuchin, 1985, p. 300). Developmental psychologists may disagree, especially if the questions asked are concerned with changes in or differences between relationships or families and are carefully phrased (Hinde, 1979).

4. Earlier, the importance of distinguishing between the objective and the subjective reality of aspects of the sociocultural structure was noted. This distinction could be important to family systems theorists. Are *family tasks*, *family myths*, and *family style* descriptive concepts useful to the therapist, or are they (consciously or unconsciously) part of the perceptions of the participants and thereby influencing process? And the *family world view*, concerned with the family's self-perceptions, may be shared by family members, but there may also be marked differences between family members in the way they perceive the family.

These somewhat academic points are perhaps tangential to the clinical achievements of the family systems approach and are intended only to supplement the important efforts made by Minuchin (1985) and others to bridge the gap between clinicians and developmentalists. In my own view, the means by which relationships affect relationships pose crucial problems for developmental psychology.

INDIVIDUAL DIFFERENCES

Developmental psychology's successes would have been impossible without the use of statistical techniques. Nevertheless, their widespread

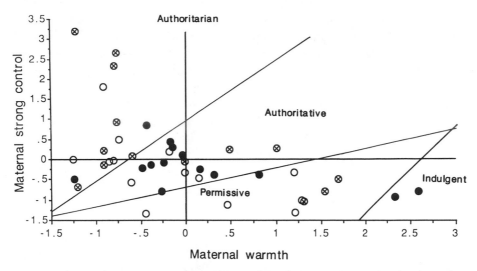

Figure 5. Relations between maternal warmth and maternal control at home and the aggression shown by 4-year-olds in preschool. (The children are categorized according to whether they were in the top third [circled crosses], middle third [open circles], or bottom third [filled circles] on aggression.)

and proper use has resulted in a focus on group means and a neglect of individual differences, although it is often differences that help us understand processes (Dunn, 1991; Rutter, 1991). Furthermore, a neglect of individual differences can lessen the value of the data to the clinician who is attempting to deal with individual cases. The advantages of a case study approach have recently been described forcefully by Radke-Yarrow (1991), for example, bringing balance to research dominated by group or variable-oriented research and greater understanding of the relations between behavioral systems; light thrown on children at the extremes and on children who show resilience in adverse circumstances or who fail in favorable ones; and the sharpening up of data on turning points in development usually obscured by group variance, thus permitting process to be studied more directly. To the biologist, individual differences raise the further question as to whether they merely represent noise in the system or whether they are adaptive. Some examples of the application of this approach to children are given in a later section.

As Radke-Yarrow (1991) pointed out, a revival of interest in individual case studies is a recent phenomenon, and statistical techniques for dealing with multiple levels of data on few individuals are at present poorly developed (but see D. H. Barlow & Hersen, 1984; Kazdin, 1982). Although this certainly does not mean that case studies should not be pursued, there is another approach that could take us some of the way. Statistical techniques that rely on linear correlational procedures can be misleading, and for many purposes it is preferable to attempt to categorize children (Hinde & Dennis, 1986). Examination of those children who appear to be exceptions to the initial categorization can lead one to new generalizations. Iteration of such a procedure can approach the individual.

An example that goes some of the way toward this goal is shown in Figure 5, which plots an index of maternal warmth against maternal strong control in 4-year-olds. The children are categorized according to whether they were in the top third, middle third, or bottom third on aggression in preschools. In three replications, aggression was found to be lower when control and warmth were more or less in balance, that is, in the central area, termed *authoritative* after Baumrind (1971), than in the authoritarian, permissive, or indulgent areas. This of course does not necessarily mean that the dimensions plotted were the crucial ones: In fact, the mother–child relationships differed between areas in many dimensions in addition to warmth and control. But there were a few high aggressives in the authoritative area and a few low aggressives in the others. These exceptions were found to differ from other individuals in the same area on some of these other aspects of the mother–child relationship. If the sample size were adequate, this procedure could be iterated to approach the individual level.

LINKS WITH ETHOLOGY

Many developmental psychologists imagine that any input biology/ ethology might have concerns parallels between animal and human behavior. Of course, parallels can be found, especially in relatively simple patterns—for instance, in rooting behavior and the Moro reflex. Some human expressive movements can be traced back to prehuman forms (e.g., Eibl-Eibesfeldt, 1975; van Hooff, 1972). But anthropomorphism is dangerous, and parallels can be misleading. In some cases, they are revealing only if one finds the right level of analysis. For example, behavioral development is disturbed by separating infant from mother for a week or two in both rhesus monkeys and humans. However, the evidence indicates that human children are more disturbed if they are away from home in a strange place during the separation period, whereas rhesus monkeys are more upset if they stay in the familiar group environment and the mother goes away. The difference seems to be that, in rhesus monkeys, the mother–infant relationship is more disturbed under the latter conditions because the mother has to reestablish her relationships with her group companions when she returns, as well as to cope with her demanding infant. What is common between monkeys and humans is that the more the mother–infant relationship is disrupted, the more the infant is disturbed (Hinde & McGinnis, 1977; cf. Rutter, 1991).

As this last example shows, rather than simple parallels, one should look for principles abstracted from animal data whose applicability to the human species can be tested. A classic example is Bowlby's (1969) use of

Harlow's data on rhesus monkeys (Harlow & Zimmerman, 1959) to show that *contact comfort*, and not just food reinforcement, as had previously been supposed, was crucial in the mother–child relationship.

Ethologists, unlike developmental psychologists, have emphasized that full understanding of a structure or behavior demands answers to four distinct questions. Thus the question "Why does the thumb move in a different way from the fingers?" could be answered developmentally (the growth of digit rudiments and nerve fibres), causally (the structure of bones, muscles, and nerves), functionally (the thumb's role in grasping, etc.), or in terms of evolution (the human species' monkeylike ancestors presumably had similar thumbs). The importance of the last two questions has been over-emphasized by some sociobiologists and neglected by most developmental psychologists. However, such issues can make a not inconsiderable contribution to understanding child development.

First, they have implications for practice. Thus the finding that, across mammals, the frequency of suckling is inversely related to the concentration of the milk and that humans have relatively dilute milk was a strong argument against schedule feeding (Blurton-Jones, 1972). The studies of Klaus and Kennell (1976; Kennell, 1986) showing that allowing mothers to have immediate postpartum contact with their infants has at least short-term (but not necessarily long-term [Fleming & Corter, 1988]) beneficial effects were influenced by comparative functional considerations. And, at a more theoretical level, Bowlby (1969) cast new light on the so-called irrational fears of childhood (fears of darkness, falling, being left alone, etc.) by arguing that they would have been functional in our environment of evolutionary adaptedness.

Second, diverse facts about human behavior, which appear initially to be isolated and independent, can be integrated from an evolutionary perspective. Thus various aspects of the mother–infant relationship are seen to form a functional whole when seen against the probable sociosexual arrangements in our environment of evolutionary adaptedness (Hinde, 1984).

Third, the links between situations and outcomes can sometimes be understood in functional terms. For example, infanticide and voluntary abortion are more common when the infant is not the putative parents' own, the infant has poor reproductive potential, or circumstances are adverse and reproductive effort might be wasted. If the incidence of infanticide or abortion is taken as an indicator of parental motivation, the data are in harmony with the view that motivation is low when further parental investment in the current offspring might decrease the mother's long-term reproductive success (Daly & Wilson, 1984).

It has even been suggested that behavior that seems maladaptive in our society may have been functional in others. Thus De Vries (1984) found that children with a "difficult" temperament were more likely to survive famine, perhaps because they were more demanding. Similarly, Main and

Weston (1982) suggested that the behavior of infants whose relationships with their mothers were avoidant permitted the maintenance of organization, control, and flexibility with mothers who do not welcome physical contact and who are restricted in emotional expression (see also Egeland & Farber, 1984). It has also been suggested that the relations between early family relationships and subsequent personality or behavioral characteristics are adaptive (Belsky, Steinberg, & Draper, 1991; Hinde, 1986, 1991b), although the evidence is far from secure.

A fourth possible payoff from an evolutionary–functional approach is that our changing adjustment to our changing culture could be greatly facilitated by an understanding of where we started. This does not imply that there are human characteristics that are independent of culture, but rather that it is helpful to distinguish biological desiderata, resulting from natural selection in our environment of evolutionary adaptedness, from the desiderata of our particular culture and to consider the relations of each to the psychological desideratum of mental health (Hinde & Stevenson-Hinde, 1990).

CONCLUSION

My plea, therefore, is for a truly multidisciplinary approach that focuses on the dialectical relations between levels of social complexity and, most particularly, on those relations among the individual, interactions, and relationships. Such an approach requires not only a descriptive base but also recognition that description can never be precise and that both descriptive and explanatory concepts are concerned with entities that are interconnected and mutually influence each other.

REFERENCES

Ainsworth, M. D. S., Blehar, M. C., Waters, E., & Wall, S. (1978). *Patterns of attachment.* Hillsdale, NJ: Erlbaum.

Andrew, R. J. (1991). Testosterone, attention and memory. In P. Bateson (Ed.), *The development and integration of behaviour* (pp. 171–190). Cambridge, England: Cambridge University Press.

Barlow, D. H., & Hersen, M. (1984). *Single-case experiential designs.* New York: Pergamon Press.

Barlow, G. W. (1977). Modal action patterns. In T. A. Sebeok (Ed.), *How animals communicate* (pp. 98–136). Bloomington, IN: Indiana University Press.

Barlow, G. W. (1989). Has sociobiology killed ethology or revitalized it? In P. P. G. Bateson & P. H. Klopfer (Eds.), *Perspectives in ethology, Vol 8: Whither ethology?* (pp. 1–46). New York: Plenum Press.

Baron-Cohen, S. (1991). Do people with autism understand what causes emotion? *Child Development, 62,* 385–395.

Barrett, J., & Hinde, R. A. (1988). Triadic interactions: Mother–firstborn–second-born. In R. A. Hinde & J. Stevenson-Hinde (Eds.), *Relationships within families: Mutual influences* (pp. 181–192). New York: Oxford University Press.

Bateson, P. (1987). Biological approaches to the study of behavioral development. *International Journal of Behavioral Development, 10,* 1–22.

Bateson, P. (1991a). Are there principles of behavioral development? In P. Bateson (Ed.), *The development and integration of behaviour.* Cambridge, England: Cambridge University Press.

Bateson, P. (Ed.). (1991b). *The development and integration of behaviour.* Cambridge, England: Cambridge University Press.

Baumrind, D. (1971). Current patterns of parental authority. *Developmental Psychology Monographs, 4* (1, Pt. 2).

Belsky, B., & Pensky, E. (1988). Developmental history, personality and family relationships: Toward an emergent family system. In R. A. Hinde & J. Stevenson-Hinde (Eds.), *Relationships within families: Mutual influences* (pp. 193–217). New York: Oxford University Press.

Belsky, J., Steinberg, L., & Draper, P. (1991). Childhood experience, interpersonal development and reproductive strategy: An evolutionary theory of socialization. *Child Development, 62,* 647–670.

Blurton-Jones, N. G. (Ed.). (1972). *Ethological studies of child behaviour.* Cambridge, England: Cambridge University Press.

Bowlby, J. (1969). *Attachment and loss. 1. Attachment.* London: Hogarth.

Bretherton, I. (1985). Attachment theory: Retrospect and prospect. In I. Bretherton & E. Waters (Eds.), Growing points of attachment theory and research. *Monographs of the Society for Research in Child Development, 50,* 1–2.

Bretherton, I. (1990). Communication patterns, internal working models and the intergenerational transmission of attachment relationships. *Infant Mental Health Journal, 11,* 237–252.

Butterworth, G., & Bryant, P. (Eds.). (1990). *Causes of development.* New York: Harvester Wheatsheaf.

Caldwell, B. M. (1969). A new "approach" to behavioral ecology. In I. P. Hill (Ed.), *Minnesota Symposia on Child Psychology, Vol. 2.* Minneapolis: University of Minnesota Press.

Carey, S. (1990). On the relations between the description and the explanation of developmental change. In G. Butterworth & P. Bryant (Eds.), *Causes of development* (pp. 135–160). New York: Harvester Wheatsheaf.

Caspi, A., & Elder, G. H., Jr. (1988). Emergent family patterns: The intergenerational construction of problem behavior and relationships. In R. A. Hinde & J. Stevenson-Hinde (Eds.), *Relationships within families: Mutual influences* (pp. 218–240). New York: Oxford University Press.

Cassidy, J., & Marvin, R. S. (1989). *Attachment organization in preschool children: Coding guidelines.* Seattle: MacArthur Working Group on Attachments.

Christensen, A., & Margolin, G. (1988). Conflict and alliance in distressed and non-distressed families. In R. A. Hinde & J. Stevenson-Hinde (Eds.), *Relationships within families: Mutual influences* (pp. 263–282). New York: Oxford University Press.

Clarke-Stewart, K. A. (1978). And Daddy makes three: The father's impact on mother and young child. *Child Development, 49,* 466–478.

Corter, C., Abramovitch, R., & Pepler, D. (1983). The role of the mother in sibling interactions. *Child Development, 54,* 1599–1605.

Craik, K. (1943). *The nature of explanation.* Cambridge, England: Cambridge University Press.

Crittenden, P. (1990). Internal representational models of attachment relationships. *Infant Mental Health Journal, 11,* 259–277.

Daly, M., & Wilson, M. (1984). A sociobiological analysis of human infanticide. In G. Hausfater & S. B. Hrdy (Eds.), *Infanticide: Comparative & evolutionary perspectives.* New York: Aldine.

De Vries, M. W. (1984). Temperament and infant mortality among the Masai of East Africa. *American Journal of Psychiatry, 141,* 1189–1194.

Dunn, J. (1988a). Connections between relationships: Implications of research on mothers and siblings. In R. A. Hinde & J. Stevenson-Hinde (Eds.), *Relationships within families: Mutual influences* (pp. 168–180). New York: Oxford University Press.

Dunn, J. (1988b). *The beginnings of social understanding.* Oxford, England: Blackwell.

Dunn, J. (1991). Relationships and behaviour: The significance of Robert Hinde's work for developmental psychology. In P. Bateson (Ed.), *The development and integration of behaviour* (pp. 375–388). Cambridge, England: Cambridge University Press.

Easterbrooks, M. A., & Emde, R. N. (1988). Marital and parent–child relationships: The role of affect in the family system. In R. A. Hinde & J. Stevenson-Hinde (Eds.), *Relationships within families: Mutual influences* (pp. 83–103). New York: Oxford University Press.

Egeland, B., & Farber, E. (1984). Infant–mother attachment: Factors related to its development and changes over time. *Child Development, 55,* 753–771.

Eibl-Eibesfeldt, I. (1975). *Ethology.* New York: Holt, Rinehart & Winston.

Emde, R. (1980). Levels of meaning for infant emotions. In W. A. Collins (Ed.), *Development of cognition, affect and social relations.* Hillsdale, NJ: Erlbaum.

Engfer, A. (1988). The interrelatedness of marriage and the mother–child relationship. In R. A. Hinde & J. Stevenson-Hinde (Eds.), *Relationships within families: Mutual influences* (pp. 104–118). New York: Oxford University Press.

Fentress, J. C. (1991). Analytical ethology and synthetic neuroscience. In P. Bateson (Ed.), *The development and integration of behaviour* (pp. 77–120). Cambridge, England: Cambridge University Press.

Feshbach, S. (1970). Aggression. In P. H. Mussen (Ed.), *Carmichael's manual of child psychology, Vol II.* New York: Wiley.

Fleming, A. S., & Corter, C. (1988). Factors influencing maternal responsiveness in humans: Usefulness of an animal model. *Psychoneuroendocrinology*, *13*, 189–212.

Getting, P. A., & Dekin, M. S. (1985). Tritonia swimming: A model system for integration within rhythmic motor systems. In A. I. Selverston (Ed.), *Model neural networks and behavior* (pp. 3–20). New York: Plenum Press.

Goswami, U., & Bryant, P. (1990). *Phonological skills and learning to read*. Hillsdale, NJ: Erlbaum.

Gottlieb, G. (1991). Experiential canalization of behavioral development: Theory. *Developmental Psychology*, *27*, 4–13.

Grossman, K., Fremmer-Bombik, E., Rudolph, J., & Grossman, K. E. (1988). Maternal attachment representations as related to patterns of infant–mother attachment and maternal care during the first year. In R. A. Hinde & J. Stevenson-Hinde (Eds.), *Relationships within families: Mutual influences* (pp. 241–261). New York: Oxford University Press.

Harlow, H. F., & Zimmerman, R. R. (1959). Affectionate responses in the infant monkey. *Science*, *130*, 421–432.

Hetherington, E. M. (1988). Parents, children, and siblings: Six years after divorce. In R. A. Hinde & J. Stevenson-Hinde (Eds.), *Relationships within families: Mutual influences* (pp. 311–331). New York: Oxford University Press.

Hinde, R. A. (1966). *Animal behavior*. New York: McGraw Hill.

Hinde, R. A. (1972). *Social behavior and its development in subhuman primates*. Eugene, OR: Oregon State System of Higher Education.

Hinde, R. A. (1979). *Towards understanding relationships*. London: Academic Press.

Hinde, R. A. (Ed.). (1983). *Primate social relationships*. Oxford, England: Blackwell.

Hinde, R. A. (1984). Biological bases of the mother–child relationship. In J. D. Call, E. Galenson, & R. L. Tyson (Eds.), *Frontiers of infant psychiatry* (pp. 284–294). New York: Basic Books.

Hinde, R. A. (1986). Some implications of evolutionary theory and comparative data for the study of human prosocial and aggressive behavior. In D. Olweus, J. Block, & M. Radke-Yarrow (Eds.), *Development of anti-social and prosocial behavior*. San Diego: Academic Press.

Hinde, R. A. (1987). *Individuals, relationships & culture*. Cambridge, England: Cambridge University Press.

Hinde, R. A. (1989a). Continuities and discontinuities: Conceptual issues and methodological considerations. In M. Rutter (Ed.), *Studies of psychosocial risk* (pp. 367–384). Cambridge, England: Cambridge University Press.

Hinde, R. A. (1989b). Reconciling the family systems and the relationships approaches to child development. In K. Kreppner & R. M. Lerner (Eds.), *Family systems and life span development* (pp. 149–164). Hillsdale, NJ: Erlbaum.

Hinde, R. A. (1991a). A biologist looks at anthropology. *Man*, *26*, 583–608.

Hinde, R. A. (1991b). When is an evolutionary approach useful? *Child Development*, *62*, 671–675.

Hinde, R. A. (1992). Auf dem wege zu einer Wissenschaft zwischenmenschlicher Beziehungen [Towards a science of relationships]. In A. E. Aulagen & R. Von Salisch (Eds.), *Zwischenmenschliche Beziehungen*. Göttingen, Germany: Hogrefe.

Hinde, R. A., & Dennis, A. (1986). Categorizing individuals: An alternative to linear analysis. *International Journal of Behavioral Development, 9*, 105–119.

Hinde, R. A., & McGinnis, L. (1977). Some factors influencing the effects of temporary mother–infant separation—some experiments with rhesus monkeys. *Psychological Medicine, 7*, 197–222.

Hinde, R. A., & Stevenson-Hinde, J. (Eds.). (1973). *Constraints on learning: Limitations and predispositions*. London: Academic Press.

Hinde, R. A., & Stevenson-Hinde, J. (1988a). Epilogue. In R. A. Hinde & J. Stevenson-Hinde (Eds.), *Relationships within families: Mutual influences* (pp. 365–385). New York: Oxford University Press.

Hinde, R. A., & Stevenson-Hinde, J. (Eds.). (1988b). *Relationships within families: Mutual influences*. New York: Oxford University Press.

Hinde, R. A., & Stevenson-Hinde, J. (1990). Attachment: Biological, cultural and individual desiderata. *Human Development, 33*, 62–72.

Hopkins, B., & Butterworth, G. (1990). Concepts of causality in explanations of development. In G. Butterworth & P. Bryant (Eds.), *Causes of development* (pp. 3–32). New York: Harvester Wheatsheaf.

Horn, G. (1985). *Memory, imprinting and the brain*. Oxford, England: Clarendon Press.

Horn, G. (1991). Cerebral function and behaviour investigated through a study of filial imprinting. In P. Bateson (Ed.), *The development and integration of behaviour* (pp. 121–148). Cambridge, England: Cambridge University Press.

Hoyle, G. (1964). Exploration of neuronal mechanisms underlying behavior in insects. In R. F. Reiss (Ed.), *Neural theory and modeling*. Palo Alto, CA: Stanford University Press.

Hutchison, J. (1991). How does the environment influence the behavioural action of hormones? In P. Bateson (Ed.), *The development and integration of behaviour*. Cambridge, England: Cambridge University Press.

Jaspers, J. M. F., & Leeuw, J. A. de (1980). Genetic–environment covariation in human behaviour genetics. In L. J. T. van der Kamp (Ed.), *Psychometrics for educational debate*. Chichester, England: Wiley.

Johnson-Laird, P. N. (1983). *Mental models*. Cambridge, MA: Harvard University Press.

Johnson-Laird, P. N. (1990). The development of reasoning ability. In G. Butterworth & P. Bryant (Eds.), *Causes of development*. New York: Harvester Wheatsheaf.

Kagan, J. (1971). *Change and continuity in infancy*. New York: Wiley.

Kazdin, A. E. (1982). *Single-case research design*. New York: Oxford University Press.

Kennell, J. (1986). *John Lind Memorial Lecture*. World Congress of Infant Psychiatry, Stockholm, Sweden.

Klaus, M. H., & Kennell, J. H. (1976). *Maternal–infant bonding*. St. Louis: Mosby.

Klinnert, M. D., Campos, J. J., Sorce, J. F., Emde, R., & Svedja, M. (1983). Emotions as behavior regulations: Social referencing in infancy. In R. Plutchik & H. Kellerman (Eds.), *The emotions, Vol 2*. San Diego: Academic Press.

Lytton, H. (1973). Three approaches to the study of parent–child interaction: Ethological, interview and experiment. *Journal of Child Psychology and Psychiatry, 14*, 1–17.

Maccoby, E. E., & Martin, J. A. (1983). Socialization in the context of the family: Parent–child interaction. In M. Hetherington (Ed.), *Mussen: Handbook of child psychology* (Vol. 4, pp. 1–103). New York: Wiley.

MacCorquodale, K., & Meehl, P. E. (1954). Edward C. Tolman. In W. K. Estes, S. Koch, K. MacCorquodale, P. E. Meehl, C. G. Mueller, W. N. Schoenfeld, & W. S. Verplanck (Eds.), *Modern learning theory* (pp. 177–266). New York: Appleton-Century-Crofts.

Main, M., Kaplan, N., & Cassidy, J. (1985). Security in infancy, childhood and adulthood. In I. Bretherton & E. Waters (Eds.), Growing points of attachment theory and research. *Monographs of the Society for Research in Child Development, 50*(Serial No. 1–2), 66–104.

Main, M., & Weston, D. R. (1982). Avoidance of the attachment figure in infancy. In C. M. Parkes & J. Stevenson-Hinde (Eds.), *The place of attachment in human behaviour*. London: Tavistock.

Markova, I. (1990). Causes and reasons in social development. In G. Butterworth & P. Bryant (Eds.), *Causes of development* (pp. 186–214). New York: Harvester Wheatsheaf.

Marks, I. M. (1987). *Fears, phobias and rituals*. New York: Oxford University Press.

Marler, P. (1991). Differences in behavioural development in closely related species: Birdsong. In P. Bateson (Ed.), *The development and integration of behaviour* (pp. 41–70). Cambridge, England: Cambridge University Press.

Mead, G. H. (1934). *Mind, self and society*. Chicago: University of Chicago Press.

Meyer, H.-J. (1988). Marital and mother–child relationships: Developmental history, parent personality, and child difficultness. In R. A. Hinde & J. Stevenson-Hinde (Eds.), *Relationships within families: Mutual influences* (pp. 119–141). New York: Oxford University Press.

Mineka, S. (1987). A primate model of phobic fears. In H. Eysenck & I. Martin (Eds.), *Theoretical foundations of behavior therapy*. New York: Plenum Press.

Minuchin, P. (1985). Families and individual development: Provocations from the field of family therapy. *Child Development, 56*, 289–302.

Minuchin, P. (1988). Relationships within the family: A systems perspective on development. In R. A. Hinde & J. Stevenson-Hinde (Eds.), *Relationships within families: Mutual influences* (pp. 7–26). New York: Oxford University Press.

Oyama, S. (1985). *The ontogeny of information*. Cambridge, England: Cambridge University Press.

Patterson, G. R., & Dishion, T. J. (1988). Multilevel family process models: Traits, interactions and relationships. In R. A. Hinde & J. Stevenson-Hinde (Eds.), *Relationships within families: Mutual influences*. New York: Oxford University Press.

Plomin, R. (1986). *Development, genetics and psychology*. Hillsdale, NJ: Erlbaum.

Plomin, R., & de Fries, B. C. (1983). The Colorado adoption project. *Child Development, 54*, 276–289.

Prechtl, H. F. R. (1950). Das Verhalten von Kleinkindern gegenüber Schlangen [The behavior of children towards snakes]. *Wiener Zeitz. f. Philosophie, Psychologie und Paedagogie, 2*, 68–70.

Radke-Yarrow, M. (1991). The individual and the environment in human behavioural development. In P. Bateson (Ed.), *The development and integration of behaviour* (pp. 389–410). Cambridge, England: Cambridge University Press.

Radke-Yarrow, M., Richters, J., & Wilson, W. E. (1988). Child development in a network of relationships. In R. A. Hinde & J. Stevenson-Hinde (Eds.), *Relationships within families: Mutual influences* (pp. 48–67). New York: Oxford University Press.

Rosenblatt, J. (1991). A psychobiological approach to maternal behaviour among the primates. In P. Bateson (Ed.), *The development and integration of behaviour* (pp. 191–222). Cambridge, England: Cambridge University Press.

Rutter, M. (1988). Functions and consequences of relationships: Some psychopathological considerations. In R. A. Hinde & J. Stevenson-Hinde (Eds.), *Relationships within families: Mutual influences* (pp. 332–353). New York: Oxford University Press.

Rutter, M. (1991). A fresh look at "maternal deprivation." In P. Bateson (Ed.), *The development and integration of behaviour* (pp. 331–374). Cambridge, England: Cambridge University Press.

Sameroff, A. F., & Chandler, M. (1975). Reproductive risk and the continuum of caretaker casualty. In F. D. Horowitz (Ed.), *Review of child development research, Vol. 4*. Chicago: University of Chicago Press.

Scarr, S., & Kidd, K. K. (1983). Developmental behaviour genetics. In J. J. Campos & M. M. Haith (Eds.), *Mussen, Handbook of child psychology* (Vol. 2, pp. 345–434). New York: Wiley.

Scarr, S., & McCartney, K. (1983). How people make their own environments. *Child Development, 54*, 424–435.

Seligman, M. E. P., & Hager, J. L. (Eds.). (1972). *Biological boundaries of learning*. New York: Appleton Century Crofts.

Simpson, E. E., & Stevenson-Hinde, J. (1985). Temperamental characteristics of three- to four-year-old boys and girls and child–family interactions. *Journal of Child Psychology and Psychiatry, 26*, 43–53.

Sroufe, L. A. (1983). Infant–caregiver attachment and patterns of adaptation in the preschool: The roots of competence and maladaption. In M. Perlmutter

(Ed.), *Minnesota Symposia in Child Psychology* (Vol. 16, pp. 41–83). Hillsdale, NJ: Erlbaum.

Sroufe, L. A., & Fleeson, J. (1986). Attachment and the construction of relationships. In W. Hartup & K. Rubin (Eds.), *Relationships and development* (pp. 51–72). Hillsdale, NJ: Erlbaum.

Stern, D. (1985). *The interpersonal world of the infant.* New York: Basic Books.

Stern, D. (1991). *Diary of a baby.* London: Fontana.

Stevenson-Hinde, J. (1986). Towards a more open construct. In D. Kohnstamm (Ed.), *Temperament discussed.* Lisse, Netherlands: Swets & Zeitlinger.

Stevenson-Hinde, J. (1988). Individuals in relationships. In R. A. Hinde & J. Stevenson-Hinde (Eds.), *Relationships within families: Mutual influences* (pp. 68–81). New York: Oxford University Press.

Stevenson-Hinde, J. (1991). Temperament and attachment: An eclectic approach. In P. Bateson (Ed.), *The development and integration of behaviour* (pp. 315–330). Cambridge, England: Cambridge University Press.

Stevenson-Hinde, J., & Shouldice, A. (1990). Fear and attachment in 2.5 year olds. *British Journal of Developmental Psychology, 8,* 319–333.

Thorpe, W. H. (1961). *Bird song.* Cambridge, England: Cambridge University Press.

Turner, P. (1991). Relations between attachment, gender and behavior with peers in school. *Child Development, 62,* 1475–1488.

Van Hooff, J. A. R. A. M. (1972). A comparative approach to the phylogeny of laughter and smiling. In R. A. Hinde (Ed.), *Non-verbal communication* (pp. 209–237). Cambridge, England: Cambridge University Press.

AUTHOR INDEX

Boles, A.J., 35, *55*

Book, B.K., 608, *613*

Booth, C., 456, *469*

Boring, E.G., 81, 83, 99, *101*

Bornstein, M., *52*, 404, *417*

Bornstein, M.H., 32, 38, *61*, 379, *382*, 555, *562*, *566*, *580*, *583*

Boston, M., 438, *463*

Bottoms, S.F., 25, *52*

Bovet, M., 275, 280, *288*

Bower, T.G.R., 348, *351*, 379, *382*, 571, *583*

Bowlby, J., 11, 19, 20, *52*, 206, 211, 212, 216, 218, 222, *225*, 431, 433, 434, 436, 437, 438, 439, 440, 441, 442, 446, 447, 448, 449, 450, 451, 453, 455, 459, 460, 461, 462, 463, 466, 468, 515, *522*, 597, *612*, 618, 629, 634, 635, *637*

Boyce, W.T., 554, *566*

Brackbill, Y., 25, 36, *52*

Bradfield, A., 32, *66*

Brainerd, C.J., 28, *52*, 377, *382*

Brassard, J.A., 11, *54*

Braungart, J.M., 457, *461*

Braunwald, K.G., 456, *469*

Brazelton, T.B., 10, 43, *52*, *61*, 218, 221, *225*, 242, *247*

Breese, F.H., 517, *520*

Breeze, K.W., 399, 410, 411, *421*

Breitmayer, B., 26, *65*

Brenner, M.W., 176, 178, *201*

Bretherton, I., 11, 22, *52*, *225*, 453, 454, 455, 458, *463*, *464*, 629, 630, *637*

Brewer, W.F., 178, 188, 189, *202*

Brody, G.H., 495, *496*

Brody, S., 413, *417*

Bronfenbrenner, U., 11, 16, 36, 40, *53*, 151, *165*, 319, *327*, 456, *464*, 479, 492, *496*, 518, *522*, 553, *566*, 579, *583*

Brooks-Gunn, J., 5, 26, 45, 46, *53*, 57, *61*, *63*, 139, *142*, 205, 221, *228*

Broughton, J.M., 128, 130, 135, 137, 138, 139, *141*, 269, *287*

Brown, A.L., 27, 40, 48, *53*, 185, 195, 200, *201*, 244, *248*, 336, 337, *351*, 352, 571, 572, 573, 575, 576, 577–578, 580, *583*, 585, *586*

Brown, B.B., 24, *68*

Brown, J.V., 43, *51*

Brown, R., 7, 20, *53*

Brownell, C.A., 221, *225*

Brubaker, T., 30, *53*

Bruner, J., 7, 22, *53*, 204, 206, 221, *225*

Bruner, J.S., 21, 70, 269, *287*, 324, 326, 327, 335, 348, *351*, 579, *583*

Bryant, P., 628, 637, *639*

Bryant, P.E., 13, *53*

Buchanan, C.M., 604, *612*

Buchsbaum, H.K., 216, *225*, 552, *566*

Buckley, K.W., 235, *248*

Bühler, C., 326, 328, 391

Buka, S., 120

Bull, N., 401, *417*

Bullis, G., 360, *384*

Burbidge, G., 559, *566*

Burgess, R.L., 95, 99

Burghardt, G.M., 95, 99

Burkhardt, R.W., 92, 99

Burnham, W.H., 105, 122, *123*

Burns, B., 413, *417*

Buss, D.M., 9, *53*

Buss, D.N., 95, 99

Bussey, K., 601, *614*

Butterworth, G., 620, 628, *637*, 640

Byng-Hall, J., 456, *464*

Cahan, E.D., 4, *53*, 74, 75, 128, 130, 138, 139, *141*, 150, *165*

Caims, R.B., *248*

Cain, A.C., 452, *464*

Cairns, B.D., 133, *141*

Cairns, R., 84, 99

Costall, A., 85, *100*

Cowan, C.P., 35, *55*

Cowan, P.A., 35, 47, *55*

Coysh, W.S., 35, *55*

Craik, K., 447, *464*, 629, *638*

Crain, W., 298, *308*

Cramer, B., 216, *226*

Crawford, C.B., 95, *100*

Cremin, L., 163, *165*

Crittenden, P., 456, *464*, 630, *638*

Crockenberg, S.B., 36, *55*

Cronbach, L.J., 193, *200*

Cross, D., 270, *290*

Crouter, A., 49, *55*

Crowell, D.H., 403, *418*

Crowley, K., 41, 48, 67, 253, 256, 578, 587

Cummings, E.M., 449, 456, *464*, 468, 606, *612*

Cuneo, D.O., 571, *583*

Cunningham, J.L., 178, 189, 190, *200*

Curtis-Boles, 35, *55*

Dahl, K., 216, *226*

Dale, P., 563, *566*

Dalton, T.C., 390, *418*

Daly, M., 94, *100*, 635, *638*

Damasio, A.R., 553, *566*

Dammann, V.T., 393, *418*

Damon, W., 264, 269, *290*

Damrosch, D.S., 394, *423*

Daniels, D., 327, *329*, 380, *385*

Danziger, K., 113, *123*

D'Arcis, U., 216, *226*

Darlington, R., 37, *61*

Darwin, C., 4, 22, *55*, 80, 83, 93, *100*

Davenport, C.B., 394, 414, *418*

Davis, F.C., *521*

Davis, W.A., 517, *523*

Day, R.L., 394, *423*

De Beer, G., 19, *55*

De Vitto, B.A., 25

De Vries, M.W., 635, *638*

Deane, K., 40, *69*

Deane, K.E., 455, *470*

deBlois, S., 582, *586*

Deci, E.L., 600, *612*

DeFries, J., 8, 64, 65, 380, *385*, 405, *422*

Dekin, M.S., 622, *639*

Delboeuf, J.L.R., 178, *200*

DeLoache, J.S., 580, *583*

Demetriou, A., 573, 574, *584*

DeMuralt, M., 216, *226*

Dennis, A., 633, *640*

Dennis, P., 402, 403, *418*

Dennis, S., 275, *287*

Dennis, W., 83, *100*

Denton, K., 94, *101*

DeVitto, B.A., 26, *57*

DeVos, J., 270, *286*

Dewey, J., 146, 147, 148, 149, 150, 151, 152, 153, 154, 155, 156, 157, 158, 159, 160, 161, 162, 163, 164, *165*, *166*, 390, 401, 409

Diamond, A., 9, 18, 46, *55*, 270, *287*, 377, 378, *383*, 578, 582, *585*

Diaz, R.M., 337, *351*

Dickstein, S., 10, *55*

Dilthey, W., 313, *328*

Dishion, T.J., 599, *614*, 630, *642*

Dix, T., 42, *55*, 606, *612*

Dixon, N.F., 452, *464*

Dixon, R.A., 269, *288*

Dobzhansky, T., 80, *100*

Dodge, K.A., 22, *55*

Dollard, J., 239, *248*, 249, 476, 477, 484, 485, 496, 497, 593, 597, *612*, *614*

Donaldson, M., 13, *55*

Donnell, F., 458, *468*

Doob, L.W., 476, 477, 496, 593, *612*

Dornbusch, S., 24, *68*

Dornbusch, S.M., 604, 605, *612*, *613*, *615*

Draper, P., 9, *51*, 94, 95, 99, *100*, 636, *637*

Dudeck, P., 314, *328*

Dunn, J., 11, 12, *55*, 322, 327, 328, 329, 456, *464*, 515, *524*, 627, 630, 633, *638*

Dvir, R., 457, *468*

Earley, L., 246, *250*

Easterbrooks, M.A., 38, *55*, 215, *226*, 629, 630, *638*

Eaton, W.O., 515, *522*

Eaves, L.J., 95, *100*

Eckardt, G., 313, 316, *328*

Edelman, G.M., 363, 380, *383*

Edwards, A., 160, *167*

Efklides, A., 573, 574, *584*

Egeland, B., 636, *638*

Eibl-Eibesfeldt, I., 634, *638*

Eichorn, D., 499, 500, *522, 523*

Eisenberg, N., 10, *56*

Ekman, P., 4, 10, 22, 43, *56*, 85, *100*, 606, *612*

Elder, G., 45, *53*, 255, *256*

Elder, G.H., 24, 27, 35, *56*, 548, 549, 552, *566*

Elder, G.H., Jr., 630, *637*

Elicker, J., *56*

Eliker, J., 11

Elkind, D., 123, *123*

Elkonin, D.B., 412, *418*

Elmer, J.D., 605, *615*

Elsberg, C.A., 394, *418*

Emde, R., 26, 67, 625, *641*

Emde, R.N., 10, 68, 211, 215, 219, 220, 221, *225, 226*, 230, 552, *566*, 629, 630, *638*

Emerson, C., 338, *351*

Emerson, P.E., 17, 36, 39, 67, 436, 448, 457, *469*

Engfer, A., 630, *638*

Englund, M., 11, *56*

Ennis, R., 278, *288*

Eppler, M.A., 380, *382*, 534, 538, 540, *542*

Erdelyi, H.M., 452, *464*

Ericsson, K.A., 41, *56*

Erikson, E., 208, *226*, 438, *464*

Espenchade, A., 506, *521, 522*

Estes, C., 32, *61*

Estes, D., 457, *468*

Etzel, B.C., 36, *56*

Evans, R.B., 112, *123*

Fagan, J.F., 379, 386, 555, 567, 580, *587*

Fairbairn, W.R.D., 206, *226*, 433, *465*

Falkner, F., 413–414, *418*

Fantz, R., 7, *56*

Fantz, R.L., 242, *248*, 368, 379, *383*

Farber, E., 636, *638*

Farran, D.C., 43, *60*

Farrar, M.J., 18, 29, *56*, 574, *584*

Fast, I., 452, *464*

Feinman, S., 10, *56*

Feiring, C., 37, *62*

Fenichel, O., 216, *226*

Fentress, J.C., 620, 621, 622, 630, 631, *638*

Ferguson, C.J., 516, *519*

Fernald, A., 606, *613*

Ferrara, R., 185, 200, 336, *351*

Feshbach, S., 621, *638*

Field, D., 195, *200*

Field, T., 8, 11, 22, 27, 40, 44, *56*

Firth, R., 458, *465*

Fischer, K., 12, 29, *56*

Fischer, K.W., 18, *57*, 571, 573, 574, *584*, *587*

Fish, M., 16, *51*, 456, 462, *465*

Fisher, D.M., 380, *386*, 506, *525*

Fisher, K.W., 378, *383*

Fitzsimmons, M.E., 122, *123*

Fivush, R., 21, *57*

Flavell, E.R., 573, 576, 585

Flavell, J.H., 12, 16, 21, 28, 29, 33, 57, 188, 200, 264, 265, 288, 571, 572, 573, 575, 576, 577, 580, 584, 585

Fleener, J., 602, 610, 615

Fleeson, J., 11, 16, 32, 44, 68, 629, 643

Fleming, A.S., 635, 639

Foch, T.T., 30, 61

Fodor, J.A., 269, 288

Fogel, A., 12, 49, 57, 244, 250, 381, 386

Folds, T.H., 13, 48, 57

Follansbee, D.J., 608, 613

Fonagy, P., 455, 465

Footo, M.M., 13, 48, 57

Forman, E., 333, 352

Foss, B.M., 444, 465

Fowler, W., 403, 418

Fraiberg, S., 216, 218, 227

Fraleigh, M.J., 605, 612

Frank, L.K., 394–395, 418, 419

Freedman, D.G., 554, 567

Freedman, N., 554, 567

Freeman-Moir, D.J., 128, 130, 137, 141, 269, 287

Fremmer-Bombik, E., 630, 639

French, L.A., 336, 351

Freud, A., 441, 465

Freud, S., 22, 30, 57, 205, 206, 207, 208, 209, 210, 211, 212, 213, 214, 227, 432, 439, 450, 453, 465

Friberg, L.T., 510, 522

Fries, B.C. de, 627, 629, 642

Friesen, W., 10, 43, 56

Frijda, N., 211, 227

Fritz, A.S., 571, 584

Frodi, A.M., 23, 61

Frodi, M., 23, 61

Fulker, D., 379, 386, 405, 422

Fulker, D.W., 580, 587

Fuller, J.L., 560, 568

Fulton, J.F., 406, 419

Furstenberg, F.F., Jr., 26, 57

Gaensbauer, T.J., 220, 226

Galanter, E., 447, 468

Gallimore, R., 336, 353

Gallistel, C.R., 575, 576, 577–578, 585

Galuzzo, D.C., 457, 466

Gandour, M.J., 515, 522

Garber, E.E., 533, 543

Garcia, J., 555, 567

Garcia, R., 276, 277, 280, 283, 289

Gardner, H., 347, 351, 508, 523, 553, 567, 575, 585

Gardner, W., 32, 48, 61, 66

Gariépy, J.-L., 139, 142

Garrett, E.V., 35, 55

Garvin, R.A., 337, 350

Gaughran, J.M., 562, 566

Gay, J., 48, 54

Gay, P., 150, 167

Geber, M., 513, 523

Geertz, C., 336, 351

Gelman, R., 187, 200, 269, 287, 379, 382, 571, 572, 573, 575, 576, 577–578, 584, 585

Gelman, S.A., 575–576, 587

Gentner, D., 198, 200

George, C., 454, 455, 465, 515, 525

Gesell, A., 40, 57, 359, 360, 361, 362, 363, 364, 365, 366, 367, 368, 369, 370, 371, 373, 374, 375, 376, 377, 379, 381, 383, 384, 396, 397, 399, 407, 410, 419

Getchell, N., 408, 419

Getting, P.A., 622, 639

Getz, K., 216, 231

Gewirtz, J.L., 16, 17, 19, 36, 39, 56, 57, 65, 591, 613

Ghiselin, M.T., 81, 85, 86, 100

Gibbs, P.K., 517, 523

Gibson, E.J., 7, 9, 17, 20, 33, 34, 57, 368, 380, 381, 382, 384, 528–542, 542, 543, 544

Gibson, J.J., 17, 20, 57, 528, 531, 533, 543, 544

Gibson, K.R., 378, *384*

Gilstrap, B., 456, *462*

Giudice, S., 554, *568*

Gladstone, W.H., 211, *228*

Glaser, R., 194, *199*, 574, *584*

Glick, J., 48, *54*, 307, *308*

Goldberg, J., 275, *287*

Goldberg, S., 25, 26, *57*

Goldberg, W., 38, *55*, 605, *613*

Goldfarb, W., 436, *465*

Goldfield, E.C., 403, *419*

Goldman-Rakic, P.S., 18, *58*, 377, 378, *384*

Goldschmidt, R., 414, *419*

Goldsmith, H.H., 8, 10, 18, *54*, 564, *567*

Goldwyn, R., 454, 455, *467*

Goodman, G.S., 12, *58*, 216, *228*

Goodnow, J., 41, 42, *58*

Goswami, U., *639*

Gottleib, G., *58*

Gottlieb, G., 6, 31, 91, *100*, 133, 139, *142*, 208, *228*, 245, 248, 380, *384*, 414, 415, *419*, 628, *639*

Gottman, J., 42, 43, *51*

Gottman, J.M., *58*, *64*

Goudena, P., 338, *351*

Gould, S.J., 80, *100*

Graber, M., 270, *286*

Graham, S., 23, *58*

Green, F.L., 576, *585*

Green, J.A., 43, 44, *53*, *58*

Greenberg, M., 455, *469*

Greenberg, M.T., 449, 456, *465*, *466*

Greenberg, R.H., 455, *470*

Greenberger, E., 605, *613*

Greene, D., 600, *613*

Greene, S., 554, *567*

Greenfield, P.M., 269, *287*, 326, *327*

Greeno, J.G., 572, *585*

Greenough, W.T., 9, 46, 47, *58*, 380, *384*, 539, *544*

Greenwald, A., 12, *58*

Griffin, N., 506, *525*

Griffin, S., 195, *200*

Grosskurth, P., 440, 441, *466*

Grossman, K., 22, *58*, 630, *639*

Grossman, K.E., 22, *58*, 630, *639*

Grossmann, K., 216, *228*, 457, 458, *466*

Grossmann, K.E., 216, *228*, 457, 458, *466*

Gruber, H.E., 77, 79, 90, *100*, 188, *201*

Grusec, J.E., 42, *55*, 602, *613*

Gunnar, M.R., 9, 27, *58*

Guntrip, H., 206, *228*

Gurtner, J., 27, *61*

Guth, D.A., 32, *66*

Guttentag, R.E., 13, 48, *57*

Hager, J.L., 628, *642*

Hagstrom, F., 337, 349, 350, *355*

Hahn, A., 216, *228*

Haith, M., 12, *58*, 242, *249*

Hala, S., 571, *584*

Halford, G.S., 29, *58*, 198, *201*, 574, *585*

Hall, G.S., 4, 30, *58*, 103, 104, 105, 106, 110, 111, 113, 116, 117, 118–119, 120, 121, 122, *123*, 124, 157, *167*

Hall, W.G., 415, *422*

Hammond, N.R., 21, *57*

Hansburg, H.G., 455, *466*

Hansl, E.B., 403, *419*

Hardesty, F.P., 314, 316, 327, *328*

Hardin, G., 89, *101*

Harlow, H.F., 30, 32, 39, *58*, 63, 440, 446, *466*, 515, *523*, 634, *639*

Harlow, M.K., 30, *58*

Harlow, S.D., 413, *423*

Harmon, R.J., 205, 219, 220, 226, *229*

Harpending, H., 94, *100*

Harper, L.V., 221, 223, 225, 607, *612*

Harper, R.M., 554, *568*

Harris, P.H., 270, *288*

Harris, P.L., 10, *59*, 261, 265, *286*

Harter, S., 5, 59, 130, 139, *142*

Hartmann, H., 221, *228*

Hartup, W.W., 11, 44, 59, 493, 496, 599, 607, *613*

Hasher, L., 30, *70*

Hauser, S.T., 604, 608, *613*, *614*

Havighurst, R.J., 517, *523*

Hazan, C., 12, *58*, 455, *469*

Heath, A.C., 95, *100*

Hebb, D., 7, 59

Heinicke, C.M., 436, 440, *466*

Heming, G., 35, *55*

Hencke, P., 560, *567*

Hendler, J., 554, *567*

Henneguy, L., 190, *199*

Henri, V., 5, *52*, 175, 176, 179, 187, 188, 189, 190, *199*, *200*

Hermans, H.J.M., 460, *466*

Hernandez, J.M., 554, *567*

Herrick, C.J., 397, *419*

Herrnstein, R.J., 83, *101*

Hersen, M., 633, *636*

Hertzog, C., 30, *59*

Hess, E.H., 84, *101*

Hetherington, E.M., 36, 45, 59, 605, *613*, 630, *639*

Hevey, C.M., 36, *54*

Hewitt, J.K., 95, *100*

Heyl, K., 394, *419*

Higgins, N.C., 94, *101*

Hill, E.W., 32, *66*

Hinde, R.A., 9, 11, 19, 35, 44, 48, 59, 438, *466*, 607, *613*, 620, 623, 624, 626, 627, 628, 630, 631, 632, 633, 634, 635, *636*, 637, *639*, *640*

Hjertholm, E., 338, *351*

Hoffman, J., 43, *61*

Hoffman, L.W., 9, *59*

Hoffman, M.L., 495, 496, 602, *613*

Hoffreth, S.L., 27, *59*

Hofstadter, R., 163, *167*

Hofsten, C. von, 367, 381, *384*

Hogan, R., 445, *470*

Hogarty, P.S., *62*

Hogerty, P.S., *37*

Holt, R.R., 435, *467*

Homma, S., 415, *422*

Honzik, M., 508, 514, *523*

Hood, K.E., 139, *142*

Hood, L., 40, *54*

Hook, S., 146, 147, 160, *167*

Hopkins, B., 620, *640*

Hopkins, H., 106, *124*

Hopkins, M., 107, 108, 109, *124*

Hoppe, S.K., 554, *567*

Horn, G., 618, 624, *640*

Horn, J.M., 580, *586*

Horowitz, F.D., 25–26, 59, 242, 244, *248*

Horowitz, M.J., 210, 212, *228*

Houlihan, J., 608, *613*

Howes, C., 25, 40, 59, 64, 457, *466*

Hoyle, G., 631, *640*

Hubel, D., 7, 31, *59*

Huber, F., 216, *228*

Hubley, P., 322, 330, 600, *615*

Hudson, J.A., 21, *59*

Hull, C.L., 21, 59, 239, *248*

Hulsebus, R.C., 6, *59*

Hunt, J.McV., 28, *59*

Hutchins, E., 35, 60, 336, *351*

Hutchison, J., 624, *640*

Huxley, J., 404, 413, *419*

Hwang, C.P., 23, *61*

Ilg, F.L., 360, 363, 364, 365, 369, 371, 373, *384*

Inhelder, B., 41, 60, 270, 272, 275, 278, 280, 288, *289*

Isabella, R., 456, *462*

Ivins, B., 515, *525*

Izard, C.E., 20, 43, 44, *60*

Jacobson, A.M., 604, 608, *613*, *614*

James, W., 134, *142*

Janet, P., 335, *351*

Janowsky, J., 220, *225*

Jaspers, J.M.F., 629, *640*

Jay, S., 43, *60*

Jemerin, J.M., 554, *566*

Jencks, C., 111, *124*

Jenkins, E., 18, 41, 67

Jenkins, W.M., 380, *384*

Jensen, A.R., 242

Jensen, J.L., 381, *386*

Jenson, A.R., *248*

Joels, T., 458, *468*

Johnson, D.L., 516, *519*

Johnson, J.E., 42, *60*

Johnson, J.S., 33, *60*

Johnson, M.M., 457, *466*

Johnson, W.F., 215, *226*

Johnson-Laird, P.N., 628, 630, *640*

Johnston, J., 540

Jones, E., 213, *228*

Jones, H.E., 501, 502, 505, 506, 507, 510, 522, *523*

Jones, M.C., 237, *248*

Just, M.A., 194, *201*

Kaas, J.H., 380, *385*

Kagan, J., 18, 23, 32, *60*, 69, 220, 223, *228*, 379, *385*, 515, *523*, 552, 554, 556, 557, 559, 561, *567*, 623, *640*

Kahn, A.J., 516, *519*

Kail, R., 198, *201*, 585

Kalhorn, J.C., 517, *520*

Kanner, L., 556, *567*

Kaplan, B., 164, *167*, 294, 301, 303, 304, 305, *309*

Kaplan, K., *467*

Kaplan, N., 454, 455, *465*, *466*, 601, *614*, 630, *641*

Kaplowitz, C., 205, *229*

Karier, C.J., 105, *124*

Karmiloff-Smith, A., 41, *60*, 378, 379, *385*, 579, *585*

Katzman, R., 560, *568*

Kaye, K., 206, *228*

Kazdin, A.E., 633, *640*

Kearsley, R., 220, 223, *228*

Keil, F.C., 18, *60*, 537, *544*, 575, 576, 577–578, *585*

Kelso, J.A.S., 244, *250*, 381, *386*

Kelso, J.S., 506, *525*

Kempen, H.J.G., 460, *466*

Kendler, H.H., 6, 16, *60*, 239, *248*, 249

Kendler, T.S., 6, 16, *60*, 239, *248*, 249

Kendrick, C., 11, *55*

Kennell, J.H., 635, *641*

Kernberg, O.F., 211, *228*

Kessen, W., 5, 7, 16, 21, 28, *60*, 67, 73, 75, 82, *101*, 128, *142*, 164, *167*, 173, 242, *249*, 359, 373, *385*, 570, *585*

Kessler, D.B., 455, *470*

Kidd, K.K., 627, *642*

Kihlstrom, J., 12, *60*

King, A.P., 380, 381, *386*

King, R.A., 602, 607, *615*

Klagsbrun, M., 455, *466*

Klahr, D., 16, 18, *60*, 61, 198, *201*

Klaus, M.H., 635, *641*

Klein, M., 433, *466*

Klein, R., 32, *60*

Klein, R.G., 562, *567*

Klein, R.P., 205, *231*

Klinnert, M.D., 10, *61*, 68, 625, *641*

Klopfer, B., 435, *467*

Klopfer, W.F., 435, *467*

Kluge, K.A., 554, *568*

Knauer, D., 216, *226*

Knobloch, H., 513, *523*

Kobak, R.R., 455, *467*

Kochanska, G., 10, *70*, 607, *613*

Kogan, N., 185, *201*, 580, *585*

Kohlberg, L., 74, 75, 137, *142*, 267, 288, 338, *351*

Kohlstedt, S.C., 110, *124*

Kohn, D., 83, *101*

Kohut, H., 216, 221, *228*

Kolb, S., 31, 37, 70, 376, *387*, 405, *423*

Konner, M., 94, *101*, 378, *385*

Kopp, C.B., 221, *225*

Korner, A.F., 505, *523*

Koslowski, B., 10, *52*, 221, *225*

Kotelchuck, M., 449, *467*

Kozulin, A., 333, 334, *351*

Krafchuk, K.E., 562, *568*

Krasnogorski, N., 237, *249*

Krebs, D., 94, *101*

Kreppner, K., 35, *61*

Kreutzer, M.A., 85

Kroonenberg, P.M., 457, *470*

Kubler-Ross, E., 442, *467*

Kuchuk, A., 38, *61*

Kuczinsky, L., 456, *468*

Kuczynski, L., 602, 607, *613*

Kuenne, M.R., 6, *61*, 239, *249*

Kunzi, R., 415, *422*

Kuo, Z.Y., 245, *249*, 396, *419*

Kurke, M., 7, 66

Kurland, J.A., 95, 99

Laboratory of Comparative Human Cognition, *308*, 347, *351*, 579, *585*

Ladd, G., 11, *64*

Laewen, H., 516, *522*

Lamb, M.E., 8, 10, 18, 22, 23, 32, *54*, *61*, 216, 223, *228*, 445, 456, 457, *467*, *468*, *470*

Lamborn, S.D., 605, *613*

Langer, E.J., 278, *286*

Langer, J., 83, *101*

Larsen, R.J., 9, *53*

Laseter, T.M., 516, *519*

Lay, K., 606, *613*

Lazar, I., 37, *61*

Learnard, B., 239, *249*

Leeuw, J.A. de, 629, *640*

Leiderman, P.H., 22, 56, 605, *612*

Lempers, J.D., 573, *585*

Leont'ev, A.A., 333, *352*

Leont'ev, A.N., 342, 345, 348, 349, *352*

Lepper, M., 27, *61*

Lepper, M.R., 600, *613*

Lerner, R.M., 30, *61*, 84, *101*, 245, 249, 319, *328*

Leslie, A., 575, *585*

Lester, B., 43, *61*

Letson, R.D., 32, *51*

Levin, H., 6, 21, 28, 35, 40, 67, 479, 482, 483, 484, 497, 517, 525, 535, *543*, 594, *615*

Levin, I., 275, *288*

Levine, J., 35, *65*

Levine, L., 455, *470*

Levine, R., 336, *353*

Levy-Bruhl, L., 343, *352*

Lewin, K., 315, 325, *328*, 412, *419*, 595, *613*

Lewis, M., 5, 10, 20, 37, 56, *61*, 62, 139, *142*, 205, 216, 221, 226, *228*

Lewis, M.L., 552, *567*

Lewkowicz, K.S., 457, *468*

Lewkowitz, D.J., 301, *308*

Lewontin, R.C., 88, *101*

Liben, L.S., 46, *62*

Lichtenberg, J.D., 211, *228*

Lieberman, A.F., 445, 449, 456, 462, *467*

Lippitt, R., 595, *613*

Lipsitt, L.P., 6, 16, 19, 39, *62*, 368, *385*, 390, 413, *417*, *419*, 500, *523*

Lisina, M.I., 412, *419*

Livson, N., 509, *522*

Llamas, C., 578, 582, *585*

Lockman, J.J., 37, *62*

Loehlin, J.C., 580, *586*

Long, L., 402, 412, *423*

Loon, R.J.P. van, 460, *466*

Lorenz, K.Z., 438, *467*

Miles, W., 112, *124*

Miller, G.A., 447, *468*

Miller, N.E., 239, 248, 249, 476, 477, 484, 485, 496, 497, 593, 597, 612, *614*

Miller, P.H., 13, 62, 358, *385*

Miller, S.A., 42, *62*

Mills, W., 36, 63, 137, *142*

Mineka, S., 625, *641*

Minick, N.J., 333, *352*

Minot, C.S., 413, *421*

Minuchin, P., 631, 632, *641*

Mischel, T., 259, *288*

Miyake, K., 457, *468*

Moberg, G.P., 557, *566*

Modell, J., 27, 56, 255, 256, 548, *549*

Molehaar, P.C., 29, *69*

Moll, L.C., 292, 308, 333, 334, *352*

Monroe, W.S., 113, *124*

Montangero, J., 259, 267, 274, *288*

Moore, M.K., 367, *385*

Morelli, G.A., 458, *470*

Morgan, C.L., 133, 134, 136, *142*

Morgan, G.A., 205, *229*

Morgan, S.P., 26, *57*

Morisett, C., 563, *566*

Morisson, F.J., 46, 47, *63*

Morrison, V., 379, *386*

Morss, J.R., 85, *101*

Moss, H.A., 556, *567*

Mounoud, P., 377, *385*

Mounts, N.S., 605, 613, *615*

Mowrer, O.H., 476, 477, 496, 593, *612*

Muchow, M., 315, *328*

Mueller, R.H., 128, 130, 131, 134, 135, 139, 140, *142*

Munger, M.P., 603, *615*

Murphy, L., 242, *250*

Murphy, L.B., 368, *386*

Mussen, P.H., 84, *101*, 128, *142*

Myers, I., 457, *466*

Nance, R.D., 235, *249*

Naus, M.J., 13, 41, 48, *63*

Neale, M.C., 95, *100*

Nelson, C.A., 22, *63*

Neverovich, Y.Z., 412, *419*

New York Times, 403, *417*

Newell, A., 198, *201*

Newell, K.M., 381, *385*

Newport, E.L., 33, *60*

Nezworski, 456, *462*

Niles, D., 533, *544*

Nissen, H., 399, *421*

Noam, G.G., 604, 608, 613, *614*

Noirot, E., 379, *382*

Novak, M.A., 32, *63*

Nowlis, V., 478, 497, 593, *615*

Nucci, L., 495, *497*

Nunes, L.R. de Paula, 246, *249*

O'Connor, J., 578, *583*

Oden, M.H., 512, *522*

Odling-Smee, F.J., 86, 94, *101*

O'Donnell, J.M., 103, *124*

O'Leary, S.E., 40, *64*

Olenick, M., 40, *59*

Olson, D.R., 261, 265, *286*

Olver, R.R., 269, 287, 326, *327*

Oppenheim, R.W., 396, 399, 404, 413, 414, 415, 421, *422*

Ornstein, P.A., 4, 6, 13, 41, 47, 48, 53, 57, 63, 128, *142*

Osborn, H.F., 134, 135, *142*

Osgood, C., 211, *229*

Osgood, C.E., 556, *567*

Osofsky, J., 20, 44, 63, 221, *229*

Osser, H.A., 531, *543*

Overton, W.F., 16, *63*

Owens, W.A., 512, *523*

Owsley, C.J., 540, 543, *544*

Oyama, S., 91, *101*, 245, 249, 627, *642*

Ozminski, S.J., 79, 99

Paden, L.Y., 242, *248*

Paikoff, R.L., 46, *63*

Palacio-Espapa, F., 216, *226*

Palincsar, A.S., 195, *201*, 337, *352*, 580, *586*

Palmer, C.F., 412, *422*

Park, K., 44, *63*

Park, K.A., 606, *613*

Parke, R.D., 10, 11, 18, 23, 25, 26, 27, 30, 34, 35, 36, 38, 40, 42, 43, 44, 45, 47, *52*, *55*, *56*, *62*, *63–64*, 65, 68, 69, 255, *256*, 456, 468, 548, 549, 552, *567*, 607, *614*

Parker, S.T., 582, *586*

Parkes, C.M., 442, *455*, *463*, 468

Parmalee, A.H., Jr., 26, *64*

Pasamanick, B., 513, *523*

Pascual-Leone, J., 574, *586*

Patterson, C., 90, *101*

Patterson, G.R., 598, 599, 607, 609, *614*, 630, *642*

Paul, H., 214, *229*

Pawl, J.H., 456, *467*

Pearlman, E.G., 265, *287*

Pedersen, N.L., 510, *522*

Pennington, B., 220, *231*

Pensky, E., 95, 99, 630, *637*

Peplau, L.A., 599, *612*

Pepler, D., 631, *638*

Perlmutter, M., 30, *64*

Perner, J., 269, *288*, 572, *586*

Perry, D.G., 601, *614*

Pervin, L.A., 40, *64*

Petersen, R., 403, 409, *417*

Peterson, A.C., 378, *384*

Phelps, 45, *53*

Phillips, D., 25, *64*

Phillips, D.A., 27, *59*

Phillips, S.J., 403, 411, *417*

Phillipszoon, E., 211, *227*

Piaget, J., 7, 64, 133, 138, *142*, *143*, 187, 188, *201*, 208, 229, 260, 261, 262, 263, 264, 266, 269, 270, 272, 275, 276, 277, 278, 280, 281, 282, 283, 287, 288, 289, 298, 308, 326, *328*, 347, 348, *353*, 439, 468, 578, *586*

Piatelli-Palmarini, M., 270, *289*

Pick, A.D., 34, 531, *543*

Pick, H.L., 7, 70, 413, *422*

Pieron, 181

Pine, F., 20, *62*, 211, *229*

Pinker, S., 379, *385*

Pinneau, S.R., 503, *522*

Pipp, S.L., 18, *57*

Pleck, J., 25, *64*

Plomin, R., 8, 18, 27, 45, 59, 64, 65, 194, *201*, 327, *328*, 329, 380, *385*, 405, 406, *422*, 510, 515, *522*, *523*, 524, 580, *586*, 627, 629, *642*

Plotkin, H.C., 94, *102*, 552, *567*

Pollack, R.H., 176, 178, *201*, 301, *308*

Pontius, A.A., 405, *422*

Pool, L., 394, *422*

Postman, L., 17, 65, 528, *544*

Potebnya, A.A., *353*

Poulson, C.L., 246, *249*

Povinelli, D.J., 582, *586*

Powell, J.S., 580, *587*

Power, T.G., 23, 43, 64, 65

Powers, S., 604, 608, *613*, *614*

Prechtl, H.F.R., 377, *385*, 413, *422*, 625, *642*

Preyer, W., 4, 19, 65, 84, *102*

Pribram, K.H., 447, *468*

Prigogine, I., 285, *289*

Provine, W.B., 80, *101*

Pruett, L., 105, *124*

Pulkkinen, L., 605, *615*

Purdy, J., 540, *543*

Putnam, H., 273, *287*

Puzerei, A.A., 333, *353*

Quine, W.V., 140, *143*

Radke-Yarrow, M., 9, 40, 41, 65, *70*, 215, *229*, 456, 468, 602, 607, *615*, 623, 626, 629, 633, *642*

Ramey, C.T., 16, *65*

Ratner, C., 333, *353*

Ratner, S., 390, *422*

Rau, L., 6, 28, 67, 474, 479, 480, 497, 594, *615*

Raughn, C.R., 603, *615*

Rayner, E., 441, *468*

Rayner, R., 236, *250*

Razel, M., 403, *422*

Rebok, G.W., 488, *497*

Recanzone, G., 380, *384*

Reed, E.S., 538, *544*

Reese, H.W., 16, *63*

Reeve, R.A., 27

Reid, J.B., 599, *614*

Reigel, K.F., 66

Reinert, G., 83, *102*

Reiss, D., 35, 45, 59, *65*

Rende, R., 580, *586*

Resnick, L., 35, 65, 336, *353*

Resnick, S.J., 379, *385*

Reve, R.A., 48, *53*

Reznick, J.S., 515, *523*, 563, *566*

Rheingold, H.L., 16, 17, 38, 39, 65, 515, *524*

Ricciuti, H.N., 22, 26, *65*

Richters, J., 623, 626, 629, *642*

Ridgeway, D., 211, *229*, 455, 463, *464*

Ridley-Johnson, R., 506, *525*

Riegel, K.F., 25, 65, 320, 326, *329*

Riegler, H.D., 246, *249*

Riese, M.L., 515, *524*

Riesen, A., 7, *66*

Rieser, J.J., 32, *66*

Riesman, D., 111, *124*

Riley, C.M., 394, *423*

Riley, M.S., 572, *585*

Ritter, P., 605, *612*

Ritvo, L.B., 206, 207, *229*

Roback, A.A., 561, *567*

Robbons, L.C., 41, *62*

Robert-Tissot, C., 216, *226*

Roberton, M.A., 408, *419*

Roberts, D.F., 605, *612*

Robertson, J., 222, *229*, 435, 436, 440, 468

Robertson, T.B., 413, *422*

Robinson, J., 206, *225*

Rochat, P., 412, *422*, 504, *524*

Rockefeller, S., 146, 147, 149, *167*

Rockwell, R., 24, *56*

Rodkin, P.C., 104, *124*, 603, *615*

Rodning, C., 457, *466*

Roe, A., 83, *102*

Rogeness, G.A., 554, *567*

Rogoff, B., 20, 21, 22, 35, 48, 66, 158, *167*, 244, *249*, 336, 340, *353*, 579, *586*, 603, *615*

Romanes, G.J., 30, *66*

Rose, D., 379, *386*

Rosen, M.G., 25

Rosen, R., 32, *66*

Rosenblatt, J., 618, *642*

Rosenblith, J.F., 513, *524*

Rosenbluth, D., 438, *463*

Ross, D., 105, 111, 112, 121, *124*, 489, *496*

Ross, G., 21, *70*

Ross, H.W., 39, *65*

Ross, S.A., 489, *496*

Rothbart, M.K., 564, *567*

Rovee, C.K., 368, *385*

Rovee, D.T., 368, *385*

Rovee-Collier, C., 246, 249, *250*

Rovine, M., 16, 25, 51, 456, 457, *462*

Rubin, Z., 11, 44, 59, 599, 607, *613*

Rubinshtein, S.L., 349, *353*

Shuttleworth, F.K., 502, *525*

Siegel, A., 27, 68, 158, *167*

Siegel, A.W., 113, *125*, 315, *329*

Siegel, G.J., 560, *568*

Siegler, R.S., 4, 5, 13, 16, 18, 21, 29, 41, 46, 48, *62*, *67*, 187, 198, *201*, 253, *256*, 571, 573, 578, 580, 581, *586*, *587*

Sigel, I., 35, 42, *67*, 68

Sigman, M.D., 379, *382*, 555, 566, 580, *583*

Silverman, W.A., 394, *423*

Silvern, L., 573, *584*

Simmel, M.L., 178, *201*

Simon, H.A., 41, *56*, 190, *200*

Simon, T., 180, 181, 183, 184, 186, 193, *200*, *202*

Simpson, E.E., 626, *642*

Simpson, G.G., 83, *102*

Sinclair, H., 275, 280, *288*

Sinclair, H.J., 270, *289*

Singbiel, C.E., 515, *522*

Siqueland, E.R., 368, *385*

Skala, K.D., 506, *525*

Skeels, H., 68

Skinner, B.F., 68, 240, 241, *250*, 596, *615*

Skinner, E.A., 6, 42, 68

Slater, A., 379, *386*

Slough, N., 455, *469*

Smith, H., 242, *250*

Smith, H.T., 368, *386*

Smith, J., 153, *167*

Smith, L.B., 253, *256*, 571, *587*

Smith, T.L., 113, *125*

Snidman, N., 18, 60, 379, *385*, 515, *523*, 554, 557, 559, *567*

Sokol, R.J., 25

Solomon, J., 455, *465*, 515, *525*

Sorce, J.F., 10, 68, 625, *641*

Sostek, A.M., 22, *56*

Spalding, D.A., 30, 68

Spangler, G., 22, *58*, 457, 458, *466*

Spelke, E.S., 12, 34, *57*, 68, 379, 386, *572*, *587*

Speltz, 456, *466*

Spencer, H., 86, *102*, 353

Spencer-Booth, Y., 438, *466*

Spieker, S., 456, *469*

Spiker, C.C., 239, *246*, *248*, *249*

Spitz, R.A., 9, 68, 206, 218, 220, 223, 229, 230, 436, 438, 441, *469*

Sroufe, L.A., 11, 16, 27, 32, 37, 44, *56*, 68, 299, 308, 449, 450, 456, 468, 469, *470*, 597, 602, 610, *615*, 629, *642*, *643*

Stacy, M., 504, *524*

Stafford, S., 246, *250*

Stahnke, M., 516, *522*

Starbuck, E.D., 105, *125*

Staszewski, J.J., 190, *202*

Stayton, D., 11, 445, 446, *461*, *470*

Stearns, S.C., 92, *102*

Stebbins, G.L., 80, *100*

Steele, H., 455, *465*

Steele, M., 455, *465*

Stein, N.L., 603, *615*

Steinberg, J., 23, *61*

Steinberg, L., 9, 24, 25, *51*, *52*, 68, 94, 95, 99, 605, *613*, *615*, 636, *637*

Stenberg, C., 8, 10, 18, *54*

Stengers, I., 285, *289*

Stern, C., 312, 314, *329*

Stern, D., 630, *643*

Stern, D.N., 10, 68, 204, 216, 221, 226, 230, *231*, 582, *587*

Stern, W., 311, 312, 314, 315, 318, 319, 320–323, 324, 327, *329*, *330*

Sternberg, 20, 68

Sternberg, R.J., 194, *199*, 574, 580, *587*

Sternberg, R.S., 198, *202*

Stevenson, H., 242, *250*

Stevenson, H.W., 6, 27, 68

Stevenson-Hinde, J., 35, *59*, 621, 622, 623, 626, 628, 629, 630, 636, 640, 642, *643*

van Hooff, J.A.R.A.M., 634, *643*

Van Ijzendoorn, M.H., 457, *470*

Varon, E.J., 177, *202*

Veysey, L.R., 110, *125*

Vibbert, M., 38, *61*

Vietze, P., 22, 56, 205, *231*

Voloshinov, V.N., 342, *354*

Vonèche, J.J., 133, *143*, 188, *201*

Vygotsky, L.S., 21, 48, 68, 139, *143*, 298, 309, 324, 325, *330*, 333, 334, 335, 336, 337, 338, 339, 340, 341, 342, 343, 344, 345, 347, 348, *354*, *355*, 579, *587*

Waddington, C.H., 92, *102*, 245, *250*, 450, *470*

Wagners, E., 41, *70*

Wahler, R.G., 36, *69*

Walk, R.D., 7, 9, *57*, 537, 541, *543*, *544*

Walker, A., 25, *52*

Walker, A.S., 536, 537, 540, *543*

Walker, R.A., 554, *568*

Wall, S., 11, *50*, 206, *225*, 441, 445, 446, 449, *461*, 624, 636

Wallace, C.S., 9, 46, 47, 58, 380, *384*

Wallace, J.G., 18, *61*

Wallage, D.B., 516, *519*

Walters, R.H., 16, 21, 39, *51*, 474, 479, 483, 484–485, 492, 496

Wang, Y.F., 554, *567*

Wapner, S., 294, 303, *309*, 315, 325, *331*

Ward, M.J., 455, *470*

Warren, D., 27, *69*

Warren, S.F., 246, *249*

Warren, W.H., 533, *544*

Wartner, U., 216, *228*

Waters, E., 11, 22, 40, 44, *50*, *52*, 63, 68, *69*, 206, *225*, 441, 445, 446, 449, 454, 455, *461*, *464*, *470*, 597, 606, *613*, *615*, 624, 636

Watson, J.B., 5, 19, 26, *69*, 235, 236, 237, 238, *250*, 369, *386*

Watson, M.W., 216, *231*, 571, *587*

Weech, A.A., 394, 395, 411, *417*, *423*

Weinbach, A.P., 414, *423*

Weinert, F.E., 37, *69*

Weinshank, D.J., 79, *99*

Weisberg, P., 36, *69*

Weismann, A., 80

Weiss, R.S., 455, *470*, *471*

Weiss-Perry, B., 608, *613*

Weissmann, A., *102*

Welch, L., 402, 412, *423*

Wellman, H.M., 12, *69*, 261, 265, 270, 289, 290, 570, 572, 575–576, 577, *587*

Welsh, M., 220, *231*

Werner, E.E., 499, 513, *525*

Werner, H., 293, 294, 295, 296, 301, 303, 304, 305, *309*, 319, 325, *331*

Wertsch, J.V., 34, *69*, *70*, 221, *231*, 292, 309, 333, 335, 336, 338, 339, 340, 341, 342, 344, 347, 349, 353, *355*, 579, *587*

Wesley, F., 176, 185, *202*

West, M.J., 380, 381, *386*

Westen, D., 9, *53*

Westheimer, I., 436, 440, *466*

Weston, D.R., 11, *62*, 216, 229, 635, *641*

Wetmore, K.E., 106, *125*

Wetzel, N.C., 413, *423*

White, B., 19, 27, 31, *70*

White, M., 149, *167*

White, R.K., 595, *613*

White, R.W., 205, *231*

White, S.H., 113, 120, *125*, 150, 158, 165, *167*

Whitehouse, R.N., 502, *525*

Whiten, A., 582, *587*

Whiting, J.W.M., 478, 497, 593, *615*

Whitt, J.K., 40, *70*

Whorf, B.L., 345, *355*

Wiebe, R.H., 105, *125*

Wiesel, T., 7, 31, *59*

SUBJECT INDEX

role of attitude in development, 400–401

sensory exploration in learning, 535–537

structural/behavioral model, 244–245

in support of attachment theory, 442–446, 449–450

typical vs. unusual behaviors, 194

Behavioral psychology. *See also* Watson, John

in Bowlby's work, 440

challenges to, 242–243

in current theory development, 244–245, 246

Gesell and, 374–375

Gibson and, 528

McGraw's twin study and, 402–403

in social learning theories, 474–475

socialization research in, 591–592, 593–595

theoretical development in, 238–241

Berkeley Growth Study, 500

Binet, Alfred, 129, 134

on characteristic tendencies in children's thinking, 195–197

cognitive research of, 175–176

contributions of, 1–2, 4–5, 192–195

developmental theory, 186–188

intellectual development of, 177–181, 192

memory research, 188–190

personal qualities, 181–182, 193

research in intelligence, 176, 179–181, 182–186, 190–192

research methodology, 2, 38, 187–188

unified theory of intelligence, 197–199

Biological science. *See also* Genetics

in current thinking on development, 8–9, 18

Darwin's contribution to, 160–161, 162, 165

developmental transformation research in, 220

in Dewey's concepts, 148

early behavior research, 4

in emotion research, 8

evolutionary concepts in, 171–172

Freud's theories and, 224

in future developmental research, 46, 47

Gesell's developmental theory and, 361–362, 366–367

in Hall's adolescent research, 116–117

in identifying mechanism of perceptual learning, 539

McGraw's research, 160–161

neurochemistry in concept of temperament, 560–561

in Piaget's theories, 268–269, 284–285

research trends, 565

technical developments in, 554–555

in Watson's investigations, 236

Body measurement, 499–503

Boston, Mary, 436

Bowlby, John, 206. *See also* Attachment theory

career, 432–434

contributions of, 428–429, 431

on Darwin, 460

in development of attachment theory, 435–442

Bühler, C., 316, 326

Bühler, K., 316

California Infant Scale of Motor Development, 504

Case studies, research role of, 709–710

Catastrophe theory, 29

Charcot, J. M., 177–178

Child abuse, 214, 216

Child psychology, 73, 160–161

Chomsky, N., 263

Circumplex model of maternal and child behavior, 514, 515

Clark University, 112–113, 121–122, 254

Classification logic, 273

Coghill, G. E., 362–364, 366–367, 390, 395–398

Cognitive processes

abstraction vs. situational thinking in, 420–421

action and, 537–538

in active development theory, 319–320

anxiety and, 210

in attachment theory, 453

Baldwin's concepts, 131–132

Bayley's measurement of, 506–512

bidirectionality in development of, 33–34

Binet's research/theories, 175–176, 184–186

biological predisposition, 263

Bowlby's organizational structure for, 453

causal thinking, 270, 277, 280–281

characteristic tendencies in children, 195–197

child competency assessment, 13, 572–573

concept of intentionality in, 261

conceptualization in, 281, 421–422

conservations of quantity, 273–276

constructive thinking in children, 570–571

as creation of possibilities, 281–282

culture and, 416–422

current conceptualization, 18, 570

current research, 12, 571–572, 581–583

defensive exclusion in, 452

desire psychology and, 577

development of research in, 4–5, 242–243

developmental elements in, 580–581

Dewey's conceptualization, 153–155, 157–160

diagnosis problem, 572

domain-specific beliefs in, 488

as egocentric/inner speech, 413–414

environmental factors in, 510–511

equilibration in, 276–277, 282–283, 578

expertise in, 574–575

figurative, 278–279

grouping operations in, 273

individual differences in, 579–580

innate knowledge and, 378–379

interpropositional thinking, 277–278

Kant's influence in conceptualization of, 294

language and, 260–262, 301–302, 596

logical operations in, 272–273

mechanisms of development, 577–579

objectivity in thinking, 160–161

perceptual development and, 532–535, 537–539

phenomenological representation of, 582–583

Piaget's functionalism, 279–284

Piaget's structuralism, 271–279

Piaget's theory of adaptation, 268–269

Piaget's work on, significance of, 258–259, 284–286

precausal thinking, 261–262

precocity in, 12

preverbal assessment, 7

processing of contradiction in, 263–264

qualitative changes in, 577

relational understanding, 262–264

representational theories, 269

scaffolding concept, 603–604

sensorimotor development in, 268

sequential development models, 576–577

in social learning theory, 485–486, 490–491

social origins of, 410–414, 417, 579

stage model for development in, 573–574

in Stern's theory, 319–320

as theory-making, 575–576

typical vs. unusual behaviors and, 194, 195

unified theory of intelligence, 197–199

Communication. *See also* Language

affective reciprocity as, 221

cultural considerations in, 224

differential-developmental concept, 323–324

nonverbal, 418, 571–572

preverbal, 7, 221, 412

Comparative psychology, 171

Conditioning, 6, 240

Context

in developmental theory, 47–49

perceptual affordance and, 533, 534–535

secular change as, 24–26

in Stern's concept of proximal space, 320–322

in Vygotsky's concept of culture, 416–422

in Vygotsky's concept of mental functioning, 410–414

Contradiction, 263

Cortisol, 557, 561

Creativity/innovation, 425

Critical period concept, 29–33

McGraw's, 403–406

in socialization theory, 609

Darwin, Charles

Bowlby on, 460

emotional expression research, 3–4

Freud's conception of ontogeny and, 206–210

Gesell and, 361–362

ideological bias against theories of, 163–166, 173

influence of, in developmental psychology, 1, 153–154, 157–162, 174

intellectual development of, 155–157

intellectual influence of, 162–163, 172

ontogeny-phylogeny concept of, 166

psychology research and, 168–174

Spitz and, 219

Defensive processes/systems, 451–452

Denver Developmental Screening Test, 371

Dependency

adolescent aggression and, 483–484

as drive, in social learning theory, 478–479

Desire psychology, 577

Dewey, John

contributions of, 74–75, 147, 164–165

developmental theory of, 147

educational psychology of, 151–157, 159–162

intellectual development of, 145–149

learning theory of, 153–154

McGraw and, 390, 394

research methodology, 148–149, 151–152

on role of attitude, 401–402

social progress in thought of, 161–163, 165

social psychology theory of, 148–151

Differential psychology, 311

Dilthey, W., 313, 316–317

Dopaminergic system, 554

Durkheim, E., 411, 419

Ebbinghaus, H., 313, 316

Ecological approach, 18–19, 20

Ecological niche concept, 321, 327

Education/training in psychology

Baldwin in development of, 129

of Gesell, 358–359

of Hall, 105–111

historical development, 103–104, 111–112

in psychoanalytic movement, 217

of Stern, 313–314

Educational psychology

Binet in, 181, 194–195

Binet-Simon intelligence test in, 190–192

Dewey in, 151–157, 159–162

interpreting signals of growth, 412

reciprocal teaching method, 580

Stern in, 314–315

Vygotsky's concepts in, 421

Embryology

Coghill's influence on Gesell, 362–364, 366–367

Coghill's influence on McGraw, 395–398

McGraw's neuroembryology, 414–415

Emotional development

affective reciprocity, 221

attitude and, 402

in classical conditioning, 240

current research, 9–11

developmental transformations in, 219–220, 224

early research, 3–4, 114–115

infantile anxiety, 209

in infants, 236–237

maternal deprivation and, 218, 222–223

neurochemical correlates in, 561–562

polarities in, 211

scaffolding concept, 206

smiling response, 219–220

social regulation and, 10–11

in socialization process, 605–607

Spitz on, 219–221

transformations in, 220

Environmental factors. *See also* Sociocultural context

in concept of affordance, 533–534

in continuum of lability, 703–704

in current conceptualizations, 243–247

in developmental systems view, 168

historical events as, 552

mental performance and, 510–512

mother-infant relations and, 517–518

in Stern's concept of proximal space, 320–322

in Stern's theory of convergence, 317–318

in Watson's behaviorism, 237–238, 240

in Werner's theory of multiple moments, 303–306

Epigenesis, 167, 172, 208

Equilibration theory, 274, 276–277, 282–283, 578

Ethical issues

in developmental theory, 172–173

in natural selection theory, 165

Ethology, 695

description of complex processes in, 697

in development of attachment theory, 438

developmental research and, 695, 710–712

evolutionary theory and, 160, 168

Evolutionary theory. *See also* Darwin, Charles

in Bowlby-Ainsworth theory, 429

developmental accommodations and, 133

developmental research and, 9, 168–172, 552

in Hall's theory of adolescence, 117

innate knowledge concept, 378–379

natural selection hypothesis in, 133, 164, 165, 172–173

ontogeny–phylogeny concept in, 166–168

in psychoanalytic theory, 210

psychology's objections to, 164–169, 172–173

in Vygotsky's concept of culture, 419–420

Exercise, sensorimotor development and, 404–405

Families. *See also* Parent-child relations

Bowlby's research, 433–434

dual-worker, 457

effect of relationships on relationships in, 706–708

Oedipal conflict theory, 214–218

Family systems theory, 706–708

Fathers, in attachment theory, 437, 456

Fear, 701–702

Fels Institute, 37, 595

Feminist thought, 457

Fixed Action Pattern, 697

Flavell, John, 307

Frank, Lawrence K., 394–395

Freud, Anna, 435

Freud, S.

Darwinian approach to individual ontogeny and, 206–210

developmental psychology and, 2, 203–204, 223–225

on nonconscious mental activity, 210–212

objections to theories of, 213–217

Oedipus complex theory, 214–218

play theory, 204–206

Frustration-aggression hypothesis, 477–478

Functionalist theories, 157–158, 162

Gender differences

androgyny/somatyping research, Bayley's, 501–502

attachment theory and, 457

in evolutionary theory, 165

in mother–infant relations, 515, 516–517

in Oedipus complex theory, 215–216

Genetics, 276

Baldwin's concepts, 2, 129–132

behavioral, Gesell and, 379–380

behaviorism in theoretical integration with, 244–245

in cognitive development, 580

current research in, 8–9

early investigations in, 156

in growth rate, 414

identifying influence of, 705

individual stability and, 703–704

in neurochemical tendency to temperament, 560–561

ontogeny-phylogeny concept in, 166–168

in sensorimotor development, 378

Gesell, Arnold L., 234, 238, 255–256

behavioral psychology and, 374–375

career, 358–360

Coghill's sensorimotor research and, 362–364, 366–367

concept of growth of individuality, 364–366

contributions of, 357–358, 375–382

embryological concepts and, 366–367

on environmental influences, 365

evolutionary theory and, 361–362

normative development standards, 367–368, 369, 371–374

research methodology, 367–370

stage theories, 377

Gestalt psychology, 294–295

Gibson, Eleanor

career, 529, 531–532, 539

contributions/influence of, 430, 537–539, 539–542

on mechanism of perceptual development, 535–537, 538–539

on perception as cognition, 532–535

perceptual differentiation research, 529–532

as researcher, 539–541

scribble experiment, 527–528

Gibson, James, 533

Goal-directed development, 317–318, 319

Goddard, H. H., 191

Gollin, Eugene, 307

Grief processes, 441–442

Habit

in Baldwin's epistemology, 131

evolution and, 156

in Hall's child development questionnaires, 113–114

Hall, G. Stanley, 359

adolescent research, 116–121, 123

child questionnaire studies, 19, 112–116

at Clark University, 112–113

contributions of, 74, 103–104, 122–123

Dewey and, 146–147

intellectual development of, 26, 105–111

at Johns Hopkins University, 103–104, 111–112

religious beliefs of, 104, 121

Hamburg Institute, 314–316

Hegelian philosophy, 147, 154

Heider, F., 315

Heinicke, C., 436

Hetzer, H., 316

Heuristic, concept of development as, 167, 296–298, 300–301

Hopkins, Mark, 3–7

Hormonal system, 46

Hull, Clark, 239–240, 476

Hullian theory, 429, 474

Hypnosis, 177–178

Imitation/modeling, 484–485, 597–598, 600–601

Imprinting, 448

Individual differences

classification of, 556–558

in cognitive development, 579–580

in developmental research, 708–710

in evolutionary theory, 157, 165, 170–171

Gesell's concept, 364–366

in Hall's child development questionnaires, 115–116

in intelligence, 185

neural processes in, 415

in psychoanalytic theory, 212–213

typical vs. unusual behaviors, 194

Information processing models

Bowlby's, 451–453

in cognitive development theory, 16–17, 18, 578

in social cognitive theory, 491–492

in social learning theory, 3, 474

Inhelder, B., 272

Inhibition, 401

cortical, 408

Instinct, 170

in Hall's child development questionnaires, 113–114

in psychoanalytic theory, 211

Institutionalization, 218

Integrative approaches, 243, 246

behaviorism and psychoanalytic theory in, 475–476, 593–595

in current developmental theory, 17–18

in Darwin's research, 170, 174

in McGraw's work, 411–412, 415–416

in research methodology, 40

in Spitz's psychology, 218

in Stern's work, 316–317

systems theory for, 49–50

Intelligence testing
  age-related patterns, 511–512
  Bayley's work, 506–512
  Binet's contribution, 176, 179–181, 182–186, 190–192
  in predictability of later mental status, 507–509, 555
  qualitative differences in, 185
  social theory and, 191–192
  sociocultural context of, 553
  socioeconomic factors and, 510–511
  Stern's contribution, 311, 313
  zone of proximal development and, 412–413
Intentionality, 261
Internal working models, 447–448, 451–452, 454, 459–460, 705–706

James, William, 134, 135
Johns Hopkins University, 103–104, 111–112

Kant, I., 294, 295
Klein, Melanie, 432–434, 437
Kohlberg, L., 74

Laboratory Temperament Assessment Battery, 564
Lamarck, J. B., 155, 156
Language
  affective communication, 221
  of children, 186–187
  in cognitive development, 263
  culture and, 418–420
  developmental psycholinguistics, 596
  differentiation processes, 301–302
  as double schematization, 304
  egocentric component of, 260–261, 413–414
  experimental primitivization of, 301

genetic predisposition, 379
of individual development, 559
memory and, 188–189
of parent-reported observational data, 562–565
Piaget's research on, 260–262
relational understanding and, 262–264
semantic "no," 219, 220
socialization and, 260–261, 414
Stern's research/theories, 311–312
theoretical, for representation of concept relations, 303
Vygotsky's egocentric/inner speech, 413–414
Lazarus, M., 313
Learning theory. See also Social learning theory
  acquired distinctiveness/equivalence in, 530
  adaptation in, 185
  behavioral theorists, 239–240, 243–244, 245–246
  in developmental psychology, 5–6, 21
  Dewey's, 153–157
  exploratory behaviors, 535–537
  Gesell's, 374–375
  Gibson's scribble experiment and, 528
  Hullian, 429
  imitation/modeling in, 484–485, 486, 597–598
  McGraw's, 397–398, 410
  mediational variables in, 6
  neuromuscular integration in, 410–411
  perception as basis for, 534–535
  perceptual differentiation in, 529–532
  psychoanalytic theory and, 475–476
  reading skills, 531, 532–533, 535
  socialization theory as, 591
  stage models, 195–197
  stimulus–response associationism in, 17

in structural/behavioral model, 244–245

types of perception in, 528–529

in Watson's behaviorism, 236

zone of proximal development and, 412–413

Lewin, K., 315, 325, 492

Life-span analysis, 47

attachment theory in, 455–456

Freud's theories and, 224

role of, 518–519

in theory development, 29–30

Lorenz, Konrad, 168

Loss/separation

Bowlby's formulation, 441–442, 450–453

Freud's observations, 206, 210

grief processes in infancy, 441–442

infant separation anxiety, 440–441

maternal deprivation, 206, 218, 222–223

Lyceum movement, 110

Malthus, T. R., 155, 157, 164

Marx, Karl, 411

Mathematical understanding, 262–263

Maturational theory

cognitive development in, 578

critical period concept and, 403–406

Gesell's, 363, 367–368, 376–382, 397

McGraw's, 397, 402–411

in McGraw's twin study, 402–403

neuromuscular studies in, 406–411

McCosh, J., 134

McGraw, Myrtle B., 255, 256, 362

career, 389–391

Coghill and, 395–398

concept of attitude, 400–402

concept of critical period, 402–406

contributions of, 411–417

Darwin and, 160–161

on embryonic development, 398–399, 414–415

at Neurological Institute, 394–395

neuromuscular integration research, 406–411

research methodology, 390–391, 404–405, 412–414

Meliorism, 163–166

Memory

assessment of, 13

Binet's research/theories, 178, 188–190

biological correlations to development in, 554

calculation feats, 190

conformity paradigm, 189–190

episodic-semantic model, 452

of ideas, 189

in model of selective repression, 452–453

in social cognitive theory, 490

Microgenesis, 306, 578–579

Moral development

in adolescents, 120

in Baldwin's theory, 137

in Dewey's psychology, 161, 163–164

in Hall's research/theories, 115, 120

in Oedipus complex theory, 215

parent-child interactions and, 602

Piaget on, 266–267

psychology and, 164

Moro reflex, 400, 408, 710

Mother–infant relations. *See also* Attachment theory; Parent–child relations

affective reciprocity in, 221

assessment of, 514–515

consistency over time in, 515

cross-cultural studies, 457–459

dependency as drive in, 478–479

description of complex processes in, 699–700

in ethological theory, 428

Freud's research, 205–206
gender differences in, 515, 516–517
identification process in, 479
later development and, 516–517
maternal deprivation, 218, 222–223,
440–441
microanalytic analysis of, 599–600
origins of maternal behavior, 517–518
social context of research/theory, 556
Muchow, M., 315
Multiple moments, 303–306

Narcissism, 216
National Longitudinal Study of Youth, 45
Neurological Institute, 394–395
Nonverbal communication, 418
Norepinephrine, 554

Object relations theory, 206
Oedipus complex, 214–218
Ontogeny
Freud's conception, 206–210
McGraw's research/theories, 398–399
phylogeny and, 17, 19, 166–168
trait canalization and, 168
in Vygotsky's genetic analysis, 415
Operational reversibility, 263
Orthogenesis, 319

Parent–child relations. *See also* Mother–
infant relations
affect in, 605–607
assessment methodology, 41–42
asymmetry in, 610–611
in attachment theory, 601–602
authoritative parenting, 604–605
behavioral psychology research, 591–
592
as bidirectional, 607–608, 609
in child language acquisition, 596

conceptual trends, 589–595, 600
cross-cultural studies, 22–23
imitative behaviors, 597–598, 600–
601, 609–610
later social behaviors of child and, 21–
22, 607–610
microanalytic analysis of, 43, 598–600
modifiability of, 32
moral development and, 602
out-of-sight compliance in, 602–603
in psychoanalytic theory, 592–593
scaffolding concept, 603–604
secular change and, 25
in socialization, 11, 590
styles of parenting in, 604–605
Parkes, C., 441–442
Paulsen, F., 313
Perceptual development
associationist theory of, 529
cognition and action in, 532–535, 537–
539
concept of affordances, 533–534
critical period concept, 31–32
differentiation in, 529–532
Gibson's work on, 430
as learning, 534–535
learning in, 7
mechanism of change in, 535–537,
538–539
nativist-empiricist approach, 6–7
recognition of meaningful properties,
532–534
theoretical concepts of, 6–7
types of, 528–529
Werner's concepts, 293–294
Personality theory
Baldwin's, 132
continuity concept, 379
stability of traits, 558–560, 703–704
Stern's conception of disposition, 317–
318
Stern's unitas multiplex, 317

observational reports, 41–44, 562–565

parent-reported data, 41–442, 562–565

photographic technology in, 43, 362–363, 369–370, 435–436

on physical development, 255–256, 502–503

Piaget's, 138–139, 212, 266, 271, 285, 571

process analysis in, 299–302

process language for, 302–303

process versus achievements in, 298–299

protocol analysis, 40–41

proximate and ultimate factors, 168–169

reductionism and, 173–174

secular change as developmental variable, 24–26

selection of samples in, 44–45

in social cognitive theory, 489–490, 492–493

social concerns in research goals, 27

in social learning theory, 479–480, 482–483

socialization, 593–595

sociocultural factors in design/interpretation, 22–24, 547–548, 552–554, 555–558

Spitz's, 217–219, 222

Strange Situation procedure, 446, 449–450

subsample validation, 45

technical developments and, 554–555, 598–599

theory-driven, 694

unit of analysis, 34–35, 555–556

Vygotsky's, 415–416

Watson's, 236–237, 238–239, 241, 246–247

Yale Institute, 593–595

Riegel, K., 326–327

Riviere, Joan, 433

Robertson, J., 435

Rockefeller Foundation, 359, 394, 395

Romanes, G. J., 128–129

Rosenbluth, D., 436

Royce, J., 135

Scaffolding concept, 21, 206, 603–604

Schaffer, R., 436

Sears, R. R.

Bandura and, 474, 483

contributions of, 481, 494, 495

psychoanalytic theory in work of, 429

research interests of, 476–477

research methodology, 479–480

Security theory, 434–435

Self-concept

Freud's observations, 205

internal working models of, 451

in Piaget's psychology, 137

in social-cognitive development, 132, 134, 137, 487–488, 491

splitting phenomenon, 216

Self-preservation, in Stern's Dialectic view, 319–320

Self-regulation

in Gesell's psychology, 366

in social cognitive theory, 132, 134, 137, 487–488, 491

in Spitz's psychology, 220

Sensori-tonic field theory, 302

Sensorimotor development

attitude as factor in, 400–402

Bayley's research, 503–504, 512–514

behavior course vs. behavior pattern in, 398–399

causal thinking and, 270, 283

cellular processes in, 415

Coghill's research, 362–363

correlatives, 504–506

critical period concept in, 404–405

in Dewey's psychology, 153

exercise and, 404–406

Gesell's concept of, 363–364

Hall's concept, 118, 119

interdisciplinary research in, 416

McGraw's research, 393–394, 395–398, 400–402, 404–405

in neonativist conception, 126–127

neuromuscular maturation in, 406–411, 412–413

perceptual development and, 535–537

in Piaget's psychology, 267–271, 283–284

reflex arc concept, 153

research in, 376–377, 378

Separation anxiety, 440–441, 450–451, 455

Sexuality/sexual behavior. *See also* Gender differences

gender identification, 215, 601

in psychoanalytic theory, 207–208, 214–218

Siblings, 456

Siegler, R. S., 578

Skinner, B. F., 6, 239–241, 474–475, 485

Smiling response, 219–220

Social cognitive theory, 474, 486–495

contributions of, 491–493, 494, 495

mechanisms of development in, 480–481, 490–491

reciprocal determinism in, 488–489

research methodology in, 479–480, 489–490, 492–493

research needs, 493, 494–495

self-efficacy in, 487–488, 491

self-regulation in, 487

Social Darwinism, 163–164

Social learning theory, 239

aggression in, 477–478

Bandura's, 474–475

dependency in, 478–479

development of, 475–476, 593–595

identification in, 479

imitation in, 485–486

Sears', 474–475, 476–477

social cognitive theory as, 474, 486–495

Social progress

as Dewey's goals for psychology, 146, 150–151, 161–163, 165

as goals of developmental psychology, 27, 580

public policy implications of attachment theory, 459

as Watson's goals for psychology, 238

Social psychology, 694–695

Baldwin's, 131–132, 139

Dewey's, 148–151

Social referencing, 10

Socialization

adaptation and, 268

affect in, 605–607

in attachment theory, 597

in behavioral psychology, 591–592

bidirectionality in, 33–34

cognitive change and, 157–158, 264, 410–414

critical period concept in, 32, 609

effect of relationships on relationships, 706–708

in Hall's theory of adolescence, 119

imitation in, 597–598

interactions within relationships, 705–706

introception in, 322

language acquisition and, 260–262

mechanisms of, 18

nonshared effects in, 9

parent-child relations in, 11, 607–610

in psychoanalytic theory, 592–593

psycholinguistics research, 596

reinforcement theory of, 17, 595–596

research trends, 589–591

scaffolding concept, 603–604

Yale Institute research, 593–595

Sociocultural context

of attachment behaviors, 457–459

of categorization in developmental research, 556–558

of communication processes, 224

cross-cultural research, 547–802

early developmental theorists on, 74–75

of fear reactions, 701–702

of intelligence testing, 183–184, 191

as level of social complexity, 696–698, 701–703

of maternal behaviors, 517–518

in mental development, 255, 510–511, 579

of research and theory in developmental psychology, 3, 22–24, 46, 154, 173, 547–548, 552–554, 555–556

secular change as, 24–26, 552

Vygotsky's use of, 410–414, 416–422, 423–424

Werner's research, 295

Special-needs children, 358

Spencer, H., 128, 161, 162

Spitz, R., 2

on affective processes, 219–221

contributions of, 203–204, 217, 221–223, 224–225

on emergence of self, 220–221

Freud and, 217

Sroufe, A., 449–450

Stability of traits, 558–560, 703–704

Stage models

Baldwin's, 131

Binet's research and, 195–197

catastrophe theory and, 29

of cognitive development, 153–154, 573–574

of developmental anxiety, 757–8

Dewey's, 153–154

Gesell's, 377

Hall's, 118

of language acquisition, 261

in learning theory, 195–197

Piaget's, 261, 264, 269, 271, 275

of psychosexual development, 207–208

sensorimotor, 269

vs. continuous models, 28–29

Stern, William, 254–255

career, 313–316

concept of egocentrism, 322–324

concept of proximal space, 320–322, 325

contributions of, 311–312, 324–327

major concepts, 316–318

process-oriented theory of development, 318–319

theory of active development, 319–320

Stimulation

in attachment theory, 439–440

critical period concept, 404–405

perceptual learning and, 17, 528–529

Stimulus–response theory, 239, 247

Dewey on, 153

improvement in perception without reinforcement, 528

psychoanalytic theory and, 476

in social learning theories, 474–475

Strange Situation procedure, 446, 449–450

cross-cultural generalizability, 457–458

Structural theories, 244–245, 258, 259–260, 271–272

Subject-object relation, 261–262, 268, 269

levels of social complexity in, 695–697

as perceptual affordance, 533–534

Systems theory

behavioral theories and, 242, 244

complex interaction of systems, 697–700

developmental systems view, 167–168, 207, 208

embryological concepts and, 366–367

family systems theory, 706–708

Freudian theory as, 207, 208, 213

in future of developmental theory, 49–50

Gesell and, 255–256, 366–367, 381

Werner and, 254

Taine, Hippolyte, 155

Tarde, G., 150

Tavistock Clinic, 434

Temperament, 18, 553–554, 560–561

   sources of evidence in research on, 564–565

Terman, L., 359

Theory development

   Ainsworth's contribution, 428–429, 431

   Baldwin's contribution, 20–21, 127–128, 129, 130–141, 137–141

   Bandura's contribution, 474, 491–493, 495, 572

   Binet's contributions, 186–190, 192–195

   Bowlby's contribution, 2, 428, 431

   concept of bidirectionality in, 33–34, 49

   concept of temperament in, 18, 553–554, 560–561

   concepts of cognition in, 570–583

   concepts of nature of change in, 28–29, 46

   contextual relationships in, 552

   continental tradition, 253–255

   critical period concepts in, 29–33

   current trends, 8–14, 547–548, 552–555, 570–583

   Darwin's contribution, 153–155, 157–162, 172, 174

   early psychology teaching, 105–109, 111–112, 121–122

   emergence of developmental psychology, 1–3

   ethical issues in, 172–173

   ethological concepts in, 168

fragmentation in, 49

Freud's contribution, 203–204, 223–225

future needs, 45–50

Gesell's contribution, 255–256, 358, 375–382

Gibson's contribution, 430, 539–542

historical course of, 1–3, 14–18, 154, 428–430, 693–695

individual continuity as assumption in, 558–560

McGraw's contribution, 391, 411–417

meliorism in, 163–166

in modern era, 428–430

needs of attachment theory, 459–460

needs of social cognitive theory, 493, 494–495

ontogeny–phylogeny concept, 166–168

Piaget's contribution, 253–255, 257–258, 284–286

problems in developmental psychology, 693–695

reductionism in, 173

research technology and, 554–555

role of theory, 18–20, 693–694

scope of theory in, 20–22

Sears' contribution, 474, 481, 494, 495

socialization, 589–591

sociocultural context of, 3, 22–24, 555–556

Spitz's contribution, 217, 221–223, 224–225

Stern's contribution, 254–255, 311–312, 324–327

structural/behavioral model, 244–245

systems approach, 49–50

types of explanatory processes in, 17–18

unified theory of intelligence, 197–199

unit of analysis in, 33–34

Vygotsky's contribution, 255, 410

Watson's behaviorism in, 241–247

Watson's contribution, 233–235

Werner's significance, 254, 306–307

Werner's tradition, 254

Thomas, W. I., 150

Tiedemann, Dietrich, 155

Tilney, F., 394

Traits

    canalization of, 167, 168

    evolutionary theory in conceptualization of, 170–171

Transactional theory, 242, 244

    Stern and, 326

Transference, developmental significance of, 211–212

Transformations, 196

    in Spitz's theory, 219–220, 224

Twin studies, 8

    Gesell's comparative behavior interview, 369

    McGraw's Johnny and Jimmy study, 400–401, 402–403, 404–406

Unconscious

    in current developmental research, 12

    in psychoanalytic theory, 210–212

von Baer, Karl, 156

Vygotsky, L., 74, 128, 139, 244, 255, 292, 295–296, 324, 325–326

    concept of culture, 416–422

    concept of mediated action, 425

    concept of zone of proximal development, 412–413

    criticism of, 422–426

    current interest in, 409–410

    Eurocentrism in thought of, 420, 422

genetic method of, 415–416

theory of individual mental functioning, 410–414

Walters, R., 429, 483

Waters, E., 449–450

Watson, John

    contributions of, 2–3, 26, 233–235

    as developmentalist, 234, 235–236

    extremist views of, 237–238

    on goals of psychology, 235, 238

    Hull and, 239

    influence of, 16, 241–247

    personal qualities, 235

    on prenatal development, 245

    research methodology, 236–237, 238–239, 241, 246–247

    Skinner and, 239–241

Werner, Heinz, 254, 315, 319, 325

    concept of developmental moments, 303–304

    cultural primitivism and, 305

    current status in psychology, 292–293

    on development as heuristic, 296–298

    intellectual development of, 294–295

    key publications of, 293–294

    on organismic representation, 302–303

    process analysis methodology, 299–302

    process vs. achievement in theory of, 298–299

    significance of, 306–307

Williams College, 105–111

World Health Organization, 436

Yale Institute, 475–476, 593

Yale University, 359–360

Zone of proximal development, 21, 412–413, 579

ABOUT THE EDITORS

Ross D. Parke is professor of psychology and director of the Center for Family Studies at the University of California, Riverside. He is a past president of Division 7, the Developmental Psychology Division, of the American Psychological Association (APA). He has been editor of *Developmental Psychology* and associate editor of *Child Development*. His research has focused on early social relationships in infancy and childhood. He is well known for his early work on the effects of punishment, aggression, and child abuse and for his work on the father's role in infancy and early childhood. His current work focuses on the links between family and peer social systems.

Peter A. Ornstein is professor of psychology and director of the Program on Developmental Psychology at the University of North Carolina as well as a member of the mentor faculty of the Carolina Consortium on Human Development. He serves as cochair of APA's Working Group on Memories of Childhood Abuse and has been associate editor of *Developmental Psychology*. His research concerns the development of memory and cognition, especially young children's long-term retention of salient, personally experienced events. His interest in the testimony of young children is paralleled by his concerns about the abilities of adults to remember accurately the details of traumatic events experienced in childhood.

John J. Rieser is professor of psychology and director of the developmental psychology area at Peabody College, Vanderbilt University. He was a member of the National Science Foundation review panel on cognition and perception and is an APA fellow and past associate editor of *Developmental Psychology*. Rieser is working on understanding how perception, representation, and action are linked and how the linkages change with development and with sensory or motor disability. He conducts research with toddlers, children, and adults to assess their perceptual-motor coordination, spatial orientation, imagining, and problem solving.